Children's Literature Review

volume 3

Children's Literature Review

Excerpts from Reviews,
Criticism, and Commentary
on Books for Children
and Young People

Gerard J. Senick
Editor

Gale Research Company
Book Tower
Detroit, Michigan 48226

STAFF

Gerard J. Senick, *Editor*

Sharon R. Cillette, *Associate Editor/Production Editor*

Linda M. Pugliese, *Manuscript Coordinator*
Jeanne A. Gough, *Permissions Coordinator*
Judith Fischer Rutkowski, *Research Coordinator*

Laura A. Buch, Thomas E. Gunton, Jacqueline Sharp,
Carol Sherman, David J. Szymanski, *Editorial Assistants*

Arthur Chartow, *Cover Design*

Special acknowledgments to Ann Block, Dedria Bryfonski,
Susan Johnson, and Phyllis Carmel Mendelson.

Contents

Preface vii

Authors Included in Volume 3

Cumulative Index to Authors
Cumulative Index to Titles
Cumulative Index to Critics

Appendix

Preface

Children's Literature Review contains selected excerpts from literary criticism concerning the fiction and nonfiction of about forty authors for children and young adults. General essays and specific reviews provide the critical opinions. Excerpts are carefully prepared to maintain the style of the critic and the quality of the original piece.

Material is selected to represent as completely as possible the criticism to date of each author and his work. Since *CLR* is an ongoing series, entries in a given volume are not definitive. An entry is subject to updating in future volumes as additional significant criticism becomes available.

It is hoped that this volume fulfills the qualifications for a good reference tool: usefulness, dependability, and respect for both the subject matter and the user. Since it is a reflection of children's literature, we hope that its use will also provide both a learning experience and pleasure. We believe, along with Walter de la Mare, that "only the rarest kind of best. . . can be good enough for the young" and for those who love their literature. We have tried to make this volume an example of that philosophy.

Organization of the Book

Author entries are arranged in alphabetical order, according to the author's surname. An entry includes the following sections: author heading, identification paragraph, author's commentary, general commentary, and title entries.

- The *author heading* consists of the full name of the author and any pseudonyms he or she has used when writing books for children, followed by birth and death dates, when available.

- The *identification paragraph* contains both biographical and background information about the author, and includes any major honors or awards.

- The *author's commentary* gives the author's viewpoint on his own work.

- The *general commentary* gives the opinion of one or more critics on the author's work as a whole.

- The *title entries* each consist of excerpts from reviews and critical pieces dealing with the author's individual works. Some title entries include both excerpts and additional references (*other citations*) to criticism not excerpted. If title entries are not used for every one of an author's works, an attempt is made to select titles which are representative of the entire body of his or her work.

New Features

We have made several changes in *CLR,* starting with the present volume.

The table of contents lists the authors included in *CLR* in alphabetical order and the page number on which their entries begin.

In order to better represent the international importance of literature for children, we have included writers of several different nationalities. More nonfiction writers are now in *CLR,* including those who work in fields such as music and architecture. A more evenly distributed time span is represented in this volume, with more emphasis given to seminal authors of literature for children as well as those whose importance is currently being established.

There has been an increase in background information given in the identification paragraphs. For instance, if an author's work has been adapted into a major motion picture, this information is included, since many readers become familiar with an author through seeing his or her name connected with a popular film.

In past volumes, we included cross-references to *Contemporary Authors* (*CA*) and *Something About the Author* (*SATA*). Now *CLR* also cross-references *Contemporary Literary Criticism* (*CLC*) and *Yesterday's Authors of Books for Children* (*YABC*), in addition to *CA* and *SATA*.

We have included an author's commentary section because we feel it can function in several ways. For instance, the commentary can provide background to the author's career or give the author's opinion of the present state of society and how children's literature reflects it. It can serve as exemplary material on writing, or list qualities and standards for children's literature which can be applied to the author's work. The author's commentary can be found in two places. It appears at the beginning of the entry when it presents an overview of the author's work as a whole. It appears before a title entry when the author comments on a specific work. The entry now lets authors speak for themselves; their statements may be echoed or countered in the criticism that follows.

Title headings now include this information: first publication date of a book in the country of its origin, followed by the date of its first publication in the United States. If the title was published concurrently in both countries, only the year is listed.

Excerpts used in *CLR* have been lengthened, where appropriate, to include more plot and/or explanation of character, since this material often gives background to the critical statements. Examples from the original text have been included when they illustrate a critical point.

Page numbers now follow each fragment, rather than being given in an inclusive note at the end of the entire excerpt, as was done in previous volumes. This method is the same as that used in *CLC*.

Beginning with Volume 3, *CLR* will contain an appendix which lists the sources from which material has been reprinted in this volume. It does not, however, list every book or periodical consulted for the volume.

Acknowledgments

The editor wishes to thank the copyright holders of the excerpts included in this volume for their permission to use the material, and the staff of the Detroit Public Library, Wayne State University Library, and the libraries of the University of Michigan for making their resources available to us.

Suggestions Are Welcome

Since *Children's Literature Review* is a reference source that attempts to maintain relevance to the needs of its users, the book will constantly be growing and changing. By expanding its scope we feel we are making necessary improvements, thus adding to its usefulness.

Several editorial changes in this volume were instituted in response to suggestions from users and reviewers of the series. We would greatly appreciate other comments for future consideration. Such suggestions and responses are invaluable in maintaining a reference tool which reflects the area of children's literature criticism and stays responsive to the desires and needs of its users.

A

ARDIZZONE, Edward   1900-

A British artist and author, Edward Ardizzone has been described by critic Marcus Crouch as the ''doyen of English illustrators.'' Born in Vietnam, Ardizzone was sent to England at the age of five. During World War II, Ardizzone was appointed by art historian Kenneth Clark to be Official War Artist in the North African and European theaters of war, an experience recorded in 1974 in his *Diary of a War Artist*. Ardizzone has illustrated many titles in his career, including the Bible, and his pictures grace the works of Shakespeare, James Reeves, Dickens, Eleanor Farjeon, Cervantes, and Walter de la Mare. His first children's books were written at the urgings of his son and daughter, the models for Little Tim and Lucy Grimes. Ardizzone's children's books are a reflection of his sharp observation of the details of daily life and his vivid recall of children's love for both adventure and security. He wrote an autobiography for children in 1970, *The Young Ardizzone*. His *Tim All Alone*, published in 1956, was the first winner of England's Kate Greenaway medal. (See also *Contemporary Authors*, Vols. 5-8, rev. ed. and *Something About the Author*, Vol. 1.)

AUTHOR'S COMMENTARY

I am not an expert. I am a man with a family who has made up stories for his children. For the past thirty-four years I have been a practising artist. . . . After so long a time, it is inevitable that one should have developed some ideas about one's craft.

The story of *Little Tim and the Brave Sea Captain*, the first of the Tim books, was invented twenty-four years ago. It did not spring ready-made to the mind, but started as a rather brief little tale made up on the spur of the moment to amuse my children. Luckily it did amuse them, so it was told again the next day and then the day after that and so on, and each time it was told again it grew somewhat in the telling until I finally found I had a story which I felt was worth illustrating and sending to the publisher.

Now this process of telling and retelling until it grows into something worthwhile has two major advantages. The first is that the script will inevitably be cast in a mould which is easily read aloud; and this is important, because the poor parents may well have to read the story over and over again. Secondly, and probably more important, the children will often make their own suggestions. They will add those

wonderful inconsequential details which only children can think of and which, if incorporated in a tale, so greatly enrich the narrative.

When it comes to making the drawings for one's tale and writing down the tale to match the drawings, then a number of special problems arise, problems which are peculiar to the production of picture books. In picture books the drawings, of course, are as important as, or more important than, the text. The text has to be short, not more than two thousand words. In fact, the text can only give bones to the story. The pictures, on the other hand, must do more than just illustrate the story. They must elaborate it. Characters have to be created pictorially because there is no space to do so verbally in the text. Besides the settings and characters, the subtleties of mood and moment have to be suggested.

Now this is where the old convention of the balloon coming out of a character's mouth, with writing in the balloon, can be invaluable. Take a passage like this from *Tim to the Rescue*. The situation so far is that Ginger, who has anointed his hair with the Mate's hair restorer and whose hair is growing alarmingly, comes up before the ship's barber to have his hair cut for the umpteenth time. In the drawing, there is poor mop-headed Ginger with the tears streaming down his face, the barber [Bloggs] with his scissors, and the Bosun. . . . [A] balloon comes out of Bloggs's mouth in which is written, 'Blimey, Mr Bosun. I just can't, my thumb aches simply 'orrible.' While out of the Bosun's mouth comes another balloon in which is written, 'Mutiny, eh Bloggs!'

You will see at once that what is said in the balloon pinpoints the characters of Bloggs and the Bosun for us, as well as describing the tension in the ship due to the deplorable growth of Ginger's hair. This would take a page or more of text to describe, and in picture books, with only sixty words to a page, there is not the room to spare. Balloons, however, must be used sparingly; otherwise one's book might take on the character of a strip cartoon, which would be sad indeed.

Now to make drawings which tell a story clearly and in which characters are portrayed convincingly and subtleties of mood conveyed is difficult. It demands some professional ability, more ability even than the writing of the text. There is an idea that the work of an amateur or inexperi-

1

enced artist is suitable for books for little children, provided they have a certain spurious brightness of colour. Though there may be exceptions, I think this idea a bad one. (pp. 347-49)

Writing the text for a picture book also has its particular difficulties, the main one being that the tale has to be told in so few words yet must read aloud easily and sound well when read. Another difficulty is that at the turn of each page, and one rarely has more than one hundred and twenty words between the turns, the text must end with a natural break, a note of interrogation or suspense. With rare exceptions, the professional writer who is no artist finds this extremely difficult, if not impossible, to do. Not being visually minded, he cannot leave out enough; he must elaborate; he cannot visualize how the picture will tell the story. And this, I think, is why the best picture books have been created by artists who have written their own text. It is a one-man job.

In what I have said I seem to have suggested that a good picture book should contain certain elements which can be defined and enumerated. Yet if somebody asked what made a good picture book, I would be hard put to say. Some genius might easily come along and break all the rules and produce a work of enduring delight. All the same, I feel sure that there is a basic quality or virtue common to all the finest work and, rather hesitatingly, I suggest it may be the quality of enjoyment. The author-artist must enjoy the act of creating his book. It must be fun for him and he must believe in it. Or rather, he must create a world in which, in spite of all sorts of improbabilities from an adult point of view, he can believe in one part of himself, the childish part.

Characters in the books must also have life. . . . This is particularly so in the drawings. One must be able to believe in them. (pp. 349-50)

Put another way, one might say that, for the childish part of [the author], the story must be both possible and true, and of course in its childish framework it must have its own formal logic. You will notice in the splendid kingdom of [Jean de Brunhoff's] Babar the Elephant how all the animals act quite logically in the given framework. Then, I think, the story might have that enduring appeal which makes it a classic. It will be a story that may well appeal to the childish element in the adults, as well as to the child.

However, let's take this question of the author's enjoyment of his work somewhat further and say the following, which sounds something of a paradox: the author-artist does not primarily create his books for children, but rather to amuse that childish part of himself. If this is so, and he may not always admit it, he will never be in danger of committing that cardinal error of writing and drawing down to children. Instead he will be writing up to himself. I am sure we are all agreed that this question of writing up or down for children is of the greatest importance. Little children love all books. They have no taste, and rightly so, and of course will read and look at anything with pleasure. All the more reason, therefore, that we should give them the best.

But what is the best, what sort of books should be given to children, what kinds of subject dealt with? I don't know, nor have I the courage or the knowledge to discuss the subject. . . . All the same, I will be brave enough to say that I think we are possibly inclined, in a child's reading, to shel-

ter him too much from the harder facts of life. Sorrow, failure, poverty, and possibly even death, if handed poetically, can surely all be introduced without hurt. After all, books for children are in a sense an introduction to the life that lies ahead of them. (p. 351)

Now in all this I may be wrong. But what I do find when I read to children, and what indeed I can be sure of, is that children, particularly little children, love the sounds of words for their own sake, which is why they so often love listening to verse. One should therefore be choosy as to the quality of the verse and prose one gives them. The prose in particular should not only be simple and lucid but should have a poetic cadence which will appeal to the ear. Long and difficult words can be used as long as they are explained as the text unfolds. Notice how cunningly Beatrix Potter does this. Children, in fact, love strange words, and I don't think it matters much if at first they don't understand them.

I am often asked why the Tim books are about the sea and not about animals or fairies or other possibly more suitable themes. The answer, of course, is they are what they are because of the kind of artist I am. (pp. 351-52)

The scenes in the books are, to a great extent, drawn from old half-forgotten memories of past experiences. Not that I have suffered shipwreck or collision or fire at sea or any such adventures; but I made, as a child, the long sea voyage from China to England and have been at sea much since then and seen a gale or two. Now for me, these old half-forgotten memories are far the best to work from. Time has removed the inessentials, while nostalgia has given them a poignancy which no close or too well remembered thing can have. (pp. 352-53)

[My own children's books] were, of course, primarily written and illustrated to amuse the children, and I hope that the poor grownups who have read them over and over again do not find them too irksome. But all the same, they were still written largely to amuse that childish part of myself. I am afraid this is an awful confession to make, but alas I am not only incorrigible but also unrepentant, and so will go on concocting new works merely for the fun of it. (p. 356)

Edward Ardizzone, "Creation of a Picture Book," in Top of the News *(reprinted by permission of the American Library Association), December, 1959 (and reprinted in* Only Connect: Readings on Children's Literature, *edited by Sheila Egoff, G. T. Stubbs, and L. F. Ashley, Oxford University Press, 1969, pp. 347-56).*

GENERAL COMMENTARY

The outstanding picture-book artist of the early 'thirties was Clifford Webb. . . . [He] was the master of a clean style, with an effectively simplified use of colour and fidelity to his animal models. . . . The weakness of Clifford Webb's books lay in the text; it seemed almost invariably as if the pictures had been drawn first and words devised to fit them. (p. 57)

This could never be a criticism of Edward Ardizzone. In his work, word and line seemed to have grown together, and it was impossible to imagine one without the other.

Ardizzone was a largely self-taught artist who had already done some illustrating when *Little Tim and the Brave Sea Captain,* in 1936, established him as a maker of picture-books who looked back to the great tradition (he looked to Caldecott rather than Crane and still more to Dicky Doyle and Leech and Rowlandson) but still drew in a style all his own. *Little Tim* was a major landmark in English picture-books, for its fine colour, vigorous action drawing, beautifully simple and vivid prose, and profound understanding of children and their dream fantasies. In this huge book, 13½ inches high and generously produced with gloriously blank pages between each pair of printed ones as a challenge to the emulating talents of young artists, Ardizzone brought fresh air into the nursery. His hero, a real boy, neither prig nor clown, was resourceful and commonplace and pleasingly modest. In 1937 the scene changed to England and the pictures focussed on a heroine, Lucy Brown. *Lucy Brown and Mr. Grimes* (which encountered opposition in the States on grounds of morality!) was a quieter story but showed as firm an understanding of children. (pp. 57-8)

Ardizzone's . . . *Paul, the Hero of the Fire* was not among his best, but in the same year [1948] he produced a big picture-book in his finest manner, *Nicholas and the Fast-moving Diesel,* an amusing, highly unconvincing story set in the richly detailed landscape which is the hallmark of his style. In the following year he returned to his 'Tim' books with *Tim to the Rescue.* This, although in a smaller format than the pre-war 'Tims', came up to the highest expectations. Written in an unobtrusively exquisite prose, and drawn with a sure line and fine colour, it was most successfully printed. This was due largely to the artist's method of colour separation which anticipated some of the printer's difficulties. (p. 100)

There was . . . in Edward Ardizzone's w)rk . . . a deep satisfaction that drawing should be . . . true and kindly. The post-war 'Little Tim' books showed none of the weakened inspiration common in sequels, only an increased certainty of draughtsmanship and a richer appreciation of people. *Tim and Charlotte* . . . , *Tim in Danger* . . . and *Tim All Alone* . . . were beautifully drawn and printed and told in a deceptively simple prose which marked Ardizzone as the best writer among artists since Beatrix Potter. (p. 115)

> *Marcus Crouch, in his* Treasure Seekers and Borrowers: Children's Books in Britain 1900-1960 (© *Marcus Crouch, 1962), The Library Association, 1962.*

Edward Ardizzone is a professional artist and illustrator. Much of his work is associated with children's books, but in no sense has he ever produced 'pictures for children'. Whether as war artist in 1940 or illustrator of Dick Whittington in 1970, his draughtsmanship is continuous and consistent, suggesting effects rather than stating exact portraits, deriving all the time from sketches stored in his personal note-books.

In this sense, he is in direct line with the great nineteenth century school of illustrators, who often produced children's books too. George Cruikshank, Kate Greenaway and Walter Crane all had a child as well as an adult following. This is an important point: pictures specially drawn for children by artists who could never compete in the adult world can very often be second rate, as well as almost always underpaid. (p. 21)

Ardizzone gets his best effects through understatement: with the minimum of line he can suggest an expression, an action. As he says, 'One shouldn't tell the reader too much. The best view of a hero, I always feel, is a back view.' In other words, these are illustrations that leave something for the child to fill in; unlike the Disney school of art, for example, where the expected audience reaction has been planned for down to the last detail. Like Caldecott—one of his most direct influences—Ardizzone's pictures are full of bustle and movement. By illustrating stories at the most exciting point of the action, the reader is fairly whisked on to the next page, and once familiar with the plot can follow it by the pictures alone. For children between five and eight years old, this can be a real advantage. (pp. 21-2)

[Ardizzone's] most famous work for children is of course the Tim series, which I shall discuss in detail since I believe it provides the best example of his extraordinary talents. . . . Tim meets adventures that nearly result in his death, from shipwreck to fire at sea. He is a tough little boy, though, and enjoys the excitement, although life can be hard sometimes. On the boat, he does a full day's work, and at times suffers from sea sickness, as well as the occasional bout of loneliness and juvenile melancholia, shown by a dejected hunch of the shoulders. Yet on the whole his essential stoicism comes through unchanged, and if there are heroics, these are never false ones. (p. 22)

Ardizzone's favourite story is *Tim all alone.* . . . It is perhaps the most emotional of his books: Tim arrives home after one of his trips at sea which are allowed so unquestionably for this five year old, only to find his home locked up and his parents gone. After dangerous adventures and forlorn searchings, he finally sees his mother sitting crying in the window of 'Sunshine Café', a hunched dumpy figure, incongruously surrounded by cakes and pastries. 'In a moment Tim was in the café and in his mother's arms.' Again, the understatement: the reunion is very quickly celebrated. Yet it has a powerful effect; one adult reader was found in tears over this book. A few critics, referred to rather testily by Ardizzone as 'silly women librarians' have found some of these Tim books hard to take. . . . [For example, in the reissue of *Lucy Brown and Mr Grimes,* a] change has been forced on Ardizzone: Mr Grimes, previously just a lonely old man in a park whom Lucy befriended, has now got to be turned into an old family friend, in case any children are encouraged to speak to old men they have never met before. What does Ardizzone think of this? 'Absolute nonsense, of course.'

In fact I have some sympathy for the critics in this last case. But otherwise, it seems to me, the laconic strength and confrontation with ideas of death and separation in the Tim stories remind me of the healthy outspokenness of nursery rhyme and folk tale. Children can only defeat fear by experiencing and overcoming it, and since it is generally agreed that all children have fantasies of separation, the Tim books can hardly be blamed for putting the idea into their heads. Rather, these stories may help a child follow Tim's example of meeting disaster as it comes and winning through by sheer perseverance. The Tim books are aimed at children roughly between the ages of five and eight; a time that coincides with the occasionally overmatriarchal atmosphere of the infant school and concomitant emphasis in books upon order, good manners and the milk of human kindness. There is a dearth of active, energetic literature for infants that in any way comes up to the drama and excitement of their own games and fantasies. Except for Ardizzone, of course: over-protective women and faint spirits come off badly in the Tim books. He writes for tough, independent little kids who run away from home against good advice and do not faint at the sight of blood. . . . (pp. 22-5)

Ardizzone . . . has . . . a prose style that is spare and lucid, in the best tradition of Beatrix Potter, perhaps. On gramophone records, narrated by David Davis for Delyse, the Tim stories make excellent reading. In the books themselves, the pictures elaborate rather than echo the text, and create the characters. Tim's resolution is perfectly expressed by the rounding of his shoulders as he sets off on his path: Ginger's weakness comes out in his spindly shape and nervous pointed face. Sometimes Ardizzone will add a speech balloon to his drawings: again, using this old device as a way of extending rather than reinforcing the plot. It becomes clear, when he is illustrating someone else's work in picture books, how much is missed in this linking of text and picture. (pp. 25-6)

But all this skill could not really work without the affection and nostalgia Ardizzone puts into his best books. . . . He has written that the artist should be able to create a world that is 'fun for him and he must believe in'. Perhaps this is why one finds in Ardizzone's works so many details drawn from his own past: a picture of a particular house where he once lived, for example, or of a park where his children played. There is no feeling of adult superiority running through these stories; they show the interests and enthusiasms of the artist himself, and of his 'childish part'. Ardizzone's slightly old fashioned boats and sailors are real. The mate, for example, will have a nice collection of buxom nudes pinned around his bunk. When there is a storm, the sea will lash as strongly as in any adult nightmare.

Like so many of the best children's books, Ardizzone's first picture book, *Little Tim and the brave sea captain,* was turned down by publishers and only accepted at last by an American branch. . . . Now that the quality of his art is generally recognized, it would be a mistake to write off his accompanying stories as just mere versions of common fantasies. Of course, with so few words at his disposal, Ardizzone has to fall back on some stock story conventions simply for the sake of economy: pirates, legacies from benevolent old men, cash rewards for heroism that just save a family from disaster and so on. But the way one adventure is topped by the next one in the same story is often extremely skilful. In *Tim and Ginger,* for example, Ginger nearly gets drowned, as usual through his stupidity, and then loses the oars after Tim rescues him, so that the boat drifts into a storm and is smashed against some strange rocks. Ginger rescues Tim, but refuses to move as he is terrified of possible cannibals, so Tim sets off and resolves the adventure. Each character, in other words, has his own moment and readers can on one page feel heroic with Tim, and on the next feel superior (and perhaps a little bit of sympathy) for the ever-popular Ginger, who with his boasting, cowardice and rather endearing weaknesses is the perfect foil for the resourceful Tim. Yet when pressed, Ginger can show a rather grudging heroism, and other characters step out of their simple stereotypes from time to time. . . . But this interesting and slightly unpredictable ambiguity is always kept well in balance with direct action. 'Dash my wig' (an Ardizzone family expression) someone will cry,

and the story will get on the move again. There are glimpses of adult preoccupations, mixed with completely childlike images; after rescue from certain death, Tim and the brave sea captain are tucked up into twin beds after nice cups of cocoa. (pp. 27-9)

Ardizzone has said that book illustrations must be secondary to the story itself, and always help it along. He has no time for pictures that in a sense stand separate from the text or even worse, threaten to swamp it altogether. His own books are a rare example of that complete marriage between picture and text. . . . (p. 29)

> *Nicholas Tucker, "Edward Ardizzone," in* Children's Literature in Education (© 1970, APS Publications, Inc., New York; reprinted by permission of the publisher), No. 3 (November), 1970, pp. 21-9.

Edward Ardizzone has sought, in his illustrations, to define and capture a paradise of domesticity. He is concerned almost always with children at play, or children in loving relations with adults. In the contemplation of these activities he discovers bliss. In this he is reminiscent of Kate Greenaway, but his world is less hermetic than hers, his children closer to the real children of the world. Her paintings are consolatory fantasy, the result of flight. His drawings are idealizations, and though he does yearn backward, his is not an invented world, merely a place purified by hope and then refined by art. His world is a place of harmony, a place of buttercup fields and croquet games, of fenced yards and spotted dogs, of families singing together, of fireplaces and warm kitchens; a world over which a child in a swing could, for an instant, hope to stand in high mastery. (p. 40)

> *Welleran Poltarnees, in his* All Mirrors Are Magic Mirrors: Reflections on Pictures Found in Children's Books *(copyright © 1972 by The Green Tiger Press), Green Tiger Press, 1972.*

JOHNNY THE CLOCKMAKER (1960)

Johnny is a handy boy with a real gift with saw and hammer. Unfortunately he has unsympathetic parents and a teacher who should know better. As for his schoolfellows, they are with the exception of Susannah uniformly horrible. When he decides to build a grandfather clock, only Susannah believes in him, but after many disappointments he is finally successful, everyone admires him, and he sets up in partnership with the village blacksmith.

The story, told with all Ardizzone's unobtrusive mastery, has a nineteenth-century success-story atmosphere. The drawings too have a period flavour—Johnny's school is of the debased Gothic style which has almost disappeared from the educational scene now—and the colouring has the softness and the subdued tones associated with the great age of Victorian colour-printing. What puts this book in a class all its own, apart from the artist's complete mastery of his material, is the consistency of his world. Every detail of each lovely picture dovetails neatly. Every character is conceived in the round and put into his setting. How much to look at, how many depths into which to peer! Ardizzone does it again. (p. 211)

> The Junior Bookshelf, *October, 1960.*

OTHER CITATIONS

Claire Huchet Bishop, in Commonweal, *November 18, 1960, p. 206.*

Jane Wylie, "Hour of Glory," in The New York Times Book Review, *December 25, 1960, p. 13.*

Ruth Hill Viguers, in The Horn Book Magazine, *February, 1961, p. 46.*

LITTLE TIM AND THE BRAVE SEA CAPTAIN (1936)

The unity of a picture book is evident when the story and the pictures carry us simultaneously to the dramatic climax of the story and then on to the denouement. Edward Ardizzone has achieved this unity to a marked degree, from both a child's and a critic's viewpoint, in his picture book *Little Tim and the Brave Sea Captain.* The pictures are a delight to the trained eye. They have an engaging sketchy looseness in the drawing and a range of fine color that portrays the changing moods of the sea. The fast-moving action, the sturdy figures of Tim and his seaman friends, and the tossing ships on a stormy sea are set before us with circumstantial detail which children never tire of exploring for some particular they may have missed.

The text is a tale of adventure on the high seas. Its essential plot is that of any story of shipwreck, but transposed here into an idiom that a little child can grasp. For him it holds tense drama, and for the time being he *is* Little Tim and shares all his adventures. Tim is a stowaway, he learns the hardships of a seaman's life, he is shipwrecked and finally his rescue by cable restores him to his family and friends. The harmony between text and pictures is complete in the mood of excitement conveyed by the simple, rhythmic and sustained telling of the story and in the rapid and vivid lines, washed with stimulating and harmonious color. (p. 127)

> *Lillian H. Smith, in her* The Unreluctant Years: Critical Approach to Children's Literature *(reprinted by permission; copyright © 1953 by the American Library Association),* American Library Association, *1953.*

Even young children need a touch of wildness now and then, which is precisely what ... Mr. Ardizzone gives them in *Little Tim and the Brave Sea Captain* . . . , his spirited account of Tim's adventures at sea. It all starts with Tim, who plays in and out of boats on the beach. How he becomes a stowaway, learns to be an efficient if reluctant deck hand, and experiences shipwreck makes a thrilling story. . . . Mr. Ardizzone's watercolors are as vigorous as his tale. Here is realism for the youngest at its most adventurous level. Tim is a do-it-yourself hero if ever there was one, and his competence and achievements through a series of stories rouse the admiration of his young devotees. Mr. Ardizzone's books introduce other heroes, but Tim is still the favorite. . . . (p. 426)

> *May Hill Arbuthnot and Zena Sutherland, in their* Children and Books *(copyright © 1947, 1957, 1964, 1972 by Scott, Foresman and Company; reprinted by permission), fourth edition, Scott, Foresman, 1972.*

OTHER CITATIONS

Judith Higgins, in Grade Teacher, *November, 1970, pp. 124, 126.*

LUCY BROWN AND MR. GRIMES (1937; redrawn edition with text augmented, British Edition, 1970; US Edition, 1971)

This book was drawn (text and pictures) for the artist's own little girl, just as *Little Tim and the Brave Sea Captain* was made for his own little boy. The artist's pictures glorify a commonplace, materialistic story of a little girl who befriends a lonely old gentleman and comes to be adopted by him away from a maiden aunt too busy to care for a child. Mr. Grimes lives to make Lucy happy in all the ways little girls are supposed to like. The artist's earlier book, *Little Tim and the Brave Sea Captain,* is a classic, but even Ardizzone pictures cannot make *Lucy Brown* important. (pp. 36-7)

> The Horn Book Magazine *(copyrighted, 1938, by The Horn Book, Inc., Boston), January-February, 1938.*

The improbabilities of *Lucy Brown and Mr. Grimes* are framed in the most appealing and recognisable of settings. This was one of the two earliest of Mr. Ardizzone's picture-books, written, as so many of the greatest books have been, for the delight of one child and finding, almost by accident, its wider audience. This is the famous book which offended the Puritan heart of America in the middle Thirties—Mr. Grimes had a little girl to stay with him, and the sex-crime rate was bad enough without this encouragement!—and unlike the other Tim and Lucy books it was not reprinted. For the new edition Mr. Ardizzone has redrawn the pictures and, if I recall the original aright, tidied up the text a little. Most of his picture-books are for boys and tomboys, but this is for little girls who will share Lucy's compassion as much as her excitement at the enlargement of her life. It is an enchanting story—and with what mastery the author deploys his brief text!—with drawings which explore lovingly the charm and the sadness of Lucy's two worlds. (pp. 273-74)

> *M. S. Crouch, "One Old, One New: A Review of Two Books from Edward Ardizzone," in* The Junior Bookshelf, *October, 1970, pp. 273-74.*

The author has completely redrawn and partially rewritten and augmented the text of this old favorite, which was published in 1937. Lucy Brown is a dear, lonely little orphan, living in early 20th-Century London with her aunt, who "was very busy and could not be bothered with her very much." Lucy has no one to play with, and gladly makes friends with Mr. Grimes, who is old and ugly, but kind. He, too, is lonely because, although he likes children, they do not like him and call him a "horrid old thing." Lucy does not make fun of him, and ultimately she goes to live with him as her guardian in a lovely house in the country. The most significant change in the text has to do with the manner in which Lucy Brown and Mr. Grimes become acquainted at the Recreation Ground. In the original version: ". . . she looked so pretty that he had to go and talk to her. 'How are you my little dear?' he said. 'You do look nice.'" Apparently this didn't sound sinister in 1937, but in the new version Lucy recognizes Mr. Grimes as an "old family friend,'' thus removing any suspicion that might have been cast—justifiably—by modern minds on this actually natural and joyful alliance of the old and the very young. The text in the original book is sparse, and although the new version is basically the same story, it is much amplified, so wordier. Visually, the original book is by far the more impressive. The pictures were all done in full, intense watercolors (the back of each page remained blank). In the new book, as in the familiar ''Tim'' series by this author, black line drawings alternate with watercolor illustrations—which are faded-looking and much diluted when compared with those in the '37 edition. The pictures show much the same content as before but have been diminished in size (from 9″ x 13¼″) to fit the smaller format (7¾″ x 10¼″). The print in the original book was likewise more appealing, being handsome, large, dark black hand-lettering; in this book, standard, ''machine-made'' large type is used. Nevertheless, the original is out of print now, and young readers of Ardizzone books will be pleased to find this along with the others on the shelf. (p. 100)

> *Melinda Schroeder, in* School Library Journal *(reprinted from the September, 1971, issue of* School Library Journal, *published by R. R. Bowker Company, a Xerox company; copyright © 1971 by Xerox Corporation), September, 1971.*

OTHER CITATIONS

John Coleman, in New Statesman, *November 6, 1970, p. 612.*

Derwent May, in The Listener, *November 12, 1970, p. 674.*

Ethel L. Heins, in The Horn Book Magazine, *April, 1971, p. 157.*

Zena Sutherland, in Bulletin of the Center for Children's Books, *June, 1971, pp. 149-50.*

NICHOLAS AND THE FAST MOVING DIESEL (British Edition, 1947; US Edition, 1959)

The wispy Daumier-like drawings of Edward Ardizzone, with their mystery and wit, always stand out in any text which they illustrate. It is very nice that someone who is such a power in children's books and book illustration in general should turn out every time to be so expert and so evocative. The children are appealingly weedy figures with large heads and minnowy bodies and the scenery is always observed with great charm. In *Nicholas and the Fast Moving Diesel* he has himself written and illustrated an attractive, school-atlas-sized story book, filled with large whimsical cartoons, some in colour. Nicholas and his friend, riding on the footplate of an engine, deftly assume the controls and avert disaster when the driver and his mate go down with an almost lethal attack of the colly-wobbles after drinking tainted tea. The incidental detail in the pictures is pleasant, from the curl of fly-paper in the kitchen of Nicholas's home to the locomotive, green with gold bands like a Ruritanian admiral (what a relief from engines with faces!). (p. 847)

> *Jonathan Miller, in* The Spectator *(© 1959 by The Spectator; reprinted by permission of* The Spectator*), June 12, 1959.*

Edward Ardizzone's latest picture story is his first in a long time that hasn't even the flash of an ocean wave or a whiff of salt in it and, much as one admires an artist for taking a new tack, I must report regretfully that something else is missing. The ingredients of the story, except for a Diesel engine, are right out of a Victorian album: a poor boy whose father is too sick to work, his friend Nicholas who comes to stay, an unplanned ride on a train, two railway men who—horrors!—drink tea on the job, and a collision averted only by the quick-witted Nicholas. Now Mr. Ardizzone has always been pretty persuasive, in his tongue-in-cheek manner, about the most unlikely adventures—and what child doesn't dream about flagging down a train just in the nick of time? But here he brings together just too many of the tried-and-true devices. His pictures are fine and free, as always, but his story lacks the unexpected which we have come to expect from him. (p. 29)

> *Ellen Lewis Buell, in* The New York Times Book Review *(© 1960 by The New York Times Company; reprinted by permission), January 17, 1960.*

OTHER CITATIONS

The Junior Bookshelf, December, 1947, p. 163.

Polly Goodwin, in Chicago Sunday Tribune Magazine of Books, *Part 4, November 15, 1959, p. 10.*

Margery Fisher, in her Intent upon Reading: A Critical Appraisal of Modern Fiction for Children, *Franklin Watts, Inc., 1962, pp. 24-5.*

TIM ALL ALONE (British Edition, 1956; US Edition, 1957)

[*Tim All Alone*] is as near perfection as we are likely to see. It has charm, style, truth; it shows an exact integration of words and pictures, so that it is impossible to dispense with either. There is real pathos in Tim's quest of his parents and joy in his ultimate success. How wonderfully Mr. Ardizzone portrays movement and thought and character, even in a back view. And he is equally successful with ships and, particularly in this volume, buildings. He has as keen an eye for architecture as Osbert Lanchester, and greater affection. . . .

Beyond question, the English picture book of the year. (p. 320)

> The Junior Bookshelf, *December, 1956.*

OTHER CITATIONS

Mary K. Eakin, in her Good Books for Children, *third edition, University of Chicago Press, 1966, p. 9.*

TIM AND CHARLOTTE (1951)

Tim is one of my favourite characters. Sensitive without being a sissy, he is as brave and resourceful as any boy could wish, he can turn his hand to anything, and he still remains a self-contained, capable and modest lad. In this story he and Ginger (former ship's boy) are walking on the beach when they come upon a little girl unconscious among the waves. This is Charlotte, who lives happily with them until claimed by a wealthy and formidable guardian. The story is too good to give away further, but its climax comes with the great battle at school known for years afterwards as "Tim's last stand."...

[Ardizzone's] stories have grown in depth and sympathy without losing their fun and high spirits. The pictures, needless to say, are superb. (p. 164)

The Junior Bookshelf, October, 1951.

Will somebody find me a windmill and lend me a cap?— Here goes, then! *I adore Ardizzone.* For years I have loved my Love with an A, and this year, with *Tim and Charlotte* before me, love has flamed into the passion born of the discovery of a Nursery Classic. *All ages,* declares the jacket-flap: how truly! I have spent a blissful afternoon introducing this one to a rather young friend, listening to his joyful ejaculations and moans of sorrow, as we turned the pages together....

Most of us already know our Tim; Charlotte appears as a little stranger washed up by the tide on the beach near Tim's house. Oh that beach with its cold exciting sea! and oh those two small boys trudging between the breakwaters, heads bent to the wind. You know that sort of seasideness so well, you believe you could draw it *just exactly* like that (only you'd have to grow up like Edward Ardizzone, if he ever has, without forgetting the look and feel of things before you did, if you know what I mean).... The tale ends with the children in that state of supreme satisfaction we so often wished—and vainly—for ourselves; reading it, we have identified ourselves with every vicissitude of joy and sorrow and victory, told and pictured by an adult genius which *knows* what childhood feels like when it is sad, glad, and victorious.

There now! I've lost my cap. Let's hope it was caught, on the other side of the windmill, by some child coming home for the holidays.

> *Eleanor Farjeon, "Cap over Windmill," in*
> The Spectator *(© 1951 by* The Spectator;
> *reprinted by permission of* The Spectator*),*
> *December 14, 1951, p. 828.*

TIM AND GINGER (1965)

Some years ago we were told that there would be no more Little Tim books. That was one promise Mr. Ardizzone was much too kind-hearted to keep, so here is *Tim and Ginger,* a picture-book in the grand tradition. Ginger, who was always big-headed, gets into serious trouble and is rescued by Tim, only to get them both into trouble again. A story like this must come easily to Mr. Ardizzone now, but he shows his customary care and mastery in laying it out on the page; no one does this kind of job better. The pictures are too full of characteristic touches, dramatic and funny. There is a lovely page, to be set beside the best of the past, in which Ginger stands up to the chin in the sea, surrounded by seagulls. Tim's expression, as he comes to the rescue, is a masterpiece of understatement.

Mr. Ardizzone, in the early 'Thirties a pioneer of pioneers, now represents the high tradition of the English picture-book. (pp. 274-75)

The Junior Bookshelf, October, 1965.

TIM IN DANGER (1953)

There is indeed one Ardizzone, and no one today so delightfully combines sweetness with strength. Those who have admired his recent work in line—notably in the Oxford Trollope and in Mr. [James] Reeves' latest book of verse—will know how his style has matured and strengthened, but he has lost none of the honesty and simplicity which first endeared little Tim to us so many years ago. *Tim in Danger* contains no surprises, and surprise is the last thing one wants from an old favourite. Instead it gives the reader what he expects as his right—rich humour, kindliness and a gallery of characters, some like Tim, Ginger and Charlotte, old friends, some new to us, but all real people who go on living their lives after the book closes. The drawings of ships and people are vigorous, true and born of ripe experience. Mr. Ardizzone knows exactly how much acid to mix with his paint. (pp. 175-76)

The Junior Bookshelf, October, 1953.

OTHER CITATIONS

Virginia Haviland, in The Horn Book Magazine, *December, 1953, pp. 451-52.*

TIM TO THE LIGHTHOUSE (1968)

How lucky we are that Edward Ardizzone has such a large family. His books are always dedicated to one or another of his cousins, nephews, grandchildren, and we may safely assume that they will never have enough of his stories; happily, we can all share the fruits of his beneficence.

The "Tim" books have been praised so often that we begin to take them for granted: it is impossible to compare them with any other author's work; hopeless to try to fit them in with any other books, as they dwarf them.

Tim to the Lighthouse is as thrilling as anything that has gone before. One stormy night Tim notices that the beam of light from the lighthouse is not shining into his room. He wakes his father and is told "Go back to bed, Tim, and stop your nonsense". But of course he cannot sleep, so he trudges off to rouse his old friend Captain McFee (looking very frail now, but still as brave as a lion) and together they row to the lighthouse. How Charlotte and Ginger appear on the scene will not be revealed, but [there is] . . . high drama [in] the moment when the wreckers burst upon the rescue party. . . .

It might be Algernon Blackwood in *Boy's Own Paper,* but Ardizzone's genius is to design the drawings and the type so simply and so elegantly that a child of three can follow every move. . . . (p. 582)

> The Times Literary Supplement *(© Times*
> *Newspapers Ltd., 1968; reproduced from*
> The Times Literary Supplement *by permission), June 6, 1968.*

OTHER CITATIONS

Mrs. G. V. Barton, in Children's Book News, *May-June, 1968, p. 183.*

The Junior Bookshelf, October, 1968, p. 291.

TIM TO THE RESCUE (1949)

If without corrosive reservations one welcomes Edward Ardizzone's *Tim to the Rescue* so happily, there must be good reasons why, and faint praise is not in order. From a spirited jacket through page after page are drawings in pen, free and vigorous, almost of Daumier bravura, well suited to a theme, the excitement of which is conveyed in fast-moving vivid *line*, and organized, not contrived for too obvious design, into rhythmic *compositions*, like well-conceived choreography. This is an effective foil for an earnest little boy of most delicate manliness. Tim versus the weather, poised birdlike in the rigging on his dancer's feet, is sketched with the utmost knowledge of little boys, as again with Ginger in a puddle before a quite comic-opera, but perfectly seaworthy, captain. All illustrations are unrestricted and compelling; mood dominates manner, and all is wit.

Form is indicated fluently in mellow line or crisp, as needed, with quick perception, and a well-rounded artist's personality is clear in composition relationships, fidelity to types and situations, not to mention excellent drawing.

Masses here are stated admirably in values, with rapid diagonal slashes and daring cross hatch. In such fulsome expression is seen no cautious niggling about for surface effects so often confused with art, affectations of any kind being blessedly missing from the work of Mr. Ardizzone.

As to depicting *types*, this artist tosses them off in a gust of sounds, tastes and smells. Their sea dog speech caught in waggish balloons, but not too often; their secret vanities (see Third Mate's cabin); the grousing and heady mixtures (in mess and galley); Tim the Scribe (see letters home); their common weakness, the common cat (seen everywhere)—all are keenly observed. And where, oh where, is a sight so hilarious as Ginger, the barber's Nemesis, transfixed under his bramble of hair, except in some of the good examples of genre illustration of the eighteenth and nineteenth centuries, including [George] Cruikshank?

Color, where used, floats in transparent washes of blues, stormy greens and sturdy siennas to umber. Reds have a song. Love's labor is saved for our enjoyment in beautiful reproductions, and informal hand lettering carries the charming and reticent text.

Finally the key to all is an *attitude*. Along with fun a sweet seriousness toward children could hardly be better shown than in drawings of sea longing (p. 1), attention to lessons, a proud home-coming, and above all in Mr. Ardizzone's conception of Tim himself. The story, the pictures, everything, reflect and bear his hero out. He is very small in such great seas, but he sparkles beautifully, and can be seen at any distance. Long life to little Tim! (pp. 210-11)

> *Helen Stone, in* The Horn Book Magazine *(copyrighted, 1950, by The Horn Book, Inc., Boston), May, 1950.*

OTHER CITATIONS

The Junior Bookshelf, *November, 1949, p. 174.*

Ellen Lewis Buell, in The New York Times Book Review, *November 13, 1949, p. 12.*

TIM'S LAST VOYAGE (British Edition, 1972; US Edition, 1973)

Tim fans need not fear that his luck has finally deserted him, once again he survives a hair-raising adventure. But it is made clear that this is the tenth and last in the Tim series, at the end of the story he promises his parents that he will not go to sea again until he is grown up (the final page gives us a glimpse of the future with Tim looking unexpectedly priggish as the 'Captain of a great ship').

This is vintage Ardizzone: Tim and Ginger on their knees scrubbing the deck, threatened by a tartar of a bosun who wields a rope's end—Storm—Shipwreck—Rescue—a colourful crew with kindly ship's carpenter, Gino the cook, McAndrew the engineer and the cowardly bosun (who retreats to his cabin with a bottle of rum and howls 'DOOM' from a porthole).

The style is characteristically vigorous and the illustrations show that the master has lost none of his sureness of touch. Scenes of action are splendidly dramatic and there are some beautiful drawings of life below decks with plenty of the sort of detail that fascinates small boys.

Few would question the classic status of the Tim books, children have enjoyed them for the past thirty-seven years and there seems every reason to predict that they will continue to delight young readers for many years to come. (p. 8)

> *Eleanor von Schweinitz, in* Children's Book Review *(© 1973 Five Owls Press Ltd.; all rights reserved), February, 1973.*

OTHER CITATIONS

Derwent May, in The Listener, *November 9, 1972, p. 646.*

Ruth Marris, in The Spectator, *November 11, 1972, p. 762.*

Paul Heins, in The Horn Book Magazine, *June, 1973, p. 256.*

THE YOUNG ARDIZZONE: AN AUTOBIOGRAPHICAL FRAGMENT (1970)

The real-life young Ted was apparently not much like the intrepid Little Tim. Perhaps young Ardizzone's fantasies were used by old Ardizzone for his fictions. But for the circumstantial details with which the illustrations to those fictions are fleshed out, he used his memory. This book confirms that it is strong and visual. Despite the tenuousness of the narrative and the modest domestic scale, this is a sharp and amusing memoir. . . .

On every spread there are drawings. One of Ardizzone's strengths is that he does not tell you too much: his drawings are like those portraits where a certain looseness of touch or ambiguity of modelling, just because it leaves something for the imagination to fill in, achieves a likeness. His illustrations don't annoy you by being too precise about the heroine's profile: instead, they establish what the light was like, how big the room was, or the exact nature of the landlady's inquisitive and supercilious stance. Like a good accompanist, he knows that his business is not to compete with the singer. He has something of [Thomas] Bewick's ability to insert in felicitously pastoral English landscapes tartly observed human goings-on. He makes concrete the details of places and things, but he does not do what the film of the book inevitably does—that is, corrupt and drive out with something stronger the images the writer has given you.

The drawings he did as a war artist of Home Guardsmen in *Dad's Army* situations, his illustrations to *The Pilgrim's Progress,* to De la Mare and to his own and other people's children's books, are all peopled with the same little figures. That they can mix in such various company, offend no one, and give something of their own, is proof of their manners, which are open, friendly and warmly sentimental, but not pushing. Who could rebuff them?

> *Peter Campbell, "Miniature Manners," in* The Listener *(© British Broadcasting Corp. 1970; reprinted by permission of Peter Campbell), December 24, 1970, p. 891.*

[*The Young Ardizzone: An Autobiographical Fragment* is a fragmentary] autobiography too, of a horse-drawn but unsteady world, a boyhood of new houses, new towns, abiding shyness. Tipped in are grandmother's purple rages and compensatory loose rein; elaborate party preparations (only the ice cream measured up) and a visit to Bruges busy in snow and ice; learning to swim (or sink) at the end of a fishing pole; gay-blade uncles back from East Asia and, infrequently, his pragmatic, adaptable father too. "Alas, poor man, the only person he could not get on with was his wife"—and Ted, who pronounces his pretty, cultivated mother probably "sexually cold," suffered from being drawn into one of their quarrels. Worst for a child "born to be teased and bullied" was school: terror induced apathy in the classroom and flight outside (once he was caught, his "poor little penis" burned). If the young Ardizzone was no indomitable Little Tim, neither does he whimper: there were good times especially on the Ipswich docks where the books had their adventure-tinged beginning. Other images endured—a man silently, ferociously strangling a woman (the scoutmaster: "Eyes front, boys"); two drunken hoydens pulling hair, ripping clothes—and increasingly Ned "took refuge in painting and drawing." Only, however, after several years of clerking at the China and Japan

Trading Company and sampling Bohemian London would a providential gift from his father turn him to full-time professional art. Enhancing the kaleidoscopic recollections on almost every page are the author-artist's spirited drawings and, given the staying power of his style, some young people will welcome the confidences of Little Tim's progenitor—confidences not so different from the first-personalizations currently dominating fiction. "I was a conformist. I tried to do the right thing but failed." Expendable, certainly (and expensive), nonetheless engaging. (p. 59)

> Kirkus Reviews *(copyright © 1971 The Kirkus Service, Inc.), January 15, 1971.*

In [*The Young Ardizzone*], Mr. Ardizzone tells the story of his childhood, often unhappy, his youth, and his early manhood, until the timely gift of £500 from his father enabled him to give up his dull office work and chance his arm as an artist. Mr. Ardizzone was an artist born and the memories he stored up were visual ones, full of sharp detail and of humour and drama. There is much in this "autobiographical fragment" which illuminates one's understanding of his work, in his selection of subjects and in his treatment of them. It is highly readable, with that direct, sensitive but unfussy style which has always been his hallmark. It belongs, for all its modesty and small scale, with such classical studies of childhood as Frank Kendon's *Small Years,* for it has the same utter honesty and a recollection which falsifies nothing and prefers reporting to analysis. An enchanting book, finding readers mainly, but not exclusively, among those who have grown up with the author during his forty-year-old career. (p. 13)

> The Junior Bookshelf, *February, 1971.*

OTHER CITATIONS

Elizabeth Minot Graves, in Commonweal, *May 21, 1971, pp. 265-66.*

Shirley Hughes, in The School Librarian, *June, 1971, p. 135.*

B

BACON, Martha   1917-

Martha Bacon is an American poet, novelist, and teacher who has traveled widely, especially in Africa, and studied in Italy. She is the daughter of New England poet Leonard Bacon, and has written for both children and adults.

IN THE COMPANY OF CLOWNS: A COMMEDIA (1973)

This reviewer tried hard to find something in this book good enough to justify the insults to the Church, the hierarchy, women—religious or secular. There is sufficient good literature to meet our needs without wasting time on this. We might quote the opening sentence of Chapter Ten: "It smelled like a sewer and looked like paradise." (p. 145)

> *Sister M. Constance Melvin, I.H.M., in* Best Sellers *(copyright 1973, by the University of Scranton), June 15, 1973.*

Although the witty dialogue and the humorous turns of phraseology [in *In the Company of Clowns*] would seem directed to a sophisticated reader, the pulsating Italian background, the incisively drawn characters, and the boisterous action all simmer and seethe in an exciting story. (p. 376)

> *Paul Heins, in* The Horn Book Magazine, *(copyright © 1973 by The Horn Book, Inc., Boston), August, 1973.*

Another imaginative historical tale by the author of *Sophia Scrooby Preserved* . . ., this is about an orphaned boy who seeks adventure with a troupe of traveling players in 18th-Century Italy. . . . Italy, particularly Venice of the period, and the life of second-rate entertainers are interestingly presented. The lively action, well-drawn characters, and satirical humor make this enjoyable reading, and the black-and-white line drawings [by Richard Cuffari] add to the story's interest. (p. 79)

> *Marcia L. Perry, in* School Library Journal *(reprinted from the September, 1973, issue of* School Library Journal, *published by R. R. Bowker Company, a Xerox company; copyright © 1973 by Xerox Corporation), September, 1973.*

OTHER CITATIONS

Kirkus Reviews, *April 1, 1973, p. 382.*

The Booklist, *September 15, 1973, pp. 114-15.*

SOPHIA SCROOBY PRESERVED (1968)

. . . Or, How The Daughter of an African Chieftain Is Kidnapped by Slavers, Sold to and Educated by a (colonial) New England Family, Transported to England Where She Makes Her Fortune Singing Italian Arias, Then Is Returned to the (just independent) States and Freedom with her Family. . . . *La Belle Sauvage* of New Haven (Connecticut) becomes the rage of Greenwich (England), carries over that inflexible moral poise suggestive of [Samuel Richardson's heroine] Clarissa Harlowe, although Sophia faces no temptation. The book has an eighteenth-century look: Sophia in cameo on the jacket; handsome, mannered illustrations and some elaborate lettering inside [by David Omar White]; a shorter-than-Fielding capsule preceding each chapter "in which the reader" is apprised of its end (but not the means—which may be just the gimmick to jostle attention spans). For mood, one of her rescuers says it straight: "You are quite worthy of the pen of the author of *The Castle of Otranto*—a very pretty romance." She's too good to be true (will girls know?) but she is viable, and the ensemble has integrity. (pp. 822-23)

> *Kirkus Service (copyright © 1968 The Kirkus Service, Inc.), August 1, 1968.*

In the mannered style of the early English novelists, [*Sophia Scrooby Preserved* is] a romantic story in which the heroine moves from one dramatic adventure to another. . . . Sophia is an engaging heroine, and her story is written with flavor; the book tends, however, to have the indefatigable quality of [Hervey Allen's] *Anthony Adverse*. (p. 2)

> *Zena Sutherland, in* Bulletin of the Center for Children's Books *(copyright 1968 by The University of Chicago; all rights reserved), September, 1968.*

Readers who enjoy the books of Joan Aiken, Sid Fleischman, and Margery Sharp will be fascinated and thoroughly entertained by the adventures of [Bacon's] indomitable heroine. . . . All the fun and fantastic adventures of Pansy Scrooby are set against a serious and vivid portrayal of the conditions of life in colonial America and of the evils of slavery. A provocative book for the perceptive reader. The illustrations are properly satiric. (pp. 561-62)

> *Diane Farrell, in* The Horn Book Magazine *(copyright © 1968 by The Horn Book, Inc., Boston), October, 1968.*

Martha Bacon has a lively style and when she is sure of her scene, writes with wit and perception. Her story opens promisingly and is most appealing when it pictures life in an African village, the peculiarities of the Elect in a Connecticut town and the fashionable foibles of the 18th-century English upper class. But the possible strength and conviction of the story are repeatedly drained by Mrs. Bacon's contrivances and, once she moves beyond the African origins, by her failure to examine more closely the black experience this side of the Atlantic. From the time that 5-year-old Nono travels across Africa to the coast with only a herd of swift impalas for company, she is Superchild soaring over every blow of fate with unflinching resourcefulness and only occasional fleeting emotion. And even with minor characters: would *any* poor mother sell her children so casually?

Mrs. Bacon clearly wanted to show that the African child forced into slavery could be at least the natural equal of his American counterpart, that slavery could be kind, and that black people, too, could exploit their own. But her story is too thin: the themes obtrude. (p. 38)

> *Jacqueline Bernard, in* The New York Times Book Review *(© 1968 by The New York Times Company; reprinted by permission), October 20, 1968.*

Sophia "Pansy" Scrooby began life as the daughter of an African chieftain. . . . She is sold to a gentle Tory family who love and educate her; her high intelligence and musical talent blossom. In time, however, they are forced to sell her. From here on the plot is extremely contrived. Pansy goes through some wild adventures and ends up among the nobility in England, singing at Drury Lane theater. The author's style is lively and her purpose is noble: to show that an African sold into slavery and given the same advantages as an American child, would, of course, be the same. But the book is too thin and she does not succeed. (p. 288)

> *Laura Polla Scanlon, in* Commonweal *(copyright © 1968 Commonweal Publishing Co., Inc.; reprinted by permission of Commonweal Publishing Co., Inc.), November 22, 1968.*

Two hundred and twenty-seven pages would, on consideration, seem few enough in a book which takes our heroine to three continents, and in which even the journeys from one continent to the next supply adventures enough for many a novel, by a lesser writer. Full marks then, to Martha Bacon for making every word tell—and for convincing one reader at least, that, to mix a metaphor, the long arm of coincidence never sleeps. . . .

Sophia is, above all, a child of great natural dignity—a dignity so striking that it gives a charismatic quality to her character. (p. 92)

> *Margot Petts, in* Children's Book Review *(© 1971 by Five Owls Press Ltd.; all rights reserved), June, 1971.*

Sophia Scrooby Preserved, is [a] real novelty. . . . How does one classify this engaging book? It is almost history, certainly fiction; it presents an original glance at life (in three continents) during the 1770s; and the bright eye that looks belongs to a very young, very curious, and extremely intelligent African miss. *Candide* is a probable ancestor; so, very likely, is Shaw's *Black Girl in Search of God.*

Sophia herself (or Pansy, as she is usually called—a sailor on the slaveship gave her the name) starts life as a chieftain's daughter, much given to asking questions. She is even ready to query that her people are the sole inhabitants of the world; and a raid that leaves her the only survivor of the village shows her that she is right. She joins a herd of impala travelling north (a superb passage, this), reaches the coast, is sold to a Portuguese slave-trader, and starts a new phase of her education in a kind Connecticut household. . . .

The war, alas, reduces the Scroobys to penury. Pansy, still technically a slave, tastes swamps and jails and pirate vessels before she reaches London (Sheridan, Siddons, Reynolds) and makes, once again, her very individual mark. She has of course the charmed invulnerable quality of a creature in fairy tale.

And if the author doesn't maintain the promise of her first idea—the picaresque encroaches on the satirical more and more—she has produced one of the most stylish and exhilarating books of the season, agreeable to read, with ideas for readers to ponder over. (p. 766)

> The Times Literary Supplement *(© Times Newspapers Ltd., 1971; reproduced from* The Times Literary Supplement *by permission), July 2, 1971.*

As this story opens one feels almost prepared not to like it, but it develops a fascination and proves to be a most unusual tale. Martha Bacon, writer of adult novels and poetry, has chosen to write her first novel for children about a girl, born of high parentage in a tribe in Africa, who was sold to slavery when the tribe was decimated. She is transported in dreadful conditions to America, gaining the name of Pansy en route. Sold again to a kindly Tory family as companion to their daughter Prudence, she becomes Sophia Scrooby. Her intelligence and perseverance are remarkable, and need to be when the Scrooby family are dispossessed and she is sold again, escapes, and her adventures continue. The variety in scene is equalled by the variety in characters. The story is both well-written and constructed. It grips. (p. 233)

> The Junior Bookshelf, *August, 1971.*

OTHER CITATIONS

Zena Sutherland, in Saturday Review, *September 21, 1968, p. 37.*

The Booklist and Subscription Books Bulletin, *October 1, 1968, p. 183.*

Elaine Moss, in The School Librarian, *September, 1971, p. 255.*

THE THIRD ROAD (1971)

The Third Road is the path taken by three children and a

unicorn to an acutely realized world of the imagination that recalls classic English fantasies but is entered from a very modern California milieu where the children are visiting their grandmother, a red-haired actress who uses choir stalls for dining room chairs, is "never short of truffles, macadamia nuts, pickled mangoes, and other necessities," and serves the children wine at table. . . . Berkeley, Fox (the girl of the trio) and Casper meet the unicorn in their grandmother's paddock, and he transports them to a garden in a 17-century Spanish court. For a while Fox is left behind and an arrogant teen-aged cardinal returns to today with the boys. Other times and places are visited, including the fabled Hy Breasil, encountered in a sand castle of their own making, where the children view all history simultaneously, before they attend the closing pageant in which grandmother's recitation works its own magic in uniting the California past, the Spanish scenes visited via the Third Road, and the lives of the viewing children. This rather tenuous resolution might disconcert the literal minded, and the later time trips unfortunately lack the crystal clarity of the original Spanish adventure. But even here, firmly sketched Old World characters and concrete locations lend reality to otherwise wispy abstractions, and the light, sophisticated tone relieves and vitalizes the awesome timelessness of the children's experiences. Despite some unmarked later stretches, it's a *Road* worth travelling. (p. 943)

> *Kirkus Reviews (copyright © 1971 The Kirkus Service, Inc.), September 1, 1971.*

Martha Bacon . . . shifts children in and out of time and space. Her *Third Road* is the one True Thomas took in the ballad: it leads three children on the back of a unicorn to the court of the King of Spain where they meet the Infanta, her dwarf companions, and her spaniel. Don Diego Velasquez, the spaniel explains, has painted them, and so they are outside of time. Further journeys astride the unicorn take them on the Camino Real of Spain overseas, and to Hy Breasil; but round the corner all the time is their grandmother's house, on a beach in California. The two elements, now and then, the real food cooked by Granny and the magic plumed serpent snatched by a Spanish grandee, are held in one frame through the precise and pedantic voice of the narrator, twelve-year-old Berkeley Craven: "We are allowed wine at table with water in it. I don't like the taste very much but the idea pleases me." There are some nice word plays—"nothing but a fig-leaf of your imagination"—but the appeal of *The Third Road* is not limited to the sophisticated literary child, it is for all who know that their dreams are as "real" as their cornflakes. (p. 26)

> *Janet Adam Smith, in The New York Review of Books (reprinted with permission from The New York Review of Books; copyright © 1971 NYREV, Inc.), December 2, 1971.*

*   *   *

BAYLOR, Byrd   1924-
(also Byrd Baylor Schweitzer)

An American writer of poetry and fiction for adults and children, Byrd Baylor spent most of her childhood in Mexico and the southwestern United States. Her affection and respect for these lands and their people pervade many of her books.

BEFORE YOU CAME THIS WAY (1969)

"You ALMOST know how it must have been." Two natives of the Southwest—the author of *One Small Blue Bead* and the artist-researcher [Tom Bahti] of *Southwestern Indian Arts and Crafts*—have made the motifs of prehistoric Indian rock paintings into *dramatis personae* without destroying their totemic nature. . . . The motifs—birds and deer and skunk, tracks and stars, men and masked figures "no longer men"—are silhouetted against a rich, rough bark paper, light brown against dark, dark brown against light; the telling is terse, energetic, empathic; the layout lets the two react against each other. The book *communicates* —that which is long gone becomes immediate and vital. (p. 991)

> *Kirkus Reviews (copyright © 1969 The Kirkus Service, Inc.), September 15, 1969.*

"You walk down this canyon, this place of high red cliffs and turning winds and hawks floating in a far white sky and you wonder: 'Am I the first one ever to come this way?'" The entire book is infused with a sense of wonder and quiet reverence, a vivid imagining of what the majestic canyons held in the days when primitive men lived in the great rocks of the Southwest, and the land was abundant with wild things. *Before You Came This Way* is based on prehistoric Indian petroglyphs, and the illustrations [by Tom Bahti], in tones of brown on handmade bark paper, are in the rugged style of cave drawings. Evocative and poetic, a distinguished book. (p. 65)

> *Zena Sutherland, in Saturday Review (copyright © 1969 by Saturday Review, Inc.; reprinted with permission), November 8, 1969.*

It is difficult to say whether [*Before You Came This Way*] should be classified as poetry, art, or archaeology. Technically, it belongs in the third category, as the subject is prehistoric Indian cave drawings of the American Southwest. But this is not a "fact" book; indeed, the few facts contained in the text are so casually mentioned that they can be easily ignored. It is rather a work that treats the drawings for what they are—the emotional expressions of a non-literate people. Both the artist and the author interpret these drawings freely; he with his original (though primitive) illustrations on bark paper; she with her perceptive but subjective comments: "The pictures are dim now, half shadow, but you search the canyon for them. And here you see young hunters leap in the morning sun. The light still gleams on their arrows." It is seldom that children are exposed to such a poignant commentary on any unfamiliar culture, past or present. The light will gleam in their eyes long after an exposure to this book. (p. 39)

> *Euple L. Wilson in School Library Journal (reprinted from the December, 1969, issue of School Library Journal, published by R. R. Bowker Company, a Xerox company; copyright © 1969 by Xerox Corporation), December, 1969.*

Children who are fond of outlining their hands in pencil, leaving footprints in wet sand or scratching stick drawings in the dirt, should enjoy this poetically stylized introduction to prehistory. The sepia woodcuts suggest what life might have been like for the prehistoric nomadic Indians of the Southwest who carved a record of their lives in stones on canyon walls. Here are enigmatic handprints and foot-prints, listening rabbits, leaping deer. A coyote howls at the moon—sharing the past with the men who hunted beside him. Simply, with great economy of line and color, this book totally succeeds in portraying the two dimensions of time in which men live. The first dimension, slow, linear historical time, separates us forever from our past. The second, the time of art, lies in the eternal present. Freezing the events of the moment, art closes the gap to bring us face to face with the minds and hearts of those people of long ago. (p. 19)

> *Gloria Levitas, in* The New York Times Book Review *(© 1969 by The New York Times Company; reprinted by permission), December 28, 1969.*

OTHER CITATIONS

The Booklist, *January 15, 1970, pp. 618, 620.*

Sidney D. Long, in The Horn Book Magazine, *February, 1970, p. 50.*

Mary Ann Wentroth, in Top of the News, *April, 1970, p. 307.*

COYOTE CRY (1972)

Among the many coyote cries that Antonio and his grand-father hear as they guard their sheep is one that sounds different, and strange. This proves to be the call of a female coyote who has lost her own puppies, and steals one from their sheep dog, not to eat but to adopt. Antonio, trained to regard the coyote as an enemy, is moved by the revelation of the maternal instinct of the predator.

This story is simply told, and shows plainly the contrast between the harsh judgments of the boy and the more temperate opinions of the grandfather. Both the characters and the animals are portrayed [by Symeon Shimin] in attractive naturalistic pictures, tinted with a light colour wash.

I should have liked confirmation of my guess that the setting of the book is Mexico and, far more important, some indication of whether a coyote would actually behave in this apparently unnatural manner. (pp. 246-47)

> The Junior Bookshelf, *August, 1973.*

[*Coyote Cry* is a] beautifully told and excellently illustrated story of a young boy's growth of understanding of the mothering instinct in the wild, as well as domestic animals. This is a picture story book . . . written with an economy of language and without sentimentality. (p. 1128)

> The Times Literary Supplement *(© Times Newspapers Ltd., 1973; reproduced from* The Times Literary Supplement *by permission), September 28, 1973.*

OTHER CITATIONS

Virginia Haviland, in The Horn Book Magazine, *June, 1972, pp. 263-64.*

THE DESERT IS THEIRS (1975)

Baylor's spare lyricism recreates the intimate relationship between Desert People and their land [in *The Desert Is Theirs*]. The message is kinship with the environment and all living things ("Papagos try not to anger their animal brothers. . . . They say, 'We share . . . we only share'"), and [Peter] Parnall's delicate line drawings, layered like sand paintings with bright color, reverberate with peace and harmony. Ready and waiting for that special, receptive moment. (p. 1059)

> Kirkus Reviews *(copyright © 1975 The Kirkus Service, Inc.), September 15, 1975.*

Emphatic, crisp, and uncompromising, Baylor tells us about the desert [in *The Desert Is Theirs*], describing selected flora and fauna, and respectfully paying tribute to the Desert People who know its secrets and would live nowhere else. Her prose poem sits amidst Parnall's encompassing scenarios, which have a mythic, even delicately surreal quality about them, and which are given bold form by dramatic swaths of brittle color. A striking mood piece. (pp. 511-12)

> The Booklist *(reprinted by permission of the American Library Association; copyright 1975 by the American Library Association), December 1, 1975.*

Peter Parnall's first book in full color may draw mixed reactions from his admirers; the composition and line of his work are no less spare, and the colors are clean hues used with restraint, but they do focus attention on themselves. The text is, like that of other Baylor books, a prose poem of lyric simplicity; it is infrequently marred slightly by attributions of purposiveness that add a note of anthropomorphism . . . but the whole is a graceful, stately tribute to the "strong brown Desert People" whose gentle courtesy toward the other life-forms of the desert, whose love and understanding for the land they occupy, and whose nature myths contribute to a harmonious way of life. (p. 74)

> *Zena Sutherland, in* Bulletin of the Center for Children's Books *(© 1976 by the University of Chicago; all rights reserved), January, 1976.*

Focusing on the theme that "[t]he desert gives what it can to each of its children," author and illustrator have brilliantly integrated myth, folklore, and factual description into a coherent whole. Each concept—from the introduction of the spare, harshly beautiful setting to the celebration in honor of the rain—subtly reinforces and extends the others so that a total way of life is presented, involving the reader as participant rather than as observer. The poetic text is simple, direct, and concrete, yet imbued with a sense of the transcendent forces which bind together the aspects of a culture. This blending of reality and mysticism is given visual expression in the illustrations, which combine meticulous drawing of animals, people, and plants with abstract impressions in color of sky, stone, and sand. The unique, multidimensional presentation is eloquent, profound, and totally absorbing. (p. 39)

> *Mary M. Burns, in* The Horn Book Magazine *(copyright © 1976 by the Horn Book, Inc., Boston), February, 1976.*

OTHER CITATIONS

Ruth M. McConnell, in School Library Journal, *February, 1976, p. 36.*

Barbara Dill, in Wilson Library Bulletin, *February, 1976, p. 485.*

Publishers Weekly, *October, 1976, pp. 86-7.*

EVERYBODY NEEDS A ROCK (1974)

The clean, crisp sparseness of [Peter] Parnall's semi-abstract drawings almost disguises the unbecomingly arch tone, reinforced by the "poetic" word arrangement, of Baylor's ten rules for finding "a / special / rock / that you find / yourself / and keep / and (sic) long as / you can—/ maybe forever." And given the validity of the basic observation—if not everybody, then at least many children will recognize the satisfaction of carrying around a rock that feels "easy in your hand" and "jumpy in your pocket when you run"—most will overlook such coy pseudoadvice as "The worst thing you can do is go rock hunting when you are worried" and "A rock as big as an apple is too big. A rock as big as a horse is MUCH too big." An attractive novelty, with a thin vein of truth. (p. 797)

> Kirkus Reviews *(copyright © 1974 The Kirkus Service, Inc.), August 1, 1974.*

The text [of *Everybody Needs a Rock*], written with the lilt and imagery of poetry, is part of the total design of the book—a design that includes beautiful black and white line drawings [by Peter Parnall], highlighted by touches of earthy browns and ocher. The illustrations move away from the literal to capture the essence of each part of this important mission—finding a personal touchstone. All ages will respond to this example of bookmaking at its best. (p. 110)

> *Amy Kellman, in* Teacher *(excerpted from the January issue of* Teacher *magazine with permission of the publisher; © 1974 by Macmillan Professional Magazines, Inc.; all rights reserved), January, 1975.*

Nobody else can ever know what is special about another person's rock, but for the owner it is perfect: just the right shape to fit the hand, just the right size and color and smell. Byrd Baylor gives the rules for finding your rock, and in a fluid, chanting text speaks of the comfort and pleasure of having a perfect rock to touch and hold. Her stripped, clean text is matched in quality and grace by Parnall's pictures—black, white, and earth browns—which have the same flowing line and restraint of composition. (p. 105)

> *Zena Sutherland, in* Bulletin of the Center for Children's Books *(© 1975 by the University of Chicago; all rights reserved), March, 1975.*

OTHER CITATIONS

Publishers Weekly, *July 29, 1974, p. 58.*

The Booklist, *September 1, 1974, p. 38.*

Virginia Reese, in School Library Journal, *December, 1974, p. 35.*

HAWK, I'M YOUR BROTHER (1976)

This is a beautiful book which reveals the values of a Third World culture in a profoundly positive way....

The setting is the Southwest, and the characters appear to be Native American or possibly Chicano (in the Southwest, Native Americans often have Spanish names like Soto [the main character in *Hawk, I'm Your Brother* is Rudy Soto] and much of Chicano culture is similar to Native American). The lack of specific identification seems intentional. The author is not interested in the "quaintness" or "color" of Native American or Chicano people but in their view of life. Instead of emphasizing dress, food or other surface aspects of culture, she focuses on values. And although the characters wear ordinary, "white" clothes and speak "regular" English, they have a profoundly Third World cultural outlook.

The oneness between human beings and nature is the core concept of the book. Unlike many animal stories for children, this book does not assign human qualities to animals or recreate a human world in animal form. The latter approach (the Walt Disney Syndrome) reflects a common attitude toward nature in U.S. society: Nature exists to be exploited—either ravaged for profit or petted for human pleasure.

Rudy's selfishness in confining the hawk is gently but firmly rejected. The message is: no one can be truly free if others are not free, and we attain our own freedom by allowing others to be free. Thus, in an uncontrived way, individualism is put down. Rudy's feelings are treated with respect, patience and a touch of mystery—it is no accident that a book which does not exploit or distort animals also does not exploit or distort children.

The theme of unity between people and nature is expressed in [Peter Parnall's] illustrations. They are full of circular patterns which, on the one hand, capture the glorious sweep of a hawk in flight and, on the other, interrelate sky and human beings. *Hawk, I'm Your Brother* should be excellent for Native American or Chicano children and should foster respect for these cultures in other children. A minor complaint: in some pictures, Rudy's features are not as sharply defined as they might be. (p. 15)

> *Elizabeth Martinez, in* Interracial Books for Children Bulletin *(reprinted by permission of Interracial Books for Children Bulletin, 1841 Broadway, New York, N.Y. 10023), Vol. 7, No. 6, 1976.*

OTHER CITATIONS

Kirkus Reviews, *May 15, 1976, p. 587.*

THE MAN WHO TALKED TO A TREE (1968)

Enormously sensitive lines, skillfully reproduced texture and shadow, grace a poeticized telling which will speak to very few. A stranger appears to talk to the boys' tree, then slowly repeats what the tree has said—about the land before people arrived, how a single seed grew, how Matt knew this was the place and sought the right tree for the right seed.... There was a boy named Jim who climbs a mountain during a drought to bring water. "But all that / Happened / Long ago...." As proof the stranger suggests the boys look, and they do find what Jim secreted in the tree: an arrowhead, a white seashell, a rock flecked with golden sand. The stranger departs: the boys examine: "'Maybe *he* was that boy once / Long ago.' / But the tree doesn't say. / It just waves / In that friendly tree way." The boys sprawl, fidget, hang all over the tree, a tree that would be a fine refuge from the hot desert sun, but the romanticizing is overbearing, especially in such an extended text and the peach and blue coloring [of Symeon Shimin's illustrations] becomes monotonous. (p. 594)

> Kirkus Service *(copyright © 1968, The Kirkus Service, Inc.), June 1, 1968.*

It's impossible for me to talk about this rare book without raising my voice. I was so impressed with another rare book Mrs. Schweitzer and Mr. Shimin created, "One Small Blue Bead" . . ., that I was afraid they couldn't do it again. It's with great joy that I report that they could and they did —with *this* rare book—a poetic remembrance that a tree evokes for an old man, a remembrance the old man shares with the small boys who perch in its branches. (p. 55)

> *Lavinia Russ, in* Publishers Weekly *(reprinted from the July 1, 1968, issue of* Publishers Weekly *by permission of the critic, published by R. R. Bowker Company, a Xerox company; copyright © 1968 by Xerox Corporation), July 1, 1968.*

OTHER CITATIONS

Polly Goodwin, in Book World, *September 8, 1968, p. 24.*

ONE SMALL BLUE BEAD (1965)

Story and arresting illustrations convey the dual theme—of the oneness of man and his resistance to new ideas even in ancient times, as understood by a prehistoric Indian boy. The small blue bead is a symbol of brotherhood that is passed from one young Indian to another. Unfortunately, the singsong poetry form of the text seems at variance with the rather somber and mystical tone of the illustrations. Such wisdom as displayed by the Indian boy seems pompous and unnatural in one so young. [*One Small Blue Bead* is a] good idea not quite consummated. (p. 59)

> *June Barker, in* School Library Journal *(reprinted from the November, 1965, issue of* School Library Journal, *published by R. R. Bowker Company, a Xerox company; copyright © 1965 by Xerox Corporation), November, 1965.*

Terribly poetic in intent, [*One Small Blue Bead*] is something less in execution—it works too hard at its message and too weakly at its verse. Like many suppositions about prehistoric peoples it caters shamelessly for modern tastes and like many picture books this is as shameless in pandering to children's self-importance. In staggering verse it conjures up a nameless Boy, hitherto lazy, who offers to do the work of the only elder of the tribe who believes other men may exist and who sets out to find proof. And when the people of the tribe are ready to cast their spears at two strangers it is the Boy who bids them to lay down their weapons and who recognises the returning elder, who brings a boy with the blue bead back as proof that their Boy is not the only one in the world. Needless to say the bead is given to the Boy and the reader is reminded he might be the one to find it today. Symeon Shimin's carefully rendered drawings underline the feeling that this is a picture book

one is supposed to read in hushed, reverent tones. It is easy to see why people make such books, less easy to guess why they expect children to like them—like the Sunday School tracts of the last century they are made by earnest people who honestly believe in what they say but seem to have forgotten how it feels to be a child. (pp. 238-39)

> The Junior Bookshelf, *August, 1967.*

OTHER CITATIONS

Ethna Sheehan, in America, *November 20, 1965, p. 638.*

May Hill Arbuthnot and Zena Sutherland, in their Children and Books, *fourth edition, Scott, Foresman, 1972, p. 495.*

PLINK, PLINK, PLINK (1971)

All sorts of night sounds—from "plink," "sliggle" and "swush" to "ka-trum, ka-trum, ka-trun"—are presented here as an imaginative child fantasizes about various creatures who lurk in the darkness of his room and the activity which might cause the noises. Of course, in the morning the child discovers that nothing at all has happened. Pen-and-ink sketches with gray-washed colors [by James Marshall] give the shadowy feeling of night and, like the rhymes, convey a light, humorous mood and add a dimension to the text. As a read-aloud, a noise or two at a time, this will be fun and perhaps helpful to the worried child. However, taken as a whole, the book will not sustain the interest level of the intended age group, and an unfortunate switch from third person to first is likely to confuse. A more comforting and realistic approach to the going-to-bed syndrome is taken by [LaVerne] Johnson in *Night Noises*. . ., while [Russell] Hoban's *Bedtime for Frances* . . . is still the funniest and most natural story on the subject. (p. 112)

> *Shirley Wayland, in* School Library Journal *(reprinted from the September, 1972, issue of* School Library Journal, *published by R. R. Bowker Company, a Xerox company; copyright © 1972 by Xerox Corporation), September, 1972.*

OTHER CITATIONS

Kirkus Reviews, *September 1, 1971, p. 933.*

Lisa Hammel, in The New York Times Book Review, *January 23, 1972, p. 8.*

Ethel L. Heins, in The Horn Book Magazine, *April, 1972, pp. 134-35.*

SOMETIMES I DANCE MOUNTAINS (1973)

Byrd Baylor has made prehistoric paintings come alive and . . . *Clay Sing* . . . but she has less success in communicating her own "private experience" of the "deep natural primitive impulse" of dance. Baylor's drive to become water, bubbles, bugs, or frogs, "all things that are OPEN, things that are CLOSED," "a hundred happy feelings loose" and "sorrows that you could never say in words" is interpreted by a graceful, attractive child dancer who floats across white pages adorned [by Ken Longtemps] with wispy painted curlicues. Children, especially other young dancers, will enjoy seeing Nancy Davis' fluid form and free, expressive postures, but though we're duly convinced that "a dance can say anything" it's unfortunately true that creativity loses much of its kick when made into a spectator sport. (p. 1151)

> Kirkus Reviews *(copyright © 1973 The Kirkus Service, Inc.), October 15, 1973.*

A once-removed quality weakens this book's effectiveness. The author tries to translate one art form into another, to express in writing the wonderful release and satisfaction a dancer feels. But the text is unconvincing. . . . The illustrations [by Bill Sears (photographs) and Ken Longtemps (drawings)] are innovative in combining photography and sweeping design. (p. 40)

> *Jean F. Mercier, in* Publishers Weekly *(reprinted from the December 3, 1973, issue of* Publishers Weekly *by permission of the critic, published by R. R. Bowker Company, a Xerox company; copyright © 1973 by Xerox Corporation), December 3, 1973.*

OTHER CITATIONS

Ethel R. Hardee, in School Library Journal, *January, 1974, p. 37.*

THEY PUT ON MASKS (1974)

Indian and Eskimo masks and the ceremonies they are used in are a natural subject for Byrd Baylor and from the start she makes us feel their power and magic: "They made their masks of / wood / and deerskin / and seashells / and cornhusks / and horsehair / and bones. // Yes, / and they made them of / magic / and dreams / and the oldest dark secrets / of life." . . . Unfortunately Jerry Ingram's flat illustrations of three to five masks per double page echo none of the magic. Resembling cutouts from cereal boxes, they float against a wave-shaped background on two-tone pages— some green or yellow, some baby blue, some (inexplicably) even pink or mauve—that recall merchandising displays more than they do the dreams and prayers and things of the earth that Byrd Baylor evokes in her lyrical text that is almost a chant. Of course the fact that Jerry Ingram is not Tom Bahti (who illustrated Baylor's *Before You Came This Way*, . . . and *When Clay Sings*...), though regrettable, does not disqualify the whole, and *They Put On Masks* remains a valuable first look at an impressive subject. (p. 428)

> Kirkus Reviews *(copyright © 1974 The Kirkus Service, Inc.), April 15, 1974.*

[*They Put on Masks* is comprised of color-filled] pages of ceremonial Indian masks pictured with verse that is both informative and evocative. Baylor tells of the uses and meanings of masks . . . through quiet, rambling verse which calls up that sense of power and mystery given to the masks by their makers. Some of the spiritual concepts may be hard to grasp. . . . However, much feeling and information of importance is communicated in the effective illustrations [by Jerry Ingram] and poetic dramatizations. (p. 1102)

> The Booklist *(reprinted by permission of the American Library Association; copyright 1974 by the American Library Association), June 1, 1974.*

OTHER CITATIONS

Karen Brown, in School Library Journal, *September, 1974, p. 53.*

Zena Sutherland, in Bulletin of the Center for Children's Books, *October, 1974, p. 22.*

Georgess McHargue, in American Libraries, *March, 1975, p. 166.*

WHEN CLAY SINGS (1972)

As in *Before You Came This Way* by Baylor and [Tom] Bahti . . . this is a lyrical treatment of archaeology and the art of Indians of the Southwest. Great immediacy is lent by the reflections on the pre-historic people who might have used these fragments and by the parallels of thought and feeling drawn between then and now. Bahti has filled the pages with evocative pen-and-ink line drawings representing the primitive figures and designs found on the pottery; these have been arranged against a background collage of subtle brown, sienna and beige. The striking effect of the illustrations is matched by Baylor's word images concerning how some pieces were used, how others were made—"Once somebody sitting on the ground outside a high cold cliffhouse thought: 'I'll make this bowl as pretty as I can.'" *When Clay Sings* echoes with it's own eloquent tune. (p. 62)

> *Alice Miller, in* School Library Journal *(reprinted from the May, 1972, issue of* School Library Journal, *published by R. R. Bowker Company, a Xerox company; copyright © 1972 by Xerox Corporation), May, 1972.*

To some eyes, a potsherd would go unnoticed, but to the Indian, "Every piece of clay is a piece of someone's life. They even say it has its own small voice and sings in its own way." And so the author brings the lore of the ancient Indians and pottery to the attention of today's children.

As a means of introducing children to the craft of ceramics and pottery, this book is unique in its excellence. Beautifully written, and illustrated throughout with motifs and fragments of the old pottery in sepia and earth tones on beige and black, the book is not only a lyrical praise of the ancient craft of pottery making, but a beautiful object itself. (p. 176)

> *Michael and Rosemary Teres, in* Instructor *(copyright © 1972 by The Instructor Publications, Inc.), August-September, 1972.*

Across the earth-toned pages the poetic and evocative brief text runs, along with a hundred drawings in bold outline, the designs all derived from prehistoric pottery of the American Southwest, from the Anasazi, Mogollon, Hohokam and Mimbres cultures. Leaping fish, strong bowmen, whirlwinds, jumpy bugs, rabbits and flute players—all are presented as the artful women drew them long ago, the women who "must have spoken to the earth as they took its clay." "Sometimes children may have said (but in that other language): 'Mama, make a bowl with pictures of big animals for me.'" "Indians who find this pottery today say that everything has its own spirit—even a broken pot. They say the clay remembers the lands that made it. Does it remember the cornfields too? And the summer rains?" This is a beautiful book. . . . Its pages will recall to many young readers over many years to come their gifted artist, whose untimely death this year we note here in sadness. (p. 120)

> *Philip and Phylis Morrison, in* Scientific American *(copyright © 1972 by Scientific American, Inc., all rights reserved), December, 1972.*

When Clay Sings by Byrd Baylor, illustrated by Tom Bahti, . . . uses a marvelous variety of designs taken from prehistoric Indian pottery of the American Southwest. Both words and pictures treat this book's subject matter with intelligence and respect. There is, however, an overly muted quality to the drawing, palette, and design, which becomes repetitive and defeats the wealth and drama of the material by casting a shadow of similarity over it. (p. 86)

> *Karla Kuskin, in* Saturday Review *(copyright © 1973 by Saturday Review, Inc.; reprinted with permission), April 14, 1973.*

OTHER CITATIONS

Beryl Robinson, in The Horn Book Magazine, *August, 1972, p. 382.*

Pat Timberlake, in Childhood Education, *November, 1972, p. 86.*

Alan Cheuse, in The New York Times Book Review, *November 5, 1972, pp. 7, 20.*

Mary Ann Wentroth, in Top of the News, *January, 1973, p. 167.*

*   *   *

BETHANCOURT, T(homas) Ernesto 1932-

T. Ernesto Bethancourt is an American writer of Hispanic descent. Besides being an author of books for children, Bethancourt is also a musician, songwriter, and performer who uses the professional name of Tom Paisley. He has previously been employed as a child actor, farm worker, music critic, and ice cream man. He describes himself as the hero of *New York City Too Far from Tampa Blues*, a novel which was written for his first daughter. (See also *Contemporary Authors*, Vols. 61-64 and *Something About the Author*, Vol. 11.)

THE DOG DAYS OF ARTHUR CANE (1976)

The lessons (in tolerance, etc.) that Arthur learns [in *The Dog Days of Arthur Cane*] are so obvious from the start as to be dismissible, and day by day his tribulations are more reminiscent of a run-of-the-alley dog story (and, where his blind friend comes in, a sentimental one at that) than they are of Gregor Samson's dilemma [in Franz Kafka's *The Metamorphosis*]; certainly there's not the vitality here that the author brought to *New York City Too Far From Tampa Blues*. . . . But there is some distressful humor in Arthur's first recognition of his plight, and throughout, his human reactions give the adventure a slightly wiggy twist. (p. 848)

> Kirkus Reviews *(copyright © 1976 The Kirkus Service, Inc.), August 1, 1976.*

With an ingenious combination of realism and imagination, Ernesto Bethancourt has changed Arthur Cane . . . into a mongrel dog and then put him through the process of learning about the world beyond Manorsville, Long Island. *The Dog Days of Arthur Cane* . . . is full of humor and pathos. This is a sensitive, contemporary story which develops the theme of true friendship. (p. 3)

> The Babbling Bookworm, *November, 1976.*

Reading the dust cover of this book and finding out that it was about a wealthy teenage kid who mysteriously turns into a dog, I said, "Aw, come on!" Skeptical, I put the book aside. But I picked it up a few days later, and it wasn't long before I was hooked.

T. Ernesto Bethancourt (I didn't think that was his real name), otherwise known as singer-guitarist Tom Paisley, has an easy, laid-back, wryly humorous style that's infused with truth and insight.

Arthur Cane's exploits as a mongrel dog find him threatened by his dog Bert in his own home, pursued by the dog catcher, and abused by almost everyone until he settles in Greenwich Village as the seeing eye dog of a young, blind street minstrel. He is saved from a wretched demise in a dog pound gas chamber in a predictable way, but predictable doesn't mean boring. The book is never boring. From the descriptions of how human mentality adjusts to four-legged performance of bodily functions to the discovery that dogs do have feelings, every page comes off as perfectly plausible.

I have this eerie feeling that Bethancourt/Paisley somehow got inside the mind of a dog for a period of time. As for me, I've developed a new sensitivity for my canine friends. (p. 47)

> *Barbara Karlin, in* West Coast Review of Books *(copyright 1976 by Rapport Publishing Co., Inc.), Vol. 2, No. 6 (November, 1976).*

[*The Dog Days of Arthur Cane* is a] first person narrative, in a somewhat brash, outspoken style, about`. . . a Long Island high school boy who found, one morning, that he had turned into a dog. . . . His transformation back to human form is gratefully accepted by the reader, who is willing to welcome any narrative device to save the dog/boy from the gas chamber. Arthur became a sadder and wiser teenager—no closer than before, however, to his conventional suburban parents. (pp. 157-58)

> *Paul Heins, in* The Horn Book Magazine *(copyright © 1977 by the Horn Book, Inc., Boston), April, 1977.*

OTHER CITATIONS

Barbara R. McCoy, in Children's Book Review Service, *September, 1976, p. 6.*

Melinda Schroeder, in School Library Journal, *January, 1977, p. 99.*

THE MORTAL INSTRUMENTS (1977)

In this sophisticated, superbly crafted SF thriller, Bethancourt has moved into a new genre. Mature teenagers *and* discriminating adults will be mesmerized, baffled and chilled by Eddie Rodriguez, a Harlem *barrio* gang leader, who suddenly changes inexplicably in appearance and intellect. (p. 83)

Sybil Steinberg, in Publishers Weekly *(reprinted from the February 14, 1977, issue of* Publishers Weekly *by permission of the critic, published by R. R. Bowker Company, a Xerox company; copyright © 1977 by Xerox Corporation), February 14, 1977.*

Composed of short clips—transcripts, memos, the thoughts of agents and others on the case—this is a staccato sci-fi thriller in the form of a federal investigation. The subject is one Eddie Rodriguez, a nineteen-year-old genius from Spanish Harlem who has gained control of the world money markets, and then disappeared. Eddie's dead body is found, but the being from the future who, we learn, has occupied it is still very much in business. Eventually he/it/Eddie takes up residence not in a human body but in ODIN, the government's top secret central computer through which he plans to run the world. The investigators' style is semi-tough ("All I had to do was explain to the President how I had turned over control of the western world to an insane Puerto Rican slum kid who thought he was God"), the mechanics of the plot and of Eddie's possession are ingenious yet easily accessible, and the whole is a proficient simulation of a popular adult form, subtly trimmed to junior proportions. (p. 289)

Kirkus Reviews *(copyright © 1977 The Kirkus Service, Inc.), March 15, 1977.*

[*The Mortal Instruments*] is can't-put-down reading. A rich combination of detective thriller and supernatural tale, this fast-paced novel for young adults offers much food for thought. Any reader who has ever given any thought to the question of ESP, telepathy, or occult science in general, and many who have not, will find this fascinating reading. (p. 88)

Nikki Grimes, in Children's Book Review Service Inc. *(copyright © 1977 Children's Book Review Service Inc.), April, 1977.*

The whereabouts of Eduardo Rodriguez, a nineteen-year-old Puerto Rican from the barrio in New York, are a subject of great interest to the Secret Service of the United States government. Eddie has become a sort of superman; starting from an unpromising beginning, Eddie led his street gang, the Barons, to become a political power, astonished his professors at the university with his utter brilliance, and made an enormous fortune on the international money market, apparently by prior and unerring knowledge of what the rates of exchange were going to be. Eddie finally no longer needs a human body and attempts to rule the world from a gigantic government computer near Washington. The twists and turns of the bizarre plot are cleverly detailed from many points of view—of the various agents covering the case, of Eddie's sister and his friend Rafael, and especially of Dr. Myra Sokolow, the psychoanalyst, who knows Eddie best. There are adroit references to the recent political scene and some wry humor. A fitting climax ends the breakneck pace of an unusual book of science fiction, and the denouement leaves the question of the future still hanging. (pp. 448-49)

Ann A. Flowers in The Horn Book Magazine *(copyright © 1977 by the Horn Book, Inc., Boston), August, 1977.*

OTHER CITATIONS

Zena Sutherland, in Bulletin of the Center for Children's Books, *September, 1977, p. 5.*

NEW YORK CITY TOO FAR FROM TAMPA BLUES (1975)

Like Tom in the novel, the author is a half-Hispanic singer-guitarist (known as Tom Paisley) who grew up in Brooklyn and Florida, and the whole book is a loose, funny, nonstop rap, mixing past and present verb tense with seeming obliviousness, that makes you feel you're listening to his spontaneous recollections. . . . When Tom battles a scrappy little "trashmouth" Italian kid for a shoeshine spot, the two end up not only best friends but "the Griffin brothers," singing in Irish bars on Sunday afternoon, making a hit at the eighth grade commencement exercises, and even cutting a record of the song they wrote—the "New York City Too Far From Tampa Blues." About Aurelio Tom says "I just can't write down what he really talks like. If I did I'd catch hell," and in the same spirit as the blanks in Aurelio's speech are all those observed street phenomena (like the chicks coming up and saying hello to his older friends on Eighth Avenue) that he claims not to understand. But granting Bethancourt's cautious approach to writing for YA's, it's more authentic to leave blanks than to pretend the kids used milder epithets, and in any case there's never a doubt that Tom was right there in the midst of it—Brooklyn street life, Spanish-American family life, New York public miseducation, rock recording, whatever was going down. (pp. 464-65)

Kirkus Reviews *(copyright © 1975 The Kirkus Service, Inc.), April 15, 1975.*

["New York City Too Far from Tampa Blues" is bitingly] real, joyously satisfying. Characters—from Tom's sour but adored father to Aurelio's older brother who helps the boys with their music—are drawn with a deft touch. The social comments are wry but similarly soft-pedaled. Far from implying that success like Tom and Aurelio's is easily had, the author (also a musician) makes it plain how hard they had to work. He makes it clear that love, nerve and discipline are required to get where they hope to arrive, and that they are as thrilled as readers will be when they make it. (p. 45)

Jean F. Mercier, in Publishers Weekly *(reprinted from the April 28, 1975, issue of* Publishers Weekly *by permission of the critic, published by R. R. Bowker Company, a Xerox company; copyright © 1975 by Xerox Corporation), April 28, 1975.*

[*New York City Too Far from Tampa Blues* is] a skillfully written, consistently irreverent commentary about life in the tenements and on the streets of the city. However, halfway through the story the nicely developed realistic mood is short circuited when Tom teams up with an Italian friend, Aurelio, to become the Griffin brothers, a singing Irish duo. Their incredibly instantaneous success . . . dominates the second half of the book. Pancho, Tom's proud and bullheaded father, is well drawn, but the many minor characters including Jewish store owners, a prejudiced policeman, and a Black street gang are stereotypes. While certain sections of this novel are insightful and entertaining, the author is as quick to categorize other groups as he is to show concern for his Hispanic central character. (p. 117)

John F. Caviston, in School Library Journal *(reprinted from the September, 1975, issue of* School Library Journal, *published by R. R. Bowker Co., a Xerox company; copyright © 1975 by Xerox Corporation), September, 1975.*

Horatio Alger is alive and well and living in Tampa, Florida. Twelve-year-old, guitar-playing Tom lives in poverty in Tampa, Florida, with his "Spanish" father, Pancho, his Anglo mother and his three sisters. "Macho" Pancho rules his brood with an iron hand and profane mouth. But notwithstanding his authoritarianism and penchant for taking the strap to his children, everyone loves Pancho. When Pancho decides (unilaterally, of course) to move the family to Brooklyn, where his relatives have found him a truck-driving job, Tom's adventures begin.

Tough youth gangs, nasty cops and sundry other slum-look "staples" parade through the pages. Tom survives all of the action, combining his wits and musical talents with those of an Italian shoe-shine boy to earn some money. . . .

Although Tom's father and numerous relatives were born and raised in Puerto Rico, they never refer to themselves as anything but "Spanish." One can only conclude that the author, described on the book jacket as the son of an Hispanic father, must have identity problems. His general mind-set is exemplified by the following:

"My Dad was an ice man when we lived in Tampa. It's a great job. You get to carry an ice pick in a holster on your belt, like Matt Dillon."

"And it don't matter what Mom thinks, because she goes along with Dad, no matter what he says."

"Well, that where Pancho is very Spanish, Tom. He feels that he's the big dog over in your yard. And when he barks, you jump. He don't figure he has to explain nothin to his own kids."

"Driving with Pancho is a lot of fun. It's like you at war with everybody else on the road."

"I never knew what Uncle Jack thought was so funny when he said Spanish people wear pointy shoes for killing cockroaches in corners. It's true. . . ."

Pancho dearly loves his only son, holds two jobs, and works very hard. He is also very proud—which means that when he goes on strike, the author describes the strike in two paragraphs and devotes pages to Pancho's resistance to welfare and food stamps.

Stereotypes abound. The three sisters, like Mom, have no personality, cry a lot and seem inept. A virago of a grandmother and an Irish prostitute have hearts of gold. So does a little Italian mother who says, "Girls are a pleasure, next to boys. I always wanted a girl. Instead, I ended up with this bunch of Indians and troublemakers." The author also stereotypes Jews with regard to money and the Irish vis-à-vis liquor, so Native Americans, women and "Spanish" people should not feel they have been discriminated against.

Escapism is evident, as well. Although Tom shares the money he earns from singing with his family, his musical

flight from poverty is the stuff of which dreams are made for Third World boys and girls in our urban ghettos and *barrios*. The story does have humor, and some cultural validity, but overall, it is a negative experience which fails to provide role models and reinforces the worst kinds of stereotypes. (p. 17)

Carmen D. Figueroa, in Interrracial Books for Children Bulletin *(reprinted by permission of* Interracial Books for Children Bulletin, *1841 Broadway, New York, N.Y. 10023), Vol. 7, No. 1, 1976.*

OTHER CITATIONS

The Booklist, *May 15, 1975, p. 963.*

*   *   *

BLAND, Edith
See NESBIT, E.

*   *   *

BOSTON, L(ucy) M(aria)   1892-

One of the most singular events in the life of English author Lucy Boston was her purchase, in 1939, of the Manor at Hemingford Grey. Boston's restoration of this twelfth-century home, and her appreciation of its great mysteries and the depth of its past, inspired the writing of two books: *Yew Hall*, an adult novel, and the first of her Green Knowe series, *The Children of Green Knowe*. Thus, when she was past sixty, she became a writer of fiction and drama for adults and children. As a child, Boston was raised by strict Victorian parents. It was not until she moved to the country at the age of eleven that she was able to abandon herself to a sensuous love of nature. Both influences are reflected in her work for children. Most of Boston's titles are illustrated by her son, Peter —an architect and the prototype for Tolly of the Green Knowe stories. *A Stranger at Green Knowe* was awarded the Carnegie Medal in 1961, and *The Children of Green Knowe* won the Lewis Carroll Shelf Award in 1969. Boston has also written an autobiography, *Memory in a House*, which was published in 1973.

AUTHOR'S COMMENTARY

Green Knowe, the house which is the underlying symbol in all my books, is where I live. . . .

I get lyrical about it. I think of it as a miracle, and nobody ever felt that they owned a miracle, so I must be acquitted of boasting. It is so old and so easily contemporary that to succeed in reconciling these two ideas is to go up in the air. One is bewitched from that moment.

I am not a historian. You would laugh if you knew the feebleness and anxiety of my research into such periods of history as I put in the books. It is not the affixing of serial numbers to years, months, and days that fascinates me; it is the total loss of that fragmentation of time. (p. 216)

Of course, when I am writing, I lie freely. It is allowed in the rules of the game. I put back at will what has ceased to exist or sweep away what has recently come. I even bring in what is somewhere else. St Christopher, for instance, is actually in Cheshire, where my son was a child. . . . (p. 218)

To all children, and particularly to small children, a love of the past is natural. It is the soil at their roots. They have but recently emerged from the stuff of it. It gives them comfort, security, and a pattern.

Of course, rising adults of fifteen and upwards are bursting out at all the seams and want to throw away everything that has been handed down to them. That is as it should be. But the young of today are suffering less from growing pains than from a racial wound. A generation that invented and used the atom bomb deserves the contempt of its heirs even while they invent more and worse. If, looking at the world they were born into, they see the evolution of man and all the sufferings of individuals from the Ice Age until now as ending in the lunacy of hydrogen bombs all round, what value is there for them in past, present, or future? For time has all its values indivisible.

These young people have passed beyond children's libraries, but I believe their ideas and feelings seep down through the age groups more than grown-ups remember. To every child the brother and sister two removes older is an oracle who lets in truth from outside, beyond the careful screening of the parents, if modern parents screen at all.

I think the present pessimism explains why all my child heroes, and one animal hero too (always considered by me as within the hierarchy), are dispossessed and looking for what they have lost. (pp. 218-19)

The young of the race continue to be born with their hope intact. They are popping into time at the rate of I don't know how many a minute. If I could be their fairy godmother, I would bring two gifts—veneration and delight, because you can't have one without the other.

Now, although an author obviously has nothing to give except what engages him, there must be no propaganda nor the faintest hint of patronage. This applies to children every bit as much as to adults. I deplore the tendency to come down to a supposedly childish level in subject and in language; to make it easy, to provide predigested food—to eliminate, in fact, the widening of the horizon. That will never form reading habits of value.

All art is an invitation to share the creator's world: a door thrown open or a mesh to ensnare. I prefer in this context the word *mesh,* because in a mesh every strand is equally important; lose one and there is a big hole in no time. In a work of art every word or pencil stroke or note has a reference to every other! They interrelate, foreshadow, recall, enlarge, and play all over each other to produce a specific feeling—*not* a moral. A word arbitrarily changed—presuming the writing to be organic—could change a book. It is difficult to calculate how much, since the whole process is so largely from the subconscious. . . .

I sense that people are unprepared to consider children's books as works of art, and, of course, one can get away with almost anything, because children are such artists themselves and transform what is given them. On the other hand, they react to style with their whole being. I want to stress this. Style has an irresistible authority. (p. 220)

> *Lucy Boston, "A Message from Green Knowe," in* The Horn Book Magazine *(copyright © 1963, by The Horn Book, Inc., Boston), June, 1963 (and reprinted in* The Cool Web: The Pattern of Children's Reading, *edited by Margaret Meek, Aidan Warlow, and Griselda Barton, Bodley Head, 1977, pp. 216-21).*

GENERAL COMMENTARY

Re-reading the four Green Knowe books recently in the light of my visit [with Lucy Boston in her home on All Fool's Day, 1962,] I have been struck by their lucidity. I had remembered them as deeply moving and magical but, from the viewpoint of the child reader, difficult. Now they seem wonderful still, powerfully evocative, but at the same time perfectly clear. In the atmosphere of the house Tolly's free movement through the centuries, so that he is able not only to see the long-dead children of Green Knowe but also to play a small part in their destinies, seems marvellous yet, somehow, not surprising. A re-reading brings home most sharply the masterly construction of the stories. There is perhaps a little uncertainty in the first book, amply compensated by its marvellous atmosphere, but the complex narrative of *The Chimneys of Green Knowe* [published in the United States as *Treasure of Green Knowe*] is supremely well handled. There is no waste, but each tiny detail of the story falls quietly into place so that the reader is led steadily, and with mounting suspense, to the climax. *A Stranger at Green Knowe,* with which Mrs. Boston wins a richly-deserved Carnegie Medal, marks a further advance. Hanno's face (cut from a newspaper print) broods over the living room at Green Knowe; the nobly savage head struck the first spark of this story, but how did this highly civilised countrywoman, with her deep sense of the past, think herself into that wild mind? In this book she has, for the first time, abandoned fantasy and told a powerful story in terms of consistent realism. It is a remarkable performance; it is moreover, for all its incongruous subject, a further exploration of the spirit of the ancient house. (pp. 304-05)

One thing seems certain, that Mrs. Boston cannot stop now. She may be a master of controlled narrative, but she is herself possessed by the spirit of the lovely, infinitely old house in which she lives. Green Knowe is waiting to dictate more of its secrets to this wise and understanding amanuensis. (p. 305)

> *Marcus Crouch, "A Visit to Green Knowe," in* The Junior Bookshelf, *December, 1962, pp. 303-05.*

As an author [Mrs Boston] appears to have sprung out of the ground fully armed. . . . It really is very surprising indeed that at sixty [she] should decide to take up her pen and wield it so actively and well. (p. 13)

[There] is one . . . obvious factor which, as must be apparent to all her readers, has had a decisive influence on her writing, and is a key to explaining how and when she came to be a writer: her house. (p. 20)

Releasing, recreating her almost immemorial house, must have acted as a most potent catalyst on Mrs Boston's mind. The more she uncovered, not only of its physique but of its history, the more she learned of its moods, its underlying climate, the greater the kinship and affection she felt for it and the more her imagination fed on it. (p. 24)

Frankly, it is a magic house. Perhaps it is this, and the fact of its immense antiquity that led Mrs Boston to writing about and for children. For what more splendid setting could there be for children's stories? In what better way could the ancient dignity of the house be enlivened than by the cheerful, unboding friendliness of children? In what better way could a child's imaginative boldness and appreciation of age and mystery be provoked than by such a time-outlasting place? (pp. 24-5)

It is one of the most obvious, it is also one of the most important, virtues of Mrs Boston as a writer that she has a fine sense of tempo. (pp. 26-7)

[There] is nothing haphazard about the organisation of the books; and they do not simply transport the reader from point A to point B along a single track. Characteristically, Mrs Boston entwines a number of different themes to form her plot. At first reading one of these themes appears to dominate the whole structure of the book—largely because she usually manages to contrive a startling dramatic climax to it. But on re-reading and pondering the books, their centres of gravity seem to shift; relationships between characters at first unnoticed impose themselves with a different dominance, the mood and colour of the stories change. Like a Persian carpet or a patchwork quilt, one can read their patterns in many ways. (pp. 27-8)

The Green Knowe books also share a major similarity in their formal structure. All are built out of a number of adventurous episodes, each with its own dramatic turning point, which are yet bound into the total development of the story. In the first two books, *The Children* and *The Chimneys*, this method of articulation is overt; the general narrative is interspersed with a set of short stories; these, though they may appear to break up the flow of the plot and stay the climax, in fact form one thread leading towards it. In *The River*—perhaps the most rambling and least well organised of the series—while all the episodes are formally submerged in a single narrative, the total effect is a bit disjointed: each adventure is finely rounded off in itself, but the final *dénouement* owes little to what has happened in most of them. *A Stranger* and *An Enemy* are simpler in structure and follow a unified story line; even so they are punctuated by a number of major pauses. . . . I am convinced that, for younger children, an important virtue of her books is that because of this structure they lend themselves so easily to being read aloud. (pp. 33-4)

The plot of *The Children* is poetic and fragile: timidly handled it might become static and uneventful; treated too brashly it would simply fail to compel attention and belief. Mrs Boston succeeds in creating momentum and suspense partly through skilful transitions; but more because she never lets her readers think of her theme as a fantasy, as a voyage into the unreal. (p. 35)

Nevertheless, compared with *The Children of Green Knowe, The Chimneys of Green Knowe* (1958) is much more ingeniously and strongly constructed. . . . This time . . . stories are evoked by an old patchwork quilt which Mrs Oldknow is repairing: they introduce us to the Oldknow family at the end of the eighteenth century. (p. 36)

For neatness of design, it would be difficult to surpass *The Chimneys;* it reminds one of those Russian dolls—there is plot within plot within plot. Yet it is not simply in its more brilliantly engineered structure that it differs from *The Children.* Susan and Jacob, kind Captain Oldknow and his flighty wife, and all the rest of the Regency characters are livelier, more fetching, and less entirely good than Linnet and her family. . . . Also, the incidents in *The Chimneys* are more exciting, build up greater suspense. (p. 37)

But this comparison is a little unfair to *The Children*. For if

The Chimneys is undoubtedly the jollier, livelier affair, this is partly because in it Mrs Boston is painting a picture of Regency England and does justice to its odd mixture of grace, humanity, sturdiness, raffishness and squalor. . . . Whereas she sees the seventeenth century . . . [with the] intense, refined, exquisitely beautiful and remote mood of the core of *The Children*. . . . Not immediately apparent, the evocation of a period of history turns out to be a basic dimension of both books. (pp. 37-8)

[In] *The River at Green Knowe* (1959) she struck out in a different direction, sweeping away her old cast of characters (except the house itself), and dethroning adventures into time past from a central position, as well as giving up the device of stories within the story. (p. 39)

If *The River* is less skilful in plot and less consistent in mood than its predecessors, there are plenty of compensations. Biggin and Bun are a couple of comic eccentrics portrayed with a mixture of farce and affection—a sort of blend of *Decline and Fall* and *Cranford*. . . . The children, too, are very rewarding. . . . And besides all their adventures, the book is rich with the glitter of dragonflies, the rustle of long grass, the clear images of clouds in the water, the scents of night, the ladened pleasures of an English river landscape. (pp. 39-40)

Ping captured one's heart in *The River*. It was a pleasure—and no surprise—when he reappeared in Mrs Boston's next book *A Stranger at Green Knowe* . . . (p. 40)

The opening of the book is a very remarkable piece of writing, for Mrs Boston has the daring to describe Hanno's life as a small gorilla in the forests of the Congo. Her account of the family life of gorillas, while it is lucid and clearly based on careful research, has a poetic insight which is very rare indeed. It is far away from the sentimentalities of *Black Beauty*, the dubious humanising of animals of *The Wind in the Willows* or even the vigorous but coarse depiction of animal character in Masefield's *Reynard,* and can only be compared to the superb animal poems of D. H. Lawrence and Leconte de Lisle. It also has a most important technical function for it establishes the titanic quality of her hero, the gorilla. . . . (p. 41)

Behind the suspense generated by Ping's perilous friendship with Hanno and its inevitably tragic ending are at least two major themes. One is the conflict in Ping's loyalties. In order to keep Hanno concealed and fed he has to indulge in many ill-mannered subterfuges, all the more painful to him because Mrs Oldknow is not only his hostess but a person he comes to love deeply. Yet he cannot divulge Hanno's presence in the thicket to her. . . . Ping emerges as a person of great integrity and moral—as well as physical—courage.

The other theme is 'displaced persons'. . . . [The] roots of [Ping's] quick sympathy and understanding lie in the affinity of their experience of life. Both have been tugged away from their homes; both have lived in loneliness and in the harsh indifference of institutions; both have had to face the prospect of an unmeaning future. (pp. 41-2)

A Stranger is an exotic book. . . . The quality of Englishness, so strong in her other books, is subdued here. And the historic past is of no importance at all. Even the house plays only a minor part in the proceedings.

Not so in *An Enemy at Green Knowe* . . . : here the house once more provides the motive force of the drama, for it is under a threat—a threat of the most dangerous and sinister kind. (p. 43)

Mrs Boston's other stories could be characterised as 'discovery' plots; like flowers they unfold a petal at a time; essentially they are harmonious. *An Enemy* is a book dominated by conflict; it is full of brimstone turmoil. (pp. 44-5)

To say that *An Enemy* is no bigger than its main plot would be wrong. The magic mirror for instance takes up the thread of one of Mrs Boston's favourite themes—time. There is a fine counterpoint in the relations between Mrs Oldknow and her brood. . . . Yet these matters are essentially embellishments to the striking pattern of the drama. The book *is* overshadowed by the baleful sneering countenance of Miss Powers, and when sunlight streaks its last pages the reader blinks in surprise. (p. 45)

The first reaction to *The Castle of Yew* of any reader who has followed carefully the course of Mrs Boston's development as a writer, is probably a mixture of bewilderment, surprise and unwilling disappointment. After the rich, agitating dramas of *A Stranger* and *An Enemy,* with their mastery of narrative suspense, their strong colouring, and their insistence upon moral problems, the tiny, dainty quality of *The Castle of Yew* is, to say the least, unexpected. (pp. 45-6)

Delicate, slight, neither highly inventive nor original in its main lines, still *The Castle of Yew* is more rewarding than might appear at first sight. . . . With its slightly quizzical tone—which the boys themselves adopt—and with its sparkling and poetic perception of a miniature world, the book offers its older readers some of the same sort of pleasure that Pope provides in *The Rape of the Lock.* The young children for whom it is specifically designed must find it both exciting and tantalising. (p. 47)

Probably Mrs Boston's books . . . owe a part of their popularity amongst children to the fact that they deal with subjects that children (and grown-ups) have always found exciting. But their real claim to distinction and originality lies precisely in the great imaginative tact and delicacy which she brings to traditional situations and topics. (p. 50)

However delightful fairy tales are, they suffer from one very serious failing; they are incredible. Too often they depend on an entire divorce between fantasy and fact. . . . [This is not true of Mrs Boston's books, which] weave the commonplace and the magical so closely together that each is touched with, and transfigured by, something of the essential quality of the other. (pp. 50-1)

It is one of [Mrs Boston's] great strengths that she never attempts to explain a mystery away. . . . At the same time she never forces her reader to believe more than he wishes to. (pp. 52-3)

If we take her books at their face value they ask us not to believe in any old thing but precisely to ponder certain problems which human beings have always found baffling. (p. 54)

To say that Mrs Boston's books have [this] philosophical undercurrent might suggest that they are tedious and stodgy. This is far from the case. Though the texture of the books is consistently thoughtful, though the children are always probing and analysing the mysteries, they do so in a casual and buoyant way. There is no hint of dry and systematic academic discourse. (p. 55)

A recurring motif of the books is the discovery of some lost relic of the past. . . . Put in comparatively formal terms, Mrs Boston seems to be saying that all human actions are incomplete in time, that for every act there remains a residue of unfilled intention which stretches out beyond the event itself. (pp. 56-7)

[This] fluidity of time enables Mrs Boston to devise exciting stories, full of surprising twists and turns; and it is possible to argue that she is less concerned to convince her readers than to amaze and delight them. . . . It enables her, too, to approach death—a stumbling block which most children's writers either evade or trip over with deplorable clumsiness—with sensitivity and realism. (pp. 57-8)

It is not that the strange happenings usurp the whole of each book. . . . Rather it is that with remarkable consistency, she portrays the whole of human existence as potentially mysterious. . . . (p. 58)

Critics have been quick to notice the closeness of Mrs Boston's books to the great classics of Victorian children's literature. Indeed there is something old-fashioned and substantial about the very format of her books. . . . The illustrations, too, add to the impression of nostalgic and leisurely solidity. Peter Boston has that uncanny and very Victorian ability to marry his drawings, particularly his modest vignettes, to the mood of his mother's text. . . . (p. 61)

The books reflect Mrs Boston's Victorian upbringing in other subtler and more important ways. . . . [One] sees her fearless evangelical conscience at work: her account of the big game hunter, Major Blair, is mercilessly reproachful. Nor does she hesitate to give vent to her awe and delight in the face of natural beauty. Victorian writers were much too robust in their appreciation of the frank splendours of things like mountains and sunsets to worry very much if they gushed and gave way to 'purple passageing' in describing them. Like them Mrs Boston is ready to respond with an opulent style to opulent effects. . . . (pp. 62-3)

[Perhaps] it is the sheer firmness of her moral judgments which more than anything else is ultimately responsible for imparting an air of the old-fashioned, of the Victorian, to her stories.

I am well aware that such epithets might easily be taken to be uncomplimentary. This is not my intention. (p. 64)

Nor . . . do I wish to suggest her books are mere repositories of moral maxims, that she is ponderously and persistently didactic. . . . On the contrary her stories are singularly free from any attempt to preach, admonish or even inform. . . . If she does allow virtue to be rewarded, the rewards are subtle and suitable and not doled out in automatic largesse. . . . To use a commonplace but apt term she is an unusually committed writer, who leaves us in little doubt about the nature of her commitments.

One of the foremost of these (and one which must particularly delight her younger readers) is a commitment to recognising and respecting children as independent, complete, intelligent and capable beings. This respect is not based on an idealised and unreal estimate of children. . . . She lets her children make mistakes—and perhaps it is this which makes them so credible and *un*-insipid.

Her attitude is mirrored in the attitudes of the grown-ups in her books. (pp. 64-6)

[A] mutual agreement not to invade each other's privacy, to trust each other's judgement, to appreciate each other's feelings [forms the basis of] the peculiarly warm and solid friendship and affection between the children and the 'good' grown-ups, which is perhaps the most impressive and moving theme of the books as a whole. (p. 67)

Friendship and concord between the old and the young; between the present and the past; between human beings and animals; between man and nature: these may seem rather an obvious and dull, if worthy, set of values. But in Mrs Boston they are not. Partly because of the passion with which she maintains them: the world she conjures up is very coherent—made so by her style and her moral sensibility—so that whether she is writing about a tuft of grass or the death of Hanno she strikes a fine balance between sympathy and objectivity. But more because she is able to show how important, how essential these values are, because she shows them in a world in which they are threatened. (pp. 68-9)

> *Jasper Rose, in* Lucy Boston: A Walck Monograph (© *Jasper Rose 1965), Henry Z. Walck, Inc., 1965.*

Many are the times I have seen them lying in their pools, or under a cliff at the lacy edge of the tide, sea eggs that are neither rock nor wave and yet somehow compact of both, stones scribbled and shaped and brooded upon by wings and feathers of water.

But I never guessed—it took L. M. Boston, the author of the *Green Knowe* books, to teach me my biology—that one of them might possibly hatch out a Triton. Well, it has happened. And we owe our knowledge of the event to two of Mrs. Boston's sensible, ordinary little boys. When I say ordinary, I do so with intent, not at all meaning commonplace but giving this great word a ghostly capital letter, knighting it, as it were, and saying Arise! For it takes the ordinary to comprehend, even to be related to, the extraordinary, just as, in order to fly, you need firm ground to take off from. In airness we lose all sense of air, let alone earth; in the poetic, poetry; in childishness, the child. It is solidity that gives us wings.

These two determined children in *The Sea Egg* . . . pursue their adventure with far more concentration and maturity than is discernible in their parents and, as a result, the impossible happens. For a short time, or a long time—all is timeless here—we accompany them and the wonderful merboy through the moving ocean world, submerging, coming up for air, exploring the intestinal tunnels under islands. . . . The writer's element is here so manifestly water that at the end of the adventure the reader himself feels a stranger to land and listens nostalgically for the clamor of waves on the shore.

It is this ability to surrender himself to his own particular data, to the world beyond the visible world, the fact beyond the newspaper fact, that is the mark of the true storyteller. He creates—no, not creates—he hearkens in to (as they call listening to the radio in Devon) and becomes an historian of the principality that interpenetrates and permeates our daily world, a country with laws and customs that are, within its own boundaries, valid and absolute. (pp. 246-47)

The Sea Egg certainly comes from this kingdom and the *Green Knowe* books are already established there among the archives, existing not merely as literature but as an exact description, five volumes long, of one particular corner of its countryside. It would need far more space than any editor would give me to list the virtues of their author but there are three—apart from the flowing, flexible prose—that I must take note of, three crowns that must be offered. To begin with, one is never aware that any of the stories has either beginning or end. It has obviously existed long before we picked up the book and will go on long after we have put it down; all goes back to Deuteronomy and forward to who knows where. Then, the point of view is always mature, here ripeness is all; sadness and evil are not minimized, nothing is glossed over, nothing made sentimental. Best of all, the books do not have the air of having been written for children. They appear to have been set down—and this is another mark of the storyteller—simply to please L. M. Boston! . . .

And then, the characters are so perfectly balanced and juxtaposed, like those in the fairy tales—the very old woman who has dropped so much of life and the young boy who has not yet taken on the burden of it are brought together at the mutual moment when each can perceive, not merely the five fingers of the hand, but what lies in the space between. (p. 247)

In the first two *Green Knowe* books—*The Children* and *The Treasure*—it was the old house and its magic garden into which the author submerged. . . . Then came *The River* and there she was, waterily winding through the meadows, flowing among ghostly apparitions, bearing the reader along with the drowned reflected moon.

There was nothing here to suggest, however—though had I been asked I would have admitted to not putting it past her —that in the next book she would become (well, practically) a gorilla. Of all the books *The Stranger at Green Knowe* is my favorite. Where else, except, perhaps, in George Schaller's *Year of the Gorilla,* will you find a more exact, more poignant, more perceptive evocation of the great sad noble "man-animal?". . . The book is a paean to all lost children, to all creatures far from home, all things caged and prisoned. The refugee child, Ping, and Hanno, the gorilla—the one so weak yet outside the cage, the other so strong but behind bars—are two creatures of one kind; in some cosmic sense, brothers. . . . When Hanno is killed we feel grateful, we experience the same catharsis as we do in Greek tragedy when the great heroes die. (pp. 247-48)

The last—though I prefer the word latest, as being less final —of the *Green Knowe* books, *The Enemy,* has none of Hanno's large simplicity. It is, indeed, the most complicated of them all, dealing as it does with magic, and black magic at that. Or perhaps it is truer to say that its theme is the struggle of black with white. . . . In life it is difficult not to make good seem sentimental, in books it is difficult not to make evil seem inadequate. But the earth has bubbles as the water has. . . . [So, without *The Enemy* we would never] have experienced the magic mirror, only equalled by Snow White's, which, having shown so much of ill throughout the book, redeems itself at the end by reflecting a happy image—Ping's father, thought to be dead, walking towards the house.

No old-fashioned recognition scene, no explanations, for nothing so banal could come from this writer.

"We have seen Ping's father and mine in the glass," says Tolly, "opening the garden gate."

"And so it was," the book ends.

And since, with L. M. Boston, nothing either begins or ends, so it still is and will be. We can go to bed happy. How fortunate! (pp. 248-49)

> *P. L. Travers, "World beyond World," in* Book Week *(copyright © 1967 by* Chicago Sun-Times*), May 7, 1967 (and reprinted in* Children and Literature: Views and Reviews, *edited by Virginia Haviland, Scott, Foresman, 1973, pp. 246-49).*

L. M. Boston's . . . fantasies are completely convincing. (p. 126)

In the first Green Knowe book, *The Children of Green Knowe,* the boy Tolly who figures in several of them comes to the house to visit his grandmother, Mrs. Oldknow. . . . Mrs Oldknow tells Tolly, during this first holiday, the story of Green Knowe's history and as she talks her tales come to life in his mind and he and the reader move backwards and forwards in time. . . . It is a fine flight of imagination, beautifully conceived and superbly executed, quite beyond criticism, and it is difficult for anyone at all sensitive to atmosphere to read it unmoved. (pp. 126-27)

Each of L. M. Boston's books about Green Knowe has a charm of its own. *The Chimneys of Green Knowe* is another time-shift story; *An Enemy at Green Knowe* is a frighteningly real story about one of the most shockingly believable witches in children's fiction; and her Carnegie Medal winner, *A Stranger at Green Knowe,* is a completely different kind of story, about a giant gorilla, escaped from a zoo, who finds a temporary sanctuary in the wilder parts of the Green Knowe garden and is befriended by a small visitor. This is one of the most remarkable of Mrs Boston's books, and perhaps hardly counts as a fantasy. The last, so far, of the Green Knowe books, *The River at Green Knowe,* is a puzzling sort of book that seems not quite to succeed by the standards set by the other books, but would be remarkable from any other writer.

Although the same children appear in several of L. M. Boston's books they are not sequels in the accepted sense, nor do the books suffer from any of the sense of strain which is too often apparent when an author is striving to spin too much from the one thread. Each book obviously has its roots in something that has stirred her passions or her sympathies. . . . Her house is an abiding passion and one imagines her brooding in her beautiful, wild garden, seeking ways to weld the latest preoccupation into a story about Green Knowe and its garden. Each book takes a long time, for she would be dissatisfied with anything but a perfect grafting of the bud onto the stem and she has in consequence not written many books, for she is above all an artist. She writes clearly, simply and well, in a controlled, spare style that neither intrudes nor fails to communicate anything that she wants her readers either to understand or to feel, and her characters always come completely alive and appear to think and feel, and be affected by atmosphere and events, exactly as one feels such people should. Her work, to my mind, almost completely disproves Helen Lourie's remark about the best fantasies being written by men, because *The Children of Green Knowe* is one of the loveliest fantasies ever written, and it could not conceivably have been written by a man. (pp. 127-28)

> *Frank Eyre, in his* British Children's Books in the Twentieth Century *(copyright © 1971 by Frank Eyre; reprinted by permission of the publishers, E. P. Dutton & Co., Inc.),* Dutton, 1971.

[Lucy Boston's novels explore Green Knowe], partly as children might explore it, with a sense of discovery which in Mrs Boston has stayed fresh through the years, and partly in the way an artist will explore and re-explore a theme that engages his mind. And her explorations have been four-dimensional, for the house is many centuries old and full of the past: the tangible stone and wood and handed-down treasures; the intangible memories and presences. (p. 28)

The action of the 'Green Knowe' stories is often dramatic, sometimes melodramatic. It is not for their plots that the books stand out. The first two—*The Children of Green Knowe* and *The Chimneys of Green Knowe*—have an awkward box-within-a-box construction. Discoveries from the past, such as the family jewels in *Chimneys* and an ancient book of magic in *Enemy,* are too easy and perhaps too obvious. The long arm of coincidence makes unlikely sweeps. Some of the action in *River* and in *Enemy* lacks credibility even in its own terms. Only in *A Stranger at Green Knowe,* which brings Hanno the gorilla to this quiet corner of England, is the story as such both audacious and successful.

Nor is Mrs Boston remarkable as a creator of human characters. Most of her people are simply good or bad in varying degree; they have their place in the moral spectrum and do not depart from it. (pp. 29-30)

Mrs Boston is not, then, in my view particularly well endowed with the standard equipment of the novelist: the ability to create characters and tell a story about them. Even so, she is a writer of distinction. To start with, she has an excellent ear and uses the English language superbly. She can be poetic and evocative. . . . But she is also strong, sharp and exact; and her style is perfectly suited to the Green Knowe setting. She is a highly intelligent writer and does not disguise it. Her sense of the past is subtle and haunting. There is deep feeling in her work, too; and she can go to the farther bounds of sentiment without taking the last, false step that would cross the brink into sentimentality. (p. 30)

Most remarkably, Mrs Boston combines sensuousness with an unusual degree of empathy. A comparison with D. H. Lawrence—especially the Lawrence of the poems—is not as absurd as it may seem. She offers a strong sense of the natural world, living and breathing, to be seen through the alert eye and felt through the fingertips. It is this sensuous awareness that she feels to be precious in children, that she wishes to share with them, and that may have led her to write for them. (p. 31)

Mrs Boston is not an explicitly moral writer, but her values are clearly to be seen. She believes in the goodness of the natural living creature, in roots, in continuity; and she is able to symbolize these values in the house, itself built of natural materials, which she has said she cannot think of as 'a thing'. She hates concrete and all it stands for. These values and the gift of empathy helped her to carry out the *tour-de-force* of *A Stranger at Green Knowe.* At first sight it seems incongruous to introduce a dangerous wild creature from the jungle into a quiet English countryside setting. Yet this clash and its resolution give the book its power, for out of striking dissonances a striking unity is achieved. And within Mrs Boston's frame of values the elements are not so incongruous after all. The gorilla and Green Knowe are both, in different ways, antitheses of the artificial urban civilization represented by the zoo. (p. 32)

Mrs Boston has written two books for younger children [*The Castle of Yew* and *The House That Grew*], both concerned with houses and both having clear family relationships with the 'Green Knowe' stories. . . . I do not myself feel that either of these books is successful. Mrs Boston seems to be consciously 'writing down' and not employing the qualities that make her the writer she is. Young children's books, I suspect, are not her true medium.

The Sea Egg . . . her one remaining book for children up to the time of writing, is greatly different from the rest in subject and setting. . . . Certainly the sea dominates *The Sea Egg*, as the house dominates the earlier books. Yet it is hard to think of the sea, even in literary terms, as a refuge. The associations are all the other way round. While the house is rooted, unmoving, reassuring, comfortable, safe, the sea is restless, perilous, inhospitable to creatures like ourselves who normally walk on land and breathe air. The sea is a challenge. . . . *The Sea Egg* seems to me to be a reaching out rather than a retreat. It demonstrates, incidentally, that the house is not so essential to her writing as was once thought. (pp. 32-3)

There is something in *The Sea Egg* of the Boston themes of growth, of the finding of freedom, of learning through the senses. But the scale and movement of the story come from the sea, as seen in its many moods. . . . In this book the power and beauty of Mrs Boston's style are fully matched by the power and beauty of what she is describing. For all the reputation of the Green Knowe books, I do not believe she has written anything finer than *The Sea Egg*. (p. 34)

> *John Rowe Townsend, "L. M. Boston," in his* A Sense of Story: Essays on Contemporary Writing for Children *(copyright © 1971 by John Rowe Townsend; reprinted by permission of J. B. Lippincott Company), Lippincott, 1971, pp. 28-34.*

THE CASTLE OF YEW (1965)

This is every child's dream come true. Two boys exploring a topiary garden where the yew trees are cut like chessmen find themselves suddenly small enough to go right inside one of the castles. Everything is as you would imagine it—branches cut to form a spiral staircase round the trunk, beds made up in abandoned birds' nests—though life in miniature has its terrors too. The invention is delightful. In the first three chapters, however, before the change in size, the author builds up a portentous atmosphere that suggests she is leading into an altogether more sinister story. The reader is left feeling he has the first third of one very good book joined to the last two-thirds of another. (p. 145)

> The Junior Bookshelf, *June, 1965.*

In this story for younger children Lucy Boston has written with the same skill and beauty as in her earlier work and with the same sincerity and belief in 'the things of the

spirit'. The strange, lovely new world which Joseph found beneath the old yew hedge is not magic, but a world created by the imagination; a world entirely credible to the mind of a child, that mind which is so perfectly understood by Mrs. Boston. (p. 380)

> *F. P. Parrott, in* The School Librarian and School Library Review, *December, 1965.*

OTHER CITATIONS

Virginia Kirkus' Service, *September 1, 1965, p. 903.*

Joan Bodger, in The New York Times Book Review, *Part II, November 7, 1965, p. 40.*

THE CHILDREN OF GREEN KNOWE (British Edition, 1954; US Edition, 1955)

Mrs. Boston is a much admired and respected writer; . . . [not] only is she much respected, but she is historically important. (p. 79)

Mrs. Boston has said publicly some interesting things about her work . . .:

> Is there a conscious difference in the way I write for grown-ups and children? No, there is no difference of approach, style, vocabulary or standard. I could pick out passages from any of the books and you would not be able to tell what age it was aimed at.

[Compare the] opening of *Yew Hall* . . ., Lucy Boston's first book, and written for adults (or, to use her word, grown-ups) . . . [to] the opening passage of her first children's book, published the same year . . .: there are unmistakable differences in approach, style and vocabulary. *Yew Hall* has an urbanity of style and approach that establishes very quickly a tone which implies a literate, adult reader. . . . The writing is confident, witty, slightly superior. . . . (pp. 79-80)

The language in *Yew Hall* tends towards the Latinate. *Green Knowe* is much more firmly Anglo-Saxon. Rain is splashing and blotching, lips are smacking, knitting needles click-clack, not to mention Tolly's own list of participial verbs describing Noah's animals. . . .

There is, however, as Mrs. Boston claims, no lowering of standard between the two books. *Green Knowe* is just as densely and richly textured—perhaps is even more richly textured—than *Yew Hall*. But the images and the words used to communicate them are quite different in the experiential demands made on the reader. . . . [To understand *Green Knowe*, you] need only to have seen some rain, have been on a train, know something about the story of Noah and the Flood, and to have observed women knitting for the text to be completely open to you. (p. 81)

At the very least the style appeals to the child-in-the-adult, possessing that very tone of voice I [suggest] is traditionally the English tone used in telling stories to children: direct, clear, polite, firm, uncluttered. And Mrs. Boston achieves it admirably.

We must discover whether or not the other aspects of her book reinforce the impression given by her style. . . .

Throughout [*Green Knowe*], the story is told from Tolly's

point of view. Only occasionally is there a brief shift for some narrative purpose. . . .

Even Mrs. Oldknow, so central a character in the story, is seen only from the outside. Her private thoughts and perceptions remain enigmatic, and influentially so: she occupies a somewhat mysteriously attractive place in the book. One wonders about her, and feels too a little daunted by her, a little afraid of her secret knowingness. The reader gets that impression from a subtly handled feature of the book. All along one cannot help feeling that it is Mrs. Oldknow who is telling the story. And probably the feeling would not be so strong were it not for the stories Mrs. Oldknow tells Tolly at night. They are about the children who lived in the house and died in the Plague of 1665. But then, the rest of the book is also about a boy in the house. Isn't the whole book therefore a story by Mrs. Oldknow? Has she, in fact, invented Tolly? Or isn't she, at the very least, telling his story, and doing it so well because she *knows*— can see into children's minds, as children so often believe some adults can, and tell what is going on in them? (p. 82)

[There is] a strong sense of alliance between Mrs. Oldknow, Tolly and the reader, thus placing the author unmistakably on the reader's side.

Before the story has gone far enough to establish the strong relationship I've just described, Mrs. Boston is signalling her allegiance. The opening paragraphs of the book reveal her sympathetic understanding of a small boy's response to the world about him. . . .

When Tolly at last meets his great-grandmother, wondering if she is a witch and whether he will be afraid of her (the terrible business of meeting strange relatives), Mrs. Boston-Oldknow (for Mrs. Boston's second self must surely be Mrs. Oldknow) declares her allegiance openly. . . . (p. 83)

Next morning, the adventure begins: it involves Tolly's long-ago child relatives—whether as ghosts or not we hope to discover—household toys, garden animals, and Mrs. Oldknow. Being cut off by the flood simply asserts actually and symbolically the private collusive world inhabited by the boy and the old woman.

But the collusion is not just a means of disposing the reader to the book: its profoundest meaning depends upon the nature of the relationship.

Game or ghost story? More than a game and not just a ghost story. Each time we think that at last Tolly is indisputably seeing apparitions of Toby, Alexander and Linnet, Mrs. Boston withdraws confirmation. (p. 84)

Mrs. Oldknow leaves Tolly alone in the house, and Boggis too is gone. Surely now the ghosts will emerge and they, Tolly and the reader can meet undeniably. But no. Despite the house being empty of others and dark coming on, so that the stage is set for a final exciting ghost-drama, our expectations raised for a climax (how many other writers have prepared us so before), Mrs. Boston will not satisfy us. . . . She has employed a device similar to Dickens's in *Oliver Twist*: reader's expectations raised, and deliberately dashed. We are forced to wonder why.

Here is the amicable halving of this book; here is a tell-tale gap which the reader must enter if the book's true meaning is to be negotiated. Whatever is going on in the story can only be enacted between Mrs. Oldknow and Tolly. Nothing

happens when they are apart. Together, their lives have followed a pattern. . . . [Mrs. Oldknow], like a superlatively wise play leader, offers opportunities for Tolly to enjoy himself through experiences that enliven the world to him. He is led to look closely, hear clearly, touch sensitively, think imaginatively. (pp. 84-5)

Punctuating these descriptions of the day-to-day activities are four stories told by Mrs. Oldknow to Tolly at bedtime. This device suits the apparently naturalistic plot: Tolly is on holiday with his great-grandmother: the house and gardens provide his daily adventures; before bed he is given his fictional adventure. But these four stories are not just any stories: they are about the three long-ago children and their horse Feste, one story for each. . . .

We are led to see things this way: Tolly and Mrs. Oldknow fantasize about Toby and Alexander and Linnet. Tolly may or may not actually see their ghosts, and enjoys the game. But the three long-ago children have undeniable reality only in the stories Mrs. Oldknow tells about them. There they live in their own right, not as spectres raised by Tolly and his great-grandmother, just as Tolly and Mrs. Oldknow have a reality in their own right only as characters in Mrs. Boston's story about them. Stories, Mrs. Boston is telling us, are the means by which we give life to ourselves and the objects around us. Stories, in fact, create meaning. (p. 85)

[In] few books has an author achieved her highest aims so certainly as Mrs. Boston does in *The Children of Green Knowe*. Through Tolly, guided by Mrs. Boston's second self, her implied reader is brought to grips with the direct sense stimulus that gives birth to life-expanding imagination. By any standard this is a fine achievement, all the more remarkable for the simplicity with which it is executed. (p. 86)

Aidan Chambers, in Signal *(copyright © 1977 Aidan Chambers; reprinted by permission of the author and The Thimble Press, Lockwood Station Road, South Woodchester, Glos. GL5 5EQ, England), May, 1977.*

OTHER CITATIONS

Jennie D. Lindquist, in The Horn Book Magazine, *October, 1955, p. 375.*

Della McGregor, in Saturday Review, *November 12, 1955, p. 64.*

AN ENEMY AT GREEN KNOWE (1964)

Even children who like books about old English manor houses and who have "no intention of shutting out the ununderstandable" might find the plot scrappy, the style precious in this book, the fifth in the Green Knowe series. . . . The bits of anthropological folklore may prove interesting to those who enjoy "a nip of otherness," but the story reveals little character development or plot motivation. The triumph of good over evil is reduced to a contest of mere oneupmanship. (p. 34)

Joan H. Bodger, in The New York Times Book Review *(© 1964 by The New York Times Company; reprinted by permission), September 13, 1964.*

Mrs. Boston grows with every book. In *A Stranger at Green Knowe* she triumphantly entered a world without fantasy and with no magic except that of her mastery of words. Now she returns with increased skill and power to fantasy in a story of the struggle between good and evil. It is an impressive experience. Some adults may fear that in the terrors of some of these pages there may be food for childish nightmares. Certainly there are terrors enough, but there are strength and comfort in Mrs. Boston's story. The evil is powerful, certainly, but it is decisively defeated by good.

Lest this should seem altogether too serious, it should be added that there is much sweetness and gaiety in the story, and Tolly and Ping, together for the first time, make a beautifully balanced pair.

Learner writers—and established ones too—might make a close study of Mrs. Boston's masterly handling of her story. Scene setting, introduction of theme, development, crisis, resolution: all is done with easy control which marks a considerable advance on anything she has done before. Here, in a book which is beautiful, terrifying, intensely exciting, is a very good writer at the height of her powers. I hope that the difficulties of the book, in concept much as in vocabulary, will not discourage young readers, and that some adults will see that here is admirable material for reading aloud to children who are emotionally ready for it but educationally unable to meet its demands.. (p. 304)

The Junior Bookshelf, *November, 1964.*

OTHER CITATIONS

Winnifred Moffett Crossley, in School Library Journal, *September, 1964, p. 114.*

Ethel L. Heins, in The Horn Book Magazine, *October, 1964, p. 497.*

THE SEA EGG (1967)

AUTHOR'S COMMENTARY

Today [the Manor at Hemingford Grey] is in suburbia . . . My darling Green Knowe has dwindled . . . There is not room for it to be. This may account for the flight to *The Sea Egg*. The sea is still real, undiminished. My approach has always been to explore reality as it appears, and from within to see how far imagination can properly expand it. Reality, after all, has no outside edge. I never start with a fantasy and look for a peg to hang it on. As far as I deliberately try to do anything other than to write a book that pleases me, I would like to remind adults of joy, now considered obsolete—and would like to encourage children to use and trust their senses for themselves at first hand—their ears, eyes and noses, their fingers and the soles of their feet, their skins and their breathing, their muscular joy and rhythms and heartbeats, their instinctive loves and pity and their awe of the unknown. This, not the telly, is the primary material of thought. It is from direct sense stimulus that imagination is born. . . .

The Sea Egg is almost wholly an evocation of sense perception. The triton is so implicit in the sea-stuff that he hardly needed to be mentioned. He gets perhaps a dozen sentences to himself in the whole book—a mere flick of sea foam—but the sound of the sea is on every page. (pp. 36-7)

L. M. Boston, extracts from a speech delivered in November, 1968 to the Children's Book Circle, in A Sense of Story: Essays on Contemporary Writers for Children *by John Rowe Townsend (copyright © 1971 by John Rowe Townsend; reprinted by permission of J. B. Lippincott Company), Lippincott, 1971.*

Two small boys and a triton hatched from a sea egg (a green stone the size of a turkey's egg) share crystal moments "outside calculation" in a brief, beautiful vignette. The triton, a sea boy their own size, frolics with them in their secret pool; on a moonbright night he lures them into a hidden cavern, a "ruined sea palace," within a rocky island. For a short time they are one with the seals and all the creatures of the sea—and then it is over; they return to their own, but satisfied. The evocation of mood and moment is what matters here, but there's also an easy compatibility between two young brothers and the understanding of parents who are content not to press their understanding. The problem is—for whom? It's too slight for the older child, too difficult for the younger child, too slow for reading aloud—and too lovely to leave, without regrets. (p. 498)

Kirkus Service *(copyright © 1967 The Kirkus Service, Inc.), April 15, 1967.*

Although I yield to none in my admiration for the acid head, the slip knife, and the purloined bra, I feel that a case ought to be made for escape literature, at least once in a while, and out of consideration for those who like it. Lucy Boston's *The Sea Egg* is a fable of two little boys on the Cornish coast who discover and befriend a young triton. The book, with illustrations by Peter Boston, is slight but beautiful. There is almost no story to it, but the seal puppies with blunt noses, the glittering scales, shining eyes, and cold lips of the triton, the sense of the sea, and the eloquent language make a book like a coral cluster, to be read as though it were a poem. The form of the children's story in this case is that best suited to what Mrs. Boston has chosen to say. I cannot imagine *The Sea Egg* expressed in any other manner. (pp. 152-53)

Martha Bacon, in The Atlantic Monthly *(copyright © 1968 by The Atlantic Monthly Company, Boston, Mass.; reprinted with permission), December, 1968.*

OTHER CITATIONS

Barbara Wersba, in The New York Times Book Review, *April 23, 1967, p. 26.*

The Times Literary Supplement, *November 30, 1967, p. 1133.*

Colin Field, in The School Librarian and School Library Review, *December, 1967, pp. 358-59.*

THE STONES OF GREEN KNOWE (1976)

Those who come fresh to this story without having previously visited Green Knowe will find much that is puzzling and unexplained. Roger the Norman boy sees his house being built in the twelfth century and then contrives by magic to see it it at stages of its life up to the horrid present. At each stage he meets people who are old friends to Mrs. Boston's admirers but who appear too briefly and, in one sense, too much out of context to make much impression on new readers. Notwithstanding Mrs. Boston's sensitive writing, this may perhaps be regarded as a fill-up in the chronicles of her house rather than a compelling novel in the mood of the five incomparable novels in the authentic Green Knowe sequence. (p. 295)

> The Junior Bookshelf, *October, 1976.*

Green Knowe is a real English manor house, the home, in fact, of Lucy Boston who has written five other novels about it. In this, the sixth, Roger d'Aulneaux finds two mysterious stones hidden in the forest that enable him to travel in time from his Norman England to meet children living at Green Knowe in other ages. The magic and the mystery combine to lay out the progress of history with all its marvels and problems. Although knowledge of the five earlier books will add a dimension to this novel, it is not essential, in fact *The Stones* will lure readers to seek out its predecessors. Boston is an effortless stylist and her magic seems as simple as breathing. (p. E6)

> *Brigitte Weeks, in* Book World-The Washington Post *(© The Washington Post), October 10, 1976.*

OTHER CITATIONS

Kirkus Reviews, *August 1, 1976, p. 845.*

Judith M. Amory, in The New York Times Book Review, *January 2, 1977, p. 16.*

A STRANGER AT GREEN KNOWE (1961)

Lucy Boston's story of an escaped gorilla and a "displaced" Chinese boy is a sterling example of what can be done with a simple plot peopled by human and wild creatures of individual character. After a fine opening which draws the gorilla hero in natural surroundings, a bond between the lonely zoo captive and the kinless child is touchingly forged. It is hard to say in the end whether the boy or the wild creature gains the reader's sympathy more. At any rate, the elderly lady who by chance befriends the boy runs a close third. They are all deftly drawn. So are the illustrations which are delightful without any hint of the terror which the main subject might be imagined by the less informed to inspire. (pp. 139-40)

> The Junior Bookshelf, *July, 1961.*

A Stranger at Green Knowe . . . is likely to form the basis of Mrs Boston's literary standing; this is the book that teachers should read aloud to children between the ages of ten and thirteen. A starting point for the author must clearly have been the shock of seeing Guy, the mournful, black Congolese gorilla, pent up in his soulless cage in the London Zoo. Her feeling of outrage and desecration has led her to give her gorilla, Hanno, the opportunity of escape and a few days of freedom in a secluded thicket behind Green Knowe. This is her gesture of atonement to him for the loss of the dense and humid jungles of the Congo so vividly realized in the first part of the book. (p. 8)

Hanno is not sentimentally humanized; he remains always a

gorilla, alarmingly powerful, potentially destructive, treated with respect as the animal he is. . . . The sadness is not glossed over, but there is also an acceptance that contains within itself an element of joy, for [through his death] Hanno has been given back his dignity and redeemed from the soul-destroying constrictions of his captivity. (p. 11)

> *Sidney Robbins, "A Nip of Otherness, Like Life: The Novels of Lucy Boston," in* Children's Literature in Education *(© 1971, APS Publications, Inc., New York; reprinted by permission of the publisher), No. 6 (November), 1971, pp. 5-16.*

OTHER CITATIONS

Patricia Beer, in The Spectator, *June 9, 1961, p. 850.*

Virginia Haviland, in The Horn Book Magazine, *October, 1961, p. 439.*

The Times Literary Supplement, *December 1, 1961, p. vii.*

*   *   *

BOVA, Ben(jamin) 1932-

An American author of science fiction and nonfiction, Ben Bova has also worked with leading scientists on lasers, artificial hearts, and other major projects. Among other professions, he has been a film writer, aerospace executive, and editor of *Analog*. His work on this highly respected science fiction magazine won him the Hugo Award in 1973 and 1974 for Best Editor. (See also *Contemporary Authors*, Vols. 5-8, rev. ed. and *Something About the Author*, Vol. 6.)

AUTHOR'S COMMENTARY

Every writer must bring three major factors to each story that he or she writes. They are: ideas, artistry, and craftsmanship. Ideas . . . are nowhere nearly as tough to find and develop as most new writers think they are. Artistry depends on the writer's individual talent and commitment to writing; no one can teach artistry to a writer, although many have tried. Artistry depends almost entirely on what's inside the writer—inborn talent, heart, guts, and drive.

Craftsmanship *can* be taught, and it's the one area where new writers consistently fall short. In most cases, it's simple lack of craftsmanship that keeps a writer from being published. Like a carpenter who's never learned to drive nails correctly, writers who have not learned craftsmanship will get nothing but trouble (and swollen thumbs) for their efforts. (pp. 2-3)

Science fiction has become known as "the literature of ideas"; so much so that some critics have disparagingly pointed out that many SF stories have The Idea as their hero, and very little else to recommend them. Ideas are important in science fiction. They are a necessary ingredient of any good SF tale, but the ideas themselves should not be the be-all and end-all of every story.

Very often it's the idea content of good science fiction stories that interests young writers in this exciting yet demanding field. It's the "sense of wonder" that turns them on. And why not? Look at the playground they have to themselves! There's the entire universe of stars and galaxies, and all of the past, present, and future to write about. There's interstellar flight, time travel, immortality, genetic manipulation, biofeedback, behavior control, telepathy and other Extra-Sensory Powers (ESP), the colonization of other worlds, the development of new technology that can turn one industry's pollution emissions into another industry's raw material.

But even more fascinating for the writer (and reader) of science fiction is the way these ideas can be used to develop stories about *people*. And that's what all of fiction is about: people. In science fiction, the "people" may look very nonhuman, and they may find themselves in strange, wild, exotic worlds. They will always face fantastic problems, and strive to surmount them. Sometimes they will win, sometimes lose. But they will always *strive,* because at the core of all good SF is the very fundamental faith that we can use our intelligence to understand the world and solve our problems.

All those weird backgrounds and fantastic ideas, all those special ingredients of science fiction, are really a set of tricks used by the writers to place their characters in the kinds of desperate situations where they will have to do their very best, or their very worst, to survive. For all of fiction deals with examining the human spirit, placing that spirit in a crucible where we can test its true worth. In science fiction, we can go far beyond the boundaries of the here and now, to place that crucible any place and any time we want to, and make the testing fire as hot as can be imagined.

That is science fiction's special advantage, and its special challenge: going beyond the boundaries of the here and now to test the human spirit in new and ever-more-powerful ways. (pp. 4-5)

Your job, as a writer, is to make the reader *live* in your story. You must make the reader forget that he's sitting in a rather uncomfortable chair, squinting at the page in poor light, while all sorts of distractions poke at him. You want that reader to believe that he is actually in the world of your imagination, the world you have created, climbing up that mountain you've written about, struggling against the cold and ice to find the treasure that you planned up at the peak.

The easiest way—in fact the *only* good way—to make the reader live in your story is to give him a character that he wants to be. (pp. 10-11)

Once you've decided who your protagonist will be, and you know his strengths and weaknesses, hit him where it hurts most! Develop an instinct for the jugular. Give your main character a problem that he cannot solve, and then make it as difficult as possible for him to wriggle out of his dilemma. . . .

The reader must be hanging on tenterhooks of doubts and suspense up until the very end of the story. Which means that the protagonist must be equally in doubt about the outcome. And in a well-crafted story the protagonist *cannot win* unless he surrenders something of inestimable value to himself. In other words, he's got to lose something, and the reader will be in a fever of anticipation trying to figure out what he's going to lose. (p. 12)

Every story you write will be at least partially autobiographical, and every protagonist you create will have more than a little of yourself in him. That's what makes writing such an emotional pursuit; you are revealing yourself, putting your heart and guts out on public display, every time you write a story. (p. 16)

How does a writer make an effective, fascinating background for a short story without going into excruciating detail? Here are a few simple guidelines.

First: Make every background detail *work*. That is, everything about the background should be important to the story. You don't have the room, and the reader doesn't have the time, to rhapsodize over multi-colored sunsets on a planet that has six suns. Not unless those gorgeous colors will affect the outcome of the story. If it's in the story merely for the sake of exotic detail, or simply because you enjoyed writing that paragraph, take it out. Only those background details that affect the story's development and resolution should be in your final draft.

Second: Don't try to explain how the machinery works; just show what it does. Thirty years ago, science fiction writers went into painstaking detail to show the reader that gyroscopes really could be used to maneuver a spacecraft on its way to the moon. Today such explanations are laughable, even though they're technically quite correct, because spacecraft don't use gyroscopes for attitude control; gas jets are lighter, smaller, and more reliable. (pp. 48-9)

Third: Feel free to invent any new devices, to make any new scientific discoveries that you can imagine—*providing they don't contradict what is known about science today*. (p. 49)

Fourth: You should be thoroughly familiar with the background of your story. (p. 51)

You must write about what you know. And what you know is a combination of hard information from the world around you, plus that special interior world of imagination that is yours and yours alone—until you share it with your audience. (pp. 52-3)

Fifth: This pointer is actually a corollary to the fourth one. It's important to learn the basics of science. The task is not difficult; in fact, it can be very exciting. Most science fiction writers are interested in science to some degree, although a good many of them are "turned off" by school classes in physics, chemistry, or math.

One of the best ways I know to learn about science on your own and at your own pace is to read the science books of Isaac Asimov and Arthur C. Clarke. Both these men are fine, vivid writers who can make any subject come alive. *Asimov's Guide to Science* should be on the reference shelf of every science fiction writer, along with Clarke's *Profiles of the Future*. At least!

Science is beautiful, and anyone can understand the basics of scientific thought. Poets who sing about the beauty of the stars, without understanding what makes them shine and how they were created, are missing more than half of the real splendor of the heavens. (p. 53)

The essence of creating a strong, exciting plot lies in building a powerful timebomb, and making certain that the reader can hear its ticking from the very first page—or even the first paragraph—of the story. The three aspects of short-story writing . . . character, background, and conflict—should all be brought into focus by the plot. The protagonist must have a problem that he must solve. To solve this problem he will come into conflict with other characters and/or the environment in which he finds himself. The background of the story must contribute to the protagonist's struggle. (pp. 108-09)

The stories that last, the stories that really stay in the reader's minds, are usually stories that have a strong interplay between a very sympathetically drawn protagonist and a powerful, overwhelming problem. The writer's task is to make the reader *care* about the protagonist. Tie him to a chair and put a timebomb at his feet; and make certain that the bomb's clock ticks loudly.

For me, as a writer, the best way to build a good plot is to begin with a strong, sympathetic protagonist and put him into action against a similarly strong protagonist.

"Strong," in this context, doesn't necessarily mean the jutting jaw, steely eyes, and bulging muscles of the typical old-time pulp magazine hero. In a novelet called "The Dueling Machine" (which I later expanded into a novel), my protagonist was a gangling, bumbling young man who could barely walk across a room without getting into trouble. His antagonist was an equally young man who had all the athletic skills and martial arts. But the protagonist had strengths that the antagonist lacked, chiefly sincerity, honesty, and a dogged, stubborn kind of heroism that could take a lot of punishment without admitting defeat. (pp. 110-11)

In writing stories of any length, the most important thing to keep in mind is "show, don't tell." This is especially true in the short story.

The moment you break the flow of the story's action to explain things to the reader, you run the risk of losing the reader. All of a sudden, instead of being *in* the story, living the role of the protagonist, the reader is listening to you lecturing him. No matter how important the information you want to get across to him, the reader is immediately reminded that he's *reading,* rather than living in the story. It's a risk that you should never run, if you can avoid it. Never give the reader an opportunity to look up from the page. (p. 115)

A really good writer convinces the reader that the protagonist had a rich and busy life before the story began, and will continue to do so after the last page of the story has been finished. In other words, the plot should be arranged so that the reader gets the feeling that this character is really *alive;* his life didn't begin on page one and end on page last; he encompasses much more than merely the events of this one short story, Perhaps we shall meet him again, someday.

Of course, if the protagonist dies at the end of the story the reader can't expect to find him again. But there should be some character mourning for the protagonist that *will* live on. A sense of continuity is a subtle, but extremely powerful, method for convincing the reader that the story is really true. (p. 119)

All the studying, thinking, idea-generating, talking, and planning in the world isn't going to get a single word down on paper. In the final analysis, it's those long, lonely hours when there's nothing in the universe except you, a typewriter, and a stack of blank paper, that will determine how successful a writer you will be.

It would be easy to wax poetic at this point and try to fill you with enthusiasm and *esprit de corps* about the wonderful profession of writing. Truth is, it's as much work as digging ditches, and emotionally it's the most demanding profession I know.

A writer is always putting his guts on paper, and allowing editors, critics, and readers to take free kicks at him. Isaac Asimov once pointed out that he could read a review of his latest book that consisted of five thousand words of closely reasoned praise and one tiny sentence of harsh criticism. It's that one sentence that keeps him awake all night. And that's the way it is for all of us. (pp. 171-72)

Writing is hard work. It is lonely work. The hazards and pains, especially at the beginning, far outweigh the rewards. But . . . but . . .

The United Nations has published a book of photographs by the greatest camera wielders in the world, called *The Faces of Man.*

One of these photographs has always stuck in my mind. It shows an African village, where most of the people have gathered around an old, withered man who is evidently the village story-teller. He is at a high point in the evening's story; his arms are raised over his head, his mouth is agape, his eyes wide. And the whole village is staring at him, equally agape and wide-eyed, breathless to find out what happens next.

That is what story-telling is all about.

There is no older, more honored, more demanding, more frustrating, more rewarding profession in the universe. If the only thing that separates us from the beasts is our intelligence and our ability to speak, then story-telling is the most uniquely human activity there can be. (p. 173)

> *Ben Bova, in his* Notes to a Science Fiction Writer *(copyright © 1964, 1966, 1967, 1975 Ben Bova; copyright © 1974 Boy Scouts of America; reprinted with permission of Charles Scribner's Sons), Scribner's, 1977.*

THE AMAZING LASER (1971)

[*The Amazing Laser* is a] non-technical, non-mathematical primer on the laser, with an extensive (almost one-third of the book) introductory survey of optics research from Galileo and Newton to Planck, Einstein and Bohr. Elementary theory is woven into a chronological report on the laser's development from Townes' maser to Javon's gas laser and beyond, and the extraneous biographical padding so common at this level is eschewed. Holography is briefly discussed in a closing chapter on laser applications. This can't compete with the fuller, more advanced coverage by [Ben] Patrusky [in his *Laser: Light That Never Was Before*] or [H. Arthur] Klein [in his *Masers & Lasers*], but youngsters who are ordinarily ill at ease with science will find that Bova anticipates their difficulties, and they'll appreciate his careful definitions of all technical terms, his down-to-earth explanations of concepts, and his frequent use of analogies—fingerprints, a "run" on a bank, etc.—to clarify his points. (p. 1261)

> *Kirkus Reviews (copyright © 1971 The Kirkus Service, Inc.), December 1, 1971.*

The title [*The Amazing Laser*] furnishes an accurate indication of the book's tone and content. While it may serve as a fairly good introduction for the young reader, the text does not live up to its billing on the dust jacket. Its emphasis is on "gee whiz" applications, and it is not balanced by sufficient information about how or why the laser works. The dust jacket promises "problems to solve and experiments to perform." In this case the problems consist of a few trivial questions, none bearing particularly on lasers; the single experiment is Young's interference demonstration, which also illustrates nothing much regarding lasers. The oversimplified treatment is not helped by confusion of the terms "power" and "energy," or by failure to define the frequently used term "Angstrom Unit." The "curious student and the inquiring adult" deserve a more carefully constructed book than this. (pp. 122-23)

> Science Books *(copyright 1972 by the American Association for the Advancement of Science), Vol. VIII, No. 2 (September, 1972).*

OTHER CITATIONS

Penelope M. Mitchell, in School Library Journal, *March, 1972, pp. 130-31.*

Zena Sutherland, in Bulletin of the Center for Children's Books, *December, 1972, p. 53.*

CITY OF DARKNESS (1976)

The world of tomorrow is a bleak and hostile place in ["City of Darkness"]; survival is the paramount concern. Ben Bova, a practiced hand at science fiction, takes a down-to-earth look at New York in the indeterminate future and finds it has become a maximum-security prison for undesirables. The city is enclosed in a dome, open to visitors from the Outside only during the summer months. Then, sanitized suburbanites from the super-healthy but boringly regulated Tracts, where even the weather is controlled, come to New York as to some down-and-dirty Disneyland. Much as they do now, some would say. On Labor Day the dome is closed, the city deserted. Except . . . people do live there, after a fashion. Warring gangs roam the filthy avenues, the shadows hide poverty, fear and death.

Into this forbidding world steps Ron Morgan, a Tract teenager rebelling against his dictatorial father. In the city for a fling, on the eve of having to choose his "career vector," Ron is trapped inside the dome on closing day. (p. 10)

Mr. Bova is a good storyteller, and "City of Darkness" is a tingling adventure until its closing chapters. The desolate dome city is beautifully evoked, the action fiercely realistic. But all this believability crumbles under an overload of portentousness. When Mr. Bova insists on turning his sprightly cautionary tale into a heavy-handed morality play, that dome is soon awash in stereo-typical nonsense. (p. 11)

> *Robert Berkvist, in* The New York Times Book Review (© *1976 by The New York Times Company; reprinted by permission), April 11, 1976.*

Inconsistencies in the story line, unfortunate stereotyping, and insufficient character motivations weaken an already overburdened plot [in *City of Darkness*]. Nevertheless, Bova's grim futuristic setting and graphic style plus the contemporary theme of youthful gangland violence should make this popular with older, reluctant readers. (p. 1521)

> The Booklist *(reprinted by permission of the American Library Association; copyright 1976 by the American Library Association), July 1, 1976.*

OTHER CITATIONS

Cheryl DeWaard, in Best Sellers, *August, 1976, p. 148.*

THE DUELING MACHINE (1969)

"The Dueling Machine" shapes up to be, by far, one of the best juvenile science fiction books seen in quite a while. Set in the future where galaxies are inhabited and peace is kept by a universal police force and a new machine that enables people to release their hostilities in a harmless way, the story combines excitement, scientific accuracy and credibility to provide thought-provoking and enjoyable reading. (p. 61)

> *Lavinia Russ, in* Publishers Weekly *(reprinted from the October 20, 1969, issue of* Publishers Weekly *by permission of the critic, published by R. R. Bowker Company, a Xerox company; copyright © 1969 by Xerox Corporation), October 20, 1969.*

The sight of the author's name, Ben Bova, on the title page gave one a feeling of keen anticipation and in his new SF story he does not let us down. His imagination, taking us with him into the distant future, gives a tale of great ingenuity, equalled by its continuous excitement. In it, man has not only had to look beyond this world for room to live but to establish himself in these five galactic territories in order to do so. Since apparently man must need quarrel and fight, the duelling machine was invented to fight realistically in imagination without harm to contestants until Major Odel discovers a bad use for it. This could upset the balance of power of the rest of the Universe, but . . . The characters seem real people with understandable feelings. This is a most enjoyable experience in imagination. (p. 314)

> The Junior Bookshelf, *October, 1971.*

OTHER CITATIONS

Paul Heins, in The Horn Book Magazine, *December, 1969, pp. 677-78.*

The Booklist, *January 1, 1970, p. 563.*

END OF EXILE (1975)

[*End of Exile*, the] last and least satisfying book in the trilogy uses the same gimmicks as *Exiled from Earth* . . . and *Flight of Exiles* . . . but is without their plot twists and fairly well-drawn characters. The ship is falling apart by now, the original highly intelligent inhabitants have been replaced by their progeny—a superstitious lot. The story of how Linc educates himself and guides the ship safely to its final destination in spite of the manipulative priestess Magda and the power-hungry Monel runs fairly smoothly along, covering occasional flaws of logic and science, stereotyped characters, and a hackneyed theme (science wins over superstition once again). At least there's enough action to keep young sci fi readers interested and involved if not challenged. (p. 57)

Sonia Brotman, in School Library Journal *(reprinted from the December, 1975, issue of* School Library Journal, *published by R. R. Bowker Company, a Xerox company; copyright © 1975 by Xerox Corporation), December, 1975.*

This is a fresh, vigorous and altogether successful reworking of one of the classic themes of science fiction. A huge spaceship, bound for a distant star with a cargo of would-be colonists, suffers a terrible disaster en route. The leaders of the expedition are killed; much of the ship is wrecked. The survivors gather in those areas where the life-support systems are intact. Their minds benumbed by tragedy and by the struggle to stay alive, they gradually revert to a primitive existence. In time they forget about the original purpose of the voyage; they forget they are on a voyage at all; they come to think of the ship as the universe itself.

In "End of Exile" the survivors are all children. As infants, they were cared for by an old man named Jerlet. Then Jerlet went away, leaving behind taped instructions that the children still obey as if they were the Ten Commandments: No violence, no tampering with machines, etc. But a boy named Linc learns the truth. Jerlet's commandments were safety-precautions for the very young. Unless the children take control of the ship and change its course, it will soon plunge into a yellow sun. Linc confronts his friends with a clear choice: Grow up and accept responsibility, or die. Monel, the fledgling dictator of the children's society, opposes all change. Magda, the priestess who leads in the worship of Jerlet, holds the balance of power. The conflict, as Bova describes it, is taut with suspense; every move that each young person makes is treated with the utmost seriousness. "End of Exile" is the third book in a trilogy, but it stands alone as a story—and towers above most of the competition in juvenile S.F. (p. 48)

Gerald Jonas, in The New York Times Book Review *(© 1976 by The New York Times Company; reprinted by permission), March 7, 1976.*

OTHER CITATIONS

The Booklist, *October 15, 1975, p. 297.*

Zena Sutherland, in Bulletin of the Center for Children's Books, *February, 1976, p. 91.*

EXILED FROM EARTH (1971)

There's a touch too much of the incredible in this Bova nova. This future earth is ruled by one World Government and the overriding concern is maintaining the status quo since the population has exploded into the twenty billions. The cities have been surrendered to street ratpacks but the World Government does keep a shaky control over the countryside. Therefore it cannot permit the latest breakthrough in genetic control—one that produces a race of supermen or zombies. The Government reluctantly decides to round up 2,000 of the world's top scientists and exile them on a manmade satellite. One of the prisoners is computer engineer Lou Christopher, held after several harrowing escapes. But Lou is given a second chance by a member of the government he believes is in sympathy with the scientists. Instead, he finds himself working for a power-mad segment that plans to overthrow the Government and enslave the Earth through genetics. The plot is as haphazard as the way Lou and a few colleagues manage to outwit almost everyone, not to mention surviving a nuclear explosion. Not the best programming. (pp. 379-80)

Kirkus Reviews *(copyright © 1971 The Kirkus Service, Inc.), April 1, 1971.*

[*Exiled from Earth* is a] rapidly paced, tightly plotted story of a not-too-distant future when the planet is ruled by a powerful World Government. . . . The author has drawn on his own scientific background to provide realistic and vivid glimpses of the sciences involved; and in the person of a young computer engineer he supplies the individual whose initiative will help foil the terrible injustice. Why not pool their immense knowledge, turn the satellite into a spaceship, and head for the stars? If they land on a planet unsuitable for human life, they have the genetic knowledge to modify future generations to meet new conditions. Ingenious motivation for man's inevitable starward thrust. (p. 488)

Beryl Robinson, in The Horn Book Magazine *(copyright © 1971 by The Horn Book, Inc., Boston), October, 1971.*

OTHER CITATIONS

Publishers Weekly, *June 28, 1971, p. 63.*

FLIGHT OF EXILES (1972)

Larry Belsen and Dan Christopher, sons of the scientists in *Exiled from Earth* . . . , both fall in love with the same girl and are also rivals for leadership of the exiles who have been in space for 50 years. A fire, which could be sabotage, and a death, which could be murder, add to the crisis brought on by the discovery that the planet where they intend to settle is unsuitable. Deciding whether a new generation should be genetically altered to live there or another 50-year journey to a more favorable world should be attempted is left to Larry and Dan—and one of them is psychotic! While the love interest may irritate some SF fans, the straightforward, suspenseful action will appeal to junior high school readers and the undemanding story is a good steppingstone to [Robert] Heinlein's more complex *Orphans of the Sky*. . . . (p. 74)

Ruth Robinson, in School Library Journal *(reprinted from the January, 1973, issue of* School Library Journal, *published by R. R. Bowker Company, a Xerox company; copyright © 1973 by Xerox Corporation), January, 1973.*

Notice the characters of Ben Bova's *Flight of Exiles*. . . . First, the situation: 20,000 exiled scientists have been for 50 years en route to another planet in a deteriorating space ship. While the ship is in the hands of amateurs, 50 cryosealed people are burned to death, the one all-knowing scientist is killed, and astronomical data are erased. Who is the murderer? By page 45 we have met 13 characters of almost equivalent development, names rather than people. We can scarcely be expected to identify the murderer, since we cannot identify the protagonist with certainty. He must be one of the two nearly interchangeable men, both of whom crave power, want control, love the same girl, and think in italics. Specialists—psychotechs, cryogenists, molecular geneticists, and an astronaut—are known only by their technical jobs. They, too, are flat—jealous and sharp-tongued, or beautiful and smart; they are angry, thoughtful, violent, and bitter in rapid succession and without clear motivation. In the terms of Henry James, character and action are not fused. Unlike real people who have reasons for their emotional shifts, Bova's shallow characters are so vacillating that, inevitably, we don't care about them, not even enough to wonder about the identity of the murderer. They are described from the outside, and are only stage props to carry action.

If we apply the same axioms of character development to science fiction as we do to other literature, we realize that believing in the reality of character makes us believe in the experience. If the experience is fantastic, as it is in science fiction, only a believable character can make us feel that the discoveries within the story have significance. Since poor character delineation limits our discovery about ourselves, action alone is left to hold our interest. However, since the action does not grow out of the nature of character, the plot seems contrived and unimportant. The failure of such a story is simply one of failure in character development. (pp. 26-7)

> *Rebecca J. Lukens, in her* A Critical Handbook of Children's Literature *(copyright © 1976 by Scott, Foresman and Company; reprinted by permission), Scott, Foresman, 1976.*

OTHER CITATIONS

Donald Goddard, in The New York Times Book Review, *November 26, 1972, p. 8.*

MAN CHANGES THE WEATHER (1973)

Prefaced by a hasty peek at the past, Bova's text describes the ways in which man has—deliberately or accidently—changed his world's atmosphere: some of the book discusses such planned activity as rainmaking, some the efforts to control violent phenomena of weather, and some (a considerable portion) to pollution. The final chapter poses the need for international weather control and the problems it might entail. Appended material includes a list of government weather modification programs and an index. The writing style is brisk and informal, the organization of material logical, and the information authoritative and interesting. This book pairs nicely with the author's fictional *The Weathermakers.* (p. 107)

> *Zena Sutherland, in* Bulletin of the Center for Children's Books *(© 1974 by the University of Chicago; all rights reserved), March, 1974.*

Deliberately changing the weather is an old dream, and this book deals with both deliberate attempts and unplanned activities of man which modify global weather patterns. Most of man's attempts at changing weather have been intended to bring rainfall. The author traces the history of rain-making from the days of medicine men dancing and beating on drums (or, later, firing cannons) to make rain

down to our present day methods of seeding clouds with dry ice or silver iodide crystals. Modern weather modification programs are aimed at redistributing rainfall and suppressing destructive hailstorms. There are also attempts to change the electrical nature of clouds and reduce lightning storms. Reducing fog—particularly at airports—and taming hurricanes are other beneficial ways of changing the weather. Unintentional weather modification may have occurred with the addition of carbon dioxide into the atmosphere (the "greenhouse effect"), although man-made cloudiness seems to counter this effect. The book is informative, but its scientific value is diminished by the author's subjective views and over-emphasis on the dangers of air pollution. Government weather modification programs are listed, and a number of drawings supplement the text. (p. 123)

> *Science Books (copyright 1974 by the American Association for the Advancement of Science), Vol. X, No. 2 (September, 1974).*

OTHER CITATIONS

Publishers Weekly, *September 10, 1973, p. 52.*

Ralph J. Folcarelli, in School Library Journal, *March, 1974, p. 102.*

THE MILKY WAY GALAXY: MAN'S EXPLORATION OF THE STARS (1961)

Ben Bova has tackled the biggest subject available to a writer—the Milky Way galaxy and our relation to it—in a fresh, brisk and even slangy style [in *The Milky Way Galaxy*]. Among other matters Mr. Bova . . . discusses the size and complexity of the heavens, the manner of bringing order to this mass of material through naming and cataloguing the stars, how we know what we do know about the Milky Way. We also receive a close-up of one star, in this case the sun, and he tells us something about the latest findings in such a field as radio telescopes.

Contemplation of the universe and the earth's place in it and of the long history of man's attempt to understand this universe has often inspired great writing. Thus it jars a little when Mr. Bova tells us that "the brilliant Greek culture sprayed ideas through the ancient world in machine-gun fashion." I suppose there is no reason why he should not call scientists' work rooms "labs" and refer to the sun as "Old Sol himself." But I wish he had not done so.

It is easy to find fault with factual information or with shortened definitions in a popular book on a difficult subject. Mr. Bova writes, for example: "Mass is not to be confused with weight," which is a valid distinction. Then he adds: "Mass is the measure of the amount of matter in an object. Weight is the relationship of one mass' gravitational pull on another mass." This definition of mass I believe to be old-fashioned; weight can be defined better in about the same number of words.

Mr. Bova has, however, covered an enormous range of human history and scientific work in a very short space. He is particularly good in telling about astronomy before the radio telescope. After the radio telescope, it becomes more difficult to discuss astronomy in a way we can all understand. There are seven appendices which contain calculations for a number of interesting problems such as the determination of the sun's distance from the earth or the mass of the earth.

As an introduction to astronomy, for the young or for the old, this is a book well worth while. Handsome photographs of the heavens, taken by major observatories, and drawings by Peter Robinson which help one's understanding and fit closely to the text, round out the study. (p. 27)

> *Robert Plumb, in* The New York Times Book Review (© *1961 by The New York Times Company; reprinted by permission), May 7, 1961.*

Here is a book that deals with the stars in all their aspects, and does so with verve and enthusiasm. There is no subject that can so easily be used to stretch the mind and rouse the sense of awe and wonder at the beauties and mysteries of the universe, and Mr. Bova goes at it with a will. In doing so, he assumes no prior knowledge on the part of the reader except a good understanding of the English language. He also assumes the reader to be sufficiently interested in the subject to expect real detail and not merely feeble stuff to read himself to sleep with. The publisher tries to describe the result by specifying the book to be for "young adults." In my opinion it can be read with profit and fascination by any bright youngster in his teens and by any "old" adult who does not feel that it is undignified to learn new things. (p. 281)

> *Isaac Asimov, in* The Horn Book Magazine *(copyright, 1961, by the Horn Book, Inc., Boston), June, 1961.*

OTHER CITATIONS

Dorothy Schumacher, in Library Journal, *March 15, 1961, p. 156.*

NOTES TO A SCIENCE FICTION WRITER (1975)

In an informal, generalizing way, Ben Bova . . . here attempts to teach aspiring young sci fi writers how to construct a well-crafted short story. In discussing basic story elements, e.g., plot, character, background, and conflict, four of the author's stories are used as models. Unfortunately, Bova's own writing leaves much to be desired as a prototype. Some worthwhile points are made, and the essentials of good story telling are covered, but oversimplified restrictive rules and a sloppy awkward style severely limit the book's usefulness. (pp. 86-7)

> *Sonia Brotman, in* School Library Journal *(reprinted from the November, 1975, issue of* School Library Journal, *published by R. R. Bowker Company, a Xerox company; copyright © 1975 by Xerox Corporation), November, 1975.*

Somewhat chatty in his approach, the editor of *Analog*—a science fiction writer himself—brings common sense to bear in his advice to would-be writers of science fiction. Recognizing that any writer must be endowed with ideas, artistry, and craftsmanship, he concentrates on craftsmanship, the only element of the three that can be taught. He divides his discussion into considerations of character,

background, conflict, and plot; and intersperses short science fiction stories of his own for the purpose of further analysis. He does not neglect to touch on the writer's need for a scientific background, but his major stress is on the fact that "all of fiction deals with examining the human spirit, placing that spirit in a crucible where we can test its true worth." Unabashedly relying upon the terms *protagonist, antagonist,* and *tragedy* drawn from classical criticism, the author has been humanistic as well as practical in his view of the aims and techniques of science fiction. (p. 175)

> *Paul Heins, in* The Horn Book Magazine *(copyright © 1976 by the Horn Book, Inc., Boston), April, 1976.*

THROUGH THE EYES OF WONDER: SCIENCE FICTION AND SCIENCE (1975)

The part played by speculation in the growth of man's scientific knowledge is frequently unrecognized and deliberately played down by preachers of pure science. Brief as it is, Mr. Bova's history and explanation of science fiction may show some readers how inaccurate their mental picture of science is. Some of the book is old stuff to the hardened science-fiction fan; much is not, since not all such fans are experts in the history of science. The author does a good job of showing that human curiosity has parallel if not identical effects on researcher and fiction writer. Each wonders "what-if" and then does something about his wondering—each predicts what would happen if. It is a matter of little consequence that one devises an experiment and the other writes. A science-fiction editor and writer, Mr. Bova is not a disinterested reporter in the field any more than I am a disinterested reviewer; but I think he presents a fair case for his thesis. (p. 492)

> *Harry C. Stubbs, in* The Horn Book Magazine *(copyright © 1975 by the Horn Book, Inc., Boston), October, 1975.*

Ben Bova attempts to discuss the relationship between science and sci fi, to validate the genre's existence, and to promote sci fi as *the* literary form for today and the future. Man's history from origin as prosimian 50 to 70 million years ago to scientist today is traced; basic human urges (to hunt and to know) and how science and sci fi satisfy them are discussed. Evolution, storytelling, pulp magazines and Asimov's "Three Laws of Robotics" are among the myriad subjects touched upon. While Bova's point—that sci fi can help today's youth deal with future change—is well taken, his argument is way too long and cluttered with many unrelated and trivial lines of thought that are pursued and then left unfinished. The author, editor of the widely read sci fi magazine *Analog,* is obviously biased: his informal conversational style will hold the interest of those already sharing his views, but the lack of solid objective argument and cohesive prose will deter the uncommitted. (p. 103)

> *Sonia Brotman, in* School Library Journal *reprinted from the October, 1975, issue of* School Library Journal, *published by R. R. Bowker Company, a Xerox company; copyright © 1975 by Xerox Corporation), October, 1975.*

OTHER CITATIONS

Kirkus Reviews, *September 1, 1975, p. 1000.*

Zena Sutherland, in Bulletin of the Center for Children's Books, *April, 1976, p. 122.*

THE USES OF SPACE (1965)

[*The Uses of Space* is a] fascinating and provocative account devoted solely to a subject treated only briefly in most books on space—the consideration of why man is involved in space exploration. The author comments on the value of space probes, artificial satellites, and men in space and then speculates on how the moon and the planets and what may be found on them can be utilized for the benefit of mankind. The lucid text is supplemented by well-captioned diagrams and photographs [by George Giusti]. Four statistical tables are appended. (p. 485)

> The Booklist and Subscription Books Bulletin *(reprinted by permission of the American Library Association; copyright 1966 by the American Library Association), January 15, 1966.*

Many readers will be fascinated and entertained by the trials and tribulations of life on the Moon, the oily vapor of Venus, the lakes of lead and sulphur on Mercury, space submarines in the atmospheres of Jupiter and Saturn, etc. The uses of space, the thesis indicated by the title, receives scant attention and the arguments are weak. Military use is covered in two pages plus one drawing. Publishers are building up a fairly good list of worthwhile space books, but this one doesn't rate a place on any list. (p. 237)

> Science Books *(copyright 1966 by the American Association for the Advancement of Science), Vol. 2, No. 4 (March, 1966).*

With somewhat less literary success [than Fred Warhousky's *Target Moon*], Ben Bova has written *The Uses of Space* . . . , but the book's shortcomings may be due to its origins—a series of articles in a magazine. There is considerable repetition, and more often than not, a chapter will end in such a dramatic and rhetorical climax that the following chapter may be felt to be unnecessary. Nonetheless, this book, as well as *Target Moon*, is highly recommended as a collection of opinions and predictions calculated to stimulate thinking and imagination. Such "brainstorming" may well inspire a young reader to wish to be a part of future space exploration, whether or not many of the ideas discussed by the author ever becomes realities.

In *The Uses of Space*, Mr. Bova discusses the prospects for exploration of the several other planets, and since his remarks should be regarded as opinions, the door is open for argument. A few of his facts are wrong (the rotation period of Mercury is not synchronized with its revolution, thus altering much of his discourse); some information has been omitted entirely, such as the rotation of Venus or the existence of the Van Allen belts around Jupiter, through which some satellites move. (p. 25)

> *K. L. Franklin, in* Natural History (© *The American Museum of Natural History, 1966; reprinted with permission), November, 1966.*

OTHER CITATIONS

Zena Sutherland, in Bulletin of the Center for Children's Books, *December, 1966, pp. 54-5.*

THE WEATHER CHANGES MAN (1974)

Ben Bova has written a most readable little book about man and his climatic environment. Using current information from a wide variety of scientific fields, he has traced the effect of climate on human evolution and on the development of some of our present characteristics. The book contains statements that specialist scientists would condemn, but it gets the story across. Beginning with a description of the present theory of the earth's climate in the first stages of its formation and the way life originated, he traces the development of early man and the effects of the Ice Ages on his way of life. The changeover from nomadic hunting to farming is related to the changes in man's physical environment, and the manner in which some of his less desirable traits may have occurred because of this change is amusingly argued. He discusses the anatomical and physiological responses of the human body to climate, the effects of climatic conditions on our behavior and the effects of our behavior on the environment. Figures include the metric equivalents where appropriate. The illustrations are interesting, well chosen and well placed. (p. 301)

> Science Books *(copyright 1975 by the American Association for the Advancement of Science), Vol. XI, No. 4 (March, 1975).*

Fascinating theories of how changing climate affected man's physical development and social organization. Bova presents information on the links between climate and human physical characteristics as well as the usual topics of climate and social customs. His discussion of race is a little heavy-handed (he goes overboard defending equality of all people), and there are a number of extraneous personal anecdotes and weak attempts at humor. However, the black-and-white photos are good, and, overall, this is an unusually interesting treatment. (p. 49)

> *Virginia Reese, in* School Library Journal *(reprinted from* School Library Journal, *April, 1975, published by R. R. Bowker Company, a Xerox company; copyright © 1975 by Xerox Corporation), April, 1975.*

OTHER CITATIONS

Publishers Weekly, *August 19, 1974, p. 84.*

The Booklist, *September 15, 1974, p. 95.*

C

COHEN, Daniel 1936-

As an author of more than fifty books for young people and adults, American writer Daniel Cohen says of himself, "I will never catch Asimov, but I am pretty fast." Cohen's varied titles have broadened the scope of nonfiction; he has written on such subjects as human and animal behavior, the occult, ancient history, natural history, and parapsychology. Cohen was a speaker at an international parapsychology conference in France, and has contributed articles to *Parapsychology Review*. Before becoming a free-lance writer, he was the managing editor of *Science Digest*. (See also *Contemporary Authors*, Vols. 45-48 and *Something About the Author*, Vol. 8.)

THE AGE OF GIANT MAMMALS (1969)

Paleontological finds and observations form the bulk of this cursory look at the rise, decline and continuation of mammals. Mr. Cohen's jovial popularization is in fact a vulgarization claiming in quasi-serious tone that certain mammals "died out from constipation" while others "succumbed to dental problems." Among other discrepancies, the author's *phenacodus* with well-developed claws contradicts the commonly hoofed *phenacodus*. Furthermore, given the fact that more than two-thirds of the history of mammals occurred prior to the so called "Age of Mammals" and that during this pre-Cenozoic era the basic mammalian pattern was formed, it is a gross understatement to say that these early mammal forms remained "insignificant and stagnant." An apology for the use of technical terms runs in the vein of [Hendrik W.] Van Loon's apologies for pedantic passages, and despite much theorizing, this does not even achieve the standing of hypothesis or assumption; it is unscientific and unsound. (p. 1003)

> Kirkus Reviews *(copyright © 1969 The Kirkus Service, Inc.), September 15, 1969.*

The combination of interesting material and good presentation make [*The Age of Giant Mammals*] a worthwhile book for student, naturalist and intelligent layman. Some of the topics require a background in elementary college biology, but the book can be recommended for the brighter high school student. This is not a course text but can be used for supplementary reading. The first two chapters dwell on the history of discoveries and interpretations of mammal bones, and the legends and myths that evolved concerning the bones. The chapter on theories on the extinction of dinosaurs and the rise of mammals is refreshingly brief and precise. Six chapters cover the geological history and evolution of mammals, beginning with the earliest species and progressing through the ancient giant forms to the more recent ones. Many representatives of the carnivores, herbivores, flying and aquatic mammals are described and their habitats and ways of life are discussed. The final chapters deal with the large present-day mammals and their futures. The scientific material appears to have been carefully checked, but the geologic time chart does not agree entirely with those appearing in other texts. This is a minor point however, when compared with the good features of this book. (p. 243)

> Science Books *(copyright 1969 by the American Association for the Advancement of Science), Vol. 5, No. 3 (December, 1969).*

ANCIENT MONUMENTS AND HOW THEY WERE BUILT (1971)

Monuments, the author believes, were constructed because the builders wanted "to show the world how powerful they were, and ensure that men would remember them long after they died." Seven monuments or groups of them constructed in ancient times are described in this book: the Tower of Babel, the Pyramids, Stonehenge, the Nazca Drawings, Sacsahuaman, the Easter Island Statues and Great Zimbabwe. Cohen tells why these monuments were built, how they were or might have been constructed, the part they played in their civilizations, and what remains of them today. A comprehensive bibliography follows the text and is divided according to the specific monuments, as are the chapters. Those items in the bibliography of particular interest to younger readers are marked with an asterisk. Information about these monuments is available elsewhere but in scattered sources, so libraries serving young people interested in archaeology and the study of ancient civilizations will want to acquire this clear, unified treatment. (p. 75)

> Barbara Gibson, in School Library Journal *(reprinted from the February, 1972, issue of* School Library Journal, *published by R. R. Bowker Company, a Xerox company; copyright © 1972 by Xerox Corporation), February, 1972.*

In rather simple language the author describes seven types of ancient monuments and gives a brief history of their discovery, the various theories concerning their construction, and a glimpse of the ancient history of each. Included among the monumental architectural structures of the ancient world are the ziggurats of Mesopotamia; the pyramids of Egypt; Sacsahuaman, the Inca fortress of Cuzco, Peru; Zimbabwe of Rhodesia; and Stonehenge of England. The latter three represent the best known examples of a particular type of architecture in the regions in which they are found. The two other subjects, the statues of Easter Island and the incredibly large life-forms or "drawings" in the desert areas of Peru, are not architectural. The author includes them in the class of monuments because much work and skill were needed to make them. Often the discussion of the monuments seems oversimplified, although alternative hypotheses about who actually built the monuments and how and why they were built are discussed. The presentation of alternative hypotheses is based on the latest scientific research. Such discussions are not ordinarily included in books for the general reader, and they increase the value of this book for the young reader. (pp. 178-79)

> *Science Books (copyright 1972 by the American Association for the Advancement of Science), Vol. VIII, No. 2 (September, 1972).*

THE ANCIENT VISITORS (1976)

Daniel Cohen, a free-lance writer whose past books have been on ghosts, sorcerers, and the like, here mounts a bold task—an impartial, objective and critical analysis of various theories that earth has been visited by "extraterrestrial intelligences" (ETIs). With a colloquial, personal writing style, Cohen skims the speculations of Fort, Lowell, Downing and other ETI believers; but he concentrates on the majordomo of ETI visitation—Erich von Däniken. Like the authors he criticizes, Cohen fails to do original research, relying instead on secondary sources and his own logic. And he detours, touching on recent UFO sightings and Bermuda Triangle legends. Cohen takes seriously the work of respected scientists such as Sagan and Shklovsky, agreeing with most reputable scholars today that ETI is indeed quite likely, yet visitation is simply unproved. With his own liberal perspective established, Cohen demonstrates numerous flaws in von Däniken's and similar writers' work. Considering the extent to which von Däniken-style pulp stories are believed, competent critiques intended for lay readers are welcome. Unfortunately, this one is cursory, rambling and not always convincing. (pp. 125-26)

> *Science Books & Films (copyright 1976 by the American Association for the Advancement of Science), Vol. XII, No. 3 (December, 1976).*

In this pleasant, timely book, an experienced science writer with a long-standing interest in the occult analyzes a large body of popular literature. The topics run from the Bermuda Triangle to Easter Island, from the huge markings in the Nazca desert to the crystal skull in the British Museum, from the Great Pyramid to Ezekiel's Wheel and the high-voltage Ark of the Covenant. Such disparate tales are brought together these days by a story that ascribes them, every one, to ancient visits of superior star folk.

The chief argument, when it is not based on overt distortion of the data, turns out to run more or less in the vein that those dull non-Europeans in Asia or Africa or the Americas could not possibly have made those grand and beautiful things. The stories are not in detail particularly new; Charles Hoy Fort had most of them before the Great Depression. But they persist. Cohen does a first-rate job of calm, skeptical analysis; "the fun of the book is in the evidence," he says. We ask big questions: questions of the universe, questions of the meaning and origin of life. We cannot get easy answers; the visitors with their UFO vehicles are too easy.

The young reader is left to make his own final judgment, but it is made pretty clear that the material is at best wildly unproved and at worst plain fake. Meanwhile Magnetic Hill is demonstrably not so magical, that Triangle does not eat planet and ships, and one would certainly like to see at least a snapshot of that boulder floating high in front of the mosque in Shivapur, the one that is supposed "to become weightless when eleven people stand around it touching it with their index fingers and chanting 'Qamar All Dervish' loudly." One welcomes this book, which is never hostile or condescending; libraries can make good use of it, and it may bring perspective to many readers. (p. 141)

> *Philip and Phylis Morrison, in* Scientific American *(copyright © 1976 by Scientific American, Inc.; all rights reserved), December, 1976.*

OTHER CITATIONS

The Booklist, *March 15, 1976, p. 1032.*

Kirkus Reviews, *April 15, 1976, p. 486.*

ANIMAL TERRITORIES (1975)

Animal Territories will serve as a useful introduction to the topic of territoriality in animals. Cohen develops the concept of territoriality from an evolutionary perspective. In spite of the brevity of the book, many interesting facts and examples are presented, including the three-spined stickleback, herring gull and Uganda kob. (Many of the examples that are discussed briefly in the text are shown in the film *Animal War, Animal Peace* . . . , and the book and film could be used to complement each other nicely.) The main weakness of the book lies in its brevity. There is a two-page bibliography and a general index. Unfortunately, references to several authors who are discussed in the text are not provided. Students might, for example, wish to do additional reading from the works of anthropologist E. T. Hall on spacing behavior in humans, but references are not given. (p. 40)

> *Science Books & Films (copyright 1976 by the American Association for the Advancement of Science), Vol. XII, No. 1 (May, 1976).*

Recent studies by animal behaviorists regarding animals' selection and defense of home territories have been translated into terms understandable to younger readers [in *Animal Territories*]. The author begins with the familiar dog and branches out into wider fields of wildlife. Included are such animals as the kob, an antelope that defends a small breeding mound; the social animals, such as wolves; the solitaries, such as tigers; and an array of birds and fishes that have differing territorial demands. The book includes much recent material and the explanations are good; even those which may be over-simplified remain reasonable. (p. 15)

> *Wayne Hanley, in* Appraisal *(copyright ©️ 1976 by the Children's Science Book Review Committee), Fall, 1976.*

OTHER CITATIONS

The Booklist, *November 15, 1975, p. 451.*

Debbie Robinson, in Appraisal, *Fall, 1976, p. 15.*

THE BLACK DEATH, 1347-1351 (1974)

Cohen's touch-all report on the morbidly fascinating 14th-century epidemic begins with a summary of Boccaccio's first-hand account, a review of previous outbreaks of bubonic plague as mentioned in the Old Testament and elsewhere, and an explanation of the nature and forms of the disease caused by the Pasteurella pestis baccilus and the role of rats and fleas in spreading it. Social preconditions for the plague and how it spread along trade routes, the helplessness of priests and doctors and the aftermath of disorder and revolt are all duly noted, but Cohen never stops anywhere long enough for more than a glance. Medical theory and practice of the time are almost totally ignored, the chapter on the wandering flagellants is never tied in with the Black Death, and—regarding the persecution of the Jews—Cohen points out that they were already resented for performing "necessary social functions as merchants and money lenders" but not that Church law effectively cast them in this role. He also refers to the belief that the Jews poisoned the wells but not to its partial cause—the Jews' relative freedom from plague due to superior sanitation in the ghettos. Minor omissions, which don't disqualify the introduction, but indicative of Cohen's quick-skim approach. (p. 111)

> Kirkus Reviews *(copyright ©️ 1974 The Kirkus Service, Inc.), February 1, 1974.*

One of the most morbidly fascinating occurrences of medieval history—the plague or Black Death—is given a thorough and balanced treatment by Daniel Cohen. Despite the scarcity of statistics and reliable accounts, this is a good overview of the plague years which cites such material as Boccaccio's description of the outbreak in Florence and papal records from the city of Avignon. Woodcuts and late medieval manuscripts graphically illustrate the horrors and dread reality of the pandemic of 1347-1351. Most interesting from the viewpoint of social history are the chapters describing the impact of the plague on the psychology and behavior of men. . . . Although Cohen tends to understate the effect of the plague years—the consciousness of death, sin, and morbidity did not entirely give way to the "enormous optimism" of the Renaissance, as he states—and does not delve into all the economic consequences, this is an interesting account and the only children's book on the subject. (p. 61)

Shirley M. Wilton, in School Library Journal *(reprinted from the November, 1974 issue of* School Library Journal, *published by R. R. Bowker Company, a Xerox company; copyright ©️ 1974 by Xerox Corporation), November, 1974.*

OTHER CITATIONS

The Booklist, *May 1, 1974, p. 999.*

THE BODY SNATCHERS (1975)

A book more likely to find a place in the black hearts of young readers than on the required reading lists of our school system is this dandy little account of the history of grave robbing. An unlikely subject for a juvenile book, I would have thought, but it works like a dream, a very bad dream. . . . "The Body Snatchers" combines first-rate storytelling with good, informal history. With a side trip into the land of the Zombies, Mr. Cohen sketches a deliciously dark portrait of grave robbing from the days of ancient Egypt through the 19th century, when grave robbing for anatomical dissection was common—Mr. Cohen calls it "the Golden Age of body snatching"—up to such present-day political manifestations of the dishonorable craft as the nocturnal disinterment of Marshall Petain by a group of right-wing Frenchmen in 1973.

What could have been a distasteful story in lesser hands becomes spritely and fascinating reading. Mr. Cohen has crafted a model of good juvenile literature. The book can be read with interest by adults and makes no condescension to young readers whatsoever beyond being written in good, straightforward declarative sentences. (p. 8)

> *Peter Andrews, in* The New York Times Book Review *(©️ 1975 by The New York Times Company; reprinted by permission), July 6, 1975.*

OTHER CITATIONS

Donald A. Colberg, in School Library Journal, *May, 1975, pp. 53-4.*

The Booklist, *May 15, 1975, p. 957.*

DREAMS, VISIONS, & DRUGS: A SEARCH FOR OTHER REALITIES (1976)

Cohen's review of altered states of consciousness—everything from meditation and religious visions to left-right brain research—has the merits of common-sense synthesis. Indeed, some aspects of the discussion, particularly the unhysterical approach to LSD, are conducted with more maturity than one expects from the juvenile literature. However, Cohen's summaries of scientific experiments can be off-handed; [Alvin and Virginia Silverstein], for example, offer a more rigorous treatment of *Sleep and Dreams* (1973). And quibblers can find evidence that Cohen's grasp of the subject is superficial: Zen koans *do* have answers; statements such as "LSD began producing more bad reactions than good ones" are purely assumptions. Readers who just want to get their bearings in a general way could do worse, but even a more extensive bibliography could have boosted this to a whole new level of usefulness. (p. 332)

In offering a straightforward historical review of human experiences known as altered states of consciousness (ASC), Cohen acknowledges both their subjectivity and their importance to the individual who experiences them. Neither belittling nor promoting, he ranges over some of the more distinct classes of ASC—religious and mystical, drug-related and visionary experiences, meditation, dreams, hypnosis, mortification of the flesh, and possession —citing specific cases from antiquity to the present. . . . [*Dreams, Visions, and Drugs: A Search for Other Realities* is a] comprehensive introductory overview for junior high and high school age readers. (p. 1251)

OTHER CITATIONS

Judith Atwater, in School Library Journal, *September, 1976, p. 130.*

GOLD: THE FASCINATING STORY OF THE NOBLE METAL THROUGH THE AGES (1976)

The singular attraction gold has held for humankind invites Cohen's consideration from a number of divergent perspectives. Amid facts about gold and its uses—in the present, recent, and ancient past—are some tantalizing thoughts: ". . . virtually every bit of gold that has ever been mined . . . is still around somewhere in some form or other. A modern wedding band, or even a gold tooth filling may contain gold that at one time was part of the death mask of an Egyptian Pharaoh . . . romantic or not, it is still possible." In addition, there is a hard look at how the South African gold mines and their largely black workers constitute "some of the ugly realities that lie behind the beautiful golden ornaments so many of us crave." Cohen's buckshot approach, ranging from alchemists and treasure fantasies to the world monetary market, is advantageous for perspective but results in thinness—each chapter could be the subject of a book. Yet itinerant browsers will be rewarded by the generalist approach, while later chapters on world finance will be useful to students seeking a simple outline of the gold standard and financial relationships that influence the present world monetary situation. (pp. 717-18)

[*Gold: the Fascinating Story of the Noble Metal Through the Ages* contains everything] that anyone could ever want to know about gold. Cohen writes enthusiastically of the early Egyptian and Roman use of gold as both money and as decoration, of medieval alchemy, and of the modern use of gold as a monetary standard. Also included are accounts of gold rushes in the United States, Africa, and Australia and refining in South Africa. The only book of its kind for this age level. (p. 66)

HUMAN NATURE–ANIMAL NATURE: THE BIOLOGY OF HUMAN BEHAVIOR (1975)

Cautioning against blind acceptance of what is only theory based upon a painfully small body of hard evidence, Cohen provides a thoughtful overview of scientific observations and theories concerning the nature and behavior of human beings and changing views on the evolution of man. In light of controversy between scientists who believe human behavior has a biological basis and those who think it stems from cultural influences, he examines the use of symbols and rituals as well as patterns of dominance and submission in both animals and man, the sexual behavior of men and animals, overpopulation, and war. Stressing the disparity of scientific opinion and the ease of interpreting evidence in more than one way, he concludes that man must, for the present, continue to get along with a nature he cannot really understand or fully control. A stimulating introduction. . . . (p. 809)

Daniel Cohen's thought-provoking, readable book deals basically with aspects of man's behavior that may be inherited from his biological past. It is conceptual in scope and especially valuable for the first chapter and for occasional passages that develop a perspective on the way man has viewed issues in the past as well as the present. The second chapter, on man's evolution, is concerned with theory rather than detail. Incorporating many of the points made by Lorenz, Nikko Tinbergen, and Desmond Morris, later chapters discuss society's dilemmas today—sex, love, and marriage; crowding and warfare. Also included are topics such as woman's equality, the origin of the kiss, and Lorenz's list of "cute" features of young children as they apply to Disney characters. A few of the arguments are hard to follow, and conjecture is sometimes stated almost as forcefully as fact. I hope a casual reader will not accept without question that an ape-like begging gesture is "surely the origin of our handshake." (pp. 400-01)

IN SEARCH OF GHOSTS (1972)

What is a ghost? Ask this question of a psychical researcher, a producer of horror movies, a practicing occultist and an average 12-year-old, and you will probably get widely divergent answers. Perhaps the definition given by Lewis Spence in his "Encyclopaedia of Occultism" is as good as any: "A ghost is a visual '*apparition*' of a deceased human being, and the term implies it is the spirit of the person it represents."

Unfortunately for the romantics among us, the current resurgence of interest in occult phenomena has produced almost no new or reliable evidence for the classic ghost (as distinct from the clairvoyant impression, the phantasm of the living and so on). Unless he or she is a true believer or a folklorist, therefore, the author of a ghost book is left with little to say. That is the apparent predicament of Daniel Cohen, who has responded by broadening the traditional definition of ghosts to include almost any alleged occurrence involving "spirits," whether seen, heard, felt, or even merely smelled. . . .

For anyone seeking an introduction to various views of life "beyond the grave" there are certainly some intriguing snippets of information (and some well-chosen illustrations) here. However, the final result is neither a history of belief in ghosts nor a thorough examination of the question of survival. For example, no mention is made of either the great California "soul trial" or the experiments in survival conducted by Dr. Ian Stevenson and others. Even more unfortunate is the fact that, for all its ambitious scope, the book has an oddly perfunctory air, as if the author had been writing to a word limit. The topic deserves better, and the reader can only sigh with Hamlet, "Alas, poor ghost!" (p. 8)

> *Georgess McHargue, in* The New York Times Book Review *(© 1972 by The New York Times Company; reprinted by permission), April 16, 1972.*

Ghosts is rife with such absurdities as, "Like most philosophers he was not a rich man"; or, in explaining the sudden growth of spiritualism, "The fact is that a lot of people were ready for spiritualism in 1848"; or "Primitive man was very logical" and "Primitive man was also profoundly conservative." These statements may be true, but Cohen offers no supporting evidence of any kind, so readers can assume only that he has been in spirit communication with primitive man. Furthermore, Daniel Cohen states, "The ghost of the newly dead man was usually considered stronger and closer than the ghost of one who died long ago." By whom? At what point in history? Why? Though Cohen holds a degree in journalism, he seems to have forgotten the time-honored journalistic checkpoints: who, what, when, where, why, and how. (pp. 129-30)

. . . . .

Unfortunately, the examination of the subject here is far less detailed than that in Georgess McHargue's *Facts, Frauds, and Phantasms.* . . . The scope of . . . *Ghosts* is not well defined and seems too large for the brief treatment accorded. The presentation is further marred by undocumented, sweeping generalizations (e.g., "During this period most people didn't have time to be afraid of ghosts") and an almost total lack of information about the state of the present-day phenomena. (p. 66)

> *Michael Cart, in* School Library Journal *(reprinted from the October, 1972, and the November, 1972, issues of* School Library Journal, *published by R. R. Bowker Company, a Xerox company; copyright © 1972 by Xerox Corporation), October and November, 1972.*

OTHER CITATIONS

Kirkus Reviews, *March 15, 1972, p. 337.*

INTELLIGENCE: WHAT IS IT? (1974)

In the first chapters [of *Intelligence—What Is It?*] Cohen runs through some of the more familiar studies of animal learning, language and intelligence—McConnell's controversial "memory transfer" work with planaria at Michigan, Skinner's box (extremely sketchy and superficial here), Lilly's dolphins and their relatives the whales, and various apes—without really zeroing in on the significance of the examples. The ape chapter, for example, goes on far too long about ancient supersititions and attitudes before coming even to the Harlows' chimp, and at the end describes Wolfe's experiments with poker chips and the chimp-o-mat without interpreting the findings at all. The second half of the book deals with human IQ—the history of IQ tests and the various kinds used today, the uncertainty as to what they actually do test, the debate over Jensen's views on heredity, race and IQ (here as elsewhere, Cohen seems unduly "objective," faulting Jensenism straight out only for its likely social and political effects), and—peripherally—Piaget's observations of how children of different ages think. These later topics have been less frequently exploited in children's books than the animal studies, but introducing children to currently splashy names (Jencks and Shockley among them) is of limited value when none of the basic concepts or current issues are elucidated in the process. (p. 6)

> Kirkus Reviews *(copyright © 1974 The Kirkus Service, Inc.), January 1, 1974.*

This is the best balanced book on this subject that this reviewer has ever encountered. It is exceptionally well written in a calm but interesting tone. It can and should be read by everyone from the seventh grade up. It certainly should be required reading for all teachers, school and university officials, employment counselors, personnel executives and mental health workers. Three themes run through the book; what is meant by intelligence; what is the evidence; and how good is the support for any statement made in this field. The author commences with the problem of assessing animal intelligence and relates its history and pitfalls. The "romance of the apes and dolphins" is gently deflated, and an accurate assessment of contemporary animal behavior research and its conclusions are presented. A history of IQ testing is given, and a description of the major features of these tests is presented. The major points of the IQ tests' detractors are presented, without the stridency of the latest popular works. The Jensen-Shockly-Herrnstein debacle is reviewed, and the inescapable conclusion is made clear; namely, we shall never know the answers to many questions about IQ and intelligence and, more importantly, that most of these answers don't matter: How many whites would trade their racial physiognomies for 50 extra IQ points? The message of the book is that it is important to study learning, perception and cognitive styles in order to understand how men and animals adapt to their worlds. (p. 186)

> Science Books *(copyright 1974 by the American Association for the Advancement of Science), Vol. X, No. 3 (December, 1974).*

OTHER CITATIONS

Mrs. John Gray, in Best Sellers, *March 15, 1974, p. 556.*

The Booklist, *April 15, 1974, p. 932.*

Isadora Kunitz, in School Library Journal, *May, 1974, p. 62.*

SHAKA, KING OF THE ZULUS: A BIOGRAPHY (1973)

Cohen doesn't ask us to admire Shaka—merely to judge him by the same standards we apply to Western military geniuses and despots like Napoleon and Ivan the Terrible. And he makes a good case for the genius of this illegitimate outcast who revolutionized Bantu warfare and molded the formerly insignificant Zulu tribe into the core of a sizable empire. Shaka had the dubious distinction of replacing a tradition of sportsmanlike skirmishing with *impi ebomvu* (or total warfare) and of cementing his power by means of terror, including frequent random executions of his loyal followers. But the Bantu peoples had already reached the end of their loosely organized nomadic way of life, and Cohen shows that Shaka's tactics were the work—not of a mad, rampaging savage as white South Africans were prone to believe—but of a cold, calculating political intelligence. Above all, the rapid rise of the Zulus shows that South Africa was a land in flux—and the home of some highly innovative societies—a view not ordinarily presented in white-oriented histories of Africa. Generally reliable sources, such as [Ernest A.] Ritter's *Shaka Zulu* have been mined to good effect, and without resorting to fictionalization. Low key and readable. (p. 198)

> Kirkus Reviews *(copyright © 1973 The Kirkus Service, Inc.), February 15, 1973.*

[*Shaka, King of the Zulus: A Biography* is an] exciting presentation of Shaka's life packed with details of his warfare methods and extensive use of murder and torture. Cohen documents Shaka's military and political genius which enabled him to form a nation from over 100 tribes in what is today South Africa. . . . Cohen skillfully points out cultural differences while presenting an objective view of this multi-faceted leader and his people. Detailed information is provided about the daily life of the Zulus: their traditions, economic, political, and social life. This same candid treatment is given to sexual customs—e.g., ". . . a form of incomplete intercourse that serves to release sexual tension but does not result in impregnation. [It] was frequently practiced—indeed, encouraged—between young men and unmarried girls." Such passages do not add significantly to an understanding of the Zulus or Shaka and may curtail the usefulness of this otherwise excellent book. (pp. 80-1)

> *Anitra Gordon, in* School Library Journal *(reprinted from the September, 1973, issue of* School Library Journal, *published by R. R. Bowker Company, a Xerox company; copyright © 1973 by Xerox Corporation), September, 1973.*

OTHER CITATIONS

The Booklist, *September 15, 1973, p. 110.*

THE SPIRIT OF THE LORD: REVIVALISM IN AMERICA (1975)

[On] the whole this is a responsible harkening back to those early frontier camp meetings which reached Americans who were, contrary to myth, not very religious and not likely to meld into the stern Calvinist company of the pre-destined elect. Cohen recognizes that, while in large part a reaction against Calvinism, revivalism never followed hard and fast theological lines and he traces the movement's evolution from muscular evangelism (Dwight Moody scorned audiences that had "too many Christians" in them) into professional showmanship that reaches an already churched public to confirm their existing religious and conservative political views. In the context of this relatively serious-minded presentation, Cohen's portraits of such evangelists and Dwight Moody and Billy Sunday are striking and his criticisms of the Billy Graham organization measured enough to give previously uncritical admirers second thoughts. (p. 577)

> Kirkus Reviews *(copyright © 1975 The Kirkus Service, Inc.), May 15, 1975.*

This fascinating history of revivalism in America traces its development from the first Great Awakening in Puritan times to Billy Graham and the Jesus movement today. The author looks at revivalism as part of the social history of the United States and sees its ebbing and flowing as part of a cycle which will probably continue into the future. The individual evangelists, whether Jonathan Edwards, Billy Sunday, Billy Graham, or others, are given large credit for beginning and giving substance to a revivalist movement, largely by their ability to arouse people's emotions. (Fundamentalist Christians may object to interpretations of some evangelists and the contention that the modern revivalist is "an agent for making men conform rather than reform.") This is an objective account, clearly and straightforwardly written, and it does a fine job of placing revivalism in the mainstream of American social and religious movements. (p. 52)

> *Jane E. Gardner, in* School Library Journal *(reprinted from the January, 1976, issue of* School Library Journal, *published by R. R. Bowker Company, a Xerox company; copyright © 1976 by Xerox Corporation), January, 1976.*

OTHER CITATIONS

The Booklist, *October 1, 1975, p. 225.*

Eileen Noonan, in Catholic Library World, *March, 1976, pp. 355-56.*

TALKING WITH THE ANIMALS (1971)

Mr. Cohen explores animal communication—within a species and also with man—in a comfortable book, entertaining and edifying, that concludes quite convincingly that "in a way we have come a full cycle. Primitive men believed that the animals could talk as well as men could, but we simply could not understand their language. . . . Now, after centuries of regarding the 'lower animals' as creatures that could not think, much less talk, we are again looking for the key to (their) secret languages. . . . At least a few scientists believe that when and if we find that key, the animals will have a lot to teach us." Among them are most of the men—and women—whose work is surveyed here after welcome preliminaries revive and reanalyze 'myths' and introduce concepts (somewhat over-simply: reaction, intelligence, instinct, adaptation). . . . As, however, a once-over, stand-alone synthesis this is a handy choice, and the package includes an index and reading list plus leavening photos and anecdotes. (p. 114)

> Kirkus Reviews *(copyright © 1971 The Kirkus Service, Inc.), February 1, 1971.*

Though aimed at younger people, *Talking with the Animals* makes fascinating reading for adults as well. Cohen recounts man's historical fascination with the notion of man-animal communication and succeeds in capturing the modern reader's imagination with his explanations of the advances being made in this field. Formerly, animal "speech" was generally regarded as magical, but in fairly recent times scientists have begun systematically investigating inter- and intra-species communications methods as well as the possibility of communication between man and animals. In this brief but comprehensive introduction to the subject Cohen covers historical cases of so-called "talking" animals and then proceeds to a discussion of modern theories and work in this area. We read of von Frisch's study of honeybee dances; of Konrad Lorenz' views on the limited communication ability of birds compared with the highly developed capacities of dogs; of Lilly's more tentative but potentially extremely exciting investigations of the sounds made by dolphins and whales; and, finally, there is an extensive discussion of studies of gorillas and chimpanzees under both natural and laboratory conditions. The study of Washoe, the chimp taught to communicate with humans by sign language, is especially captivating. In the process of discussing these various animals, Cohen further elucidates concepts introduced earlier in the book: instinct, learning, reaction, abstraction, adaption, intelligence, etc. The photographs, especially those of apes, are charming and enhance this attractively written, clear, but not simplistic overview of animal communication. (p. 245)

> Science Books *(copyright 1972 by the American Association for the Advancement of Science), Vol. VIII, No. 3/December, 1972).*

OTHER CITATIONS

Julian May, in Book World, *Part 2, May 9, 1971, p. 14.*

Frances Postell, in School Library Journal, *September, 1972, p. 128.*

VACCINATION AND YOU (1969)

"Every once in a while you are taken to the doctor for a vaccination. You have been getting vaccinations since you were very young. You don't remember the first ones you had. . . ." First you read about Jennings and Pasteur. Then you survey the history of vaccines until you get to Salk and Sabin. You see a caricature of a cannibal called "witch doctor driving away evil spirits" and some other artless, thoughtless drawings [by Haris Petie]. You see nothing at all about the new gun-type injection. And even though it keeps saying you don't have to be afraid, this book doesn't even redeem the old shot. (p. 1004)

> Kirkus Reviews *(copyright © 1969 The Kirkus Service, Inc.), September 15, 1969.*

Mr. Cohen clearly and simply describes Jenner's discovery of the vaccination for smallpox; Pasteur's contributions to the understanding of germs; Robert Koch's isolation of bacteria; Ehrlich and Behring's conquest of diptheria; virus study and the work of Fleming and Enders with penicillin; Salk, Sabin and the polio vaccines; and new vaccines for measles, mumps, and rubella. The information is, on the whole, general, with just enough detail provided to make the text interesting and comprehensible. Written in a pleasant, easy-to-read style, this book is a good addition to middle-grade collections and will be useful with reluctant readers. (p. 70)

> *Isadora Kunitz, in* School Library Journal *(reprinted from the May, 1970 issue of* School Library Journal, *published by R. R. Bowker Company, a Xerox company; copyright © 1970 by Xerox Corporation), May, 1970.*

OTHER CITATIONS

Science Books, *March, 1970, p. 337.*

WATCHERS IN THE WILD: THE NEW SCIENCE OF ETHOLOGY (1971)

[*Watchers in the Wild: The New Science of Ethology* is a] well-organized, very well-written elementary text, designed to provide an over-view of ethology. A sufficient amount of methodological detail is blended with a qualitative treatment of selected data to give the reader a broad, digestible impression of the way in which systematic observations of animal behavior should be conducted. The book begins with a vigorous scientific approach and attempts to articulate several basic mechanisms (e.g., competing responses) which appear to underlie complex behaviors. As the chapters proceed through a phylogenetic hierarchy, however, the approach is unevenly applied and the attempts to integrate material become more vague. The author often suggests that observation of animals under natural conditions is a useful precursor to laboratory observation. He does emphasize, however, that errors in interpretation of underlying biological mechanisms could be avoided when behavior is observed under more controlled conditions. He neglects to provide good examples of this phenomenon and, indeed, is cavalier in his own evaluation of forest "experiments." Nevertheless, he describes the study of animals in their natural habitat from a critical perspective, and demonstrates a healthy enthusiasm that could motivate many young readers toward a thoughtful and inquiring study of their environment. (p. 101)

> Science Books *(copyright 1971 by the American Association for the Advancement of Science), Vol. VII, No. 2/September, 1971).*

OTHER CITATIONS

Kirkus Reviews, *April 15, 1971, p. 444.*

The Booklist, *June 1, 1971, p. 830.*

Mrs. John Gray, in Best Sellers, *June 15, 1971, p. 150.*

Margaret Bush, in School Library Journal, *September, 1971, pp. 171-72.*

COLLIER, James Lincoln   1928-

A prolific American author of children's books, James Lincoln Collier has written adult fiction, nonfiction, and hundreds of articles for magazines as varied as *Soviet Life*, *The Village Voice*, and *Reader's Digest*. He is also well-versed in the subject of music due, in part, to his experience as a professional trombonist. Two of Collier's historical novels, *My Brother Sam Is Dead* and *The Bloody Country*, were written in collaboration with his brother, Christopher, an author and historian. (See also *Contemporary Authors*, Vols. 9-12, rev. ed. and *Something About the Author*, Vol. 8.)

BATTLEGROUND: THE UNITED STATES ARMY IN WORLD WAR II (1965)

The Second World War was such an unconfined sprawl that even 20 years later its history cannot be compassed in a book of ordinary length, but must be broken down as Mr. Collier has done with the Army, into its fighting branches. He uses an anecdotal approach to the theaters and the battles in which the Army carried the heaviest responsibility for defeat or victory, and his stories are shared out among the officers and the men. He hasn't Irving Werstein's flair for organizing the overall political and military factors that affect campaigns. Nevertheless, [*Battleground*] will be of interest to boys for the same reasons that adult books on this subject sell so well; a lot of veterans are willing to read these books and they have a lot of sons. (p. 765)

> Virginia Kirkus' Service, *August 1, 1965.*

[*Battleground* is a] history of the U.S. Army in World War II with special emphasis on individual heroes and their deeds.... One of the best and simplest explanations of why it was necessary to destroy Monte Cassino makes the book worthwhile. In addition to his treatment of personalities, the author provides an easy-to-follow overview of the war as it affected the U.S. Army ground forces. The book is well written and factual. Except for the Monte Cassino incident it contains little more than Don Larson's *The U.S. in World War II*. (p. 241)

> *Robert Kinchen, in* School Library Journal *(reprinted from the October, 1965, issue of* School Library Journal, *published by R. R. Bowker Company, a Xerox company; copyright © 1965 by Xerox Corporation), October, 1965.*

THE BLOODY COUNTRY (with Christopher Collier, 1976)

In this expository novel the Colliers highlight the troubles that befell eighteenth-century Connecticut settlers who migrated to the Wyoming Valley area of Pennsylvania around Wilkes-Barre.... There's a noteworthy story thread that explores the relationship between Ben and their family slave Joe Mountain and functions to chart Ben's evolving belief that freedom belongs to all. The smooth storytelling in modern speech patterns is sharp and speedy. It's pleasing that the authors have chosen to avoid rerunning the bleakness of *My Brother Sam Is Dead;* here it would have been sensationalized. (pp. 1403-04)

> The Booklist *(reprinted by permission of the American Library Association; copyright 1976 by the American Library Association), June 1, 1976.*

The co-authors of *My Brother Sam Is Dead* bring to life another aspect of America's past, the main events of which are based on actual occurrences [in the] mid-18th century.... As Ben describes the natural and man-made disasters that befall his people, the reader attains a better understanding of what it really meant to be a pioneer. The authoritative, honest look at brutal fighting and killing over land make this, in many respects, a disturbing book. Ben's relationship with Joe Mountain, the family slave, will remind many of the more idyllic adventures of Huck and Jim. But Ben's course is more difficult, as he and his father tangle over Joe's future. "No one wants to be a slave, whether it's the kind Joe Mountain was with a master who owned him, or the kind I almost got to be—having to work for somebody else . . . to be a slave feels about the same for everybody." A real feeling for the times as well as Joe's poignant struggle for freedom imbue the book with the stuff of history. (p. 83)

> *Ruth M. Stein, in* Language Arts *(copyright © 1977 by the National Council of Teachers of English), January, 1977.*

OTHER CITATIONS

Willard M. Wallace, in The New York Times Book Review, *May 2, 1976, p. 26.*

Publishers Weekly, *May 10, 1976, p. 84.*

DANNY GOES TO THE HOSPITAL (1970)

If an operation other than a tonsillectomy is in prospect, Danny might be your model boy—assuming relatively ideal hospital conditions . . . and a relatively untroubled patient. The operation is to correct an eye muscle and it involves, after a sunny Admissions, taking a blood sample, X-rays, and repeated check-ups ("As you can see from the look on Danny's face, he is getting pretty tired of check-ups"); betimes Danny goes to the well-equipped playroom and we go behind the scenes—to kitchen, repair shop, laundry, gift shop, library. Comes the operation, the doctor dons rubber gloves, Danny inhales an anesthetic—and mother waits (across the hall, it appears from the expressive layout) to see him when it's over. Also when it's over, the doctors rest—"Performing an operation is tiring because you must be so careful." The explanations could be more thorough (and for an older child, should be) but the people couldn't be more human. Yale Joel's photos crackle with concern, with suppressed joy, with concentration or curiosity. [Arthur Shay's] *What Happens When You Go to the Hospital* and [Billy N. Pope's] *Let's Visit* . . . and others narrow in on tonsils out; this could serve even when nothing specific is in the offing. (p. 457)

> Kirkus Reviews *(copyright © 1970 The Kirkus Service, Inc.), April 15, 1970.*

Photographs [by Yale Joel] and text show a small boy's progress through hospital routines from admittance to discharge. Danny has a minor eye operation, and the pictures show his intermittent nervousness with commendable candor. Not as entertaining as the [H. A.] Rey book on a hospital visit (*Curious George Goes to the Hospital* . . .) or as well-organized as the [Arthur] Shay (*What Happens When You Go to the Hospital* . . .), but useful. (p. 23)

Zena Sutherland, in Bulletin of the Center for Children's Books *(© 1970 by the University of Chicago; all rights reserved), October, 1970.*

OTHER CITATIONS

Isadora Kunitz, in School Library Journal, *September, 1970, p. 92.*

Mary Reed Newland, in The New York Times Book Review, *October 25, 1970, p. 38.*

GIVE DAD MY BEST (1976)

The plot [of *Give Dad My Best*] unfolds with little imagination and even less enthusiasm, and the climax is crystal clear from page one. Characterization is anemic except for Jack who possesses a dynamite conscience and the ability to daydream vividly. *Give Dad My Best* can't compare with [Robert] Burch's *Queenie Peavy* as a realistic novel depicting the anguish, the hope, and the spirit of the 1930's depression era. (p. 1)

North Carolina State Library Book Reviews, *February, 1977.*

The 14-year-old hero of James Collier's spirited new novel, who has been struggling to hold his motherless household together, frets at one point, "I didn't want to treat my own father like a kid." Readers will protest that Jack has no choice; his dad is an incurable kid at heart—a down-and-out musician. . . .

It's all suspensefully plotted, with false starts, discoveries and last-minute hesitations.

The novel has its amusing moments too, since Jack fantasizes as compulsively as other teen-agers chew gum. In one Walter Mittyish sequence he single-handedly sews up the World Series for the Red Sox, then flings his bountiful earnings at his family's feet. . . .

Still, what gives the novel its distinctive texture is not the son's imaginings but the father's love affair with music. The care he denies his children, he lavishes on his trombone. Money earmarked for food, he squanders on records. Though he hasn't landed a good-paying "gig" for months, he refuses day work in order to reminisce with the children about the 20's jazz scene and to conjure up images of himself as another Dorsey or Goodman. You have to admire his blind persistence, crazy and selfish though it clearly is. That's why, when he finally parcels the children out to various homes so that he can hit the road, Jack is resigned. It's hard to dislike a talented child, even if he is your father. (p. 25)

Joyce Bermel, in The New York Times Book Review *(© 1977 by The New York Times Company; reprinted by permission), February 13, 1977.*

OTHER CITATIONS

Jody Berge, in Children's Book Review Service, *December, 1976, p. 36.*

THE HARD LIFE OF THE TEENAGER (1972)

[Collier] assures teen-agers there is nothing abnormal about

their raging and contradictory emotions; such feelings are inevitable during adolescence in all but the most phlegmatic. ["The Hard Life of the Teenager"] explores the need for young adults to rebel against their parents, or society or both, and the roots of their need to be popular; he offers advice on how to cope with their major concerns, including acne and anxieties over sex. It's a helpful book but slow going; reading it and absorbing the message takes patience and perseverance, like getting along with one's parents. (p. 260)

Jean F. Mercier, in Publishers Weekly *(reprinted from the January 29, 1973, issue of* Publishers Weekly *by permission of the critic, published by R. R. Bowker Company, a Xerox company; copyright © 1973 by Xerox Corporation), January 29, 1973.*

"The Hard Life of the Teenager" by James Lincoln Collier . . . lucidly discusses the problems that face most teen-agers today: identity and self-image, sex, relationships with parents, popularity, rebellion, etc. I found the author's position most often sober and informed (with the exception of his lack of appreciation of the potential medical complications of the oral contraceptives). His psychological sophistication is apparent throughout and his ability to see a situation from the adolescent's vantage point will certainly enhance his appeal. But his book does not differ significantly from other advice-and-reassurance titles published within the last few years. (p. 10)

Richard A. Gardner, in The New York Times Book Review *(© 1973 by The New York Times Company; reprinted by permission), February 25, 1973.*

OTHER CITATIONS

Alice G. Smith, in Top of the News, *January, 1974, p. 192.*

INSIDE JAZZ (1973)

To paraphrase Louis Armstrong, Collier's greatest of the greats, if you don't know what jazz is Collier can't tell you. Though he starts by defining jazz in terms of rhythm and improvisation, he projects neither these qualities nor the color and feel of the music. That said, however, it must be pointed out that his introduction is knowledgeable, balanced and competently businesslike. Collier is not afraid to mention chord progression, syncopation or blue note bends for those who know just a little music, but any tin ear novice can follow his reconstruction of the beginnings of jazz and his chronologically ordered analysis of different schools and styles. Surveyed are King Oliver (who imposed his own formal order on his band), white Chicago jazz (Bix, Benny Goodman) and Dixieland ("on the whole a dead end"), Armstrong's solos and Ellington whose "real instrument is the orchestra," Bop (a harmonic and rhythmic departure developed after hours at Minton's and Monroe's in Harlem), cool (an arranger's music, more "symphonic" than bop) and today's "free" style represented by Ornette Coleman and the late John Coltrane. Collier makes the point that jazz grew up with recording technology, and perhaps his most valuable service to serious beginners is the extensive, generously annotated list of recordings—from a Folkways reissue of prejazz sounds (holler, work song, etc.) and a Riverside reissue of Armstrong with Oliver up through Coleman, Monk and Coltrane—which, once gathered together (and Collier points out that many public libraries have most of the lot) can really bring the reader *Inside Jazz*. (p. 1214)

> Kirkus Reviews *(copyright © 1973 The Kirkus Service, Inc.), November 1, 1973.*

It's a risky proposition writing books for young readers about rock, the word used to describe every kind of contemporary popular music from hard blasting rock'n'roll to soft, lilting folk. With radios and records forming the sound backdrop of their existence, kids have been hearing this music for a good part of their lives and so know a lot more about the subject than most of their elders.

As our most popular form of music today, rock is therefore the most accessible, a circumstance that has inspired books by a great many writers whose only qualifications are having two ears. Jazz, on the other hand is more esoteric, and so it's not quite so easy—and certainly not so profitable—to jump on its bandwagon. It's not surprising, then, that of this quartet of music books [the others include Brian Van Der Horst's "Rock Music," Jane Schiesel's "The Otis Redding Story," and Hettie Jones's "Big Star Fallin' Mama: Five Women in Black Music"], the most informative, intelligent and well-written is "Inside Jazz" by James Lincoln Collier. . . . Wisely Mr. Collier, a part-time jazz musician, reminds us in the first chapter just how difficult it is to translate musical sounds into words. Yet, he provides as good a verbal explanation as I've seen about jazz and its distinguishing features. After laying this groundwork, Collier sensitively outlines the history of jazz, which he calls an American music created by blacks. Without moralizing about drink and drugs in his "Jazz Life" chapter, the author lets the words of addicts like Charlie Parker underline the bad effects of those highs. Not only for younger readers, but for older ones as well who want to get acquainted with the various sounds of jazz, Collier's book concludes with a superb discography that provides a listening guide with each recommended album. (p. 10)

> Loraine Alterman, *in* The New York Times Book Review *(© 1973 by The New York Times Company; reprinted by permission), December 30, 1973.*

OTHER CITATIONS

Zena Sutherland, in Bulletin of the Center for Children's Books, *May, 1974, p. 140.*

THE MAKING OF MAN: THE STORY OF OUR ANCIENT ANCESTORS (1974)

In [*The Making of Man,* an] introduction to man's evolutionary pre-history, the reader is dragged (by the hair, as it were) into the bushes of the past to view an adolescent male Australopithecus Africanus who is quaking in his bare feet as he is about to confront a charging jaguar and, with his superior intelligence, set pre-mankind ahead another few million years. Collier breaks into this scenario with the announcement that he, the writer, is going to lead you, the reader, along "that wandering line through the four major stages in man's development" (and some minor stages as well), through those "achingly long millions of years." And

wander he does, through this achingly long 160 pages which detours into a diatribe against overpopulation, pollution, war and race prejudice. "Our" naked adolescent reappears from time to time with larger brain to show how our common ancestors developed. Though Collier attempts to give the reader "helpful hints" in understanding terminology "one of the biggest nuisances you are going to face in this book," a glossary might be of more use in understanding these "jaw-crackers." Possibly the reader may emerge with a general picture of primate life over the past 75 million years or so, but he is more likely to enjoy and profit from F. Clark Howell's *Early Man* in the Life Nature Library. (p. 435)

> Kirkus Reviews *(copyright © 1974 The Kirkus Service, Inc.), April 15, 1974.*

Collier writes about a heavy subject in a fascinating style. He has demonstrated throughout the book that he can distinguish between fact and theory, yet he presents his basic assumptions as if they were fact. On page 29 we read, "Human history begins in that immensely ancient past three billion years ago when a few bits of chemicals floating in the vast warm oceans somehow combined to form living things." . . . Meanwhile no mention is ever made of a Supreme Being who might have planned, created, or even permitted. The final chapter is strongly urging the reader's generation to limit population of mankind in the future. While a large proportion of this work is acceptable and useful, the reviewer believes that the forementioned failings should be seriously considered before the book is purchased. (p. 149)

> Sister M. Constance Melvin, I.H.M., *in* Best Sellers *(copyright 1974, by the University of Scranton), June 15, 1974.*

The author has done a fine job of synthesizing a diversity of facts and theory into a concise, logical and very readable story line. The book is not without flaws—there are some inadequate distinctions between facts, theories, and suppositions; and some might accuse the author of showing "sexist" tendencies in drawing broad-brush conclusions regarding typically male and female behavior patterns. Yet the overall approach to the complex subject of human physical, technological, emotional and behavioral evolution is an innovative one, and one that provides many valid insights into the biological bases of contemporary mankind. Adolescent readers are certain to recognize many of their own characteristics, emotions, frustrations and motivations among the verbal pictures of prehistoric people and events that the author has so skillfully drawn. (p. 13)

> Ronald J. Kley, *in* Appraisal *(copyright © 1975 by the Children's Science Book Review Committee), Spring, 1975.*

OTHER CITATIONS

Heddie Kent, in Appraisal, *Spring, 1975, pp. 12-13.*

MAKING MUSIC FOR MONEY (1976)

Helpful tips on all aspects of professional musicianship from picking sidemen and equipment to managing rehearsals, getting publicity, and finding jobs are presented in a friendly, informal manner [in *Making Music for Money*].

Collier mentions how many well-known musicians got started in the business as well as his own experiences. Some of his suggestions (e.g., using only professional demos; not allowing other musicians to sit in on gigs) apply more readily to city and suburban bands than to small town groups, but on the whole his advice is excellent and widely applicable. (p. 111).

> *Diane Haas, in* School Library Journal *(reprinted from the March, 1976, issue of* School Library Journal, *published by R. R. Bowker Company, a Xerox company; copyright © 1976 by Xerox Corporation), March, 1976.*

[In *Making Music for Money,* an] experienced musician gives tips on starting and leading a group. Collier's advice is light-handed and sensible: pick people who are reliable and easy to work with, be firm but flexible in reaching decisions, experiment with secondhand equipment, stick to the musical point in rehearsals, find a sound and develop it, perform as often as possible, and keep gigs and publicity smoothly organized. There could have been more examples from current rock (most are from jazz and dance bands) and elaboration on tuning into the energy exchange between performers and audience—not to mention "overlearning" to counteract stage fright—but basically, despite some insultingly cute black-and-white cartoons [by Robert Censoni], this is a direct management guide that could save beginners some costly mistakes. (p. 1262)

> The Booklist *(reprinted by permission of the American Library Association; copyright 1976 by the American Library Association), May 1, 1976.*

MY BROTHER SAM IS DEAD (with Christopher Collier, 1974)

"My Brother Sam Is Dead" . . . is . . . ambitious pedagogically and presents . . . ably the complex factors that helped determine political choices. . . . The narrator, young Tim Meeker, looks on as his Loyalist father and older brother Sam, a "rebel" partisan, confront each other but can never make much sense of the political controversy. . . . At first the conflict seems to set an authoritarian and calculating parent (who claims war isn't worth the cost of a few taxes) against an idealistic son. This might symbolize the dispute between England and her colonies; but the book is not content with a simple allegory. . . .

The book's occasional descriptions of violent death are physically detailed and more disturbing than run-of-the-mill television shoot-outs. But the violence is never sensational or excessive. The violence is necessary to a question the book leaves for readers to resolve: "Could the United States have made its way without all that agony and killing?" This dilemma was of great concern to colonial leaders in the mid-1770's. Raising it anew suggests the past is full of living issues. It also assumes for once that children can think. (p. 26)

> *Pauline Maier, in* The New York Times Book Review *(© 1974 by The New York Times Company, reprinted by permission), November 3, 1974.*

Collier inadequately explores the tragedy of family mem-

bers siding with opposing armies in the American Revolution [in *My Brother Sam Is Dead*]. Tim, the narrator, is caught between his older brother, Sam . . . and their father. . . . Although Tim is well drawn, the other characters pale by comparison. Well-known historical figures, among them Benedict Arnold and Israel Putnam, are thrown in as window dressing; several spirited discussions between Sam and his family are meant to bring the larger issues into focus but such a major event as the Declaration of Independence goes unnoticed. (p. 45)

> *Roberta Rogow, in* School Library Journal *(reprinted from the December, 1974, issue of* School Library Journal, *published by R. R. Bowker Company, a Xerox company; copyright © 1974 by Xerox Corporation), December, 1974.*

Based in large part on actual events, the first-person story of a Connecticut family during the Revolutionary War is told by Tim, a young adolescent whose father is not sympathetic toward the Patriot cause but whose chief purpose is to maintain a neutral attitude. . . . The authors explain that they have used contemporary speech patterns because "nobody is really sure how people talked in those days," and while the modernity is occasionally obtrusive, it is never really jarring. Well-paced, the story blends fact and fiction adroitly; the characterization is solid and the writing convincingly that of a young boy concerned more with his own problems and family in wartime than with issues or principles. (pp. 108-09)

> *Zena Sutherland, in* Bulletin of the Center for Children's Books *(© 1975 by the University of Chicago; all rights reserved), March, 1975.*

With its sharp revelation of the human aspects of Revolutionary War life and its probing of political views and divided loyalties, this stirring and authoritative novel earns a place beside our best historical fiction. The authors—one a professional writer and the other, according to the dust jacket, a university professor of early American history—have collaborated well. The three vitally drawn chief characters belong to the Meeker family, who live in the Tory village of Redding Ridge, Connecticut. They are Tim, who narrates the account; his father, who is against war and only nominally a Loyalist; and Sam, who angers his father by leaving Yale at sixteen to join the Patriots. Tim is perplexed: "'The way Sam explains it, it sounds right to be a Rebel. And when Father explains it, it sounds right to be a Loyalist. Although if you want to know the truth, I don't think Father really cares. He's just against wars.'" The authors provide an unromanticized picture of the Revolution, a look at the sort of deprivations, cheating, and barbaric behavior that made Tim admit he "didn't feel brave nor like bearing up. All I felt was angry and bitter and ready to kill somebody. If I only knew who." . . . A memorable piece of writing. (p. 152)

> *Virginia Haviland, in* The Horn Book Magazine *(copyright © 1975 by the Horn Book, Inc., Boston), April, 1975.*

OTHER CITATIONS

The Booklist, *October 15, 1974, pp. 241-42.*

Amy Kellman, in Teacher, *May-June, 1975. p. 90.*

PRACTICAL MUSIC THEORY: HOW MUSIC IS PUT TOGETHER FROM BACH TO ROCK (1970)

["Practical Music Theory"] is a book intended for the young reader that attempts to explain, as the subtitle has it, "How music is put together, from Bach to Rock." Apart from a few instances where the author presupposes some knowledge of musical ideas, it seems to me that it is quite intelligible for the average young reader. The book, illustrated with musical figures and diagrams, places its major emphasis upon harmony and chord structure. However, other aspects of music, such as melody and voice-leading, are also well covered. It is not a book that can be read at a single sitting. Rather, the reader should work through it employing a musical instrument (e.g., guitar or piano) and possibly, as the author suggests, with a friend. (p. 297)

> *Robert F. Young, S. J., in* Best Sellers *(copyright 1970, by the University of Scranton), October 15, 1970.*

[*Practical Music Theory* is a] lucid, step-by-step exposition of musical theory for dedicated music students. The versatile author of the immensely popular *Teddy Bear Habit . . .* claims that by the time earnest students have finished the book and done the exercises tailored for every chapter, they will know "enough to write songs, make arrangements and analyze scores of symphonies . . ." The five appendixes give music terms and information on transposing instruments, the ranges of instruments, music and chord symbols. Clear and challenging; for the students who stick with it, invaluable. (p. 58)

> *Loretta B. Jones, in* School Library Journal *(reprinted from the December, 1970, issue of* School Library Journal, *published by R. R. Bowker Company, a Xerox company; copyright © 1970 by Xerox Corporation), December, 1970.*

OTHER CITATIONS

The Booklist, *March 1, 1971, p. 554.*

RICH AND FAMOUS: THE FURTHER ADVENTURES OF GEORGE STABLE (1975)

Groomed by his agent as "The Boy Next Door," singing and strumming his way into the hearts of American mothers, 13-year-old Greenwich Village resident George Stable continues his quest for pop music stardom begun in *The Teddy Bear Habit Or How I Became Rich and Famous. . . .* Only an inadvertent discovery that "Superman," a recording company bigwig, is a cocaine dealer, deters George from wealth and fame and, but for a gripping rescue in the 19th-Century tradition, almost costs his life. Although the secondary characters are one-dimensional stereotypes—moralizing parent, goody-goody cousin, cynical public relations men—George is an average boy's Holden Caulfield in his consistently perceptive, and often humorous, observations of people and situations. Wildly improbable at times, this mixture of slice-of-life realism, melodrama, and mystery will still hold readers' interest. (p. 72)

> *Donald A. Colberg, in* School Library Journal *(reprinted from the November, 1975,*

issue of School Library Journal, *published by R. R. Bowker Company, a Xerox company; copyright © 1975 by Xerox Corporation), November, 1975.*

The fast pace, flip humor, and smooth suspense [in *Rich and Famous*] will draw readers, and there's no little food for thought for preadolescent top-ten consumers in Collier's nailing down the music PR racket right where it belongs. (p. 451)

> The Booklist *(reprinted by permission of the American Library Association; copyright 1975 by the American Library Association), November 15, 1975.*

OTHER CITATIONS

Kirkus Reviews, *September 1, 1975, p. 997.*

ROCK STAR (1970)

Even if lots of would-be musicians can identify with Tim Anderson's plight, few will relate to Tim himself—except with despair: he sounds like he's hiding a face full of adolescent pimples under his story, which takes place smack in the gap between generations. Flunking math kicks off the conflict that's been latent since he first got going on the guitar; Dad has doctor-lawyer ambitions for him and forbids him to play until he can muster a passing grade. Lucklessly, now, because there's a national contest in the offing that could bring Tim's group to Wolf Records' attention, but he has a strong sense of honor that in anyone else would be impressive—in him it comes across as miserable cowardliness. Tim grooms sub, sub takes sick, Tim does play, group wins the locals; Dad's furious but Tim's privately glorying in scout Mr. Jurgens' words (Do you have any idea how good you are? If you ever come to New York . . .). . . . Dad and Mr. Jurgens, long conference, okay no college, but no dropping out either: the compromise is a conservatory education—the obvious solution to the specious dichotomy of music *or* school that's prevailed all along. The gig is up as they say, *and so forth* (which is the book's most favorite locution). (pp. 1104-05)

> Kirkus Reviews *(copyright © 1970 The Kirkus Service, Inc.), October 1, 1970.*

Except for the high interest subject matter, there isn't much in this contrived novel that can't be found in most other junior novels. Tim Anderson is a good guitarist who wants to enter his band in the National Battle of the Bands Contest being sponsored by a recording company. However, he is flunking math in school, and his father (who wants him to go to college) forbids him to play the guitar. When he disobeys his father, Tim finds the gulf between them too great for reconciliation and so takes off for New York to find his fortune. There, he encounters enough obstacles to convince him that Dad, after all, is right. Tim decides that he might go into music, but he first must go to college. Although the characters are not believably portrayed and the treatment of the problems superficial, the theme might attract some pre-teeny-boppers. Nat Hentoff's *Jazz Country . . .* deals more realistically and more successfully than this with the problem of father-son conflict in a similar setting. (p. 127)

> *Jack Forman, in* School Library Journal *(re-*

printed from the March, 1971, issue of School Library Journal, *published by R. R. Bowker Company, a Xerox company; copyright © 1971 by Xerox Corporation), March, 1971.*

THE TEDDY BEAR HABIT OR HOW I BECAME A WINNER (1967)

If you think a book about a teddy bear and a kid in Greenwich Village is apt to be silly, you've got another think coming. "The Teddy Bear Habit" develops into a heck of an exciting story with a combination of humor and suspense, and a lack of fake sentiment, that is refreshing to find in a children's book. George tells the tale himself, with just the right kind of low-key artlessness. The urban setting makes it all the more interesting, while the drawings by Lee Lorenz are utterly cool. A modern book for modern kids—and let's have more of 'em! (p. 28)

> *Jerome Beatty Jr., in* The New York Times Book Review (© *1967 by The New York Times Company; reprinted by permission), March 12, 1967.*

Like Dumbo unable to fly without his feather, George can't maintain his cool without having his teddy in sight; this is next to impossible for a would-be entertainer at auditions. George has been surreptitiously balancing out his classical voice training with rock'n roll lessons at the guitar shop of the marvelously menacing Wiggsy; it's there that George gets a part in a TV special and wicked Wiggsy packs the teddy with stolen jewels. What appears to be a novel about a psychological kink (the Christopher Robin complex?) shifts into high comic adventure, culminating in a hectic, heart-stopping chase scene over Manhattan rooftops. George's observations on his Bohemian Greenwich Village neighbors, TV practices and personnel, and living motherless with a pop artist father, come over as ingenuous satire on the New York scene. An urban tall tale told in casual contemporary. (Sorry about that, idiom haters). Bears reading. (p. 84)

> *Lillian N. Gerhardt and Jean C. Thomson, in* School Library Journal *(reprinted from the April, 1967, issue of* School Library Journal, *published by R. R. Bowker Company, a Xerox company; copyright © 1967 by Xerox Corporation), April, 1967.*

This is a romp! A topical, hilarious satisfying romp! With a nonfiction hero (after all, a twelve-year-old boy who is still attached to his Teddy Bear—Dr. Freud would have worried!) who lives in Greenwich Village with a thoroughly bewildered non-hero of a father, who studies guitar from a local tough, who dips into the wild world of television and who, to his and the reader's satisfaction, ends up a winner. How satisfying can a story be? (p. 64)

> *Lavinia Russ, in* Publishers Weekly *(reprinted from the May 22, 1967, issue of* Publishers Weekly *by permission of the critic, published by R. R. Bowker Company, a Xerox company; copyright © 1967 by Xerox Corporation), May 22, 1967.*

D

DONOVAN, John 1928-

John Donovan, an American author and playwright, is the Executive Director of the Children's Book Council, an association of publishers that sponsors Children's Book Week. Several of his books for young people were forerunners in their inclusion of sophisticated topics such as death, homosexuality, and alienation.

FAMILY (1976)

In several astonishingly innovative novels for discriminating young readers, John Donovan has conveyed ideas and feelings about things which matter. His new book has the impact of a Greek tragedy; it is bound to invoke an emotional and (we hope) thoughtful response. Sasha narrates the story of apes whose lives are spent at various experimental institutions. Like most of the other apes, Sasha has been born in captivity. He is drawn to great Moses, a "natural" who has been brought from Africa. They agree that the humans are engaged in an atrocious experiment and they escape, taking with them baby Lollipop and a female adult, Dylys. Their experiences, as they try to exist on their own, are often wildly funny and exciting but the end is disaster. The book will enthrall readers of *all* ages. (p. 60)

> *Jean F. Mercier, in* Publishers Weekly *(reprinted from the April 26, 1976, issue of* Publishers Weekly *by permission of the critic, published by R. R. Bowker Company, a Xerox company; copyright © 1976 by Xerox Corporation), April 26, 1976.*

Can one say a novel is in first person when the narrator is an ape? Sasha, one of the apes in an experimental laboratory, is so convincing a voice that he seems a person—yet he remains, always, a primate, an intelligent being that is used by man.... [*Family* is] serious in tone and convincing; there are some passages that move slowly, as Sasha ponders history or problems of the ape community, but the drama of the situation and the cohesion of the plot are impressive, and the style and characterization of the story most effective. (p. 173)

> *Zena Sutherland, in* Bulletin of the Center for Children's Books *(© 1976 by the University of Chicago; all rights reserved), July-August, 1976.*

[*Family* is a] singular work—as are all of this author's creations—a story that an intelligent, reflective young person will find provocative and haunting.... The clear, simple, first-person narration, based on an understanding of human language by characters who are sharply individualized, presents an unsentimentalized and convincing view of ape thoughts and behavior and projects much about animal and human nature. (p. 404)

> *Virginia Haviland, in* The Horn Book Magazine *(copyright © 1976 by the Horn Book, Inc., Boston), August, 1976.*

[This] book is a puzzling one. Although the animals behave as apes, they seem to think and feel as humans, especially in their comment on human behavior and human ignorance. The theme is the interdependence of all living things, but Donovan seems pessimistic about the human link in the chain. Hope may be symbolized by Dylys' carrying Moses' child, when she and Sasha head back willingly to captivity. Sasha comments, "I would remember forever Moses and Lollipop, and would hope that Man is not lost." Amen. Thanks to graceful writing, this book is difficult to put down once begun, but it is for mature readers. (p. 582)

> *Ruth M. Stein, in* Language Arts *(copyright © 1977 by the National Council of Teachers of English), May, 1977.*

GOOD OLD JAMES (1975)

What would have made a funny/sad double-page cartoon strip for the *New Yorker* (indeed, the illustrator [James Stevenson] is a popular cartoonist for that magazine) is ... presented [in *Good Old James*] as a children's book. Donovan's experiment—to tell a fable about universal loneliness and the need for structure to lend form and substance to life without taking it over—is a respectable, even important one. But the medium he has chosen for this message is for all the good old Jameses. Not for their grandchildren. (p. 51)

> *Marjorie Lewis, in* School Library Journal *(reprinted from the April, 1975, issue of* School Library Journal, *published by R. R. Bowker Company, a Xerox company; copyright © 1975 by Xerox Corporation), April, 1975.*

["Good Old James"] is spare, charming and, by its subject, undelightful. Donovan . . . here deals with those outposts of alienation—old age, retirement, loneliness. The tone is understated, sophisticated and precisely reflected in James Stevenson's drawing. . . .

The book is labeled "for all ages," and is, as that suggests, available at different levels. Mentally recyclable. What a good idea. (And what a good category—allowing original books, mavericks, to find their level.)

This one, I think, is for adults and kids to share. It's thin-nish, too spare to engage adults straight. And, obviously, bringing nothing more to it, it's this story about a man who makes a pet of a fly. (p. 40)

> *Louise Armstrong, in* The New York Times Book Review *(© 1975, The New York Times Company; reprinted by permission), May 4, 1975.*

OTHER CITATIONS

The Booklist, *May 1, 1975, p. 912.*

Ernest van den Haag, in Psychology Today, *September 1975, p. 76.*

James A. Norsworthy, Jr., in Catholic Library World, *November, 1975, p. 188.*

I'LL GET THERE. IT BETTER BE WORTH THE TRIP. (1969)

Here is a remarkable book. Don't be put off, by its being written in the historical present—as your reviewer was, for the first page. By the second page the author of this moving story of a lonely boy had captured me and didn't let me go until the last word on the last page. And don't be put off when you hear—and you *will* hear—that it is a story about homosexuality, because it isn't. Among the many incidents which the author describes with such insight and compassion, incidents to illustrate the boy's loneliness and his attempts to overcome it, is an incident with homosexual ingredients. But it is only one of many which add up to a perceptive, funny, touching story, a remarkable book. (p. 57)

> *Lavinia Russ, in* Publishers Weekly *(reprinted from the March 17, 1969, issue of* Publishers Weekly *by permission of the critic, published by R. R. Bowker Company, a Xerox company; copyright © 1969 by Xerox Corporation), March 17, 1969.*

The contribution this book makes, giving reason why it should be available wherever young people read, is that it touches, with lyricism and simplicity, upon a spontaneous sexual relationship between two adolescent boys. Author Donovan side-steps the problem somewhat, but does at least say that homosexuality is to some degree a natural occurrence among close friends old enough for sexual desires but without heterosexual outlets. And he makes it clear that the best way to counter such desires is to face them honestly for what they are: something beautiful at the moment, but to be replaced in the natural course of life with interest in the other sex.

However, while anticipating the encounter of David and Altschuler, Donovan wades into deep—and sometimes muddy—psychological waters. That both boys are sons of divorced parents, reared by women, is asking the reader to be once again led into the foggy belief that only in fatherless homes do boys become infatuated with other boys. (That simply isn't true.) By implying that "affairs" at puberty are the result of an "unnatural" home life, Donovan commits a disservice to his own admirable stand and throws the subject back into the dark again—where most people have foolishly kept it all along.

The story, as told with wit and charm by David in what might be called Breathless First Person, fails to face squarely other aberrations more profound than the narrated tender relationship with Altschuler. David is also a victim of zoophilia and coprolagnia: that is, he loves his dog, Fred, more than he does any human (after his grandmother's death); and has an absolute fascination with Fred's fecal and urinary functions.

Lacking (or not choosing) the usual boyhood activities, David concentrates his affection on his dog almost to the point of bestiality. As Freud emphasized, scatologic interest is not an uncommon erotic symbol in childhood, nor is it to be considered abnormal. It is with this murky material, however, that Donovan is in danger of losing the audience for which his book was written, because he makes no attempt to clarify, as he does with other relationships.

It is through playing a game with the dog that the two boys are led into their first hesitant amorous experience. Because, indirectly, David's homosexual engagements result in the death of Fred the dog, he is forced to assume a heavy mantle of guilt that could conceivably affect him forever. It seems an extravagant way to bring him to knowledge of himself. Given such burdens to carry at 13 (plus an alcoholic mother who makes little effort to understand him, and a father whom he sees only occasionally), the chances against David's surviving to adulthood seem greater than the optimistic title would indicate. (pp. 8, 10)

> *John Weston, in* The New York Times Book Review, *Part II (© 1969 by the New York Times Company; reprinted by permission), May 4, 1969.*

In my judgment this book might be useful for adult counselors and guidance directors, but I see little value of placing it in the hands of the young reader. The author seems to try to make his hero into another Holden Caulfield, isolating an initial sexual experience between two boys. (p. 100)

> Best Sellers *(copyright 1969, by the University of Scranton), June 1, 1969.*

In the last few years we have seen the rise of a singular form of problem novel pointed primarily at people in their mid-teens, although this year the age level seems to have been slightly lowered. *I'll Get There. It Better Be Worth the Trip* (a contender for the longest title award if nothing else) by John Donovan . . . has a hero who is a scant thirteen. The novel celebrates the child's homosexual encounter with a schoolfellow. Davy Ross has multiple problems: his parents are divorced, his mother is alcoholic, his grandmother dies, and his dog is killed by a car. He tells it all in the language of *The Catcher in the Rye,* and the book is craftsmanlike and competent. But its purpose and execution pose a number of questions. The loss of innocence is an adult's subject. Once we have put it behind us, there is no return to the world or the speech of childhood. The language of children is inadequate to it, and the application of grammar school jargon to corruption and passion is neither natural nor comforting. A young person who has experienced a romantic encounter of the sort described by Davy Ross is probably best served by *David Copperfield* or even [Thomas Mann's] *The Magic Mountain,* in which such relationships are seen in the context of a larger life. I am also inclined to think that a book focused on a love affair between schoolfellows might have just the opposite effect on this age group from that which the author intended. It would not meet the needs of the initiated and might arouse in the unconcerned unnecessary interest or alarm or both. (p. 150)

> *Martha Bacon, in* The Atlantic Monthly *(copyright © 1969 by The Atlantic Monthly Company, Boston, Mass.; reprinted with permission), December, 1969.*

[*I'll Get There. It Better Be Worth the Trip*] features [a] lady lush whose marriage has collapsed. Her only child, a boy, has been living a wholesome *Saturday Evening Post*-ish life with his grandmother and his dog, Fred, in yet another provincial East Coast town. On Grandmother's death the mother claims the boy for her own and takes him off to her apartment in brownstone New York. It is the boy who tells the story: the predictable failure of the attempt at co-existence of mother, son and dog; his own edgy relationship with Father and his new wife; and his emotional entanglement with his classmate. . . . The danger of having a boy of 12 as narrator is a dual one—of the *faux-naif* on the one hand and the impossibly precocious on the other. John Donovan has contrived to avoid either fault, although he does occasionally fall into the cliché of the 'and . . . and . . . and' type of narrative. But on the whole, this is a sensitive and convincing picture of the miseries of a child—not a socially depressed child either—forced to live in a city and a society unfit for boy or dog. (p. 519)

> *Stuart Hood, in* The Listener *(© British Broadcasting Corp. 1970; reprinted by permission of Stuart Hood), April 16, 1970.*

John Donovan's *I'll Get There. It Better be Worth the Trip* is about an adolescent boy, left without useful adult guidance or steady affection, learning to find a path towards his own kind of maturity.

The part of the story which has made a mild sensation in the United States, and may do the same here [in Britain], is the homosexual episode between Davy and Altschuler; they exchange kisses on the floor, and, two days later in Mother's apartment, they "make out" together. (The toppling of taboos in books on the children's list has grown wearisome by now, but at least there is the consolation that the process must soon end through lack of further taboos to topple. Only rape and incest remain, and we have been pretty close to both of them.) It seems to be implied that in these two boys' circumstances—no girls; no other affectionate relationships—there is nothing terribly unnatural or even terribly important about a passing homosexual attachment; but in fact the story cannot carry it lightly, especially as it occurs at the point in a rather slack plot at which some kind of crisis seems due.

I'll Get There etc., like most first-person narrations by male teenagers, stands in the shadow of *The Catcher in the Rye*. That is not a fault, since it would be silly for authors to avoid an obvious form merely because others have already used it successfully, but it does invite comparisons which Mr. Donovan's book cannot stand up to. Moreover, the hero may seem less likeable to readers than he apparently does to his creator; while conversely Mother, whose life is only tolerable when she has had a few drinks and then a few more, may seem to deserve more sympathy than she gets. Readers who liked Barbara Wersba's *The Dream Watcher* may like this book; those who detested *The Dream Watcher* almost certainly will not. It is not a good novel but it is readable and interesting, and it stays in the mind—and not only because boy meets boy instead of girl, or because of the personal habits of Dog Fred. (p. 712)

> The Times Literary Supplement *(© Times Newspapers Ltd., 1970; reproduced from* The Times Literary Supplement *by permission), July 2, 1970.*

John Donovan . . . in *I'll Get There (It Had Better Be Worth the Trip)*, suggests that teenage homosexuality is so totally unacceptable, socially and psychologically, that any young homosexual is likely to have his fears and worries increased rather than reduced, and the prejudice of the heterosexual reader against homosexuals is reinforced. (p. 86)

> *David Rees, in* Children's Literature in Education *(© 1977, APS Publications, Inc., New York; reprinted by permission of the publisher), No. 25 (Summer), 1977.*

OTHER CITATIONS

Kirkus Reviews, *April 1, 1969, p. 385.*

Bruce L. MacDuffie, in School Library Journal, *May, 1969, p. 98.*

Laura Polla Scanlon, in Commonweal, *May 23, 1969, p. 300.*

Robert Bell, in The School Librarian, *September, 1970, pp. 330-31.*

Aneurin Rhys, in The Junior Bookshelf, *October, 1972, p. 293.*

REMOVE PROTECTIVE COATING A LITTLE AT A TIME (1973)

There will be no protective coating left for the reader of this novel. The hero was conceived out of wedlock on the first page and reveals much of his sexual interests and practices with and without others through age fourteen. The good writing and interesting relationship with an old female tramp did not need the overloading with sex. To paraphrase the text: You have a fixation that's unnatural. . . . It's not becoming to have you talk about private matters, John. (p. 333)

> *Sister M. Constance Melvin, I.H.M., in* Best Sellers *(copyright 1973, by the University of Scranton), October 15, 1973.*

"No man is an island," said John Donne. "Every man is an island," says John Donovan; or so it seems to me from his three novels. As an islander you can build your makeshift boats, make brief risky voyages, visit with other islanders; but at nightfall you must return to your own.

This is not a cheering thought for teen-agers, most of whom, in intention at least, are highly social beings, but many of whom have times when they are terribly aware of being islanded. And the lukewarm comfort Donovan offers, at first sight anyway, is little more than "Accept, resign yourself, it's the same for everyone."

In "I'll Get There. It Better Be Worth the Trip" and again in this new book, Donovan seems concerned with a special kind of isolation that is often felt by young people in our time. This is the state of noncommunication resulting from the failure of the parental generation to say anything to the young. (It is misleading to see it as the refusal of the young to listen.) We now have an uneasy void where, in less "advanced" societies, there would be a whole web of intimate relationships and a great handing-down of essential advice and information.

Harry, the hero of "Remove Protective Coating a Little at a Time," cannot even fight with his parents Bud and Toots. Young themselves in the flabby fifties, married too soon, missing their way in life, lacking conviction and confidence, not knowing how to solve their own problems, Bud and Toots are hardly parents at all. Floundering through the puberty of the emotions, Harry makes friends with 72-year-old Amelia. (Significantly, Barbara Wersba in "The Dream Watcher" and Paul Zindel in "The Pigman" also showed teen-agers relating to people of their grandparents' rather than their parents' generation.) Amelia lives rough in a condemned building and calls herself a bum, "a good and honorable bum." But "bums don't have anything to do with lives like yours." The wrecking crane moves in on Amelia's block; she disappears. A contact between islanders is over. Nevertheless, Amelia has given Harry something to replace the protective coating (of childhood? of innocence? of self-absorption?) which his parents could not have given.

John Donovan has the reputation of a taboo-buster: homosexuality in "I'll Get There," death in "Wild in the World." And the new book will give some people wrong impressions, for which he himself is to blame. He begins with the introduction of Harry to "one of the great indoor sports" (you play it by yourself) and with Harry's first attempt to make out with a girl (a flop). And almost the first thing that 72-year-old Amelia says to him is:"I read somewhere that about ninety percent of American male babies are circumcised at birth, automatically. Is that right, from your observation?"

But these are false trails. The book is hardly at all about sex, and (unless I'm too straight to recognize a kink when I see one) it's not substantially about a kinky young-boy-old-woman affair.

"Remove Protective Coating" is a slight-seeming book that slips down with deceptive ease. There is more to it than appears: arguments about freedom and responsibility are important, yet are only hinted at; and there is a sense that life continues beyond the edge of the page and that the author could tell you far more about Bud and Toots and Amelia if he chose. John Donovan is not so casual as he appears. Maybe he gives the impression that adult life is hardly worth the trip; you have to put up with it but don't gain much by bothering. Yet his ending is not entirely negative. And after all, Mr. Donovan has bothered to write the book. (pp. 34, 36)

John Rowe Townsend, in The New York Times Book Review (© *1973 by The New York Times Company; reprinted by permission),* November 4, 1973.

Donovan's *Remove Protective Coating a Little at a Time* . . . has . . . for its main character—Harry, aged fourteen, the child of parents who are barely in their thirties. We are told in the third paragraph of the book that "Harry's dad slipped it to his mother that glorious night, on the beach in front of the hotel, and she got pregnant with Harry." Other sexual episodes of mutual masturbation and unsuccessfully trying to make it with a camp girl at thirteen are reported with the same lack of delicacy, which may be the author's intent to define the male attitude toward sex.

The primary relationship in the book is that between Harry and Amelia, a seventy-two year old female derelict whom he meets in the park and visits in her condemned apartment house hideaway. This is a relationship that is far more fantasy than probability. There is, however, an interesting contrast depicted in the honesty and straightforwardness of Harry's relationship with Amelia and his relationship with what seems to be mere cardboard caricatures of Bud and Toots, his parents. One gains almost no feeling of what goes on between Bud, a professionally successful, pal-like father, and Harry; between Harry and Toots, the emotionally disturbed and depressed mother, nothing much at all goes on. The protective covering of all the characters is so thick that it is hardly worth the reading; one is left to wonder if perhaps this is not what the author is cynically saying about adolescents, families, people, dogs, and life itself. (pp. 177-78)

Eleanore Braun Luckey, in Children's Literature: Annual of The Modern Language Association Seminar on Children's Literature and The Children's Literature Association, *Vol. 4, edited by Francelia Butler; all rights reserved),* Temple University Press, 1975.

OTHER CITATIONS

Paul Heins, in The Horn Book Magazine, *February, 1974, p. 54.*

WILD IN THE WORLD (1971)

After an initial desolation that stretches belief, this becomes a natural and gently persuasive story of an inarticulate mountain boy and the animal that preoccupies his last days. . . . Children who would cry if the animal [the wolf-dog, Son] died will accept the rightness of John's death; Son clearly enlarged the boy's life in a dimension other than time. Though the seemingly gratuitous deaths are a shock at first, their use to underline the value of the friendship results in a quietly convincing affirmation. (p. 682)

Kirkus Reviews *(copyright © 1971 The Kirkus Service, Inc.),* July 1, 1971.

You could also call ["Wild in the World"] "Death Comes to the Little Ones"—written by the Executive Director of the Children's Book Council. Or, "Another Page, Another Death." . . .

We are so messed over, and up, by violence, so used to the

ubiquitous particulars, that the event of death shrivels easily on a sidestreet of our consciousness. And life itself hardly ever arouses more than the ego of loneliness. Is that the truth, and is that what Donovan is trying to prove to kids? Do kids accept such an "adult" view of things? Do they need such guidance into gloom?

"Wild in the World" opens, page 1, by presenting a family in demise. First there were 13 Gridleys, including Mom and Dad. But then, this and that killed him and her and him and him and her and her and him, off, until only three brothers were left. These Gridley survivors live on Rattlesnake Mountain in New Hampshire, but after a few pages, two more Gridleys have died, and that leaves John. Our hero. Let's recapitulate that body count: Twelve human beings have been listed as dead or killed in the opening pages. Is this a joke?

No: It is to explain the solitude of the hero. It is to explain the love that John, the hero, develops for a wolf. It is to explain why he names the wolf "Son." It is a metaphorical something or other to let kids know that when your folks die, and you have no more family anywhere, you could still be lucky and find a wolf that will be your friend.

Are you kidding me? . . .

Near the end, the wolf named Son is bitten by a rattlesnake and John, for the first time, is allowed to show some wish against death.

It's nice that John doesn't want his wolf to die. If you have lasted this far, through flat exposition of a weird, isolated life indifferent to the dead, and to the living, a life content to shuck corn, milk cows, can beans and make no effort to know and touch other lives, well, then, you may feel relief about John and his wolf.

Maybe the author thought that kids would finally scream and insist on life and survival and, therefore, insist on the definite loss that human death signifies. But kids have to make that scream for the living, when they turn off the tele-news, and turn to a book, kids hope to find reassurance there. They want the books they read to slow down the cameras so that there is time for tears, and grief, and memory, and new love. "Wild in the World" doesn't help. It is a horror story told in monotone. Nobody screams for anyone else. (p. 8)

> *June Jordan, in* The New York Times Book Review (© *1971 by The New York Times Company; reprinted by permission), September 12, 1971.*

Several years ago John Donovan unsettled the children's book world by publishing a "young adult" novel in which a moment of sexual affection takes place between two adolescents. The adolescents happened to be boys, and although the episode was brief, and beautifully written, it caused a considerable uproar. . . . "I'll Get There. It Better Be Worth the Trip" was so plainly a book conceived out of idealism and love that it seemed not to take into account the conservatism of many parents and librarians. Mr. Donovan has now published a second novel ["Wild in The World"]—and like its predecessor, it pays little respect to popularity. It is, however, one of the most moving books ever written for children. . . .

From the first chapter of the book, an atmosphere of bleak-

ness and silence is invoked; and this aura grows as we watch John living alone on what was once the family homestead. He has been inadvertently responsible for the death of his mother, one sister, and a brother—and his emotions are atrophied. There is a blankness to the quality of his mind, and an attitude toward life so harsh that the reader is at first alienated. When an animal wanders onto his property—a dog or a wolf, we are never sure—the encounter seems brief and of little consequence.

It is here that Mr. Donovan reveals the intention of his story; for out of this casual meeting something strange occurs. . . . A physical, almost sensual connection begins to grow between the boy and the animal. Both need each other with an intensity all the more painful because it is understated. John decides to keep the dog, and in one of the most affecting moments of the book, names him Son. . . . [When] Son is bitten by a rattlesnake, . . . the vigil that John keeps while the dog suffers is the vigil that all human beings keep over those they love. The writing in this section of the story is flawless, and classic in its restraint. . . .

There are some experiences whose depth can never be plumbed, and love is the most complex of these. The attempt that "Wild in the World" makes to explore the nature of love—and the nature of man's isolation—is very close to being noble. Some people will say that the book is not for children, and they will come to this conclusion because from the first page to the last there is a total lack of sentimentalism. The sadness in every line of the story is unremitting—and the protagonist's vision of the world is crude and incomplete. But this novel, like Mr. Donovan's previous one, is more suited to contemporary children than almost any kind of literature I can think of. (p. 8)

> *Barbara Wersba, in* The New York Times Book Review (© *1971 by The New York Times Company; reprinted by permission), September 12, 1971.*

Reading John Donovan's new novel is an eerie experience. Like the major character, John Gridley, the reader is trapped in a funnel-like existence constantly moving toward the smaller opening. Living is a complex process at best, but when a human being is forced to provide for all of his own necessities the process seems to become larger than the capabilities of a human actor. As John Gridley's family decreases a reader seems to become more intimately associated with the major character. And when John Gridley becomes the last living member of his family accompanied only by a half-wild wolf dog a reader waits helplessly while John plays out his small span of life's stage. . . .

I am tempted to provide my interpretation of *Wild in the World*, but I won't. You and your students will have exciting hours exploring the social manifestations and psychological motives inherent in John Donovan's new book. I urge you to read it and speculate. I believe *Wild in the World* may create as much literary interest as Julia Cunningham's *Dorp Dead* did a few years ago. (p. 138)

> *John. W. Conner, in* English Journal (*copyright* © *1972 by The National Council of Teachers of English), January, 1972.*

Despite the spare beauty of the writing, the feeling for the New Hampshire countryside, and the sympathetic and sensitive portrayal of the companionship between the surviving Gridley and his animal companion, [*Wild in the World*] is unimpassionedly lugubrious; and one is left wondering why such a book is at all published for children. Of course, it could appeal to an adolescent who had the makings of a congenital pessimist. (p. 57)

> *Paul Heins, in* The Horn Book Magazine *(copyright © 1972 by The Horn Book, Inc., Boston), February, 1972.*

OTHER CITATIONS

Publishers Weekly, *August 2, 1971, p. 64.*

Brooke Anson, in School Library Journal, *October, 1971, p. 119.*

Zena Sutherland, in Bulletin of the Center for Children's Books, *November, 1971, p. 41.*

The Booklist, *November 1, 1971, p. 240.*

G

GOFFSTEIN, M(arilyn) B(rooke)   1940-

M. B. Goffstein is an American author, artist, and illustrator who writes for both children and young people. Her pen-and-ink and watercolor drawings have been exhibited in several one-woman showings. Many of Goffstein's illustrated books have used simplicity of word and picture to present the values underlying creativity, daily routine, and familial love. She is married to Peter Schaaf, the pianist on the record accompanying *A Little Schubert.* **(See also** *Contemporary Authors,* **Vols. 21-24, rev. ed. and** *Something About the Author,* **Vol. 8.)**

GENERAL COMMENTARY

While M. B. Goffstein's recent works *Goldie the Doll-maker* . . . and *Two Piano Tuners* . . . are not, strictly speaking, fairy tales—they are more folk fables for our time—they confront the question of personal happiness in strikingly similar terms. In *Goldie,* an orphaned young toy-maker earns enough from the fabrication of beautiful wooden dolls to live comfortably in her own small house in the woods, satisfying every material want. She suffers, however, from an overwhelming loneliness until she realizes that, through work lovingly done, one individual being can speak—across national boundaries and even the centuries—to all others who appreciate quality and craftsmanship. It is not what one is able to take from life that provides fulfillment, but what one is able gratuitously to give from within himself.

Two Piano Tuners is still more concerned with the particulars of what constitutes human fulfillment. Here the locale is decidedly urban United States. Mr. Weinstock, a piano tuner by profession, is bringing up his young, orphaned granddaughter, Debbie. Like all American parents before him, he wants "something better" for Debbie, more exalted certainly than being a mere piano tuner. He dreams of her becoming a concert pianist. But the child, full of admiration for her grandfather's skill and in awe of the mysterious powers of the tools of his profession, wants only to be a piano tuner, too. The moral of the Goffstein tale is that "Everybody should take the responsibility for finding out what it is he really wants to do" and that there is greater virtue in being a good piano tuner than a mediocre concert pianist. Parting company with the grandiose generalities of the American Dream—that everyone can reach the highest pinnacle of fame and fortune—the author stresses the inher-

ent beauty and fulfillment of finding the right niche, regardless of its elevation on the status scale. (pp. 109-10)

> *Selma G. Lanes, in her* Down the Rabbit Hole: Adventures and Misadventures in the Realm of Children's Literature *(copyright © 1971 by Selma G. Lanes; reprinted by permission of Atheneum Publishers, New York), Atheneum, 1972.*

ACROSS THE SEA (1968)

Something delightful is happening to M. B. Goffstein. From her earlier self-consciously simple little books, she is coming through with truly simple little books—clean, straight stories, clean, straight drawings that are truly appealing. These three stories are her three best. (p. 64)

> *Lavinia Russ, in* Publishers Weekly *(reprinted from the September 9, 1968, issue of* Publishers Weekly *by permission of the critic, published by R. R. Bowker Company, a Xerox company; copyright © 1968 by Xerox Corporation), September 9, 1968.*

It's good to have a Goffstein! While too many mine the antic and frantic in picture books, she unearths the treasure of simplicity. Miss Goffstein's talent has steadily increased: from "The Gats!" through the purposefully somnolent "Sleepy People" to "Brookie and Her Lamb." And now her best, "Across the Sea," a book of five brief stories all of which are pervaded by quiet contentment and touches of Old World ways and wisdom. The title story speaks of old men sitting in doorways on sun-warmed benches carving small figures from blocks of wood; another of love between father and daughter and the world around them. In "Sophie's Picnic" a peasant girl packs bread and sausage, steps into her wooden sabots and walks "clap, clap, clap" to a sweet field of grass, eats, lies blissfully in the sun and then, "clap, clap, clap," home again. There never was a better picnic. It's good to have a Goffstein, because she writes of elemental joys and draws in a style that is simple yet skilled and charming. (p. 62)

> *George A. Woods, in* The New York Times Book Review *(© 1968 by The New York Times Company; reprinted by permission), November 17, 1968.*

The five stories in this small picture book are captivating. Told from a child's point of view, they are a blend of whimsy and order, of fancy and a down-to-earth appreciation of "sun-warmed benches" and hard green pears. The book's design, size, and illustrations perfectly complement the uncluttered simplicity and gentle humor of the stories. Pen-and-ink figures wearing wide trousers or full skirts, and wooden shoes are set with artistic precision against backgrounds of white or light blue. Red, rose, blue, and gray washes contrast vividly with areas of white, and the overall effect is one of refreshing clarity and cleanness. The book will be a favorite with young children and, if possible, they should have it for their own. (p. 680)

> Sidney D. Long, in The Horn Book Magazine (copyright © 1968 by The Horn Book, Inc., Boston), December, 1968.

OTHER CITATIONS

Kirkus Service, October 1, 1968, pp. 1105-06.

Polly Goodwin, in Book World, March 16, 1969, p. 12.

DAISY SUMMERFIELD'S STYLE (1975)

The author-illustrator has endeared herself and won honors for such notable picture books as "Me and My Captain," "A Little Schubert" and others. Now, in her novel about a newcomer to Manhattan, M. B. Goffstein is just as entrancing and believable even though the story sounds like wish fulfillment. . . . Daisy . . . [is] determined to become an honest artist, and the detailing of her life, culminating in a sweet surprise, makes the book a real page-turner. (p. 60)

> Jean F. Mercier, in Publishers Weekly (reprinted from the September 8, 1975, issue of Publishers Weekly by permission of the critic, published by R. R. Bowker Company, a Xerox company; copyright © 1975 by Xerox Corporation), September 8, 1975.

[Daisy Summerfield's Style is an] unsubstantial, unsatisfying novel about 19-year-old Daisy Summerfield's first year alone in New York City. Daisy is immature and unsophisticated at the beginning, but neither she (nor readers) has gained in strength, growth, or awareness by the end. There is a ridiculous and unresolved emphasis on clothes and appearances, beginning with Daisy switching her Ivy League wardrobe for the "artsy" rags of a girl she observes and envies on the train—an incident which ends, of course, extremely unrealistically. In fact, the worst reality Daisy has to contend with (in New York City, no less!) is a nasty storekeeper. Her parents do not approve of her dropping out of fashion design school to become an artist, but they remain a seemingly unending source of money for Daisy. Except for the descriptions of Daisy's artistic endeavors, the book mainly catalogues all of her purchases for the year. It's unfortunate that such apt subjects as art and independence are given such shallow and uncreative treatment. (p. 89)

> Cyrisse Jaffee, in School Library Journal (reprinted from the November, 1975, issue of School Library Journal, published by R. R. Bowker Company, a Xerox company; copyright © 1975 by Xerox Corporation), November, 1975.

OTHER CITATIONS

Zena Sutherland, in Bulletin of the Center for Children's Books, February, 1976, p. 96.

FISH FOR SUPPER (1976)

[One] day in one child's grandmother's life is described [in Fish for Supper] with simple and straightforward language and illustrations. . . . There are few adjectives in the text or in the illustrations, making it hard to tell whether or not Grandmother enjoys her life. It is equally difficult to know how the grandchild/narrator feels about Grandmother. And it is just this absence of emotion that I object to and find so unsatisfying in this book. I think the intended audience will want to know if Grandmother is happy or sad. In fact, so do I. (p. 66)

> Lauren L. Wohl, in Children's Book Review Service (copyright © 1976 Children's Book Review Service Inc.), March, 1976.

Simplicity is all in this prim little picture book. . . . Artfully spare pen drawings feature a bespectacled, superficially expressionless figure going about her business, yet nuances of personality shine through in touches like the big sun hat or the tilt of grandmother's head as she cleans her fish. An affectionate, masterfully understated recollection. . . . (p. 1045)

> The Booklist (reprinted by permission of the American Library Association; copyright 1976 by the American Library Association), March 15, 1976.

"When my grandmother went fishing she would get up at five o'clock in the morning . . ." to spend the day catching, cleaning, and eating fish. "Then fast, fast, she cleaned up the dishes and went to bed, so she could get up at five o'clock in the morning to go fishing." A spare life, well suited to Goffstein's spare line drawings which never sentimentalize the dumpy grandmother's lonely pleasures. (Veraciously, her expression doesn't even signify that she's enjoying her meal—though the tea and hot fresh rolls make a contrary impression.) Utterly simple, unmistakably individual, implicitly touching—in short, a Goffstein. (p. 385)

> Kirkus Reviews (copyright © 1976 The Kirkus Service, Inc.), April 1, 1976.

I suppose I like M. B. Goffstein for her consistent simplicity. . . . I like all the white space surrounding the little pictures in the middle of the page. I like the uncluttered sketches of uncluttered people. I like the black and whiteness. And, I like the "straight to the point" story. Fish for Supper fulfills all my requirements for consistent simplicity: Grandmother's day of fishing is detailed, including what time she gets up, what she uses for bait, and what she catches. Good things do come in small, simple packages! (p. 2)

> The Babbling Bookworm, May, 1976.

OTHER CITATIONS

Publishers Weekly, March 8, 1976, p. 65.

Marjorie Lewis, in School Library Journal, April, 1976, p. 60.

Ethel L. Heins, in The Horn Book Magazine, *June, 1976, pp. 279-80.*

THE GATS! (1966)

The gats . . . are shapeless creatures that look like a cross between Piglet and the Goops. The very minimal text [of *The Gats!*], which more or less follows the tribe of gats on their search for a home, reads like a child's narrative based on nothing more cohesive than the rhymes which can be made with gat—cravat, hat, that, vat, bat, etc. The illustrations are very simple black and white ink sketches with some little green leaves. The pictures are in silly greeting card style, which is about all the book amounts to. (p. 299)

> *Virginia Kirkus' Service (copyright © 1966 Virginia Kirkus' Service, Inc.), March 15, 1966.*

This slight 32-page story about a group of amorphous, schmoo-like creatures who find a tree-top home, then destroy it by dancing (the gamba) on its limbs, has a comic-strip type of humor and illustration. But whatever prompted its publication in book form? The sketches are pedestrian, the characterization nil, the whimsy flimsy, and whatever irony there is (e.g., the use of the adjectives "fattest," "smartest," or an article of clothing to distinguish among utterly homogeneous creatures) will be lost on children. Not recommended. (p. 142)

> *Evelyn Geller, in* School Library Journal *(reprinted from the May, 1966, issue of* School Library Journal, *published by R. R. Bowker Company, a Xerox company; copyright © 1966 by Xerox Corporation), May, 1966.*

OTHER CITATIONS

Lavinia Russ, in Publishers Weekly, *May 2, 1966, p. 57.*

GOLDIE, THE DOLLMAKER (1969)

Like the smile on the dolls that Goldie Rosenzweig makes, this little book is captivating. Never mind that there's a lot more story than the small size would suggest, that, unlike the earlier Goffsteins, there's much more text than illustration; never mind even (though children may, a little) that the first two illustrations don't jibe with the text. The more you know Goldie, the more you appreciate her: going about her dead parents' house continuing their work of making dolls, oblivious of day and night until each one is complete; ordering a crate from Omus Hirschbein and explaining why she uses only pristine sticks of wood, not his clean, square scraps; visiting the bakery where a little girl buys a sugar cookie to share with a Goldie Rosenzweig doll. . . . Worth finding the right child or family for and then, again like Goldie's dolls, it will sell itself. (p. 995)

> *Kirkus Reviews (copyright © 1969 The Kirkus Service, Inc.), September 15, 1969.*

Children, too, [like Goldie] will realize that they are not alone—for once again, M. B. Goffstein has spoken to them in their language. With the simplest of words and the plainest of illustrations, she manages to transform Goldie—an ageless creature—into the essence of childhood solitude;

and if there is an elusive quality to the book, all the better. An artist as gentle and serious as Miss Goffstein needs little definition. (p. 34)

> *Barbara Wersba, in* The New York Times Book Review *(© 1969 by The New York Times Company; reprinted by permission), October 19, 1969.*

Although the stiff, bare illustrations break the mood somewhat, here is a story that has a genuine sweetness, a wistful Luise Rainer charm. Living alone, Goldie lavishes her love on the dolls she makes, painting into each little wooden face her own gentle smile. Shopping one day, Goldie sees an expensive Chinese lamp and extravagantly buys it. A friend tells her she's crazy, but Goldie is consoled by a dream of the man who made the lamp. "I made the lamp for you, whoever you are," the voice says, and the little dollmaker, listening, is comforted, knowing well that happiness can lie in the making of beauty. Not a childlike theme, but so simply told a tale that children can appreciate the delicacy, which is in the concept rather than the writing. (pp. 67-8)

> *Zena Sutherland, in* Saturday Review *(copyright © 1969 by Saturday Review, Inc.; reprinted with permission), November 8, 1969.*

What seems at first to be a simple picture story about dolls is really an attempt to define the nature of art and to explain the compulsion that forces the artist to be faithful to his own inner vision. . . . The story requires some sophistication on the part of the reader to comprehend how little Omus and Goldie share, to understand why Goldie will probably continue to work and live alone. . . . *Goldie the Dollmaker* is a significant book for the discerning child. (p. 41)

> *Diane Farrell, in* The Horn Book Magazine *(copyright © 1970 by The Horn Book, Inc., Boston), February, 1970.*

OTHER CITATIONS

Linda L. Clark, in School Library Journal, *December, 1969, p. 52.*

Ned O'Gorman, in The Nation, *December 15, 1969, p. 671.*

A LITTLE SCHUBERT (1972)

Like the nicest people, the best books don't need occasions. They make them. If you know a young, musical child, make an occasion by giving him *A Little Schubert*. . . . Or just look at it yourself. The title suits the drawings, the drawings suit the words, and the small recording (by Peter Schaaf) of five delicate "Noble waltzes" tucked inside the back cover suits it all. . . . The drawings are gracefully plain. They are also funny and endearing and should not be seen without the words, which should not be read without the pictures. And that, to my mind, is a quality of a well-illustrated picture book. I had three slight regrets about this book: 1) that Franz's nose and fingertips weren't touched blue with cold (the illustrations are black line and wash); 2) that his clothes, which are described as shabby, don't look shabby; and 3) that it all ended so soon. (p. 79)

Karla Kuskin, in Saturday Review *(copyright © 1972 by Saturday Review, Inc.; reprinted with permission), November 11, 1972.*

The story line [of *A Little Schubert*]—as sparse, simple, and bare as Schubert's living quarters—has been perfectly set off by line drawings of frumpy Schubert freezing, writing, and dancing. And the recording of five of the "Noble Waltzes," which has been included with the book, adds a final touch of gaiety to an ingenious and delightful multimedia package. Truly, a painless introduction to music. Bring a little Schubert into your life . . ., and dance and dance and dance. (pp. 582-83)

Anita Silvey, in The Horn Book Magazine *(copyright © 1972 by The Horn Book, Inc., Boston), December, 1972.*

Small framed pictures, with Schubert or two friends stiffly gesturing in each, illustrate a slight but engaging tale of how the composer in old, cold Vienna forgot the dreary privation of his bare room because his head was so filled with music he couldn't get it all written down. . . . Despite the brevity of [Goffstein's] text and the frugality of [her] illustrations, the book can give small children an impression of the composer's absorption in his creative work—and fortunately, it does not attempt to do more. (p. 90)

Zena Sutherland, in Bulletin of the Center for Children's Books *(© 1973 by the University of Chicago; all rights reserved), February, 1973.*

As light and gentle as a waltz, this brief book with simple, cartoon-like illustrations is merely a pleasant introduction which supplies just what the title suggests, a little information on Schubert. . . . The enjoyable story is enhanced by the inclusion of a durable plastic recording of five of his waltzes, which is clear in sound reproduction and played by a competent musician. The total experience is lovely. (p. 63)

Lillian Canzler, in School Library Journal *(reprinted from the May, 1973, issue of* School Library Journal, *published by R. R. Bowker Company, a Xerox company; copyright © 1973 by Xerox Corporation), May, 1973.*

ME AND MY CAPTAIN (1974)

Me is a she, a little wooden doll on the shelf. The Captain, wooden, too, is master of a model fishing boat anchored on the window sill below. She dreams of him coming up to see her, marrying, showing him her treasures, eating the plaster figurine food, laughing, joking. . . . But if the dream never comes to pass, just looking down at the Captain's boat on the sill below makes her "feel happy because he is there."

Find fault if you will, say that Miss Goffstein offers here profound *adult* concepts of love, longing and contentment. Besides, we know that they are only dolls, inanimate things. But children, remember, aren't so sure; they give life to dolls. As a child were you convinced it was only an errant breeze that had moved your doll in the night? You believed dolls had an existence, a world of their own. Childhood continues and so does love. Miss Goffstein is

the advocate pointing this out with an efficient, expert simplicity in text and illustration. Her pen-and-ink-drawn dolls stand sturdy and stanch. They remain dolls. Only their hearts are true. (p. 8)

George A. Woods, in The New York Times Book Review *(© 1974 by The New York Times Company; reprinted by permission), September 29, 1974.*

Goffstein's rather dowdy wooden doll reveals, with an affecting directness that fits her humble form, her dreams of marrying the captain of a fishing boat that sits on the window sill below her shelf. . . . The doll, the captain and the dog are all firmly attached to round wooden bases and after the first view of their cozy imagined dinner both humans are seen to be standing stiff and upright on their chairs, arms immobile at their sides—a touch which somehow underlines their poignancy at the same time that it emphasizes their make believe character. (p. 1058)

Kirkus Reviews *(copyright © 1974 The Kirkus Service, Inc.), October 1, 1974.*

The *Me* . . . of the title is a tiny wooden doll who harbors a little girl's dream of finding love and happiness. She imagines the captain of the toy fishing boat coming to visit her and proposing marriage. They eat a doll's dinner of painted plaster food, "a feast for the eye"; the captain then sails away on a long voyage; and the doll waits for him with her dog—and a new baby. Both the text and the small ink drawings portray this traditional "womanly" wish for marriage and a family with wit, delicacy, and understatement. (p. 37)

Cherie Zarookian, in School Library Journal *(reprinted from the December, 1974, issue of* School Library Journal, *published by R. R. Bowker Company, a Xerox company; copyright © 1974 by Xerox Corporation), December, 1974.*

OTHER CITATIONS

Publishers Weekly, *September 23, 1974, p. 156.*

The Booklist, *October 15, 1974, p. 242.*

Mary M. Burns, in The Horn Book Magazine, *February, 1975, p. 38.*

MY CRAZY SISTER (1976)

With her customary economy of line and elliptical sense of composition, the author-illustrator unfolds a Thurber-like series of incidents [in *My Crazy Sister*], which are presented in rectangular panels elegantly but simply framed in black and red. . . . The two sisters and the baby lived in perfect harmony, and their preposterous experiences are joyously conveyed by means of visual and verbal understatement. (p. 38)

Paul Heins, in The Horn Book Magazine *(copyright © 1977 by The Horn Book, Inc., Boston), February, 1977.*

Goffstein's bare-essential drawings, framed and tiny, illustrate three episodes in a slight book that has action, affection, and humor. Yet it may be limited in appeal because each incident is a gag, presented but not developed. . . .

Readers-aloud may lift eyebrows at forgetting the baby or putting him in a dangerous place, but the story is warm and often funny. (p. 107)

> *Zena Sutherland, in* Bulletin of the Center for Children's Books *(© 1977 by the University of Chicago; all rights reserved), March, 1977.*

"My crazy sister came to live with me and turned my whole house upside-down." From these opening lines on, "my crazy sister" proceeds to accomplish that feat by losing her baby (she forgets she placed him on a high shelf between the clock and the vase), buying a real railroad car instead of a toy train, and bringing home an abandoned airplane. Yet, the two sisters are so happy being together that these peculiar habits of the "crazy sister" are affectionately overlooked. The story, which is divided into three episodes, is simply told and simply illustrated. Sparse, black and white line drawings, that are enclosed on each page by red and black rectangular frames, complement the text. Overall, an appealing and attractive picture book, although some parents may be uncomfortable with the unusually close relationship between the two sisters. (p. 2)

> North Carolina State Library Book Reviews, *April, 1977.*

OTHER CITATIONS

Publishers Weekly, *July 12, 1976, p. 72.*

SLEEPY PEOPLE (1966)

The purpose of this volume is to induce slumber. Soft, gray, pencil drawings show a family of sleepy people, eyes closed, stretching, who perhaps "live in one of your old bedroom slippers." They are very cozy there in warm nightshirts and hats (yawn). The sleepy father goes to find them warm cocoa and cookies for a bedtime snack (yawn), and the sleepy mother sings the children a soft soothing song as they drowse off (yawn). Don't read it unless you're ready to sleep. It's (yawn) infectious—Zzzzzzzz. (p. 34)

> *George A. Woods, in* The New York Times Book Review *(© 1966 by The New York Times Company; reprinted by permission), October 9, 1966.*

The appeal of a book like M. B. Goffstein's *Sleepy People* can only be explained in terms of the artist-author's unique conception. The notion of a minuscule, droopy-lidded race, some of whose members may be "living in one of your old bedroom slippers," is inspired, helping to make her small work a rival to the sandman in summoning slumber. (pp. 183, 185)

> *Selma G. Lanes, in her* Down the Rabbit Hole: Adventures and Misadventures in the Realm of Children's Literature *(copyright © 1971 by Selma G. Lanes; reprinted by permission of Atheneum Publishers, New York), Atheneum, 1972.*

OTHER CITATIONS

Virginia Kirkus' Service, *August 15, 1966, p. 825.*

Evelyn Geller, in School Library Journal, *October, 1966, p. 216.*

TWO PIANO TUNERS (1970)

Not more story but more text and fewer pictures, perhaps too much text and too few pictures (holding *Goldie the Dollmaker* as the *perfect* example). Quite simply and sublimely, Reuben Weinstock is a master piano-tuner and his orphaned granddaughter Debbie, who wakes hm-m-m-m-m-ing middle C, would be another. . . . For those who are not attuned, illustrations of the enumerated implements and the manner of their use would have been helpful; the occasional drawings are almost incidental, affecting the read-aloudability too. But Debbie is totally disarming—walking down the street thinking "Hello, dogs, here comes the piano tuner"—for a select audience. (p. 449)

> Kirkus Reviews *(copyright © 1970 The Kirkus Service, Inc.), April 15, 1970.*

The author-artist's previous book, "Goldie the Dollmaker," explored the isolation of the artist. This one pays tribute to the dedication of the craftsman. . . .

As in all the Goffstein books there is an almost tangible appreciation for the simple things in life, the small acts and gestures that can convey emotional depth and define a characterization. But in this book the careful construction seems overdone; the plot does not warrant the lovingly evoked sounds and textures and feeling for objects. It is hard to imagine a child whose attention will be held by Debbie's story. "Everybody should take the responsibility for finding out what it is he really wants to do," says the wise pianist, but there is something too tidy about the way the child achieves her vocation. The sense of finality in the end is almost unnerving: Debbie and Grandfather Reuben getting up every day at the same time, eating the same wholesome breakfast, and tuning pianos into the infinite void. (p. 114)

> *Sidney D. Long, in* The New York Times Book Review *(© 1970 by The New York Times Company; reprinted by permission), May 31, 1970.*

OTHER CITATIONS

Zena Sutherland, in Bulletin of the Center for Children's Books, *October, 1970, p. 25.*

THE UNDERSIDE OF THE LEAF (1972)

In clinically affectless prose, [*The Underside of the Leaf* contains] the pubescent daydreams of twelve-year-old Paula as she passes a summer on the lake painting watercolors, designing clothes for paper dolls, and imagining that Tom Kadrie, her neighbor's jazz musician boyfriend, is secretly in love with her. Five years later, when she's in New York for a weekend, Paula calls Tom (who hardly remembers her) and makes a date. His seedy apartment, his sexual expectations, his ineffectually half-hearted friendliness all intrude on her carefully cultivated fantasies, but there's none of the morally uplifting, psychologically improbable instant maturity so common in teenage fiction. Paula's unenviable innocence remains intact, and on the plane out of New York we see her interest beginning to shift to the Princeton student sitting in front of her. The illusions and vulnerability of adolescence are depicted with an unflinching accuracy, and young women will find this a moving and sensitive examination of the painful side of growing up. (p. 485)

Kirkus Reviews *(copyright © 1972 The Kirkus Service, Inc.), April 15, 1972.*

Known previously for her bedtime stories and wise fables, [M. B. Goffstein] in *The Underside of the Leaf* . . ., ventures into fictionalized biography for an older reader. This latest work is a thoroughly honest—if ambivalent—account of the coming of age of a cosseted, Midwestern Jewish-American princess. We meet Paula Nathanson at age 12, during the summer she develops an adolescent crush on a jazz flutist, Tom Kadrie. We see her again as a college freshman, when she doggedly pursues this childhood Prince Charming and makes him part of her only slightly more mature reality. M. B. Goffstein beautifully captures that curious back-and-forth quality of adolescence—playing with paper dolls one moment and imagining vague sexual encounters the next. She achieves a memorable portrait of a callow, self-willed girl who knows exactly how to get what she wants—even if she has no idea why she wants it. The author may even have succeeded too well. Few girls in the early years of adolescence are likely to have the perspective necessary to appreciate her accomplishment. And older readers, for whom it might make perfect sense, are unlikely to be caught dead reading a children's book about the end of childhood and the tentative beginnings of maturity. This odd, painfully perceptive work is unlikely to get its just deserts. (p. 15)

Selma G. Lanes, in Book World, *Part 2* (© *The Washington Post), May 7, 1972.*

M. B. Goffstein is one of the few "originals" in children's literature. Her tiny, delicate picture books have a Middle-European flavor and a gentle reverence for life. In both words and illustrations, she blends gravity with humour, and the effect has always been disarming. Lately, however, Miss Goffstein's work has been growing more complex—and now we have a full-length novel from her. I regret to say that it is a disappointment.

The main problem with "The Underside of the Leaf" is its protagonist, Paula Nathanson. Carefully drawn, scrupulously described, she is nonetheless a shallow girl who is forever imagining how she looks to others. The first part of the story finds her at the age of 12, an incipient painter and madly in love with the boy next door. This rather limp character, Tom Kadrie, is irresistible because he is older, and also an artist. In the second half of the book, Paula has grown up, gone off to college, and is still in love with Tom. When, after many years, they finally confront each other in New York and have a thwarted sexual encounter, the reader is strangely unmoved. Why?

The first reason is that Miss Goffstein's current prose lacks tension: that elusive quality which keeps the reader turning the page. And the second reason is that she describes every single thing that involves her heroine, whether it be a sunset or a sandwich. Thirdly, one is extremely nonplussed halfway through the book, to realize that the story is set in the 1940's. Not only does this come as a surprise, but it makes one turn back to earlier references to saddle-shoes and pedal-pushers with a new (and irritable) awareness. Last but not least, the division of the book into two such disparate parts makes us wonder what age reader it was intended for.

But all of this is quibbling. What I really object to in "The Underside of the Leaf," is that the *soul* of the story is missing. We have characters and conflicts and events, but the spirit of the author is not there—and it is a tremendous loss. It is natural for a writer to want to experiment, changing his inner landscape and altering his angle to the sun. But some writers are more suited to perfecting a special, very personal style—and I think this is true of Miss Goffstein. The quiet sadness and beauty in her small book, "Goldie the Dollmaker" are more valuable than all the young adult novels on the current book scene. (p. 8)

Barbara Wersba, in The New York Times Book Review (© *1972 by The New York Times Company; reprinted by permission), May 28, 1972.*

Goffstein does understand the emotional dichotomies of pre-teens, but her endless descriptions of fishing, the weather and Paula's clothes make this slow going. The nostalgic evocation of college life in the '50s has meaning only for those who lived it; today's kids will find Paula self-conscious, posturing and snobbish, and are unlikely to spend the time to analyze what may lie on the underside of Paula's leaf. (p. 75)

Alice Miller Bregman, in School Library Journal *(reprinted from the November, 1972, issue of* School Library Journal, *published by R. R. Bowker Company, a Xerox company; copyright © 1972 by Xerox Corporation), November, 1972.*

This gentle spoof of an adolescent girl's infatuations is delightful reading if an adolescent reader has outgrown her own immature infatuations and can view this stage in an adolescent girl's development somewhat dispassionately. How old must one be before he can laugh at himself? That is the question that must be answered before *The Underside of the Leaf* becomes good reading. (p. 1385)

John W. Conner, in English Journal *(copyright © 1972 by The National Council of Teachers of English), December, 1972.*

OTHER CITATIONS

Publishers Weekly, *May 15, 1972, p. 53.*

The Booklist, *September 15, 1972, p. 86.*

Zena Sutherland, in Bulletin of the Center for Children's Books, *October, 1972, p. 25.*

H

HASKINS, James 1941-
(Jim Haskins)

James Haskins is a Black American author for adults and children. A versatile writer, he has published works which cover diverse areas exemplified by his *Revolutionaries: Agents of Change* and his *Jokes from Black Folks*. Haskins has also lectured and taught many subjects, including folklore and literature, urban education, and the psychology of Black language. (See also *Contemporary Authors*, Vols. 33-36.)

ADAM CLAYTON POWELL: PORTRAIT OF A MARCHING BLACK (1974)

If asked about Adam Clayton Powell, Jr., most young readers today would answer, "Adam, Adam who?" Such an answer can not be too surprising given the clouds of controversy that always blocked any real understanding of Adam Clayton Powell. It is almost three years since his death and it is time to look back over his life and fill in the years between 1908 and 1972—to see the man behind the clouds. . . .

Mr. Haskins' book is a necessary addition to libraries serving young readers; unfortunately, the author fails to create a sense of excitement for the reader. Mr. Haskins gives the facts, but there is no intensity as he explores Adam's contributions and his seemingly self-destructive behavior. Nevertheless, the facts need to be told, and Mr. Haskins' book has done that. (p. 5)

> *Ray Anthony Shepard, in* Interracial Books for Children *(reprinted by permission of* The Bulletin—Interracial Books for Children, *1841 Broadway, New York, N.Y. 10023), Vol. 5, No. 6, 1974.*

"The right-size box for each gift"—this system permits the reader to put the Powell biography in a very small package. Adam Clayton Powell was a strong, magnetic, intelligent Negro with a rich heritage and monumental charisma, who worked, often very successfully, for the black man. But a goodly portion of his bounty was given to wine, women, double-dealing, and succumbing to the Achilles heel of many charismatic leaders—depending on charm to balance the indolence of their days. The author's blindness to any shortcomings reduces the book's value to almost nothing—certainly of little value as an objective look at a Negro giant.

Grades 7-up. (The publisher's age 9-12 suggested level seems unreal.) (p. 285)

> *Mrs. John G. Gray, in* Best Sellers *(copyright 1974, by the University of Scranton), September 15, 1974.*

As interesting as a facet of black history in the United States as it is as a biography, this is based in part upon the reminiscences of Powell's friends and relatives, of whom brief sketches are given at the back of the book. It is therefore understandable that the writing often has a note of reverence and always a tone of affection for the black leader who came to be a controversial public figure. The material is carefully organized and is written in a vigorous style, with many quotations from Powell or others. An index and Powell's legislative record are appended. (p. 63)

> *Zena Sutherland, in* Bulletin of the Center for Children's Books *(© 1974 by the University of Chicago; all rights reserved), December, 1974.*

OTHER CITATIONS

Kirkus Reviews, *May 1, 1974, pp. 492-93.*

The Booklist, *September 15, 1974, p. 100.*

THE CREOLES OF COLOR OF NEW ORLEANS (1975)

This non-fiction work describes the past and present of Louisiana's so-called free men of color, better known as Creoles—a conglomeration of octoroons, quadroons and mulattoes whose origins date back to the founding of the territory. (p. 12)

[The] author openly discusses the prejudice and snobbery of the Creoles—their alienation from Blacks and their pride in liaisons with whites—as a point of distinction and pride. Yet, he does not pursue these matters in a context that would help readers place the Creoles' self-hating and elitist values in the proper perspective. Such a framework is necessary to foster understanding of the Creoles' value system as the product of a racist environment.

Instead, the author presents the Creoles' negative opinions and beliefs about Blacks, Native Americans and others with little interpretive commentary, which has the effect of extolling the virtues of the Creoles at the expense of others. . . .

[The] final section, which discusses the Creoles' contributions to U.S. society, would no doubt elicit total disinterest following as it does 107 pages of racist, elitist, and conformist drivel.

Although the mediocre black-and-white illustrations [by Don Miller] are compatible with the text, they do not enhance it. (p. 13)

> *Patricia Spence, in* Interracial Books for Children Bulletin *(reprinted by permission of* Interracial Books for Children Bulletin, *1841 Broadway, New York, N.Y. 10023), Vol. 7, No. 5, 1976.*

[*The Creoles of Color of New Orleans*] was written for the purpose of tracing the history of the Creoles . . ., their contributions and their culture that remains strong as they enter the American mainstream. . . .

Prior to American control over New Orleans (1803), the Creoles had the same rights and privileges as Europeans and they were determined to keep themselves separate and distinct from the non-French Black population.

Light skin, Caucasian features and "silky" hair were treasured blessing in the Creole world and the goal of every generation was to ensure that the next generation was even lighter. This was done by Creole girls entering into a "placage" with French men. . . .

Haskins rationalizes this irrational behavior as being the likely thing for Creoles to do as an "accommodation to the values of the predominant white society, . . . the closer to white a person is, the 'better' he is, the more opportunities he has, the more wealth he can acquire." The closest Haskins comes to a condemnation of this very sad self-hatred is to call it "nonsense." He even implies throughout the book that Creoles are not denying their Blackness because, indeed, they are not Black! Terms such as octaroon, quadroon, griffe (the offspring of a Black person and a "mulatto") are used to explain the un-Blackness of Creoles. . . .

How Haskins can force his pen to romantically portray such ridiculous and shameful attitudes and practices is beyond me. In a time when we are trying to provide the most positive and constructive images for our young, he chooses to glamorize an age that we should be attempting to give a truer assessment to. It would be understandable if he were presenting these facts to be examined and criticized from a Black/Afrikan frame of reference, but the Brother still uses the word *negro*! Toward the end of the book he says that Creoles are now becoming conscious of their Blackness and that ". . . the ideal skin color now is not almost-white, but a light-brown." It is hard to believe that Haskins is serious about this. This book would be useful in teaching children what not to write and how not to think. Other than that, it is only another example of mis-education of the negro. (p. 63)

> *Hazel Copeland, in* Black Books Bulletin *(copyright © 1976 by the Institute of Positive Education), Fall, 1976.*

OTHER CITATIONS

John F. Caviston, in School Library Journal, *September, 1975, p. 104.*

FIGHTING SHIRLEY CHISHOLM (1975)

Much of a soothsayer's prophecy about Chisholm's political career is played out here in a factual history which provides readers with a picture of Chisholm's precocity and early independence. . . . Haskins' account is straightforward; succinct quotes give insight into his subject's thinking, and he enlarges on the reasons behind some of her determined, independent political stands. (p. 692)

> The Booklist *(reprinted by permission of the American Library Association; copyright 1975 by the American Library Association), March 1, 1975.*

A biography of the first black woman to serve in the United States Congress gives a good balance of personal and professional material, is written with vigorous admiration, and is candid about incidents not included in other Chisholm biographies written for young people. All her biographers have made it clear that Shirley Chisholm is honest, courageous, and forthright; Haskins stresses the decisions she has had to make about paramount causes: would she take a stand on an issue as a black or as a woman when the stands conflicted, for example. Like [Susan] Brownmiller's *Shirley Chisholm,* for slightly younger readers, this is a lesson in political structure and in the necessity for practical compromise to achieve idealistic goals. (p. 10)

> *Zena Sutherland, in* Bulletin of the Center for Children's Books *(© 1975 by the University of Chicago; all rights reserved), September, 1975.*

OTHER CITATIONS

Publishers' Weekly, *January 20, 1975, p. 77.*

Kirkus Reviews, *May 15, 1975, p. 578.*

FROM LEW ALCINDOR TO KAREEM ABDUL JABBAR (1972)

All too obviously drawn from the same clipping file mined by the Burchards [in *Sports Hero: Kareem Abdul Jabbar,* by Sue and Marshall Burchard], the same career highlights written up for the 9-12 set and with the addition of more candid material on the friction with coaches Donohue and Wooden, the boycott of the '68 Olympics and a not always friendly press. The few first-person insights are apparently drawn from previously published *Sports Illustrated* material and Haskins' no-hype approach may not please those addicts who demand voluminous statistics, but Kareem Jabbar's evident seriousness as a player and as a person gives the narrative its staying power. (p. 805)

> Kirkus Reviews *(copyright © 1972 The Kirkus Service, Inc.), July 15, 1972.*

A brief, informative biography of the life of a popular sports hero is certain to attract younger adolescent readers. And when that hero is Kareem Abdul Jabbar, basketball fans rejoice. James Haskins recounts highlights of the popular professional basketball player's life from the time he started school until he joins the Milwaukee Bucks. (p. 825)

Although Lew Alcindor's life story is the principal subject of the book, basketball fans will be delighted by exciting retellings of some of the important games in Alcindor's career which dot the book. Alcindor's thoughtful and quiet conversion to the religion of Islam occurs while he is a student at UCLA. His legal change of name occurred in the summer of 1971. And so Kareem Abdul Jabbar became the official name of one of the greatest basketball players of our time. Excellent photographs provide a pictorial history of the basketball star, enhancing James Haskins' fine commentary. *From Lew Alcindor to Kareem Abdul Jabbar* will delight the star's young fans. (p. 826)

> *John W. Conner, in* English Journal *(copyright © 1973 by The National Council of Teachers of English), May, 1973.*

OTHER CITATIONS

School Library Journal, *December, 1972, p. 77.*

Zena Sutherland, in Bulletin of the Center for Children's Books, *January, 1973, p. 76.*

JOKES FROM BLACK FOLKS (1973)

Haskins' selections [in *Jokes from Black Folks*] don't really clarify his introductory distinction between the old black humor (you laughed at them) and the new (you laugh with), and if several of the lines are up to the level of the TV shows he cites as examples of the new *(Flip Wilson, Sanford and Son, All in the Family)*—that only demonstrates the value of actors and canned laughter. A fair proportion of the jokes center on the variously black subjects of preachers and church, landlords and rent, and lunch counter integration; then there are the Little Moron variations that seem close enough to laughing at (father to son: "ain't they found that lowest common denominator yet? Why they was looking for it when I was a boy") and a few aphorisms (among the best, Satchel Paige's "Don't ever look back; something might be gaining on you"). The mere existence of a black joke book for kids is to be welcomed, but considering the sharper wit that goes free on any ghetto street corner, this one is a let-down. (p. 602)

> Kirkus Reviews *(copyright © 1973 The Kirkus Service, Inc.), June 1, 1973.*

Inadequate as a presentation of Negro humor, this collection of ethnic jokes mainly includes the type heard on TV variety shows rather than the folk humor implied in the title. A short introduction gives some background as well as comments on the current scene but fails to penetrate beneath the surface. The subject divisions—religion, school, intelligence, crime, poverty, landlords, food—seem arbitrary, and the final section containing African riddles, short sayings and rhymes from other sources, and two stories by Langston Hughes contrasts sharply with the contemporaneity of the rest of the book. The collection is definitely not suitable for a young audience: the jokes are overly slick and sophisticated; words like "rape" and "bastard" are used unnecessarily; and the humor in the last section is subtle to the point of being obscure. [Harold] Courlander's *Terrapin's Pot of Sense* . . . and collections of Negro folktales better portray black humor. (pp. 62-3)

> *Margaret Blue, in* School Library Journal *(reprinted from the November, 1973, issue of* School Library Journal, *published by R. R. Bowker Company, a Xerox company; copyright © 1973 by Xerox Corporation), November, 1973.*

THE LIFE AND DEATH OF MARTIN LUTHER KING, JR. (1977)

[*The Life and Death of Martin Luther King, Jr.* is a] respectful biography of King that describes his youth, significant influences, and early Movement domination, plays down the mid-Sixties opposition, and dwells extensively (as the title indicates) on the theories of his assassination. The biographical section includes childhood distinctions, adolescent distractions (which conflicted with the demands of the ministry), and the gradual assumption of leadership. Haskins ignores neither Hoover's blatant hostility nor the FBI bugging (although he doesn't specify what was overheard), but he fails to acknowledge the extent of the challenge from Malcolm (unmentioned), the Panthers, and others. The last section—a third of the book—follows habitual liar James Earl Ray through the months before the assassination and examines numerous theories of his involvement, using his own testimony and recanting and the works of other authors. These speculations, which require a highly attentive reader, distinguish this most recent life of King from comparable juvenile biographies, such as Edward Preston's *Martin Luther King. . . .* (p. 583)

> Kirkus Reviews *(copyright © 1977 The Kirkus Service, Inc.), June 1, 1977.*

[This] book from the astonishingly prolific Haskins is a straightforward nuts and bolts account of the King story that would inform readers of any age. The rather militant tone of the section on King's Atlanta childhood is muted as events become too horrifying for rhetoric. Haskins does not ignore the chinks in the leader's armor although he does not dwell on them unduly. The going gets pretty heavy for 10-year-olds when the conspiracy theory and the legal battles of James Earl Ray are described in detail, but the book is a valuable source, written lucidly but without any talking down. (p. E6)

> *Brigitte Weeks, in* Book World—The Washington Post *(© The Washington Post), September 11, 1977.*

OTHER CITATIONS

Nikki Grimes, in Children's Book Review Service, *July, 1977, p. 129.*

A PIECE OF THE POWER: FOUR BLACK MAYORS (1972)

[*A Piece of the Power* is another] of Haskins' competent but totally non-interpretive collective biographies. Unlike the disparate subjects of his recent *Profiles in Black Power* . . . , all four mayors are moderates who dissociate themselves from militant slogans and movements. Only Charles Evers, whose tiny Fayette, Mississippi, is known solely for his election, makes interesting reading; Haskins whitewashes neither the viciousness of Mississippi racism, nor Evers' dabbling in prostitution, numbers and bootlegging along with shopping centers and civil rights, nor the coercive methods used by black leaders to ensure that their boycott of white merchants was a success. The other profiles are flatly similar, though a few distinct impressions emerge: the political ambitiousness of Carl Stokes of Cleveland whose sad story ends with the defeat of his chosen successor; the statement by Hatcher of Gary, Indiana (re his problems with white resistance which went as far as attempted "disannexion") that "What's on trial in Gary is the American system''; the overwhelming financial troubles of Ken Gibson's Newark which illustrate that without the power of state and federal pursestrings an honest and able black mayor is impotent. The unintentionally ironic title is an indication of Haskins' lack of incisiveness, but his material even in this unprocessed state probably has a place. (p. 631)

> Kirkus Reviews *(copyright © 1972 The Kirkus Service, Inc.), June 1, 1972.*

[Haskins'] sketches [of four black mayors] are written in a competent style and with objective approach, but are perhaps more interesting as studies of the intricacies of political life than as revealing biographies. An extensive divided bibliography and an index are appended. (p. 77)

> *Zena Sutherland, in* Bulletin of the Center for Children's Books *(© 1973 by the University of Chicago; all rights reserved), January, 1973.*

OTHER CITATIONS

Mrs. John G. Gray, Best Sellers, *July 15, 1972, p. 199.*

The Booklist, *October 15, 1972, pp. 189-90.*

PROFILES IN BLACK POWER (1972)

Haskins' noncommittal biographical sketches of men associated with the black power slogan, from Adam Clayton Powell to Rap Brown, maintain a decidedly low profile. While stressing the slogan's elasticity (''definitions of black power range from simply 'an equal share' to 'armed revolution,'''), Haskins tends to see similarities more than differences—even with Ron Karenga, who receives the harshest judgment here. Haskins accepts the *Wall Street Journal*'s assessment that Karenga is ''typical of many militants . . . eager to gather influence for quiet bargaining with the predominantly white power structure.'' For the most part, polemics, allegations and defenses are impartially transcribed (though the more salacious details on the Newton-Cleaver feud are omitted). The summaries give a good overview of each individual's career and will be useful for checking facts, but they are not synthesized to reflect the dynamics of the movement. Finally, while the inclusion of the Reverend Cleage, Floyd McKissick and Dr. Nathan Wright add breadth to the discussion, the omissions—Bobby Seale, George Jackson and Angela Davis—considerably diminish its topical value. (p. 1220)

> Kirkus Reviews *(copyright © 1971 The Kirkus Service, Inc.), November 15, 1971.*

Eleven brief chapter-length articles covering such black leaders as Adam Clayton Powell, Malcolm X, Eldridge Cleaver, Stokely Carmichael, and H. Rap Brown. Also included is useful, not easily come by material about the Reverend Albert B. Cleage, Floyd McKissick, James Forman, Huey Newton, and Ron Karenga. Unfortunately, Haskins omits Bobby Seale, Angela Davis, George Jackson, and some of the writers who express the ideas of Black Power such as Don Lee, Nikki Giovanni, and James Baldwin. An excellent set of notes for each chapter is provided in the back of the book, and there is an excellent bibliography including books and periodical articles. While little new is presented about these men, each is portrayed

sympathetically and the short format biographies read smoothly. (p. 146)

> *Janet G. Polacheck, in* School Library Journal *(reprinted from the April, 1972, issue of* School Library Journal, *published by R. R. Bowker Company, a Xerox company; copyright © 1972 by Xerox Corporation), April, 1972.*

OTHER CITATIONS

The Booklist, *June 15, 1972, p. 903.*

RALPH BUNCHE: A MOST RELUCTANT HERO (1974)

[*Ralph Bunche: A Most Reluctant Hero*] helps to fill a yawning informational gap. While it is light on the political and social substance of Bunche's activities, the book successfully communicates his character and something of his contributions, the best sections dealing with early schooling and time spent as UN mediator between Arabs and Israelis in 1948-49. Haskins pays attention to his subject's role in American struggles for black-white equality, frequently comparing and contrasting Bunche's personal successes to the situation of most blacks. (p. 1253)

> The Booklist *(reprinted by permission of the American Library Association; copyright 1974 by the American Library Association), July 15, 1974.*

This excellent biography captures the personal style of its subject. Haskins doesn't shout praises but, instead, compellingly shows evidence of Bunche's greatness by describing his activities, quoting his speeches, and relating anecdotes which show the man in action. . . . The material is well chosen and presented, integrating Bunche's life with the political and social movements of his day. Haskins' readable account updates and replaces [J. Alvin] Kugelmass' *Ralph J. Bunche: Fighter for Peace.* . . . (p. 105)

> *Anitra Gordon, in* School Library Journal *(reprinted from the September, 1974, issue of* School Library Journal, *published by R. R. Bowker Company, a Xerox company; copyright © 1974 by Xerox Corporation), September, 1974.*

OTHER CITATIONS

Kirkus Reviews, *June 15, 1974, pp. 641-42.*

RELIGIONS (1973)

A neutral, succinct summary of the five major religions' basic tenets, [*Religions*] makes clear organizational distinctions between the generally accepted beliefs regarding each faith's founding, its historical evolution, and current trends. Haskins is strongest when sketching the broad outlines of religion's sociohistorical impact—attitudes towards women, towards class differences, and tolerance of outsiders (stressing, for example, Islam's belief in the brotherhood of man, an aspect unfamiliar to most Christians raised on stories of fanatic Holy Wars). . . . Such a vast overview necessarily leads to generalizations, but Haskins is always fair. This is a different approach from that taken by those bland offerings which discuss religions totally outside their cultural context, yet easy and undogmatic enough to be understood by youngsters with diverse religious backgrounds. (pp. 127-28)

> Kirkus Reviews *(copyright © 1973 The Kirkus Service, Inc.), February 1, 1973.*

[*Religions* is a] brief and generally clear account of the origins, tenets, and practices of five major contemporary religions: Hinduism, Buddhism, Judaism, Christianity, and Islam. The author appreciates non-western religion and explains the appeal to some young people today of what he calls their "simple" spirituality (in fact, it is complex). Nazareth is erroneously reported as Jesus' birthplace (according to the Bible it was Bethlehem) and some interpretations are controversial (e.g., that the prevalence of mysticism in Eastern religions means greater spiritual richness; that Jesus was recognized as a rabbi by the Jewish community; that there was a revival of faith in the 19th Century; etc.). However, on the whole, this is a useful introduction for young people. (p. 124)

> *Bernard Poll, in* School Library Journal *(reprinted from the October, 1973, issue of* School Library Journal, *published by R. R. Bowker Company, a Xerox company; copyright © 1973 by Xerox Corporation), October, 1973.*

REVOLUTIONARIES: AGENTS OF CHANGE (1971)

[*Revolutionaries: Agents of Change* contains eleven] individual biographies that don't, collectively, afford any grasp of the nature of revolution or revolutionaries. That, in another vein, they demonstrate "the impossibility of placing different revolutionary characters into any but very general categories" is incontrovertible; indeed, any categorization is suspect, including that based, as the author suggests, on vague "kinds of and causes for revolutions." Complicating the problem is the application of the tag "revolutionary" to George Washington on the basis, ostensibly, of the difficulties he overcame as military commander and his later advocacy of a strong central government; Patrick Henry fills his niche somewhat better but while his revolutionary utterances are quoted, their significance is not pointed out. Neither, except for his selfless commitment to land reform, is the uniqueness of Zapata or his movement conveyed. Of the other accounts, each of which, save one, appears to be based primarily on a single secondary source (not necessarily the foremost authority), the best in terms of clarity, interest and judiciousness is that of Ho Chi Minh; the treatment of Malcolm X is flat—unattuned and unrevealing; re Karl Marx, the complex is reduced to the simplistic (as is Hegel's thought, which we are then told—twice—Marx and his acquaintances had difficulty understanding). Moreover, and this is a serious deficiency, there is no critique of Marx's theories; in a generally admiring presentation, no distinction is made between the still-useful, the inherently dubious and the discredited. A similar degree of simplicism attends the portrayal of Che Guevara as "a sort of political Robin Hood," a characterization that's repeated and retained without qualification; on the other hand Castro is considered an opportunist, again without modulation. Meanwhile Mao's "ruthlessness" is explicitly extenuated. Actually, the fault is not just in the judgments (and their

inconsistency) but in the crude imposition of moral standards on political behavior, the result being particularly distortive in the case of Robespierre. (The course of the French Revolution is anyhow incomprehensible here.) Atatürk is more justly drawn though one might question the rationalization excusing *his* dictatorial rule—especially since Turkey today is far from being "truly democratic." Informative to a degree then, but only in the narrow sense of arranging facts in sequence. (p. 61)

> Kirkus Reviews *(copyright © 1971 The Kirkus Service, Inc.), January 15, 1971.*

A novel company of revolutionaries meet in these pages. . . . The portraits are sympathetic but are balanced by evaluations which show the tendency of some revolutionists to rely on dictatorship while working toward a democracy whose day never dawns. Needed, accurate information is included (except that the Bastille was attacked on July 14, not on July 17). Short sketches of such people as Atatürk and Zapata are not easily come by. However, the style is early *World Book*—the real people never do stand up. And each chapter seems to make use of only a couple of sources, secondary ones at that, so that at best readers are given just a digest of books already available. The bibliography is merely a good list of beginning readings, while the magazine list is a group of sketchy articles in an average run of popular magazines: *Life*, *Newsweek*, *Ramparts*, the *New Republic*, the *New York Times*, and *Time*. As a last warning, even a limited use of this book will be curtailed unless your cataloger does analytics. (p. 75)

> *Janet G. Polacheck, in* School Library Journal *(reprinted from the May, 1971, issue of* School Library Journal, *published by R. R. Bowker Company, a Xerox company; copyright © 1971 by Xerox Corporation), May, 1971.*

THE STORY OF STEVIE WONDER (1976)

Quotes enliven the narrative [of *The Story of Stevie Wonder*] which also takes time to impress upon the reader the special problems Wonder faced as a blind person. Some of Haskins' interpretive comments and characterizations are open to dispute: . . . it's a gross generalization to say that white rock music in the early seventies lacked meaning, and white audiences were dissatisfied until Stevie Wonder introduced them to black music "which did have meaning." Commentary like this hardly implies a basic understanding of the music of that time. But Stevie Wonder's life is what's important here, and the basics of it come across. (p. 38)

> Booklist *(reprinted by permission of the American Library Association; copyright 1976 by the American Library Association), September 1, 1976.*

Casual and conversational in tone, astute in analysis of the musician's work, and objective although admiring, Haskins' biography should appeal to all Stevie Wonder fans and inform those not familiar with his career. Born blind, Steveland Morris changed his name when he became a phenomenal star, at the age of twelve, with his first hit record. Despite a failed first marriage and a serious automobile accident, the singer and composer has been resilient enough to retain the ebullience that, with his range and vocal control, have won a vast audience and many awards. A discography and an index are appended. (p. 125)

> Zena Sutherland, in Bulletin of the Center for Children's Books (© 1977 by the University of Chicago; all rights reserved), April, 1977.

OTHER CITATIONS

Kirkus Reviews, *May 15, 1976, p. 604.*

Diane Haas, in School Library Journal, *January, 1977, p. 92.*

Children's Book Review Service, *February, 1977, p. 69.*

STREET GANGS: YESTERDAY AND TODAY (1974)

In *Street Gangs,* Professor James Haskins offers a study that could easily serve as a sourcebook for a high school or college sociology course. Gangs have had attention over the years, in books, articles and films—Marlon Brando in "The Wild One." But Haskins's attention goes deeper than this. He believes that "participation in gang activities is one way of feeling like 'somebody.' Identity, a sense of belonging, a sense of importance—for many in the lower economic classes gang activity has seemed the only way to fulfill these very important needs. This has been true, in urban centers across the United States, throughout its history."

The strength of Haskins's book is in its historical material, its account, for example, of runaways in the 1790s when the suddenly liberated colonies were without the money or institutions to care for homeless children, or of the battles between the Bowery Boys and the Dead Rabbits in New York between 1830 and 1860. . . .

Haskins argues persuasively that "when you get down to basics, the conditions that have fertilized the soil for gang violence throughout American history exist, essentially unchanged, today. The human needs of the new street gangs are no different from the gangs of the past, the difference is that today's gang members are more politically aware and their potential for violence is much greater." (p. 8)

> Colman McCarthy, in Book World—The Washington Post (© The Washington Post), November 10, 1974.

A sober and sobering history of street gangs from colonial times to the present is based on newspaper accounts and sociological studies. Well-researched and organized, written in strong, direct prose, the book makes clear the facts that street gangs are not a new phenomenon, that there have long been ties of political and criminal nature, and that there are no easy solutions. (p. 78)

> Zena Sutherland, in Bulletin of the Center for Children's Books (© 1975 by the University of Chicago; all rights reserved), January, 1975.

[In *Street Gangs: Yesterday and Today*] James Haskins presents a consistently absorbing overview of disorderly conduct and violence by organized youth gangs. The book's historical perspective forces the modern reader to view gangs not as an invention of Blacks and Puerto Ricans, but as a phenomenon endemic to urban ghettos. . . .

The author tells his story dispassionately. He neither condones nor condemns gangs but allows the facts and the people to speak. (p. 18)

> Jane Whittaker, in Interracial Books for Children Bulletin (reprinted by permission of Interracial Books for Children Bulletin, 1841 Broadway, New York, N.Y. 10023), Vol. 5, Nos. 7 & 8, 1975.

OTHER CITATIONS

Mrs. John G. Gray, in Best Sellers, *October 15, 1974, p. 330.*

Kathleen Roedder, in Childhood Education, *April-May, 1975, p. 329.*

THE WAR AND THE PROTEST: VIET NAM (1971)

Unincisive and even ingenuous in comparison to Hal Dareff's *Story of Vietnam* . . . and its recent sequel *From Vietnam to Cambodia* . . . , this is an unsearching newssummary, variously erroneous, distortive, and subjective. While Haskins does cite the destructive socio-political influences of French colonialism and trace the growth of the ambiguous Communist (nationalist?) movement whose implications were misinterpreted if not ignored by a singleminded America, he questions only the wisdom—never the facts—behind Congress' adoption of the Tonkin resolution ("In August 1964 the United State [*sic*] destroyers *Maddox* and *C. Turner Joy were attacked* [our italics] by North Vietnamese torpedo boats . . ."). Johnson announced his retirement "in the interests of world peace and international unity" as the "protest tree" blossomed, the Major Organizations Against the War being SANE, Women Strike for Peace, the Resistance, and Mobe. Subsumed under the third of these is "the burning of draft files by nine persons in Catonsville, *Ohio* (!)," and profiled in the following section on Major Leadership Against the War are Julian Bond, Martin Luther King, Jr., William Sloane Coffin, Jr., and Benjamin Spock (if the choices are odd, the annotations are odder still). Among the hawks ("A famous Indian chief was named Black Hawk") was George Wallace, who—due to one of all too many misprints—"led (left?) the Democratic party and formed his own . . ."; and among the Effects of the Campaign on the Peace Talks there is no mention of the more significant effects of the Parish machinations (the holding tactics of the South Vietnamese delegation) on the campaign. Before the lame bibliography—seven peripheral books and a slew of conventional periodicals—and limp glossary ("civil disobedience: action or resistance that openly breaks the law but is *polite* and *disciplined*"), comes Mr. Haskins' unenlightening and unenlightened conclusion: "The Nixon administration is growing tired of making all the offers and bitter that the bombing halt, the increased troop withdrawals, and the appointment of Bruce, have gotten the United States nothing in return." (p. 563)

> Kirkus Reviews (copyright © 1971 The Kirkus Service, Inc.), May 15, 1971.

Although the title implies that Haskins' book deals with the domestic protest against the war, almost one-third of the text concerns events leading up to and including the war itself. But [Hal] Dareff, in his two books, provides more thorough coverage of the war and its history. In writing about the protest to the war, Haskins effectively isolates from the mass of material now available some of the major groups and persons involved in the peace movement. But his seemingly studied attempt to write on a fifth-grade level impedes the flow of his text. In addition, there are minor inaccuracies (for example, Haskins states that most Kennedy supporters went over to McCarthy after the assassination. No mention is made of McGovern, whose candidacy is the result of Kennedy supporters' disenchantment with McCarthy). Haskins' sympathies lie with the peace movement, though he goes to great lengths to be fair to all sides. At the end of the book, this attempt to be fair results in a failure to apply to Nixon the critical criteria which he used earlier in the book in relation to Johnson. An ambiguous and not very helpful glossary follows the text. (pp. 158-59)

> *Jack Forman, in* School Library Journal *(reprinted from the September, 1971, issue of* School Library Journal, *published by R. R. Bowker Company, a Xerox company; copyright © 1971 by Xerox Corporation), September, 1971.*

WITCHCRAFT, MYSTICISM AND MAGIC IN THE BLACK WORLD (1974)

"Witchcraft, Mysticism and Magic in the Black World," by James Haskins, has responded to the present interest with a well-researched book about a people to whom magic is no fad. This is for children in the sense that it is written with clarity and liveliness. Its introductory part surveys the new American mysticism—black masses, churches of Satan, astrology, ESP, and so on—so neatly that it serves the reader as background to all the literature. He then points out that magic has always been an important part of the black world. . . .

In a narrative as vivid as a film documentary Haskins traces these beliefs from their sources in the West African slave-supplying nations of the eighteenth century, in which religious practice and daily life were identical, through bondage in the West Indies and our Southern American states, to practices and beliefs among blacks today. . . .

Haskins's study of magic and witchcraft in the United States today is . . . absorbing reading. We learn about "turning the trick," voodoo, hoodoo, *gris-gris,* "the drugstore" (love powders, war powders), charms, the established churches ("As in slavery times the Catholic Church service is too strict and too rigidly defined for blacks to embroider upon it."), and at last about contemporary Northern black affluent cults, which are, of course, close brother to the white ones. This book, to which the omnibus review [nine books are reviewed here] can do no justice, is the one to read first. (p. 22)

> *Christopher Davis, in* The New York Times Book Review *(© 1974 by The New York Times Company; reprinted by permission), May 5, 1974.*

Haskins' intent [in *Witchcraft, Mysticism and Magic in the Black World*] is to discuss the African origins of New World black witchcraft, mysticism, and magic and to show the lasting qualities of these beliefs and practices as revealed in today's black American scene. Unfortunately he seems overcome by the complexities of this huge undertaking and spends much of his book listing voodoo and hoodoo practices, leaving too little space for real analysis and insight. Perhaps because of dealing with the subject at a juvenile level, his analysis itself is frequently oversimplified, e.g. "The most noticeable aspect of black life throughout the New World is the great importance of the supernatural." Nevertheless, much valuable information is presented, and such a serious treatment of this aspect of black culture should be welcomed. (p. 1099)

> *The Booklist (reprinted by permission of the American Library Association; copyright 1974 by the American Library Association), June 1, 1974.*

OTHER CITATIONS

Kirkus Reviews, *February 15, 1974, p. 193.*

John F. Caviston, in School Library Journal, *April, 1974, p. 66.*

*   *   *

HINTON, S(usan) E(loise)   1950(?)-

S. E. Hinton is an American writer of fiction for young adults. At the age of 17, she wrote *The Outsiders*, a story of high school gang rivalry with characters loosely based on her own acquaintances. Its realistic style and subject matter brought praise, criticism, and indisputable popularity with young adults. Hinton's perceptive understanding of the male viewpoint in her novels has often led to the assumption that she is a man.

AUTHOR'S COMMENTARY

The trouble is, grownups write about teen-agers from their own memories, or else write about teen-agers from a standoff, I'm-a-little-scared-to-get-close-they're-hairy view. Teenagers today want to read about teen-agers today. The world is changing, yet the authors of books for teen-agers are still 15 years behind the times.

In the fiction they write, romance is still the most popular theme, with a-horse-and-the-girl-who-loved-it coming in a close second. Nowhere is the drive-in social jungle mentioned, the behind-the-scenes politicking that goes on in big schools, the cruel social system in which, if you can afford to snub every fourth person you meet, you're popular. In short, where is reality? On the other side of the coin, there are the hair-raising accounts of gangs, motorcycle and otherwise; gangs hold a fatal fascination for adults. Adults who try to write realistically seem to mix up the real with the dirty. (p. 26)

Adults who let small children watch hours of violence . . . on TV scream their heads off when a book written for children contains a fist fight. But violence too is a part of teen-agers' lives. . . . Only when violence is for a sensational effect should it be objected to in books for teen-agers. Such books should not be blood and gore, but not a fairyland of proms and double-dates, either. Sometimes I wonder which extreme does the most harm.

Teen-agers should not be written down to; anyone can tell when his intelligence is being underestimated. Those who are not ready for adult novels can easily have their love of reading killed by the inane junk lining the teen-age shelf in the library. . . .

Teen-agers know a lot today. Not just things out of a textbook, but about living. . . . They know that persons in high places aren't safe from corruption, that some men have their price, and that some people sell out. Writers needn't be afraid that they will shock their teen-age audience. But give them something to hang onto. Show that some people don't sell out, and that everyone can't be bought. Do it realistically. Earn respect by giving it. (p. 29)

> *Susan Hinton, "Teen-Agers Are for Real,"* in The New York Times Book Review (© *1967 by The New York Times Company; reprinted by permission), August 27, 1967, pp. 26-9.*

THE OUTSIDERS (1967)

It is rare-to-unique among juvenile books (where even the non-fiction concentrates on positive aspects of American life and ignores its underside) to find a novel confronting the class hostilities which have intensified since the Depression. The setting of the story is a small Oklahoma city, which underscores the national scope of a current problem and by-passes the subliminal reactions that attach to major cities. The boys in this book are neither unimaginable urban sophisticates nor unassimilated Puerto Ricans or Negroes running berserk; they are the pioneer-stock legatees of Huckleberry Finn. Ponyboy, the 14-year-old narrator, tells how it looks and feels from the wrong side of the tracks and of guerrilla raids into his territory by the traditional, well-heeled enemy from the residential district, and the beating that led to a murder charge and two deaths. The story is exciting and those difficult-to-serve kids at the culturally detached bottom of society can respond to this book, with its revelations of the latent decency of the urban slum characters, who are nearly but not yet hopeless. The book is a good bet to select for discussion with young teens, especially if you ask them to contrast it to [John Rowe] Townsend's *Goodbye to the Jungle*. . . . Compassionate understanding sometimes crosses into sentimentalization and the story could have used some strong comic relief. The jacket says the author is a teenager. A writer not yet practiced in restraint perhaps, but nevertheless seeing and saying more with greater storytelling ability than many an older hand. (pp. 64-5)

Critic's Note: The cover-up initials stand for Susan Hinton, who wrote *The Outsiders* at the age of 17. The book was read for review before this information arrived from the publisher and the author's skirts didn't hang in the story. Compassion was certainly evident throughout, but women have no corner on this quality. In retrospect the obvious clue is that maybe only a girl could broadcast, without alibi, the soft centers of these boys and how often they do give way to tears. (p. 65)

> *Lillian N. Gerhardt, in* School Library Journal *(reprinted from the May, 1967, issue of* School Library Journal, *published by R. R. Bowker Company, a Xerox company; copyright © 1967 by Xerox Corporation), May, 1967.*

Can sincerity overcome clichés? In this book by a now 17-year-old author, it almost does the trick. By almost any standard, Miss Hinton's performance is impressive. At an age when most youngsters are still writing 300-word compositions, she has produced a book alive with the fresh dialogue of her contemporaries and has wound around it a story that captures, in vivid patches at least, a rather unnerving slice of teen-age America. . . .

Apparently in Tulsa, where Miss Hinton sets her story, the poor guys don't beat up the rich guys. It works the other way around—and she uses this switch to build up quite a head of self-pitying steam for her hero and his friends.

This, I must admit, runs somewhat counter to my own teen-age experience; in my old home town, even *semi*-socs were the ones who got their lumps. But Hinton's fire-engine pace does not give the reader much time to manufacture doubts. And the final confrontation between Ponyboy and the Socs, in which he realizes they too are pretty mixed-up kids, is a comforting if not quite believable ending. (pp. 10-11)

> *Thomas Fleming, in* The New York Times Book Review, *Part II (© 1967 by The New York Times Company; reprinted by permission), May 7, 1967.*

Is it possible . . . to reach these children of McLuhan in that old-time medium, the novel? I believe it is, because their primary concerns are only partially explored in the messages they get from their music and are diverted rather than probed on television. If a book is relevant to those concerns, not didactically but in creating textures of experience which teenagers can recognize as germane to their own, it can merit their attention.

One such book, written by a seventeen-year-old girl from Tulsa, is Susan Hinton's *The Outsiders*. Any teenager, no matter what some of his textbooks say, knows that this is decidedly not a classless society, and *The Outsiders* examines the social and physical warfare between a group of slum youngsters, 'the greasers', and the progeny of the upper middle class in Tulsa, 'the Socs'. Miss Hinton, with an astute ear and a lively sense of the restless rhythms of the young, also explores the tenacious loyalties on both sides of the class divide. Her plot is factitious at times, but the book has been widely read among heterogeneous sections of the young because it stimulates their own feelings and questionings about class and differing life-styles. (pp. 401-02)

> *Nat Hentoff, in* The Atlantic Monthly *(copyright © 1967 by The Atlantic Monthly Company, Boston, Mass., reprinted with permission), December, 1967 (and reprinted in* Only Connect, *edited by Sheila Egoff, G. T. Stubbs, and L. F. Ashley, Oxford University Press, 1969).*

[*The Outsiders*'] author is seventeen and capable of interesting a wider audience than the group she writes about. She reports on the class, social and physical warfare of two city gangs, the Greasers and the Socs. . . . Both lots suffer from parental absence or neglect and seek to realize themselves in feats of strength which lead to disaster and death. The violence is unrepressed, but less significant than Ponyboy's struggle to express the nature of gang loyalty and family affection in a world which is hostile to Greasers, who have even less chance than Socs to sort out desirable goals and less hope of ever attaining them. Ponyboy is a credible character, but the plot creaks and the ending is wholly factitious. The author's determination to "tell it like it is" means that the language, wholly group-coded, is both arresting and tiring to read in its repetitiousness. (p. 1258)

The trusted adult (who, it seems, is envisaged as the ideal reader) may find the unrelieved seriousness, a kind of literary egocentrism, too monotonous. Young readers will waive literary discriminations about a book of this kind and adopt Ponyboy as a kind of folk hero for both his exploits and his dialogue. (p. 1258)

> *The Times Literary Supplement (© Times Newspapers Ltd., 1970; reproduced from The Times Literary Supplement by permission), October 30, 1970.*

[*The Outsiders* is an] American novel which, without regard to the fact that it was written when the author was seventeen, has remarkably interesting qualities. . . .

The only major flaw is that the book is written with self-indulgence, and could profitably have been cut. Apart from this, even the over-didacticism of its first person narrative —it is as didactic as modern pop songs—comes off the page with such absorbed conviction, such persuasive truth and emotional power that one accepts it. The story has humour, passion, tenderness, intelligence, action a-plenty and, best of all, compassion. It is worth a place in any secondary school or public library. (p. 280)

> *A. Chambers, in* Children's Book News *(copyright © 1970 by Children's Book Centre Ltd.), November–December, 1970.*

The author is seventeen and perhaps this shows in the romanticism of some aspects of the story, but he gets under the skin of a 'greaser' with remarkable insight. Their world is limited by deprivation and convention but it is also enlarged by affection and humour. Ponyboy has little chance of breaking free, but he grows in understanding and perception. And perhaps there is nowhere to escape to, for as one of the 'Socs' says: 'Things are rough all over.' (p. 455)

> *C. E. J. Smith, in* The School Librarian, *December, 1970.*

S. E. Hinton . . . was in her teens when she wrote *The Outsiders* . . . , a novel of violence and feuding between greasers and socialites. The book is technically remarkable for so young a writer; its background appears authentic; but true feeling is hopelessly entangled with false, bad-film sentimentality, and the plot is creakingly unbelievable. It may be noted that, just as slum children in novels by middle-class writers can easily be nice middle-class children under the skin, so the greasers in this book by 'a seventeen-year-old whose best friends are greasers' sometimes look like sheep in wolves' clothing. (p. 295)

> *John Rowe Townsend, in his* Written for Children: An Outline of English-Language Children's Literature *(copyright © 1965, 1974 by John Rowe Townsend; reprinted by permission of J. B. Lippincott Company), revised edition, Lippincott, 1974.*

OTHER CITATIONS

Kirkus Service, *April 15, 1967, pp. 506-07.*

Publishers Weekly, *May 22, 1967, p. 64.*

Geraldine E. LaRocque, in English Journal, *February, 1969, p. 295.*

The Junior Bookshelf, *February, 1971, pp. 60-1.*

RUMBLE FISH (1975)

As gut-wrenching as the "sneaky pete" her hero guzzles down, S. E. Hinton's latest novel won't sit well with book selectors who demand that children's fiction end hopefully, if not happily. No hard-nosed punk, young Rusty-James rapidly loses everything meaningful to him—his girl, his "rep" as number one tough guy, and, most important, his idolized older brother—a James Dean look- and act-alike known only as the Motorcycle Boy. And, although it is the Motorcycle Boy who is gunned down at the end after breaking into a pet store, it is Rusty-James, emotionally burnt out at 14, who is the ultimate victim. Stylistically superb (the purposely flat, colorless narrative exactly describes Rusty-James' turf of pool halls, porno movie houses, and seedy hangouts), this packs a punch that will leave readers of any age reeling. (p. 106)

> *Jane Abramson, in* School Library Journal *(reprinted from the October, 1975, issue of* School Library Journal, *published by R. R. Bowker Company, a Xerox company; copyright © 1975 by Xerox Corporation), October, 1975.*

The dialogue and the boy's monologue are vibrant and authentic, and the narrative moves quickly and dramatically from one event to another. But essentially the material of [*Rumble Fish*] remains undeveloped, and the commentary glib and superficial. . . . Amy Lowell once asked, "how far has the condition of authorship (at least in its more mature state still to come) been hampered by . . . [an] early leap into the light?" By her third book, the outcome for S. E. Hinton appears to be unpromising; her writing has the same style and the same perception as it had when she was seventeen. Instead of becoming a vehicle for growth and development, the book, unfortunately, simply echoes what came before. She is no longer a teenager writing about teenagers today, and the book raises the question whether, as an adult, she will ever have much of importance to say to young readers. (pp. 601-02)

> *Anita Silvey, in* The Horn Book Magazine *(copyright © 1975 by the Horn Book, Inc., Boston), December, 1975.*

"Rumble Fish" (the title refers to Siamese fighting fish, which must be kept in separate tanks or they will tear one another to shreds) makes its bleak points tellingly enough, despite a curiously remote quality. Much of the latter, I think, stems from . . . Motorcycle Boy, who clanks through the story like a symbol never quite made flesh. (p. 8)

> *Robert Berkvist, in* The New York Times Book Review *(© 1975 by The New York Times Company; reprinted by permission), December 14, 1975.*

S. E. Hinton's *Rumble Fish* was disappointing. Hooked on Mr. Hinton since I discovered how popular *The Outsiders* and *That was then, this is now* are with adolescents, this came as a let-down. The earlier two books also deal with the American delinquent scene, but in both the central character has an intelligence and sensitivity which set him apart from his peers. . . .

The detachment of the central figure is lost in *Rumble Fish*. This time the narrator, Rusty-James, is a product (and victim) of his environment, and the world is a grey, sordid and destructive place. The bright values of literature and loyalty have faded, the best friend is a minor figure who lapses into gross insensitivity, and the book is filled with failures, drunks and junkies. In the foreground is the doomed Motorcycle Boy, the narrator's brother and hero, a near-zombie as a result of many crashes on stolen bikes. . . . Rusty-James has always wanted to be like his brother and that's how he turns out. The narrative is retrospective—the boy is reminded of things he'd like to forget when he meets an old friend—and this perspective emphasizes Rusty-James's hopelessness; there can't even be a glimmer of hope for the future. (p. 388)

> *Jane Powell, in* The Times Literary Supplement *(© Times Newspapers Ltd., 1976; reproduced from* The Times Literary Supplement *by permission), April 2, 1976.*

Those distant and unjustly derided tales of adolescent emotion, the school stories of Talbot Baines Reed, were almost the last to do justice to an emotion still and always important in the 'teens—hero-worship. Susan Hinton gives it due prominence in *Rumble Fish*, as she did in that remarkable story, *That was then this is now*, and once more in a fraternal context. Rusty-James, though he has a reputation of his own for toughness, will not be satisfied till he has measured up to the ideal figure of his older brother the Motorcycle Boy. . . . But Rusty learns the terrifying extent of his brother's disorientation from life when he also realises how useless and unpractical his own behaviour is, his habit of attacking blindly, as the tropical rumble fish will attack even its own shadow. Here once more is an author who stands back and invites her hero to put his own case—evasively, in words all the more forceful because they snatch at meaning:

> "I had been feeling funny all day. It had started the night before, when the Motorcycle Boy told me why I was scared to be by myself. It sort of felt like nothing was solid, like the street would tilt all of a sudden and throw me off . . . All my life, all I had to worry about was real things, things you could touch, or punch, or run away from. I had been scared before, but it was always something real to be scared of—not having any money, or some big kid looking to beat you up, or wondering if the Motorcycle Boy was gone for good. I didn't like this being scared of something and not knowing exactly what it was. I couldn't fight it if I didn't know what it was."

Here once more is the American urban scene in a book as uncompromising in its view of life as it is disciplined in form. Told in flashback, with a carefully placed final chapter, the story has a tight, compact shape within which dialogue and event develop as though with the random order of reality. Of the three striking books by this young author, *Rumble Fish* seems the most carefully structured and the most probing. (p. 2894)

> *Margery Fisher, in her* Growing Point, *May, 1976.*

Rumble Fish belongs, essentially, to one of the established forms of children's books, the animal story, in which the child is given the opportunity of living in the skin of the grizzly bear or the wild horse. The experiences of the animal are felt by the child, though in a different way from that in which the animal feels them. So in *Rumble Fish* the boy's emulation of his older brother, his alienation from his father, his rejection of school and authority—the things many children feel—are projected onto the terrible dangerous animals who live in the concrete jungle. They are sufficiently distanced for the child to identify with them without being overwhelmed. This is a story about an alien way of life, just as the animal stories are, and like most of them it falls into the trap of sentimentalising its subject. But it is an improvement on S. E. Hinton's earlier books, better constructed and more restrained. I think it is an Action Man; a dolly, in spite of its combat gear and fierce armoury of weapons. (p. 335)

> *Dorothy Nimmo, in* The School Librarian, *December, 1976.*

OTHER CITATIONS

Martin Amis, in New Statesman, *May 21, 1976, p. 690.*

David L. Rees, in Children's Book Review, *October, 1976, pp. 17-18.*

THAT WAS THEN, THIS IS NOW (1971)

Using the background and a sprinkling of the characters from her first book, *The Outsiders,* the author tensely builds up an atmosphere of violence, catalyzed constantly by the vicious cycle of justice which demanded that every score be personally settled by some means of retribution, whether by verbal derision, a beating, or the cutting off of a girl's hair. The scenes portrayed are sometimes ugly; the decisions forced on the characters are often motivated by basic survival needs, emotional as well as physical; and Bryon's final commitment to himself and to his future is harshly and realistically underlined in an ending that offers no pat promises. This is a disturbing book and perhaps in some senses a too contemporaneous one, but it will speak directly to a large number of teen-agers and does have a place in the understanding of today's cultural problems. (p. 389)

> *Sheryl B. Andrews, in* The Horn Book Magazine *(copyright © 1971 by The Horn Book, Inc., Boston), August, 1971.*

There are many similarities between this second book by S. E. Hinton and her first, "The Outsiders." Both are powerful, realistic stories about being young and poor in a large Oklahoma city. But instead of a gang of rich kids spoiling for a fight, the antagonist in this more ambitious novel is time.

"That Was Then, This Is Now" attempts to show how

time changes 16-year-old Bryon Douglas and his relationships with those he loves. These include Mark, his adopted brother, who, unlike Bryon, tries to make time stand still; Cathy, the girl friend who makes Bryon think of the future; M&M, a flower child, gentle and trusting, for whom time means nothing once he has become tragically involved with acid.

The phrase "if only" is perhaps the most bittersweet in the language, and Miss Hinton uses it skillfully to underline her theme: growth can be a dangerous process. As Bryon moves toward maturity he faces the dangers of the emotional vacuum that waits to be filled after loss of innocence. But "if only" is also a tricky device, encouraging an easy descent from pathos to bathos, and if there is fault to be found with "That Was Then, This Is Now" it is that at its end, when love and hate have run their course, all that is left to Bryon is not honest and believable grief but life-denying self-pity. Despite Bryon's difficult education in maturity, his central decisions—turning Mark in to the police and breaking off with Cathy—are made not intellectually but emotionally. It is unfortunate that Miss Hinton has indulged herself in this way, for otherwise she has written a mature, disciplined novel, which excites a response in the reader. Whatever its faults, her book will be hard to forget. (p. 8)

> *Michael Cart, in* The New York Times Book Review (© *1971 by The New York Times Company; reprinted by permission), August 8, 1971.*

For all its weaknesses, this young writer's first novel *The Outsiders* made a considerable impact and offered an uncomfortable glimpse into the world of teenage violence in America.

We are still in that world, but here it is even more strikingly drawn. Sixteen-year-old Bryon Douglas is finding himself becoming oddly disturbed by all the fights and retaliations. There is more to life than this. His best friend Mark finds it hard to understand his attitude and continues doing exactly what he wants, relying on his charm to wriggle out of the awkward moments that inevitably arise. Death, beatings up, and a terrifying encounter with drugs dog the pages. The knowledge that Mark, whom Bryon has grown to love, is helping to push the drugs creates a crisis. The police are told and Mark will be beyond redemption.

As with the earlier book I found myself becoming curiously involved. The death of Charlie came over wincingly well and all the time there was the uneasy feeling that I was eavesdropping on a world that did not welcome intruders. Impressive. (p. 194)

> *David L. Rees, in* Children's Book Review (© *1971 by Five Owls Press Ltd., all rights reserved), December, 1971.*

Perhaps the title does not suggest strongly enough the theme of disillusionment among young people which the text realistically drums into the reader without any implication of sentimental compensation or romantic conclusion. One of the teenagers portrayed ends in jail, his attitude hardened even against family life; another, still categorically a child, has begun a protracted trip from which remedial medicine will probably never rescue him. A barman friend is shot to death while trying to protect the youngsters

in an alley brawl. The setting of the tale in America does not provoke the smug reaction of "it can't happen here" [in Britain]; it can and does and one prays it will not get worse. One other thing is sure; I do not recollect reading the same author's *The Outsiders*, written at seventeen years of age, but I do agree with the comment on it made in the [London] Sunday Times: "A name to watch". (p. 398)

> The Junior Bookshelf, *December, 1971.*

There are certain problems which it is difficult to deal with successfully; an obvious example is the drug problem. The underlying aim has got to be to explore the rights and wrongs of the situation, but finally to come out with the conventional view without too much didacticism or moralising. This is a topic which has really got to be examined in a contemporary setting and this is perhaps why I favour S. E. Hinton's *That was Then, This is Now,* where the American setting, for English readers at any rate, provides the distancing factor. (p. 21)

> *Sheila Ray, in* The School Librarian, *March, 1977.*

OTHER CITATIONS

Brooke Anson, in School Library Journal, *September, 1971, p. 174.*

Robert Bell, in The School Librarian and School Library Review, *March, 1972, p. 64.*

The Best in Children's Books, *edited by Zena Sutherland, 1973, p. 182.*

*   *   *

HOBAN, Russell   1925-

A self-taught artist, painter, poet, and writer of fiction and nonfiction for children and adults, Russell Hoban is best known for his series of picture books on Frances the Badger and for his odyssey of two indomitable toys, *The Mouse and His Child,* which he calls "a world picture . . . in . . . a microcosm." The idea for the story came from a toy that danced each Christmas under the tree of his friends, Harvey and Marilyn Cushman. It was filmed in 1976. A full-time writer since 1967, Hoban has been a Western Union messenger, teacher, animator, and art director. He has published over thirty children's books, many in collaboration with illustrator Lillian Hoban, herself a creator of picture books. In 1972, Hoban received the Lewis Carroll Shelf Award for *Emmett Otter's Jug-Band Christmas.* (See also *Contemporary Authors,* Vols. 5-8, rev., ed., *Something About the Author,* Vol. 1, and *Contemporary Literary Criticism,* Vol. 7.)

AUTHOR'S COMMENTARY

'The poet must surrender himself as he is at the moment to something which is more valuable,' says Eliot. 'The progress of the artist is a continual self-sacrifice, a continual extinction of personality.' Well, it takes a real high-flying intellectual to come up with something that elementary. What else, really, could the progress of an artist possibly be? Art, like babies, is one of the things life makes us make, and the strongest, most passionate affirmation of the self is necessarily the losing of the self in that continuous stream of being in which we change the past and the past changes us. The babies don't belong to us and neither does the art, because what can the most powerful integration of self with life be but the dropping of that precious fussy little identity that we wear like morning dress and a bowler hat? For goodness' sake forget it. And once it's forgotten, time and the light are now. And the next moment and the moment after that.

Well, here we are in the stretto. . . . Life continues its changing balance of war and peace, famine and plenty, hope and despair, and the devaluation of currencies and people. Are writers moving forward towards time and the light? Are they achieving that affirmative extinction of personality, that necessary symbiosis with the past? Some are, I think, particularly those who write for children and young people.

I don't read many contemporary novels, but sometimes I talk to people who do. It seems to me and some of my friends that more and more adult novels are not essentially literary. Many of them simply communicate experience, and that of itself is not art. To attempt to define the literary art is not my purpose here, but I think it always . . . makes us be equally present in a continuous flow of time and being and it evokes vital resources in us. There are empty spaces now in literature, vacated by the so-called adult novel, and some of those spaces now become new territory for children's writers. (pp. 70-1)

As we move forward in this stretto of time the distinctions between children and adults blur and fade: today's children do not live in an expurgated world. With their elders they must endure sudden deaths and slow ones, bombs and fire falling from the sky, the poisoning of peaceful air and the threatened extinction of this green jewel of Earth. They must endure the reality of mortal man. Like Mr Fast in Leon Garfield's book [*The Ghost Downstairs*] we have sold the self that must at all costs be preserved and not betrayed. New selves arise each moment, and we must offer them a friendly hand of innocence and encouragement.

If in my meandering I have seemed to offer tangled thinking more than worked-out thoughts, it has not been through self-indulgence; I have wanted to join the action of my being with that of my readers in a collective being. Collectively we must possess and be repossessed by the past that we alter with our present, must surrender the vanity of personal identity to something more valuable. We must with our children go into the dark and through it to a place where time and the light lie before us. (pp. 75-6)

> *Russell Hoban, "Thoughts on Being and Writing," in* The Thorny Paradise: Writers on Writing for Children, *edited by Edward Blishen (© 1975 by Russell Hoban), Kestrel, 1975, pp. 65-76.*

GENERAL COMMENTARY

Russell Hoban has been well known for years as an author not of novels for grown-ups but of admirable children's books, a series about a young badger named Frances, and an especially memorable character study of a runaway beaver called *Charlie the Tramp*.

These books are unique, first, because the adults in their pages are usually humorous, precise of speech, and understandingly conversant with general life, and second, because the author confronts—not unfancifully but without

kinky secret garden stuff—problems with which ordinary parents and children have to cope. (The problems include reluctance to accept one's lot, too many sweets, disloyal friends, non-permissive grandparents, etc.) The lessons taught to Frances—for example, that a child's best friend may cheat her—are widely applicable, and learning them under Russell Hoban's tutelage entails no sacrifice of, say, one's right to pay back a dirty deed in kind. This writer's world is dense with small jokes and large appreciations, not alone with moral realities. (p. 84)

> *Benjamin DeMott, "The Way You Slide," in* The Atlantic Monthly (copyright © 1976 by The Atlantic Monthly Company, Boston, Mass.; reprinted with permission), *August, 1976, pp. 83-4.*

[Of] those who pursued [depicting family life] none were more successful than the Hobans.

Bedtime for Frances was the start, and Frances, to look at, is a badger. "Obviously, human children will feel far superior to Frances, and know that only a little animal could possibly act this way. And when their bedtime comes, they will be ready to get into bed and stay there, sleeping as soundly as Frances finally did." It is the language of the blurb for [Margaret and H. A. Rey's] *Spotty*, and there will always be some truth in it; but even less than the raccoons in [Margaret Wise Brown's] *Wait Till the Moon Is Full* are Frances and her sorely tested parents distinguishable from you and me. More intriguing, though, and funnier, the way it's funnier at any time—in Ylla or Garth Williams—to see ourselves in animal guise. (p. 472)

From *Bedtime for Frances* onward, Russell Hoban situates his families in the material world—as natural to a child as grass and trees—where not to get to work on time means not to have a job (a mouthful more than 'Daddy goes to work in the morning'), where a trademark is a byword and (in *A Birthday for Frances*) a Chompo Bar is candy covered with glory. (p. 474)

Gloria apart, and the songs momentarily aside, [*A Baby Sister for Frances*] is a different book than *Bedtime*, one that makes Frances less the object, more the subject; and less to be laughed at, more to be laughed at-with. . . .

[Frances, in *Bread and Jam for Frances*] is . . . the kindergartner's Russell Baker. (p. 475)

Bread and Jam for Frances marks . . . the emergence of the songs, either sotto voce or in solitude, unheard, as the still small voice of Frances speaking out (where before they were occasional ditties, pastimes or performances). In picturebooks there is little place for the omniscient narrator, reader of minds, hence the customary *He thought*, followed by quotes, for what is not actually said but might as well be, a kind of talking to oneself. The other kind of talking to oneself is of course the first-person voice when it is—in [Janice May Udry's] *A Tree Is Nice* as in [Marie Hall Ets'] *Play With Me*—more reverie than recital. Russell Hoban is preeminently a dramatist but he is also a poet, and his solution, an original one, is the songs, Frances's private thoughts manifest.

Altogether the action, dramatic and emotional, is in the words. Let us acknowledge that Lillian Hoban, who can draw people as states of being, is no badger-master; it is a measure of the text that the illustrations need only position the characters for the message to carry. Little things, internal things, help: concrete nouns, active verbs, and—for emphasis, for fun—repetition. . . .

A Birthday for Frances was published in 1968, and the flap copy speaks, lightly, of Frances's struggle "to set mind over matter"—meaning will she or will she not give Gloria the Chompo Bar she bought for her. It is the post-enlightenment era, for picturebooks and for the Hobans (the year before brought Russell Hoban's philosophic fantasy *The Mouse and His Child*), and the central issue is not adjustment but right action: whatever her resentments, Frances should not use them as an excuse for keeping the Chompo Bar. Put another way, when Frances is sitting under the sink, in *A Baby Sister for Frances,* or in the broom closet, she is all psyche—which is to say also all-vulnerable, all-malleable; and in *A Baby Sister for Frances,* that is chiefly what she is. In *A Birthday,* once past the pitiable Alice, Frances is engaged in a struggle *with herself,* quite another matter—one that allows, within a psychologically valid setting, for ethical choice. (p. 477)

> *Barbara Bader, in* American Picturebooks from Noah's Ark to the Beast Within *(reprinted with permission of Macmillan Publishing Co., Inc.; copyright © 1976 by Barbara Bader), Macmillan, 1976.*

A BABY SISTER FOR FRANCES (1964)

Bedtime for Frances is one of the few post-war picture books which have already become "classics." Its gentle, truthful charms are truly beyond race and time. The sequel, *A Baby Sister for Frances,* has the same qualities. Again there is no hint in the exquisitely serious text to suggest that Frances and her family are badgers. Lillian Hoban, who draws the pictures this time, is no Garth Williams but she conveys satisfactorily the homely uncloying sweetness of the enchanting story. (pp. 26-7)

> The Junior Bookshelf, *February, 1966.*

A BARGAIN FOR FRANCES (1970)

[*A Bargain for Frances* is another] Frances the Badger story, . . . with all the warmth and perceptive plot line of its predecessors. The author, as always, explores naturally a situation familiar to childhood, with an ear cocked to the language and logic of children. The story centers around friendship and trust, as Frances is tricked into buying her friend Thelma's plastic tea set with the red flowers instead of the china set that she's been saving for. Even though Thelma has insisted on "'no backsies'" (a significant clue for any child), the story ends happily with a more sophisticated Frances, the proud possessor of Thelma's new china tea set, singing, "'Being careful isn't nice. / Being friends is better!'" Slightly more heavy-handed than some of the earlier books, this one still attains the easy humor that children delight in. (p. 475)

> *Sheryl B. Andrews, in* The Horn Book Magazine *(copyright © 1970 by The Horn Book, Inc., Boston), October, 1970.*

In an examination of children's trade books for both their explicit and implicit approaches to consumer education,

first prize goes to Russell and Lillian Hoban's *A Bargain for Frances.* In this recent . . . addition to our favorite badger series, Frances' "friend" Thelma cons her into buying an ugly plastic tea set with red flowers, when she had her heart set on a real china set with pictures in blue of "trees and birds and a Chinese house and a fence and a boat and people walking on a bridge." Thelma tells her that that kind breaks, is very expensive, and besides, the stores no longer sell them. She kindly sells Frances her own ugly set for $2.17, all the money Frances has in the world. Agreeing to a policy of "no backsies," Frances pays her money and trots home with her acquisition, only to discover that the set she wanted is readily available at $2.07. Using the same psychological trickery that was used on her, Frances eventually gets the tea set with the blue pictures, plus a dime left over. Along the way, the first or second grade reader for whom the book is designed receives several valuable lessons in consumerism. An analysis of Thelma's sales pitch shows that Frances was taken in by: 1) the immediate availability of the ugly tea set; 2) the misrepresentation of the saleslady (Thelma) about the availability of the competing product; and 3) the desire for a bargain without bothering to find out first if it indeed is a bargain.

Frances and Thelma agree to give up trying to trick each other because it's a big nuisance having to watch each other so closely when they play together. "Do you want to be careful or do you want to be friends?" asks Frances, and the implication is clear that the buyer-seller relationship automatically precludes friendship. (p. 77)

> *Katherine M. Heylman, in* School Library Journal *(reprinted from the October, 1971, issue of* School Library Journal, *published by R. R. Bowker Company, a Xerox company; copyright © 1971 by Xerox Corporation), October, 1971.*

OTHER CITATIONS

Jane Yolen, in The New York Times Book Review, *November 15, 1970, p. 42.*

Trevelyn Jones, in School Library Journal, *December, 1970, p. 68.*

BEDTIME FOR FRANCES (1960)

The exasperated humor of this book could only derive from actual parental experience, and no doubt parents will enjoy it. Children who have mastered their own nighttime fears will probably be vastly amused, too, since the very process of "getting it" implies their superiority to the child-bear (see quotation from dust jacket . . .) and also to their younger selves. However, for children who are still in the grips of a struggle at bedtime the book is not likely to be either funny or helpful. For these youngsters the story may be real to a point of discomfort and entail the further risk of confirming or extending existent fantasies and concerns. Not a choice to be made lightly. (p. 40)

> Saturday Review *(copyright © 1960 by Saturday Review, Inc.; reprinted with permission), May 7, 1960.*

Russell Hoban's theme [in *Bedtime for Frances*] is universal rather than American, and he tells the story of little Frances going to bed with beautiful economy. This is the rarest kind of picture-book text, rhythmic, natural, unalterable. That superb artist, Garth Williams, takes us by surprise. He has chosen to interpret the story, so characteristic of human children, in terms of badgers. Frances is irresistible with her buttony nose and striped back. Mother and father, blending most happily badger anatomy and human characteristics, are drawn with beauty and understanding. This is a little work of art, but it is literally flawless. (pp. 126-27)

> The Junior Bookshelf, *July, 1963.*

In all of Russell Hoban's stories about Frances, the small badger, there is affection for and understanding of children. In *Bedtime for Frances* . . . the bright-eyed heroine goes through all the techniques of stalling with which every child save the most sanctimonious is familiar. She wants a glass of milk. She asks to be carried to her room. May she sleep with her doll? Mother gives her the doll. "Did you kiss me?" Yes, but Mother and Father kiss her again. She wants the door open, she sees a tiger in the corner and goes to report on this, and then she sees a giant, and thinks it would be nice to stay with her parents and watch television. She remembers that she forgot to brush her teeth. By then her parents are in bed, and Father cocks a leery eye when she comes in to tell him that something is moving the curtains. Finally Father asserts himself and tells Frances the train of consequences that may possibly, just possibly, result in a spanking. These characters are indeed ourselves in fur: the fact that Frances is a badger makes the story applicable without being didactic, but in each of the stories about Frances (*A Baby Sister for Frances, Best Friends for Frances* [1969], *A Bargain for Frances,* and others) there is some very familiar childhood situation used as a basis for an amusing story—with beguiling illustrations—that can contribute to a small child's understanding of himself, his relationships with other people, and the fulfillment of his emotional needs. (pp. 396-97)

> *May Hill Arbuthnot and Zena Sutherland, in their* Children and Books *(copyright © 1947, 1957, 1964, 1972 by Scott, Foresman and Company; reprinted by permission), fourth edition, Scott, Foresman, 1972.*

BREAD AND JAM FOR FRANCES (1964)

Perhaps parents will appreciate this even more than children, as it deals with a phase of child behaviour all too familiar. Yet children will enjoy it too, and it does not just poke fun at Frances' sudden refusal to eat anything but bread and jam but shows real sympathy for her reaction to other food. Descriptions of food often enthral children, and here is plenty of it, both meals at home and the exotic American fare in the school lunches, made over-exotic to add to the humour of the situation. Frances' talk of eggs may put any child off them for a few days—sunnyside-up they "look up at you in a funny way," the others "just lie on their stomachs and *wait*"—but her lines are the best in the book, and her expression in [Lillian Hoban's] pictures provide half the fun. For a little badger she has an astonishing range of human expressions. Some of the text is a bit too "cute" and the father seems to over-act his part, but in

the main this is a most acceptable import from America and a very valid piece of child psychology. (p. 304)

> The Junior Bookshelf, *October, 1966.*

OTHER CITATIONS

Virginia Haviland, in The Horn Book Magazine, *December, 1964, p. 605.*

EGG THOUGHTS, AND OTHER FRANCES SONGS (1972)

Besides the favorite "Soft-Boiled" from *Bread and Jam for Frances* . . . [*Egg Thoughts and Other Frances Songs* contains] 21 new poems with the same fresh but familiar appeal of the Frances stories. Who won't get a shock of recognition from "Homework sits on top of Sunday, squashing Sunday flat"? or sympathize with Frances' troubles with her little sister: "No one ever thinks she's tricky. / She spilled honey on the floor— / Mother found me very sticky. / Gloria was out the door. / When I caught her no one hit her. / I got spanked because I bit her / Ear, that little Gloria sister. / Still, I guess I would have missed her."? As is evident above (and elsewhere—"I know kids who do not kick / Stones down roads or even pick / Sea-glass up on beaches"), Frances likes to end her rhymed lines in midsentence, which gives them a comfortably bumpy feel that nicely maintains her amateur status. Frances' songs will make new friends for the little badger, and keep some old ones who are outgrowing the picture books. (p. 396)

> Kirkus Reviews *(copyright © 1972 The Kirkus Service, Inc.), April 1, 1972.*

Poems for the young are very hard to bring off. Two and a half cheers, then, for Russell Hoban's *Egg Thoughts and Other Frances Songs.* . . . They are well-observed, wistful, laconic—closer to Seuss than Milne. The trochaic rhythms and dry enjambements cleverly convey the sense the reader has of a little girl reciting them. I could have done without the drawings of a cute badger [by Lillian Hoban]. I suppose the idea was to give hard-to-sell poems a boost from the popular Hoban series, but they are not obviously concerned with anything other than six-year-old *human* life and should have stood on their own:

> Sometimes when I lose a kite
> Far away and out of sight,
> Then the string that I rewind
> As I walk until I find
> Where my kite is, takes me through
> Places I might not get to.
> If I didn't like string.

Which perhaps is a moral lesson for us all. (p. 780)

> *John Fuller, in* New Statesman *(© 1973 The Statesman & Nation Publishing Co. Ltd.), May 25, 1973.*

OTHER CITATIONS

Linda Silver, in School Library Journal, *May, 1972, p. 64.*

Ruth Crossley-Holland, in The Spectator, *April 14, 1973, pp. 462-63.*

EMMET OTTER'S JUG-BAND CHRISTMAS (1971)

The best of this year's [Christmas] offerings—a winner for

any year—is *Emmet Otter's Jug-Band Christmas* by Russell and Lillian Hoban. . . . This fairly long but very well written story presents sentiment—the mutual love of a parent and child—without sentimentality, and reflects a refreshingly pragmatic, clear-headed view of life. . . . The parallel activities and aspirations of Emmet and Ma are cleverly and tightly constructed; the many, delightfully expressive, softly colored crayon and watercolor drawings are attractively laid out on the pages along with the well-spaced print. Despite the old-fashioned garb worn by the protagonists, *Emmet Otter's Jug-Band Christmas* is a thoroughly modern Christmas story: the characters are "tired of just getting by"; their best efforts fail to win them reward; they manage to make it only through luck—by being in the right place at the right time. (p. 126)

> *Diane Gersoni Stavn, in* School Library Journal *(reprinted from the October, 1971, issue of* School Library Journal, *published by R. R. Bowker Company, a Xerox company; copyright © 1971 by Xerox Corporation), October, 1971.*

["Emmet Otter's Jug-Band Christmas"] is by the authors of "Charlie the Tramp" and "Bread and Jam for Frances" —my two all-time favorite children's books. The Hobans' old-fashioned, down-home books delight my pseudo Yankee bones, and Emmet Otter is no exception. Emmet's mother takes in washing and Emmet does odd-jobs (somehow, I don't even mind the male-female role assignments, which are altogether too comfortingly old-fashioned) and this Christmas will be a hard one, because "money's hard to come by.". . . Emmet and his mother each risk the other's tools of trade for a chance to win a talent contest prize and buy each other presents. They both lose, but of course virtues—thrift, hard work, common sense, love and courage—triumph. I am not usually fond of animals as people, but I often wish the Hobans' animals were my kin, so I could wish them a Merry Christmas. (p. 90)

> *Jane O'Reilly, in* The New York Times Book Review *(© 1971 by The New York Times Company; reprinted by permission), December 5, 1971.*

OTHER CITATIONS

Kirkus Reviews, *September 15, 1971, p. 1013.*

Zena Sutherland, in Bulletin of the Center for Children's Books, *November, 1971, p. 44.*

The Junior Bookshelf, *April, 1974, p. 83.*

GOODNIGHT (1966)

It is almost impossible to find anything to praise in this unbearably arch production. From its coy, sugar-almond colouring to its sickly verse, it is exactly what one most deplores in books for children. Intended, one would imagine, to soothe the over-imaginative child with a fear of the dark, it may produce exactly the opposite reaction. What three-year-old (for only a three-year-old could conceivably enjoy the book) would be reassured by: "Maybe just outside my door / Where I hear a creaking floor, / MAYBE IT'S GHOSTS."? This is accompanied by vague, formless heads in nasty custardy colours. [Illustrations are by Lillian

Hoban.] No! Not for me or the children, imaginative or not, of my acquaintance. (p. 211)

> *Mrs. G. Maunder, in* Children's Book News *(copyright © 1969 by Children's Book Centre Ltd.), July-August, 1969.*

OTHER CITATIONS

Virginia Kirkus' Service, *January 15, 1966, p. 53.*

Arlene Mosel, in School Library Journal, *April, 1966, p. 82.*

HERMAN THE LOSER (1961)

Mother, Father and Sister Sophie were all accomplished finders—especially of things like cowboy hats and mittens which Herman was so good at losing. Eventually he lost Father's watch (not the *good* one) and an expedition to recover it proved that Herman really found much more than he lost—especially detritus like green glass and tyre valve caps.

It appears that this is the first English edition of what was Russell Hoban's second book (it was published in the U.S.A. in 1961, a year after *Bedtime for Frances*). It has none of the glamour usually associated with picturebooks of the sixties—Lillian Hoban's monochrome drawings being homely, rather in the manner of Ardizzone's pen-drawings in *Little Tim*—and fitting round—accompanying—the text, not dominating it. The result of course is not immediately spectacular but that is because this is a book to live with, to *read* and to glean more from on the second occasion than on the first. Russell Hoban's fluent conversational prose is a constant pleasure, better indeed here than in some of his later, more overdone tales like *Tom and the Two Handles*, and one regrets only that ten years' worth of English children have missed it. (p. 109)

> *Brian W. Alderson, in* Children's Book Review *(© 1972 by Five Owls Press Ltd.; all rights reserved), September, 1972.*

[*Herman the Loser* is a] charmer, warm, snappy, full of 'humors and reflections'; and withal—but withal?—a cautionary/salutary tale. (p. 473)

We can see the wheels turning, ever so gently: it is an 'enlightened,' constructive treatment of childhood, careful to value Herman's independent proclivities, equally careful to inculcate in him reasonable responsibility and demonstrate how to use it. Implicitly, parents are not to be arbitrary, neither are children to be left undirected, the one productive of fear, the other of guilt; and both destructive of the child's individual personality. The last is critical: behavior-model that it is, for parents and their offspring (who "will rejoice with Herman in his new role of finder and . . . want to become finders too"), it is not, finally, mechanical—any more than are the psychological profiles of an Eriksen or a Fraiberg, or what one sees in the raw in a sandbox. The nub and, caught and held, the special pleasure, is Herman's personality. Loser or finder, he is a serious looker—per a typical Hoban throwaway line, "Different places." (pp. 473-74)

> *Barbara Bader, in* American Picturebooks from Noah's Ark to the Beast Within (*reprinted with permission of Macmillan Pub-*

lishing Co., Inc.; copyright © 1976 by Barbara Bader), Macmillan, 1976.

HOW TOM BEAT CAPTAIN NAJORK AND HIS HIRED SPORTSMEN (1974)

Russell Hoban by now needs no introduction to the parents of young children. The astonishing thing about this writer is the sheer variety of his output, and the consistently high standard he produces in a wide range of literary forms. *How Tom Beat Captain Najork and his Hired Sportsmen* is a romp, a tongue-in-cheek saga of juvenile triumph in the face of adult oppression. . . . Tom is a buoyant character, whose irrepressible passion for fooling around stands him in good stead when Captain Najork and his sportsmen turn up to teach him a lesson. Tom vanquishes these dedicated professionals at their chosen sports of sneedball, womble and muck, and finishes up with a delightful new aunt called Bundlejoy Cosysweet, while Captain Najork and Aunt Fidget marry and live happily ever after. Quentin Blake has a lot of fun interpreting into visual terms the mad, incomprehensible jargon of Captain Najork's games, and he produces a splendidly zany set of illustrations. (p. 718)

> The Times Literary Supplement (© *Times Newspapers Ltd., 1974; reproduced from* The Times Literary Supplement *by permission), July 5, 1974.*

Were the author not American one might assume that the details of the plot and the mysterious, newly-forged antique nouns and proper names [in *How Tom Beat Captain Najork and His Hired Sportsmen*] owed their existence to a Goon-lit childhood. ["The Goon Show," a British radio program of the 1950's, was popular for its nonsensical humour.] The speech of each character rings true and presents a real opportunity for storytellers with a repertoire of funny voices. Although the story is amusing, its humour lies largely in the invented words and in the tone which the dialogue and narration demand. The only problematical area lies in the matching of verbal and visual descriptions of the weird sports; either mode of description on its own would be fine, but the two kinds seem, here, to work against one another. If the verbal description had been reduced, almost to a single phrase, I think fewer children would become detached at this point, indeed, they might have become more involved had they been able to project their own interpretation onto the visual evidence of, say, wimbling in action. (p. 144)

> *Clive Phillpot, in* Children's Book Review *(© 1975 Five Owls Press Ltd.; all rights reserved), Winter, 1974-75.*

OTHER CITATIONS

Bronnie Cunningham, in New Statesman, *May 24, 1974, p. 741.*

The Junior Bookshelf, *August, 1974, p. 202.*

Derwent May, in The Listener, *November 7, 1974, p. 617.*

THE LITTLE BRUTE FAMILY (1966)

There hasn't been anything in ages that concentrates on etiquette and interfamily courtesy. Of course, the Hobans

can be relied on never to attack the subject in sobersided formation; as they did in their Frances books, they tease their way to the point. [Illustrator Lillian] Hoban's Brutes are arresting and in full color—blob-nosed, bristle-haired, snaggle-toothed, they combine the worst features of Wallace Beery and W. C. Fields. The result is paradoxically appealing. . . . (p. 621)

> Virginia Kirkus' Service (*copyright © 1966 Virginia Kirkus' Service, Inc.), July 1, 1966.*

Children will enjoy this short story about the Brute family. The Brutes—Mama, Papa, Brother, Sister, and Baby are pleasantly ugly. They eat gravel porridge and stick and stone stew. The young Brutes sink rather than swim, their kites don't fly, and in winter they fall off their crooked clumsy sleds and land upside-down in snowbanks screaming and howling. And all because they are so mean and "No one said, 'please.' No one said, 'thank you,' and no one said, 'How delicious,' because it [the porridge] was not delicious." Then baby Brute tucks a little wandering lost good feeling in his pocket one afternoon. . . . All ends happily and the family changes its name to "Nice." The moral is presented in a straightforward and funny way which children will appreciate. Those who know *The Three Bears* will enjoy this light parody even more. This small book's format is attractive, and the pictures are as amusing as the text. (p. 235)

> School Library Journal (*reprinted from the September, 1966, issue of* School Library Journal, *published by R. R. Bowker Company, a Xerox company; copyright © 1966 by Xerox Corporation), September, 1966.*

THE MOUSE AND HIS CHILD (1967)

AUTHOR'S COMMENTARY

Often I'm asked if [*The Mouse and His Child*] really is a children's book. When I wrote it I didn't think it was. I was writing as much book as I was capable of at the time. No concessions were made in style or content. It was my first novel and at the age of 41 it was the fullest response I could make to being alive and in the world. . . .

When I began to write about the clockwork toy I'd never completed anything longer than 12 typewritten pages of picture-book text. I thought the story might run to 30 or 40 pages but as I got deeper into it I found there was more writing than that to be done. I had a very good editor at Harper & Row, Ferd Monjo, himself a writer, who challenged me to find what was in my material, to find what the thing wanted to be and let it be that, to find the level and depth of the action and observe it correctly. As I worked on I came to feel that I wasn't making up a story but revealing one that had its own existence independently of me. I still feel that way when I write a book. . . .

During the three years I spent writing *The Mouse and His Child* my small protagonists assumed large proportions for me. I believed in them and in the world that came out of my typewriter day by day and night by night. I believed that the winning of a dolls' house was truly a victory and I believed that victory might be a permanent thing. That's why the book is a children's book.

Now I know that the winning of a dolls' house may be a

proper triumph for clockwork mice in a story but for human beings in real life it won't do. Nor can any victory be permanent. Indeed the only thing that can be won is the capacity to go on fighting. And that's the only thing that can be lost because nothing else is one's own to lose. Even that isn't one's own really—it is the reciprocating energies of life and death within us driving us to make and unmake, put things together and tear them apart, change whatever is into what isn't. That's a hard and heavy thought but it's a thought that needs to be dealt with. That's why I'm writing about people now instead of toys, and no dolls' houses.

Within its limitations and because of them I think *The Mouse and His Child* is suitable for children. Its tin heroes and heroines found out what they were and it wasn't enough, so they found out how to be more. That's not a bad thought to be going on with.

> *Russell Hoban, "'The Mouse and His Child': Yes, It's a Children's Book" (© Russell Hoban), in* Books for Your Children, *Winter, 1976, p. 3.*

This book begins with a metaphysical quotation from W. H. Auden, and we know at once that we are in for a puzzle. Now, puzzles can be exciting—but only if the pieces fit. Imagine two toy mice who begin life in a toyshop and then are buffeted from place to place as they seek the lost paradise of their first home—a doll house—and their first "family," a toy elephant and seal. Imagine further that these mice land in the town dump, flee a villainous rat, are told a mysterious fortune by a psychic frog, find portents in the label on a can of dog food and eventually meet a group of forest creatures who speak in philosophic conundrums. Alas, these pieces do not fit even when the author has pushed them into place and resolved his plot. It is the mouse, his child and their search we care about—not metaphysics—and the intellectual trappings of this story are unnecessary. The writing is beautiful, the satire often profound—but the puzzle remains unworked. (p. 26)

> *Barbara Wersba, in* The New York Times Book Review *(© 1968 by The New York Times Company; reprinted by permission), February 4, 1968.*

Russell Hoban is known best in [England] for his gentle bedtime stories about little Frances, who is so like little girls all over the world but who turns out in the illustrations to be a badger-cub. They are charming picture-books, distinguished from others of their kind by the shrewdness which lies below the surface sentimentality. Excellent as they are, they give no hint that the author had in him such a blockbuster of a book as *The Mouse and his Child*. . . .

Each stage of the toys' odyssey is purposeful, and the author brings the threads together with the greatest skill. . . .

The story is rich in memorable invention, but this would count for nothing if the style were not so exquisitely apt. There is no fine writing, but Mr. Hoban matches every nuance of his narrative with words so completely right as to be quite unobtrusive. This is a perfection so flawless as to pass unobserved until, the turmoil and passion of the story over, one thinks back to the masterly means by which these ends were reached.

Nothing could be farther than the untidy muddle of this anguished world from the miniature perfection of the Borrowers, but it is to Mrs. [Mary] Norton, together with even more distinguished and "adult" writers, that the mind returns again and again in the course of *The Mouse and his Child*. It is partly a matter of scale. Everything in the story is precisely to size. There is a marvellous consistency in each one of a multitude of details. There is something too in the nature of the fantasy. Like Mrs. Norton, Mr. Hoban rides his fantasy with a tight rein. Granting himself one single improbable assumption—that among the rubbish dumps and the wildernesses beyond the urban world there is a world of animals and toys made in its distorted image—he pursues the implications of his invention with remorseless logic.

This is to take quite seriously a story which deserves and demands such a reception. The story is also, for full measure, hugely funny, provocative, pathetic and heroic. Some of the fun is satiric with adult overtones. The metaphysics—however mock—may be beyond the range of those who revel in the knockabout. Like the best books it is a book from which one can peel layer after layer of meaning. It may not be a Children's Book but, my goodness, it is a *Book*.

> *"What Toys Endure: A Clockwork Odyssey," The Times Literary Supplement (© Times Newspapers Ltd., 1969; reproduced from The Times Literary Supplement by permission), April 3, 1969, p. 357.*

Demanding, disturbing, memorable, like all the best children's books [*The Mouse and His Child*] is a book for anybody. I am sure it is a classic: *The Wind in the Willows* of this post-Buchenwald generation. Buy it and read it aloud by firelight to children warmed with mugs of . . . malted bedtime drink. Alone, in a cold bedroom, it could be too hard for them to take. (p. 701)

> *Ann Thwaite, in* New Statesman *(© 1969 The Statesman & Nation Publishing Co. Ltd.), May 16, 1969.*

"'War,'" muttered the father. "'The dustbin the dump, murder, robbery, and war.'" Fit subjects for children's fiction? *The Mouse and his Child,* a masterpiece by the standards of whatever age-group you consider it for, asks the fundamental questions about writing for children. What age, if any, what sex if either, what group or class does it address? . . . [Just] where would you fruitfully plant a book about life and death as deeply pondered as this one? That's where a knowledge of child rather than age-group comes in. Maybe more adults than children will come to know it, as the word gets round. But even adults are human, and this is addressed to humans (size immaterial).

Not that a single human (except a tramp, on the first pages and the last) intrudes into this perfectly envisaged landscape where nature is as red as riot and where passions are as terrible, as wilful and as sublime as they are in the larger human landscape above it. Everything exactly fits the size of the small animals whose intelligence, taste and attitudes are wholly human. In their world of rubbish dump or undergrowth or pond, each animal has his place and his fellows, his natural defences, his way of life. But let loose in this ordered if jungly existence are the displaced persons of another species, broken clockwork toys that look like animals but don't function like them, that have nowhere and nothing, no allies, no way of life; crippled 'windups' preyed upon by anyone who likes to use them as slave labour, a subspecies.

Pursuing what seems the mirage of security and love and a place in the world—modest enough goals to those who have achieved them—while escaping their pursuer, the tycoon scrapdealer Manny Rat, the clockwork mouse and his child wander through a world of human values and behaviour, burningly conjured, fearsomely alive. . . .

Brilliantly plotted, so that everything is satisfactorily linked and coincidence seems like destiny, *The Mouse and his Child* is more than a spellbinder. It keeps you spellbound in the sense that you sit on and read, but it has much to offer beside its galloping adventure, danger and suspense. It has mystery, and jokes, and a sense of the almost awesome nature of happiness; it has an absolute respect for its subject—which means its readers as well; it has a style that glows and crackles when it needs to but never seems to strain for it, as if what happens couldn't be put across otherwise. I'm still not sure just who is going to read it but that hardly seems to matter at the moment. It will last. (pp. 654-55)

> *Isabel Quigly, "Nice Mice," in* The Spectator *(© 1969 by* The Spectator; *reprinted by permission of* The Spectator*), May 16, 1969, pp. 654-55.*

The Mouse and His Child distressed me almost as much as any book I've read. Indeed at times I had to stop reading it because I could not bear the continuing images of cruelty and decay. Such images might well have gone straight over a child's head. The dynamic of the book, as with Andersen, Disney and Carroll, seems to me to be impermanence, decay, cruelty. It is like Beckett for children and no one will say that Beckett is an optimistic writer.

Indeed the more I consider *The Mouse and His Child,* the more similarities I can see with Andersen. I am reminded of *The Little Fir Tree* left mouldering in the attic after its Christmas glory, just as the mouse and his child, new and shiny in the toyshop at the beginning of the book, find their way to the rubbish dump. I am also reminded of *The Steadfast Tin Soldier.* Indeed there are a great many Andersen stories involving inanimate objects, toys and ornaments, in which the more elaborate despise lesser ones. Usually they point the moral that 'pride comes before a fall' or 'golden lads and lasses must as chimney sweepers come to dust'.

I am not sure that Russell Hoban does not share Andersen's sweetness as well as his bitterness. Of course he is much too modern and sophisticated to show the kind of overt sentimentality that Andersen does, but for me the ending of *The Mouse and His Child* seems just as fundamentally soft-centred as anything in Andersen. The conversion of Manny Rat, the rehabilitation of the toys and of the doll's house, seemed convention to me, as if the heart was not really in the writing any more. For me, cruelty and decay are what the book is really about. (p. 36)

> *Penelope Farmer, in* Children's Literature in Education *(© 1972, APS Publications, Inc., New York; reprinted by permission of the publisher), No. 7 (March), 1972.*

Russell Hoban's *The Mouse and His Child* . . . is such a

strange, haunting and distinguished book that it is very difficult to classify. It is about toy mice, yet the clockwork father and son move through a world in which small animals act out human dramas. The happy ending does not dispel the lingering sadness of the clockwork pair, the father doomed to travel forward through the world and the son (who is joined to him) backwards. Helpless when they are not wound up, unable to stop when they *are,* they are fated like all mechanical things to breakage, rust and disintegration as humans are to death. . . . As an adult, it is impossible to read it unmoved. (p. 186)

> *Margaret Blount, in her* Animal Land: The Creatures of Children's Fiction *(copyright © 1974 by Margaret Ingle-Finch; abridged by permission of William Morrow & Co., Inc.), William Morrow, 1974.*

Russell Hoban's *The Mouse and His Child* . . . was published in the United States in 1967 and in England two years later. In England it is widely seen as a modern classic, one of the three or four outstanding children's books of the thirty years since World War II. In the United States it had a lukewarm reception, and opinion about it has remained lukewarm ever since. . . . I have seldom met an American who was enthusiastic about it. For once, minds failed to meet in mid-Atlantic. (pp. 449-50)

I share the British view that this is a splendid book. It operates on several levels; it can be read as a simple adventure story, packed with incident. . . . On this level it is accessible to any child who reads willingly. (p. 450)

There is a good deal of not-too-difficult verbal humor; and there is much satire, some of which again is of a fairly obvious kind: the armies of shrews that almost wipe each other out, leaving the survivors to be eaten by weasels; the bluejay reporter who screams the news in headlines to the world. And the allegory of the toys' longing to be self-winding is well within children's comprehension.

But there is also a wry, dry wit for those who are ready for it. And beneath the book's bright, busy surface lie philosophical and psychological depths. There is, for instance, the matter of the dogmeat cans that keep cropping up. On their labels is a picture of a dog carrying a can that has a picture of a dog carrying a can that has a picture of a dog carrying a can . . . and so on until the dogs are too small to be seen. A phrase that echoes through the story is "beyond the last visible dog." For a long time the mouse and his child are stuck in the mud at the bottom of a pond, contemplating infinity in the form of one of these cans. This, I think, is the deepest point of the book, illuminated by Hoban's remark [in his "Thoughts on Being and Writing"; see excerpt above] that

> In all of us, I think, there remains some awareness, rudimentary and inchoate, far down, dim in green light through the ancient reeds and tasting of the primal salt, in which there is no "I", no person, no identity, but only the passage, moment by moment, of time through being undisturbed by birth or death. . . . I think we have to . . . dive for it and touch it before returning to the sunlight and the present.

The mouse child sees that beyond the last visible dog is

nothing; but the nothing is "nothing but us." And he finds a way to the surface.

It's an extremely rich and crowded book. Though there are no human characters except the tramp who sets the toys in motion near the beginning and who tells them to "be happy" at the end (and you may well wonder who *he* is), it is, in fact, a deeply human story. The mouse and his child clearly are loving *people*, totally interdependent. The author's sense of the pathos of a toy's life—the sadness of rusted metal and rotting plush, the decline from freshness and efficiency toward the rubbish dump—is, of course, a sense of the pathos of human life. But there's hope as well as pain in this pilgrimage; and, significantly, it's the child who hopes, the child who perseveres when the father would give up. This is a book that can be returned to many times at many ages, and there will always be something new to be found in it. (pp. 450-51)

> *John Rowe Townsend, "A Second Look: 'The Mouse and His Child'," in* The Horn Book Magazine *(copyright © 1975 by the Horn Book, Inc., Boston), October, 1975, pp. 449-51.*

OTHER CITATIONS

Kirkus Service, *September 15, 1967, p. 1134.*

Joan Murphy, in The School Librarian, *June, 1969, p. 210.*

Marcus Crouch, in his The Nesbit Tradition: The Children's Novel in England 1945-1970, *Ernest Benn, 1972, pp. 119-20.*

Where, *March, 1974, p. 76.*

Margery Fisher, in her Who's Who in Children's Books: A Treasury of the Familiar Characters of Childhood, *Holt, Rinehart and Winston, 1975, p. 243.*

Books for Your Children, *Summer, 1976, p. 15.*

Anne S. MacCleod, in Children's Literature in Education, *No. 21 (Summer), 1976, pp. 96-7.*

A NEAR THING FOR CAPTAIN NAJORK (1976)

Fooling with a chemistry set, Tom invents an "anti-stick" substance, constructs a "two-seater jam-powered frog" and uses both inventions to circumvent the jealous Captain and to disconcert the fat, sadistic headmistress of a girls' school, who has incurred the suspicious attention of Tom's bossy Aunt Fidget. A somewhat cynical text which is hardly lightened even by Quentin Blake's sprightly and ingenious visualisation of a nasty jumble of snake, people and general stickiness. It seems a pity even to try to repeat the fresh, appealing nonsense of Tom's first exploit. (p. 2858)

> *Margery Fisher, in her* Growing Point, *April, 1976.*

A sequel to *How Tom Beat Captain Najork and His Hired Sportsman* . . . [*A Near Thing for Captain Najork*] is just as delightfully daft a tale, with Blake's vigorous paintings a medley of ersatz Victoriana and *Punch* cartoon style. Tom, the boy who knows how to putter about, builds a jam-powered frog vehicle; he is spotted and followed by the captain (traveling, with his stalwarts, in a mechanical snake) who is still smarting from the defeat suffered in the first book.

Somehow the chase gets complicated by the fact that the captain's militant wife suspects him of dallying with the headmistress at a girl's school and challenges her supposed rival at arm wrestling. And through it all, Aunt Bundlejoy Cosysweet amicably drifts about with flowers springing wildly from her hat and her long, long hair floating in the breeze. Written and illustrated with comic genius. (p. 175)

> *Zena Sutherland, in* Bulletin of the Center for Children's Books (© *1976 by the University of Chicago; all rights reserved), July-August, 1976.*

OTHER CITATIONS

The Junior Bookshelf, *February, 1976, p. 15.*

Pamela D. Pollack, in School Library Journal, *February, 1976, p. 39.*

THE PEDALING MAN, AND OTHER POEMS (1968)

Describing a poem as a "writer's attempt to hold on to what world he has and to grab a little more if he can" that may "help the reader do the same thing," Hoban has selected 16 of his poems that represent personal incidents and thoughts he felt impelled to record for himself and possible kindred readers. . . . [*The Pedaling Man* is a] collection of unusual poems which, though varying in quality, are distinguished by originality of concept and imagery. (p. 1234)

> The Booklist and Subscription Books Bulletin *(reprinted by permission of the American Library Association; copyright 1968 by the American Library Association), July 1, 1968.*

The black-and-white drawings are kept to a minimum, an occasional bird, boat, etc. to decorate a page. Of the 28 poems in this book, the title selection is the best, its jazzy rhythm resulting from a free-wheeling beat, the stringing of accented syllables serving to spring the rhyme and meter. The majority of poems, however, are less fortunate. "The Crow" asks inconsequential questions, then ends with the too precious image: "Loaves of blue heaven under each wing." "The Friendly Cinnamon Bun" is innocently sinister: "I smiled back at that cinnamon bun and ate him, one two three, / And walked out with his friendliness inside." Other poems show a mastery of form—and a bland handling of tired themes and images. This collection is a disappointment from the Hobans. (p. 191)

> *Steve Rybicki, in* School Library Journal *(reprinted from the September, 1968, issue of* School Library Journal, *published by R. R. Bowker Company, a Xerox company; copyright © 1968 by Xerox Corporation), September, 1968.*

I recently had the privilege of hearing Russell Hoban read some of these verses to an audience of small children. Any doubts I had about their relevance to the young went scuttling into hiding. With *The Pedaling Man* Mr Hoban joins that very select company of poets who, writing from the heart, speak directly to the hearts of children.

Mr Hoban's subjects are the ageless ones, youth and the coming of age, the sky and the wind, and the animal kingdom. His eye is keen and his perception sharp and original. Others have seen hunter and hunted; only he sees sparrowhawk and mouse as highwayman and victim, the latter holding 'fast the small purse of his life'. He shares this tender, shrewd and humorous vision generously, and seasons the poems with a Yankee toughness. With this enchanting collection Mr Hoban strengthens his position as one of the most outstanding and original writers for the young. (p. 248)

> *Marcus Crouch, in* The School Librarian, *June, 1970.*

OTHER CITATIONS

Walker Gibson, in The New York Times Book Review, *Part II, May 5, 1968, p. 44.*

B. W. Alderson, in Children's Book News, *March-April, 1970, p. 87.*

The Junior Bookshelf, *June, 1970, pp. 151-52.*

Edward Blishen, in Children's Book Review, *February, 1971, p. 8.*

John Rowe Townsend, in his Written for Children: An Outline of English-Language Children's Literature, *revised edition, Lippincott, 1974, p. 302.*

THE SEA-THING CHILD (1972)

Flung up on the beach in a howling storm, the sea-thing child engages in delightfully grave conversations with a complaining fiddler crab ("Oh, if only I had a bow, what music I could play!") and a passing eel and albatross before turning to the ocean he was born in. This tiny but resonant book is probably what the word exquisite should have been saved for, and only Hoban could bring it off. (p. 1412)

> Kirkus Reviews *(copyright © 1972 The Kirkus Service, Inc.), December 15, 1972.*

The sea-thing child is a thing of the sea swept up on to the beach in a storm and forced to wait until growing up allows him to return. Not that he minds staying in the beginning: there are sea-stone igloos to build and a crab to talk to. But a crab so hard to please—self-pitying and patronising, showing all the self-willed illogic the Red Queen directs at Alice. And, like Alice, the sea-thing child must be moving on, for the sea calls him back and destiny cannot be changed. The beach is a place for becoming and this book is about such a beach: the crab finds honesty and stays, the sea-thing child finds wings and goes. You're at liberty to see it as a fable, yet you know it's other things too. Hoban's words are for readers not age groups, and it's a good thing occasionally to start at the beginning again with books like this. A memorable reader-thing book. (p. 13)

> *C. S. Hannabuss, in* Children's Book Review *(© 1973 Five Owls Press Ltd.; all rights reserved), February, 1973.*

OTHER CITATIONS

Publishers Weekly, *November 13, 1972, p. 45.*

Zena Sutherland, in Bulletin of the Center for Children's Books, *February, 1973, p. 92.*

Diane Gersoni-Stavn, in School Library Journal, *February, 1973, p. 68.*

Donald F. Pfau, in Childhood Education, *May, 1973, p. 422.*

THE SONG IN MY DRUM (1962)

Eavesdropping on children at play has become the basis for a new genre of picture books. Sometimes—as in [Ruth Krauss's] "A Hole Is to Dig"—the result is both *of* children and *for* them, but Russell Hoban's duologue of a brother and sister will baffle and bore young listeners.

"Bup diddy bup," says the girl beating her drum. "I could gobble up people with my shoes," says the boy, wearing Father's shoes. "He is the mysterious protein dog," they say inexplicably of their dog, Maxie. On it goes, without any support from Lillian Hoban's vague repetitious sketches. The team who created "Herman the Loser" is capable of far better.

Mr. Hoban has caught the curious phrases and non-sequiturs of children's imaginative world but, quoted without insight or story, the result neither entertains nor sparks the imagination. Nor is it universal enough for children to have the fun of recognition. Like a private joke, it is meaningless to all but the originators. (p. 22)

> *Alice Low, in* The New York Times Book Review *(© 1962 by The New York Times Company; reprinted by permission), June 17, 1962.*

OTHER CITATIONS

Virginia Kirkus' Service, *January 15, 1962, p. 55.*

THE SORELY TRYING DAY (1964)

A family quarrel and its inevitable chain reaction are delicately and deliciously portrayed in this picture book. Father comes home at night after a bad day only to find that life on the home front doesn't look so good either. "The cat was on top of the grandfather clock and the dog was barking and trying to climb up after her. All of the children were striking one another. . . ." But it wasn't really their fault at all. Adults will relish the delightful Victorian prose and both children and adults will enjoy the progressively funny comedy and the subtle humor in the detailed Victorian drawings [by Lillian Hoban]. This is the best creative effort of this author-artist team. (p. 169)

> *Irene Davis, in* School Library Journal *(reprinted from the September, 1964, issue of* School Library Journal, *published by R. R. Bowker Company, a Xerox company; copyright © 1964 by Xerox Corporation), September, 1964.*

I don't quite know what to make of the Hobans' deadpan Victorian cautionary tale. It is beautifully done. The grave, elegantly phrased story is precisely right for these pencil drawings of a domestic setting against which a charming, slightly deformed family play out their drama. It is a perfect period piece, flawless to the last detail. But was it worth doing anyway? And what will modern children make of its sobriety and concealed humour? The shelf on which one puts the "sports" of the publishing world is one to which one returns often with pleasure; it is on this shelf the *The Sorely Trying Day* belongs. (p. 276)

> The Junior Bookshelf, *October, 1965.*

OTHER CITATIONS

Virginia Kirkus' Service, *April 1, 1964, p. 361.*

THE STONE DOLL OF SISTER BRUTE (1968)

At the end of *The Little Brute Family*, the Brutes change their name—and nature—to Nice; bringing 'em back bad poses problems that don't apply to most repeats. . . . [In *The Stone Doll of Sister Brute*] Sister Brute, wanting something to love, adopts a stone—she draws it a face, dresses it, and names it Alice Brute Stone; she is adopted by an ugly dog wearing hob-nailed boots who wants someone to love him. But the doll is hard and heavy and the dog keeps kicking and Sister Brute has only tiredness and bruises for her love. Mama Brute, confronted with the problem, is stymied until she looks at Alice Brute Stone's face; it is just like hers. "You could love me," she says, "and I will give you soft hugs and sing you lullabies." Each of the family, Sister Brute learns, has a special offering; she will love them all and Alice Brute Stone and the ugly kicking dog too. . . . In the perfunctory introduction to the family, Mama and Papa seem typical impatient, preoccupied parents, funny-looking but not loutish enough to be funny to the child who's meeting them for the first time. On the other hand, the youngster who remembers their reform will wonder how come they're so nice before becoming Nice. It's a questionable parallel of the original with some undeniably touching images—Sister Brute fondling Alice Brute Stone; the buck-toothed yellow dog, really a rejected toy, claiming her affection because she pays attention to him; and Mama Brute seeing her own face in the stone. (p. 2)

> Kirkus Service (*copyright © 1968 Virginia Kirkus' Service, Inc.*), January 1, 1968.

OTHER CITATIONS

Carolyn A. Hough, in School Library Journal, *March, 1968, p. 128.*

TOM AND THE TWO HANDLES (1965)

Tom and the Two Handles is . . . an almost perfect allegory of the current world situation as seen by the well-meaning liberal Republican mind. Tom gets into a fist fight with his friend Kenny, and is beaten. He complains to his father, who is full of wise sayings and good advice ("Every problem has two handles," "You can't win them all," "It's time to call a spade a spade."), but each time he goes back to Kenny's house and tries to apply the advice, they begin to quarrel and Kenny beats him up again. Finally Tom gets a punching bag; practices on it, and goes and beats Kenny up; then they are friends again. The story has everything—the idea that coexistence is only possible between military equals; the lack of any real reason for conflict; and the inane political platitudes and bad advice of elderly statesmen. Most striking of all, though the book is full of [Lillian Hoban's] pictures, none of them show Tom and

Kenny actually fighting. The five battles described in the text take place invisibly; as it were, on another continent. (pp. 27-8)

> *Alison Lurie, in* The New York Review of Books (*reprinted with permission from* The New York Review of Books; *copyright © 1966 NYREV, Inc.*), December 15, 1966.

OTHER CITATIONS

Virginia Kirkus' Service, *April 1, 1965, p. 376.*

WHAT DOES IT DO AND HOW DOES IT WORK? (1959)

As they grow, children move steadily from the small world of home into the wider world around them. Despite their increasing competence, even at six or eight or ten they sometimes feel, and are, quite small and powerless. Learning how things work is one way of gaining a hold on the world and replacing fear with mastery. Knowledge brings self-respect and a measure of the control over their world that these young people seek. In "What Does It Do and How Does It Work?" . . . Russell Hoban tells about power shovels, dump trucks, and other heavy machinery. This book differs from many others on the same topic in its assumption that the child wants serious, straightforward information that respects his ability to understand. The book also acknowledges the child's need to be powerful and strong: "Here is where you sit . . . when you want to dump the load, you shift the lever to raise the body . . ." The pictures are distinctive for their strength and force—no merry blue-and-red tractors here, but powerful, massive machines. (pp. 74-5)

> *Irma Black, in* Saturday Review (*copyright © 1959 by Saturday Review, Inc.; reprinted with permission*), October 17, 1959.

Dump trucks, bulldozers, and other heavy machines are pictured in realistic action; sometimes a section of a machine is shown. Most of the text describes the action of the machines, not their uses. Illustrations are artistic but not instructive, and descriptions without diagrams lead to confusion and disappointment. Not recommended. (p. 38)

> *Olive Mumford, in* Junior Libraries (*reprinted from the November, 1959, issue of* Junior Libraries, *published by R. R. Bowker Company. A Xerox Publishing company. Copyright © 1959*), November, 1959.

*   *   *

HOUSTON, James   1921-

James Houston is a Canadian artist and an author for adults and children. Living for 12 years with the Eskimos of the Canadian Arctic influenced both his fiction and the world of visual art. It was Houston who "discovered" and promoted the sculpture of the Eskimos and introduced print-making to them. He has twice won the Canadian Library Association Award, in 1966 for *Tikta'liktak* and in 1968 for *The White Archer*. Houston's *The White Dawn*, an adult novel, was filmed in 1974 using a primarily Eskimo cast. (See also *Contemporary Authors*, Vols. 65-68.)

GENERAL COMMENTARY

Were it not for the success of James Houston's *Eagle Mask*

... and *Ghost Paddle* ..., it might seem that Canadian historical fiction for [younger children] was foredoomed to failure. It is true that in these tales of West Coast Indian life Houston has not had to concern himself with recording historical fact, but out of a wealth of available evidence he has been able to choose exactly those details of Indian life that give meaning to the background and that advance an original story. Within sixty-four pages, highly illustrated, he has produced two gems, although *Ghost Paddle* is more tautly contrived and exciting than *Eagle Mask*. *Ghost Paddle*, the story of a young prince of the Raven Clan who accompanies his father on a peace mission to a neighbouring tribe and saves the mission by his courage, moves swiftly to a climax but preserves a mythic quality. (p. 115)

James Houston has not only been the most prolific spokesman for the Eskimo in children's literature, but the most artistic writer. In *Tikta'Liktak* ..., *The White Archer* ..., *Akavak* ..., and *Wolf Run* ... he has distilled the essence of the heroic in Eskimo life, as in a broader sense the stories of King Arthur, Roland, and Beowulf bring to a culmination the essence of the civilizations they represent. Legend is by definition 'some wonderful event handed down for generations among a people and popularly believed to have historical basis, although not verifiable: distinguished from myth'. Certainly all the events that James Houston records in his stories *could* have happened, and he has clothed them in the dignified language that befits a legend. But in the timeless world that he describes, his heroes are as modern as those in Roderick Haig-Brown's *Starbuck Valley Winter* or David Walker's *Pirate Rock* or Jean Mackenzie's *River of Stars*. As Houston's Eskimo characters complete their quest, they have changed, become aware of themselves and their environment, and so achieve a new inner power.

Tikta'Liktak is closest to legend. The story of the young man (less than twenty years of age) who escaped from his floating prison to equal danger and hardship on a barren Arctic island, and who then, by courageous and ingenious means, made his way back to the mainland, had become famous in the Arctic when James Houston first heard it. ... The boy's long period of loneliness and isolation in *Tikta'Liktak* and his knowledge that there will be no rescue search on his behalf make his story more powerful than that previous classic of the North, Wilfred Grenfell's *Adrift on an Ice-Pan* (1909).

Stories of Eskimo life have little internal variety. The basic needs of food and shelter are at the root of all those we have for children, whether written in another era, such as [Vilhjalmur] Stefansson's *Kak the Copper Eskimo* (1924), or Doug Wilkinson's *Sons of the Arctic* (1965). The harsh realities of the northern landscape and climate cannot be denied. The traditional antipathy between Eskimo and Indian, which forms a minor theme in [Farley] Mowat's *Lost in the Barrens* and in legendary material, is the major one in Houston's *The White Archer*. Survival, however, is still the underlying ingredient. The plot is a simple one—although, as is usual with James Houston, it is designed more for the insight it gives into the Eskimo people and their ways than for narrative interest. An Eskimo family is forced by its laws to offer hospitality to three strangers (also Eskimo) who had just returned from Indian territory—the Land of Little Sticks—where they had desperately hunted game and robbed an Indian camp. The Indians, following their trail,

retaliate by mass murder of the Eskimo family who sheltered the strangers. Twelve-year-old Kungo escapes and his young sister is carried off by the Indians. Kungo trains himself for revenge under the guidance of an old, wise, nearly blind archer. Four years later Kungo, now 'the white archer', sets out on his odyssey of hate, his all-white clothes perhaps signifying the North as much as the purity of spirit that is to come to him in the final moments of his revenge. At any rate the story is charged with a mysticism not usual in Eskimo stories. The motif—man's finding himself—is of course basic to all literature.

Akavak and *Wolf Run* are simpler stories but are all the more welcome as books of quality and integrity for younger children. (pp. 161-63)

In all his writing Houston continues to show a people who overcome their problems of living in a frozen land by an inner warmth and love. (p. 189)

> *Sheila Egoff, in her* The Republic of Childhood: A Critical Guide to Canadian Children's Literature in English (© *Oxford University Press, Canadian Branch, 1975*), *second edition, Oxford University Press, 1975.*

AKAVAK: AN ESKIMO JOURNEY (1968)

"Your grandfather must see his brother before he dies," said Akavak's father. "Long ago he promised to do this. Now he grows old and there is only a little time. You are the one who must help him."

So the boy and the old man set out together away from the coastal plateaus of the sea hunters to the northern land of the great river. Akavak was young and courageous and strong but his grandfather had a lifetime of experience and great wisdom to guide them. They encountered disaster after disaster; their food cache was raided by a bear, all their dogs but one were lost in a deep blue abyss in the glacier; tempest and hunger and weariness beset them until they dreamed strange dreams of soaring up together among the stars. But they survived all these and at last the old man cried out: "Look, look, the river, the Kojuak."

This is the most stirring and vivid of all James Houston's books. The pictures and the simple narrative blend together with an unbearable intensity. The hard land, the bitter wind, the majestic spaces and the bright stars are as real and strong as the terrifying hardship. The wisdom and strength of the old man are reassuring and credible, and as he falters and the boy develops his own wisdom and resourcefulness it is expected and true. The tale moves on to a sad but triumphant ending as they reach their goal and the old man dies.

James Houston has an almost magical power of making the strange, hard world of the Eskimo believable to the city dweller and never more so than here. (pp. 26-7)

> *Alice E. Kane, in* In Review: Canadian Books for Children, *Winter, 1969.*

The story of [Akavak and his grandfather's] terrible time, of Akavak's battle with the musk ox, and of the last wild-sled ride down the mountain makes exciting readings [in *Akavak: An Eskimo Journey*]. But it is the portrayal of the relationship of the Eskimos to each other—especially that of the boy and the old man—and their attitude toward themselves and their environment that make the story more than just a tale of an adventure. In harmony with the elements, often controlled by them, the characters do not lose their sense of personal destiny. At the end of his journey Akavak experiences a feeling of exultation when he looks up at the mountains— "From those great heights, he had looked down at the world like a wind spirit and had seen all of the land and the vast distances of the frozen sea. After that he had come down . . . now, like his grandfather, he had a strong secret feeling for the white plateau." (p. 54)

> Sidney D. Long, in The Horn Book Magazine (copyright © 1969 by The Horn Book, Inc., Boston), February, 1969.

OTHER CITATIONS

Betty L. Ryder, in School Library Journal, November, 1968, p. 87.

Digby B. Whitman, in Book World, November 3, 1968, p. 10.

The Best in Children's Books, edited by Zena Sutherland, University of Chicago Press, 1973, p. 198.

EAGLE MASK: A WEST COAST INDIAN TALE (1966)

The author . . . has for many years lived and traveled in the Canadian Arctic and the Northwest. His knowledge of the West Coast Indians is basic enough to keep the cultural details of his story from being obtrusive; his quiet writing has a simplicity that is eminently appropriate for the rich and dignified living patterns of the Eagle clan. (p. 50)

> Zena Sutherland, in Saturday Review (copyright © 1966 by Saturday Review, Inc.; reprinted with permission), November 12, 1966.

In an eloquent story emphasizing the Canadian Northwest Indian's sense of kinship with nature, the author . . . describes the coming-of-age trials, rituals, and celebrations of a young Eagle-clan prince and explains their significance within the framework of tribal customs, beliefs, and legends. Although the tribe is not identified, their culture is basically the same as that of the Indians discussed in [Christie Harris' Raven's Cry] and this tale affords an elucidating introduction to the Northwest coastal clans for younger readers. Illustrated with vigorous black-and-white sketches. (p. 418)

> The Booklist and Subscription Books Bulletin (reprinted by permission of the American Library Association; copyright 1966 by the American Library Association), December 1, 1966.

Mr. Houston's artistic skill combined with his mastery of prose has again produced a vivid picture of a life and time other than our own, and has set against this background the uncertainties and aspirations of youth. If Skemshan, the young prince, is less fully realized than was the Eskimo youth in Tikta'liktak, the author's previous book, this is primarily due to the fact that most of Skemshan's perils and trials take place in the company of others so that the ele-

ment of solitude is missing. However, where Skemshan walks alone, we feel the challenge of his dream.

Caught up in the adventure with bear and whale, the excitement of totem pole and potlach, many a boy will lay down the book with a complete comprehension of Skemshan's feeling ". . . he seemed to be in tune with all the world like a carved wind flute that sings to the mountains and is answered by them." (p. 32)

> D. M. Reid, in In Review: Canadian Books for Children, Winter, 1967.

OTHER CITATIONS

Phyllis Meras, in The New York Times Book Review, Part II, November 6, 1966, p. 40.

Ethel L. Heins, in The Horn Book Magazine, December, 1966, p. 716.

GHOST PADDLE: A NORTHWEST COAST INDIAN TALE (1972)

In the same vein as Eagle Mask . . . , [Ghost Paddle is] another quietly compelling story of a chief's son among the Indians of the Northwest coast. Using a specially designed paddle—recreated from his father's dream—Hooits becomes part of a peacemaking party sent out to end his group's protracted war with the Inland River People. Before the truce is agreed upon there's a David and Goliath battle between Hooits and the River People's giant slave in which the ghost paddle becomes a deadly weapon. In spite of this confrontation, the story has little of the drama and momentum of Houston's Eskimo tales; still the many details of culture and custom combine with Hooits' own sense of wonder to create a sense of mythic solidarity, and the strong, sweeping drawings make up for any action the tale itself lacks. (p. 1027)

> Kirkus Reviews (copyright © 1972, The Kirkus Service, Inc.), September 1, 1972.

Houston's writing, like his illustrations, has a stark and dramatic simplicity that is eminently right for the dignity of the Indian peoples he describes. The protagonist who wields the ghost paddle is Hooits, an adolescent prince who has never known peace in his lifetime, and yearns for it. He is delighted when his father decides to take a small band of young people to the mainland, to prove to the Inland River people that they come as peacemakers and that the hostility between them had been craftily engendered by a third tribe. The story is so deftly imbued with the spirit and the cultural details of Hooits' people that the incorporation seems effortless, and the theme has a pertinence for today. (p. 43)

> Zena Sutherland, in Bulletin of the Center for Children's Books (© 1972 by the University of Chicago; all rights reserved), November, 1972.

James Houston in Ghost Paddle embroiders portraits of historical Indians with a modernist flare. Hooits (Grizzly Bear) becomes a peacenik as the book progresses from preoccupation with tribal warfare to a reverence for shrewd diplomacy. James Houston, in keeping with a noticeable Canadian trend, derived his inspiration from specific visual impression, in this case from the legendary Indian carvers of the Northwest coast of Canada. Appropriately, Houston serves as his own illustrator. . . . His award winning Eskimo books, unlike the Indian volumes, attempt to reflect Eskimo life without recourse to modernism. (p. 148)

> *Leonard R. Mendelsohn, in* Children's Literature: Annual of The Modern Language Association Seminar on Children's Literature and The Children's Literature Association, *Vol. 4, edited by Francelia Butler (© 1975 by Francelia Butler; all rights reserved), Temple University Press, 1975.*

OTHER CITATIONS

Publishers Weekly, *October 9, 1972, p. 113.*

Marge Grnya, in School Library Journal, *January, 1973, p. 69.*

Virginia Haviland, in The Horn Book Magazine, *February, 1973, p. 48.*

KIVIOK'S MAGIC JOURNEY: AN ESKIMO LEGEND (1973)

If it were not for the descriptive passages, James Houston's *Kiviok's Magic Journey: An Eskimo Legend* . . . might have stepped from the pages of the Brothers Grimm, with its theme of the beautiful girls whose cloaks of goose feathers are stolen while they bathe. Here the girls are snow geese, the thief who steals the feathers of one of them is Raven in his wicked manifestation, and the hero who travels far to recover his wife and children is Kiviok the Eskimo. The axe of a friendly giant flings out bright chips of ivory and Kiviok is carried beneath the frozen sea on the back of a sea trout. In calling the silvery fish he chants: 'Bubbles, bubbles / End my troubles. / Help me now, / Oh magic fish.' Here is evidence of the commonality of folklore: while plots and themes are similar, the details and perhaps an attitude to life can signify the country of origin. Russian folklore produces an image of vast plains and fleet horses, while German tales are usually played out in dark and mysterious forests. In the French version of 'The Sleeping Beauty' the prince kisses the princess awake, but in the Spanish version it is the prince who is asleep.

James Houston has long been known for his authentic legend-type stories of the Eskimo—spare narratives that in style, detail, and impact are honed to the essence. He has diverged from that style in *Kiviok's Magic Journey*, probably to interest quite young children for whom this picture-storybook is intended. His illustrations are softer than his usual severe, sculptured pictures based on Eskimo carvings; they swirl and dance. Like the text, they give the story a European atmosphere. (pp. 47-8)

> *Sheila Egoff, in her* The Republic of Childhood: A Critical Guide to Canadian Children's Literature in English (© Oxford University Press, Canadian Branch, 1967, 1975), second edition, Oxford University Press, 1975.*

OTHER CITATIONS

Publishers Weekly, *November 19, 1973, p. 61.*

Zena Sutherland, in Bulletin of the Center for Children's Books, *April, 1974, p. 130.*

Virginia Haviland, in The Horn Book Magazine, *April, 1974, p. 146.*

SONGS OF THE DREAM PEOPLE: CHANTS AND IMAGES FROM THE INDIANS AND ESKIMOS OF NORTH AMERICA (1972)

Chants and poems, some so brief as to be impressions, have been chosen from the songs of the Eskimos and Indians of North America and are illustrated with handsome drawings of art objects and artifacts. The selections are grouped regionally: Eastern Woodland, Central Plains, Northwest Coast, and Eskimo. The song-poems reflect their cultures; all are interesting, many are beautiful, some dignified and strong and other delicate in their tenderness. A lovely example of the reverence for natural things is the Tewa song, "Weave us a garment of brightness / That we may walk fittingly where birds sing / That we may walk fittingly where grass is green / Oh, our mother the earth / Oh, our father the sky." (p. 125)

> *Zena Sutherland, in* Bulletin of the Center for Children's Books (© 1973 by the University of Chicago; all rights reserved), April, 1973.*

James Houston's *Songs of the Dream People* . . . is a sensitively chosen collection of 'chants and images from the Indians and Eskimos of North America'. Many have the delicacy of the Japanese haiku and others express with extraordinary neatness an aspect of the Eskimo character that is often overlooked:

> I want to laugh, I, because my sledge is broken.
> Because its ribs are broken I want to laugh.
> Here at Talviuyaq I encountered hummocky ice, I
>   met with an upset.
> I want to laugh. It is not a thing to rejoice over.
>
> (Central Eskimo)

Songs of the Dream People is not specifically a book for children; but the poems are a part of the Indian and Eskimo oral traditions and are as closely related to their legends as the English ballad is to English folklore. Their appeal therefore spans the gap between adulthood and childhood. (pp. 245-46)

> *Sheila Egoff, in her* The Republic of Childhood: A Critical Guide to Canadian Children's Literature in English (© Oxford University Press, Canadian Branch, 1967, 1975), second edition, Oxford University Press, 1975.*

OTHER CITATIONS

Dee Brown, in The New York Times Book Review, *Part II, November 5, 1972, p. 7.*

Mary I. Purucker, in School Library Journal, *March, 1973, p. 108.*

Ethel L. Heins, in Top of the News, *June, 1973, pp. 356-57.*

Elizabeth Minot Graves, in Commonweal, *November 23, 1973, p. 220.*

TIKTA'LIKTAK: AN ESKIMO LEGEND (1965)

[*Tikta'liktak: An Eskimo Legend* is a] short story, economically written, with the sharp realism of an actual, stark adventure. The young Eskimo Tikta'liktak, seeking food for his hungry people, one day finds himself drifting away from the mainland on an ice floe cut off when a crack on the coastline ice widens. Near starvation, he finally reaches the uninhabited granite island called Sakkiak where, in a trancelike dream and then in reality, he encounters dangerous Arctic wildlife. His courage and ingenuity in surviving and returning to humanity make a true hero tale, distinctively and forcefully illustrated in pencil line by the Canadian artist, who lived for twelve years among the Eskimos. (p. 633)

> *Virginia Haviland, in* The Horn Book Magazine *(copyright © 1965 by The Horn Book, Inc., Boston), December, 1965.*

James Houston retells an Eskimo legend that celebrates man's will to survive.... In Mr. Houston's hands, this short tale tells much about the tenacious, spirited people who inhabit the far North. The author's distinctive drawings help make this a memorable book. (p. 12)

> *Robert Berkvist, in* The New York Times Book Review *(© 1965 by The New York Times Company; reprinted by permission), December 19, 1965.*

The qualities of courage, daring, and adroitness with which the Eskimo faces the perils and precariousness of life in the Far North are depicted in the story of a young hunter's struggle for survival when cast adrift on an ice floe. Although the rather flat narrative style makes the story more interesting than exciting, the arctic setting is vividly portrayed and enlightening details of Eskimo life and customs are unobtrusively woven into Tikta'liktak's adventures. (p. 450)

> The Booklist and Subscription Books Bulletin *(reprinted by permission of the American Library Association; copyright 1966 by the American Library Association), January 1, 1966.*

An Eskimo legend is told as straight fiction in a book that has all the appeal of the Crusoe situation plus the embellishment of the exotic setting. The illustrations, strong and stark in black and white, enhance the mood of solitude and isolation. (p. 59)

> *Zena Sutherland, in* Bulletin of the Center for Children's Books *(copyright 1966 by the University of Chicago; all rights reserved), December, 1966.*

OTHER CITATIONS

Beatrice M. Adam, in School Library Journal, *November, 1965, p. 63.*

THE WHITE ARCHER: AN ESKIMO LEGEND (1967)

[*The White Archer* is a] strong, spare evocation of Eskimo life—of stalking caribou, skinning a seal, settling into an ice house in winter, a skin tent in summer—with moral and mythic overtones: only a good man "who obeys the rules of life" gets game, the animals "will not give themselves" to

one who is cruel and stupid. Mr. Houston won applause with *Tikta'liktak* . . .; he should find a larger audience with this less constricted story. (We're calling it fiction despite the subtitle because it has all the essential attributes of characterization, motivation, resolution.) (p. 694)

> Kirkus Service *(copyright © 1967 Virginia Kirkus' Service, Inc.), June 15, 1967.*

In this timeless, dramatically illustrated story, the windswept ice contrasts with the hospitable snowhouse; the stark simplicity of the telling contrasts with the depths of the wisdom imparted. (p. 589)

> *Helen B. Crawshaw, in* The Horn Book Magazine *(copyright © 1967 by The Horn Book, Inc., Boston), October, 1967.*

There is an epic quality to this short book telling an Eskimo legend in spare words and strong illustrations. James Houston's story of a boy's obsession for revenge against the Indians who killed his family also suggests echoes of the Arthurian legend: the boy, Kungo, could be an Eskimo Arthur; Ittok, a Merlin-like old hunter, and Kigavic, the great bow, could be Excalibur. Ittok teaches the boy the arts of hunting, tracking and survival and, fortunately, wisdom about life as well. His feeling for revenge is tempered and anger is buried in "whirling drifts of snow." In this rugged tale by a Canadian author and artist who has lived and worked among the Eskimo, the reader sees a primitive yet dignified and poetic civilization and a land where the air is "still and sharp like the thinnest crystal." (p. 38)

> *Margaret McCloskey, in* The New York Times Book Review *(© 1967 by The New York Times Company; reprinted by permission), October 8, 1967.*

James Houston's quiet stories and tumultuous pencil drawings, good from the start, get better and better. Both are crowded with the most vivid and intimate details of Eskimo life. Rudyard Kipling wrote only one Eskimo story ("Quiquern") but, as usual, left a high and solitary mark for others to shoot at. In my judgment, *The White Archer* hits that mark. For all ages. (p. 22)

> *Digby B. Whitman, in* Book World *(© The Washington Post), November 5, 1967.*

The author of "Tikta'liktak" has written another Eskimo legend [in "The White Archer"]—a stark legend of the power of hatred, a power that can only be defeated by the power of love. He tells it with dramatic and moving fervor, which makes it a mighty legend and a proud one. (p. 56)

> *Lavinia Russ, in* Publishers Weekly *(reprinted from the November 20, 1967, issue of* Publishers Weekly *by permission of the critic, published by R. R. Bowker Company, a Xerox company; copyright © 1967 by Xerox Corporation), November 20, 1967.*

OTHER CITATIONS

Zena Sutherland, in Bulletin of the Center for Children's Books, *October, 1967, p. 28.*

Constantine Georgiou, in his Children and Their Literature, *Prentice-Hall, 1969, p. 239.*

Margery Fisher, in her Who's Who in Children's Books: A Treasury of the Familiar Characters of Childhood, *Holt, Rinehart and Winston, 1975, p. 168.*

WOLF RUN: A CARIBOU ESKIMO TALE (1971)

It's curious that Punik, thirteen and as culture-bound as the rest of his isolated family, can perceive that incantations will not fill their bellies and that only action, initiative, will. And there are other unanswered questions in this unrelieved account of one boy's lonely hunger as he marches "half-mad" through the snow and has "to pull his hair . . . to make himself feel a different kind of pain"; after a while "in wild excitement" he finds and eats "the scattered black droppings of an Arctic hare" and then, "to make a meal of it," he cuts away the top of a boot and chews off the skin. In the absence of dialogue, Mr. Houston supplies stark description and a sort of monologue—the loose meanderings of Punik's mind: he sees his sister Seela and his father, drowned last year, his mother, uncles, and revered grandparents; he recalls their words about the spirits and indeed he feels their spirits at the end. Two wolves approach him, don't attack but head instead for caribou—the late and long-awaited herd; they chase and kill one while, exhausted, Punik watches—"He could scarcely believe what he saw. They ate not one bite," just stood staring, "until the female gave a low whine and leaped across the fallen caribou, bumping her mate . . . as a signal." Punik helps himself to the warm liver, removes the hide and swathes himself in it planning for tomorrow's hunt: remembering the fresh human tracks he'd crossed earlier (one set identified as his grandmother's—no explanation; the other as his very own—he'd retraced his steps), Punik "knew now that his grandfather and his grandmother had sent their spirits with the wolves to help him." A small and internally illogical climax to what is inescapably a horror story, mispackaged besides: it looks around nine, reads considerably older, and speaks with an adult intensity that will disturb the child not otherwise put off. (pp. 365-66)

> *Kirkus Reviews (copyright © 1971 The Kirkus Service, Inc.), April 1, 1971.*

Houston's distinctive literary style and his understanding of Eskimo life and character enrich this story of Punik, a young Eskimo boy of the caribou-hunting people who defies the traditional custom of waiting for the magic of the drum to bring the caribou by setting out alone to hunt for food for his starving family. The taut narrative vividly pictures the hardships of Punik's arduous but ultimately successful trek across an uninhabited white wilderness, the reveries and hallucinations which comfort and torment him, and his strange encounter with wolves that helps to save his life. A moving and memorable story of human determination and courage. (pp. 701-02)

> *The Booklist (reprinted by permission of the American Library Association; copyright 1971 by the American Library Association), April 15, 1971.*

The author of *Akavak: An Eskimo Journey* writes vividly of another hazardous journey across the bitter Arctic tundra, this one undertaken alone by a thirteen-year-old boy. . . . The dreadful loneliness of the journey, the savage and unremitting hunger, the fright and desperation that increased during the six days of his struggle to survive are described with intense and sometimes painful attention to detail. But at the same time, in Punik's thoughts and memories, the way of life of his people is revealed, their admiration and affection for each other, and the strength of their unwavering belief in the interrelationships of man and animal. This belief is stronger than the hostile environment and brings the story to a dramatic and deeply satisfying climax. Strong black-and-white drawings increase the intensity of the experience. An unforgettable story. (p. 287)

> *Beryl Robinson, in* The Horn Book Magazine *(copyright © 1971 by The Horn Book, Inc., Boston), June, 1971.*

Houston, in this short moving novel, has vividly conveyed the essence of suffering and the courage and endurance which his hero must draw upon to overcome it. His writing is compelling with a starkness and simplicity which complement his theme. His illustrations are perfectly suited to the text. This will be another deservedly popular story, and an excellent addition to our small collection of Eskimo tales. (p. 28)

> *Marilyn McCullough, in* In Review: Canadian Books for Children, *Summer, 1971.*

The bleak strength of the illustrations complements the direct portrayal of a primitive people's dignity and courage [in *Wolf Run: A Caribou Eskimo Tale*]. And, as in each of James Houston's stories, an integrity of conception provides a firm base on which the tautly structured, vigorously executed plot rests. (p. 27)

> *Zena Sutherland, in* Saturday Review *(copyright © 1971 by Saturday Review, Inc.; reprinted with permission), August 21, 1971.*

OTHER CITATIONS

Publishers Weekly, *March 8, 1971, p. 71.*

Margaret N. Coughlan, in Childhood Education, *May, 1972, p. 422.*

*　　*　　*

HUGHES, Ted   1930-

Ted Hughes is an English poet, dramatist, lecturer, critic, short story writer, editor, and myth-maker who is regarded as one of the most significant poets of his generation. Hughes's books for children are noted for the same brevity of writing, strong imagery, and imagination that he brings to his adult works. They contain a lightening of, but not a departure from, his explanation of the intensity of the forces both within and outside of man which order his place in the natural world and the universe. Hughes received his degree from Cambridge in archaelogy and anthropology. Before he became a full-time writer and married American poet Sylvia Plath, Hughes was a rose gardener, teacher, and zoo attendant. He has published poems and stories in several international magazines, and has received many awards for his work. (See also *Contemporary Authors*, Vols. 1-4, rev. ed. and *Contemporary Literary Criticism*, Vols. 2 and 4.)

AUTHOR'S COMMENTARY

[Imagination] isn't merely a surplus mental department meant for entertainment, but the most essential piece of machinery we have if we are going to live the lives of human beings. (p. 57)

[Hughes's next point concerns the classic function of stories as "the deliberate education of imagination." He uses the example of the poets of the Heroic Age in Ireland, who "had a strong intuition of the therapeutic effect of simple narratives." Their stories had a "semireligious function," giving life to the fears and problems of their audience and then, subsequently, dispelling them. Without full operation of imagination, especially as it is represented in the framework of a fantasy, Hughes says that we can become "sick, mechanical monsters."]

And so, . . . children's literature assumes new importance. There's no question of reversing the trend, abandoning science, though that seems to be what a lot of people would like to do. But a technological civilization is useless, and dangerous, unless it is handled by imaginative minds, or by minds that can move as freely in their imaginations as they can move among facts. But what is the right kind of literature to correct this? When we tell a story to a child, to some extent we have his future in our hands insofar as we have hold of his imagination. That's the key; what affects a person's imagination affects their whole life. . . . When we tell a child a story, the child quickly finds his role; as the story proceeds the child enters a completely imaginative world, and it has to be a completely imaginative world or he jibs. If you try to introduce too much extraneous material, or connect the story too obviously to his own outside world, he resists. He doesn't want it. He wants to be enclosed completely in a totally coherent imaginative world. So to some extent he goes into a condition of trance and what he is really resisting is being jerked out of this trance. This trance is a dangerous place; a person in a trance is in a hypnotized condition and so he is completely at the mercy of any kind of suggestion. And so whatever happens to him in the story happens under conditions of hypnosis. In other words, it really happens. (pp. 60-1)

There's a blind faith that just mental, imaginative activity somehow will trigger off the right effects and put the power into the child's hands and open up the inner worlds and make the connections, that just sheer stories of any kind will do this. It's possible, maybe, to be more deliberate. And, coming down to actual cases, to illustrate what I have been talking about, I'll analyse a story constructed quite deliberately with this notion in mind.

When I was in the States ten years ago I saw a series of children's books which just recounted very simply a child's visit to the supermarket, the post office and the station and so on and they read like primers for men from outer space, men who didn't know how to put one foot in front of another. And these books reflected it seemed to me very sharply what I encountered of neurosis in the students that I was teaching. It seemed to me that the whole education of these students, based on something like these little books, or on the general outlook that produced these little books, or that thought these little books were the ideal, necessary literature for children, had completely neglected the real major experience of their lives, namely the collision with the American technological world and, beyond that, the opening up, by physics and so on, of a universe which was completely uninhabited except by atoms and the energy of atoms. It seemed to me then that what they should have been taught was a mythology where all these things would have had a place and meaningful relationships one with another, the student, the technology and the chaos, and his terror of the two.

So when I began to tell [the story of *The Iron Man*] to my own children later, I shaped it in a particular way. (pp. 62-3)

If I had been concerned to write an ordinary monster story, I would have had my little boy destroy the Iron Man, maybe. . . . He would have been a Hercules freeing society from this tremendous threat and, in fact, this is what he does. In psychoanalytical terms, for there are no others that you can really use, he enters, at that point, into a sort of neurotic condition. (p. 65)

If this were an ordinary monster story again, if I were trying to bring it back into ordinary, traditional terms, as in the St George story, my little boy and his Iron Man would be like St George in his armour, you see, this innocent, virginal being inside this mechanized protective, aggressive, defensive case. And he'd destroy the monster or send it rolling back into space. But the story of St George is one example of the sort of story that you do not tell to children —it's a suspect story. And for teachers interested in using imaginative literature for educational purposes, it is a forbidden story. It records, in fact, and it sets up as an ideal pattern for any dealing with unpleasant or irrational experience, the complete suppression of the terror. In other words it is the symbolic story of creating a neurosis, and as it's the key symbolic story of Christianity, it's the key to the neurotic-making dynamics of Christianity. . . . In fact, this story of St George and the dragon is exactly the story and exactly the symbolic condition that . . . educationists . . . are trying to undo, and that in this particular story of mine I'm trying to reverse. And so my little boy with his Iron Man, instead of destroying the dragon, makes friends with the dragon; he includes the dragon in the world, he doesn't shut off and close the world back into a narrow prison. He keeps space open. . . . So I have made a plan, a sort of imaginative blueprint, in which all these things are connected together in your mind as you read the story. You read the story and see the facts of the story as I give it, but in your mind, because it's completely free of any realistic points to pin it down and hold it, it works as a metaphor. And so you make metaphorical interpretations of it. It has complete liberty to be interpreted in every level of experience in your mind. So it stands purely as a blueprint for connecting your ordinary life with a supernormal, practical energy and with the energy of space, connecting them all together in a friendly way. (pp. 65-6)

When you tell a story to a child, this is the kind of shadow that you are putting over him. Every story you tell is a whole kit of blueprints for dealing with himself and for dealing with his own imagination. And so you have to be careful what the blueprints are and what the kit is. I think if you are to think of imaginative literature as an educational tool, you are finally up against the fact that imaginative literature is therapeutic and does have a magical effect on people's minds and on their ultimate behaviour. This is the appeal of great works of imaginative literature to us as adults, that they are hospitals where we heal, where our imaginations are healed, that when they are evil works they are also battlefields where we get injured. To think of children's literature in this way, although it seems very extreme and remote and generalized, sharpens your sense of what kind of thing you are playing with when you use children's literature as an educational thing. Imaginative works of any kind whatsoever have enormous effects and it's as well to be aware of it, to make sure, insofar as it is possible, that they have good effects. (p. 67)

Ted Hughes, "Myth and Education," in Children's Literature in Education *(© 1970, APS Publications, Inc., New York; reprinted by permission of the publisher), No. 1 (March), 1970, pp. 55-67.*

There are all sorts of ways of capturing animals and birds and fish. I spent most of my time, up to the age of fifteen or so, trying out many of these ways and when my enthusiasm began to wane, as it did gradually, I started to write poems.

You might not think that these two interests, capturing animals and writing poems, have much in common. But the more I think back the more sure I am that with me the two interests have been one interest. . . . Maybe my concern has been to capture not animals particularly and not poems, but simply things which have a vivid life of their own, outside mine. (pp. 9-10)

[At] about fifteen my life grew more complicated and my attitude to animals changed. I accused myself of disturbing their lives. I began to look at them, you see, from their own point of view.

And about the same time I began to write poems. Not animal poems. It was years before I wrote what you could call an animal poem, and several more years before it occurred to me that my writing poems might be partly a continuation of my earlier pursuit. Now I have no doubt. The special kind of excitement, the slightly mesmerized and quite involuntary concentration with which you make out the stirrings of a new poem in your mind, then the outline, the mass and color and clean final form of it, the unique living reality of it in the midst of the general lifelessness, all that is too familiar to mistake. This is hunting and the poem is a new species of creature, a new specimen of the life outside your own. (p. 11)

How can a poem, for instance, about a walk in the rain, be like an animal? Well, perhaps it cannot look much like a giraffe or an emu or an octopus, or anything you might find in a menagerie. It is better to call it an assembly of living parts moved by a single spirit. The living parts are the words, the images, the rhythms. The spirit is the life which inhabits them when they all work together. It is impossible to say which comes first, parts or spirit. But if any of the parts are dead . . . if any of the words, or images or rhythms do not jump to life as you read them . . . then the creature is going to be maimed and the spirit sickly. So, as a poet, you have to make sure that all those parts over which you have control, the words and rhythms and images, are alive. (pp. 11-12)

[Imagine] what you are writing about. See it and live it. Do not think it up laboriously, as if you were working out mental arithmetic. Just look at it, touch it, smell it, listen to it, turn yourself into it. When you do this, the words look after themselves, like magic. If you do this you do not have to bother about commas or full-stops or that sort of thing. You do not look at the words either. You keep your eyes, your ears, your nose, your taste, your touch, your whole being on the thing you are turning into words. The minute you flinch, and take your mind off this thing, and begin to look at the words and worry about them . . . then your worry goes into them and they set about killing each other. So you

keep going as long as you can, then look back and see what you have written. After a bit of practice, and after telling yourself a few times that you do not care how other people have written about this thing, this is the way you find it; and after telling yourself you are going to use any old word that comes into your head so long as it seems right at the moment of writing it down, you will surprise yourself. You will read back through what you have written and you will get a shock. You will have captured a spirit, a creature. (pp. 12-13)

Ted Hughes, "Capturing Animals," in his Poetry Is *(copyright © 1967 by Ted Hughes; reprinted by permission of Doubleday & Co., Inc.), Doubleday, 1970, pp. 9-24.*

GENERAL COMMENTARY

[Ted Hughes], I suggest, has had more influence on children through his own writing and his selection of material for BBC schools programmes than any other living poet. His poetry, especially the animal poems of *The Hawk in the Rain* and *Lupercal,* have an immediate and sensational vitality that appeals as much to the eight-year-old as to the adolescent; there is a freshness and a precision in his language which sharpens the reader's perception of certain animals; and since he writes (or used to) mostly about animals it was natural that his poetry should often be the starting point of a child's experience of poetic realism. His work, too, fitted with the mood of encouraging a child's intuitive response to things, an emphasis on strong feeling in oppostion to the mechanistic formalism of society. As a stimulant to creative writing, his poetry is very successful; and in his talk "Capturing Animals", Hughes has helped to increase a child's awareness of how someone begins to write poetry [see excerpt from *Poetry Is* above]. (p. 65)

Ted Hughes is against falsity, especially false writing. In *Poetry in the Making* [published in the United States as *Poetry Is*] he condemns the practice of asking children to copy Keats or Milton in their own writing. . . . He offers new models instead. In the chapter "Writing about people" he recommends Keith Douglas's *Behaviour of Fish in an Egyptian Tea-Garden,* a stylish performance with clever metaphor but not profound, and primarily exhibiting detachment; Philip Larkin's *Mr. Bleaney,* flat and homiletic; and Hughes's own chip serenade, *Her Husband.* Against these uninspiring pieces (and they are presumably meant to inspire or stimulate children to write) Hughes does recommend *You're* by Sylvia Plath and *Elegy* by Theodore Roethke, which both have some warmth and vitality (in the accepted sense) of people writing as they want to about others in a sympathetic way.

Cutting children off from the literary tradition of England may free them from certain stylistic inhibitions, as Hughes intends, but it also leaves them severed from the accumulation of poetry that is distinctively English in terms of cultural growth. This is a falsity, because Hughes, while acknowledging his own debt to Shakespeare, Lawrence, Blake and others, would make available to children mainly modern poets drawn from a wide sweep across Europe and America, in an attempt to keep them free from "the terrible suffocating, maternal octopus of ancient English poetic tradition". He believes in the internationality of poetry—"a universal language of understanding''—but unlike Pound he seems to have no historical view. (p. 66)

The poetry he has written for children is in a distinctive style of fantasy and surrealism. *Meet My Folks!* is the nearest he has come to writing about people close to him, and although he has acknowledged the difficulty of writing about certain close relationships—in his case, his mother—one has to admit that the results are a curious mixture of lolloping rhymes. They are too particularized to have any universality, and yet there's hardly a hint of feeling towards the characters he writes about. These are, he says in *Poetry in the Making,* not his real relatives but invented ones. In one way Hughes is suggesting that children (and he himself) should disguise their family pen-portraits to minimize embarrassment; in another way he is implying that you can be more honest under a veneer of invention. *So My Sister Jane* is a portrait of a crow:

> At meals whatever she sees she'll stab it—
> Because she's a crow and that's a crow habit.

There is something harsh in these lines, both in sound and sense, that is at variance with the jokey style of semi-nonsense. ''All these poems are a sort of joke,'' he says; ''. . . the best jokes are about real people: one does not have to be fantastic.'' It would seem that Hughes does need to be fantastic to cope with real people, but the results are not a success. It is true that children enjoy the momentary meeting with these poems, but they are not likely to return to them as they are to Lear or Old Possum because there is virtually no sympathetic power in them. In *The Earth-Owl and Other Moon-People* [a volume of poetry published in Britain in 1963 containing poems later included in *Moon-Whales and Other Moon Poems*] Hughes explores a surrealist landscape inhabited by the creepy and the deeply disturbing fears at the bottom of dreams: the phantasmagoric ambience has a dream reality that every child knows, but the preoccupation or obsession with animal energy and its corollary of human weakness stands out crudely and with a strangely didactic note, not really as good as Swift. On this moon, earthly order is inverted: in the *Moon Manhunt* when foxes have the upper hand, man writhes in fear. . . . As a piece of verse, whether for children or adults, this is obsessionally narrow and heavy-handed, and in a way sadistic.

The paradox of Ted Hughes is that on one side he has been promoting creativity in children's writing and emphasizing the vitality of his own verse, while on the other he shows little sympathy for humanity and tends towards a narrower and blacker view of life to the point of chaos. Here, I think, is the nature of Hughes's influence: momentarily it is for a burst of creativity, without any sustaining power; there is no development or growth of his poetry, but a fierce burning-out. (pp. 70-1)

> *John Adams, "Dark Rainbow: Reflections on Ted Hughes,"* in Signal *(copyright © 1971 John Adams; reprinted by permission of the author and The Thimble Press, Lockwood Station Road, South Woodchester, Glos. GL5 5EQ, England), May, 1971, pp. 65-71.*

A guiding myth of our time is that art—''good art''—humanizes, the case that it *should* being linked to the unproven hypothesis that it *can* or *does.* The impassioned

work of men like George Steiner would seem to have gone much of the way towards exploding this concept. Art makes us aware, opens up the possibilities of behaviour and attitude, gives us insight into our own lives and others': it may make us better lovers or philanthropists or citizens; as likely it will make us better murderers or torturers or thieves. The same set of circumstances is as likely to debase one man as to enlighten another. . . .

[In the] face of such a conclusion the artist cannot be held responsible for the deficiencies or limitations of his fellow citizens. Even the clearest writers can be misread—and have been, and will be, misread. . . . All a writer can do is be as unambivalent as possible, and then *hope* he is read properly. This is as likely to operate on the level of the individual—child or adult—as on the level of whole societies, for the reading of, say, a poem involves much more than the mere fact of the poem.

To mention the name of Ted Hughes in this context may seem, on the face of it, ridiculous, except that the judgements Mr. John Adams made in his article in the last *Signal* [see excerpt above] were based directly on the assumptions Steiner so devastatingly questions. Mr. Adams contended that the vitality of Hughes's poetry is spurious and exhibits a cynical and negative view of life such as denies man his full humanity. (p. 102)

If art has any purpose, it is to supply a ritual need for the imaginative exploration of our surroundings and emotions and to enhance the quality of the exploration. Though nothing, of course, guarantees the use to which such a liberation of the mind is put, the better the literature the better this function is performed. And since art always operates in the context of a life history, a classroom, a contemporary culture, and since all that it can truthfully be said to do is strengthen our awareness of this context, it seems to me that when we question whether or not a piece of art is ''good'' for children, goodness ought to lie in the specifically literary merits: quality of imagination, sense of language, rhythm, choice of imagery, clarity and control of thought. These, more than the subject, are the hallucinatory, the beguiling elements in a work of literature: these are what shape the mind and it is here we should be looking for our positives.

Apart from the obviously traumatic or incomprehensible, what, above all, we should *not* be giving children is the boring, the second-rate, the confused, the outworn, the shrill—anything that will kill an interest in literature or muddy one's reactions to it. These, like our popular trash art, are more corrupting to the imaginative life than violence intelligently placed and articulated. . . .

Boring, second-rate, confused: these things Hughes's poems are not; and, as it happens, they do not seem to me to be cynical either. (p. 103)

[The] literature [the child] reads ought to be giving him an experience equally distinctive and be articulating at least a part of what he feels and knows about. Not literature that shocks, but literature that takes its place with vividness beside the headlines. By no means is this kind of literature necessarily about war, violence and corruption—it will need to be known by virtue of its language, imagination, emotional intensity, clarity of thought, immediacy of theme. If the subject is contemporary, it need not be so in the obvious way. Hughes's poetry is a good example:

though about nature, it has the feel of the present, of being written in history. Like a far greater poet's, Rimbaud's, Hughes's poems often share the sharp perception and intensity of childhood, flooded with energy, occasionally without discrimination, but reflecting a man who does not run away from his deepest experiences. (pp. 105-06)

> *Brian Morse, "Poetry, Children and Ted Hughes," in* Signal *(copyright © Brian Morse 1971; reprinted by permission of the author and The Thimble Press, Lockwood Station Road, South Woodchester, Glos. GL5 5EQ, England), September, 1971, pp. 102-13.*

[Ted Hughes is] a major poet of the first rank, a worthy successor to the great English poets of the first half of the century, Yeats, Lawrence and Eliot. (p. 1)

I believe Hughes to be a great poet because he possesses the kind of imagination which issues in the purest poetry, charged poetry, visionary, revelatory poetry that sees into the life of things, that takes over where all other modes of apprehending reality falter. Words, though controlled up to a point, are allowed to retain a life of their own and express more than the poet consciously knows. His imagination, which draws on his unconscious, on the racial unconscious, on his sixth sense and perhaps innumerable further senses, speaks through him. He is, in a word, 'inspired', though the word is not now fashionable. He performs a function essential to the race, a function analogous to that performed in more 'primitive' cultures by the shaman, whose function is to make the dangerous journey, on behalf of his society, into the spirit world, which is to say, into his own unconscious. . . . (p. 3)

> *Keith Sagar, in his introduction to his* The Art of Ted Hughes *(© Cambridge University Press 1975), Cambridge University Press, 1975, pp. 1-5.*

HOW THE WHALE BECAME (British Edition, 1963; US Edition, 1964)

Young children love nothing better than the mythical explanation of scientific fact; the legend serves to feed their sense of fantasy and discloses a poetic truth which in itself is revealing of life and intensely satisfying. Ted Hughes, for the first time leaving verse for prose, has not in fact left the world of poetry. His collection of eleven short stories is about the days just after the Creation when the air sparkled 'because it had never been used,' and the animals had to decide what they wanted to be. The situation suits the imagination of the poet-author. Economically told and wittily, without condescension, in a language which is vivid and precise, the stories never preach, yet they comment upon the vain, the treacherous, the proud and the cunning, and children will delight to know why the bee must still go from flower to flower seeking sweetness to stop his sorrow and why the elephant remained himself, shy, but strong and clever and kind. Excellent for reading aloud. . . . (p. 98)

> *Laurence Adkins, in* The School Librarian and School Library Review, *March, 1964.*

These 11 enchanting stories deserve to take their place among the classic fables. They come alive because they are rooted in the fundamental truth of the need for identity, and they illustrate the happiness that comes when we stop pretending to be something we are not and start being ourselves. The animals in each allegory emerge with humanness. . . . From the haunting beauty that tells about Hare's courtship of the Moon to the deliciously funny tale of Polar Bear with a crowd of young admirers hanging around her cave—mainly seals and all very giddy—every reader will find a particular favorite. Rick Schreiter's illustrations are strong and handsome. (p. 38)

> *Gloria Vanderbilt, in* The New York Times Book Review *(© 1964 by The New York Times Company; reprinted by permission), November 8, 1964.*

OTHER CITATIONS

Margaret Sherwood Libby, in Book Week, *November 22, 1964, p. 20.*

Janet Adam Smith, in The New York Review of Books, *December 3, 1964, p. 14.*

THE IRON GIANT: A STORY IN FIVE NIGHTS (1968)

This stark "Story in five nights" has the concentration of mood and the economy of detail belonging to poetry; it could be defined as an anti-war poem with the theme implied through the story and openly stated at the end. With the simplicity of myth Ted Hughes describes the giant who stalks through a seaside village chewing up farm machinery until young Hogarth, the farmer's son (a nice substitute for the fairy-tale younger son), remembers the nearby rubbish-tip. Pacified by a generous supple of rusty metal, the iron man is ready to help mankind when a space-bat-angel appears and the duel that follows is described in forceful terms which do not conceal the important meaning. This is a fantasy which invites thought through feeling and the drawings [by George Adamson] are as strong as the text. (p. 1176)

> *Margery Fisher, in her* Growing Point, *March, 1968.*

Ted Hughes's new book *The Iron Man* [British title] is . . . designed for bedtime reading. It is subtitled "A Story in Five Nights" and was told to the writer's children, who must be tougher than most. Faber [the publisher of the British edition] rightly murmur in the blurb: "Some parents will think it too exciting for bedtime reading." Exciting it is indeed, and frightening too. . . .

This is obviously not a book to appeal to every child, but it is the best in the batch [which also includes Gladys Williams's *Semolina Silkpaws*, Katjia Beskow's *The Astonishing Adventures of Patrick the Mouse*, and Dorothy Carnegie's *Kako the Cockatoo*]—the only one, really, that *had* to be published, that will indeed make children think and feel. It is the only one which could not have been written by anyone else. This is true novelty. If only the young would be eager for it. (p. 256)

> The Times Literary Supplement *(© Times Newspapers Ltd., 1968; reproduced from* The Times Literary Supplement *by permission), March 14, 1968.*

"The Iron Man came to the top of the cliff". With the first sentence of this story, Ted Hughes demands attention, and he holds it to the end. The style is vigorous, the language rich but not beyond the understanding of children who will be gripped by the story.... [*The Iron Man* is] the most original fable to have appeared for some time.

One point: the sub-title describes the book as "A Story in Five Nights"; but because the story is frightening in the telling, it should be gone through in one reading. It is well worth the time. (p. 139)

> *Mrs. P. M. Royds, in* Children's Book News *(copyright © 1968 by Children's Book Centre Ltd.), May-June, 1968.*

The robot of science fiction becomes the dragon slayer of traditional literature in this unconvincing pastiche. The Iron Giant, a self-perpetuating horror with a voracious appetite for metal, frightens earth until an even larger space-bat-dragon with an even bigger appetite appears.... In a lame and pretentious conclusion, the vanquished dragon reveals himself to be a pacifistic singer of the music of the spheres, momentarily confused by greedy, warring mankind. Despite the authentic chill developed by the foraging robot and a fine description of the dragon, this reads exactly as the jacket copy describes it, the bedtime improvisations of a fond father—which do not survive the translation to print. (p. 45)

> *Elva Harmon, in* School Library Journal *(reprinted from* School Library Journal, *December, 1968, published by R. R. Bowker Co., a Xerox company; copyright © 1968 by Xerox Corporation), December, 1968.*

The antagonists in this extraordinary, concentrated narrative are symbols rather than characters, for each means something different to every reader. For some, the crux of the story is the fact that the space-creature's singing turns aggressive man towards the idea of peace. For others, there is significance in the theme of the enemy who is seen to be a friend. Others may interpret the idea of reconciliation intellectually (as the growth of wisdom, perhaps) or emotionally, as the balance of ego and id. The 'seasoning' of 'an inner personality by fantasies' is the core of Ted Hughes's work. The metaphor, as large as the Iron Man himself, suggests that we need to discover the wholeness in life, to accept as essential the duality of good and evil, and above all, to see as a guiding force the power of imagination. In Ted Hughes's personal myth, created for himself and for his own children, each reader must find his own myth. (p. 142)

> *Margery Fisher, in her* Who's Who in Children's Books: A Treasury of the Familiar Characters of Childhood *(copyright © 1975 by Margery Fisher; reprinted by permission of Holt, Rinehart and Winston, Publishers), Holt, 1975.*

OTHER CITATIONS

Timothy Rogers, in The School Librarian, *July, 1968, p. 252.*

Polly Goodwin, in Book World, *February 23, 1969, p. 20.*

"Extracts from the Discussion Session with Ted Hughes,"

in Children's Literature in Education, *No. 1 (March), 1970, pp. 67-70.*

John Rowe Townsend, in his Written for Children: An Outline of English-Language Children's Literature, *revised edition, Lippincott, 1974, pp. 236-37.*

Fred Inglis, in The Times Literary Supplement, *March 25, 1977, p. 362.*

MEET MY FOLKS! (British Edition, 1961; US Edition, 1973)

From the sheer absurdity of Uncle Dan's useless inventions (a bottomless glass, a toothless saw, a rubber ladder) to the playful grotesquerie of a tearful octopus grandmother, the tone and the pace of Hughes' eccentric family album is brisk and jaunty; still, the casting of sister Jane as a crow is not the only hint that this is indeed the same blood-and-terror Ted Hughes—albeit on holiday. Although Mother's wildest feature is—disappointingly—her creativity in the kitchen (with such dishes as curried rattlesnake in Creme de la Cactus), Dad has a few hairy moments as Chief Inspector of Holes, and weirder yet are Aunt Dora who grows a prize weed that responds by devouring her, Uncle Mick who paints a tiger—and his roar—so lifelike that Uncle Mick is seen no more ..., and the "horrible ... yet very ordinary" Aunt Flo whose two personalities, the proper tea party-church choir spinster and the witch who hangs dried human parts in her attic, are described in alternate chapters that regularly break free of the rhyme scheme just as Aunt Flo breaks free of propriety.... Overall, both the regular form and the naughty grisliness give Hughes' folks an old-fashioned British tone, but that doesn't really reduce the fun of making their dotty acquaintance. (pp. 815-16)

> Kirkus Reviews *(copyright © 1973 The Kirkus Service, Inc.), August 1, 1973.*

OTHER CITATIONS

Margaret A. Dorsey, in School Library Journal, *September, 1973, p. 69.*

William Cole, in Saturday Review/World, *December 4, 1973, p. 29.*

John Rowe Townsend, in his Written for Children: An Outline of English-Language Children's Literature, *revised edition, Lippincott, 1974, p. 305.*

MOON-WHALES AND OTHER MOON POEMS (1976)

The poet has chosen the moon as a base for grossly exaggerated earthly forms, which he imagines living there.... Similar in theme or atmosphere, the poems, with their wit, fantasy, and richness of words and images, should be taken in small doses to permit the full savoring of the author's brilliance. The ink-line drawings of the specters and the monsters are completely in tune with the poetic conceptions. For young adults. (pp. 181-82)

> *Virginia Haviland, in* The Horn Book Magazine *(copyright © 1977 by the Horn Book, Inc., Boston), April, 1977.*

In an explosion of fantasy, the eminent British poet envisions the creatures, the customs, and the landscape of a lunatic world; his icy, eerie imagery is echoed by the grotesque, adroit pen and ink drawings of [Leonard] Baskin. The title poem begins, "They plough through the moon stuff / Just under the surface / Lifting the moon's skin / Like a muscle . . ." Here, and in some others of the poems, there is a sonorous felicity of phrase and conception. There is, however, a less familiar playfulness in some selections, an extravagance of concepts that almost leads to a suspicion that Hughes is having one on. It's not an even collection, but it is ebullient in a mood that is often macabre. Intriguing, at times awesomely splendid. (p. 143)

> *Zena Sutherland, in* Bulletin of the Center for Children's Books *(© 1977 by the University of Chicago; all rights reserved), May, 1977.*

OTHER CITATIONS

Booklist, *January 1, 1977, p. 667.*

NESSIE THE MONSTER (British Edition, 1964; US Edition, 1974)

Ted Hughes' poem about the Loch Ness monster [published in Britain as *Nessie the Mannerless Monster*] is aggressively contemporary and vulgar, with sprawling verses and harsh assonances, and a kind of rough wit. . . . They have drama and rude health, but much less than usual of the poetry of which he is capable. Children who are with it will love this book; most parents and teachers will wince. (p. 145)

> The Junior Bookshelf, *July, 1964.*

Though without the easy outrageousness of his *Meet My Folks* . . . , this unastonished chronicle of the Loch Ness monster's preposterous roadside encounters is likely to appeal both to very young children who will take it straight and to others who appreciate a more subtle kind of playfulness. (For a start, the lines don't regularly rhyme, but any five or ten or so consecutive ones will end with the same consonant.) . . . Jan Pyk's black and white line towns and people have a suitably straightfaced and self-important silliness, and his green-curlicue-on-green saurian Nessie brightens the pages in a spiffy, decorative use of one-color illustration. (p. 105)

> Kirkus Reviews *(copyright © 1974 The Kirkus Service, Inc.), February 1, 1974.*

OTHER CITATIONS

The Booklist, *April 1, 1974, p. 874.*

POETRY IS (British Edition, 1967; US Edition, 1970)

When (as happens only too rarely) one or two textbooks rise so far above the general level as to be worth while, even distinguished, in themselves—and perhaps even readable by adults for their own sake—there is reason to rejoice.

Ted Hughes's *Poetry in the Making* [British title] is one such book. It is simply a collection of scripts delivered in the B.B.C. Schools "Listening and Writing" series, with one or two additional teachers' notes. But as an introduction for children to the point of poetry and the practice of

writing, and as a revelation of this poet's own outlook and methods, it is of special interest and value.

Beginning with a warning to teachers against setting any kind of stylistic ideal, Mr. Hughes proceeds to demonstrate that *not* "How to write" but "How to try to say what you really mean" should be the guiding principle. In a series of chapters built around poems by a number of writers including himself (he was given an autobiographical brief) he explores, colourfully and intensively, themes such as "Capturing Animals", "Wind and Weather" and "Writing about People". The purpose throughout is to lead on, via a discussion of the poems (which he does with riveting skill) to some direct encouragement to the children to think and write for themselves. He makes the whole venture seem enjoyable, and somehow urgent. . . .

[Hughes] does also ask a combination of intellectual rigour and near-Dionysian fervour, which makes writing seem a very dedicated, as well as a fascinating task. "Head-long, concentrated improvisation on a set theme" and "all-out flowing exertion" are his own methods, and ones which he repeatedly recommends to children. This book, with its excellent selection of poems and the poet's constantly stimulating commentaries, should prove valuable alike for teachers and—one ought to say it—very capable and imaginative children. (p. 262)

> The Times Literary Supplement *(© Times Newspapers Ltd., 1968; reproduced from* The Times Literary Supplement *by permission), March 14, 1968.*

Ted Hughes, whose powerful nature poems are known from his three adult books, presents in "Poetry Is" . . . the text of his talks on poetry for young people given over the B.B.C. It includes as illustration poems by Mr. Hughes and others which makes up a compact anthology. Mr. Hughes's prose, however, is rather metaphysical and sometimes murky; it appears to be aimed at the child who wants to write rather than read. The book is valuable, though, in asserting once again that there are no *poetic* subjects, that the stuff of poetry comes out of the stuff of living. (p. 55)

> *Thomas Lask, in* The New York Times Book Review, *Part II (© 1970 by The New York Times Company; reprinted by permission), November 8, 1970.*

All teachers of English who have searched for appropriate texts for teaching creative writing know how difficult it is to find helpful texts which do not prescribe rigid writing forms. For this reason, welcome *Poetry Is*. . . .

The low-keyed ease with which Hughes presents his ideas and his obvious reliance upon content rather than form as the basis for instruction should appeal to adolescents. I think a teacher may be tempted to distill Hughes' material and present it rather than allow the author to speak to students. Don't. The magic in this brief book is in the method of delivery as well as the material presented. Hughes is a master of prose style as well as poetry. Let the author speak to your students. I think poetry writing taught a la Hughes may be very exciting for adolescent writers. (p. 406)

> *John W. Conner, in* English Journal *(copyright © 1971 by The National Council of Teachers of English), March, 1971.*

OTHER CITATIONS

Julian Symons, in New Statesman, *February 9, 1968, pp. 178-79.*

Eve Merriam, in Book World, *Part II, November 8, 1970, p. 5.*

Publishers Weekly, *November 16, 1970, p. 77.*

Paul Heins, in The Horn Book Magazine, *February, 1971, p. 57.*

SEASON SONGS (1975)

What a team the painter [Leonard Baskin] and the poet make. It's hard to think of a better place to put $10 than this exquisite book, even if you have to skip lunch. Ted Hughes has written six songs for each of the four seasons. He begins appropriately with Spring, the time of birth, and the lyrics are fresh, underivative, equaled only in imagination by the splendor of Leonard Baskin's watercolors. . . . This treasure of a book continues through Summer, Autumn and Winter in words and pictures one absorbs like music. (p. 85)

> *Jean F. Mercier, in* Publishers Weekly (*reprinted from the October 6, 1975, issue of* Publishers Weekly *by permission of the critic, published by R. R. Bowker Company, a Xerox company; copyright © 1975 by Xerox Corporation), October 6, 1975.*

[In] "Season Songs," [Hughes] has written a cycle of children's poems—a category I would be hard put to defend for this book—that is a kind of modern shepherd's calendar. It reviews the year from spring through winter: the birth of a calf, the death of a lamb, sheep shearing, the turbulent winds of March, the growing and cutting down of the wheat, the death of leaves in autumn, the search for salmon in the frigid waters of December.

The verse could not be more spare, compact. There is little easy music in these lines, no Tennyson's "Brook." Single syllabled words mark the stanzas as sharply as incised lines on stone. But more notable than the texture of the verse is the poet's unbending vision. Describing the death of the lamb, he writes:

> Death was more interesting to him.
> Life could not get his attention.
> So he died,
>   with the yellow birth-mucous
> Still in his cardigan. . . .

Not all the poems are in [a] violent vein. "The River in March" with its refrain, "Now the river is rich," "now the river is poor" suggests the lovely meandering quality of the stream, and in "Snow and Snow," snowfall transforms and pacifies all that it covers. But "Season Songs" is not a tranquil volume nor a benign one. The young reader who responds to "The Stag" may flinch from the image of the winded buck fleeing the hounds. But he will remember the poem. The same judgment can be made for the entire book.

"Season Songs" is beautifully printed, and Leonard Baskin, long associated with Mr. Hughes, has provided the illustrations in his characteristic vein—a fact that many will consider an added virtue for the book. It is a volume of genuine originality and distinction. (p. 8)

> *Thomas Lask, in* The New York Times Book Review (© *1975 by The New York Times Company; reprinted by permission), December 21, 1975.*

Old and new poems by the eminent British poet are grouped by seasons and are superbly illustrated by paintings and drawings that have a grand simplicity of composition, subtle use of color and line, and a felicitous evocation of mood. The latter quality is one of the most notable achievements of the poems as well; in the autumn poem, "The Seven Sorrows," for example, Hughes creates a vivid picture of the faint melancholy, the stillness of dying life forms, the end of the golden time of year. All of the poems have a singing quality and an awareness of the natural world that is communicated through sharp, illuminating phrases and concepts. (p. 98)

> *Zena Sutherland, in* Bulletin of the Center for Children's Books (© *1976 by the University of Chicago; all rights reserved), February, 1976.*

The temptation [with *Season Songs*] is to quote, but there would be no end of quotations because this is one of those books encountered once in a generation. And Hughes is not easy to classify. He belongs to no school. He is his own man and apparently adheres to no popular literary movement. The poems included here are, as the title suggests, distilled from the Devon countryside, a region of unique charm and natural beauty. They are more than image, color, sound: they are alive with whatever it is that vibrates on the downs of Devon. Hughes does not describe; he evokes and enchants. The one book that comes most vividly to mind as one reads these pages is Blake's *Songs of Innocence*. (p. 1572)

> Choice (*copyright © 1976 by American Library Association), February 1976.*

Celebrating the four seasons of the year, the poet has written sensitive, meditative, and lyrical verses about animals, plants, birds, fish, weather, and personal moods. . . . Close to the phenomena of nature, faithful to the freshness and imminence of the poet's observations, the poems are deftly woven webs of words that call for a reader attuned to their subtleties of expression and form. The watercolor paintings are neither illustrations nor decorations but modulated color equivalents of the moods and creatures held captive by the verses. (pp. 172-73)

> *Paul Heins, in* The Horn Book Magazine (*copyright © 1976 by the Horn Book, Inc., Boston), April, 1976.*

The jaded calendar revolves, as MacNeice said long ago. Yet, all things considered, the seasons' greetings continue to be most welcome, and their rotating sights and sounds persistently affecting. The repetition of their wonders, the surefire message in their growing up and dying back, and the quarterly pull of the heart-strings, annually charge the imagination, and the mistake. It is not at all surprising that poets see in them the ideal format for containing messages and conceits, and that words made to circle around in monthly patterns should prove to be so accessible to poetry readers. It is said that the most famous of *Seasons*, [James] Thomson's, was among the most civilising factors of the 18th century. But long before and long after this, poets have been driven to 'take the measure of the year', as Keats put it.

Ted Hughes began to do this when asked to write the words for Richard Drakeford's *Five Autumn Songs,* sung by children at the harvest festival at Little Missenden in 1968. With *Crow* out of the way, in 1970, Hughes could return to the addition of spring, summer and winter for boys and girls. Children retain more of the old seasonality than adults. Their year is very, very long and its changes are still heavily incised with the old metaphor. Hughes allows all the traditional treats, but typically sets them on edge with shots of acid. Life is sweet but death is likely. As Beatrix Potter remarked, when telling the truth and not one of her tales: 'Every lamb that is born, is born to have its throat cut.' There speaks the shepherdess.

For Hughes, too, from January to December there is plenty of murder about, and don't let the idyllists tell you otherwise. But—he adds—see, watch, hug to yourself the glory of beast and plant before the knives flash. . . .

Hughes's seasons are cheerfully agrarian. The agricultural clock rotates his vision, both keeping nature in check and seeing that it makes a profit. Animals and shoots grow up in order to be mown down, but all around are insects, birds and weeds caught in a different action. Everything is fair, but nothing lasts. For so much and so many, there is no second spring. The actual rural detail is frequently reminiscent of [John] Clare in his *Shepherd's Calendar.* . . .

To use Clare's fine description, 'young things of tender life' enter Hughes's west-country acres much as they have always done; it is their exits which have a 20th-century difference. Abattoir, spray, combine-harvester and the genteel brutalities of the Exmoor hunt attack seed and bone, and then it all begins again. The young, immersed in these brilliant pages, might well blanch at the thought of such a roundabout. Particularly when it starts off with the wild mares who

> Stand stupid with bliss
> Among the first miraculous foal-flowers. . . .

In 'The Golden Boy', his Frazer poem, when the corn is miserably buried so that it can be born, nursed by the Lord's mother until it is tall and strong, and petted and made much of by men until the harvest morning, Hughes enters the dancing ruthlessness of the child as he bites off the head of gingerbread and jelly-baby.

> With terrible steel
>   They slew him in the furrow
> With terrible steel
>   They beat his bones from him
> With terrible steel
>   They ground him to powder
> They baked him in ovens
>   They sliced him on tables
> They ate him they ate him
>   They ate him they ate him. . . .

A juvenile vocabulary to suit such pragmatism is introduced throughout these poems to roughup the mature language, words like *cronks, wobbles, buzz, skid, bang, goggles, honked, lobs, bulges* and—often—*bounce.* And such things as a child's ennui in a car, either when it is jerking along in the car-serpent from the day by the sea, or following a stag hunt in the pouring rain, are made to reveal that the country holiday has its hell when you are small.

The collection ends elegiacally and magically. Conkers are ravishingly elevated—

> The chestnut splits its padded cell.
> It opens an African eye.
>
> A cabinet-maker, an old master
> In the root of things, has done it again.

A dreaming boy's skies, 'the vast soft armistice, like an Empire on the move', make way for what is to come and declare what is to go. Leaves first. ('O leaves,' Crow sang, tremblingly, 'O leaves . . . ') Soon 'carols shake your television' and 'the worst cold's to come.' The four quarters of the year are passed times. Everyone, except children, sleep, wait.

> *Ronald Blythe, "The Grass Is Happy," in* The Listener (© *British Broadcasting Corp. 1976; reprinted by permission of Ronald Blythe), May 20, 1976, p. 651.*

OTHER CITATIONS

Merrie Lou Cohen, in School Library Journal, *December, 1975, p. 52.*

Dennis Dunn, in Encounter, *November, 1976, pp. 78-80.*

THE TIGER'S BONES, AND OTHER PLAYS FOR CHILDREN
(British Edition, 1970; US Edition, 1974)

Because of the very special demands involved in constructing a play (one is a playwright, but not a poemwright or novelwright, etc.), it is simply not enough to be a good writer, not enough to be a sensitive and thoughtful poet, not enough to have a "significant" message handed down to an audience from a mountaintop upstage center. One must know how to put a play together. And Ted Hughes does not. His words are often lovely; but, with rare exception, his characters show little growth; and, with no exception, his plots are gratuitous.

Something happens, not because the events worked out that way, but because it seemed like a good idea at the time, as if one were free to develop a children's play by tossing in whatever the fancy pumps up. Even in children's theatre, where fantasy can have a different kind of run, the work needs to develop organically from end to end, one step following the next, not one step left out.

But, in this collection of ex-radio plays, there are tremendous gaps. The plays begin and end, but lack a middle. Sometimes, as in *The Tiger's Bones* [published in Britain as *The Coming of the Kings, and Other Plays*], there seem to be two different plays. We know much more about the peripheral characters in *Beauty and the Beast* than the central ones, so love and transformation become a mere change of costume. A wonderfully bizarre devil enters midway through *Sean, the Fool, the Devil, and the Cats* for a three-page monologue, then we never see him again. It's no wonder. The monologue is, essentially, narrative. In three pages, we never see this devil act on anything or with anyone. His being there affects nothing. He simply talks himself out of the play.

Hughes' promiscuous use of a narrator, in one guise or another, in every single play, is like hunting hummingbirds with a howitzer. It might be fine for radio; but, on stage, the play is blown away. It would be so simple to convert just about every narrative passage into a real scene. In Story Theatre, the narrator is actually a part of the drama, weaving in and out of every scene, totally and actively involved (somewhat like Tevye in *Fiddler on the Roof,* to choose another style). Language is dialogue, a part of the dramatic process, but never used for its own sake. One of the ironies of theatre is that beautiful words, unless they are an integral part of the entire theatrical package, can ground a play as surely as pig-iron.

Mr. Hughes makes the mistake of telling us practically everything, including the message; and, in case the slower children don't get it, he'll often tell it again. His words do all the work. Either he doesn't trust the machinery of the stage, or he doesn't know how to use it, for theatre becomes poetry only when every one of its elements actively combines to form the image, not otherwise. Pure poetry is filet mignon; theatre is poetry on the hoof.

Ted Hughes must be given credit for attempting to create intelligent, imaginative and gutsy plays for children. Though he often mistakes bald ideology for dramatic substance, compared to Clutch Cargo and all the other kiddie garbage oozing out of our culture, his work is a relief. Unfortunately, that isn't enough. Only one play is more: *Orpheus.* There is mystery in this work, transcendence. It grows beyond the earth; and, for all its flaws, it moves us within whispering distance of the life-song. Death, distant as a sunset, close as a dawn, sings, too. It is a play to make a child wonder. Orpheus' music becomes the music of the universe, and that is an exquisite thing. (pp. 210-11)

> *Stephen Howard Foreman, in* Children's Literature: Annual of The Modern Language Association Seminar on Children's Literature and The Children's Literature Association, *Vol. 3, edited by Francelia Butler (© 1974 by Francelia Butler; all rights reserved), Temple University Press, 1974.*

OTHER CITATIONS

"Acting Words," in The Times Literary Supplement, *October 30, 1970, p. 1253.*

The Junior Bookshelf, *December, 1970, pp. 372-73.*

Kirkus Reviews, *January 1, 1974, p. 7.*

Paul Heins, in The Horn Book Magazine, *April, 1974, p. 155.*

The Booklist, *April 1, 1974, pp. 874-75.*

* * *

HUNTER, Kristin   1931-

Kristin Hunter is a Black American author of fiction and short stories for adults and children, as well as a lecturer and a teacher of creative writing. Starting at the age of 14, she wrote a regular column for the *Pittsburgh Courier* for six years. Her novel *The Soul Brothers and Sister Lou* was awarded both the 1968 Council on Interracial Books for Children Award and the 1971 Lewis Carroll Shelf Award. Hunter's *The Landlord,* an adult novel, was filmed in 1970. (See also *Contemporary Authors,* Vols. 13-16, rev. ed.)

AUTHOR'S COMMENTARY

[Top of the News]: Why do you write for older children?

[Kristin Hunter]: To avoid succumbing to the temptation to write down and be overly cute or condescending, therefore false. Older children can be addressed on an adult or near-adult level. I can literally "level" with them without watering down or falsifying my style or my content.

[TN]: Can a writer be too realistic?

[KH]: Yes, if he emphasizes "facts" at the expense of the deeper truths of felt life and the creative imagination. I deplore both the adult non-novels which are really compendiums of facts on airports, advertising, drugs, etc.—and the new children's books which emphasize rockets and computers instead of fantasy or people. Dull, dull, dull!

[TN]: Did you ever meet Sister Lou?

[KH]: No, except in my imagination, where large chunks of me and smaller chunks of all the other people I've known reside and occasionally combine in a mysterious way to generate fictional characters with a life of their own. . . .

[TN]: Contrast what you read as a child with books about black children today.

[KH]: There were no black children in the books I read as a child, though I remember a racist incident in one of the *Bobbsey Twins* books (involving their servants) that enraged me for months. I haven't seen any of today's books about black children except my own, but I hope they're peopled with three-dimensional characters, not just black-faced Dicks and Janes.

[TN]: What advice have you for future writers?

[KH]: Read all you can till you're 20, live all you can till you're 30, and write all you can after that. And fight all your life against regimentation, automation, and standardization—all the forms of the Machine which want to make you obsolete. (pp. 217-18)

> *"Kristin Hunter—Profile of an Author," in* Top of the News *(reprinted by permission of the American Library Association), January, 1970 (and reprinted in* Authors and Illustrators of Children's Books: Writings on Their Lives and Works, *edited by Miriam Hoffman and Eva Samuels, Bowker, 1972, pp. 217-19).*

BOSS CAT (1971)

A small issue of zoological racism divides the thoroughly and proudly black Tanner family (residents of the Benign Neglect Apartments) when Dad brings home a black cat and Mom maintains that it will bring bad luck. Though perhaps the contrast between well-informed Dad and superstitious, hysteria-prone Mom builds the image of black masculinity at the expense of the good name of motherhood (he consults the library, she goes to the House of Occult Help), the good natured domestic squabbling is believable enough. The family relishes their own ethnic jokes; relevance, for once, doesn't preclude humor; and Pharaoh the cat, an excellent mouser, turns out to be a real winner. (p. 1212)

> Kirkus Reviews *(copyright © 1971 The Kirkus Service, Inc.), November 15, 1971.*

With some suspense, humor and the pervading warmth of a close-knit family, [*Boss Cat*] is an account of the anxieties, fears, and frustrations of ghetto life, with an underlying sense that this family will survive. [Harold] Franklin's line drawings effectively illustrate the affection and spirit of this above-average family. However, the characters are one-dimensional: daddy is the courageous male yet tells romanticized stories about the good old days "Down Home in Georgia"; mom is called a "Doctor of Potsology" and, in her determination to keep her family well-fed, she is described in the most sexist terms possible; the twins are rotund ninnies; Tyrone, the only son, is brave and strong; and Baby Jewell does nothing but cry. Unfortunately, this blatant stereotyping seriously weakens the book. (p. 132)

> *Clare D. Rizzolo, in* School Library Journal *(reprinted from the September, 1972, issue of* School Library Journal, *published by R. R. Bowker Company, a Xerox company; copyright © 1972 by Xerox Corporation), September, 1972.*

OTHER CITATIONS

Publishers Weekly, *December 13, 1971, p. 43.*

Zena Sutherland, *in* Bulletin of the Center for Children's Books, *May, 1972, p. 140.*

Anne C. Weaver, *in* Childhood Education, *October, 1972, p. 28.*

GUESTS IN THE PROMISED LAND (1973)

Hunter seems to be sniping at everyone [in *Guests in the Promised Land*]: the whites who try so complacently to "help," the brothers and sisters who enforce conformity to a soul lifestyle, the striving oreos who lock their children out of both worlds. The most successful of these eleven variations on the theme of growing up black is the least heavy—an amusing first person account of a little boy's frustrated attempts to bury his white dog (named Bee-Gee for Brown Girl) in a cemetery for white people's pets. Elsewhere though, when the stories are not preoccupied with making racial points, they are most noticeable for their neatly constructed short story workshop quality—as in "Debut," which begins patly with "'Hold *still*, Judy,' Mrs. Simmons said around the spray of pins that protruded dangerously from her mouth" and goes on to document Judy's instant transformation from an innocent girl untouched by her mother's relentless upward-pushing to a cool bitch "dazzling (her date) with a smile of sweetest cruelty." In the title story some ghetto boys on a fresh air outing react to their benefactors' (white Jaycee's) hypocrisy by trashing their country club, but the piano-playing loner who touches off the violence is not fully enough realized to vitalize all the other stereotypes. . . . Which is not to say that the stories lack interest for YA readers or that they are below the level of "quality" teen magazine fiction. (p. 567)

> Kirkus Reviews *(copyright © 1973 The Kirkus Service, Inc.), May 15, 1973.*

[Kristin Hunter] has produced a series of short stories superb for their exploration of Black experience as well as for their art. . . . Ranging from humor and satire to indignation, the stories present various facets of lives that have been warped by a frustrating racial milieu and—at the same time—have gone beyond it into universal humanity. Most of the accounts have been presented in the first person, and Black English is freely used in their telling. (p. 386)

> *Paul Heins, in* The Horn Book Magazine *(copyright © 1973 by The Horn Book, Inc., Boston), August, 1973.*

This collection of short stories deals with black children who must come to terms with themselves and their lives. The stories are usually somber but never self-pitying and, by the end of each, the main character has a firm grip on the future, whether it's a positive ("The Scribe") or a negative one ("Debut"). The dialogue is perfectly suited to the characters, from street talk in "Hero's Return" to suburban patter in "Come Out of That Corner." Characterizations are well fleshed out, particularly in "Debut," "You Rap, I'll Reap," and "The Scribe," and the stories invite reader involvement. A good choice for slow junior high readers, Hunter's new book deserves a place on library shelves along with her *Soul Brothers and Sister Lou*. . . . (pp. 69-70)

> *Lynn B. Reamer, in* School Library Journal *(reprinted from* School Library Journal, *September, 1973, published by R. R. Bowker Co., a Xerox company; copyright © 1973 by Xerox Corporation), September, 1973.*

Kristin Hunter is an excellent storyteller and she does it with such an economy of words that she makes the form seem easy. But more important, she uses her terse style to speak to younger children and teenagers of limited attention spans with a directness and freshness which makes her a joy to read.

In *Guests in the Promised Land* . . ., Ms. Hunter has included 11 short stories which might be sub-titled vignettes of black life with a message. There is no way that one can overlook the point of these stories for the author never fails to drive home the thesis that humanity is the only consideration that matters in this topsy-turvy world—a deep abiding concern for one's fellowman and ultimately the human condition.

The stories linger in your sub-consciousness long after you have finished reading them. One such story is about a young girl dressing for her debut who reacts to her mother's fussiness by making the dance analogous to a battle. Mother replies: "It is a battle. It starts tonight and it goes on for the rest of your life. The battle to hold your head up and get someplace and be somebody." Or consider the 13-year-old lad, who, after tiring of seeing Blacks pay to have checks cashed, letters addressed, read or written, decides to open a free Public Scribe firm right in front of the established place of business. Or the young Black who discovers that he cannot dance, which is worse than sin among his own.

The absentee father, the grandmother figure, the social worker, the gossip, as well as the potentially dangerous subject of young Black-white relations, are all handled deftly by Ms. Hunter. One may even be led to sympathize with the small Black lad who plunges his pocket-knife into a beautiful piano at the all-white country club. Especially when the explanation lies in the fact that "it ain't no Promised Land at all if some people are always guests and others are always members."

In short, here are some thoroughly delightful stories that young readers of both races might read with pleasure and profit. (p. 91)

> *Huel D. Perkins, in* Black World *(copyright © September, 1974, by* Black World; *reprinted by permission of Johnson Publishing Company and Huel D. Perkins), September, 1974.*

OTHER CITATIONS

Mrs. John G. Gray, in Best Sellers, *April 15, 1973, pp. 45-6.*

Zena Sutherland, in Bulletin of the Center for Children's Books, *June, 1973, p. 156.*

Christina Carr Young, in Childhood Education, *October, 1973, p. 29.*

Elizabeth Minot Graves, in Commonweal, *November 23, 1973, p. 216.*

THE SOUL BROTHERS AND SISTER LOU (1968)

AUTHOR'S COMMENTARY

I've been asked to give some background of my book "The Soul Brothers and Sister Lou."

When it came to writing my first juvenile after two adult novels, I had some doubts and misgivings. For one thing, I thought my style was too adult for teenagers, and as it turns out, this *is* a rather adult book, but I'm glad. I've done a lot of speaking to teenagers in recent months, and I find they have pretty adult minds. Also, I was made to see this book as a comedown; while I was working on it, my adult-book writing friends teased me constantly about my "kiddie book." But now that it's done, I'm very pleased with the results. For me it represents the kind of personal growth any new venture produces when you go into it deeply and thoroughly and with complete commitment, and I think it represents a degree of professional growth as well, growth that will serve me well in future projects. And by writing about a lonely little light-skinned girl named Louretta Hawkins and the growth of her self-confidence and pride in her black identity, I feel I've been able to exorcise some of my own adolescent demons, some of which have persisted unconsciously into adulthood.

There is a lot of talk these days about "identity crises," but I don't think it's generally known that the most acute of them all is currently being gone through by black people. I don't mean black youth; I think the youngest black people have already gone through this crisis and come out whole. But it is my generation—people of my age, give or take ten years—who are having the most acute conflicts and fomenting the most violent rebellions. We are the last in line of generations of efforts to produce *white* black people—what Franz Fanon calls "black skins with white masks." Our parents mated selectively to produce offspring with white characteristics, in values and in appearance, and their parents did the same before them. Thus my generation was the last to make an all-out effort to be white, and as the last in line of this thrust, we traveled the farthest and suffered the most when we were eventually, inevitably, brought up short. We went to Ivy League schools; we spoke almost too-perfect English as well as French; we traveled in Europe; we socialized with whites; some of us even married them. Then came the inevitable day when we realized, individually and collectively, that it had all been to no avail. For me both events coincided. The public event was the failure of the Democratic convention to seat the Mississippi Freedom Democratic Party in Atlantic City in 1964; the private event that same year was much too painful and catastrophic to discuss. At any rate, all of us learned somewhere along the line that the white society would not let us be white. In its eyes we were still, in spite of our efforts, niggers. . . .

But we still had developed a white part that we could not amputate or deny, and the frustrations it caused kept us angry. This is the agony and the conflict of the people of my generation which may destroy this nation if it cannot be resolved.

But the aware young people—those in their early twenties and under—are not in that schizophrenic bag of trying to be white and digging being black at the same time. They are black, they are beautiful, they know it, and they are not divided about it, though they are united in their opposition to anyone who tells them that black is not beautiful and that their God-given personalities and preferences are wrong. It is for them I have written this book. (p. 30)

The nation within a nation that is called Negro America has suffered . . . indignities. It is constantly deplored, clucked over, studied and reformed, but never admired and appreciated for its own worth. When this kind of patronizing, condescending attitude lies behind programs for "improving" the ghetto, the programs won't work—and the children, being the most sensitive and the most all-out idealists, will be the first to rebel.

What they *will* accept right now is anything that confirms them in their new and rather desperate belief that in spite of all the things that have been said about them, in spite of all the racist assumptions held by the majority of this country's population, they *do* have worth and value. My book, in addition to being a work of fiction, with all the complexity that implies, is an attempt to confirm young black people in their frail but growing belief in their own self-worth.

For I have tried to show some of the positive values existing in the so-called ghetto—the closeness and warmth of family life, the willingness to extend help to strangers in trouble, even to take strange children into the home and care for them, the natural acceptance of life's problems and joys—and there is a great deal of joy in the ghetto—and the strong tradition of religious faith. All of these attitudes have combined to create the quality called "soul," which is the central theme of the book. . . .

In my book I have also shown some of the much-publicized negative side of ghetto life, of course, and I think the most out-and-out militants will not find it negative enough, particularly since I have allowed my heroine to halt the destructive course of her friends at one point. But I have never considered violence and destruction to be valuable in themselves, any more than I am convinced that success and acceptance in white America's terms are valuable enough to be worth *any* price. In the long run, of course, my opinions will not matter; if we are going to be destroyed, we will be. But I do feel that if all-out destruction is to be prevented, we cannot accomplish it by going to troubled people with smug attitudes that will only enrage them further. The sore point of racial inequality has to be eliminated at the source—the basic attitudes of superiority and inferiority cited in the recent Riot Commission Report. It has to be eliminated by treating all people, and particularly young black people, with the kind of respect for their integrity that is based on true appreciation of their worth. My book represents one small effort to accord them this respect and this appreciation. (p. 31)

> *Kristin Hunter, "'The Soul Brothers': Background of a Juvenile," in* Publishers Weekly *(reprinted from the May 27, 1968, issue of* Publishers Weekly *by permission of the critic, published by R. R. Bowker Company, a Xerox company; copyright © 1968 by Xerox Corporation; reprinted by permission of Harold Matson Co.), May 27, 1968, pp. 30-1.*

[*The Soul Brothers and Sister Lou* concerns the] misery and sweetness of growing up black—and if it sells *soul*, it also talks sense. Louretta Hawkins, at fourteen, is a nice girl who lives [Longfellow's] "Learn to labor and to wait" until the police raid the teenage club in her brother's print shop and, without provocation, shoot one of the boys; then she discards the homilies she's learned in school and adopts the hostile stance of an Outsider.... What saves her, however, is soul: she finds it in music; at a stomping, shouting funeral; finally in herself. The story could end here and perhaps should; the quick success of Louretta and three of the boys as a singing group, performing blues she and another boy have written, is no more than an appendage that allows for a few extra ironies. Subsumed within the story is the whole range of white and black attitudes, and Miss Hunter doesn't mince words: whites expecting gratitude, older Negroes awaiting the next world, militants welcoming a martyr—all get a going over. Not all-time literature, maybe, but in 1968 *this is it*. (p. 765)

> Kirkus Service *(copyright © 1968 The Kirkus Service, Inc.), July 15, 1968.*

Sister Lou is a girl you won't want to miss. And her story is one you'll be glad to know. Glad because Lou is quite a girl, a girl who faces loneliness in a northern city with courage, solves it with love—love for her family, love for music. It's a story that will be a revelation to many—it will reveal to them the heart of a black girl. [This is the] first novel for young readers by an author with two adult novels ["God Bless the Child" and "The Landlord"] to her credit—we hope from our heart it will not be the last. (p. 61)

> *Lavinia Russ, in* Publishers Weekly *(reprinted from the September 30, 1968, issue of* Publishers Weekly *by permission of the critic, published by R. R. Bowker Company, a Xerox company; copyright © 1968 by Xerox Corporation), September 30, 1968.*

Lou and the boys [being] tabbed for a successful career when they sing at the funeral of the slain gang member [is] a too-pat ending for a book that is honest, convincing, and incisive. Actually, the plot is of less importance than the depiction in the book of the maturing of a young girl who learns to appreciate her racial heritage during those difficult years when self-acceptance and self-identity are problems

for all adolescents. This is indeed a book for our times. (p. 37)

> *Zena Sutherland, in* Saturday Review *(copyright © 1968 by Saturday Review, Inc.; reprinted with permission), October 19, 1968.*

With mixed success, this novel jumps head-on into the main concerns of ghetto youth today: Black identity and militancy.... Unfortunately, militancy is unpersuasively made to seem the result of personal failure, merely a stage to be passed through, and militants are portrayed in superficial terms which reinforce fears aroused by the mass media: girls wear Afros and "huge earrings swinging like knives," men are "hairy figures," the friend's death is not regretted by Fess who thinks it beneficial to the movement. Though militancy plays a large part in the story, it is a fictional fragmentation, far from a complete presentation of the philosophy or the motivations of its adherents. Such a flaw is especially regrettable since this is one of the few juvenile books attempting to present the culture of the ghetto rather than merely its economic impoverishment. The language, music, family relationships, joys and problems will be familiar to many readers from the ghetto and will give others insight through the sympathetic and believable characterization of Lou. (p. 101)

> *Susan O'Neal, in* School Library Journal *(reprinted from* School Library Journal, *November, 1968, published by R. R. Bowker Co., a Xerox company; copyright © 1968 by Xerox Corporation), November, 1968.*

In *Soul Brothers and Sister Lou,* the ghetto culture is graphically depicted and the main character and her search for self-identity are realistic. The drawbacks lie in the one-dimensional treatment of the minor characters, an unrelenting series of melodramatic situations, a hastily compiled ending, and a kind of immediacy of response to pleasure and pain that cheats the reader of the experience of real tragedy. These flaws weigh more heavily for some readers than for others, but many readers can use this story as a bridge from pure pulp fiction to the excellent black fiction written for adults. (p. 423)

> *Judith Thompson and Gloria Woodard, in* Wilson Library Bulletin *(copyright © 1969 by the H. W. Wilson Company), December, 1969.*

The author has tried too hard in this reasonably accurate picture of life in a Negro ghetto in one of the American cities. Her aim seems directed against the Black Power Movement (though she never names it) and the alternative she proposes for the salvation of her young characters is through the formation of a successful pop group; yet at the end of the book she admits that this is not the answer either. In short, here is a writer, anxious to turn her talents to improving the lot of the black American, fumbling for a solution which none of us has yet found. And while it is refreshing to find a story in which the Cinderella myth with its happy-ever-after ending is questioned, the manner in which this author expresses her doubts merely adds an awkward finish to an otherwise well-rounded book. However, ignoring the wider issues, young teenagers may well enjoy the story which has some exciting moments as well as a few dulled ones like Mr. Lucitanno's music lesson, and tension builds up to a climax with the brutality of the police and the reaction of the gang of boys, making the reading easy and the reader likely to devour it in one sitting. Of course, as in most tracts, the characters are pegs on which to hang a bit of special pleading, and none of them really comes to life, neither Lou the heroine nor her tarty sister who finds the dust and ashes of Hollywood, nor her good brother Will nor even the fanatical Fess whose ''reformation'' is hardest of all to give credence to. Notwithstanding all this, if there are any readers of any age who in spite of television have not the slightest inkling of what black America is like, this story will begin to tell them. (p. 111)

> *The Junior Bookshelf, April, 1971.*

For the teacher who is attempting to introduce aspects of Black culture to students who have limited racial experiences, I would recommend using the adolescent novel *The Soul Brothers and Sister Lou* by Kristin Hunter. The novel touches on the following areas in Black culture that could be explored by the class as a whole or by small groups which could then share their findings: general ghetto conditions, folklore, literature, media, and levels of Black awareness or thought.

In terms of general ghetto conditions, the novel points to institutional racism (crowded living conditions, prevalence of diseases, lack of balanced diets), the nature of gangs, survival means (welfare, numbers racket, illegal wine), and ''outsiders,'' those who have totally succumbed to the forces of oppression. Folklore and ''soul'' are illustrated in the characters' verbal dexterity, dancing, and music, especially the blues. The history of Black music is conveyed through the character of Blind Eddie Bell, an old blues singer. When challenged to name Black authors, Lou cannot, thus displaying the mis-education that occurs in literature courses. Two questions emerge: Who are the Black authors? and why is their literature not taught? In the novel, the media plays both negative and positive roles. Lou is struck by the unreality of what is shown on television in comparison to her own life. On the other hand, the newspaper serves as a tool for education (Black history and Black literature) and for action (community reaction to Jethro being killed by a policeman). Many levels of Black awareness or thought are portrayed through the characters including: attitudes toward religion, social positions, and education; inter- and intra-racial tensions; reactions toward the police; militancy; and the ignorance of many whites.

Focusing on these areas would provide an adequate base for the teacher to build a beginning understanding of Black culture. There are, however, some limitations in the novel that the teacher should be aware of, the major one being that it does not present the Black dialect. The teacher should supplement or follow up this novel with another that does portray Black speech patterns, such as *His Own Where* by June Jordan, *A Hero Ain't Nothing But a Sandwich* by Alice Childress, or *Snakes* by Al Young. Other limitations are the attitude presented toward Black women, the comments directed against mothers, and the somewhat datedness of the novel (e.g., drugs are not mentioned).

Because it is easy reading and because it presents elements of Black culture in a non-threatening but realistic manner, *The Soul Brothers and Sister Lou* is an excellent device for developing students' cultural awareness. After reading it, students will be prepared and eager to move on to more complex and more forceful works. (p. 61)

> *Nedra Stimpfle, in* English Journal *(copyright © 1977 by The National Council of Teachers of English), March, 1977.*

OTHER CITATIONS

Best Sellers, *October 1, 1968, p. 277.*

Polly Goodwin, in Book World, *November 3, 1968, p. 20.*

Robert Bell, in The School Librarian, *September, 1970, p. 260.*

Ann Thwaite, in New Statesman, *March 5, 1971, p. 312.*

May Hill Arbuthnot and Zena Sutherland, in their Children and Books, *fourth edition, Scott, Foresman, 1972, pp. 467-68.*

James A. Banks, in Educational Leadership, *April, 1974, pp. 593-94.*

THE SURVIVORS (1975)

[*The Survivors* is a] sentimental ghetto tale about a lonely middle-aged dressmaker and a thirteen-year-old street boy and how the two independent ''survivors'' find each other and themselves.... In spite of the heavy hand of coincidence, and the Valentine ending (admittedly with a wry twist), the author saves a damp tale from mawkishness with some grainy inner-city insights. A *Good Times* lift for hard times escape. (p. 322)

> Kirkus Reviews *(copyright © 1975 The Kirkus Service, Inc.), March 15, 1975.*

Kristin Hunter, whose *The Soul Brothers and Sister Lou* ... proved a hit with adolescent readers, has here created a novel sure to attract film and/or television production.... One is not surprised that Hunter teaches creative writing, so gifted is she in ''specificity,'' though some characters tend to be flat, for example B. J.'s incredible wino father Jayjay, and the junior Superfly, Bobo. Were the book conceived from a ''central intelligence,'' its motivation might be more convincing, but the comic sense throughout saves the story, which usually manages to avoid sentimentality. (pp. 999-1000)

> Choice *(copyright © 1975 American Library Association), October, 1975.*

Scribner's is marketing *The Survivors* as an adult novel and no doubt Kristin Hunter meant it as such, but for all its realism, it is essentially a long junior novel. The theme—friendship between an adult and a child—has by this time become familiar, but not so familiar that it fails to delight. Miss Lena Ricks, middle-aged industrious dressmaker, and B. J., 13-year-old street kid, meet when B. J. is sent to stake out Miss Lena's home and business establishment for a robbery. From that initial meeting their lives become more and more interdependent. Because these two characters are so well drawn and fleshed out, most readers will care about Miss Lena's and B. J.'s shared experiences and growing need for each other. Inspiring in the best sense of the word, *The Survivors* should appeal to many people, from junior high school age to adult. (pp. 115, 175)

> *Gary Bogart, in* Wilson Library Bulletin *(copyright © 1975 by the H. W. Wilson Company), October, 1975.*

When a street-wise thirteen year old kid named B.J. (short for Bond Jewelers) enters the comfortable dress shop of Miss Lena Ricks and adopts her, a new life begins for both; and an appealing story unwinds for Kristin Hunter's readers.

Hunter gives us two main characters who represent very different manners of survival in the black inner city and a glimpse of the spectrum of lifestyles in between. But what she really provides is a character study of Miss Lena, a successful but otherwise drab, self-made entrepreneur whose justifiably hardened personality cracks and mellows under B. J.'s omnipresence. A theme of understanding people's many needs and ways of coming to grips with life develops.

Although B. J. and Lena do not always seem believable, and other characters suffer from considerable stereotyping, their story and its gentle humor will probably appeal to most young adult readers of black and/or city life—except perhaps those who read *Down These Mean Streets* portrayals exclusively. Recommended for secondary schools and public library young adult collections. (p. 9)

> *Janet Leonberger, in* Young Adult Cooperative Book Review, *October, 1975.*

OTHER CITATIONS

The Booklist, *May 15, 1975, p. 941.*

Melody E. Hardy, in Best Sellers, *October, 1975, p. 197.*

K

KRAHN, Fernando 1935-

Fernando Krahn is a Chilean artist and writer whose formal training was in stage design. He illustrates his own, often wordless, picture books as well as children's books by other authors. He has also drawn cartoons for national magazines, such as *The New Yorker* and *The Atlantic Monthly*. Maria de la Luz Krahn, his wife, has collaborated with him on several books. (See also *Contemporary Authors*, Vols. 65-68.)

GENERAL COMMENTARY

An exception [to wordless books that "are slight, with nothing to convey that extends beyond their covers"] is the work of Fernando Krahn, the Chilean cartoonist active in New York in the Sixties. *Journeys of Sebastian*, Krahn's first independent effort, takes place entirely in Sebastian's head; or rather as fancy takes him, so he goes. . . . There was a bee buzzing around his head to start with; and at the close, after flying off with the mum-mum-men (or whatever you like) to a giant garden and falling from a cut flower, he is on the floor holding the flower in his hand. What do you think of that! The second journey moves through mirrors; and the third finds him finding a string hanging from a hole . . . that, pulled, becomes the tail of a rubbery monster . . . that takes Sebastian, along with the mum-mums (mounted on like monsters), on a steeple-chase over rivers and rooftops to victory, and a victor's cup . . . that the monster slides into, until only the end of his tail hangs over the edge. Inexplicable? ask a child.

There's a little of Edward Gorey in *Journeys of Sebastian*, and a little of Dr. Seuss: Krahn is an original who can make the oddest twain meet. A natural mimic besides. *Gustavus and Stop* . . . is broad old-time cartooning (pre-*Night Kitchen*) set up with brief captions—worded like silent film titles—to tell, mostly in pictures, about a little boy, Gustavus, and his dog, Stop, and their efforts to become circus clowns. Dog beats boy, that's the story; but the interest is, one by one, in the sobersides comedy of the cartoon frames.

With or without words, the books make something individual of their particular form. The least venturesome but, not surprisingly, the one with the widest appeal is *How Santa Claus Had a Long and Difficult Journey Delivering His Presents*. Krahn uses color emblematically too, and economically. *How Santa Claus . . .* looks as if it belongs under the tree by virtue of vivid red endpapers, just-as-green sheets opposite the illustrations and—when a bell-ringing bear wakes Santa and helps him dress—a red, naturally, Santa Claus suit. A merry Christmas book of drawings. . . .

What happened was that the traces snapped and the reindeer flew off without the sled; and the toy airplanes tried and couldn't get it off the ground; and the dolls and animals marched out of the sack and picked Santa up; and the sled, righted, ran into a snowbank; *and what shall we do now?* The answer is angels but there's no hurry about finding it: each of the drawings, displayed singly, is to look at and laugh at and look over: to 'read,' in other words, not like a road sign but like a book. (pp. 540-42)

> Barbara Bader, in American Picturebooks from Noah's Ark to the Beast Within *(reprinted with permission of Macmillan Publishing Co., Inc.; copyright © 1976 by Barbara Bader), Macmillan, 1976.*

APRIL FOOLS (1974)

Fernando Krahn's story in pictures of two boys who put on their fellow citizens with a homemade monster has more narrative interest and incidental wit than most wordless picture books. From the boys' secret construction of a dragon-like head on a long green neck, which then surfaces in several sly but conspicuous appearances around town, to their triumphant autocade return after the creature has rescued them from being lost in the woods—kids won't take their eyes off that silly inert beast except to check the reactions of the spectators and the ingenuity of the two young perpetrators. (p. 419)

> Kirkus Reviews *(copyright © 1974 The Kirkus Service, Inc.), April 15, 1974.*

OTHER CITATIONS

Jean Mercier, in Publishers Weekly, *May 6, 1974, p. 69.*

The Booklist, *May 15, 1974, p. 1057.*

THE FIRST PEKO-NEKO BIRD (with Maria de la Luz Krahn, 1969)

I saw and laughed at the oddball line drawing of Fernando

Krahn when his work first arrived here from Chile about half a dozen years ago. As far as I'm concerned, it is the country's major export. Nitrate isn't very funny, anyway, whereas a Krahn interpretation of just a tree or a rock is a joke in itself. He has applied his sense of humor to "The First Peko-Neko Bird" . . ., which he and his wife, Maria de la Luz, wrote to accompany his cartoony illustrations. The bird is hatched in a forest where no bird has ever been before. Without precedent, he knows not who or what he is. He finds out. Children should giggle at this shaggy-bird story. (p. 69)

> *Jerome Beatty, Jr., in* The New York Times Book Review, *Part II (© 1969 by The New York Times Company; reprinted by permission), November 9, 1969.*

A FLYING SAUCER FULL OF SPAGHETTI (1970)

["*A Flying Saucer Full of Spaghetti*" is another] superbly silly book; the title gives fair warning there are giggles waiting within its covers. The illustrations need no captions, so Fernando Krahn omitted them. The pictures of the effect a flying saucer full of spaghetti has on a little girl and on the town in which she lives can spark laughter very well on their own, as those who remember Mr. Krahn's illustrations for other people's stories know. . . . (p. 50)

> *Lavinia Russ, in* Publishers Weekly *(reprinted from the August 17, 1970, issue of* Publishers Weekly *by permission of the critic, published by R. R. Bowker Company, a Xerox company; copyright © 1970 by Xerox Corporation, August 17, 1970.*

[*A Flying Saucer Full of Spaghetti* is a] story without words, and a good one. For once this is no gimmick but a story finding its natural form for expression. A family of rather horrid gnomes take pity on a hungry poor girl. They visit a poor little rich girl who refuses to eat her spaghetti, entertain her with some hilarious tricks, then take spaghetti and saucer and deliver them to the hungry child. The drawing has a badness which is so complete as to become a virtue. The humour is the greater for being presented without a flicker of a smile. A nice book. (pp. 369-70)

> The Junior Bookshelf, *December, 1972.*

HILDEGARDE AND MAXIMILIAN (1970)

There's economy (viz. M. B. Goffstein) and then there's penury . . . as per the courtship, aborted moon probe and contented parenthood of Lord Maximilian Bug and Lady Hildegarde Bug [in *Hildegarde and Maximilian*]. Known—and colored—as Maximilian the Yellow and Hildegarde the Red until their ceremonial dubbing by Queen Bee, a sample of Mr. Krahn's ready wit as the drawings are indicative of a considerable talent that has not as yet found a comparable story. Ostensibly (i.e. according to the jacket) domestic bliss dims a longing for the moon; in fact, the moon flight appears as Maximilian's sudden whim, and the children—notwithstanding a brief pause on a branch—as somehow the issue of it. Altogether up in the air. (p. 100)

> Kirkus Reviews *(copyright © 1970 The Kirkus Service, Inc.), February 1, 1970.*

Fernando Krahn, the Chilean cartoonist, has one of the drollest senses of humor in the picture-book world. *Hildegarde and Maximilian . . .*, his latest, evokes such adjectives as "whimsical" and "precious" and even, from my three-and-a-half-year-old, "cute." And none of this in the pejorative sense. This very slight tale of the meeting and mating of two ladybugs even has a small moral: that though you reach for the moon and fail, there is plenty to keep you busy enough here on earth. The pictures add charm, and the moral is of the velvet-glove variety. (p. 7)

> *Jane Yolen, in* Book World—Chicago Tribune, *Part 2 (© 1970 Postrib Corp.), May 17, 1970.*

OTHER CITATIONS

Susan Stanton, in School Library Journal, *April, 1970, p. 110.*

HOW SANTA CLAUS HAD A LONG AND DIFFICULT JOURNEY DELIVERING HIS PRESENTS (1970)

[*How Santa Claus Had a Long and Difficult Journey Delivering His Presents*] adds up to a lot of paper and not much story, the middle of which bogs down as often as Santa's sleigh. The berry-nosed characters are cute in Krahn's rendering, but they all look alike (except for the bear, and he stays home). This lack of variety and color compounds the repetition of the story and makes that a device which, in this case, is detrimental to rather than effective in the building of interest. (p. 147)

> *Marilyn R. Singer, in* School Library Journal *(reprinted from the October, 1970, issue of* School Library Journal, *published by R. R. Bowker Company, a Xerox company; copyright © 1970 by Xerox Corporation), October, 1970.*

A long title with lots of words for a book with none—which is right and proper when the pictures are by Fernando Krahn, the artist with the laughing pen. (Even his angels are funny. And *that* takes a hilarious pen to achieve.) A funny, funny book. (p. 60)

> *Lavinia Russ, in* Publishers Weekly *(reprinted from the November 9, 1970, issue of* Publishers Weekly *by permission of the critic, published by R. R. Bowker Company, a Xerox company; copyright © 1970 by Xerox Corporation, November 9, 1970.*

Puckered with worry and quite chap-fallen, Father Christmas is marooned·in the tundra. With the aid of a solemnly efficient brown bear he had made a good start to his annual deliveries, but the traces of the sleigh had broken in mid-flight and the reindeer gone off on their own affairs. . . .

[It] takes a couple of passing angels to set matters to rights. The gormless reindeer are found, grazing on a snow-covered roof; the angels depart, flapping brawny wings; our hero, still somewhat bemused, descends the first chimney.

This collection of twenty-two pictures, with never a word from beginning to end, contains the quintessence of the Father Christmas tradition. Here is no bleary pensioner, reeking of double-X, dispensing gift-wrapped plastic in the local store. The chunky, worried features, the blob of a nose, over which tears will at any moment fall—these are the marks of kindly innocence, and when the angels turn up, they prove to be a couple of all-in wrestlers *manqués,* rather than the refulgent nothings of the fourpenny Christmas cards.

The warm-heartedness and simplicity which are at the heart of Mr. Krahn's 'story' are exactly caught in his unaffected drawing and in his telling use of grey and red in the pictures and emerald green by way of decoration. If the humane tradition of the family Christmas is to remain, then this book ought to be an indispensable part of it. (p. 190)

> *Brian W. Alderson, in* Children's Book Review *(© 1971 by Five Owls Press Ltd.; all rights reserved), December, 1971.*

[*The*] picture book of the year must be the inspired book without words *How Santa Claus Had a Long and Difficult Journey Delivering His Presents.* Mr. Krahn has sent from Chile 22 perceptive grey drawings embellished only by the cherry red hero and their own brilliance, and each is set off by a blank facing page of emerald green. The effect is so striking and descriptive that to introduce words would be an intrusion and totally alien to the spirit of the tale. The solemn brown bear clangs his bell to awaken Father Christmas for his annual journey, but when the sleigh and reindeer part company the combined efforts of all the toys fail, in spite of their ingenious if unscientific efforts at mass propulsion. However, salvation is at hand in the form of two angels whose bulging muscles were certainly not gained playing a harp on a cloud. [It is a] rare gem of a book that will give countless hours of browsing and conversation in any family. (p. 89)

> The Junior Bookshelf, *April, 1972.*

OTHER CITATIONS

Kirkus Reviews, *September 15, 1970, p. 1029.*

JOURNEYS OF SEBASTIAN (1968)

Fernando Krahn made very funny pictures last year to illustrate the words by Alastair Reid for "Uncle Timothy's Traviata". . . . This year he has told his own story by pictures alone. And so fantastic and so witty are his pictures that words would be redundancies. Don't let your children miss the fun of this one. Don't *you* miss it! (pp. 49-50)

> *Lavinia Russ, in* Publishers Weekly *(reprinted from the November 4, 1968, issue of* Publishers Weekly *by permission of the critic, published by R. R. Bowker Company, a Xerox company; copyright © 1968 by Xerox Corporation), November 4, 1968.*

[*Journeys of Sebastian* is a] book of drawings without words, divided into three chapters, each comprising a different episode from Sebastian's imagination. In the first, a bee buzzing around Sebastian's head sparks an imaginary sightseeing trip which concludes with Sebastian perilously parked on a flower; a peek through the mirror initiates a journey to an imaginary kingdom preoccupied with mirrors; a tug on a string brings into being a lovable monster which Sebastian rides to win a race. The first episode is a bit

complicated for young children to follow and doesn't supply the necessary ingredient of humor; while the second is more successful, it is the third that superbly combines straightforward adventure and subtle comedy. The excellent pen drawings are often splashed with a different color (yellow, blue, red) in each chapter to reinforce the change of episode. An enjoyable addition to the small but growing collection of textless picture books. (p. 67)

> *Lena Dame, in* School Library Journal *(reprinted from the February, 1969, issue of* School Library Journal, *published by R. R. Bowker Company, a Xerox company; copyright © 1969 by Xerox Corporation), February, 1969.*

OTHER CITATIONS

Sister Marie O'Donnell, S.J., in Catholic Library World, *October, 1969, p. 141.*

THE MYSTERY OF THE GIANT FOOTSTEPS (1977)

Krahn's latest wordless put-on starts with giant footprints in the snow outside an isolated log cabin, shows a small boy and girl hurrying off in curious pursuit, and has a worried looking Ma and Pa following close behind with a shotgun. As the trail passes other houses the tracking party grows; guns, pitchforks, and axes are shouldered; and the prints lead on—across a frozen lake, over a canyon which the giant appears to have spanned (the posse crosses on a fallen tree), and around an upright evergreen like Charles Addams' weirder ski marks. Krahn ends the search in a cave, where the original two children have already found the "monster" and appropriated it for a pet—except that it isn't one monster but two unlikely, furred creatures, each consisting of a giant foot connected to a leg—or a long neck, as you will, and topped by a small foxlike head. . . . All told, their closest relative might be the shaggy dog. Still, the expedition has its droll distractions. (p. 422)

> Kirkus Reviews *(copyright © 1977 The Kirkus Service, Inc.), April 15, 1977.*

Krahn is known and appreciated as the creator of wordless books. This is a crazy story, told in scenes of rare artistry and imagination. In the far north, a family is cosily at home in their cabin, set among tall pines in deep snow. Little brother and sister spot monster footsteps outside and rush to investigate. Father and mother spread the alarm when their children are lost and everyone in the remote settlement joins in the search. It takes them far afield and into events which become funnier on each page. Young readers will be absolutely delighted with the mystery of the giant footsteps, when their makers are revealed at last and become community pets. (p. 63)

> *Jean F. Mercier, in* Publishers Weekly *(reprinted from the May 16, 1977, issue of* Publishers Weekly *by permission of the critic, published by R. R. Bowker Company, a Xerox company; copyright © 1977 by Xerox Corporation), May 16, 1977.*

THE SELF-MADE SNOWMAN (1974)

Krahn is quoted on the jacket [of *The Self-Made Snowman*]

as saying that he enjoys making "humorous illustrations of public catastrophes." Despite the intriguing detail of Krahn's black and white drawings which resemble soft pencil sketches, the wry, sophisticated absurdity of this particular catastrophe won't necessarily tickle everyone the same way. Appreciation is probably more a matter of sensibility than of age, but it's more likely to take the form of solitary smiles and silent laughter than public story hour success. (p. 737)

> *Kirkus Reviews* (copyright © 1974 The *Kirkus Service, Inc.), July 15, 1974.*

No words are needed and none used to tell a fast-moving suspense story [in "The Self-Made Snowman"] of how a ball of snow rolls down a mountain and acquires a head, arms and feet—even clothes—as it gathers speed. The pictures of the woodland creatures and town people that the snowman startles in his wild careening are always funny and sometimes truly hilarious. "Readers"—young and old —should get as big a kick out of of the book as the artist obviously did in its creation. (p. 307)

> *Jean F. Mercier, in* Publishers Weekly *(reprinted from the August 26, 1974, issue of* Publishers Weekly *by permission of the critic, published by R. R. Bowker Company, a Xerox company; copyright © 1974 by Xerox Corporation), August 26, 1974.*

For devotees of a white Christmas there's a snowman that's free of drippy personification.... A run of luck worthy of its Horatio Alger prototype builds up *The Self-Made Snowman* ... from ball to behemoth. Fernando Krahn's cartoons without text follow the mammoth mound as it crashes through trees, routs bear and moose on-lookers, topples a trapper's tent, sets an unhitched cart hurtling into town, and, crowned with a Christmas wreath, plows through a crowd turned out for a parade. Krahn uses accelerating speed and size to funny advantage, but the deadpan destruction won't stir an avalanche of interest. (pp. 90-1)

> *Pamela D. Pollack, in* School Library Journal *(reprinted from* School Library Journal, *October, 1974, published by R. R. Bowker Co., a Xerox company; copyright © 1974 by Xerox Corporation), October, 1974.*

OTHER CITATIONS

Zena Sutherland, in Bulletin of the Center for Children's Books, *November, 1974, p. 46.*

WHAT IS A MAN? (1972)

"So the blind man took Orestes in his arms and began to tell him of the virtues of man...." If only we had been spared this self-conscious ending, Orestes' attempt to visualize a man might have stood forth both as clever satire and inspired silliness. Piecing together the fragments of information he gets from other animals (man, said the hen, "has a soft little beak which he doesn't use too much"), Orestes imagines a series of composites—each more ridiculous, but also uncomfortably more anthropoid, than the last. Krahn's hypotheses on the nature of man unfold luxuriously—with the cameo drawings on the right-hand pages facing versos alternately colored bright pumpkin and brown, but the mix

of sophisticated wit and unctious sentimentality fails to answer either Orestes' question or ours—why this provocative Latin American artist so often fails to complete his stories on key. A puzzlement. (pp. 669-70)

> *Kirkus Reviews* (copyright © 1972 The *Kirkus Service, Inc.), June 15, 1972.*

The two fastest-selling forms of greeting cards today are studios and heartsies. Studio cards usually feature well-drawn grotesques saying something slightly racy or mildly insulting, and heartsies attempt to say something Awful Nice with such stunners as: I thanked God for you again today! This book is an odd combination of both greeting card approaches. The illustrations are finely detailed animal grotesques while the last sticky line aims straight for your heart but hits you right in the gulp. Orestes, a small, unidentifiable, fur-covered creature creeps from jungle to barnyard to city streets asking various animals, "'What is a man?'" Each names a different physical characteristic or clothing preference—the giraffe says it's someone with a short neck and the hen says he has a soft beak, etc.—and on each following page Orestes' wild imaginings of the conglomerate of features and dress are shown. It goes on like this in simple words until the joke begins to wear thin for adults but it's still on target for average middle graders until Orestes puts his question to a blind man. The blind man can't describe what a man looks like, but he fondles Orestes while listing the virtues of man and Orestes falls asleep thinking, "A man is someone who can love." When humor is used to produce heartburn, it isn't good for any age level. (p. 55)

> *Lillian N. Gerhardt, in* School Library Journal *(reprinted from the December, 1972, issue of* School Library Journal, *published by R. R. Bowker Company, a Xerox company; copyright © 1972 by Xerox Corporation), December, 1972.*

WHO'S SEEN THE SCISSORS? (1975)

No one will have trouble seeing these runaway scissors as both they and their path are conspicuously colored red when they cut a mischievous swath across town.... Like [Krahn's] *April Fools* ... this takes off from the merest snippet of an idea, and (though it's distracting to follow the scissors flying backwards from right to left across the page) Krahn fills out the wordless joke with truthful detail—from the pencil drawn house facades and interiors to the chagrined faces of the victims. A very private chuckle. (p. 445)

> *Kirkus Reviews* (copyright © 1975 The *Kirkus Service, Inc.), April 15, 1975.*

Wordless picture books have been much in vogue, but few of them have been as successful as this new one in telling a simple tale with clarity and ease.... The quiet slapstick is revealed in expressive, soft-pencil drawings, in which the capricious, soaring scissors are colored bright red. (pp. 369-70)

> *Ethel L. Heins, in* The Horn Book Magazine *(copyright © 1975 by the Horn Book, Inc., Boston), August, 1975.*

This wordless picture book is truly inspired. Children will laugh and love the adventurous antics as pleasantly shown in the soft pencil drawings. Highly recommended. . . . (p. 93)

Catholic Library World, *September, 1975.*

OTHER CITATIONS

Hayden Atwood, in School Library Journal, *September, 1975, p. 85.*

L

LANGSTAFF, John   1920-

John Langstaff is an American concert soloist, music teacher, and recording artist who is noted for his edited compilations for children of traditional British and American folk songs and ballads. He became interested in these forms through hearing the music of Southern Appalachia. His first retelling of a folk song in picture book form, *Frog Went A-Courtin'*, was awarded the 1956 Caldecott Medal. Langstaff is the co-editor of two collections; one was compiled with his wife, Nancy, and one with his daughter, Carol. (See also *Contemporary Authors*, Vols. 1-4, rev. ed. and *Something About the Author*, Vol. 6.)

FROG WENT A-COURTIN' (1955)

A favorite old nursery ballad now appears in resplendent new dress. Many of us know it as "The frog he would a-wooing go," but that is a Johnny-come-lately compared to its earlier forms. From the many variants John Langstaff has put together his own version, one with a happy ending. And why not, since folksongs are never set in a permanent mold? So the frog and his mouse-wife sail gaily off to France on their honeymoon, which ought to please children more than the old catastrophic ending.

The tune is a simple one from the Southern Appalachians and the phrases and rhythms of the song have the hearty, old-fashioned flavor of that region. Illustrator Feodor Rojankovsky somehow manages to combine quaintness with sophistication and his doughty frog, the coy mouse, the greedy chick and others of the wedding party make a high-spirited, charming company. (p. 26)

> *Ellen Lewis Buell, in* The New York Times Book Review *(© 1955 by The New York Times Company; reprinted by permission), March 20, 1955.*

If you and your young companions like good splashy color and lots of active animals, you will be captivated by *Frog Went A-Courtin'* retold by John Langstaff and pictured by Feodor Rojankovsky. . . . Perhaps you will say as I did, "That's not the way *we* heard the old rhyme"—but no matter. The full-page illustrations are nothing short of stunning, and I predict that this will be a lasting favorite in the nursery. (p. 82)

> *Margaret Ford Kieran, in* The Atlantic Monthly *(copyright © 1955 by The Atlantic Monthly Company, Boston, Mass.; reprinted with permission), June, 1955.*

OTHER CITATIONS

Virginia Haviland, in The Horn Book Magazine, *April, 1955, p. 108.*

Elizabeth Mitchell, in Library Journal, *April 15, 1955, p. 102.*

Frances Lander Spain, in Saturday Review, *May 14, 1955, p. 47.*

HI! HO! THE RATTLIN' BOG: AND OTHER FOLK SONGS FOR GROUP SINGING (1969)

Not a distinguished collection, this, yet it see-saws deceptively: up on the novel Anglo-American material, down on the over-used old-standby categories (Soldier Songs, Sea Songs, Ballads, etc.); up on the sensitive guitar explanations by Happy Traum, but down on the brevity of Langstaff's commentary; up on those piano arrangements that are skillfully imaginative and simple at once, but down, of course, on those that are not; neutral on the illustrations [by Robin Jacques] that neither contribute nor detract. Ruth Seeger's classic *American Folk Songs for Children* far outshines this book in its scope of purpose and content and in its invaluable suggestions for songleaders and teachers, but Langstaff has indeed filled something of a gap—he's organized a book for the young, not-too-accomplished pianist or guitarist himself, and done so without condescension or pretension. Could be better, but fun for beginning folk(ophiles) of any age to explore. (p. 781)

> Kirkus Reviews *(copyright © 1969 The Kirkus Service, Inc.), August 1, 1969.*

Here is poetry to sing: sea-chanteys, lullabies, dance songs, ballads, ghost and soldier songs. Here are the tunes to sing them to, the harmonies for guitars, the arrangements for pianos. Here is a rollicking, rich collection for all families, all groups who like to sing together, collected by a singer who has been singing them to the vast delight of audiences everywhere. (p. 56)

> *Lavinia Russ, in* Publishers Weekly *(re-*

printed from the September 8, 1969, issue of Publishers Weekly *by permission of the critic, published by R. R. Bowker Company, a Xerox company; copyright © 1969 by Xerox Corporation), September 8, 1969.*

OTHER CITATIONS

Mary Reed Newland, in The New York Times Book Review, *November 9, 1969, p. 67.*

Sister Mary Ethelreda Smeltzer, in Catholic Library World, *February, 1970, p. 385.*

JIM ALONG, JOSIE: A COLLECTION OF FOLK SONGS AND SINGING GAMES FOR YOUNG CHILDREN (with Nancy Langstaff, 1970)

A concert singer, collector and interpreter of folk music, and eminent teacher—together with his wife, another experienced musician and teacher—has compiled a generous collection of traditional songs that reflect their conviction "that music for young children should be tremendous fun and of the best quality." The pure melodic line of folk songs as well as the rhythmic vigor of the words and music make them particularly suitable as an early introduction to both music and poetry. Traditional for centuries and basic to childhood, singing games like "Oats and Beans" and "Captain Jinks" combine dancing and dramatic play with singing; while action songs like "This Old Man" invite improvisation. Guitar chords are given with simple alternates when necessary, making the book ideal for use by a guitar teacher with groups of young beginners. A detailed Preface contains a splendid discussion of the subject of music and children, including advice on the teaching of songs and singing and on the use of simple percussion instruments. The book is a delight to look at, with its spacious pages and large, clearly printed notation. Beautifully executed silhouettes [by Nancy Winslow Parker] decorate the pages and point out the inherent humor in the songs. (p. 625)

> *Ethel L. Heins, in* The Horn Book Magazine *(copyright © 1970 by The Horn Book, Inc., Boston), December, 1970.*

OH, A-HUNTING WE WILL GO (1974)

Devoid of a strong story line, the song [*Oh, A-Hunting We Will Go*] has been arranged on the pages in such a way that the reader is at least kept interested in turning the pages to discover what will happen to the creatures captured in the hunt. And the simple crayon illustrations [by Nancy Winslow Parker] . . . have been imbued with marvelously ludicrous details. . . . [The] book contains an excellent choice of stanzas, which provide delightful creatures to be illustrated. Even though the book could be used in singing, rhythmic, and wordplay activities, it is also, in its own right, a true picture book—accessible to even the most tone-deaf. (pp. 45-6)

> *Anita Silvey, in* The Horn Book Magazine *(copyright © 1975 by the Horn Book, Inc., Boston), February, 1975.*

OTHER CITATIONS

Kirkus Reviews, *August 1, 1974, p. 799.*

Publishers Weekly, *October 7, 1974, p. 63.*

OL' DAN TUCKER (1963)

Ol' Dan Tucker is a popular song of the last century, and allegedly the favourite song of Abraham Lincoln—it is easy to believe. John Langstaff has had the kind of fun with it that he had with *Frog Went A-Courtin'*, and Joe Krush, making his Dan look uncommonly like Abe, has provided a set of frolicsome pictures. It is all very funny, very professional, and pure Yankee. (pp. 336, 338)

> The Junior Bookshelf, *December, 1963.*

Ol' Dan Tucker, a legendary character who grew out of American pioneer life, is immortalized in a book full of the humor and boisterous exaggerations that are a vital part of an American tradition. From the many existing versions of this 120-year-old banjo dance tune, Mr. Langstaff has chosen the verses he likes best and with the interpretive assistance of Mr. Krush, has made this into a picture book as gay and lively as the song itself. (p. 462)

> *Constantine Georgiou, in his* Children and Their Literature *(© 1969; reprinted by permission of Prentice-Hall, Inc., Englewood Cliffs, New Jersey), Prentice-Hall, 1969.*

OTHER CITATIONS

Ethel L. Heins, in School Library Journal, *March, 1963, p. 165.*

ON CHRISTMAS DAY IN THE MORNING! (1959)

[*On Christmas Day in the Morning!* is an] unusual song book which will bring both beauty and fun into the Christmas season. Gay and tuneful are the verses and musical versions which Mr. Langstaff has chosen for his four carols: "On Chris-i-mas Day in the Morning," "Dame, Get Up and Bake Your Pies," "The Friendly Beasts," and "I Saw Three Ships." For the last, a familiar English May-dance tune is the traditional one selected; it fits the words even better than the more familiar airs usually heard and will easily set children to dancing. The piano arrangements are simple enough for many piano-playing children. The volume's distinction lies especially in [Antony Groves-Raines's illustrations]. Doublespread scenes, alternately in glowing full color and a bright red with black, have fascinating medieval details appropriate to the antiquity of the songs. Some are as full of moving figures as a Breughel painting; others have small floral embellishments for an early illuminated effect. (p. 471)

> *Virginia Haviland, in* The Horn Book Magazine *(copyright, 1959, by the Horn Book, Inc., Boston), December, 1959.*

To our modern, economical, Puritanized tastes this collection of four carols seems at first glance to miss the point of the season: "On Chris-i-mas Day in the Morning," "Dame Get Up and Bake Your Pies," "I Saw Three Ships" and "The Friendly Beasts" make no direct mention of the incarnation. But on second glance we welcome them—for they remind us that Christmas was once upon a time an occasion for dance and mime. Marshall Woodbridge's musical settings tempt us to join Joseph and his "fair ladye" in whistling and singing about Christmas. And Antony Groves-Raines's illustrations catch the frivolous mood of the minnow and drake that winnowed and raked on Chris-i-mas day. The whole creation groans in travail awaiting the final fruits of redemption: why shouldn't the beasts, friendly and all, have a place in the heralding of the coming of our Savior? A collection of quality, overpriced. (p. 1405)

> *The Christian Century (copyright 1959 Christian Century Foundation; reprinted by permission from the December 2, 1959 issue of* The Christian Century), *December 2, 1959.*

The rich glow of the Christmas season thru hundreds of years shines out of this many-faceted jewel of a volume. Dancing, singing, rejoicing, the merriment of a mummers' procession, the fragrance of puddings and pies, the prickle of red-berried holly, the swelling chords of an angels' choir, the reverent wonder of man and beast kneeling beside the rude manger are all here, captured both in the four carols and in the brilliantly detailed pictures mindful of Flemish miniatures. Antony Groves-Raines worked for three years to create the exquisite settings for "Dame Get Up and Bake Your Pies," "I Saw Three Ships," "Chris-i-mas Day in the Morning," and "The Friendly Beasts," sending songs and pictures into the endless future. (p. 17)

> *Polly Goodwin, in* Chicago Sunday Tribune Magazine of Books, *Part 4, December 6, 1959.*

OTHER CITATIONS

The Booklist and Subscription Books Bulletin, *November 1, 1959, p. 73.*

Saturday Review, *December 19, 1959, p. 430.*

The Times Literary Supplement, *November 28, 1963, p. 989.*

SAINT GEORGE AND THE DRAGON: A MUMMER'S PLAY (1973)

John Langstaff's adaptation of *Saint George and the Dragon: a Mummer's Play* . . . goes back to the heathen origins of Christmas celebration in the death and rebirth of one who represents the waning of the old and the rising of the new year. Most readers in the intermediate grades are as removed from this symbology as from the rhythm of the seasons; but, this evocation of harmony with nature harbors meaning which has been processed out of our ordinary merrymaking. The book is strikingly designed with forceful color woodcuts [by David Gentleman] which give impetus to the burlesque and to the giant vs. dragon/dragon vs. hero action; scores and clear directions for staging, costuming, and performing the sword dance make this a practical as well as a graphic hit. (p. 95)

> *Pamela D. Pollack, in* School Library Journal *(reprinted from the October, 1973, issue of* School Library Journal, *published by R. R. Bowker Co., a Xerox company; copyright © 1973 by Xerox Corporation), October, 1973.*

There are many variants of the folk play about Saint George and the dragon, which used to be performed traditionally at Christmas time in England by local actors or mummers. It is no wonder, then, that the present version coincides only in part—as to characters, speeches, and staging—with Katherine Miller's *Saint George: A Christmas Mummers' Play . . .*; the essence of folklore is its freedom in the treatment of inherited, traditional material. If Katherine Miller envisioned her *Saint George* as a domestic performance, John Langstaff associates his version with a performance for a sizeable audience and invokes music and dancing to bring to life "the play's boisterous broad humor and fun mixed with the solemn moments of mysterious magic." Five traditional musical selections accompany the verses of the text; and there are costume suggestions for performance and a "very abbreviated" set of directions for the sword dance. The unsophisticated woodcut illustrations—overlaid in appropriate places with patches of blue, green, purple, and pink—capture the bold, good-humored fooling of the text, but fail to suggest the solemn resurrection ritual on which the core of the play rests and which is, in some degree, effectual in a live performance. (p. 584)

> *Paul Heins, in* The Horn Book Magazine *(copyright © 1973 by The Horn Book, Inc., Boston), December, 1973.*

Saint George and the Dragon. . . , a folk play that is more than a thousand years old, offers an original approach to the traditional holiday pageantry. This version by John Langstaff, with glowing woodcuts by David Gentleman, is meant to be performed, not just read. There's everything to delight both audience and young actors: a dragon, a comic hobby horse, dancers, a noble knight, and a magical fool.

The mixture of ritual and good-natured buffoonery makes this ancient mummer's play very appealing.

Author Langstaff has provided text and music, as well as suggestions for costuming and props, and instructions for the sword dance which is the climax of the play. His "Saint George" is part of the annual Christmas Revels in Cambridge, Mass., and is always a great success. (p. 14)

> *Jennifer Farley Smith (reprinted by permission from The Christian Science Monitor; © 1973 by The Christian Science Publishing Society; all rights reserved), in* The Christian Science Monitor, *December 12, 1973.*

OTHER CITATIONS

Kirkus Reviews, *September 15, 1973, p. 1041.*

Publishers Weekly, *November 12, 1973, p. 36.*

The Booklist, *February 15, 1974, p. 657.*

THE SEASON FOR SINGING: AMERICAN CHRISTMAS SONGS AND CAROLS (1974)

[*The Season for Singing* is an] interesting, broadly ethnic-American collection of songs which nevertheless bears the mark of twentieth-century neutralization. Among the folk carols are three Puerto Rican songs, while a section grouping Shaker, Moravian, and Indian works has one Huron song of doubtful native influence. Under the heading

"Black Tradition, Spirituals, and Gospel" there are 12 familiar numbers; the next large section adds shape-note songs and well-known works composed over several centuries. Part songs old and new conclude the volume. While the hand of the once-removed adaptor is felt most strongly in the section on black songs and throughout in the piano parts, moderately easy instrumental accompaniments are lively. Moreover, the book will supplement collections exclusively devoted to all-time favorites, providing entertainment and a few diminished lessons in our diverse cultural heritage. (p. 571)

> The Booklist *(reprinted by permission of the American Library Association; copyright 1975 by the American Library Association), February 1, 1975.*

OTHER CITATIONS

Publishers Weekly, *October 6, 1974, p. 48.*

Patricia Mahoney Brown, in School Library Journal, *April, 1975, p. 54.*

SHIMMY SHIMMY COKE-CA-POP! A COLLECTION OF CITY CHILDREN'S STREET GAMES AND RHYMES (with Carol Langstaff, 1973)

[The] title is the name of a handclapping game in this collection of 48 or more (many more with their variations) modern street games.... Although the collection is open-ended leaving plenty of room for improvisation and invention, it is in the tradition of "the classics" in game books: Lady (Alice Bertha) Gomme's *Traditional Games of England, Scotland, and Ireland* (1894-98 1st ed. ...); *London Street Games* (1916 ...) by Norman Douglas; *The Lore and Language of Schoolchildren* (... 1959) by Iona and Peter Opie. The authors' rationale is that of the physician friend of Swift and Pope, Dr. Arbuthnot, that tradition was nowhere "preserved pure and uncorrupt but amongst school-boys (and girls one should add), whose Games and Plays are delivered down invariably from one generation to another." Don MacSorley's action-filled photographs are in black and white. (p. 255)

> *Iris Vinton, in* AB Bookman's Weekly (© *1973 by AB Bookman Publications, Inc.), July 23, 1973.*

The streets of Boston and New York and Rapid City, no less than the more homogeneous districts of the Old World, sound to the gibes and rhythms of all kinds of children, forever newly recruited to a culture as old as the harvest and newer than yellow submarines. This feast for eye and voice presents name-calling ("Eddie Spaghetti with the meatball eyes" and "Ringo, Ringo, Ringo Starr") and ball, tag, rope, circle, action, drawing, dramatic and follow-the-leader games, all transcribed in our land and in our time. Tune and handclap rhythm are noted for many, such as the trochaic little rhyme, "I don't want-a let you go. / Just because I kissed you once doesn't mean I love you so." Vigorous, as authentic as the rearing bike and the kicked can, the text and [Don MacSorley's] photographs are full of life and action, by no means prettified. The book is both a record and a guide to emulation, provided that the way is genuinely freed and that the adults, forever alienated by the years, manage to stay far off on the sidelines.... The

collectors, incidentally, come from the world of music theater, dance and film. (p. 135)

> *Philip and Phylis Morrison, in* Scientific American *(copyright © 1973 by Scientific American, Inc.; all rights reserved), December, 1973.*

Recent books on children's play and games, such as Bess Hawes' and Bessie Jones' *Step It Down* and Brian Sutton-Smith's *The Folkgames of Children* . . . constitute fine contributions to the field [of folklore literature]. They reproach volumes like *Shimmy Shimmy Coke-Ca-Pop! A Collection of City Children's Street Games and Rhymes*, by John and Carol Langstaff.... The authors offer the texts of fifty rhymes and games, some minor directions for the games, a too brief introduction with scholarly pretensions, and fine, but unlabeled, photographs throughout. They never define an audience, and the book thus has dubious value as a beginning for scholars or as an end for kids. The introduction is not unintelligent. The authors know something about transmission theory, variation, form, function, origin, classification. They comment briefly on ethnic syncretisms in the city and on the creativity and tradition children exhibit in their games. But all these things receive short shrift in the introduction. The text offers little that is not mere rhyme. The photographs are beautiful, but, since they are unlabeled, they are of little use. Better to see Bess Hawes' wonderful film, *Pizza Pizza Daddy O*, and inspire children and parents to understand and create games. This book appears to want parents to understand just enough about games so they can instruct the children in using the book. At $4.95, parents had best rely on their own child's creativity and go to Sutton-Smith or Hawes if they want to understand gaming. Perhaps scholars ought to produce "popular" works to offset books like this. (p. 104)

> *Rayna Green, in* Journal of American Folklore *(copyright © 1974 by the American Folklore Society; reprinted by permission), January-March, 1974.*

OTHER CITATIONS

Kirkus Reviews, *May 1, 1973, p. 518.*

Zena Sutherland, in Bulletin of the Center for Children's Books, *October, 1973, p. 30.*

Donald F. Pfau, in Childhood Education, *November, 1973, p. 100.*

Judith Schneider, in School Library Journal, *November, 1973, pp. 40-1.*

SOLDIER, SOLDIER, WON'T YOU MARRY ME? (1972)

The familiar folksong charmingly elucidated by Anita Lobel's fresh and lively pictures, each a framed portrait of the bustling old-time town. Her "sweet maid" is a small child in old fashioned bonnet and ribboned gown who answers the jaunty soldier's every objection ("Oh no, sweet maid, I cannot marry you / For I have no hat/shirt/tie/coat/boots/gloves to put on") by running off (over flowered fields and cobblestone streets) to the appropriate shop for a plumed hat, scarlet coat, etc.—and then, after the clinching "Oh, no, sweet maid, I cannot marry you / For I have a wife at home," is seen on the last page, her tears already dried, returning the lot to the merchants. Musical score appended, rhythm and bounce throughout. (p. 534)

> Kirkus Reviews *(copyright © 1972 The Kirkus Service, Inc.), May 1, 1972.*

The decrepit gallant who led his sweetheart such a traipse [in *Soldier, Soldier, Won't You Marry Me?*] may have been a deceiver, but no more so than Anita Lobel. She moves towards setting up the pay-off line of the song most charmingly, but when it arrives she will not confront its cynicism. The workmanship of her framed drawings, her command of design and colour are much to be admired. They convince us that the 'sweet maid' may possibly be a child, and that—in John Langstaff's version—she may just as well get the soldier's new outfit from the shops as from her grandfather's chest. But surely the point of the whole thing is that the soldier then departs to 'the wife of his own' in a posh new uniform (including breeks, which modesty has here left unchanged); it is against all custom that he should pile up his new garments in the village street and march off in his rags.

One other little device also disappoints, and thereby emphasizes the need for illustrators' *ad lib* contributions to the events of their story to be apposite. Throughout the sequence of events Mrs. Lobel runs a pictorial theme of her own: two old ladies who are clearly shocked at the wanton generosity of the sweet maid and who, in other circumstances, will meet the fate reserved for interfering busybodies. Here, however, their mean suspicions of the soldier's motives are almost entirely justified, and their final appearance in an attitude betokening 'I-told-you-so' supplies a triumph for characters who are just not worthy of it. (p. 117)

> *Brian W. Alderson, in* Children's Book Review *(© 1973 Five Owls Press Ltd.; all rights reserved), September, 1973.*

OTHER CITATIONS

The Booklist, *May 15, 1972, p. 821.*

Publishers Weekly, *May 22, 1972, p. 51.*

Tally Gilkerson, in School Library Journal, *September, 1972, pp. 67-8.*

*   *   *

LEE, Dennis   1939-

Publishing his first poem at the age of four, Dennis Lee has become a respected Canadian poet for children and adults. He has been actively involved in Canadian arts and education, a teacher, and a founder of both Rochdale College and a major Canadian publishing firm, the House of Anansi Press. "In short," writes Clare MacCulloch, "he sits front and centre in our cultural core." Lee won the Governor General's Award for Poetry in 1973. *Alligator Pie,* **his second book of poetry for children, was the recipient of the Canadian Library Association Awards Books of the Year prize in 1975. (See also** *Contemporary Authors,* **Vols. 25-28, rev. ed.)**

AUTHOR'S COMMENTARY

I would very much like to share [my concept of the essence of children's poetry], unfortunately, I can't. For the essence of children's poetry went clean out of my head about two years after I started writing those poems ["nursery rhymes for my children," Lee calls them], and today for the life of me I can't remember what it was. All I recall is that I used to know what constitutes a good kid's poem, and now that I write and read them aloud all the time, I don't. At least not the way I used to.

For most of my doctrinaire notions went kaplooey, boring the children I foisted them on even more than they were boring me. (p. 28)

At the same time, some improbable notions for poems jelled tolerably well, even though they made hash of my hardest-won critical dogmas about children's poetry. Something, I began to realise, was out of synch. There seemed to be no direct connection between knowing what a poem should be and being able to write it. . . . Eventually I lost interest altogether in the Essence of Poetry, since it was no use in writing poems. And I wound up with a completely promiscuous, catch-as-catch-can sense of the thing. If a notion or an approach works, it's good; if it doesn't, it isn't; and you never know which will happen till you try. That is now the sum of my theoretical wisdom about children's poetry. (pp. 28-9)

Like any other kids' poet worth his salt, I act as if children's verse in English existed for the sole purpose of letting me rummage through it for rhythms, ideas, and starting points for poems of my own. I try not to borrow or imitate, of course. Rather, I try to steal: to assimilate completely what the masters in the field have done, to make it my own so I can go and do otherwise, pursue my own proper necessities. It is like a child's relation to his parents. (My "parents", though it may not show in any extensive way, are Carroll and Milne—master of the lunatic muse, and master of the domestic, inward muse.) . . .

[A] poet's most cogent commentary on other literature comes in the poems he writes. (p. 29)

I write as a 35-year-old child. That is a paradox, I suppose, but it's the only way I can say what I mean. In fact, to really say it I have to make the statement more outlandish still: namely, "I write as a 35-year-old children."

What does that mean?

Like most adults, I have a number of children trapped, held in suspension, in my nervous system. I can't find the right physical image for this, so I have trouble expressing the notion. But it is such an everyday experience that I don't question it. . . .

And the key to writing for children, for me at least, is to get in touch with one of those children in myself and then follow his nose, going wherever the child's interests lead me. . . .

That often leads to neat poems. On the other hand, if I start from my adult notions of what a child will enjoy, or should enjoy, I wind up writing something very pompous, or condescending, or dull: something pasted onto the child's inner life from the outside, like a taxidermist's label. (p. 30)

Sometimes, though, I can start directly from some refrain or character or rhythm that intrigues me and feels in touch with one of the kids suspended in my system. Then I'm able to follow it wherever it wants to go and to play directly on the page. This involves using the instinct of the child and the craft of the adult.

If people ask me afterwards, "What age was this poem written for?" I usually scratch my head. It was never calculated for the reading level of a specific age group. Some kid in me was just enjoying the thing as it happened. I'm as much interested as anyone else, after the fact, to find out what age *does* get off on it—how old the engaged child in me was.

Still, that is only half the picture. I've been talking about writing as a 35-year-old *children*—taking one's lead from the impulse of the kid. The point about writing as a *35-year-old* children, which is the other half, is that as a grown-up who writes I have a certain amount of experience, a fairly strong sense of craft, and the like. I do want the child in question—the one that's perched somewhere in me—to find a voice in the poem. But, given that, I'm quite unwilling to surrender any of the adult's prerogatives. Thus, the thing has to be written well, It may be very simple, but simplicity is usually more demanding than complexity anyway. And while the child's way of perceiving the world may be incomplete (from the adult's vantage-point), I can't accept that it be simplistic or untrue. (pp. 31-2)

To write as an adult children . . . means reconnecting with the capacity to feel directly.

It means experiencing a partial integration of the adult and the children in oneself—which is what many grown-ups discover when they return to children's books with their kids. (pp. 34-5)

About 1965, when I was starting to read Mother Goose to my older daughter, . . . I found myself starting to chafe. I could hardly believe the subversive thoughts that were stirring in my brain. In one way they seemed ludicrous to me, not worth taking seriously. In another way, I had no choice.

What I was thinking was this. "Here is a little girl, not quite two, and she is getting bounced and tickled to the rhythms of tuffets and millers and pipers and pence, of curds and whey, of piglets and plum pudding and pease porridge hot, and she hasn't the slightest idea what a single one of them is. For shame! Thought control! Mother Goose is an imperialist conspiracy!"

But that seemed pretty silly—if only because, had she been getting bounced to the rhythm of fire hydrants and hockey sticks and T-4 slips, she wouldn't have known what *they* were either. (p. 39)

"Still," I went on to myself, "isn't it bizarre that before she's two years old this child should be learning the lessons we Canadians know by heart in our cells and bloodstreams: that the imagination leads always and only to the holy city of elsewhere, that we enter it as barbarians from outside the gates? 'The imagination can never play on what is immediate in our lives': do I really want to teach my daughter that? At the age of two?"

Well, I thought, that's not entirely true either. Mother Goose, or *King Lear, is* about our lives. About the delight in rhythms and words chasing themselves in and out, about the destiny on earth we share with people in Renaissance England. There's something portable in them.

But while I agreed with this, and still do, I couldn't escape the sense that you are poorer if you never find your own time and place speaking words of their own. Finally I made

a dim, murky discovery, which struck me with the full force of the banality it possesses, and yet felt momentous and almost illicit to me, since I had never heard it said out loud before.

The nursery rhymes I love, and that my daughter loves, are necessarily exotic to us. . . . But they were in no way exotic to the people who first devised them and chanted them. . . . The air of far-off charm and simpler pastoral life which now hangs over Mother Goose was in no way a part of those rhymes' initial existence. I don't want to wish away that aura now: it is part of their enduring in time. Nor do I want to "modernize" them, that supreme impertinence! But the people who told those nursery rhymes for centuries would be totally boggled if they could suddenly experience them the way children do here and now, as a collection of references to things they never see or do, to places they have never heard of and may never visit, told in words they will sometimes meet only in those verses. Mother Goose never meant those things till the twentieth century. And to look for living nursery rhymes in the hockey-sticks and the high-rise that my children knew first-hand would not be to go on a chauvinistic trip, nor to wallow in a fad of trendy relevance. It would be nothing but a rediscovery of what Mother Goose had been about for centuries.

So I began writing nursery rhymes. I was rather puzzled where to start, but I scrambled about and tried this and that. The most simple-minded thing to do, in a sense, was just to play with the place-names that dot the country. (pp. 39-40)

A lot of things I tried in this vein were pretty pedestrian—they had nothing going for them but the purity of their programmatic intent—and I threw them out. Gradually I realised that the externals didn't have to be so self-conscious. If it seemed right to include something that was explicitly Canadian, fine. If it didn't seem right, equally fine. (p. 41)

There was a mounting sense of excitement as I abandoned the more crusading aspects of the thing, and discovered that there really was a music and a cluster of themes in the lives of the children I knew and was. (p. 42)

What I was trying to do in these books [*Alligator Pie* and *Nicholas Knock and Other People*] was to go back and rehearse new gestures of being human. "New," not in the sense that they were unheard of, that no one had ever used this emotional musculature before; but new in the sense of breaking taboos I felt subject to—against play, against rage, against rejoicing. (p. 46)

I'm pleased with these two books, but like most other writers I really revolve around the things I haven't written yet. They're my centre of gravity. And when I look back at the books from that obscure perspective, I'm anything but satisfied.

Not so much because of what is in the books, but because of what isn't. I spent so much energy just clearing a way towards rooted play, it seems to me, and so little time making its poems. And I think: there are terrors, and joys, and states of daily despair and amazement which I was barely making passes at here. How could I take this as anything but a first flirtation? trying to pass off mischievousness as bawdy vitality, and a timid sense of discomfort as holy terror?

Then I read the books with grown-ups and kids again, and they do trigger the things out loud I was reaching for, and I no longer know what to think. I don't want to dump on these poems, for some of them are good. Nor do I want to accord them any more respect than they deserve. Finally I turn away from them, back to other poems that are waiting to be written, which I still don't know. They are always what compels me, though I know that once they're written they will slide away from me too, leaving me confused and exultant and depressed.

I remember what I said at the beginning, that the only cogent commentary a poet makes on other literature comes in the poems he writes. That is true of his own work too. (p. 58)

> *Dennis Lee, excerpted from "Roots and Play: Writing as a 35-Year-Old Children" (originally a speech delivered at the Lough-borough Conference in Toronto, August, 1975), in* Canadian Children's Literature, *No. 4, 1976, pp. 25-58.*

GENERAL COMMENTARY

[A man of letters] is Dennis Lee, . . . [the] creator of the newest entrants into the world of rhythm and rhyme for children. The verses from his first book, *Wiggle to the Laundromat . . .* , are now included in his new book, *Alligator Pie,* which was published simultaneously with his collection for slightly older children, *Nicholas Knock,* in 1974. Dennis Lee makes considerable use of things Canadian. His avowed intent has been to give Canadian children (his own at first) a sense of their particular time and space —a feat that obviously cannot be accomplished in writing from other countries, no matter how excellent it is. Northrop Frye once pointed out that 'In what Canadian poets have tried to do there is an interest for Canadian readers much deeper than what the achievement itself justifies.' Fortunately Lee can hold his own with the best of the modern nonsense versifiers, as is shown by these quotations from *Alligator Pie:*

> In Kamloops
> I'll eat your boots.
>
> In the Gatineaus
> I'll eat your toes.
>
> . . . . .
>
> or
>
> Yonge Street, Bloor Street,
> Queen Street, King,
> Catch an itchy monkey
> With a piece of string.

Much of the appeal of the poems is due to Lee's colloquial diction, his sense of the incongruous, and to the internal rhyme and strong beat. . . . (pp. 243-44)

Nicholas Knock has a wider range than *Alligator Pie.* The title poem is a drama in seven parts—a celebration of the youthful imagination in the face of adults and their institutions. Amoral Harry in the cautionary 'Oilcan Harry' is a modern Struuelpeter. . . . The drawings by Frank Newfeld, many of them in four colours, and the attractive layout, make *Alligator Pie* and *Nicholas Knock* two of our few thoroughly delightful illustrated books.

Nonsense verse such as that of Dennis Lee can be deceptively simple. . . . [It] requires skill, sensitivity, and a kind of controlled playfulness. . . . (p. 245)

> *Sheila Egoff, in her* The Republic of Childhood: A Critical Guide to Canadian Children's Literature in English *(© Oxford University Press, Canadian Branch, 1975), second edition, Oxford University Press, 1975.*

ALLIGATOR PIE (Canadian Edition, 1974; US Edition, 1975)

At the end of this volume of poems Dennis Lee has written "A Postlude" in which he describes how his verses came into being. For his own Canadian children, he could find no nursery rhymes that were relevant to their everyday lives, so he set out to remedy the lack. He also found that "words should never be sacred"; children should be free to add their own words and verses to poems, and he urges children to recreate his poems using the words they choose to charm and amuse their own ear and their own tongue. This is rare generosity and the poems themselves ring out with the same invitation. They are light but not empty, nonsensical but not farcical, bubbling but of lasting pleasure. The well-designed pictures both in line and colour interpret to the full all the qualities of the poems and add a perceptive delight.

The whole book shows children to themselves reflecting for children and adults alike the spirit and blitheness of present-day childhood. (p. 35)

> *Margaret E. Johnston, in* In Review: Canadian Books for Children, *Winter, 1975.*

Singa Songa . . . Bouncing Song . . . Willoughby Wallaby Woo . . . Tony Baloney . . . If the titles aren't enough to convey the tone of Lee's rhythmic, repeatable nonsense rhymes for very young listeners, here's a longer excerpt: "Billy Batter, / What's the matter? / How come you're so sad? / I lost my cat / In the laundromat / And a dragon ran off with my dad. . . ." Lee, a Canadian poet, says he wrote these to supplement the old nursery rhymes which "kids still love" but whose references to pigs, pence and jolly millers have become exotic. Very likely his Toronto street and store names and Canadian towns will be just as exotic below the border, but as the rhymes are almost all sound and no sense that won't matter any more than those references to St. Ives and London. Lee has read a bit too much Milne and maybe a little Laura E. Richards, whom he hasn't assimilated with anything like the wit of [Mary A.] Hoberman's *Raucous Auk.* . . . Nor do [Frank] Newfeld's harsh, designer-like cartoons pick up the rhymes as did [N. M.] Bodecker's pictures for his own, jauntier verses in *It's Raining Said John Twaining.* . . . (In fact the pictures are a real handicap and may well turn you off before you even begin to read.) Still, just the fact that such comparisons come to mind puts Lee in pretty good company. (p. 912)

> *Kirkus Reviews (copyright © 1975 The Kirkus Service, Inc.), August 15, 1975.*

A slender volume, containing more than three dozen poems, introduces American children to a fresh, new voice from Canada. Percussive rhythms, an acrobatic use of language, and a fine variety of form, meter, and subject matter distinguish the verses.... The first part of the book consists of poems for younger children, [in which echoes] of traditional rhymes can be heard.... Included in the second half of the book, for somewhat older children, are many poems which are as dexterously nonsensical as those of Laura E. Richards. Although the overall design of the colorful book is original and attractive, the humor in the exaggerated, somewhat mannered pictures is not nearly as spontaneous as that in the verses. (p. 608)

> *Ethel L. Heins, in* The Horn Book Magazine *(copyright © 1975 by the Horn Book, Inc., Boston), December, 1975.*

An eminent Canadian poet, Dennis Lee wrote the first poems in this collection for his own children, and the published book won the award for the most outstanding children's book published in Canada in 1974. There are nonsensical narrative poems, rhymes for games, humourous and rhythmic four-liners, tongue-twisters, and verses based on Peter Rabbit and Winnie-the-Pooh. Jingly, sunny, silly poems. The illustrations have verve and variety, although some may be limited in appeal because of the dull greens that are combined with white. Not great poetry, but facile poetry that is great fun. (p. 113)

> *Zena Sutherland, in* Bulletin of the Center for Children's Books *(© 1976 by the University of Chicago; all rights reserved), March, 1976.*

OTHER CITATIONS

William Cole, in Saturday Review, *November 29, 1975, p. 33.*

Barbara Thiele, in School Library Journal, *December, 1975, p. 47.*

NICHOLAS KNOCK AND OTHER PEOPLE (Canadian Edition, 1974; US Edition, 1976)

The other day I saw something I'd missed by holidaying in October—Dennis Lee reading his poetry to the children of Thunder Bay. How sad to miss the real thing! But how marvelous the ways of videotape! And how the children enjoyed it.

Back I went to *Nicholas Knock* to try again to write a review. Oh how simple it is to say, of course I'll review it. To review poetry of any sort—nonsense, lyric or what have you—is just not that simple. It's not simple at all.

Neither is the poetry in this delightful *Nicholas Knock*. There are story poems and singing poems and funny poems and joyous poems. Through them all there is a sense of gaiety, an appeal that shouts for reading aloud. (p. 35)

There is something for everyone in this book—colour, imagination, lilting verses full of Canadian allusions. And those allusions belong; there is no straining to make them fit.

The poems' delights are enlarged by Frank Newfeld's gorgeous illustrations and fine design. To see Mr. Hoobody is to fall victim to his charms—there he is, pink beard and all, dancing through the flames of the furnace with his whiskey keg under his arm.

Just so that we do not go mad with the joys of Grundiboobs and Hoobodys there are quieting bits, like "Summer song," "The coat" and my favourite, "You too lie down."

If you haven't bought *Nicholas Knock* for your library yet, rush right off to your nearest bookseller and purchase some. You won't regret it. (p. 36)

> *Betsy English, in* In Review: Canadian Books for Children, *Winter, 1975.*

This Canadian poet's latest batch of nonsense rhymes bounces along less evenly than last year's *Alligator Pie*. The Milne-ish rhythms of the title poem and others, the outlandishness of scrubbing one's eyes with a toothbrush, and such pure silliness as "The Poodle and the Grundiboob," recall the first collection; and their audience will easily go along with "Attila the Hun / Is eating a bun / At the corner of Yonge and Bloor" despite unfamiliarity with Attila and Toronto—but what will they make of "1838," which begins the "The Compact sat in parliament" and ends "Mackenzie, come again"? And though it probably isn't necessary to catch the allusion in "There are wombats in the bureau of my uncle," there's no excuse for the subtitle "Robert Service Meets Martin Heidegger" to the rhyme about "the Thing-Which-Is-Not." Borderline—and the harsh illustrations don't place it anywhere. (p. 786)

> *Kirkus Reviews (copyright © 1977 The Kirkus Service, Inc.), August 1, 1977.*

OTHER CITATIONS

Publishers Weekly, *September 5, 1977, p. 73.*

Paul Heins, in The Horn Book Magazine, *December, 1977, p. 675.*

WIGGLE TO THE LAUNDROMAT (Published exclusively in Canada, 1970)

The fourteen poems and rhymes which comprise this picture book suggest a Canadian Mother Goose. Dennis Lee ... has endeavored to transmit a feeling of Canada and in particular of Ontario to his reader. Four poems are based on the sounds and flavours of Canadian place names and two are about distinctly Canadian animals. The tone and rhythm of the poems vary from rollicking nonsense verse and street rhyme to whimsical song.

Unfortunately the quality of the poetry also varies. Although most of the poems succeed in delighting and stirring the imagination, one or two appear to be the contrived result of an adult playing a game of 'let's pretend'. Some of the poems are quite sophisticated in both idea and language and might possibly be unappreciated by the young child attracted to the book by its large format.

However, Charles Pachter, the designer-illustrator, has greatly enhanced the book's appeal with vibrant double page sketches illustrating each poem. The size of these black and white spreads make the book especially suitable for story hour use, as the careful unity of visual and mental images carries through to the last detail of differing type faces. (p. 25)

> *Margot Montgomery, in* In Review: Canadian Books for Children, *Spring, 1971.*

Le GUIN, Ursula K(roeber) 1929-

Ursula Le Guin, daughter of anthropologist A. L. Kroeber, is an American writer of science fiction for adults and fantasy and fiction for young adults. Le Guin conceived an inimitable world of fantasy in her Earthsea trilogy and makes it the battleground for the awesome forces of good and evil. *The Farthest Shore*, the last book of the three, was given the National Book Award for Children's Literature in 1973. (See also *Contemporary Authors*, Vols. 21-24, rev. ed., *Something About the Author*, Vol. 4, and *Contemporary Literary Criticism*, Vol. 8.)

AUTHOR'S COMMENTARY

All my life I have written, and all my life I have (without conscious decision) avoided reading How-to-write things. . . . However in reading and teaching and talking with other writers one does arrive at a certain consciousness of technique. The most different technique to my own, the one that starts from the point farthest removed, is . . . one of preliminary plans and lists and descriptions. The technique of keeping a notebook and describing all the characters in it before the story is begun: how much William weighs and where he went to school and how his hair is cut and what his dominant traits are. . . .

I do have notebooks, in which I worry at plot ideas as if they were old bones, growling and snarling and frequently burying them and digging them up again. (p. 6)

But I don't write out descriptions beforehand, and would indeed feel ridiculous, even ashamed, to do so. If the character isn't so clear to me that I know all *that* about him, what am I doing writing about him? . . . [After] all he is myself. Part of myself.

If William is a character worthy of being written about, then he exists. He exists, inside my head to be sure, but in his own right, with his own vitality. All I have to do is look at him. I don't plan him, compose him of bits and pieces, inventory him. I find him. (pp. 6-7)

This attitude towards action, creation, is evidently a basic one, the same root from which the interest in the *I Ching* and Taoist philosophy evident in most of my books arises. The Taoist world is orderly, not chaotic, but its order is not one imposed by man or by a personal or humane deity. The true laws—ethical and aesthetic, as surely as scientific—are not imposed from above by any authority, but exist in things and are to be found—discovered.

To return circuitously to Earthsea: this anti-ideological, pragmatic technique applies to places, as well as people. I did not deliberately invent Earthsea. . . . I am not an engineer, but an explorer. I discovered Earthsea. (p. 7)

The history of the discovery of Earthsea is something like this:

In 1964 I wrote a story called "The Word of Unbinding" about a wizard. . . . I don't recall now whether the fact is made much of in the story, but it was perfectly clear in my mind that it took place on an island, one among many islands. I did not give much attention to the setting . . .; and developed only such rules-of-magic as were germane to the very small point the very minor story made.

Soon after, I wrote a story, "The Rule of Names," in which both the islands and the rules of magic were considerably more developed. . . . It was set on an island called Sattins, which I knew to be one of an outlying group East of the main archipelago. (pp. 7-8)

Along in 1965 or 66 I wrote a longish story about a prince who travels down through the archipelago from its central island, Havnor, in search of the Ultimate. He goes southwest out into the open sea, beyond all islands, and finds there a people who live on rafts all their lives long. . . . This story wasn't submitted for publication as it never worked itself out at all well; but I felt strongly that the basic image—the raft-colony—was a lulu, and would find itself its home somewhere eventually. It did, in the last of the Earthsea books, *The Farthest Shore*.

I explored Earthsea no further until 1967, when the publisher of Parnassus Press, Herman Schein, asked me if I'd like to try writing a book for him. He wanted something for older kids, . . . and gave me complete freedom as to subject and approach. . . . For some weeks or months I let my imagination go groping around in search of what was wanted, in the dark. It stumbled over the Islands, and the magic employed there. Serious consideration of magic, and of writing for kids, combined to make me wonder about wizards. Wizards are usually elderly or ageless Gandalfs, quite rightly and archetypically. But what were they before they had white beards? How did they learn what is obviously an erudite and dangerous art? Are there colleges for young wizards? . . . And so on.

The story of the book is essentially a voyage, a pattern in the form of a long spiral. I began to see the places where the young wizard would go. Eventually I drew a map. Now that I knew where everything was, now was the time for cartography. Of course a great deal of it only appeared above water, as it were, in drawing the map. (pp. 8-9)

People often ask how I think of names in fantasies, and again I have to answer that I find them, that I hear them. This is an important subject in this context. From that first story on, *naming* has been the essence of the art-magic as practiced in Earthsea. For me, as for the wizards, to know the name of an island or a character is to know the island or the person. Usually the name comes of itself, but sometimes one must be very careful: as I was with the protagonist, whose true name is Ged. I worked (in collaboration with a wizard named Ogion) for a long time trying to 'listen for' his name, and making certain it really was his name. This all sounds very mystical and indeed there are aspects of it I do not understand, but it is a pragmatic business too, since if the name had been wrong the character would have been wrong—misbegotten, misunderstood. (p. 9)

Much the same holds for the bits of invented languages in the text of the trilogy. . . .

[In] *The Farthest Shore* there are several whole sentences in the Language of the Making, as dragons will not speak anything else. These arrived, spelling (formidable) and all, and I wrote them down without question. (p. 10)

I said that to know the true name is to know the thing, for me, and for the wizards. This implies a good deal about the 'meaning' of the trilogy, and about me. The trilogy is, in one aspect, about the artist. The artist as magician. The Trickster. Prospero. That is the only truly allegorical aspect it has of which I am conscious. If there are other allegories in it please don't tell me: I hate allegories. A is 'really' B, and a hawk is 'really' a handsaw—bah. Humbug.

Any creation, primary or secondary, with any vitality to it, can 'really' be a dozen mutually exclusive things at once, before breakfast.

Wizardry is artistry. The trilogy is then, in this sense, about art, the creative experience, the creative process. There is always this circularity in fantasy. The snake devours its tail. Dreams must explain themselves.

It was interesting, trying to write for children (i.e., people over twelve years old). It was hard. (pp. 10-11)

There is seldom big quick money in kiddylit, but a successful children's book has an unusually long life. It sells to schools, to libraries, and to gift-giving adults, and it goes on selling, and making money, for years and years and years. This is not reflected in the advances or the royalties. It is a very badly paid field, in general.

But the economic discrimination is only an element, as usual, of the real problem: a reflection of a prejudice. The real trouble isn't the money, it's the adult chauvinist piggery.

"You're a juvenile writer, aren't you?"
Yeth, mummy. . . .
"It must be relaxing to write *simple* things for a change."

Sure it's simple, writing for kids. Just as simple as bringing them up.

All you do is take all the sex out, and use little short words, and little dumb ideas, and don't be too scary, and be sure there's a happy ending. Right? Nothing to it. Write down. Right on.

If you do all that, you might even write *Jonathan Livingston Seagull* and make twenty billion dollars and have every adult in America reading your book!

But you won't have every kid in America reading your book. They will look at it, and they will see straight through it, with their clear, cold, beady little eyes, and they will put it down, and they will go away. Kids will devour vast amounts of garbage (and it is good for them) but they are not like adults: they have not yet learned to eat plastic. (pp. 11-12)

The most childish thing about *A Wizard of Earthsea*, I expect, is its subject: coming of age.

Coming of age is a process that took me many years; I finished it, so far as I ever will, at about age 31; and so I feel rather deeply about it. So do most adolescents. It's their main occupation, in fact.

The subject of *The Tombs of Atuan* is, if I had to put it in one word, sex. There's a lot of symbolism in the book, most of which I did not, of course, analyse consciously while writing; the symbols can all be read as sexual. More exactly, you could call it a feminine coming of age. Birth, rebirth, destruction, freedom are the themes.

The Farthest Shore is about death. That's why it is a less well-built, less sound and complete book than the others. They were about things I had already lived through and survived. *The Farthest Shore* is about the thing you do not live through and survive. It seemed an absolutely suitable subject to me for young readers, since in a way one can say that the hour when a child realizes, not that death exists—children are intensely aware of death—but that he/she, per-

sonally, is mortal, will die, is the hour when childhood ends, and the new life begins. Coming of age again, but in a larger context.

In any case I had little choice about the subject. Ged, who was always very strong-minded, always saying things that surprised me and doing things he wasn't supposed to do, took over completely in this book. He was determined to show me how his life must end, and why. I tried to keep up with him, but he was always ahead. I rewrote the book more times than I want to remember, trying to keep him under some kind of control. . . . If you insist upon discovering instead of planning, this kind of trouble is inevitable. It is a most uneconomical way to write. The book is still the most imperfect of the three, but it is the one I like best. It is the end of the trilogy, but it is the dream I have not stopped dreaming. (pp. 12-13)

> *Ursula K. Le Guin, excerpted from "Dreams Must Explain Themselves," in* Algol *#21 (copyright © 1973, 1975 by Ursula K. Le Guin; reprinted by permission of the author and the author's agent, Virginia Kidd), November, 1973 (and reprinted in* Dreams Must Explain Themselves, *by Ursula K. Le Guin, Algol Press, 1975, pp. 5-13).*

GENERAL COMMENTARY

[Ursula Le Guin's] . . . fiction is closer to fantasy than naturalism, but it is . . . grounded in ethical concerns . . ., despite its apparent distance from present actualities. (p. 39)

There are few writers in the United States who offer fiction as pleasurable and thoughtful as Ursula Le Guin's. It is time for her to be recognized beyond the special provinces of fantasy and science fiction or feminism as simply one of our best writers. (pp. 39-40)

> *Robert Scholes, in* The New Republic *(reprinted by permission of* The New Republic; *© 1976 by The New Republic, Inc.), October 30, 1976.*

THE EARTHSEA TRILOGY: A Wizard of Earthsea; The Tombs of Atuan; The Farthest Shore

Mrs. Le Guin has an intricate imagination, and children ages 11 and up who enjoy series of books which set out to chronicle fantastic worlds in detail will not be disappointed by the way she contrives to sustain interest. All the same, "A Wizard of Earthsea" is the best of the three, its attention to physical detail effectively and exactly representing young Ged's reactions to the strange world about him. The subsequent volumes take too much for granted, including an addition to their subject-matter which allows the author to indulge herself in lengthy passages that become tedious. Attentive children may also find that Ged's character scarcely achieves a credible consistency or continuity; indeed he seems a different person in each, unwise in the first, reticent in his magic in the second, wise but at the same time adventurous in the third.

Now that the series is complete, it cries out for comparisons. Tolkien's "Lord of the Rings" and C. S. Lewis's

Narnia books will doubtless be mentioned, but in my opinion Mrs. Le Guin lacks the energy of the former or the underlying and informing theology of the latter. She has been well served by her illustrators, especially Gail Garraty, but good black-and-white decorations cannot disguise a certain absence of clear vision in the texts. The true myth is like a dream—it speaks straight from the unconscious. Mrs. Le Guin's myths, with the exception of much of "A Wizard of Earthsea," seem rather too conscious of themselves, too near the surface of contrivance.

> *Robert Nye, "Doings in Earthsea," in* The New York Times Book Review (© *1973 by The New York Times Company; reprinted by permission), February 18, 1973, p. 8.*

[Ursula Le Guin] always shows a concern with the dignity of man, which she communicates to us through her artistic skill. She is an elegant, but not a light writer: not to be trifled with.

Superficially her work charms because it has all the glitter of high intelligence and efficiency. Mrs Le Guin is extremely gifted. . . . [Her] narrative gift, her wide-ranging intellect, her good clean prose, her pathos, the sympathy she can win for all her characters, even the villains, her ability to evoke the look of a place in vivid clear colours, and the poetic resourcefulness with which she manipulates language and symbols, would guarantee her an honourable place in any company. Her one weakness, it seems, is a certain inability to devise her own launching-pad. *A Wizard of Earthsea* is the tale of the sorcerer's apprentice; . . . *The Tombs of Atuan* is Theseus and Ariadne. Still, Mrs Le Guin never makes the least attempt to disguise her borrowings, and she handles them in a manner which makes them all her own. . . .

Probe a little deeper, and it is her originality and fecundity that are most impressive. Writers of fantasy commonly create their own universe, and make it as solid as they can; but Ursula Le Guin, whose worlds are all as solid as Middle-earth or Frank Herbert's Dune (and a great deal solider than Narnia) is unusual in her ability to multiply her creations. (p. 43)

To anyone who cares for the art of fiction, the writer's skill will give almost as much pleasure as the exciting and moving tale on which she lavishes it.

Yet there are other charming and convincing storytellers. Their very gifts sometimes betray them: power and variety become ends in themselves, books mere playthings. Mrs Le Guin is safe from such a fate: her danger is far greater, for she is playing for the highest stakes. Underlying all her work, . . . is an obsessive vision and concern. Fantasy, for her, is even more than a personal expression. Her ambition goes beyond that: she is a religious writer, and her success must ultimately be measured by the degree to which she affects the religious views of her readers. . . .

Ursula Le Guin has great literary tact; but she is greatly helped by the nature of Taoism. It is a religion without a god, without a church, without promises of immortality. (p. 44)

Taoism appeals to Mrs Le Guin at least in part because it is a supremely elegant expression of the sort of wisdom that characterised the Red Indian shamans she knew, through her father, as a child. The principal inhabitants of Earthsea are red men, and their day-to-day acquiescence in the ways of nature owes as much to the way of life of the North American Indians before the whites destroyed it as to the nostrums of Lao-Tse and Chuang-Tse. Yet the Taoist view is there. The essential principle underlying the true magic of Earthsea is equilibrium. . . .

It is Taoism that provided her with her wizards, guardians of the equilibrium. . . .

Mrs Le Guin sets them to work in the bright and dangerous world she has imagined. The satisfaction of her stories is that her heroes and heroines are constantly on the brink of doing the wrong thing, and sometimes do: a reader holds his breath at every turn. . . . In short, the young will never be bored, and seldom be perplexed; this is high, heroic narrative. Yet, at the root of all, is the covert Taoist questioning. In a primary world where, through the greed, cowardice, cruelty and restlessness of men, the equilibrium is far indeed from being maintained, Mrs Le Guin takes pains to suggest notions of a different order. "In Tao the only motion is returning; the only useful quality, weakness." Behind the brilliance of her books are some very subversive notions indeed. (p. 45)

> *Fantastes, "Enchantress of Earthsea," in* Cambridge Review: Fantasy in Literature, *November 23, 1973, pp. 43-5.*

[If] I were to choose one writer to illustrate the way in which it is possible to unite speculation and fabulation in works of compelling power and beauty, employing a language that is fully adequate to this esthetic intention, that writer would be the Good Witch of the West.

In the Land of Oz, all the good witches come from the north and south, the wicked witches from the east and west. But we do not live in the Land of Oz and must take our witches as we find them. Ursula Kroeber Le Guin, born in California and a resident of Oregon, is very much of the west, and the literary magic she works is so dazzling as to make the title of "good witch" almost literally appropriate. . . . She has been compared to C. S. Lewis, with some appropriateness, expecially as concerns her juvenile trilogy, but that comparison fails ultimately because she is a better writer than Lewis: her fictions, both juvenile and adult, are richer, deeper, and more beautiful than his. She is probably the best writer of speculative fabulation working in this country today. . . . (pp. 79-80)

The Earthsea trilogy . . . [has] been compared to C. S. Lewis's chronicles of Narnia, especially by English reviewers, for whom this constitutes considerable praise. But the comparison is misleading. Lewis's books are allegories in the narrow sense of that much abused word—his Lion *is* Christ, and the whole structure of the chronicles is a reenactment of Christian legend. . . . The ultimate value of such allegorizing, then, must reside in the permanent value of the legendary pattern itself, raising the question of how the story of Christ functions cognitively to help us understand our world and live in it. . . . [This] kind of allegory is leading its readers toward a stock response based on a pre-established and rigidly codified set of values. But there is another kind of allegory—allegory in a broader sense—which is more speculative and less dogmatic. Ursula Le Guin, in the Earthsea trilogy, relies on the mythic patterns of sin and redemption, quest and discovery, too, but she places them in the service of a metaphysic which is entirely responsible to modern conditions of being because its perspective is broader than the Christian perspective—because finally it takes the world more seriously than the Judeo-Christian tradition has ever allowed it to be taken.

What Earthsea represents . . . is the universe as a dynamic, balanced system, not subject to the capricious miracles of any deity, but only to the natural laws of its own working, which include a role for magic and for powers other than human, but only as aspects of the great Balance or Equilibrium, which is the order of this cosmos. . . . Ursula Le Guin works not with a theology but with an ecology, a cosmology, a reverence for the universe as a self-regulating structure. This seems to me more relevant to our needs than Lewis, but not simply because it is a more modern view—rather because it is a deeper view, closer to the great pre-Christian mythologies of this world and also closer to what three centuries of science have been able to discover about the nature of the universe. No one, in fact, has ever made magic seem to function so much like science as Ursula Le Guin. . . . (pp. 81-3)

A Wizard of Earthsea is the story of the making of a mage, the education and testing of a young man born with the power to work wonders but lacking the knowledge to bring this power to fruition and to control its destructive potential. (p. 83)

Ged's quest, [after he has unleashed a shadow of terror] is to find the shadow and subdue it, to restore the Balance that he has upset by working his power in a way beyond his knowledge. His quest is both an adventure story and an allegory which clearly raises the parallel to Lewis's Narnian allegory. For Ged must try to redeem his world, too, He must struggle with an evil power and suffer in the process. The difference is that Ged himself is the sinner who has made this redemption necessary. In C. S. Lewis's universe, which is the traditional Christian universe, God functions like Maxwell's demon, to distort the natural balance of the universe. God accepts the blame for man's sin without accepting the responsibility, leaving the world forever unbalanced, with man forever burdened by a debt that cannot be repaid. In the case of Ged, however, the redemption of the individual will restore the Great Balance, making the world harmonious again. Ged's final sacrifice will save both himself and the world equally, and at once. There is no eternity, no heaven in this universe, though the spirits of the dead are not lost; there is only the balance, in which death defines life as the darkness defines the light. (p. 85)

The shadow was himself, his own capacity for evil, summoned up by his own power. To become whole, he had to face it, name it with his own name, and accept it as a part of himself. Thus by restoring the balance in himself, he helped to restore the balance of his world. (p. 86)

Is this magic? Religion? Science? The great gift of Ursula Le Guin is to offer us a perspective in which these all merge, in which realism and fantasy are not opposed, because the supernatural is naturalized—not merely postulated but regulated, systematized, made part of the Great Equilibrium itself. And of course, this is also art, in which the sounds of individual sentences are as cunningly balanced as the whole design, in which a great allegory of the destructive power of science unleashed, and a little allegory of an individual seeking to conquer his own chaotic impulses, come together as neatly as the parts of a dove's tail. (pp. 86-7)

Robert Scholes, in his Structural Fabulation: An Essay on Fiction of the Future *(copyright © 1975 by University of Notre Dame Press), University of Notre Dame Press, 1975.*

[Creation] of relevance from what appears to careless readers as unbridled fantasy is embodied as well as anywhere in modern literature by Ursula K. Le Guin's trilogy of books, *A Wizard of Earthsea, The Tombs of Atuan, The Farthest Shore:* and significantly enough it is based on a semantic point. The archipelago-world of the trilogy (we never find out where or when it is) is devoid of science, but based on magic. Mrs. Le Guin identifies the workers of magic reasonably indifferently as wizards or witches or sorcerers, but there is one term she does not use, and that the commonest of all in Modern English: a worker of magic is never described as a "magician" [but rather as a "mage."] The reason, of course, is that this term has a familiar current sense, deprecatory if not pejorative, "a practitioner of legerdemain." . . . The point may seem a trivial one, and yet is close to the trilogy's thematic centre. The continuous and consistent use of words *not* familiar to the modern reader reminds him to suspend his judgement: his ideas, like his vocabulary, may be inadequate, or wrong.

This, indeed, is the basic point repeated through the first half of the first book in the sequence, *A Wizard of Earthsea.* Definitions of magic are repeatedly implied, or stated, and then turned down or disproved: the definitions bear a close resemblance to those current in our world. . . . [One] theory of magic, the anthropological one, stated most clearly by B. Malinowski, [is] that magic is in essence a cathartic activity, called forth by stress, and working in so far as it produces confidence. . . . Ged understands perfectly well the difference between desire and fulfillment, hope and fact. He is, in short, not the self-deluding savage whom Malinowski regards as the appropriate and natural practitioner of magic.

Ged is in fact at all times rather precisely placed within a framework of anthropological theory. For Malinowski's "cathartic" notion is not the only influential modern explanation of magic. Even more widespread were the "intellectualist" theories of Herbert Spencer, E. B. Tylor, Sir James Frazer, and others, by which magic was, as it were, a crude and mistaken first step in the evolution of man towards science and the nineteenth century, a "monstrous farrago" indeed, [a quotation from Tylor's *Primitive Culture,* Vol. I] but nevertheless one based on observation and classification, if not experiment: something closer to science than to religion (so Frazer argued) because based on the assumption that the universe ran on "immutable laws" [quoted from Frazer's *The Golden Bough*]. It may seem that the magic of Earthsea can be reduced to a kind of unfamiliar technology in this way, since it depends on knowledge and has severe limits to its power, but that too would be wrong. For the very first thing that Mrs. Le Guin does in the trilogy is to show us one way in which magic differs profoundly from science: it all depends on who does it! . . . A mage . . . is knowledgeable, like a scientist; but his knowledge needs to be combined with personal genius, a quality we tend to ascribe to artists. And unlike both, his skill (or art, or science) has some close relationship with an awareness of ethics—something we expect, not of a priest perhaps, but of a saint.

It is the oscillation between concepts of this kind . . . which draws one on into *A Wizard of Earthsea,* searching for conclusions; and the book is evidently a *Bildungsroman,* a story of a sorcerer's apprenticeship, where one's attention is simultaneously on the growth of personal maturity, as one would normally expect, but also on the acquisition of technique. Once again, the basic processes of magic in Earthsea depend on a concept brought to prominence by early modern anthropology: what one might call the "Rumpelstiltzkin" theory. This is, that every person, place, or thing possesses a true name distinct from its name in ordinary human language; and that knowing the true name, the *signifiant,* gives the mage power over the thing itself, the *signifié.* . . . What Mrs. Le Guin is clearly suggesting . . . is that this promotion of the thing above the word has philosophical links with materialism, industrialisation, the notion that, to modern men, "Nature is a machine to be worked, and taken to bits if it won't work as he pleases." In her imagined world, the devotion to the word rather than the thing is bound up with an attitude of respect for all parts of creation (even rocks), and a wary reluctance to operate on any of them without a total awareness of their distinct and individual nature. (pp. 149-52)

[The] semantics and the explanations and the detailed apprenticeship of Ged are all necessary preparations to allow the author to approach a theme which cannot be outranked in importance by those of the least "escapist" of "mainstream" fictions, and which can perhaps nowadays only be expressed in fantasy: matters, indeed, of life and death. (p. 152)

For the temptation which runs as a thread through the account of Ged's apprenticeship is to act, to exploit his power, to reject the wise passivity of the true mage. . . . It is dangerous not just because it breaks the rules of magery, including the often-mentioned but dimly-defined concept of Equilibrium, but because light and speech draw their opposites, shadow and silence: which are, quite overtly, terms for death. In seeking to preserve and aggrandise himself (and others) Ged draws up his own extinction. . . . Nevertheless, it is not that which is frightening, but the land of the dead itself . . .: a conception lonelier and less humanised than the Styx which Aeneas crosses with his golden bough, and yet closer to Classical images than to the familiar Christian ones of Heaven and Hell.

It may be said that the fear of this dim place underlies the whole of the *Earthsea* trilogy, to be faced directly in the last book. But the land of the dead also acts as an ultimate support for the structure of ideas already outlined. Ged's temptation is to use his power; it is a particularly great temptation to use it to summon the dead or bring back the dying. . . . And yet the respect for separate existences within the totality of existence, which is inherent in magic dependent on knowing the names of things, resists the diminution of others which comes from prolongation of the self, extension of life. One might say that the darkness has rights too. So the nature of his own art is against Ged, and his attempts to break Equilibrium with his own light only call forth a new shadow. . . . The questions that agitate Ged and the reader from then till the end of the book are: "What is it? Has it a name?" (pp. 152-53)

The puzzle is resolved in the only possible compromise when Ged, after being hunted by the beast and then turning to hunt it instead, catches up with it in the desolate waters beyond the easternmost island. . . . Here man and shadow fight, *and fuse;* the land turns back to sea; for each has spoken the other's name simultaneously, and the names are the same, "Ged." The shadow, then, is equal and opposite to the man who casts it; it does have a name, but not one of its own. . . . The story then makes a clear final point, needing almost no critical exegesis. What should be realised further and more consciously, however, is first that this point about the nature of existence is in harmony with the earlier discussion of the nature of magic, with its restrained if not submissive philosophy; and second that all the philosophical implications of *A Wizard of Earthsea* exist in defiance of twentieth-century orthodoxys, whether semantic, scientific, or religious. It is an achievement to have created such a radical critique and alternative, and one so unsentimentally attractive.

One final way in which the book may be considered is indeed *as* an alternative, one might say a parody or anti-myth if the words did not sound imappropriately aggressive. [Ged re-enacts] the scene of Helen and Dr. Faustus [and] his return from the land of the dead [is] reminiscent of the *Aeneid* in its difficulty . . . though different in being done without a golden bough. To these one might add the final scene. For one of Sir James Frazer's great achievements in *The Golden Bough* was to create a myth of wasteland and fertility rite and king who must die, a myth mighty yet, as one can see just from book-titles. The regenerative aspect of that myth, as Miss Jessie Weston restated it, was the "freeing of the waters," the clearing of the dry springs. . . . The weakness of Sir James's myth was that it asked us to accept a cyclic process as rebirth; and Mrs. Le Guin knows the limits of such consolation. More positively, there is another aspect in which *The Golden Bough* is rejected by *A Wizard of Earthsea.* Sir James entitled his third volume—which contains the discussion of names—"Taboo and the Perils of the Soul"; and his account of true- and use-names was accordingly entirely about psychic dangers and the universal mistrust of savages. But Ged and his companions, once again, are no savages, for all their habits of nomenclature. Repeatedly in the book we have moving scenes where characters, instead of concealing their names as is normal and advisable, *reveal* them to each other in gestures of trust and affection. . . . And [this] is the final impression that Earthsea gives: a world surrounded by the ocean in space and by the dry land of the dead in time, but still bright, warm, and fearless, removed from both the insecure exploitativeness of modernity and the meaningless murderousness of Frazerian antiquity. It offers a goal rather than an escape.

In a story so concerned with the fear of death and the assertion of life, one must expect to find strong statements of pathos, as with the pointless and unstoppable death of Ioeth, the little son of Ged's fisherman-friend. Throughout *A Wizard of Earthsea,* however, pathos is very rarely caused by deliberate, human cruelty; and what cruelty there is comes not from the Inner Lands, but from the eastern empire of Karego-At. . . . It is an extreme move, then, to set the second book of the trilogy in Atuan, one of the four islands of the empire; and to use it as a setting for discussion of another element not represented in the first book, the nature of religion. . . . [The] Kargs are more like us than are Ged's people from the Inner Lands. They are white, for one thing, while Ged is brown. They are fierce, hierarchic, imperialistic, slave-owning. They have an organised state religion, and indeed an organised state, both unfamiliar in the rest of Earthsea. And officially at least, they do not believe in magic. (pp. 153-55)

The real fear beneath Kargish religion [of the Nameless Ones] is to have that assurance taken away, to have the whole thing exposed as a tragic mistake, or swindle, and the threat which Arha, accordingly, fears most is that of atheism—even if this is a warm and affectionate atheism like that of Earthsea mages or many modern agnostics. (p. 156)

As with the anonymity or otherwise of the shadow-beast earlier, there are questions with quite objective answers at the core of *The Tombs of Atuan*. Nor are the new answers very dissimilar. Ged's central statement is that the Nameless Ones are powers, but not gods, and that their strength has two sources. One is the innate cruelty of the universe—a concept familiar to us since the time of Darwin. The other is the human reaction to that fact, the impulse to propitiate and sacrifice and offer scapegoats.... Ged's essential point, and Mrs. Le Guin's, is that though the universe cannot be denied, and loss of one kind or another is therefore inevitable, what can be controlled is the placatory impulse which seeks to control death but in practice makes an institution of it. Pathos is always with us, in short, but cruelty can be stopped. (p. 157)

The movement of the first two books of the trilogy is then on the whole downwards, into a deepening gloom, and towards us, towards familiarity. It is continued and even accelerated in the last book, *The Farthest Shore,* which describes what things are like when the magic starts to run out. Earthsea begins to resemble America in the aftermath of Vietnam: exhausted, distrustful, uncertain.... Earthsea, in a word, has grown secularised; and we recognise the condition.

The root of the process is told us many times, and is entirely predictable from the two preceding books. It is the fear of death.... The new if related factor in *The Farthest Shore* is more precisely the hope of life. (pp. 158-59)

[In] Earthsea the one who brings the promise is a destroyer; the Christian of *Pilgrim's Progress,* who flees from his family with his hands over his ears, shouting "Life, life, eternal life!," now reappears as the wizards who abandon their trade and turn the world to shoddiness and gloom.... [There] is a consistent image which underlies *The Farthest Shore,* and which seems to be taken from another book about the failure (and reattainment) of belief, Dostoyevsky's *Crime and Punishment*. There the morbid, sensual, ghost-haunted *roué* Svidrigaylov propounds his personal theory of eternity. Raskolnikov has just said "I do not believe in a future life"—a statement that holds no terrors. But Svidrigaylov replies:

> "And what if there are only spiders there, or something of the sort.... We're always thinking of eternity as an idea that cannot be understood, something immense. But why must it be? What if, instead of all this, you suddenly find just a little room there, something like a village bathhouse, grimy and spiders in every corner, and that's all eternity is."

... Ged's enemy seems close to Svidrigaylov, especially in

that both have an abnormal terror of death; and his promise of eternity is inextricably spidery. His use-name, to begin with (he has forgotten his true-name) is Cob, the old English word for spider. . . . There are many other contributory references. All suggest the entrapment of life in something powerful yet tenuous: if Cob has his way, both the lands of the dead and of the living will become like Svidrigaylov's bath-house, dry, dusty, covered by his personal web.

In both works faith (whether in magic and Equilibrium or in Christianity and eternal life) is wrecked by doubt, a parallel which ought to clear Mrs. Le Guin of the charge of wilful blasphemy. She is implying, not that Christianity leads to morbidity, but rather that the present inability of many to believe in any supernatural power lays them open to fear and selfishness and a greedy clutching at hope which spoils even the present life that one can be sure of.... Mrs. Le Guin has no trouble in convincing us that loss of faith is unfortunate, nor that joy in life is a proper goal. What is difficult is persuading us that the latter can co-exist with the former, or (to put it in the symbols of her trilogy) that magic is worthwhile even when it promises no immortality. The solution, for the last time, turns on an objective realisation, about names. (pp. 160-61)

For the simplest way to describe the shades in the land of the dead is to say that they are names, which go there and must stay there.... Perhaps one should say that a man's name is his self, his sense that he is who he is; once the man is dead this never returns. (p. 162)

We are on our own; living is a process not a state; reality is to be endured not changed: precepts of this nature underlie the *Earthsea* trilogy.... [It] has to be said that these three books clearly aim at having some of the qualities of parable as well as of narrative, and that the parables are repeatedly summed up by statements within the books themselves. Mages appear to think in contrasts. "To light a candle is to cast a shadow," says one; "to speak, one must be silent," says another.... [*A Wizard of Earthsea* is] not just a parable, but a parable for our times.

It is tempting to lead on and declare that Mrs. Le Guin is a "mythopoeic" writer (an adjective many critics find easy to apply to fantasy in general). The truth, though, seems to be that she is at least as much of an iconoclast, a myth-breaker not a myth-maker. She rejects resurrection and eternal life; she refutes "cathartic" and "intellectualist" versions of anthropology alike; her relationship with Sir James Frazer in particular is one of correction too grave for parody.... As was said at the start, she demands of us that we reconsider even our basic vocabulary, with insistent redefinitions of "magic," "soul," "name," "alive." . . . One might end by remarking that novelty is blended with familiarity even in the myth which underlies the history of Earthsea itself, the oldest song of *The Creation of Éa* which is sung by Ged's companions in at least two critical moments. "Only in silence the word," it goes, "only in dark the light...." By the end of the trilogy we realise that this is more than just a rephrasing of our own "Genesis" as given by St. John. Mrs. Le Guin takes "In the beginning was the Word" more seriously and more literally than do many modern theologians; but her respect for ancient texts includes no great regard for the mythic structures that have been built on them. (pp. 162-63)

T. A. Shippey, "The Magic Art and the

Evolution of Words: Ursula Le Guin's Earthsea Trilogy, in MOSAIC X/2 *(copyright © 1977 by The University of Manitoba Press), Winter, 1977, pp. 147-63.*

OTHER CITATIONS

The Economist, *April 13, 1974, p. 70.*

Margery Fisher, in her Growing Point, *May, 1977, pp. 3118-19.*

THE FARTHEST SHORE (1972)

As always, there can be no quarrel with the world [Le Guin] creates: She walks the paths of fantasy much as Sparrowhawk traverses the Dark Land—in full awareness and with a certain awe of the power that is hers. But in [*The Farthest Shore*] the scope of what is being dealt with is greater than what either the story or the characters can handle. The characters themselves are somehow flat. The author is a myth-maker, and as such her territory rightly spans life, death, philosophy, history, and religion. But because she is such a consummate myth-maker, the vehicle she chooses to carry her creation must be exceptionally strong. This book is not such a vehicle. Yet, the language is evocative, the world created absolute, and the "dragons on the wind of morning" will burn in the imagination. (p. 600)

> *Sheryl B. Andrews, in* The Horn Book Magazine *(copyright © 1972 by The Horn Book, Inc., Boston), December, 1972.*

Opinions may always differ on whether *A Wizard of Earthsea* or its current sequel, *The Farthest Shore*, is the greater book. . . . But few will dispute that both Le Guin books are cut from the same cloth, offer the same heady range of scene and plan, pose and meet no less audacious problems, in no less seductive style. . . .

At its very simplest level [*The Farthest Shore*] is a major adventure yarn: heroic, anguished, desperate, noble, demanding to the uttermost. (What would yesterday's boy readers have made of it?) But the wounds and scars don't come from the usual battlefields. . . . The author does not even resort to that hallowed and useful convention of fairy tale, which comfortably packs all evil into nonhuman creatures, cyclops, troll, or beast. When she deals with ultimates—the greatest mage, the farthest edge of the world (and this is a major element in Le Guin)—she carries total belief. . . . Unlike Kingsley, MacDonald, Kipling, C. S. Lewis, she does not take any overt political or theological stance. Indeed her own voice (again, compare that crotchety set of geniuses) does not seem to be heard at all. But the ideas are inescapably there, intrinsic to the whole, and with sure contemporary relevance. . . . Earthsea is not the only place with a secret name for every thing or being; with a choice in the personal road that every one must take.

After Earthsea-lore, with its weight and substance, most other modern fantasies must ring thin.

> *"A Hole in the World," in* The Times Literary Supplement *(© Time Newspapers Ltd., 1973; reproduced from* The Times Literary Supplement *by permission), April 6, 1973, p. 379.*

OTHER CITATIONS

Sada Fretz, in Book World—The Washington Post, *Part 2, May 13, 1973, p. 6.*

Shirley Toulson, in New Statesman, *May 25, 1973, p. 780.*

Peter Nixon, in an interview with a student, in Children's Literature in Education, *No. 14 (September), 1974, pp. 18-20.*

THE TOMBS OF ATUAN (1971)

As in *A Wizard of Earthsea* . . ., the author has created a successful high fantasy which may be read on a number of levels. But the storytelling is so good and the narrative pace so swift that a young reader may have to think twice before realizing that the adventures that befell Tenar were really the experiences that marked the growth of her personality. . . . Somber, but never quite reaching the depths of tragedy, [*The Tombs of Atuan*] is the story of the transformations that link life and death, and it bridges the chasm that separates the simulated reincarnation of Arha from the spiritual resurrection of Tenar. Some of the characters, like the High Priestesses Kossil and Thar, are monolithic in concept; and some, like Manan the eunuch and the novice "called Penthe," are touched with human traits. But Arha, or Tenar, who first learns to accommodate herself to death, darkness, and silence is always at the center of the book; and what began as a monodrama becomes—with the introduction of Sparrowhawk—a duet of personalities. And Atuan, like Earthsea, is located in the mind of its maker, but was created out of the very stuff of mythology and reflects universal patterns that were once embodied in Stonehenge and in the Cretan labyrinth. (p. 490)

> *Paul Heins, in* The Horn Book Magazine *(copyright © 1971 by The Horn Book, Inc., Boston), October, 1971.*

OTHER CITATIONS

"Earthsea Revisited," in The Times Literary Supplement, *April 28, 1972, p. 484.*

C. S. Hannabuss, in Children's Book Review, *June, 1972, p. 78.*

The Junior Bookshelf, *August, 1972, p. 251.*

VERY FAR AWAY FROM ANYWHERE ELSE (1976)

[In *Very Far Away from Anywhere Else*, published in England as *A Very Long Way from Anywhere Else*, seventeen-year-old] Owen fancies himself an intellectual, and a misunderstood one at that. He feels alienated from his father, who is so proud of the new car he bought for his son. He feels alienated from all his peers . . . that is, until he meets Natalie, a young woman who lives for her music and seemingly nothing else. Owen is a bore, which is saying a lot, since the characters are so flat it is difficult to say anything at all about them. This is, over-all, just a poor book. (p. 47)

> *Marilyn Darch, in* Children's Book Review Service *(copyright © 1977 Children's Book Review Service Inc.), January, 1977.*

[The] voice of an introspective youth, articulate mainly in

his mind and not at all like the average American 'teenager (though trying hard to conceal this from his peers) sounds through this compressed first-person tale, its off-hand self-depreciation giving it humour and depth. . . . In his efforts to define sex, love and friendship in his relations with Natalie, Owen may be said to have discovered himself, or at least to have come to see a future for them both that differs from conventional expectations or his own forecast. This is a subtle tale and an immediate one. The offhand voice Owen uses is managed so skilfully by the author that it helps us to hear far more than he is prepared to remember and to place him and his girl both in the world of everyday and the world of their private feelings. In this quiet, ironic, compressed story readers in the 'teens should find much to concern them. (pp. 3041-42)

> *Margery Fisher, in her* Growing Point, *January, 1977.*

OTHER CITATIONS

Ethel L. Heins, in The Horn Book Magazine, *February, 1977, pp. 57-8.*

Alleen Pace Nilsen, in English Journal, *September, 1977, p. 86.*

A WIZARD OF EARTHSEA (1968)

It is never important to pigeonhole works of fiction nor to insist that a certain book should belong, in a child's estimation, in this category or that. . . .

[I am thinking here, specifically, of the term "high fantasy." . . . Works of high fantasy reveal a striking attitude regarding the human condition and our relationships with one another. For within these tales lies the essence of their creators, the philosophy of their lives subtly woven through the pages of a story that children love and remember, and which may, quite unbeknown to the children themselves, become a lasting influence.

A Wizard of Earthsea is a fantastical tale . . . which strikes me as being a rare book that not only moves with vividness and power, but embodies the philosophic point of view of its creator. And the expression of that point of view, as in any fine piece of fiction, never for a moment stills or even momentarily impedes the movement, because this expression lies within the action and determines it.]

If, as I believe, the tests of [good] high fantasy (and certainly of any outstanding piece of fiction) lie in strength and cleanness of structure, the overwhelming sense of reality, the pervading sense of place, the communication of the visual perceptiveness of the writer, exactness of detail, the originality and discipline with which materials are handled, excellence of style, richness of character portrayal and depth of vision, then I can say with assurance that *A Wizard of Earthsea* is indeed [superb] high fantasy. (p. 333)

[Knowledge] of anthropology . . . is everywhere apparent in *A Wizard of Earthsea,* making itself felt not as a science but aesthetically as a mood of the writer. . . . [Mrs. Le Guin] feels that certain elements of [this attitude] must be "a curiosity about people different from one's own kind; interest in artifacts; interest in languages; delight in the idiosyncrasies of various cultures; a sense that time is long yet that human history is very short—and therefore a sense of kinship across seas and centuries; a love of strangeness; a love of exactness." It is these very loves and interests which enrich the quality, the texture, and the spirit of *A Wizard of Earthsea.*

A Wizard of Earthsea is, above all, a book of magic and of learning; its theme is the misuse of the power magic bestows. . . . In fact one is moved to believe, as one turns the pages of the book that surely this is one of the most complete pictures of a world immersed in magic ever written for youth. . . . (pp. 334-35)

[Names and shadows] haunt the book, they are woven through all its patterns, they lie at the heart of every scene. Recalling Ursula Le Guin's knowledge of anthropology, it is not surprising that she has used these two ancient and potent subjects to underlie and illumine her meanings. . . .

Jung, in discussing archetypes and the collective unconscious, calls the inferior side of ourselves, which is to be found in the personal unconscious, the *shadow.* And the shadow represents, for him, all that we do not allow ourselves to do, all that we do not want to be. . . . It is useless to repress it. Man must recognize it and either wrestle with it or try to change those situations which provoke it. So [the hero] Ged's shadow-beast, which he himself had released, must be sought out, recognized, and wrestled with. Concerning Ged's final struggle, we are reminded of Jung's individuation process, neither a neurotic nor a pathological phenomenon, but a struggle which all who are becoming self-aware will gradually engage in. It is an effort to become whole, to recognize and to give wise expression to both sides of one's being. (p. 337)

As for the little names of *A Wizard of Earthsea,* the names of plants and birds and fish and places and people, it would seem that Ursula Le Guin must herself be a wizard at naming. (p. 338)

The dragon whom Ged defeats with a single stroke of knowledge is called Yevaud. *Yevaud!* Do you feel what I feel in those syllables? The sound of these names falls upon my ear with ease and a sense of complete appropriateness, given the nature and atmosphere of Earthsea, but I cannot explain my satisfaction as, ideally perhaps, I should not be able to. (p. 339)

To me, it is as if Ursula Le Guin herself has lived on the Archipelago, minutely observing and noting down the habits and idiosyncracies of the culture from island to island. . . . Nothing has escaped the notice of her imagination's seeking eye, but always she has chosen her details with the discrimination of an artist for whom economy of style is the ideal. We know that the essence of any novel is its human situation, but essence without a superbly convincing context is nothing. It is only the beginning, only an idea. (p. 340)

Like all the great fantasies, *A Wizard of Earthsea* leaves an echoing in our minds, that sense of having experienced something we can never quite put into words—a divine discontent, more to be desired, C. S. Lewis believed, than any possible satisfaction. The great fantasies leave with child readers a scarcely realized sense of something beyond their reach, which gives another dimension to the world of reality. They help children to orient themselves, help them to distinguish good from evil, and to learn how the forces of good and evil work. . . . Very often danger and horror are made harshly vivid, but because these dangers and horrors occur in timelessness and in the world of magic, children learn to face without shock what otherwise might be unendurable: the force of that dark message which both dreams and fantasy so often bring. Finally, it is not only facts about the world that children need to know, Joanna Field says in *A Life of One's Own,* but facts about themselves, and only through the imaginative symbols of fantasy and fairy tales and legends can they at first express themselves and understand something of their own deeper natures. (pp. 340-41)

Gore Vidal [in his *Rocking the Boat*] has something to say about fiction which reminds me of *A Wizard of Earthsea.* "[N]ovel writing goes, at its best, beyond cleverness to that point where one's whole mind and experience and vision *are* the novel and the effort to translate this wholeness into prose *is* the life: a circle of creation." This kind of wholeness is, I believe, what Mrs. Le Guin has accomplished. . . . For *A Wizard of Earthsea* is a work which, though it is fantasy, continually returns us to the world about us, its forces and powers; returns us to ourselves, to our own struggles and aspirations, to the very core of human responsibility. (p. 341)

> Eleanor Cameron, "High Fantasy: 'A Wizard of Earthsea'" (originally published in a different version in The Horn Book Magazine, *April, 1971; copyright © 1971 by Eleanor Cameron; revised by the critic for publication in* Children's Literature Review), in Crosscurrents of Criticism: Horn Book Essays 1968-1977, *edited by Paul Heins, The Horn Book, Inc., 1977, pp. 333-41.*

OTHER CITATIONS

C. S. Hannabuss, in Children's Book Review, *April, 1971, p. 53.*

Wendy Jago, "'A Wizard of Earthsea' and the Charge of Escapism," in Children's Literature in Education, *No. 8 (July), 1972, pp. 21-9.*

*   *   *

LEWIS, C(live) S(taples)   1898-1963

An Irish-born British mediaevalist, poet, novelist, and author of books on Christian apologetics and literary criticism, C. S. Lewis is well known for his scholarly *Allegory of Love,* a study of courtly love and its manifestation in the literature of the Middle Ages. According to Cecil Beaton and Kenneth Tynan, Lewis "combines the manner of Friar Tuck with the mind of Saint Augustine" in his writings. Lewis's reputation in children's literature rests on his seven-volume saga of Narnia. He received the 1956 Carnegie Medal for the final book in that series, *The Last Battle.* An autobiography, *Surprised by Joy,* was published in 1955. (See also *Contemporary Literary Criticism,* Vols. 1, 3, and 6.)

AUTHOR'S COMMENTARY

I think there are three ways in which those who write for children may approach their work; two good ways and one that is generally a bad way.

I came to know of the bad way quite recently and from two unconscious witnesses. One was a lady who sent me the

MS of a story she had written in which a fairy placed at a child's disposal a wonderful gadget. I say 'gadget' because it was not a magic ring or hat or cloak or any such traditional matter. It was a machine, a thing of taps and handles and buttons you could press. You could press one and get an ice cream, another and get a live puppy, and so forth. I had to tell the author honestly that I didn't care for that sort of thing. She replied, 'No more do I, it bores me to distraction. But it is what the modern child wants.' My other bit of evidence was this. In my own first story I had described at length what I thought a rather fine high tea given by a hospitable faun to the little girl who was my heroine. A man, who has children of his own, said, 'Ah, I see how you got to that. If you want to please grown-up readers you give them sex, so you thought to yourself, "That won't do for children, what shall I give them instead? I know! The little blighters like plenty of good eating.'" In reality, however, I myself like eating and drinking. I put in what I would have liked to read when I was a child and what I still like reading now that I am in my fifties.

The lady in my first example, and the married man in my second, both conceived writing for children as a special department of 'giving the public what it wants'. Children are, of course, a special public and you find out what they want and give them that, however little you like it yourself.

The next way may seem at first to be very much the same, but I think the resemblance is superficial. This is the way of Lewis Carroll, Kenneth Grahame, and Tolkien. The printed story grows out of a story told to a particular child with the living voice and perhaps *ex tempore.* It resembles the first way because you are certainly trying to give that child what it wants. But then you are dealing with a concrete person, this child who, of course, differs from all other children. . . . In any personal relation the two participants modify each other. You would become slightly different because you were talking to a child and the child would become slightly different because it was being talked to by an adult. A community, a composite personality, is created and out of that the story grows.

The third way, which is the only one I could ever use myself, consists in writing a children's story because a children's story is the best art-form for something you have to say. . . . This method could apply to other kinds of children's literature besides stories. I have been told that Arthur Mee never met a child and never wished to: it was, from his point of view, a bit of luck that boys liked reading what he liked writing. This anecdote may be untrue in fact but it illustrates my meaning. (pp. 22-3)

Where the children's story is simply the right form for what the author has to say, then of course readers who want to hear that, will read the story or re-read it, at any age. I never met *The Wind in the Willows* or the Bastable books till I was in my late twenties, and I do not think I have enjoyed them any the less on that account. I am almost inclined to set it up as a canon that a children's story which is enjoyed only by children is a bad children's story. The good ones last. A waltz which you can like only when you are waltzing is a bad waltz. (p. 24)

[Of] the three methods, I know by experience only the third. I hope my title did not lead anyone to think that I was conceited enough to give you advice on how to write a story for children. There were two very good reasons for not doing that. One is that many people have written very much better stories than I, and I would rather learn about the art than set up to teach it. The other is that, in a certain sense, I have never exactly 'made' a story. With me the process is much more like bird-watching than like either talking or building. I see pictures. Some of these pictures have a common flavour, almost a common smell, which groups them together. Keep quiet and watch and they will begin joining themselves up. If you were very lucky (I have never been as lucky as all that) a whole set might join themselves so consistently that there you had a complete story: without doing anything yourself. But more often (in my experience always) there are gaps. Then at last you have to do some deliberate inventing, have to contrive reasons why these characters should be in these various places doing these various things. I have no idea whether this is the usual way of writing stories, still less whether it is the best. It is the only one I know: images always come first. (pp. 32-3)

[Everything] in the story should arise from the whole cast of the author's mind. We must write for children out of those elements in our own imagination which we share with children: differing from our child readers not by any less, or less serious, interest in the things we handle, but by the fact that we have other interests which children would not share with us. The matter of our story should be a part of the habitual furniture of our minds. This, I fancy, has been so with all great writers for children, but it is not generally understood. . . . Nothing seems to me more fatal, for this art, than an idea that whatever we share with children is, in the privative sense, 'childish' and that whatever is childish is somehow comic. . . . The child as reader is neither to be patronized nor idolized: we talk to him as man to man. But the worst attitude of all would be the professional attitude which regards children in the lump as a sort of raw material which we have to handle. We must of course try to do them no harm: we may, under the Omnipotence, sometimes dare to hope that we may do them good. But only such good as involves treating them with respect. We must not imagine that we are Providence or Destiny. (pp. 33-4)

Once in a hotel dining-room I said, rather too loudly, 'I loathe prunes.' 'So do I,' came an unexpected six-year-old voice from another table. Sympathy was instantaneous. Neither of us thought it funny. We both knew that prunes are far too nasty to be funny. That is the proper meeting between man and child as independent personalities. Of the far higher and more difficult relations between child and parent or child and teacher, I say nothing. An author, as a mere author, is outside all that. He is not even an uncle. He is a freeman and an equal, like the postman, the butcher, and the dog next door. (p. 34)

. . . . . .

Some people seem to think that I began by asking myself how I could say something about Christianity to children; then fixed on the fairy tale as an instrument; then collected information about child-psychology and decided what age group I'd write for; then drew up a list of basic Christian truths and hammered out 'allegories' to embody them. This is all pure moonshine. I couldn't write in that way at all. Everything began with images; a faun carrying an umbrella, a queen on a sledge, a magnificent lion. At first there wasn't even anything Christian about them; that element pushed itself in of its own accord. It was part of the bubbling.

Then came the Form. As these images sorted themselves into events (i.e., became a story) they seemed to demand no love interest and no close psychology. But the Form which excludes these things is the fairy tale. And the moment I thought of that I fell in love with the Form itself: its brevity, its severe restraints on description, its flexible traditionalism, its inflexible hostility to all analysis, digression, reflections and 'gas'. I was now enamoured of it. Its very limitations of vocabulary became an attraction; as the hardness of the stone pleases the sculptor or the difficulty of the sonnet delights the sonneteer.

On that side (as Author) I wrote fairy tales because the Fairy Tale seemed the ideal Form for the stuff I had to say.

Then of course the Man in me began to have his turn. I thought I saw how stories of this kind could steal past a certain inhibition which had paralysed much of my own religion in childhood. Why did one find it so hard to feel as one was told one ought to feel about God or about the sufferings of Christ? I thought the chief reason was that one was told one ought to. An obligation to feel can freeze feelings. And reverence itself did harm. The whole subject was associated with lowered voices; almost as if it were something medical. But supposing that by casting all these things into an imaginary world, stripping them of their stained-glass and Sunday school associations, one could make them for the first time appear in their real potency? Could one not thus steal past those watchful dragons? I thought one could. (pp. 36-7)

The Fantastic or Mythical is a Mode available at all ages for some readers; for others, at none. At all ages, if it is well used by the author and meets the right reader, it has the same power: to generalize while remaining concrete, to present in palpable form not concepts or even experiences but whole classes of experience, and to throw off irrelevancies. But at its best it can do more; it can give us experiences we have never had and thus, instead of 'commenting on life', can add to it. I am speaking, of course, about the thing itself, not my own attempts at it. (p. 38)

> *C. S. Lewis, "On Three Ways of Writing for Children" and "Sometimes Fairy Stories May Say Best What's to Be Said," in his Of Other Worlds: Essays and Stories, edited by Walter Hooper (copyright © 1966 by The Executors of the Estate of C. S. Lewis; reprinted by permission of Harcourt Brace Jovanovich, Inc.), Harcourt, Brace & World, 1966 (and reprinted by Harcourt Brace Jovanovich, 1975, pp. 22-34, 35-8).*

THE CHRONICLES OF NARNIA: *The Lion, the Witch and the Wardrobe; Prince Caspian: The Return to Narnia; The Voyage of the Dawn Treader; The Silver Chair; The Horse and His Boy; The Magician's Nephew; The Last Battle*

Within limitations, it is not hard to suppose that Peter's shield with the great red lion on it is the Christian armor, that Aslan's breath which brings greatness is like Christ's breath imparting the Holy Spirit, that Susan's magic horn is a symbol of prayer, and that the Noble Order of the Table is intended to suggest the Eucharist. (p. 138)

[But there] are some satiric and other implications beyond the Christian in the Narnia books. There is just a hint at the beginning of *The Last Battle* that Shift, the ape, hopes to set up a socialistic state in Narnia. Uncle Andrew's experimentation on guinea pigs is satirized in *The Magician's Nephew* and progressive education in *The Silver Chair*. There are psychological as well as Christian implications in the fact that dragonish thoughts turn Eustace into a dragon in *The Voyage of the Dawn Treader,* and there are Platonic overtones in the idea that earth was nothing more than a shadow-land to the glorious new Narnia.

Lewis manifests his usual realism even in these children's stories. There are numerous quarrels and backbitings among the characters, both human and animal, and not even conversion turns anybody into a goody-goody.... Perhaps the most realistic touch in all the stories is Susan's failure to get into the new Narnia at the close of *The Last Battle.* When King Tirian discovered the seven glittering kings and queens inside the happy land, he asked about Susan. Peter answered shortly and gravely, ''My sister Susan is no longer a friend of Narnia.'' (pp. 139-40)

One senses the pleasure Lewis must have had in his invention of creature and place names. Few can approach the vast accomplishment of Lewis's friend J. R. R. Tolkien in this regard, but Lewis has no mean array of them himself. In both Lewis's and Tolkien's naming of things we find a singular combination of philological astuteness and creative imagination, and, in Lewis in particular, a love of nature which gives him insight into good onomatopoeic names also....

Narnia is indeed a world in itself—again not so deep and profound a cosmos as that created by Tolkien, yet with few exceptions whole and consistent. In one respect Lewis's Narnia may be more properly called a cosmos, for he more than Tolkien takes account of our world, the world of Narnia, and the heavens themselves. Tolkien's is a neater world, more consistent and logical, but Lewis's contains paradox and in that sense is firmer. As one might expect, Lewis's Narnia is essentially original.... Lewis's Christian theme is ancient, fixed, and orthodox. His events, on the other hand, are created from the rich world of fantasy. It is no small accomplishment to merge these two effectively. (p. 141)

As everywhere else in Lewis, the Narnian stories contain the motif of joy and longing, both joy-in-longing and the greater joy-in-possessing. There is a good deal of romping and joking both among the people and animals, yet there is a deeper happiness and wonder which is ''too good to waste on jokes.'' The latter is far the more prominent sort of joy depicted. (p. 144)

A dominant idea in these stories is that of an earlier time when things were more a harmony and unity.... Always there is the notion of an older and better world, and very often that world in Lewis is simply the Garden of Eden. On the other hand, there is not only the Eden that was but also the Eden to come, the new Narnia of *The Last Battle.* (pp. 144-45)

Excellent as are the Narnian stories, I feel that they are not entirely without defects. There are minor errors, as when Digory's last name is spelled both Kirk and Kirke, Calormen is spelled Kalormen, and Ettinsmore called Ettinsmuir. More serious are some lapses in structural unity such as the unmotivated appearance of the underwater people toward the end of *The Voyage of the Dawn Treader* and the uncharacteristic conversation of the Tarkeena Lasaraleen in *The Horse and His Boy.* ...

Yet the defects are as nothing compared to the excellencies. (p. 145)

> *Clyde S. Kilby, "The Kingdom of Narnia," in his* The Christian World of C. S. Lewis *(copyright © 1964 by Wm. B. Eerdmans Publishing Co.), Eerdmans, 1964, pp. 116-46.*

[As] an imaginative writer Lewis seems to me to be completely and satisfyingly English. He himself has told us of his boyhood entrancement by the sagas of Iceland, and in his work he must have read the books of almost every medieval writer in Europe, but while the impact of foreign culture may have widened a mind already wide enough to take in the conception of Deep Heaven, it did not affect his native bluntness and fresh poetry.

These qualities come out forthrightly—as if, with a sigh of pleasure, all the brakes had been taken off—in his seven books for children, the Narnia stories.

All the things that he seems to have liked best are here: magic, talking animals, a group of friends having adventures, the over-riding moral sense, danger and courage in face of it, and, of course, allegory. (pp. 98-9)

In the ... Narnia books [following *The Lion, the Witch and the Wardrobe*] the allegory is much stronger and more plain, so strong that when, in *The Last Battle,* the final book of the series, I found the great lion who has haunted the former stories given a capital H—'and as He spoke He no longer looked to them like a lion'—I felt a shock: not, of course, with any implication of disapproval, but pure shock, as if cold water had spouted up from the page....

Most of us modern Christians are poor weak creatures, and tend to be over-conscious of two thousand years being a very long time; even if we have not been trained in scientific thinking we have unconsciously absorbed some of the half-baked and one-sided thinking that floats uneasily around in this most unhappy age, and we tend to see Christ as pictured and static and *past.* I do not believe that Lewis was thus hampered. I believe that his reading in medieval literature and his painfully-acquired faith conspired to give him a personal feeling for Christ and an intellectual conception of His immediacy that was exceedingly strong; it would be a commonplace, to Lewis, to conceive of Christ under the likeness of a Lion, a Lamb, a Fish. (p. 100)

This is very bold. Its boldness makes that of some contemporary writers look inept.

Yet I confess that I do not altogether *like* it, and it could be argued that the tremendousness of the allegory mars the artistry of the tale.

I imagine the accusation would pass Lewis by completely. He would not have thought that it mattered....

C. S. Lewis [created a world], a beautiful and dangerous world lit by hope. I suppose that in his imaginative writing he might be accused of ignoring the travails and discoveries and ethos of the contemporary scene. In my opinion at least, it is all, as an imaginative writer, that he can be accused of. (p. 101)

Stella Gibbons, "Imaginative Writing," in
Light on C. S. Lewis, *edited by Jocelyn
Gibb (© 1965 by Geoffrey Bles Ltd.), Bles,
1965 (and reprinted by Harcourt Brace Jovanovich, Inc., 1976), pp. 86-101.*

There can be few authors more earnestly recommended by
adults to children than C. S. Lewis, and yet I wonder just
how many adults have sat down and read all the 'Narnia'
books right through? And if those who do, emerge as disturbed, even as sickened, as I have . . . ? (p. 126)

The books are, of course, Christian apologia—allegories on
the messianic legend combined with some kind of highly
mystical personal statement about the nature of Good and
Evil. Now there is no reason in the world why Lewis, or
anyone else, should not write stories for children in such a
form, if they are good stories. I would attack them on two
counts: firstly, that in writing with a 'message' he makes
the cardinal error of condescension towards children and
that this produces books that have been written *at* rather
than *for* children, and secondly, and most seriously, that
the moral itself, and hence much of the content, is distasteful and alarming.

The first book, *The Lion, the Witch and the Wardrobe,* introduces the four child characters (in the later books some
more are added), and takes them into the land of Narnia
where the subsequent adventures take place. It is also an
allegorical account of the Crucifixion and the Resurrection,
with even a Judas-figure thrown in for good measure. To an
adult reader the symbolism is crude in the extreme, making
it at times almost unreadable—and surely one of the tests of
a good children's book is whether or not adults can enjoy it
as well? . . .

At the level of pure story-telling [the 'Narnia' books] are
susceptible to a number of criticisms. The child characters
are never more than cardboard figures: we are not told how
old they are or what they look like and they remain indistinguishable except for their names, since what they say or do
does nothing to develop them as characters but is merely
what is convenient to keep the story moving. Their speech
is totally unreal—they are made to exclaim 'By Jove' and
'Great Scott' at regular intervals. It is the writing of one
who has not listened to how children really talk. (p. 127)

The other leading character is the Lion—Aslan, Christ, or
what you will—whose appearance in each story is marked
by a sudden change of tone from the brisk, cheerful, lets-
get-on-with-the-story note of the main narrative to a solemn, awesome atmosphere which tells us that this is where
the author is really taking things seriously. I'm sure I
cannot be alone in finding Aslan's effect on the children
quite nauseating. (pp. 127-28)

For [his] is the Christianity of the Old Testament, the awful
warning of an unrelenting and all-powerful God. It is the
Christianity of violence, the Christianity of the middle ages,
the Christianity of the Crusades, a theology in which the
only good Infidel is a dead Infidel and the sooner battle is
joined the better, the theology of a world in which Good
and Evil are locked in an eternal struggle which can only be
resolved by violence. And violence pervades the
books. . . . (p. 128)

It is this underlying savagery that, to me, makes the books
so sinister, and the more so because this is what emerges as

the most convincing thing about them. There is something
perfunctory, even condescending about much of the writing, as though the author doubted his readers' capacity to
appreciate truly thoughtful description. Many of the descriptive passages are cliché-ridden and limp and were it
not for Pauline Baynes' illustrations (in the Puffin edition),
which do evoke a magical, Ucello landscape, we would
have no very clear picture of what Narnia is meant to be
like. In places there is even something arch about the use of
language: if you want to describe a voice as 'pale' there is
no need to add 'I hope you know what I mean by a voice
sounding pale' (*The Lion, the Witch and the Wardrobe,* p.
96). That is what I mean by condescension in the writing.
But above all, the children's adventures have no real urgency, because all the creative energy in the books has
been saved up for the appearances of Aslan, and the presentation of the Christian message behind the stories. (p.
129)

*Penelope Lively, "The Wrath of God: An
Opinion of the 'Narnia' Books," in* The Use
of English *(© Chatto and Windus 1968),
Winter, 1968, pp. 126-29.*

To describe the Chronicles of Narnia is to give little idea of
their quality. At the most obvious level they are a series of
adventure stories told by a master story-teller with an excellent sense of construction. . . . Looking a little deeper,
we find that the magic is not only that of the wonders themselves: there is a 'glamour' in the old sense that falls upon
us as we enter Narnia, like the softest dew, but growing as
we venture deeper and deeper in. This is the subtle creation
of atmosphere, of which the sights, the sounds, the smell
and taste and feel grow upon us until Narnia becomes a
place that we remember or recognise rather than learn
about.

Deeper still, and we realise a difference between these stories and most other children's books: though the White
Witch or Miraz may represent the evil power, just as there
are good powers culminating in Aslan, the real villains as
well as the real heroes and heroines are among the children
who find their way or are drawn into Narnia. . . . But, . . . a
deeper reversal is taking place in them all the time, so that
the plot seems suddenly to be concerned with their own
internal battles rather than the external adventures. (pp.
135-36)

The adult characters are of much less importance [than the
children], except in *The Magician's Nephew,* where Uncle
Andrew is perhaps slightly caricatured though still acceptable, and Frank the cabby is a beautiful little miniature of
simple goodness. The Narnian Kings and Calormenes are
much more shadowy: Rilian and Tirian are less distinct
than Caspian, and the rest loom a little larger than life in
the bewildering mist with its stirring background of music
that is our general vision of Narnia.

Out of that mist come character after character for magic
moments of their own, gleaming suddenly into life in the
midst of an incident and then fading once more into the
moving pageant of the background. . . . (p. 150)

The sense of wonder and discovery, the feeling of awak-
ened memory rather than of cunningly drawn mind-pic-
tures, is helped greatly by the descriptions of scenery and
of even the smallest facet of nature—always growing naturally out of the narrative and never superimposed. (p. 151)

[There is a] slightly episodic nature [to] the earlier books, and the brilliant scenes and incidents . . . occasionally hang together rather than [grow] out of each other. (pp. 151-52)

[This is most apparent in] *The Lion, the Witch and the Wardrobe,* though the general suspense and the steady heightening of interest and expectancy prevents it from breaking the 'glamour' for the child reader, though the critical adult cannot help feeling from time to time: 'Here are superb incidents, vivid moments, thought-provoking ideas —but they have come separately and been fitted together: oh, so cunningly—but there *is* a trace of the cement.' . . . *The Voyage of the 'Dawn Treader'* triumphs completely since it is intended to consist of consecutive adventures as the ship sails among unknown islands towards the World's End—and some of the separate incidents in their settings are among the best and most memorable in the whole series.

The Horse and his Boy combines the picaresque with the plot pleasantly and excitingly, but less memorably. Only with *The Silver Chair* does Lewis come fully into his kingdom—or into all the provinces of his kingdom—both constructing a complete and single unity with each incident growing naturally as part of the whole, and conjuring up the characters, strange or ordinary, against marvellous and unexpected backgrounds, as if the circumstances and not the author had called them into being. *The Magician's Nephew* is just as perfect a unity and as rounded and satisfying an experience, and it is very much a matter of opinion whether it or *The Silver Chair* is the best of the series. . . . (p. 152)

There is no slackening of power in *The Last Battle,* but its nature does not demand an involved plot; the great movement is as of a slowly rising wave or the final surge of the music rising to a solemn climax and fading away into a hushed and awe-filled silence.

Here we come nearest to the deep core of the stories: the moral, or the religious truth which is, in the highest sense, their inspiration. (p. 153)

The truest, the unique strength of the Chronicles of Narnia, the spirit incarnating them, the breath of Aslan which gives them life so that they will, I believe, live to take their permanent place among the great works of children's literature, is 'the whole cast of the author's mind' which has gone into their making. The mind of a true scholar, of one of the best-read men of his age; of a superb craftsman in the art of letters, with a gift for story-telling; of a thinker, logician and theologian who has plumbed the depths of the dark void of atheism and come by the hardest route on his pilgrimage back to God. (p. 154)

> *Roger Lancelyn Green, "C. S. Lewis"* (© *Roger Lancelyn Green 1963), in* Henry Treece, C. S. Lewis and Beatrix Potter, *by Margery Fisher, Roger Lancelyn Green and Marcus Crouch, revised edition, Bodley Head, 1969, pp. 109-58.*

Lewis accepted myth and miracle in the same way that others accept fact. There was no question in his mind concerning the validity of myth, even as a religious experience. There is no avoiding it: his books for children are religious. They are meant to be religious. However, they are not designed to proselytize for one system of faith, doctrine, or worship. Lewis writes of the religious experience that transcends the dogmatic boundaries of a particular sect, and aims for a universal response from within the hearts of all men. It is only natural, in doing this, that he draw upon Christian symbolism, for that is the symbolism he knows best. (p. 45)

Children are capable of grasping the significance of the *Narnia* stories even if they have not recognized Aslan as a Christ-symbol. Aslan is like Christ not for the reader's sake, but for the writer's sake; this was his medium. Children certainly should not be expected to recognize the symbolism; but they will recognize the quality of divine goodness which pervades the stories, even if this recognition can never be verbalized. Unlike most adults, children find their meaning solely within the story, and most often they absorb the significance through a passion below the tier of cognizance.

Lewis says quite clearly that he never intended the *Narnia* books to be allegorical. He doesn't ask his readers to make allegorial comparisons, and there is no promised deepening of appreciation for those who do. The reader is merely asked to open the eyes of his heart so that he can truly respond to the sufferings and joys of Aslan. And this the child can do far better than the adult. This is the reason why these are children's books, no matter who may read them. (p. 47)

> *James E. Higgins, in his* Beyond Words: Mystical Fancy in Children's Literature *(Teachers College Press, New York, 1970), Teachers College Press, 1971.*

Readers of Lewis's fairy tales are not likely to understand, simply from reading these books, how deeply his imagination slept as a boy, or how momentous was his liberation in losing "the desire to be very grown up." His boyhood was, nevertheless, a period of great fecundity: he wrote many stories about his invented world of Animal-Land at the time, and was, without knowing it, training himself to be the future chronicler of Narnia. (p. 277)

In Lewis's autobiography, *Surprised by Joy,* we get the impression of two lives—the "outer" and the "inner," the life of the intellect and the life of the imagination—being lived over against each other, albeit at the same time. The "outer" life is chiefly concerned with those things which he spoke and wrote about openly: namely, Animal-Land. The "inner" life—and this is what *Surprised by Joy* is mainly about—is essentially the story of Joy (i.e. intense longing) working on his imagination. Narnia would never have come into existence had Lewis not come to understand the meaning and purpose of Joy. (p. 278)

[It] is important at this point to say something about Joy. In his autobiography Lewis defines Joy by first recording three experiences from his early childhood. While standing by a flowering currant bush on a summer day there arose in him the memory of a yet earlier morning in which his brother had brought into the nursery a toy garden. The memory of this memory caused a sensation of desire to break over him. Before he could know *what* he desired, the desire itself was gone and he was left with a "longing for the longing that had just ceased". . . . The second glimpse of Joy came through [Beatrix Potter's] *Squirrel Nutkin.* This book troubled him with the "Idea of Autumn" . . . , and again he was plunged into the experience of intense desire. The third glimpse came to him while reading Long-fellow's translation of *Tegner's Drapa*. . . . [His] mind was uplifted into huge regions of northern sky. At the very moment he was stabbed by desire, he felt himself falling out of that desire and wishing he were back in it.

Lewis tells us that Joy, the quality common to these three experiences, is an unsatisfied longing which is itself more desirable than any other satisfaction. (p. 280)

I could not in this short paper recount how, one by one, his reservations about accepting the Christian faith were swept away (it is all admirably recounted in *Surprised by Joy*). But so they were. . . . He who is the Joy of all men's de-siring came upon him and compelled him by divine mercy to surrender a long-sieged fortress. . . . After that, the old bitter-sweet stabs of Joy continued as before. But he never gave them the importance they once had. That would have been impossible: he knew to what—or, rather, to *Whom*—they pointed.

Now, what is the relevance of all this to the Narnian Chronicles? (p. 283)

I said earlier that it would be difficult to know what kind of "dressed animals" Lewis was writing about in his boyhood stories without the benefit of his illustrations. In the Narnian books his animals appear in their natural beauty and interesting differences. They are the real thing. Al-though you will not have read Lewis's juvenilia, chances are you will have seen a Walt Disney film. I find much of Walt Disney's work very pleasant, but his dressed animals do not seem to me much like the animals they are intended to represent. Perhaps they are not supposed to. Neverthe-less, it cannot be claimed, I think, that Mickey Mouse is very mousy, or Pluto very doggy. If we sat in the cinema with our eyes closed and *heard* a Walt Disney film, would we be able to guess what kinds of animals the characters are? On the other hand, the Narnian animals, whether they can talk or are dumb, retain the qualities that endear them to us. Anyone who has owned a dog will recognize the real-istic touch when he reads about the adventures at the Giants' Castle, where there are "wagging tails, and bark-ing, and loose, slobbery mouths and noses of dogs thrust into your hand". . . . (p. 314)

[Some] of Lewis's ideas on animal immortality [in *The Problem of Pain* have] application . . . in the Narnian sto-ries. Nevertheless, we must remember that we are talking about imaginative fiction, and I think it would be disastrous to push the analogies too far. It would appear that part of Lewis's purpose was to create a world in which the relation between men and beasts is as nearly as possible like that which might have existed before both were corrupted at the beginning of this world. He even gives us an idea of what the Narnian animal kingdom was like before men or evil came into their lives (the people are there only as witnesses at first). Instead of animals being subordinate to men, the dumb beasts are subordinate to the Talking Animals. . . . After the Creation, Asian chooses from the beasts (all of which are dumb) two of every kind and gives them speech and reason. . . . (p. 316)

However, after the Coronation of King Frank I, all Narnian beasts become subordinate to Man. Though Man is responsible for the corruption of Narnia (Digory brought the evil Jadis there on the day of Creation), the Kings and Queens of Narnia must always be *human*. This is not their

privilege, but their responsibility: "As Adam's race has done the harm, Adam's race shall help to heal it." It is, then, part of Man's redemptive function to help raise the beasts to their derivative immortality in the eternal Narnia. And—who can deny it?—the beasts play some part in the redemption of Man. . . . (pp. 316-17)

There is never any doubt in anyone's mind that Aslan is the Lord of that world. Even his enemies believe this. . . . If I had not read the Narnian Chronicles, I could not have be-lieved an author could concentrate so much goodness into one being (I am not forgetting the author's Model). None of the mushy, goody-goody sort of thing we sometimes find in people we feel we ought to like, but cannot. Here, in this magnificent Lion, is absolute goodness beyond anything we could imagine. Qualities we sometimes think of as oppo-sites meet in him and blend. (p. 323)

Aslan is Christ. It is, however, with reluctance that I men-tion this fact, whether you already knew it or not. I am re-luctant because I do not want in any way to damage Lew-is's success in getting "past those watchful dragons" which freeze many people's feelings about Christ and orthodox Christianity. . . . It is often precisely because many readers do *not* know who Aslan is that the Narnian stories have been so successful in getting into the bloodstream of the secular world. Hints about who is what and so forth have already caused many readers to regard the fairy tales as codes that need deciphering. They were written to give pleasure and (I think) as an unconscious preparation of the imagination. And this they do most effectively without our extra efforts. (p. 325)

We will not find an exact, geometrically perfect equivalent of Christ's incarnation, passion, crucifixion, and ascension in the Narnian stories. We are not meant to. This is why we should not press the analogies too closely, or expect to find in the fairy tales the same logic we find in the Christian story. If we do press the analogies too closely, we will, I think, go a long way toward spoiling our receptivity for what the stories have to give us. (pp. 325-26)

I think we can appreciate fully the use Lewis made of bib-lical parallels when we consider the two opposite dangers into which he could have fallen. Had the biblical parallels been very obvious, he would not, I think, have nearly so many readers. Nonbelievers would have felt they were being "got at" and rejected them at once. On the other hand, our imaginations would not have been attuned to the Everlasting Gospel had he been too subtle—especially as so many people today have never read the Bible. Some middle way was needed. This *via media* came easily to Lewis because he did not begin with morals or the Gospels at all, but wrote stories in which those ingredients pushed themselves in of their own accord. (p. 330)

One of the excellences of the fairy tales is that their ability to entertain and edify does not depend on "explanation" from outside the books. Indeed, I am inclined to believe that the kind of essay I am writing at the moment could, in some hands, have a detrimental effect. It is better to read *nothing* more into the books than to view them as a vast complex of "ideas," "influences," "images," "allego-ries," and "symbols" which we are expected to explain. (p. 332)

Professor Kilby, in his excellent book, *The Christian World of C. S. Lewis* [see excerpt above], draws our attention to the "motif of joy and longing, and the greater joy in possessing" which runs through the Narnian books. You may recall from my preliminary remarks about Joy, that Lewis believed that if we find in ourselves a desire no experience in the world can satisfy, the most probable explanation is that we were made for a different world. In *The Last Battle* the faithful Narnians pass through the Stable door into the world of their hearts' desire. I am quite aware that some nonbelievers use Lewis's reasoning about desire, and the fulfillment of that desire in the real Narnia, to illustrate their stock argument that "people *want* heaven to be real, so they make up religion and try to believe it." But there is good reason for distrusting the nonbelievers' argument.

(1) Like Lewis, most Christians have found that in their search for one thing they were being *sought* by Something else. The Hound of Heaven was tracking them down even as they were sniffing along the path that led to him. . . . There is not nearly so much in it about man's search for God as there is about God's persistent wooing of man, his efforts to give man some great richness without which he will die of poverty. (p. 334)

(2) Is it, then, a lucky accident that God turns out to be what we want more than anything in the world? It is neither luck nor accident. Our appetite for God is one of his gifts. (p. 335)

My reason for discussing this here is that something very similar happens in the Narnian stories and is articulated on several occasions. But before we think of them, it might be illuminating to look at a passage that I find (though it says nothing of *mutual* desire) stabs with "sweet desire"—stabs me, at any rate—more powerfully than do any other words in the fairy tales. After the White Witch is dead, Aslan leads the children to Cair Paravel. The castle towered above them and "before them were the sands, with rocks and little pools of salt water, and seaweed, and the smell of the sea and long miles of bluish-green waves breaking for ever and ever on the beach. And oh, the cry of the seagulls! Have you heard it? Can you remember?"

I can, of course, speak only for myself, but, taken in their context, these words—especially the questions—set me yearning for that "unnameable something" more powerfully than any bluish-green waves and the cry of seagulls in this world have ever done. In this particular instance I do not feel sorry for the children in Narnia (they remain there for five years), but for myself. I can tell from the feel of the book in my hands that, for me, the adventure is almost at an end. And (forgetting the other fairy tales momentarily), how can *I* live never meeting Aslan? What I am suggesting is that, for both the reader and those who get into Narnia, the joys of that world (the place, the people, the castles, the landscape) are inseparable from the joy of knowing the Lion. We want to be there because *he* is there. We desire the Lion because—well, not only because Aslan is in himself desirable, but because the desire is one of the things he has given us, one of the things of which we are made. (pp. 335-36)

[In *The Last Battle* the] old Narnia flows, as it were, into the real Narnia. Jewel the Unicorn, arriving on the other side of the Stable door, expresses the feelings of the others. He stamped his hoof, neighed, and cried, "I have come home at last! This is my real country! I belong here. This is

the land I have been looking for all my life, though I never knew it till now". . . .

The Unicorn's words recall for me Lewis's own reaction to death at a crucial time in his life, and I end on this personal note. (p. 338)

Observing his peaceful acceptance of death—there was nothing regretful about it—I said, "You know, you really do believe all the things you've written." He looked a bit surprised. "Of course!" he said. "That's why I wrote them." (p. 339)

> *Walter Hooper, "Past Watchful Dragons: The Fairy Tales of C. S. Lewis," in* Imagination and the Spirit: Essays in Literature and the Christian Faith, *edited by Charles A. Huttar (copyright © 1971 by Walter Hooper and the Trustees of the Estate of C. S. Lewis; used by permission), Eerdmans, 1971, pp. 277-339.*

One cannot, I think, escape [the] question [of violence in the Chronicles of Narnia] by saying that there is violence in all myth and fairy tale. There is also love in many fairy tales. In C S Lewis there is a particular emphasis on a *continual* aggressive stance: indeed, in a sense, nothing happens in the Narnia books except the build-up and confrontation with paranoically conceived menaces, from an aggressive posture of hate, leading towards conflict. . . .

[Lewis's] Narnia is the place where spiritual battles are fought: and in the end it is the place where (everlasting) life begins. But taking the symbolism in the way it derives from *Alice in Wonderland* and George MacDonald, it seems legitimate to find this other world as the 'inner world' of 'psychic reality'. (p. 5)

Taking clues from the philosopher of surrealism, Gaston Bachelard, from psychoanalysis, and from my work on Sylvia Plath, I believe that C S Lewis's Narnia stories have their origins in the fact of his life that his mother died when he was a baby. I believe that this left him a psychic hunger —to be nurtured by the mother he had lost. It left him (as a similar fate left George MacDonald, by whom Lewis is evidently much influenced) needing to find his way *into the other world where the mother was:* the world of death.

How do we get there? Since we came into the world through mother's body, we could go back there, through her body: and the Wardrobe is her body (or, to be more specific, her birth passage). (p. 6)

But now another problem arises. If we go into that other world of death where the mother is, we shall perhaps encounter a mother who has not been humanized by us, as a mother normally is, over the long years of knowing her as a child. She may be the all-bad, all-hate mother we were capable of phantasying as an infant. . . . She may be what Melanie Klein called the 'castrating mother'. . . .

In Narnia she is the white witch, whose major antecedent is Lady Macbeth. . . .

How do we take all this? We can take it as a pantomime story, and as such it would perhaps be harmless. We can take it at the level of C S Lewis's theology, and it will then imply that a pagan sensuality and selfishness (Turkish Delight) will make us treacherous to our own natures and to others. Or we can take it at the level of unconscious phantasy, when it will imply that in the world there is a hostile female figure who seeks to thrust evil and hate into us, and so distort our natures. . . . What we are dealing with is deep primitive symbolism, such as a very young infant experiences, and because so many bodily feelings are involved this imagery is very sexual. (p. 7)

[There is a] strange dissociation in Lewis's phantasies. The 'spiritual enemies' are not within *human beings:* they are *inhuman.* . . .

Evil . . . belongs to a non-human world, of demons, and justifies one's immediate hostility. The dehumanization feared by the schizoid individual is projected into these imagos, which are inimical. The appeal is in arousing schizoid-paranoid fears (as do many cultural artifacts, such as horror films, etc.)—of demonic possession. (p. 10)

In *The Voyage of the Dawn Treader,* Eustace becomes a dragon—perhaps the weirdest episode in all C S Lewis's Narnia books. He becomes a dragon because of greed. (p. 14)

[This] is a psychotic nightmare belonging to the dread of being 'taken over'—the kind of fear Winnicott describes as belonging to 'unthinkable' anxieties. It is, of course, a specifically schizoid fear, of being taken over, or becoming something else, non-human, and terrible. (pp. 14-15)

[The] cure, at the deepest level, is to get rid of one's beastly, greedy disgusting body altogether: the sin snake. When Lewis spoke of adopting a children's story form 'for something you have to say' there seems no doubt that one of his motives was to export his guilt into children, the guilt being that about the body and bodily hunger, and, I think, at a deep level, masturbation. (p. 17)

Nowhere in the Narnia books are there causes to be served, in terms of the mysteries of this world, the possibilities of man, or the satisfactions of interpersonal encounter between human beings: love. There is only plotting, marching, moving about the terrain, and killing—in opposition (mostly) to non-human creatures, helped by magic, in world after world in which events are already *determined.* The children never escape from magical control and determinism: they never question what they do, or their motives —and they never make existential choices. They never suffer. . . . Aslan is often exercising a disguised predatoriness, which is a form of hate, too, since its most harmful effect is to rob human beings of their autonomy—and so of their freedom, and their quest for authenticity. (pp. 23-4)

> *David Holbrook, "The Problem of C S Lewis," in* Children's Literature in Education *(© 1973, APS Publications, Inc.; reprinted by permission of the publisher), No. 10, March, 1973, pp. 3-25.*

[The chronicles of Narnia] are guarded from criticism by certain protective misconceptions. Chief of them is the notion that they form a continuous religious allegory. Allusions to Christian doctrine and symbolism are scattered haphazardly through all the stories, but the doctrinal content is really important in only three: *The Magician's Nephew* (the creation, Adam and Eve, the forbidden tree); *The Lion, the Witch and the Wardrobe* (the Crucifixion and Resurrection, the Judas-figure) and *The Last Battle* (the destruction of the world, Judgement Day, Paradise). In these books the parallels are clear if inexact. In *The Horse*

and his Boy the doctrine is very clear and very exact, though the religion it celebrates is not Christianity but Old Testament theology at its most crudely vicious. *The Voyage of the 'Dawn Treader'* offers an experience of the numinous which is more directly linked to the Grail legends than to Christian orthodoxy. The religious content of *Prince Caspian* and *The Silver Chair* is negligible.

It is a mistake, then, to view the Narnia books as a coherent work of Christian exegesis. They are not coherent, and some of the time they are not Christian. (p. 17)

A second misconception is that the Narnia stories, attractive to children in the first place as the beguiling fantasies of a compelling storyteller, have an underlying moral function in harmony with their religious content. Not only do they create a modern myth which revives the awe and mystery of worship, but they appear to show a group of contemporary children gaining in stature and understanding, and outgrowing childish spite and selfishness. In outward terms it can certainly be argued that (apart from Susan) they do. They become 'Kings and Queens' in Narnia and Archenland, they learn to fight heroically on Aslan's behalf, and if they were once disposed to selfishness and treachery, they are duly reformed—either by the suffering that treachery entails or by the lion's stern teaching.

The reality is rather different. Aslan is not a *tame* lion, as we are often reminded, and he is not a kindly teacher either. His purpose is not reformation but transformation, and his method is retribution and punishment. Minor transgressors and quick learners, such as Digory and Lucy, are just made to feel ashamed. More serious offenders, major and minor, are punished by ridicule and physical degradation. (p. 18)

Nor is it only Aslan's divinely sanctioned vengeance that makes people smart for their failures. Edmund, briefly the traitor of *The Lion, the Witch and the Wardrobe,* is goaded with the whip and almost has his throat cut. Eustace is beaten with the flat of a rapier by the very parfit gentil mouse Reepicheep. (p. 19)

The nature of this moral world is clear. Bad and good are sharply differentiated, and children do not grow with experience from the one to the other. Rather they are dismantled and reconstructed: after their chastening experiences they are different people. In a rigidly authoritarian and hierarchical society, the supreme virtues are conformity, submission and obedience—to Aslan above all, but also to his chosen stewards, whether Narnian princes or English schoolchildren. The worst sin of all is to question or ignore the revealed will of Aslan and the expressed will of his kings: independence, initiative, scepticism and even common sense are reprehensible if they mean that obedience falters. The structure of power in Narnia, with Aslan at its head, is enforced by battle, violence, retributive justice, pain and death. Anything which challenges the power is either evil or stupid, and frequently both.

In the Narnian world the English children exist at the fulcrum of this power structure. When they are wise, they recognise with awe and fear the power in Aslan to which they must meekly submit. Yet they also love the power that rules them, and feel joy in its revealed presence. In turn they are entrusted by Aslan with power second only to his, holding regal and mystical authority in Narnia. (This balance of fear, love and power is the key to a crucial paradox of feeling in the books: Aslan's appearances and other phenomena are repeatedly described as inspiring simultaneous fear and gladness, being 'terrible and beautiful', awakening solemn joy.)

Lewis's revelation of the power-system at work is peculiarly erratic in language and feeling, sliding abruptly from sublimity to bathos, from innocence to childishness, from awesome ceremonial to high jinks. We can never be quite sure how seriously to take it, because its author obviously isn't. (pp. 19-20)

Most frequently, however, it is power as it existed in the life and literature of medieval England which is truly re-enacted, and sometimes the effect is very beautiful. Sometimes, on the other hand, it is barbaric. Narnia is a world of religious and secular tyranny, demanding absolute obedience to god and king. The warlike superstructure of that world is essential to its nature: battles and crusades, forays, sieges and quests, tournaments, duels and hunting, tests of courage and cowardice, the majestic embroidery of death. Realism and romance combine in Lewis's scholarly imagination to create a world for which he clearly has a deep nostalgia, however tongue-in-cheek and rich in parody he sometimes makes it seem. (p. 20)

It is not hard to see what children find so compulsive in such books. . . . It is a violent, immature and enticingly simple world, one that young children commonly inhabit for a time, but one which benevolent grown-ups are constantly trying to destroy. How gratifying for young readers to find a storyteller who actually *shares* their prejudices and gives to their daydreams a local habitation and a name.

Perhaps it is not hard, either, to see what some of us find so offensive. The 'religious allegory' which everyone notices tends to obscure the political allegory that no one does. Aslan's kingdom is also a model of feudal dictatorship, with all its barbarous simplicities. Perhaps children notice this no more readily than they do the religious content, but it is there. Such a world-view cannot endure the realities and complications of modern life, which the child is encouraged to detest. In particular, the books mount a systematic and continual assault on schools and education. . . . (pp. 20-1)

Lewis's attitude towards his young readers is by turns avuncular and conspiratorial: he claims the privilege of adult wisdom when it suits his purposes, yet coyly aligns himself with the child's own fantasies. The Narnia books reveal a startlingly immature and vindictive sensibility. The writer prescribes his own standards of moral and spiritual failure—standards which are questionable in themselves— and presents such failures in a tone which is not as a rule austere or compassionate but spiteful and gloating. For children this sequence of books, which seems outwardly enriching and fertile, is actually a regressive experience, presenting a world of seductive and brutalised simplicities. Its one real complexity is the ambiguity of the lion-hero himself: the warmth of Aslan's breath is loving but menacing, his speech intimate but savage, his strength both awesome and brutish. The image of the divine power is, in the end, the unedifying image of a beast. (p. 21)

> *Peter Hollindale, "The Image of the Beast: C. S. Lewis's Chronicles of Narnia," in* The Use of English, *Spring, 1977, pp. 16-21.*

David Holbrook's strongly stated critique "The Problem of

C S Lewis" [see excerpt above] charges that Narnia is a paranoic world full of lurking malignancy, expressed by violent sexual imagery sprung from Lewis's subconscious which, it is alleged, is morbidly obsessed by the early death of his mother. Holbrook's arguments are humanistic, pacifist, and, most notably, psychoanalytic. In my opinion, his arguments are wrong. . . .

[To call Narnia an "inner world"] is to misunderstand the nature of Narnia. The moral problems of a Narnian's life are identical with those in a life in our world. . . . Narnia is precisely as "spiritual" as, and no more "spiritual" than, Earth.

Then follows Holbrook's specific premise [that Lewis's loss of his mother in infancy led to his search for the world of death where she was.] (p. 51)

However, the "fact of Lewis's life" is that his mother died when he was 9 years and 9 months old, which it would be hard to label as "baby" or "infant." . . . If Lewis was that old when his mother died, what trauma was there? We have Lewis's own answer, from his autobiography [*Surprised by Joy*].

> For us boys [Lewis and his brother] the real bereavement had happened before our mother died. We lost her gradually as she was gradually [with cancer] withdrawn from our life into the hands of nurses and delirium and morphia . . . With my mother's death all settled happiness, all that was tranquil and reliable, disappeared from my life . . . no more of the old security.

This is not trauma, repressed into the subconscious, only to emerge in obsessive imagery and haunted themes. This was a grief consciously understood at the time and, as the tone of the extract suggests, coped with by Lewis as an adult. (p. 52)

Lewis was not a baby when his mother died, his response to her death was conscious and even constructive, given his age, and he was familiar with [Freud and the] psychological analysis of mother-figures, death, sex, and the like. All this demolishes the foundation of Holbrook's psychoanalytic criticism. But, within itself, Holbrook's analysis is inherently flawed. . . .

[Holbrook sees the White Witch as the "castrating mother" found in Narnia. He] says the "major antecedent [of the White Witch] is Lady Macbeth" (p. 7), but the only common factors are gender and morals. Fairy stories are full of such characters, to be accepted at the immediate level of the narrative. . . .

At first glance there could be something in Holbrook's view of the White Witch as some kind of mythic castrating female, power-crazy and viciously destructive. (p. 53)

Indeed it is because the White Witch wields phallic [objects such as wands and an iron bar] that she can be considered a form of male being. . . .

[But the] White Witch must be understood in the whole context of the Narnia stories. . . . Repeatedly she attempts to deprive all Narnians of their self-determination, independence and individual being. . . . The Witch's role thus parallels that of Lucifer, or the Devil. (p. 54)

[Another] of Holbrook's objections to Narnia [is the control by Aslan which rarely allows the characters to use their capacity for choice]. . . .

Such existential limitations would severely mar the Narnia stories, if Holbrook were correct. However the characters repeatedly demonstrate their free choices. The White Witch tells us [in *The Magician's Nephew*] how she chose to be evil in Charn, before she enters Narnia.

Later in Narnia, she chooses to eat the forbidden magic apple. . . . The lack of freedom is self-inflicted, and is the natural consequence of her earlier choices. (p. 55)

Indeed an aspect of this free will of characters is one of the most attractive things in the books. This is that most of the main characters are tested and, as a consequence of their testing, grow morally through the narrative. (p. 56)

All of [the] examples of free choice are the same kind as can happen in our real world. But because of the physical as well as visionary presence of Aslan in Narnia, there is another kind of free choice (which is much rarer in the real world), in which the consequences of a bad choice are worked out or revealed by magic or "divine" intervention. (pp. 56-7)

The major example of divine revelation of moral consequences is in *The Voyage of the Dawn Treader* where the boy Eustace is turned into a dragon. This incident is one of Holbrook's worst misreadings of Lewis. . . .

Eustace is a bad boy. This may partly be a result of his upbringing, but certainly he likes and chooses to be bad. (p. 57)

[Through the punishment of becoming a dragon], the awakening of Eustace's human sympathies is complete. Lewis's purpose in this episode is clear, even if Narnian dragon-magic has replaced the conventional rejection of an unpleasant person which would serve the same purpose in a story where magic was not invoked.

But Holbrook has completely missed the point of moral growth in his haste to discover subconscious fears and perversions in the Narnia stories. He claims to find several in this episode. (pp. 58-9)

Eustace's consciousness and will remain human and, indeed, intensely his own. He is not afraid of, or despairing about becoming a dragon. . . . Clearly this is not a psychotic nightmare of Eustace's or Lewis's.

At this point, Holbrook mistakenly says that "to become evil [like Eustace] is to become non-human." . . . However there are many evil humans—King Miraz, Rabadash, Uncle Andrew, Pug, Rishda Tarkaan, etc.—and many good nonhumans—beavers, unicorns, centaurs, horses, etc. —in Narnia. (p. 59)

(Holbrook's approach to Lewis could be turned around against Holbrook to ask what fears and guilt so drive Holbrook that he misreads and distorts to arrive at his particular and seemingly obsessive interpretations of perversions and guilt? Why is he continually preoccupied with *deeper* levels and meanings? Perhaps those of his sentences which are most technically turgid indicate an approach to subjects which are emotionally charged and guilt-laden). Such sexual interpretation besmirches the purpose and achievement of the story. (pp. 60-1)

Holbrook claims that Lewis is preoccupied with preparation for and performance in battles, that Lewis emphasises the importance of a continual aggressive stance. . . . However two of the books have no fighting at all . . . , one has only a slight scuffle . . . and two have only small battles. . . . [Many of the] books share an almost Aristotelian structure of Exposition/Approach to the climax/Climax/Consequences and Conclusion. Holbrook's "nothing . . . except conflict" does not allow for the lengthy conflictless beginnings and endings of these books. . . .

I have criticised salient points of Holbrook's article on Lewis, but there are many other details which could well be criticised further. It is not enough for a reader of Holbrook to say, "I don't like what he says, he takes this sex business too far, but it's a question of taste I suppose." Holbrook's article is not merely idiocyncratic, it is bad scholarship, false information, and so internally contradictory as to verge now and then on incoherence. Holbrook concludes that Narnia "is so personal a myth that it is barely reconcilable with Christianity at all, surely?" Yet Holbrook's is so personal an interpretation that it is not reconcilable with Narnia at all, surely? (p. 61)

John Gough, "C S Lewis and the Problem of David Holbrook," in Children's Literature in Education (© *1977, APS Publications, Inc., New York; reprinted by permission of the publisher), No. 25 (Summer), 1977, pp. 51-62.*

OTHER CITATIONS

M. S. Crouch, "The Chronicles of Narnia," in The Junior Bookshelf, *November, 1956, pp. 245-53.*

John W. Montgomery, "The Chronicles of Narnia and the Adolescent Reader," in Religious Education *54, September-October, 1959, pp. 418-28.*

Richard B. Cunningham, in his C. S. Lewis: Defender of the Faith, *Westminster Press, 1967, pp. 152-56.*

Margaret Blount, "Fallen and Redeemed: Animals in the Novels of C. S. Lewis," in her Animal Land: The Creatures of Children's Fiction, *William Morrow & Co., Inc., 1974, pp. 284-306.*

Kathryn Ann Lindskoog, in her The Lion of Judah in Never-Never Land: The Theology of C. S. Lewis Expressed in His Fantasties for Children, *William B. Eerdmans Publishing Co., 1974.*

Richard Purtill, in his Lord of the Elves and Eldils: Fantasy and Philosophy in C. S. Lewis and J.R.R. Tolkien, *The Zondervan Corp., 1974.*

THE HORSE AND HIS BOY (1954)

"The Horse and His Boy" is relatively uninspired. It does not glow as much as the incomparable first book of the series, "The Lion, the Witch and the Wardrobe." It has not as much gay satire and plain excitement as several of the others. Just possibly the Narnian fields are suffering from overcropping, and could stand lying fallow while other fields are put back into cultivation. (p. 44)

Chad Walsh, in The New York Times Book Review (© *1954 by The New York Times*

Company; reprinted by permission), October 17, 1954.

This is the fifth book about the wonderful country of Narnia and, since C. S. Lewis is to children of today what E. Nesbit was to an earlier generation, its coming has been hailed with delight. . . . It is a good story, well written and true to the land of fancy, but it lacks some of the richness of the first four. Children who have already read those will want to read this, too; but to introduce C. S. Lewis to a child I should begin with the first book, *The Lion, the Witch and the Wardrobe,* and let him have the others in their proper sequence. (p. 435)

> *Jennie D. Lindquist, in* The Horn Book Magazine *(copyrighted, 1954, by The Horn Book, Inc., Boston), December, 1954.*

OTHER CITATIONS

Virginia Kirkus' Bookshop Service, August 1, 1954, p. 484.

Margery Fisher, in her Who's Who in Children's Books: A Treasury of the Familiar Characters of Childhood, *Holt, Rinehart and Winston, 1975.*

THE LAST BATTLE (1956)

[The] greatest service Lewis does childhood . . . is to elicit a sense of the numinous. At least as great a service is *The Last Battle's* confrontation, in terms the child can understand, of the ineluctable fact of death. In this volume the door which admits the earth children to Narnia's strange realm is at once a more usual and a more terrible portal than the ones we have encountered before in the earlier stories; and Dr. Lewis' use of it involves him in what is probably the most audacious gambit in children's literature since George MacDonald sent little Diamond to the back of the North Wind. In a word, this door through which one enters Narnia and, after Narnia, the "real Narnia," is a door children's books have chosen to avoid ever since the pool of funeral tears which used to inundate the Victorian nursery offerings. (pp. 104-05)

What Dr. Lewis has done, on this plane, has long needed doing. Death, as a psychological experience on the part of the child who undergoes the loss, is a trauma from which there is no surcease but one: the surcease of religious belief in the survival of the individual human personality. This is the path down which in symbol Dr. Lewis leads his child readers up to, through and gloriously after the miniature Armageddon of *The Last Battle.* (p. 105)

> *Charles A. Brady, "Finding God in Narnia," in* America *(© America Press, 1956; all rights reserved), October 27, 1956, pp. 103-05.*

OTHER CITATIONS

Chad Walsh, in The New York Times Book Review, *September 30, 1956, p. 46.*

Heloise P. Mailloux, in The Horn Book Magazine, *October, 1956, p. 352.*

THE LION, THE WITCH AND THE WARDROBE (1950)

[*The Lion, the Witch and the Wardrobe* is a] vigorous and

fascinating book. . . . The fairy-story is admirable at fairy-story level; but also at the deep, unformulated level of myth. It never loses its vitality, its fantasy, its emotional vividness; it never becomes that tiresome thing, allegory, which can be worked out like a code or a crossword puzzle; but awareness grows that the frozen kingdom thawing with the arrival of the wild and loving Lion, his death in exchange for Edmund's life, his return, his setting the statues free, emblazon in a fabulous and holy heraldry the theme of redemption. (p. vi)

> *The* Times Literary Supplement, *(© Times Newspapers Ltd., 1950; reproduced from* The Times Literary Supplement *by permission), November 17, 1950.*

Striking as [*The Lion, the Witch and the Wardrobe*] and its sequels are—they frankly imitate E. Nesbit's methods and techniques—they come nowhere near taking [Nesbit's] place. To me, [Lewis'] children have no particular individuality. Prince Caspian is, no doubt, admirable, but he is completely blotted from my recollection by the self-reliant child, King of Plurimiregia, who sailed out on a sea of boiling toffee with a Lee-Metford rifle to do battle with one of E. Nesbit's interesting dragons. (p. 338)

> *Earl F. Walbridge, in* The Horn Book Magazine *(copyrighted, 1953, by The Horn Book, Inc., Boston), October, 1953.*

OTHER CITATIONS

Eleanor Graham, in The Junior Bookshelf, *November, 1950, p. 198.*

Chad Walsh, in The New York Times Book Review, *November 12, 1950, p. 20.*

C. S. Lewis, "It All Began with a Picture . . . ," in Of Other Worlds: Essays and Stories, *edited by Walter Hooper, Harcourt Brace Jovanovich, 1975, p. 42.*

THE MAGICIAN'S NEPHEW (1955)

In some ways [*The Magician's Nephew*] is the best of the Narnia books since *The Lion, the Witch and the Wardrobe,* though like all the series it is oddly disappointing. . . . Aslan is just singing Narnia into being and a pleasant paraphrase of the first chapters of Genesis follows, degenerating badly when the newly created animals take the uncle for a plant and smear him with mud, water, and honeycomb with the bees in it. This kind of physical indignity inflicted on unpleasant characters has appeared more than once in the series and suggests the author thinks that is the only kind of 'fun' children can understand (though there is some humour on another level). Some of his explanations are rather condescending too, and references to the more holy aspects of Narnia are often given in a hushed voice and read rather like Victorian Sunday School books. There is much that is entertaining, but not much that is convincing in the way presumably intended. The allegorical trials and temptations of the nephew are quite well devised but somehow fall flat. . . . Some of the situations in earlier books are neatly explained, like the presence of the Witch, but the suspicion grows that Narnia has been created largely to allow the author to include all his pet theories. He seems to have begun with quite a strong framework based on his great knowledge of religion and mythology and of literature, but he couldn't resist adding anything else that caught his fancy, traditional themes, literary conventions, private ideas on society, education, or what have you. This will doubtless prove very useful to later scholars studying his life and work, but it does not make entirely satisfactory children's reading. The series is well-written and very attractively presented, and probably more worth reading than three-quarters of other books for children written today, but cannot be numbered amongst the best of our time. This is particularly sad since the author would seem so admirably qualified for writing something really special, comparable to his work in other fields. As one of the few surviving specimens of Old Western Man he should be able to leave a better legacy to the children of our age. It does seem likely that some of the Narnian imagery will endure for a time, the Wood between the Worlds, perhaps and maybe the memory of a land under a lion's governance, but probably not the nature of that lion, which is, after all, the whole reason for the books. The vision is not kept steady enough, and some of its surroundings are too disparate for that. (pp. 147-49)

The Junior Bookshelf, July, 1955.

"The Magician's Nephew" is as good as the first volume of the [Narnia] series—"The Lion, the Witch and the Wardrobe"—and praise can scarcely go further. . . .

"The Magician's Nephew" glows with the sort of mythology that C. S. Lewis created at his best, replete with religious and philosophic implication. At the same time, it held my children, and me, spellbound from start to finish. (p. 40)

> *Chad Walsh, in* The New York Times Book Review (© *1955 by The New York Times Company; reprinted by permission), October 30, 1955.*

OTHER CITATIONS

Eulalie Steinmetz Ross, in Saturday Review, *November 12, 1955, pp. 64-5.*

Margery Fisher, in her Who's Who in Children's Books: A Treasury of the Familiar Characters of Childhood, *Holt, Rinehart and Winston, 1975, p. 287.*

PRINCE CASPIAN: THE RETURN TO NARNIA (1951)

This sequel to an earlier adventure in fairyland, "The Lion, the Witch, and the Wardrobe," has the same down-to-earth qualities. The cuteness and archness that mar so many books written for children is blessedly lacking here. The story is for boys and girls who like their dwarfs and fauns as solid as the traffic policeman on the corner. The present book has a more complicated structure than the first one. I suspect that some children will have difficulty following the story-within-a-story that develops. . . .

Anyone who has studied C. S. Lewis' life and books is aware of how deeply influenced he has been by the Scottish writer George MacDonald. The sense of poetic magic and wonder which MacDonald could evoke is not found in "Price Caspian," but both writers share a deep respect for children and the world of the child's imagination. (p. 26)

> *Chad Walsh, in* The New York Times Book Review, *Part II (© 1951 by The New York Times Company; reprinted by permission), November 11, 1951.*

The theme of this fantasy is the restoration to his rightful throne of Prince Caspian and the overthrow of the usurper; aided of course by the four children from the other world. It is a picturesque, romantic story, with hints here and there of Dr. Lewis's erudition and deeper facts of his talents. The canvas is a little crowded, but the colourful story and fine writing carry the reader over all obstacles. This is a notable book in some ways which will appeal to the imaginative child who allows himself to be borne away on wings of fantasy. (p. 276)

The Junior Bookshelf, December, 1951.

OTHER CITATIONS

Virginia Kirkus' Bookshop Service, August 1, 1951, p. 393.

Bertha Mahoney Miller, in The Horn Book Magazine, *December, 1951, p. 412.*

THE SILVER CHAIR (1953)

This is the fifth book [sic] in the Aslan-Caspian series . . . , so most people will be prepared for the powerful quality of the imagination, the good writing, and the allegory. Perhaps they will also expect that strange lack of tenderness which, to my mind, weakens the effect and the value of the work. It is striking in the descriptions of human character and behaviour, seeming to imply great contempt for the human race. Mr. Lewis calls the boy and girl on whom his story depends (one can hardly describe them as hero and heroine) "Scrub" and "Pole". He makes them as unattractive as those names sound. They are poor, despicable creatures, serving as guinea pigs for the demonstration of an idea. The author displays their weaknesses, their shabby conduct, and exposes them to indignities, without pity. I felt this was a bad approach if he wished to stir young readers, for in real life and to critical eyes, they themselves are probably as scrubby and unglamorous as this boy and girl—as indeed we all are, seen without sympathy from a sufficiently lofty standpoint. But while we are children we see neither ourselves nor others with such appraising eyes. Children do not regard each other with just that ruthless scrutiny, though their eyes may be searching. They are, perhaps unconsciously, more aware of human kinship, and have a simpler sense of values. To them, I feel sure, C. S. Lewis's portraiture will appear unjust, unkind. Also, it offers little inducement to read on through the book, and is not likely to fire the imagination to the point at which the meaning of the allegory will become plain and sink in. (p. 199)

The Junior Bookshelf, October, 1953.

Eustace plays as much of a hero's part as he is allowed [in *The Silver Chair*], but he and Jill, though they work hard at arms drill and try to conquer their fear of the enchantress and her allies, are really manipulated by Aslan through the rules he has given them. Since the other children in the Narnia stories are 'good' (Edmund's lapse being single and brief), Eustace and to a lesser degree Jill, as they argue and squabble their way through the land of the giants, seem superficially to be more interesting as characters; but in fact they have only a limited freedom of action in the grand design over which Aslan presides. (p. 106)

> *Margery Fisher, in her* Who's Who in Children's Books: A Treasury of the Familiar Characters of Childhood *(copyright © 1975 by Margery Fisher; reprinted by permission of Holt, Rinehart and Winston, Publishers), Holt, 1975.*

OTHER CITATIONS

Virginia Haviland, in The Horn Book Magazine, *October, 1953, p. 362.*

The Times Literary Supplement, *November 27, 1953, p. iv.*

THE VOYAGE OF THE DAWN TRADER (1952)

[*The Voyage of the Dawn Treader*] is rich with incident and adventure, colourful, vivid and pulsating with the breath of life. This strange and allegorical fantasy is no mere myth or fairytale, but one that is charged with spiritual insight and significance. The story as a whole is a picture of life and each event heightens and illumines our knowledge and understanding of spiritual truths and values. Perhaps the loveliest piece is that where Lucy, reading in the magicians book, comes upon a spell, "for the refreshment of the spirit." She reads entranced but all too soon the page is turned and Lucy finds she cannot turn back. She remembers a story, however, the loveliest story she had ever known, a story about a sword, a cup, a tree and a green hill. The adult can find riches and food for thought here while the child will enjoy the story for itself. It is a fast moving one that fascinates and attracts by its ingenuity of thought and originality of theme, and excitement enough to lure children on. Meanwhile as they read, much may be gleaned unnoticed for spiritual stores and the book will leave a much needed bequest. (pp. 181-2)

The Junior Bookshelf, *October, 1952.*

[Caspian's] journey is conducted, and described, in the spirit of one of those tests of knightly worth which abound in the work of Malory and Spenser. A certain dignity accrues to Caspian from the circumstances of his endeavours in battle and in the exploration of strange archipelagoes, but in another sense he is just a goldenheaded youth, sharing adventures with the Pevensies, who speak and act like children even though they have been called back from the distant past of their reign in Cair Paravel. This ambiguity of age, stature and behaviour is found in all the Narnia books, with their mixture of chatter and formal speech, hoydenish romps and medieval combat, schoolroom feasts, high table ceremonies and the symbolic sharing of food. C. S. Lewis's firm hand on his plots and his simple, energetic narrative style reconcile the disparate elements in the stories. But we must accept that his characters—and in particular his princely heroes—cannot be drawn in depth but must be, as occasion warrants, regal figureheads or hearty lads. (p. 289)

> *Margery Fisher, in her* Who's Who in Children's Books: A Treasury of the Familiar Characters of Childhood *(copyright © 1975 by Margery Fisher; reprinted by permission of Holt, Rinehart and Winston, Publishers), Holt, 1975.*

OTHER CITATIONS

The Times Literary Supplement, *November 28, 1952, p. vii.*

Margery Fisher, in her Who's Who in Children's Books: A Treasury of the Familiar Characters of Childhood, *Holt, Rinehart and Winston, 1975, p. 302.*

M

MACAULAY, David   1946-

Born in England, David Macaulay studied architecture at the Rhode Island School of Design, where he now teaches. Long an admirer of the Gothic cathedral, Macaulay has traveled widely in Europe, observing architectural design. His books are a reflection of both his interests and his talents. Macaulay's *Cathedral: The Story of Its Construction* was awarded the Deutscher Jugendbuchpreis in Germany for the best nonfiction picture book of 1975. (See also *Contemporary Authors*, Vols. 53-56.)

GENERAL COMMENTARY

"Overwhelming praise and international recognition" are the powerful words from the blurb of David Macaulay's latest book on early architecture aimed at children of an uncertain age. Such phrases must make us pause for a moment to consider the state of our visual culture and look more closely at the three volumes *Cathedral, City* and *Pyramid*.

The original book by this young English illustrator working in America was the story of the construction of an imaginary French cathedral. Its success led to the repetition of the formula for studies of an imaginary Roman city and an imaginary Egyptian pyramid. The central idea is to illustrate the way these large structures came to be built and to give some insight into the actual problems of early technology, materials and tools. The illustrations are large, often full page (12" x 9"), or even double spread. There is none of the patchwork collage familiar in some school books where three or four small pictures, diagrams, or photographs jostle together on a page like a Sunday supplement that will not hold the handling.

One laudable purpose of these books is to awaken children to the technical problems of building in earlier civilizations. The processes of cutting rock, moving heavy materials with winches and pulleys, preparing foundations, making wooden centerings for vaults and flying buttresses or coffering domes, are conveyed with substantial clarity. Children can participate *imaginatively* in certain areas of the work. I should like the Chinese Dotheboys Hall approach to education to develop from these books, where children participate *in reality* in small technological problems. History, geology, technology, and craftsmanship could be fused much earlier in the child's life than at present. The trouble is that the spectator's experience of mixing cement or splitting rock has little to do with the workers', and it is difficult to bridge the gap as our society is constructed. Mr. Macaulay has chosen rather remote and time-hollowed examples so that the imaginative experience dominates. Visits to quarries, masons' yards, and old craftsmen could reinforce the material of these books.

The vigorous black-and-white illustrations are all drawn by the author, which gives a unity to the books and must be a godsend to the publisher. It could be argued that the variety of visual experience offered to a child would be greater if he had to interpret mediaeval plans, or make sense of a reproduction of a real mediaeval window, or compare drawings and photographs of pumiced Pompeii. A good teacher or parent would naturally supplement the book with other illustrations and have his own views about what children prefer. (pp. 12, 14-15)

Many illustrators of children's books seem to be aiming at other adults rather than at children. Adult reaction to David Macaulay's work is generally enthusiastic, especially among people with little art training who may feel they have the eye of childhood. John Ruskin has turned more than once in his grave. Mr. Macaulay has certain devices which produce immediate response as we turn the pages. The high angle shot or helicopter view is more lucid than an aerial photograph and as exciting as trembling on the scaffolding or spending the night with that sweet thing perspective. This device is most effective in his first book on the soaring French Gothic . . ., but there are lively moments in his Roman city, such as the voyeur's view of the public lavatory . . . or the gods' own view of the amphitheatre. Mr. Macaulay's own love of building is vividly conveyed.

The style ranges from careful explanatory diagrams through steady architectural observation . . . down to poor, hairy figure-drawings. . . . The confidence and ease of his best effects may be necessarily built on light-hearted springboards and areas of casual vagueness. Occasionally, it seems that a watered-down cartoon style echoing [Saul] Steinberg is felt to be less intimidating to the young than the clarity and precision [shown in some of Macaulay's work]. At times, therefore, the cathedral appears to have been knitted in string, the stonework mortared in running ink, and the craftsman hamfisted. It is interesting that the odd birds' nests in the scaffolding or the sleeping cat and mouse in the blacksmith's workshop do not occur in the later books. Some editor, no doubt worried about high-seriousness, has forgotten the way a child explores a picture. He should remember the torturer's horse scratching his innocent behind on a tree. The figure drawings lack all individuality and character. One child described them as "dummies arranged in a museum". They all have the same eyes and limbs and are clearly incapable of any movement. They certainly could never shin up the Gothic scaffolding or lift a stone. As the books are narrative (in the minimal sense that events unfold through time) it does seem to me that a figure from Chaucer or Cicero deserves a real face and form even if they are totally subsidiary to their workmanship. In *City*, several characters are mentioned by name but they die on the page instantly. It is interesting to compare the mediaeval workers . . . and their perfunctory shading with the cleaned up Romans. . . . Neither are better than an average teenager's drawing and compare unfavourably with the skilful albeit mass-produced faces of certain comics.

It would be easy to build up a list of vaguenesses in Mr. Macaulay's work. Any structuralist would conclude that his training in architecture leaves him uneasy about animate things. The underparts of the ox in *City*, for instance, the dissected rabbit used for omens, the giant sandals in the peristyle, the unconvincing postures of the road builders and the bulge of the glassblower's cheeks, the joyless encounter in the wicked baths—all lead me to suggest that he should use another artist for the "animation" work.

The children who could get most from these books are probably those who do not read easily but learn through deep absorption in pictures. . . . These children value precision. They are inspired by drawings which give them examples to copy or imitate. They haven't crashed the realism barrier. I have watched children draw mechanical objects with rulers in case their souls should leak into their visual passion or because they fear the wiry bounding line which they cannot control. The vagueness in these pictures will offend them.

As we are looking closely there are more details where care was needed. In *Cathedral* [between the years 1280 and 1281] the cottage roofs suddenly change from chimneyless thatch to tiles with chimneys. On page 40 a reference is made to mortice and tenon with only a tiny example in the accompanying picture. Further on, the illustrations to stained glasswork are too vague to hold the child's interest.

In *City*, the important area of water supply is presented unevenly because the illustrations don't connect. The position of the reservoir is obscure and the reason for the height of aqueducts is given as pollution rather than as pressure. I am not sure that using an imaginary town is an advantage. Indirect references to Pompeii and other places make it difficult to fix the location in the imagination. I would argue that the generalised approach to a typical Roman city is of less value historically than the study of a *representative* city. If young students are expected to absorb a good number of Latin namings of parts without benefit of English connections these students are mature enough to be given historical actuality. In the same way, architecture itself cannot be generalised too far. The great excitement of remaining ruins like the Pont du Gard, the Colosseum or the Arch of Constantine is easily dissipated.

However, the text gives a good general picture of life in a

Roman provincial town. There is a real sense of a growing town filling out to the confining walls. There are nice details about roads and shops and building restrictions.

I like Macaulay's sense of purpose in making links with modern town planning and traffic in *City*, and heartily regret the backward step to Egypt. The surplus wealth and slaves of Egypt were squandered on structures almost totally devoid of intellectual interest. . . . After *City*, the Egyptian study is not really worth a whole book. It has to be filled out with details about burying the King. Architecture is one of the most important things man can turn his hand and mind to—most children until recently have rarely got beyond a start at Gothic, and *Georgian* means the more-expensively fitted houses on the new estate. Future county councillors and the power seekers who presume to decide the environment will not learn much from *Pyramid* except the idea of moving large numbers of people about.

Publishers should be turning their attention where the young are: Victorian Architecture, Art Nouveau, Art Deco, Bauhaus, New Towns, Geodisic Domes and Intermediate Technology. Let us all re-read William Morris on the *Prospects of Architecture in Civilisation*:

> Though the days worsen and no rag of the elder art be left for our teaching, yet the new art may yet arise among us, and even if it have the hands of a child with the heart of a troubled man, still it may bear on for us to better times the tokens of our reference for the Life of Man upon the Earth.

Cathedral and *City* make a good attempt to preserve aspects of "the elder art". Now for the new. (pp. 15, 17-18, 20)

> *Geoffrey Hoare, "The Work of David Macaulay," in* Children's Literature in Education *(© 1977, APS Publications, Inc., New York; reprinted by permission of the publisher), No. 1 (Spring), 1977, pp. 12-20.*

CATHEDRAL: THE STORY OF ITS CONSTRUCTION (1973)

The relatively speedy 86-year construction of an imaginary Gothic cathedral, from the hiring of the Flemish architect and various master craftsmen to the installation of the bells, statues, and stained glass windows, is traced in workmanlike prose (from two to sixteen lines per oversized page) and black and white drawings that invite poring over. This has none of the richness and passion of Abbe Suger's true story told by Anne Rockwell in *Glass, Stone and Crown* . . . , and the absence of definitions for words like transept and vaulting, let alone tympanum and voussoirs, is a minor stumbling block. However, browsers attracted by Macaulay's lovingly detailed inside, outside and off-site sketches will most likely be intrigued as well by the equally detailed text (right down to the winter coating of straw and dung to keep the new mortar from cracking) of his solidly based reconstruction. (p. 689)

Kirkus Reviews (copyright © 1973 The Kirkus Service, Inc.), July 1, 1973.

For readers of all ages—and particularly those who believe that man's greatest achievements are to be found in the age of space and automation—[*Cathedral*] might well be an introduction to the remarkable perseverance, courage, religious fervor, ingenuity, and engineering acumen of the medieval laborers and craftsmen whose incredible architectural monuments are still standing. . . . [Macaulay's] brief but lucid text supports [his] splendid, meticulously detailed drawings which soar and spread over the ample pages. (pp. 478-79)

> *Ethel L. Heins, in* The Horn Book Magazine *(copyright © 1973 by The Horn Book, Inc., Boston), October, 1973.*

The Middle Ages were a time of faith—faith in God and faith in man under the guidance of God. Evidence of this faith and justification for it can be seen in the great cathedrals of England and the Continent, monuments to the spiritual insights and material achievements of mankind over the centuries.

In "Cathedral" David Macaulay describes in clear and fascinating detail the 86-year-building of one such Gothic edifice—an imaginary one in 13th- and 14th-century France —and how its construction to the glory of God, inspired and united a community. Mr. Macaulay's Cathedral of Chutreaux, as so many others, was built on the site of an earlier church—a site which may well have been (though the author does not say this) a religious one from pre-Christian times. Just as the beauty and craftsmanship of Gothic derived from earlier forms, so the faith of medieval Christendom developed from earlier concepts and beliefs.

The contribution of the planners and architect and of each of the many artisans—workers in stone, wood, glass and metal—involved in this long and complex project is both explained in the text and shown in Mr. Macaulay's large, eye-catching drawings. These drawings, some from ground level, some from high in the building itself, reveal the ongoing stages of construction, the interrelation of the parts and the ingenuity and skill of medieval craftsmanship.

Solidly built of stone, except for the timbers and lead of the roof and the stained-glass of the windows, the fictional Cathedral of Chutreaux—as those real cathedrals of Chartres, Canterbury, Vienna, Ulm, Paris, York, and all the others—achieved that essential blend of beauty and utility that marks all truly functional architecture of the highest order. It is the great virtue of Mr. Macaulay's book to reveal this in a pleasing and convincing way. (p. 10)

> *Nash K. Burger, in the* New York Times Book Review *(© 1973 by the New York Times Company; reprinted by permission), December 16, 1973.*

Cathedral, by David Macaulay, is a book to treasure. It is an account of the building of an imaginary gothic cathedral, stage by stage and illustrated by the most haunting pen drawings I have ever seen in a so-called picture book. Through page after page the structure rises; gaunt walls enclose their ordained space, arches are fashioned, bells are cast, and strange gargoyles are carved; and everywhere ant-like craftsmen labour on tiny details. On the last page of all the huge cathedral rises above the town, a mighty monument to faith and craftsmanship which together have produced a work of art. In its own way, so is this book. (p. xi)

> *Leon Garfield, in* The Spectator *(© 1974 by The Spectator; reprinted by permission of The Spectator), September 14, 1974.*

The building of a medieval cathedral hardly sounds a topic likely to set young minds a-tingle but David Macaulay's combination of succinct text and versatile drawings has just that quality. The people, the builders, the cathedral, the course of its construction are imaginary: planning and preparation, buttress and beam, vaulting and voussoir are authentic enough, and illustrate clearly how, step by step, a Gothic cathedral was constructed.

The drawings have a depth and sense of perspective, a meticulous concern for a hundred tiny details: they convey something of the grandeur of the building—almost a reflection of the pride in workmanship that the thirteenth century craftsmen must have felt. Indeed, it is a similar precision and enthusiasm in Mr. Macaulay himself that helps to make this book so rich an experience. (p. 67)

> The Junior Bookshelf, *February, 1975.*

The idea of this book is a little better than the performance. David Macaulay follows all the stages in building a typical French cathedral, in words and more especially in illustrations, which range from wide comprehensive pictures through isometric drawings to the working plans and drawings which the medieval craftsmen might have used. It is all precise, carefully researched and convincing. It is perhaps too much to wish that it might also be a beautiful book. The drawing is too clinical to convey the passion and excitement, and the daring gambles with gravity, which produced the great buildings of the Middle Ages. The words too are accurate without eloquence. The result is a book which never attempts to reach beyond its grasp, admirable but unexciting. (p. 60)

> *Marcus Crouch, in* The School Librarian, *March, 1975.*

The Gothic cathedral is one of the triumphs of western civilization. In this spectacular book David Macaulay takes the reader through every stage of the construction of an imaginary cathedral from the planning of the architect, through the labours of every type of craftsman whose work was part of the magnificent edifice, to the supreme moment 86 years after its conception "when the choir began to sing, the building filled with beautiful sounds and the people, most of them grandchildren of the men who had laid the foundation, were filled with a tremendous awe and a great joy." Line drawings vary from architectural cross sections to vertiginous views—a visual commentary on the sum of craftsmanship which adds up, miraculously, to emotional exultation. (p. 87)

> *Elaine Moss, in her* Children's Books of the Year 1974 *(© Elaine Moss 1975), Hamish Hamilton, Ltd., 1975.*

OTHER CITATIONS

Publishers Weekly, *September 10, 1973, p. 52.*

V'Anne Didzun, in School Library Journal, *December, 1973, p. 50.*

Zena Sutherland, in Bulletin of the Center for Children's Books, *January, 1974, p. 81.*

Top of the News, *April, 1974, p. 247.*

Eliot Fremont-Smith and Karla Kuskin, in New York Magazine, *December 16, 1974, pp. 108, 111.*

Where, *August, 1975, p. 221.*

CITY: A STORY OF ROMAN PLANNING AND CONSTRUCTION (1974)

[In *City*] Macaulay focuses on one aspect of the Roman world—the achievement of efficient and rational city planning. His brilliantly individualistic drawings capture the essential quality of the Roman character, the ability to organize. Although his men and women are awkward, rough-hewn, and earthbound, the temples, arenas, and aqueducts rise with grace, precision, and awesome magnitude. A fascinating celebration of man's works. (pp. 119-20)

> *Shirley M. Wilton, in* School Library Journal *(reprinted from the October, 1974, issue of* School Library Journal, *published by R. R. Bowker Company, a Xerox company; copyright © 1974 by Xerox Corporation), October, 1974.*

David Macaulay's "City" is about urban planning as practiced by the ancients. The book raises questions it doesn't ask about the authentic functionalism of contemporary planning. And the author seems to leave no stone unturned. It's a story of stucco, drains and granaries. But another tale emerges—of a life-style devised by enlightened central authority, engineered by the military and built by skilled craftsmen for bourgeois business and family life. . . .

There are even real people—notably one Marcus Licinius, a former slave who prospers as a baker and builds an attractive townhouse, described from peristyle to water closet. History has but lately resumed a healthy preoccupation with plumbing—unaided by the intervening centuries of northern European domination.

Macaulay's book is as appealing and revealing as last year's "Cathedral." And it's a great deal more important to the young who may never have been confronted by such a statement as, "The Romans knew that well planned cities did more to maintain peace and security than twice the number of military camps." (p. 8)

> *Richard Peck, in* The New York Times Book Review *(© 1974 by The New York Times Company; reprinted by permission), October 6, 1974.*

David Macaulay's *City* is the work of an artist/architect but though visual material occupies the greater part of the book, it is in the precise, intelligent marriage of text and illustration that it excels. . . . His is a book crammed with information. . . . But above all it is a book to make you think—to wonder, for example, at the simple, militaristic grid system on which Verbonia was planned and the way Roman thought seemed to follow the same structural pattern, to speculate on the fortunes of those who did not entirely fit the pattern. Informative as the book is, it is not only a treatise on streets and buildings, but a study of people whose way of life both dictated and was dictated to by the plan of this imaginary but reasonably representative Roman city. (pp. 2742-43)

> *Margery Fisher, in her* Growing Point, *November, 1975.*

[*City*] is designed to show "children of all ages" the problems involved, the needs of . . . an autonomous community and the way in which they were all met. David Macaulay describes the first nucleus [of Verbonia], planted by Augustus with a force of two thousand veterans, and how they marked out the limits and street system of the city as they already envisaged it, when it would reach its fullest extent. He thinks of it as a commercial city, a clearinghouse for the products of the region, as occupying a rectangle of 720 by 620 yards inside its walls and as capable, at its fullest, of holding 50,000 people—surely rather an excessive number for this space. The first half of this book shows how in the first few years the planners and their force of soldiers and slaves completed the walls, the grid of streets, the drainage system and the aqueducts, and settled the sites of the forum, public buildings and places of recreation. The second half shows how the skeleton of the city was filled in with houses, shops and public buildings, which included the markets, the baths, the theatre and the amphitheatre.

The book is obviously a considerable enterprise. David Macaulay draws everything clearly and honestly, and makes a special effort to elucidate technical processes—the way in which everything is made. Only rarely does he omit something important such as the ditch in front of the town hall. His greatest strength, perhaps, is his almost Roman power of picturing complicated *ensembles* and making his pictures wholly convincing—provided that one does not worry about the finer points. Finesse, indeed, an appreciation of the details of Roman culture, is the one virtue lacking in this otherwise admirable book—a book which shows brilliantly how the "Roman kind of planning is the basis of any truly successful city". One hopes that next time Mr Macaulay will seek the advice of a few specialists, and so produce something even better. I offer a few criticisms of his present work, I hope in no unhelpful spirit.

First, he shows too few inscriptions, and those inadequate. One "Augusta Verbonia DCCXXVIII", like the stele on which it is cut, seems hopelessly bald. So also does the senator's tomb. It is a pity that no Latinist helped the author over "valarium" (for the correct "velarium") or "castrum" (for the normal "castra"), or gave him the Latin names for his various tools. Again, while he knows and admires Roman construction, he shares the insouciance still, alas, so fashionable about Roman aesthetics.

So schools will need to supplement even his pictures with some of real Roman works. For instance, the buildings around his forum are very crowded, with far too few surrounding courts; and few of the typical Roman axial relations are established. This is partly because his drawings make too little use of separate enclosures for separate trades. The axis joining theatre and amphitheatre is hopelessly blocked by an inexplicable building, large but pinched. Nor does Mr. Macaulay always take pains with his temples. They sometimes lack cornices. The *Capitolium* is too crude; but the Temple of Augustus is better.

Of smaller cavils, the following seem worth making. I half-sympathize with him for not identifying those "city planners" who legislated about the height of street-frontages. Later he seems to make the kerbs of his road too high. Rain would not have run off. Despite his interpretation, are aqueducts near towns made so lofty chiefly to stop people stealing or poisoning the water? Is not their height due to the slightness of the gradient by which they descended from their springs in the mountains? But then Mr Macaulay has no space in which to discuss such things, and omits the inspection-points ("castella") from which cleaners crawled along the channels. The gallery above the town gate is given too few windows.

Contrast Trier and Autun. While the ancient bakeries are admirably illustrated, there are surely unreasonable liberties taken with the plan of the *atrium* house. The *atrium* has only one *ala*, and that is given the improbable use of a dining room; while there is no *tablinum* between *atrium* and rear-peristyle, only a thin corridor. It is also mildly surprising that a mere baker should have a separate room as "library", as Mr. Macaulay states. Finally, one could argue for a long time about the "thermae", or public baths, which are even dated as AD 42. The changing-room is a little remote and is not situated (as it so often was) at the crossroads between the cold bath and the tepid bath. The architecture, as shown here, suggests to me a date *c* AD 250 rather than AD 50. On the other hand, the external colonnades so numerous in this town—not only in the public baths—are nearly all Doric, pre-Augustan rather than Augustan or later. But surely in an Augustan foundation they would have been Corinthian from the outset.

Were Mr. Macaulay to agree about these details, he would need to alter a fair number of his drawings, some of them considerably. But to my mind the labour would seem worth while.

> *W. H. Plommer, "Lovingly Reconstructed" in* The Times Literary Supplement *(© Times Newspapers Ltd., 1975; reproduced from* The Times Literary Supplement *by permission, December 5, 1975, p. 1458.*

OTHER CITATIONS

Kirkus Reviews, *August 1, 1974, p. 807.*

Paul Heins, in The Horn Book Magazine, *October, 1974, p. 149.*

Zena Sutherland, in Bulletin of the Center for Children's Books, *December, 1974, pp. 65-6.*

The Economist, *December 20, 1975, p. 103.*

The Junior Bookshelf, *February, 1976, p. 50.*

PYRAMID (1975)

Another tour de force from [David Macaulay]. This time Macaulay skillfully reconstructs the building of a representative pyramid—from approval of the site (2470 B.C.) to laying in the capstone (2442 B.C.)—and contiguous structures in the funerary complex, e.g., a smaller queen's tomb, valley and mortuary temples, boat pit, mastabas. He dispels the mystery surrounding these magnificent edifices with clear, methodical explanations of the rudimentary but ingenious technology devised to overcome seemingly insurmountable obstacles—e.g., water-filled trenches cut into the foundation rock were used to level the site; sand and rubble fill were used as a platform on which to lower the stone sarcophagus into the tomb—and attends to details which reinforce readers' sense of how slowly the laborious work progresses, e.g., the pharaoh is interred before work on the complex is complete. The illustrations, which are, appropriately, more geometrical and panoramic than those in the earlier titles, offer a glimpse of this early desert civilization which makes the pyramids seem all the more monumental. (p. 107)

> *Leah Deland Stenson, in* School Library Journal *(reprinted from the October, 1975, issue of* School Library Journal, *published by R. R. Bowker Company, a Xerox company; copyright © 1975 by Xerox Corporation), October, 1975.*

On the subject of Egyptology, youthful generations have had to make do with the highly colored tableaux in The National Geographic's pages, augmented by Saturday matinees of Mummy's Curse movies. Such romance and mystery are missing from David Macaulay's "Pyramid," but the raising of man's mightiest monument is told in a sort of countdown that encapsulates the years of labor and the many skills involved in building a pyramid, circa 2500 B.C. . . .

We learn some, though not enough about this early empire to suggest the impetus behind the building of monumental tombs that towered over their time to cast a shadow well into ours. . . .

The author-artist's illustrations are, as always, instructive, though more lifeless and less crisp than in his earlier books. The problem may well stem from our perceptions of ancient Egypt: a misty culture of worker-insects creating astounding anthills. A more pictorial treatment of Egyptian artistry—the bejeweled sway of the sarcophagus, the awesome sculpture, the frescoes—would tell a more vibrant story. Perhaps we still need those pages from The National Geographic to enliven this part of the past. (p. 10)

> *Richard Peck, in* The New York Times Book Review *(© 1975 by The New York Times Company; reprinted by permission), October 5, 1975.*

With finely detailed, black-and-white drawings and a clear, objective text, the construction of an imaginary pyramid on the west bank of the Nile is the subject of a volume as distinctive as *Cathedral* and *City*. . . . Every step in the process is explained, beginning with the reasons why the ancient Egyptians attached so much importance to the building of permanent, magnificent tombs. Information about selection of the site, drawing of the plans, calculating compass directions, clearing and leveling the ground, and quarrying and hauling the tremendous blocks of granite and limestone is conveyed as much by pictures as by text. It is interesting to note that although the author mentions the many thousands of people recruited to work on the pyramid and the ceremonies conducted from time to time during its construction and after its completion, he makes no attempt to dramatize either the labors of the workers or the pomp and circumstance of the ceremonies. This restraint adds strength to a notable presentation. (p. 603)

> *Beryl Robinson, in* The Horn Book Magazine *(copyright © 1975 by the Horn Book, Inc., Boston), December, 1975.*

Pyramids hold a special place perhaps in everyone's mind who has studied even a minute amount of ancient history, but Macaulay has taken their building and transformed a historical event into the true wonder which pyramids are. Step by step with complete but not boring explanations to relate in order just what was done, through text and illustrations Macaulay takes the reader back to Ancient Egypt. As with his earlier books *Cathedral* and *City*, *Pyramid* is a must title for every media center both for study and enrichment. This is one of those rare nonfiction titles that can be read with just as much excitement and enjoyment as fiction. (p. 410)

> *James Norsworthy, in* Catholic Library World, *April, 1976.*

What a beautiful book! We follow the building of the pyramid, step by step. The drawings explain the complex preparations elegantly and lucidly. The author is an architect and his understanding of the stupendous project includes a feeling for the people who did the actual work. I think all age groups will be fascinated and entertained by this elegant and original approach to a subject that has so often been dealt with in an uninspired way. (p. 68)

> *Charles Hannam, in* The School Librarian, *March, 1977.*

OTHER CITATIONS

Publishers Weekly, *August 25, 1975, p. 294.*

Kirkus Reviews, *September 1, 1975, p. 1001.*

Barbara Dill, in Wilson Library Bulletin, *November, 1975, p. 195.*

Stefan Kanfer, in Time, *December 8, 1975, p. 88.*

Donald J. Bissett and Ruth E. Moline, in Language Arts, *May, 1976, p. 503.*

UNDERGROUND (1976)

It's hard to imagine an artist better qualified to explore the maze of pipes, piles, and tunnels that lies *Underground* beneath a big city, and if this recreation lacks the utopian clarity of Macaulay's imaginary *Cathedral . . .* and *City . . .*, there are compensating flashes of humor and playful solutions to the problem of illustrating what can't be seen. Explanations of the four major kinds of foundations for large buildings, the layout of sewer systems and underground cables, and the building of a subway tunnel require a more substantial and more challenging text than previous volumes, but the visual experience can stand by itself. In addition to the predictable surface views, diagrams and cutaway cross sections, Macaulay strips away pavement and soil to show us how the superstructure of a city street would look if we could stand on bedrock, below. The perspective is mind boggling, and though we've seen parts of the picture elsewhere—in [James E.] Kelly and [William R.] Park's *Tunnel Builders . . .*, for example—Macaulay gives us a breathtaking and entirely original insight. (p. 908)

> Kirkus Reviews *(copyright © 1976 The Kirkus Service, Inc.), August 15, 1976.*

I don't think David Macaulay's fourth book is going to attract as many readers as did his three previous books, *Cathedral, City,* and *Pyramid.* Thirty-four pages on foundations is a bit difficult to get through. It's an interesting network beneath the city streets that he has painstakingly researched, visited and detailed for us, but I don't need to know *that* much about it. Nor, do I think, would any child; short of a future engineer.

His graphics, as usual, are impeccable, and there's a new addition here that I like. He's injected some sly humor into his artwork. There's an alligator in the sewer system and a

fire hydrant is never pictured without a dog somewhere in the vicinity. Subtle.

The text is informative and thorough. If there is such a thing as too thorough, that may be the weakness in this visually splendid book. (p. 44)

> *Barbara Karlin, in* West Coast Review of Books *(copyright 1977 by Rapport Publishing Co., Inc.), Vol. 3, No. 1, (January, 1977).*

Perhaps nowhere is the complexity of today's civilization more evident than in the intricate support systems hidden beneath metropolitan streets. However, average city dwellers are unlikely to appreciate such subterranean phenomena as subways, building foundations, water mains, or electrical conduits until a malfunction occurs. Only then may people realize that the modern city is in many ways an artificial organism dependent for its survival upon the services provided by a series of sophisticated networks. Because of their complexity, these systems are difficult to envision, let alone describe. That such information is conveyed accurately, concisely, and artistically is the triumph of an unusual book which achieves clarity through an imaginative and ingenious approach. Introduced by a visual index—a bird's eye view of a busy, hypothetical intersection with colored indicators marking the specific locations analyzed in subsequent pages—detailed illustrations are combined with a clear, precise narrative to make the subject comprehensible and fascinating. The use of two- and three-dimensional cutaway views, diagrams, and a variety of unusual perspectives creates the illusion of a guided tour beneath as well as through the underground maze. Touches of humor—a wistful canine gazing across a ditch toward an unattainable hydrant or an alligator swimming lazily toward two sewer rats—lighten the tone of a prodigious work. (pp. 63-4)

> *Mary M. Burns, in* The Horn Book Magazine *(copyright © 1977 by the Horn Book, Inc., Boston), February, 1977.*

Unless somebody builds a giant X-ray machine, we will never see the spindly foundations of a skyscraper or the snaky landscape of sewer pipes and subways under a city street. David Macaulay has an exciting way of showing us all that in factual architectural drawings that somehow evoke the mood of science fiction. The drawing technique itself is not new; it was much used in the '40s and '50s, particularly in the British *Architectural Review.* What is original is Macaulay's choice of subject matter. He is a born teacher with an interest in things nobody before had the skill or the courage to try to explain. Until he came along with this book, we had no clear idea what we were living on. Children now have more information on this particular subject than you can easily find in adult literature—even in the working libraries of engineers and architects.

The author's use of a second color to separate elements and clarify structure is worth careful study; second color is normally used as an ornament. Here it makes a strong contribution to the understanding of the complex subject matter. (p. 80)

> *Alvin Eisenman, in* Children's Book Showcase *(© 1977 The Children's Book Council, Inc.), Children's Book Council, 1977.*

OTHER CITATIONS

Publishers Weekly, *July 26, 1976, p. 79.*

*　　*　　*

MANLEY, Seon

Seon Manley is an American writer, editor, anthologist, and student of folklore. Among her associates she has numbered Edgar Varese, Anaïs Nin, and Ernest Hemingway. Two of Manley's strongest interests are her Scottish heritage and New York City, about which she has written two atmospheric autobiographies, *My Heart's in the Heather* and *My Heart's in Greenwich Village*. Many of her anthologies for children were compiled in collaboration with her sister, Gogo Lewis.

ADVENTURES IN MAKING: THE ROMANCE OF CRAFTS AROUND THE WORLD (1959)

Combining fiction, fact and a great many stunning photographs, Seon Manley has produced a striking book about crafts and craftsmen. It is not a do-it-yourself manual—no one today is expected to run up a feather cloak Hawaiian style or illumine a parchment manuscript in the medieval manner. It is rather an account of some of the lovely, curious and useful things that people all over the world have made and are making today.

Brief fictional sketches, some based on history, introduce the various crafts: a tale of Paul Revere's son leads off the section on silver working; the section on puppetry begins with a Balinese boy's delight in that centuries-old art; and so on. . . . The book is really a dual invitation—to discover and appreciate the handicrafts and to try some adventures in making. (p. 36)

> *Ellen Lewis Buell, in* The New York Times Book Review *(© 1960 by The New York Times Company; reprinted by permission), February 14, 1960.*

Featherwork, ivory carving, mask making, silversmithing, patchwork, glassmaking, sand painting, book illumination, and tapestry making are some of the crafts described in a survey of handcrafts, past and present, around the world. Although somewhat weakened by the unnecessary use of contrived narratives to introduce the factual descriptions and histories of the various crafts, the book is stimulating and worth adding to the collection if only for the many well-selected, excellent photographs of craft objects and craftsmen at work. A list of books for further reading is included; no index. (p. 457)

> The Booklist and Subscription Books Bulletin *(reprinted by permission of the American Library Association; copyright 1960 by the American Library Association), March 15, 1960.*

OTHER CITATIONS

Polly Goodwin, in Chicago Sunday Tribune Magazine of Books, *February 14, 1960, p. 8.*

LADIES OF THE GOTHICS: TALES OF ROMANCE AND TERROR BY THE GENTLE SEX (with Gogo Lewis, 1975)

The stories in *Ladies of the Gothics* have, as the title implies, two things in common: they are gothic and they were written by women. The editors, Seon Manley and Gogo Lewis, have clearly endeavored to cover the field—yoking classic ladies such as Emily Brontë and Mary Shelley unchronologically to modern practitioners such as Celia Fremlin and Ruth Rendell—and the team does not pull well together. Beginning with stylistically simple modern short stories, the book moves abruptly into formidable gobbets of *Wuthering Heights* and *The Mysteries of Udolpho*, material which is widely available elsewhere and hardly benefits from being fragmented. The editors have stationed modern tales at the edges of the book, presumably as sugar coating for the nineteenth-century pill within, but this strategy hardly mitigates the inconsistency of the material; it rather sacrifices such coherence as chronological order would lend the book. There is, however, an apparent reason for all of this: the anthology, with its charming biographical introductions, is a girl's book, a feminist document intended to inspire pride in young women by praising the literary accomplishments of their gender. In this purpose, the anthology is quite successful; but it is doubtful that anyone, male or female, will read with enthusiasm all of the stories and snippets assembled by force between its covers. (pp. 292-93)

> *William H. Green, in* Children's Literature: Annual of The Modern Language Association Seminar on Children's Literature and The Children's Literature Association, *Vol. 5, edited by Francelia Butler (© 1976 by Francelia Butler; all rights reserved), Temple University Press, 1976.*

OTHER CITATIONS

The Booklist, *November 15, 1975, p. 445.*

Kirkus Reviews, *November 15, 1975, p. 1296.*

MISTRESSES OF MYSTERY: TWO CENTURIES OF SUSPENSE STORIES BY THE GENTLE SEX (with Gogo Lewis, 1973)

If anyone in this age of feminism still believes that women are "the gentle sex," they need only glance through this volume to see that men don't exclusively control the macabre. In nine stories of hating and haunting, treachery and terror, the authors—E. Nesbit, Dorothy Sayers, Edith Wharton, Monica Dickens—demonstrate their expertise at spine-tingling storytelling. As is often the problem with anthologies, the selections vary tremendously in the quality of the writing, but the situations conjured up—women being poisoned by caps placed on their teeth, Lizzie Borden's activities a year after the famous murders—make for excellent reading on a cold, windy night when the branches scrape against the windows or at a storytelling session. Edmund Wilson once asked, "Why is it that when we all have electricity, radios, and the telephone, we still return to antiquated tales of horror?" Reading Edith Wharton's "All Souls" and Marjorie Bowen's "Cambric Tea" should give the reader a partial answer to that question. (p. 472)

> *Anita Silvey, in* The Horn Book Magazine *(copyright © 1973 by The Horn Book, Inc., Boston), October, 1973.*

OTHER CITATIONS

Kirkus Reviews, *May 15, 1973, p. 568.*

The Booklist, *July 1, 1973, p. 1018.*

Joan Joffe Hall, in Children's Literature: Annual of The Modern Language Association Seminar on Children's Literature and The Children's Literature Association, *Vol. 2, edited by Francelia Butler, Temple University Press, 1973, pp. 235-36.*

MY HEART'S IN GREENWICH VILLAGE (1969)

Charming, delightful, entertaining, amusing, even instructive, this nostalgic view of Greenwich Village of 25 years ago will go right over the heads of the Young Adults for whom the publisher intends it. But their parents will savor it and anyone who knew the Village "when" or who does not equate "Village" with "East." It's a sort of "My Sister Eileen" with the girls and their beaux and the wonderful and innocently entertaining things that happen to them. There may be some in the Village for whom life is still like this; but most of the Young Adults are over in the East Village wearing the clothing of a long-gone generation and oblivious to what happened to anyone 25 years ago. So, let the older generation read and enjoy Seon Manley's reminiscences and save it for the Young Adults ten years from now. (p. 314)

Edith C. Howley, in Best Sellers *(copyright 1969, by the University of Scranton), November 15, 1969.*

Occasionally slow-moving memorabilia by a fine children's book author . . ., this begins with some false-sounding graffiti purportedly found in a Greenwich Village subway station, and reads for the first couple of chapters like a mother's tour of Alexandria, Virginia, with dull, quaint allusions to architecture and history. Modernization takes place by the third chapter, however, as Mrs. Manley humorously describes the first apartment she shared with five other girls, one her sister, Gogo, during World War II. Village living is the central theme: in an endless search for the right apartment in which to house their printing press, Seon and Gogo are befriended by Spanish anarchists, boys without funds, four elegant French sisters, an old woman who wears nothing but ancient furs, and, in the end, by Henry Miller, Kenneth Patchen, Anais Nin. They even encounter Ernest Hemingway. In context, these great names are not the most memorable; the author, via vivid writing, has given such characters as Polychronos, Agatha, and Joey the Rat equal importance. This book has more than regional appeal; its very appearance marks the achievement of the author's goal and this will satisfy future artists. (p. 59)

Jean C. Thomson, in School Library Journal *(reprinted from the December, 1969, issue of* School Library Journal, *published by R. R. Bowker Company, a Xerox company; copyright © 1969 by Xerox Corporation), December, 1969.*

The author and her sister, as young unmarried women, lived in Greenwich Village for some years; this is the anecdotal record of their mild adventures there, reminiscent of *My Sister Eileen* but lacking its vigor, and occasionally forced in the semi-humorous dialogue. There is enough color and variety in the Village to sustain the account, most of which consists of sisterly sparring, descriptions of people, and running battles with inadequate housing. (p. 84)

Zena Sutherland, in Bulletin of the Center for Children's Books *(© 1970 by the University of Chicago; all rights reserved), January, 1970.*

OTHER CITATIONS

Kirkus Reviews, *July 1, 1969, p. 682.*

Publishers Weekly, *October 13, 1969, p. 55.*

Mary Silva Cosgrave, in The Horn Book Magazine, *February, 1970, p. 62.*

MY HEART'S IN THE HEATHER (1968)

This charming autobiographical sketch comprises a series of vignettes of life in New York City during the period when the parents and grandparents of many children still had strong ties to European countries. The orphaned author and her younger sister lived with their grandparents in a Scotch-Irish neighborhood, where they absorbed the never-ending homesickness along with the songs, food, and customs of the old country, as they learned Gaelic and listened to stories of the old country. Beautifully written, the book is, unfortunately, too static to have general appeal, but it could be successfully introduced to young people who enjoy dipping into nostalgic reminiscences. (p. 151)

Madalynne Schoenfeld, in School Library Journal *(reprinted from the March, 1968, issue of* School Library Journal, *published by R. R. Bowker Company, a Xerox company; copyright © 1968 by Xerox Corporation), March, 1968.*

Places and times do not alleviate problems, as Seon Manley verifies in her story of a Scottish-American family that makes great contributions to the development of our nation. New York is the setting; Papa, a Scot, Mama, an American, and the two sisters, Gogo and Seon, give the reader many a laugh as they relate their experiences with well-known writers, anthologists and just plain human beings. Throughout one becomes well acquainted with traditions of the past, the ups and downs of adolescence and in the unending joys of a happy family, in which there is wit as well as understanding. (p. 155)

Best Sellers *(copyright 1968, by the University of Scranton), July 1, 1968.*

Whether or not a single drop of Gaelic blood flows in your veins, you'll be liking this loving memoir. It stems from the author's childhood in a Scottish-American neighborhood in New York City, where the older folk felt nostalgia for the Old World and the young people, though rooted in that past, were becoming absorbed into America and "hunting for their own tomorrow."

The poetry and fire of the Scots are captured in these recollections. In a series of delightful vignettes, Mrs. Manley gives hilarious accounts of a Sunday school performance of *Macbeth* (Shakespeare, said the director, was, of course, really a Scot!) and of letters written to Scottish shopkeepers for free tartan samples, as well as lively portraits of a variety of friends and neighbors, both Scottish and Irish—who with her family made up the rich fabric of a long-gone world. (p. 12)

Polly Goodwin, in Book World (© The Washington Post), *July 7, 1968.*

NATHANIEL HAWTHORNE: CAPTAIN OF THE IMAGINATION (1968)

Although adult studies of Hawthorne abound, little is available for younger readers except . . . [the] florid and sentimental *Romantic Rebel* . . . [written by his granddaughter, Hildegarde Hawthorne]. Mrs. Manley's book, while covering the same information—childhood influences, sources of literary inspiration, idyllic marriage to Sophia Peabody, friendship with leading writers and reformers of his era—has a more contemporary beat but is less revealing of the personalities of Emerson, Thoreau, and others of that era. Shy, introverted Hawthorne is a difficult subject for juvenile biography; still, determined students who can assimilate the lengthy quotations and extensive descriptive passages in this biography will find their reading of Hawthorne enhanced and they will find the extensive chronology that is appended most helpful. (p. 91)

> *Priscilla Moxom, in* School Library Journal *(reprinted from the February, 1969, issue of* School Library Journal, *published by R. R. Bowker Company, a Xerox company; copyright © 1969 by Xerox Corporation), February, 1969.*

The author of *Rudyard Kipling, Creative Adventurer* . . . quotes extensively from Hawthorne's notebooks and letters in a well-researched biography of the shy, introverted writer who "opened the way to the paths of science fiction, the Gothic, the psychological novel, and, greater than all of these, perhaps, the romance." . . . Manley traces the development of Hawthorne's writing, including appreciative descriptions and appraisals of his works, and vividly portrays the times and Hawthorne's relationships with his contemporaries, although the other literary figures do not come to life in the account. An interesting introduction to Hawthorne and his works, this may stimulate further reading. A chronology and an extensive list of books by and about Hawthorne are appended. (p. 1005)

> The Booklist and Subscription Books Bulletin *(reprinted by permission of the American Library Association; copyright 1969 by the American Library Association), May 1, 1969.*

OTHER CITATIONS

Best Sellers, *April 1, 1969, p. 21.*

RUDYARD KIPLING: CREATIVE ADVENTURER (1965)

Mrs. (Seon is a lady) Manley's "biography for young adults" is no significant addition to the meagre list of Kipling studies. Simply written and quite obviously a labor of love, it may, however, lead some "young adults," and some old ones too, to the writings of Kipling himself: no bad thing, for the Anglo-Indian author suffered for far too long from a "bad press." Mrs. Manley, of course, is quite *au courant* since Kipling has in recent years been dignified by the approval of such distinguished contemporaries as T. S. Eliot, and Randall Jarrell.

Unfortunately, this biography never comes to life. Mrs. Manley, for one thing, indulges in the vicious practice of manufacturing dialogue; and never does she suggest the complexity of Kipling's character. Far more serious, however, is her insistence upon the more pleasant side of the man and her refusal to see any of Kipling's many weaknesses as author. It must be remembered, at the same time, that the book is addressed to a juvenile reading level; and the standards expected of an adult-directed critical biography may not be applied too rigidly.

As an introduction to Kipling and his work, *Rudyard Kipling: Creative Adventurer* is satisfactory enough; and if Mrs. Manley does stir up a revival of interest in her subject, her biography has provided its own excuse for existence. (p. 53)

> *Stephen P. Ryan, in* Best Sellers *(copyright 1965, by University of Scranton), April 15, 1965.*

A new biography of Kipling has arrived for his centennial year. It tells of the chief events and influences in his life, pointing out their effects on his writing. Miss Manley is a conscientious author who seems to have a great and genuine enthusiasm for Kipling's writings, but I found the book disappointing. It did not seem to compel the reader to start rereading Kipling but rather to afford information useful for a student. It belongs to that amorphous form, the "biography for young adults" (an irritating phrase which should mean youthfulness of body and maturity of mind but which has come to mean physical maturity and mental immaturity). If a person is old enough to be interested in a great writer's life and its relation to his work, there is no need to offer interpolated conversations, fictionalized trimmings and paragraphs chopped up to make the page look lighter.

Any reader over 11 will find Rosemary Sutcliff's monograph on Kipling a far more satisfactory introduction. Literate, lively and sympathetic, it gives a masterly ten-page summary of Kipling's life, telling succinctly much that is in Miss Manley's book, and then adds percipient and interesting comments on Kipling's books for children (*Stalky & Co.,* the *Just-So Stories,* both Puck books, both Jungle books, *Kim* and *Captains Courageous*). Then he might turn to Miss Manley's book, especially the chapters on Kipling's life in India and his early writing career, or to the adult books both Miss Sutcliff and Miss Manley mention, C. E. Carrington's and J. M. S. Tompkins' books and Kipling's own autobiography, *Something of Myself.* Whatever books are used, may they lead back to the short stories of a master stylist and celebrate the 100th year of Kipling's birth by giving more readers, especially young ones, a chance to come under his spell. (p. 24)

> New York Sunday Herald Tribune Book Week (© The Washington Post), *May 9, 1965.*

Fortunate children are still growing up with *Just So Stories* and *The Jungle Books,* then going on into *Captains Courageous* and *Kim.* It is to be hoped that young people will enjoy Mrs. Manley's fine—albeit romantic—biography, and will read it for the vivid pictures it gives of Kipling's childhood, of his India, of England and the Sussex Downs, of American interludes and Brattleboro, Vermont. There are glimpses of events older people may have forgotten, younger people never known. . . .

Rudyard Kipling has been given a format that is adult and dignified in appearance and worthy of the hundredth anniversary. Only the beginnings of chapters, speeded up to catch interest—and a few "asides" by the author on writing in general—let us know that it is aimed at a younger audience. How seriously young people will take the Empire of Kipling and Queen Victoria remains to be seen. But all the roots of today's turbulent society are in it; the book is an excellent picture of that period of colonial "glory," which now seems so far away. (p. 39)

> *Alice Dalgliesh, in* Saturday Review *(copyright © 1965 by Saturday Review, Inc.; reprinted with permission), May 15, 1965.*

OTHER CITATIONS

Morton N. Cohen, in The New York Times Book Review, *February 7, 1965, p. 26.*

John Gillespie, in School Library Journal, *March, 1965, p. 196.*

Zena Sutherland, in Bulletin of the Center for Children's Books, *October, 1965, p. 36.*

TEEN-AGE TREASURY OF THE ARTS (with Gogo Lewis, 1964)

After a couple of generations of being cozzened and generally catered to, those young people inclined or committed to the creative arts have been getting short shrift lately in a labor market that pants after science and math talent. An inspired search of fiction, biography and autobiography have led the concerned editors to collect these sections of longer works that deal with the moments that adolescents have determined on careers in art. From *Act One,* comes the story of Moss Hart's start in the theater. From *My Sister Eileen,* comes the always delightful "Hungah." (Delightful as it is, this was a poor choice. It shows a confrontation with "Culture" as funny as Ruth McKenney can make it, but she has told of her early dedication to writing in other sketches.) Louisa May Alcott, through the chapter on Jo's literary efforts from *Little Women,* is still wry commentary on the difference between an author's desire and commercial considerations. "Drowne's Wooden Image" by Hawthorne reveals the artistic discipline of a craftsman and there is a morale building excerpt for young dancers and choreographers from Agnes DeMille. One could carp about sources that are missing, nevertheless this is an honest effort that should lead readers to full length books in the areas of their special interests. (p. 660)

> Virginia Kirkus' Service, *July 15, 1964.*

[*Teen-Age Treasury of the Arts*] is not just another collection of prose works and poetry; it is definitely directed along lofty intellectual channels to encourage the young person to contemplate the fine arts. Selections are taken from the old familiars, such as Moss Hart, Alcott, Hawthorne, West, Day, Shakespeare, Whitman and a host of other masters in the fields. The arrangement of alternating a section of prose with a section of poetry prevents boredom. Terminating the book is a three or four line description of nearly all the contributors. No index, but the Table of Contents in this book will suffice. This is a must purchase for the High School library. (p. 291)

> Best Sellers *(copyright 1964, by the University of Scranton), October 15, 1964.*

OTHER CITATIONS

Thomas Lask, in The New York Times Book Review, *November 1, 1964, p. 63.*

TEEN-AGE TREASURY OF GOOD HUMOR (1960)

The anthologist who compiles a book for young people has a dual advantage. Not only has he a considerable body of material written especially for them but he also has the opportunity—and the satisfaction—of leading his readers into the larger world of adult literature, of introducing them to writers whom they will enjoy all their lives—or at least for a long time. Thus in her "Teen-Age Treasury of Good Humor" . . . Seon Manley leads off with James Thurber's "The Night the Bed Fell"—and I have yet to meet a teen-ager who doesn't think that perfect—goes on to Clarence Day, Saki, Robert Benchley and includes also such favorites as Mark Twain (the white washing scene from "Tom Sawyer,") Edward Lear and Lewis Carroll. Giving her audience due credit for sophistication, in the right sense, and taste, she has put together a generous collection to cheer any reader. (p. 38)

> *Ellen Lewis Buell, in* The New York Times Book Review *(© 1961 by The New York Times Company; reprinted by permission), February 12, 1961.*

TEEN-AGE TREASURY OF OUR SCIENCE WORLD (with Gogo Lewis, 1961)

[This anthology] including excerpts from Teal's "Dune Boy," Ley's "Satellites, Rockets and Outer Space," a Gertrude Friedberg story from "New World Writing" (very good, but hardly fighting the stereotypes), a Max Shulman story (!); a selection from Gamow's "Birth and Death of the Sun," Poe's "Balloon-Hoax," a selection from Eisenberg's "There's One in Every Family," a bit of "20,000 Leagues Under the Sea" a snippet of "Life on the Mississippi" re piloting, a dab of Eugenie Clark's "Lady With a Spear," etc. There appears to be no unifying element in the book at all, other than some vague relationship, often very vague, to science. Some poetry (and some verse) is included. Why Wordsworth's "To A Butterfly," surely one of his worst non-science poems? Or Keats "On the Grasshopper and the Cricket"? Or Shelley's noted poem on science "To a Skylark?" Not recommended despite the excellence of some of the selections simply because it is not a "treasury of our science world." (p. 173)

> *Theodore C. Hines, in* School Library Journal *(reprinted from the October, 1961, issue of* School Library Journal, *published by R. R. Bowker Company, a Xerox company; copyright © 1961 by Xerox Corporation), October, 1961.*

Interpreting the term science in the broadest possible way, the editors have compiled an unconventional, immensely provocative anthology. Side by side with excerpts from the writings of such men as Gamow, Faraday, Schliemann and Darwin, and trenchant quotations from other thinkers and discoverers, there are humorous stories and verse—gently kidding aspects of science and scientists—serious fiction and poems, all put together to provide a way of looking at science. Certain of the selections seem a little far-fetched but the volume succeeds admirably in prodding the reader, who may have thought of science as a remote field for geniuses, into a realization of its breadth and immediacy. (p. 32)

The New York Times Book Review (© 1961 by The New York Times Company; reprinted by permission), October 8, 1961.

*   *   *

MATHIS, Sharon Bell   1937-

A Black American author of children's books, Sharon Bell Mathis has also been a special education teacher, a school librarian, and a columnist for *Ebony, Jr!* **magazine. In 1970, she was presented with the Council on Interracial Books for Children Award for her novel** *Sidewalk Story.* **(See also** *Contemporary Authors,* **Vols. 41-44 and** *Something About the Author,* **Vol. 7.)**

THE HUNDRED PENNY BOX (1975)

The Hundred Penny Box is a thoughtful and sometimes touching story about a Black family trying to adjust to the presence of their one-hundred-year-old Aunt Dew. The father, an authoritarian figure who rarely appears in the story, has invited her to live with them in appreciation to Aunt Dew for having raised him when he was orphaned.

The mother, Ruth, has problems with Aunt Dew. . . . Throughout the story, she threatens to burn Aunt Dew's hundred penny box. The battered wooden box holds one penny for each year Aunt Dew has lived and she has a story for every penny.

The threat to the penny box elicits Michael's protective feelings towards his aunt. Unfortunately, however, much of the relationship between Michael and Aunt Dew is dependent upon the mother's hostility. Must it be this way?

The conflicts that arise in the book are never really resolved. The ending is ambiguous, with Michael lying peacefully next to his sleeping aunt. He sees the box through different eyes and decides that it is a bit scruffy. Does this mean he has come to agree with his mother's plan to throw the box away?

The strength of the book lies in Aunt Dew's brief but vivid accounts of her life and in her relationship with Michael. Its weakness lies in the unexplained hostility of the mother and the absence of the father.

The illustrations [by Leo and Diane Dillon] are warm and eloquent, carrying the theme of the hundred penny box throughout the story. (p. 8)

Lydia Bassett, in Interracial Books for Children Bulletin *(reprinted by permission of* Interracial Books for Children Bulletin, *1841 Broadway, New York, N.Y. 10023), Vol. 6, Nos. 3 & 4, 1975.*

What is so fine about ["The Hundred Penny Box"] is that it does not set out in that kind, condescending, nervous way to acquaint its young readers with the concepts of Old Age and Death, to make them less fearful and perhaps less wonder-full. It is a quiet work of art, not an educational project. And so it presents an experience to which both children and the adults who may read them this story can relate and compare their own experience. (p. 20)

Annie Gottlieb, in The New York Times Book Review *(© 1975 by The New York Times Company; reprinted by permission), May 4, 1975.*

The best parts of Mathis' overpraised *Teacup Full of Roses* . . . were the observations of neurotic family dynamics, and this much smaller, more closely focused story (which benefits immeasurably from the trimming) shows that she can be as sensitive to more positive attachments. The only false note occurs in an early conversation between Michael's parents, too obviously designed to project a strong black family image; the rest is a loving evocation of the relationship between the little boy and his hundred-year-old great-great-Aunt Dew. . . . [When] Aunt Dew says "Them's my years in that box. That's me in that box," Michael understands what his mother doesn't. The Dillons' shadowy brown watercolors, dark like old memories, set ghosts of those hundred years behind the child and the wrinkled, almost fleshless old woman. (p. 568)

Kirkus Reviews (copyright © 1975 The Kirkus Service, Inc.), May 15, 1975.

The Hundred Penny Box is an excellent story of the family life and love that transcends generations and paints a very warm picture of human interactions that many of us only hear about. Too many of our children miss out on the wonderful world of grandmothers and even grow up having negative attitudes about their elders and about growing old themselves. Although the reading of one book cannot rectify that situation, *The Hundred Penny Box* is definitely a step in the right direction toward literature that entertains and provides some positive direction for our children. This is a must for every child who can read and can be read to. (p. 19)

Hazel Copeland, in Black Books Bulletin *(copyright © 1975 by the Institute of Positive Education), Winter, 1975.*

A poignant vignette rather than a story, describing a remarkable love between a young boy and his one hundred-year-old great-great aunt. The author has handled this fragile episode with "tender-loving care," resulting in a heart-warming tribute to the very young and to the very old. Each character is dealt with realistically and with great depth of understanding. (p. 154)

Christina Carr Young, in Childhood Education *(reprinted by permission of the Association for Childhood Education International, 3615 Wisconsin Ave., N.W., Washington, DC 20016; copyright © 1976 by the Association), Vol. 52, No. 3 (January, 1976).*

OTHER CITATIONS

Ethel L. Heins, in The Horn Book Magazine, *June, 1975, pp. 268-69.*

Zena Sutherland, in Bulletin of the Center for Children's Books, *November, 1975, p. 51.*

Teacher, April, 1976, p. 119.

———————

LISTEN FOR THE FIG TREE (1974)

Beneath the insistent, if only sketchily relevant, black consciousness raising lies a very traditional moral victory for Muffin [in *Listen for the Fig Tree*], who in spite of blindness, an alcoholic mother and her father's murder the previous Christmas manages to attend the Black Museum's identity affirming Kwanza/Christmas celebration in an ego-affirming dream outfit of pale pink suede. In the weeks before Kwanza Muffin copes more or less bravely with her mother's self pity, stresses the righteousness of patronizing black owned stores (a theme which receives a disproportionate share of dialogue), is taught to sew by a charming homosexual neighbor and saved from rape by another, and wonders briefly how to reconcile the blackness of her attacker (and her father's murderers) with her growing racial pride. This last problem is dismissed rather offhandedly considering how much it seems to trouble Muffin at first; nor can we ever be sure how much wishful thinking has gone into her dreams of marrying her sighted, silent boyfriend Ernie. In all Muffin's wardrobe grows faster than her maturity, but if sober observers, like Ernie, think that the blind girl's determination to overcome her problems with beautiful clothes is "like riding a horse backward," Muffin's stunning appearance at Kwanza would be enough to boost anyone's pride. It seems to promise much more, but that fulfillment depends more on the reader's own response to the symbols of black liberation than to Muffin's. (p. 121)

> *Kirkus Reviews (copyright © 1974 The Kirkus Service, Inc.), February 1, 1974.*

[*Listen for the Fig Tree*] is an obvious updating of "Cinderella" with Momma playing a watered-down wicked stepmother; and Mr. Dale, a homosexual neighbor, filling in for the fairy godmother (he designs Muffin's Kwanza dress and makes sure she gets to the festival). The characters, however, are more full-blooded than their fairy tale counterparts: Momma supplies some much needed humor with her slurred but sly mutterings; mincing Mr. Dale turns out to be a sensible father figure; and Muffin is not merely a victimized martyr (e.g., she selfishly uses Kwanza to block out her mother's drinking). Mathis also has a fine ear for the syncopation of Black speech, but her soap operatic story drags with too many scenes rehashing what's already happened. Moreover, the plot panders to those who thrive on other people's hard luck tales, however pathetic or degrading, e.g., there's a scene in which Muffin fumbles around cleaning up the "foul flow" of her mother's vomit. Kwanza's message of endurance is thus apt, for most readers will need lots to wade through this inner-city sob story. (p. 120)

> *Jane Abramson, in School Library Journal (reprinted from the March, 1974, issue of School Library Journal, published by R. R. Bowker Company, a Xerox company; copyright © 1974 by Xerox Corporation), March, 1974.*

It is the duty of the Black writer to portray and reflect images of our lives as Afrikan people, from the depths of our despair to the heights of our joy. At the same time he should lead us to see that which is positive and beautiful about the way we live while also pointing out that which should be changed. A responsible black writer will not only seek to entertain, but teach and enlighten as well.

Sharon Bell Mathis has done her job well, as a responsible black writer, in her new book for young people entitled *Listen for the Fig Tree*. Throughout the story we witness the struggle of a tiny family, mother and daughter, to remain intact. The mother, Leola, is half out of her mind with grief over the murder of her husband. Muffin, the daughter, is blind; but she is a proud and strong girl who works hard to soothe her mother's sorrow and pull her from the clutches of alcoholism. We are left with the feeling that she will succeed.

I hope that young readers will realize that Muffin's struggle is necessary and that the family has been of prime importance to us historically as it will continue to be.

Although Muffin is strong and works hard, she could not do what must be done without neighbors who reached out to help. . . . This should illustrate the importance of Ujima, collective work and responsibility, which means that our brothers and sisters' problems become our problems and we must solve them together. We as a people have practiced Ujima historically and must continue to do so if we are to survive, develop, and progress as a strong black nation.

Muffin is portrayed as a teenager whose knowledge about her Afrikan identity, which intially began with her father, is being heightened constantly by those around her. The focal point of the story is the Kwanza celebration. This is a good chance for young people to learn about this important Afrikan holiday. It is explained well. Through Muffin we feel what Kwanza means to black people. It is the celebration of the harvest of the first fruits—it could be the first fruits of a real crop harvest as it was celebrated by our ancestors, or it could be the fruits of our labor to rebuild our nation. During Kwanza, Muffin realizes that her efforts to keep her mother together are necessary and are exactly what Kwanza is all about. The family is the smallest unit of the nation.

Mrs. Mathis has mastered her craft. Her characters are clearly defined and warm. She did a superb job of relating to us how it feels to be blind; she did a superb job of relating to us how it is to be black. The story is suspenseful and should hold the interest of young people. (pp. 39-40)

> *Rochelle Cortez, in Black Books Bulletin (copyright © 1974 by the Institute of Positive Education), Spring, 1974.*

"Listen for the Fig Tree" is a beautiful black book about beautiful black people, achingly poignant and fierce and proud. Mathis has a talent for the music of black speech and for conveying the togetherness of black people.

But she has a more important talent, characterization and the ability to describe delicate relationships. Unfortunately for the last part of the novel, she lets these go for a panegyric about Africa. Concentrating on Muffin would have been a more successful call to arms. (p. 8)

> *Dale Carson, in The New York Times Book Review (© 1974 by The New York Times Company; reprinted by permission), April 7, 1974.*

OTHER CITATIONS

The Booklist, *May 15, 1974, p. 1058.*

Sister Mary Columba Offerman, in Best Sellers, *July 15, 1974, p. 202.*

Zena Sutherland, in Bulletin of the Center for Children's Books. *July-August, 1974, p. 182.*

RAY CHARLES (1973)

[In her *Ray Charles*] Mathis offers no particular insight into the experiences or personal qualities that led to his success, and the emphasis (whether the author's or the subject's) on possessions is a further barrier to our getting to know the man, but the combination of black and blind makes Ray Charles' a success story with a built-in audience. (p. 1208)

> Kirkus Reviews *(copyright © 1973 The Kirkus Service, Inc.), November 1, 1973.*

In this short, inspiring biography, Mathis successfully juxtaposes past and current events in the life of Ray Charles, the blind Black jazz musician. The lively text emphasizes Charles' strength, independence, and determination to succeed in spite of his race, his blindness, and his impoverished childhood. Enhanced by [George] Ford's two-color charcoal drawings, this will broaden Black biography collections. (p. 56)

> *Betty Lanier Jenkins, in* School Library Journal *(reprinted from the May, 1974, issue of* School Library Journal, *published by R. R. Bowker Company, a Xerox company; copyright © 1974 by Xerox Corporation), May, 1974.*

This book is about as good as a short biography of Ray Charles could possibly be. The musician, blinded as a child from an eye disease, emerges from Ms. Mathis' skillfully crafted book as a gentle, strong, competent man, husband, father, Black man. The black and white illustrations by George Ford are sensitive and excellently complement the text. (p. 7)

> *Barbara Walker, in* Interracial Books for Children *(reprinted by permission of* The Bulletin—Interracial Books for Children, *1841 Broadway, New York, N.Y. 10023), Vol. 5, No. 5, 1974.*

OTHER CITATIONS

Anita Silvey, in The Horn Book Magazine, *April, 1974, p. 166.*

SIDEWALK STORY (1971)

Lilly Etta's story is told with mild humor, a refreshing absence of sentimentality, and lively dialogue that places her convincingly in both the black ghetto culture and the nation of nine-year-olds everywhere. Five double-page black-and-white illustrations [by Leo Carty], along with a mostly brownish street (or stoop-and-sidewalk) scene on the jacket, authentically recreate Lilly Etta's world. (p. 434)

> Kirkus Reviews *(copyright © 1971 The Kirkus Service, Inc.), April 15, 1971.*

[Fiction is the] most demanding genre, it reveals flaws and virtues quickly; and a miss is more than a mile, it is an infinity. Sharon Bell Mathis does not miss in "Sidewalk Story" . . . Obviously Miss Mathis knows what she is about. . . . Her inner-city story of Lilly Etta, who decides to do something about her friend's eviction to the pavements, smoothly avoids the quivering-lip-amid-dirty-old-slum syndrome as well as the Hooray-I-found-a-lovely-nest-of-magic-roaches-in-my-dirty-old-slum virus. Her Lilly is a real little girl and, confronting real problems, she behaves like a child, bull-headed, pro-life and charming. It is a lovely book, warm but not sticky, serious but not relentlessly grim and it certainly deserves better than its "honest" (read oppressive) illustrations. (p. 43)

> *Toni Morrison, in* The New York Times Book Review, *Part II (© 1971 by The New York Times Company; reprinted by permission), May 2, 1971.*

[*Sidewalk Story*] is written by a black author and for that very reason the black characters and background are more rounded, convincing and relaxed. . . . It has something to say about friendship to children of any color and is written with pace, humor and a fine ear for the cadences of speech. (p. 265)

> *Elizabeth Minot Graves, in* Commonweal *(copyright © 1971 Commonweal Publishing Co., Inc.; reprinted by permission of Commonweal Publishing Co., Inc.), May 21, 1971.*

[This] story of black poverty was the 1970 winner in its age category of the Council on Interracial Books for Children contest for manuscripts by black writers. But little of the black experience is revealed in the book. The specter of eviction has always haunted the urban poor—black or white. Moreover, expediency—even in times of crisis—can scarcely be substituted for literary depth and quality. The writing is reportorial; characterizations hover on the surface; and the traumatic occurrences fail to leave their mark on the reader's emotions or sensibilities. (p. 385)

> *Ethel L. Heins, in* The Horn Book Magazine *(copyright © 1971 by The Horn Book, Inc., Boston), August, 1971.*

OTHER CITATIONS

Publishers Weekly, *April 19, 1971, p. 48.*

Zena Sutherland, in Bulletin of the Center for Children's Books, *November, 1971, p. 48.*

TEACUP FULL OF ROSES (1972)

Sharon Bell Mathis weaves her plots with sure authority and creates her characters with economy and veracity. Like the late Lorraine Hansberry, whom she calls to mind, she is young, gifted and black. Yet the slice of life she describes has a familiar flavor to "ethnic-Americans." Joe's milieu and his values [in "Teacup Full of Roses"] are very like those of the last generation of hyphenated-Americans, the children of Eastern European immigrants. Here are the overriding family loyalties; the pride in appearances— "Don't wear no wrinkled shirts," Joe warns Davey; the faith in education, hard work; the hope for a better life through sacrifice. The author says the book is "a salute to black kids," and she is right—but it has a lot to say to white ones, too. (p. 8)

> *Janet Harris, in* The New York Times Book

Review (© *1972 by The New York Times Company; reprinted by permission), September 10, 1972.*

Sharon Bell Mathis has perception, and she is incisive, selective, precise. Her style is lean and taut in a book that is composed chiefly of dialogue which not only evokes, without explanation, the identity of the person speaking, but develops his singularity and furthers the action. Movingly, with a beautiful sense of aesthetic distance, Sharon Mathis brings all her characters alive in a situation which speaks truth in a black world, but which would speak truth just as clearly were this novel about a white family. For what she is talking about is the human condition. (p. 83)

> *Eleanor Cameron, in* The Horn Book Magazine *(copyright © 1973 by The Horn Book, Inc., Boston), February, 1973.*

This book is filled with love messages from author Sharon Bell Mathis to every black child who reads it. The messages tell the children of their beauty, of their talent, of their strength and of their ability to survive even in the hostile environment created by racism.

Mrs. Mathis writes of the positive aspects of Black life without ignoring the fact that problems do exist. Rather, she explores alternative ways of dealing with these problems.

Teacup Full of Roses is the story of Joe, 17-year-old pillar of the Brooks family. Despite his youth, Joe is depended on by a younger brother, a drug addicted older brother, a sick father and an anguished mother. How Joe handles this responsibility is sensitively dealt with by the author in a deeply moving, well-paced story told in a language of strong Black images.

In addition to being an excellent choice for young people, this book should be put on the *must* reading list of every black filmmaker. If *Teacup Full of Roses* is overlooked in this era of growing popularity for black films, it will be a great loss to those in the motion picture industry and to their audiences as well. (p. 69)

> *Eloise Greenfield, in* Negro History Bulletin *(copyright 1973 by the Association for the Study of Negro Life and History Inc.), March, 1973.*

Ms. Mathis has great talent; therefore, we hope her next novel's *denouement* will be soundly based. Two faults plague this plot. A kid as smart as Joe would hardly have withdrawn the money and instructed Dave to open an account; why not take Dave to the bank and transfer the account to him? The premise that a member of the *confirmed* drug addict's family would leave a large amount of money anywhere in the house is an unlikely device. Moreover, some readers will object to the stereotyped black matriarch. The combination of these doubtful elements with the contrived ending weakens the whole.

Therefore, read the structurally flawed story for the insights it can give suburbanites learning about the city's traps of vice and cruelty, and for the appealing strong young people Ms. Mathis has pictured for us. (p. 422)

> *Lois Belfield Watt, in* Childhood Education *(reprinted by permission of the Association for Childhood Education International, 3615 Wisconsin Ave., N.W., Washington, DC 20016; copyright © 1973 by the Association), Vol. 49, No. 8 (May, 1973).*

This short novel packs a real wallop. It appears to be the most useable book thus far written about a family that is both black and impoverished. . . . The story moves with the steadiness of a Greek play toward the inevitable tragedy. For some readers it may even produce catharsis as they watch the trap, which they seem powerless to spring, closing around the characters. The book is not just about black families. It is about every family where a parent lavishes affection on a prodigal to the detriment of the other children. (pp. 90-1)

> *G. Robert Carlsen, in* English Journal *(copyright © 1974 by The National Council of Teachers of English), February, 1974.*

OTHER CITATIONS

Mary M. Burns, in The Horn Book Magazine, *February, 1973, pp. 58-9.*

Judith Rosenfeld, in Childhood Education, *May, 1973, p. 422.*

Rochelle Cortez, in Black Books Bulletin, *Summer-Fall, 1973, p. 35.*

N

NESBIT, E(dith) 1858-1924

E. Nesbit was a British author beloved by children for the books she wrote for them. She was, as Eleanor Graham calls her, "the modern woman of her time." She smoked and cut her hair short, and her house served as a meeting place for such writers as H. G. Wells and George Bernard Shaw. Throughout her life, Nesbit considered herself primarily a poet, although she also wrote stories and novels, verses for greeting cards, and adaptations of Shakespearean tales. At the age of forty, Nesbit wrote the first of her children's books, *The Story of the Treasure Seekers,* to raise money for her family and her husband, Hubert Bland, a founding member of the Fabian Society. Hers were among the first children's books free of didacticism—they were stories, not costumed morals. They talked to and respected children, not as miniature men or women, but for what they were. As critic Noël Streatfeild writes, "She wrote about intelligent children for intelligent children, [and] understood the essence of childhood." In 1970, a film was made of her book *The Railway Children.* (See also *Yesterday's Authors of Books for Children,* Vol 1.)

GENERAL COMMENTARY

Probably the sincerest compliment I could pay [E. Nesbit] is already paid in the fact that my own books for children could not even have existed if it were not for her influence. And I am always careful to acknowledge this indebtedness in each of my stories; so that any child who likes my books and doesn't know hers may be led back to the master of us all.

For just as Beatrix Potter is the genius of the picture book, so I believe E. Nesbit to be the one truly "great" writer for the ten-, eleven- and twelve-year-old. (p. 349)

[Her] books for children were never the mere potboilers she claimed they were. Every page shines with the delight the writer took in fashioning it, and this is a thing that cannot be faked. I know. In truth it is her "adult" writing that bears a synthetic stamp. Her poems and novels are mere self-conscious attitudinizing, the little girl playing "lady" in borrowed clothes, and all of them have long been forgotten. It was when the child in her spoke out directly to other children that she achieved greatness.

I do not mean to equate genius with arrested mental or emotional development. But there are lucky people who never lose the gift of seeing the world as a child sees it, a magic place where anything can happen next minute, and delightful and unexpected things constantly do. Of such, among those of us who try to write for children, is the kingdom of Heaven. And in that kingdom E. Nesbit stands with the archangels. (p. 351)

> *Edward Eager, "Daily Magic," in* The Horn Book Magazine *(copyright, 1958, by the Horn Book, Inc., Boston), October, 1958, pp. 349-58.*

The background and personality of a writer of adult fiction is not necessarily revealed in their books, but something of the background and personality of a good children's author is almost always discernible, for it is their ability to remember with all their senses their own childhood, and what it felt like to be a child, that makes their work outstanding. E. Nesbit, because she has been read and loved by many generations of children, has established herself as one of the great, and today her books are ranked as classics. What made them classics? What had she to give, that causes her books to be read and loved and sold widely a hundred years after her birth? (p. 11)

What makes E. Nesbit so fascinating a writer to study is that her children's books, with one exception, are divorced from the life she lived as an adult, for they have their roots in her childhood. . . . Was it possible that the E. Nesbit the world knew was an invention of the real Nesbit's, built originally for an insecure, shy girl to hide behind, but into whose skin she grew, and out of which she only emerged when she was writing for children, and at the very end of her life? It is not unusual for those in need of support to build a facade behind which to hide, to accept that E. Nesbit was such a person makes E. Nesbit the writer for children wholly understandable. (pp. 11-12)

E. Nesbit had a gift, shared by other great children's writers, for recapturing the timelessness of childhood, the vast tracts of time that lie between one Christmas and the next, from birthday to birthday. . . . (p. 14)

[She] almost certainly helped all her children readers to escape from their own particular enchanter's castle. There is, even in the magic books, such a wind of sanity blowing through their covers that it must have helped many children to forget what befell them in their dark hours. That is the best of being a magician. (p. 51)

Perhaps E. Nesbit's greatest gift as a writer for children was her naturalistic amusing dialogue. With the exception of a few words she is quite undated, for she avoided to a large extent the slang of her day and used instead family expressions and words, which curiously enough so seldom find their way on to paper, although they exist in every family. . . . [Clearly] she never forgot what family language should be, and its importance in family life, so she gave words and expressions to all her fiction families, and how right she was, for it is the family atmosphere more than perhaps any other quality that makes her books live. (pp. 52-3)

A feature of E. Nesbit's children's books which makes her almost unique amongst children's writers is that her boys are as well drawn, sometimes better drawn than her girls. Few indeed have been the women writers of whom that could be said, or indeed vice versa, few are the men writers whose girls are as well drawn as their boys. (p. 62)

Amongst all the characters authors have invented to tell their stories in the first person, Oswald Bastable holds an honourable place, if for nothing else than for his original approach to his story.

From the moment he introduces himself Oswald is no character in a book, but the most amusing of all the boys the reader knows. He never describes his looks clearly, a hint here and there but no more, yet he is quietly confident, and rightly, that everybody who reads about him would recognise him instantly, should they have the fortune to meet him. (p. 82)

There is scarcely a page of the Bastable books which has not some gem on it which shows the Oswaldishness of Oswald. Few could argue that he is by far the most original of the children in the Nesbit portrait gallery. (p. 87)

Perhaps nothing shows E. Nesbit's gift for writing for children more clearly than the ability she has for making her children live. It is not possible to find out how long she existed with her characters before she put pen to paper. The time this takes varies from author to author, but one thing is certain, she never wrote a word of the Bastables until she knew them better than the children around her, for only by knowing everything about her characters, infinitely more than she had any intention of using, could she have made them live and breathe to such an extent that when Oswald wrote at the end of *The New Treasure Seekers* that this was the last story that the present author was going to write, it did not mean for her readers that the Bastable Saga had come to an end. It was more as if a family of children who lived next door, and were so well known they were like part of the family, had moved to another place where, though you might not see them they were still enjoying their vivid and exciting lives. To be able to do this is a quality possessed by the very few, and so it is no wonder that E. Nesbit's books still live and will live for countless children yet unborn. (p. 89)

> *Noël Streatfeild, in her* Magic and the Magician: E. Nesbit and Her Children's Books *(copyright © Noël Streatfeild 1958; reprinted by permission of Thomas Y. Crowell Company, Inc.), Abelard-Schuman, 1958.*

[E. Nesbit's] books are modern—or rather, timeless—because the children in them ring true to childhood of any time. She does not do it by removing her characters to a dateless nonsense or fantasy world of their own; when the most remarkable and magical things happen to them, they happen against a background of everyday life in that world now sixty years away in time, even further by any other measure of change. Any but the very best children's books of that time are now period pieces. (p. 14)

[E. Nesbit's] real strength was the balanced, objective outlook of a comic prose writer. (p. 35)

[Because] E. Nesbit laughs at . . . moral stories, one may overlook the fact that there *is* quite a strand of moralising in her own books. In fact, a child probably will overlook it, because of the skill with which she wove it in. (p. 42)

She will put a few remarks on selfishness or thoughtlessness into the Bastable stories, arising from the situations the children get into, and usually made with engaging solemnity by Oswald himself. Or she weaves the moral into the plot. The magic of *The House of Arden* is conditional on good behaviour. Elfrida and Edred can find the room with the magic chests only when they have gone a day without quarrelling. In a way the whole of *Five Children and It* is a moral story, on the vanity of human wishes. (p. 43)

But E. Nesbit did not make her books a pulpit, either for obtrusive moralising in general or for personal views of her own—one can read them all without getting much idea of the author as a person. (p. 44)

E. Nesbit used [memories of her childhood experiences] in her stories—but there is no trace of the nerve-racking terrors of her imagination. If the children in her books get into a frightening situation, at any rate it is not a private nightmare. Even in the much-criticised episode of the Ugly-Wuglies, in *The Enchanted Castle,* Gerald and Mabel face the uncanny creatures together. She selected skilfully, leaving aside her distressing personal memories, picking on details that would strike a cheerful answering note in her readers. (p. 48)

There is a strong family likeness between all Nesbit children. They are all given to scoring off each other in this way. They are enterprising and love adventure and romance. At the same time they are to some degree realists. In a large family, brothers and sisters do not scruple to say plainly when someone is making a fool of himself, so there is bound to be a certain amount of common-sense about. They are all remarkably free from adult interference—not because their parents neglect them, but because E. Nesbit found it more convenient to get parents out of the way. (The best-remembered adult in any of her stories is not a parent at all, but Albert's good-natured uncle.) They hate the very thought of being bored, and if they feel boredom approaching, have plenty of ideas to ward it off. They all invent their own games, and are never happier than when playing at *The Jungle Book,* 'reproducing the attitudes of statues seen either in the British Museum, or in Father's big photograph book', or even playing all alone, like Mabel in *The Enchanted Castle. . . .* (p. 50)

Besides this family likeness, each Nesbit child also has a definite character of its own. And this means that in all the books, including the magic stories, the children themselves are as interesting as anything that happens to them, however startling. E. Nesbit herself really put her secret in a nutshell, describing one of her families to her readers, when she wrote [in *The Phoenix and the Carpet*], 'They were not particularly handsome, nor were they extra clever, nor extraordinarily good. But they were not bad sorts on the whole; in fact, they were rather like you.' (p. 52)

The Bastables, E. Nesbit's first important creation, immediately showed her powers of describing lifelike children. They are absolutely convincing both as a family unit and as individuals. . . . [Oswald's] style carried E. Nesbit over what might otherwise have been some sticky moments. The reconciliation with the rich Indian uncle, for instance, might easily have made uncomfortably sentimental reading, but seen through Oswald's eyes it is a thoroughly satisfactory happy ending, with a touch of fairy-tale about the sudden abundance of presents and good food. In fact, E. Nesbit was never to do this kind of thing quite so successfully again. (p. 53)

While still writing stories about the Bastables, E. Nesbit had launched out into her fantasies, in *Five Children and It* and its sequels, *The Phoenix and the Carpet* and *The Story of the Amulet*. Part of the secret of her success in this vein is that the human children who are the central figures—and with whom the child reader will identify itself—are themselves as lively as the children in the everyday-life books. She does not let her powers of fantastic invention run away with her at their expense. Cyril, Robert and their sisters have not, of course, so much scope simply to be themselves as the Bastables had, because strange adventures take up a good deal of their time. But they are far from being mere pegs for the author's imaginings. (pp. 58-9)

[The] magic creatures were among E. Nesbit's most brilliant and original ideas. 'Before Anthea and Cyril and the others had been a week in the country they had found a fairy', she writes at the beginning of *Five Children and It*. But her fairy was not one of the 'painty-winged, wand-waving, sugar-and-shake-your-head, company anathematised by Kipling's Puck. Nor did she try her hand at the true fairies of tradition, the uncanny and malicious Good People. Her gift was not for poetic fantasy; although later she inclined a little more in the poetic direction, her real feeling was for comic fantasy, the spirit in which she imagined the endearing, bad-tempered, slightly grotesque Psammead. (pp. 59-60)

[The Phoenix] provided E. Nesbit with plenty of opportunities to make magic collide with real life, and this meeting of the familiar and the fantastic was the particular *forte* of her imagination. She establishes the point of meeting, with an eye always open for a comic situation, and then describes the results. (p. 61)

Besides being so closely connected with each other, [*The House of Arden* and *Harding's Luck*] stand rather apart from the rest of E. Nesbit's stories. The plot is on much more melodramatic lines than usual. Lost heirs, kidnappings, an *Oliver Twist*-like incident when Dickie is made to be a burglar's accomplice—these do not occur seriously in E. Nesbit's other books. The melodramatic touches are neatly done; even the necessary strawberry mark, in this case an old-fashioned baby's rattle, is cleverly worked into the story. Dickie himself is partly responsible for this difference in tone from the other fantasies. . . . As a slum child who is the rightful Lord Arden, he is a fictional child rather than a startlingly real one like the middle-class children of E. Nesbit's other books. In this new vein Dickie,

rather surprisingly, does come off. Even giving him a lame leg, E. Nesbit only occasionally approaches mawkishness; most of the time she manages to steer clear. In particular, she presents his life on the open road with the tramp Beale with much imaginative sympathy. (p. 73)

E. Nesbit's great gift was to remember just what it felt like to be a child—witness her vivid reminiscences, written when she was in her late thirties [published in book form as *Long Ago When I Was Young*]—to know exactly what would amuse and entertain a child, and to be able to put it down on paper. She did not write above her readers' heads, but nor did she write down to them. Oswald Bastable, for instance, often suggests the use of a dictionary; she was not afraid of introducing children to new words. On the other hand, she does not indulge in jokes aimed only at adult readers.

Indeed, she seldom went to any extremes in her children's books. The children in them are real—neither improbably virtuous or wicked, as Victorian story-book children sometimes were, nor improbably clever and intrepid, as the tendency is today. She had of course limitations; her poetic imagination was much more limited than her comic imagination. But at her best her limitations are quite set off by her other qualities. She had at her command two great steadying influences; realism and humour. They leaven the most fantastic adventures in her books—and the conversation and homely adventures of the children who do *not* have the luck to meet with magic rings or carpets, Sand-Fairies or Phoenixes, are just as entertaining as the travels of those who do. After amusing children for sixty years, there is every reason to think that E. Nesbit's books will go on amusing new generations of children for another sixty years or more. (pp. 74-5)

> *Anthea Bell, in her* E. Nesbit (© *The Bodley Head Ltd 1960), Bodley Head, 1960.*

The 'nineties were years of turmoil and change, the years of Wilde and Beardsley, of *Jude the Obscure*. The old century died painfully, under its cover of imperial splendour. It was clear that the new age would bring many changes, among others in the attitude towards children and children's books. These changes were foreshadowed in a series of stories appearing during 1898 in the *Pall Mall* and the *Windsor* magazines and published in book-form in the next year under the title *The Story of the Treasure Seekers*. The author was E. Nesbit. (p. 11)

E. Nesbit is the key figure of the decade. Although she had written much in Victorian days, she was by intelligence and instinct very much a person of the new age. (p. 12)

[All] her best work was done between 1899 and 1911. Within this short span she reshaped the family story, the fantasy and the historical romance so fundamentally that there is scarcely a writer in these fields who does not, directly or indirectly, owe her a debt. (p. 13)

> *Marcus Crouch, in his* Treasure Seekers and Borrowers: Children's Books in Britain 1900-1960 (© *Marcus Crouch, 1962), The Library Association, 1962.*

After Lewis Carroll, E. Nesbit is the best of the English fabulists who wrote about children (neither wrote *for* children), and like Carroll she was able to create a world of magic and inverted logic that was entirely her own. Yet

Nesbit's books are relatively unknown in the United States. Publishers attribute her failure in these parts to a witty and intelligent prose style (something of a demerit in the land of the dull and the home of the literal) and to the fact that a good many of her books deal with magic, a taboo subject nowadays. (p. 174)

[Simply] to support her five children, Nesbit began to write books about children. In a recent biography, *Magic and the Magician* [see excerpt above], Noël Streatfeild remarks that E. Nesbit did not particularly like children, which may explain why those she created in her books are so entirely human. They are intelligent, vain, aggressive, humorous, witty, cruel, compassionate . . . in fact, they are like adults, except for one difference. In a well-ordered and stable society (England in the time of the gross Edward), children are as clearly defined a minority group as Jews or Negroes in other times and places. Physically small and weak, economically dependent upon others, they cannot control their environment. As a result, they are forced to develop a sense of communality; and though it does not necessarily make them any nicer to one another, at least it helps them to see each other with perfect clarity. Nesbit's genius is to see them as clearly and unsentimentally as they see themselves, thus making for that sense of life upon the page without which no literature.

Nesbit's usual device is to take a family of children ranging in age from a baby to a child of ten or eleven and then involve them in adventures, either magical or realistic (never both at the same time). *The Story of the Treasure Seekers, The Wouldbegoods,* and *The New Treasure Seekers* are realistic books about the Bastable children. They are told by Oswald Bastable, whose style owes a great deal to that of Julius Caesar. Like the conqueror, Oswald is able through a cunning use of the third person to establish his marked superiority to others. Wondering if his younger brother H. O. is mentally retarded, he writes, "H. O. is eight years old, but he cannot tell the clock yet. Oswald could tell the clock when he was six." Oswald is a delightful narrator and the stories he tells are among Nesbit's best. (pp. 175-76)

To my mind, it is in the "magic books" that Nesbit is at her best, particularly the trilogy which involves the Five Children. In the first volume, *Five Children and It,* they encounter the Psammead, a small bad-tempered, odd-looking creature from pre-history. The Psammead is able to grant wishes by first filling itself with air and then exhaling. ("If only you knew how I hate to blow myself out with other people's wishes, and how frightened I am always that I shall strain a muscle or something. And then to wake up every morning and know that you've got to do it. . . .")

But the children use the Psammead relentlessly for their wishes, and something almost always goes wrong. . . . Without moralizing, Nesbit demonstrates, literally, the folly of human wishes, and amuses at the same time. In *The Phoenix and the Carpet,* they become involved with the millennial phoenix, a bird of awesome vanity ("I've often been told that mine is a valuable life"). With the use of a magic carpet, the phoenix and the children make a number of expeditions about the world. Yet even with such an ordinary device as a magic carpet, Nesbit's powers of invention are never settled easily. The carpet has been repaired, and the rewoven section is not magic; whoever sits on that part travels neither here nor there. Since most intelligent chil-

dren are passionate logicians, the sense of logic is a necessary gift in a writer of fantasy. Though a child will gladly accept a fantastic premise, he will insist that the working out of it be entirely consistent with the premise. Careless invention is immediately noticed; contradiction and inconsistencies irritate, and illusion is destroyed. Happily, Nesbit is seldom careless and she anticipates most questions which might occur to a child. Not that she can always answer him satisfactorily. A condition of the Psammead's wishes is that they last only for a day. Yet the effects of certain wishes in the distant past did linger. Why was this? asked one of the children. *"Autres temps,"* replied the Psammead coolly, *"autres moeurs."*

In *The Story of the Amulet,* Nesbit's powers of invention are at their best. It is a time-machine story, only the device is not a machine but an Egyptian amulet whose other half is lost in the past. By saying certain powerful words, the amulet becomes a gate through which the children are able to visit the past or future. Pharaonic Egypt, Babylon (whose dotty queen comes back to London with them and tries to get her personal possessions out of the British Museum), Caesar's Britain—they visit them all in search of the missing part of the amulet. Nesbit's history is good. And there is even a look at a Utopian future, which turns out to be everything a good Fabian might have hoped for. Ultimately, the amulet's other half is found, and a story of considerable beauty is concluded in a most unexpected way. (pp. 176-77)

My own favorites among Nesbit's work are *The House of Arden* and *Harding's Luck,* two books that comprise a diptych, one telling much the same story as the second, yet from a different point of view. The mood is somewhere between that of *The Enchanted Castle* and of the *Five Children,* not midnight yet hardly morning. Richard Harding, a crippled boy, accompanies an old tramp about England. The Dickensian note is struck but without the master's sentimentality. (p. 177)

As a woman, E. Nesbit was not to everyone's taste. H. G. Wells described her and Hubert Bland as "fundamentally intricate," adding that whenever the Blands attended meetings of the Fabian Society "anonymous letters flitted about like bats at twilight" (the Nesbit mood if not style is contagious). Yet there is no doubt that she was extraordinary. Wanting to be a serious poet, she became of necessity a writer of children's books. But though she disdained her true gift, she was peculiarly suited by nature to be what in fact she was. As an adult writing of her own childhood, she noted, "When I was a little child I used to pray, fervently, fearfully, that when I should be grown up I might never forget what I thought and felt and suffered then." With extraordinary perceptiveness, she realized that each grown-up must kill the child he was before he himself can live. Nesbit's vow to survive somehow in the enemy's consciousness became, finally, her art—when this you see remember me—and the child continued to the end of the adult's life. (pp. 178-79)

E. Nesbit's failure in the United States is not entirely mysterious. We have always preferred how-to-do to let's-imagine-that. As a result, in the last fifty years we have contributed relatively little in the way of new ideas of any sort. From radar to rocketry, we have had to rely on other societies for theory and invention. Our great contribution has been, characteristically, the assembly line.

I do not think it is putting the case too strongly to say that much of the poverty of our society's intellectual life is directly due to the sort of books children are encouraged to read. Practical books with facts in them may be necessary, but they are not everything. They do not serve the imagination in the same way that high invention does when it allows the mind to investigate *every* possibility, to set itself free from the ordinary, to enter a world where paradox reigns and nothing is what it seems. Properly engaged, the intelligent child begins to question all presuppositions, and to think on his own. In fact, the moment he says, "Wouldn't it be interesting if . . .?" he is on his way and his own imagination has begun to work at a level considerably more interesting than the usual speculation on what it will be like to own a car and make money. As it is, the absence of imagination is cruelly noticeable at every level of the American society, and though a reading of E. Nesbit is hardly going to change the pattern of a nation, there is some evidence that the child who reads her will never be quite the same again, and that is probably a good thing. (p. 179)

> *Gore Vidal, "E. Nesbit's Magic," in* The New York Review of Books; *copyright © 1964 NYREV, Inc.), December 3, 1964 (and reprinted in* Homage to Daniel Shays: Collected Essays 1952-1972 *by Gore Vidal, Random House, 1972, pp. 174-80).*

It is difficult to describe the excellence of E. Nesbit's best books. The only way to appreciate them is to read them, and, as is the case with all the really great children's books, they are as enjoyable by the adult as by the child. They may be 'escapist' literature, but the escape is to the healthy stimulation of a game in the fresh air before returning to the stuffy schoolroom of life. They are irresistible because they seem to be the irresistible outpourings of the author's mind: often untidy and inarticulate, but always vividly alive and eager, with a joyous enthusiasm that disarms criticism. (p. 214)

[One] or two of her books and stories may be selected as the crown of her achievement, but all the eighteen volumes from *The Treasure Seekers* and *The Book of Dragons* even to *Wet Magic* and *Five of Us—and Madeline* are so good that to lose a single one would be a matter of real regret.

Although she has had her followers, and although her influence is apparent in the work of such diverse writers as Kipling and C. S. Lewis, there is only one E. Nesbit—and the result of all our assaying is merely to demonstrate afresh that, though we may criticize some or all of her books in detail, she has left us an imperishable and a precious heritage, a shelf of books which we show no sign of outgrowing. (p. 215)

> *Roger Lancelyn Green, "E. Nesbit," in his* Tellers of Tales *(copyright 1946, 1953, 1956, © 1965 by Edmund Ward (Publishers), Ltd); revised edition, Franklin Watts, Inc., 1965 (and reprinted by Kaye and Ward Ltd., 1969), pp. 206-15.*

Knowing that works of art are often produced, like pearls, as a means of enduring an irritant in the system, we ought not to be surprised to learn that E. Nesbit's books for children owe their particular lustre and humour to the despairs of her own childhood. But we are more than that; we are taken aback. Surely those sunlit adventures cannot be anything but the reflections of youthful happiness?

On the contrary, they are a brilliantly successful dispersal of long-menacing shadows. (p. 9)

[E. Nesbit's rhymes for her own children] afford almost the first clear prophecy of what was to be her real province as a writer. It is true that she [contributed] numerous verses and stories to children's gift books; but in these she did not let herself go; they contain little that sets them apart from what a hundred other efficient writers were producing for the same purposes. It will hardly be denied that the most shining charm of her first great success, *The Treasure Seekers,* lay in its apparent ease of manner, its ingenuous fluency. Like Jane Austen, she learned ease of manner by experimenting in her family circle, where all artificial restraints might be abandoned. (p. 121)

She knew that her books for children were good books; she was thoroughly conscientious and thoroughly conscious in her artistry while she worked at them; but she never imagined that they were the highest manifestation of her literary capacities. It was because those capacities were numerous and unequal that her efforts to win fame—for she did want fame—were long protracted, and not at best as successful as the efforts of several greatly inferior writers in the same field. (pp. 140-41)

E. Nesbit looked upon herself first and foremost as a poet. No one can say that it was necessity alone which compelled her to write prose—indeed, it is hardly likely that she would have been able to suppress a talent so lively and abundant; but it is very improbable that she would have written prose as often and as diversely without the ever-present need of money to spur her on. It is very improbable, in short, that she would have attempted those simple, rudimentary forms of juvenile fiction from which, after some ten years of practice, she rose to the creation of a magic world. (pp. 141-42)

[In 1898] she was engaged with the first set of Bastable stories. . . . Superior though it was to anything she had ever done before, she seems to have taken this work entirely in her usual stride. The only mention of it that I have found in her correspondence is one bald statement, casually slipped in among references to her incessant toil at stories, articles, verses, and reviews. "I am writing a children's book," she says to her mother, "called 'The Treasure Seekers.'"

If she suddenly attained any new consciousness of brilliant powers as a humorist, of unflagging ingenuity, and a limpid fluency in providing those "constant slight surprises" which are said to be the secret of good style, she kept the joy of the discovery to herself. (pp. 147-48)

Edith drew [the "games and pretences" of the Bastable children] from memories of her own young days strengthened by discussion and comparison. Oswald Barron, to whom she dedicated the book, had conversed with her often and at length on their respective childhoods, "identical," she said, "but for the accidents of time and space." She had been working towards the achievement of the Bastables for years. She had studied children's literature extensively—George MacDonald, Mrs. Ewing, and Mrs. Molesworth, for instance, were writers whom she admired fervently; but she owed few direct debts to any precursor.

One of these few was the ingenious device of half-concealing the identity of the supposed narrator, Oswald—of letting it be guessed only when in boyish egotism he gives himself away. It is one of the happiest things in children's fiction, and she had found it in Dickens, whose works she knew extensively and revered. He had used it in *A Holiday Romance,* but there is not a page of *The Treasure Seekers* that lacks the magic vividness only to be imparted by an original mind. The plausibility of the manner is remarkable. (pp. 148-49)

Virtue after virtue unfolds itself as the book proceeds. There is not a dull paragraph. No woman writer, surely, has ever been able to induce laughter so often and so wholesomely! (p. 149)

[Although] all these books abound with ironical humour and wisdom too subtle for a child's comprehension, they mysteriously succeed in remaining children's books *par excellence.* She never patronizes, never appears to be insinuating as—say—Charles Kingsley does: "Now I know this is just a trifle above your head." And neither does she go to the other and still more objectionable extreme. Describing her method to her friend, Berta Ruck, years later, she said: "I make it a point of honour never to *write down* to a child. Sometimes I deliberately introduce a word that it won't know, so that it will ask a grown-up the meaning and learn something by it." When she conveyed instruction overtly, it was always in some new and interesting way.

Altogether *The Treasure Seekers* and its sequels are as free from flaws as anything of their kind that has ever been done. (p. 151)

[In 1901] a series of delightful tales was appearing in the *Strand,* under the title of "The Psammead"—later to be changed to *Five Children and It*—illustrated . . . by H. R. Millar, an artist so entirely congenial that even (or especially) her warmest admirers must be willing to acknowledge her indebtness to him. . . . He fulfilled to something near perfection the exacting demands she made upon him; one has only to compare the books containing his pictures with those in which the work of other draughtsmen was used to perceive at once how marvelously sensitive he was to her requirements. She herself shared this view, and was so surprised at the skill with which he had expressed the very essence of her ideas that she frequently insisted there must be some sort of telepathy between them. Mr. Millar was not of this opinion; she forgot, he said, her power to suggest in a few words as much as most writers would take a page to describe. But she, who had known how far astray an artist can go even with a full description before him, maintained that telepathy was the basis of their co-operation. (p. 165)

With their successors, the tales of the Phoenix and of the Amulet, and later on the Arden books, the Psammead stories represented something entirely new in the realm of children's fiction: no such curious and unheard-of fairies had ever been portrayed before in contact with a family of hearty English children. Each of the supernatural characters has its own vivid, convincing personality. The traditional fairy queen, gracefully waving her wand and uttering noble sentiments in a silvery voice, is a pale, meaningless cipher to those who have known the cantankerous Psammead, the lovable but outrageously conceited Phoenix, and the Mouldiwarp who talks in dialect. They are neither "good fairies" who moralize, nor fiendish ones who, without motive, work evil spells; they belong to the rarer and much more engaging species of fairies who, while lacking nothing of magical power, are yet made credible

and familiar by human weaknesses and vanities. In ordinary fairy-tales, it is the magic and its consequences alone that excite interest; here we have not only magic most wonderful and denouements queerer than have often been conceived, but subtle distinction of character in mortals and immortals alike, and a humour so lively that eagerness to unravel the plot is repeatedly forgotten in laughter, even when the reader is a child.

Five Children and It was the first of a series of books in which the waking dreams of children are realized and crystallized as their sleeping dreams are crystallized in *Alice in Wonderland.* No one has ever been able to imitate them. . . . They were the production of a mind capable of throwing off in an instant all the shackles of adulthood while yet retaining all the skill of experience. In their own sphere they were without parallel. . . . (pp. 167-68)

Taking all the enormous body of her work together, there is undoubtedly a great deal that has not, and never can have, any value except to the student of her development as an artist. We who belong to a generation not far from her own in time may deplore the fact of her ever having written so much that was unworthy of her, but the generations of the distant future will have no such grievance, since only her best is likely to survive. And if that best is, indeed, handed down from parent to child for many and many a year to come—as who can doubt it will be?—at least a dozen volumes bearing the cherished name "E. Nesbit" will be read and treasured by our descendants. No other English writer for children has produced an equal quantity of wholly admirable work. (p. 292)

> *Doris Langley Moore, in her* E. Nesbit: A Biography *(copyright © 1966 by Doris Langley Moore; reprinted with permission of the publisher), revised edition, Chilton Book Company, 1966.*

Edith Nesbit's novels for children were inspired by her memories of childhood, conditioned by the beliefs of Fabian Socialism and coloured by the poetic style of the nineties. However, they belong wholly to the twentieth century, not to the nineteenth. They depict a change in attitudes to children which, because it was less dramatic than the contemporaneous revolution in women's lot, has received less attention, but which is just as far-reaching.

"Emancipation" was in vogue in the Edwardian era. It seems puzzling that Edith Nesbit did not, like her friends Olive Schreiner and Laurence Housman, throw her weight behind the suffragette movement. . . . [Energy] that more fashionably went into the emancipation of women was directed by her to another social revolution—the emancipation of children. . . . Over-control or over-protection alike prevents a child's full development. She therefore actualizes in her fiction the conditions in which children can attain full dignity as human beings. She provides a charter for children: "Sympathy and justice, leisure and liberty."

The emancipated child was a new concept in society as well as in literature. Since culture often follows the patterns laid down by art, Edith Nesbit, by bringing home to Edwardian adults and children what children could achieve personally and socially, may well have helped to bring about the social revolution she advocated. No convincing reasons have ever been given for the rapid amelioration of children's lot at the beginning of this century. It was a shift so radical that Victorian children seem, by comparison, utterly remote to modern consciousness. It may well be that Edith Nesbit was one of the most powerful agents of this change. (pp. 51-2)

[Victorian views of childhood] were either extremely repressive or romantic. Edith Nesbit's realism prevents her from subscribing to either. To her, children are neither devils nor angels: they are people. She is aware of the damage the first belief can inflict on a child's psyche and of the failure to mature which is the result of the second. She is not content, therefore, merely to offer alternatives to these. She attacks both mercilessly. (p. 52)

A theme in many novels and short stories is the reclamation of repressed, poor-spirited children by those who are free of such treatment by adults. The view that authoritarianism is evil in its effects was put forward by other Edwardian writers. Edith Nesbit is the first to voice it in children's literature.

One offshoot of this belief was the idea that the guilty child could expiate his original sin by undergoing salvation and expressing this in good works. But the condemnation of such complacent virtue is seen clearly in *The Wouldbe-goods*, where all the children's helpful acts go uproariously wrong and create far more havoc than mere unthinking naughtiness would.... When in *The New Treasure Seekers* they are constrained to behave like Victorian children because they are staying with a missionary, they simply have to escape to the beach to let off steam: "Then we had another yelling competition and Noel won with that new shriek of his that is like railway engines in distress."

The children in Edith Nesbit's novels are wonderfully uninhibited. They are not burdened by a sense of guilt; their good deeds are motivated by kindness, not a need for expiation. The impulse to make every act a moral choice is firmly rejected. Indeed, as F. Harvey Darton says, she turns "unmorality into a kind of inverted laughter". The Puritan image of a century is shattered by this laughter. (pp. 52-3)

This quality of expansiveness, rather than restriction, is Edith Nesbit's contribution to the Edwardian concepts of childhood. Its foundations lie partly in her own experience as a child and as a mother, partly in what she derived from authors she admired, partly in her political beliefs and partly in her theories of education. Her work reflects some of the most advanced ideas on child care which were held in her age, ideas which are only now gaining general acceptance in education. The qualities of childhood which she valued most highly are now to be seen in some of the country's best primary and middle schools, a fact which makes her particularly relevant for today. Group activity, the development of initiative and the fostering of imagination are all found in her work. (p. 54)

Edith Nesbit's intention of making her characters typical of an emancipated Socialist generation leads to certain limitations. In the first place, the children are, by definition, ordinary children, typical of their generation: "The children were not particularly handsome, nor were they extra clever, nor extraordinarily good. But they were not bad souls on the whole; in fact they were rather like you" (*The Phoenix and the Carpet*). So they live in cities or suburbs, in semi-detached houses, going to local schools, visiting the sea every summer. Their achievements, their delights and

their futures are average ones, within reach of all children. Edith Nesbit does not write about unusual children, but about ordinary children. It is her triumph to make them so extraordinarily interesting.

A second limitation is one that can be argued against all Socialist writers—[William] Morris, Wells and Shaw among them. It is that their view of life is unduly optimistic and over-rational. Edward Bellamy wrote in 1888 in a postscript to *Looking Backward* that this Utopian work "was written in the belief that the Golden Age lies before us and not behind us and is not far away. Our children will surely see it".... This belief attached to children an importance unknown in Victorian literature.

The children in Edith Nesbit's work are no longer enslaved by the repressive or over-indulgent adult domination of an earlier age. They converse freely with their elders, are at liberty to develop as they will and have the freedom of personal awareness given by a rich imaginative life. Added to this, they have the freedom of being citizens of the future, moving towards goals undreamt of by their forbears. They are indeed an emancipated generation. (p. 63)

> Mary Croxson, "The Emancipated Child in the Novels of E. Nesbit," in Signal (copyright © 1974 Mary Croxson; reprinted by permission of the author and The Thimble Press, Lockwood Station Road, South Woodchester, Glos. GL5 5EQ, England), May, 1974, pp. 51-63.

[It] is true that Nesbit is one of the first children's writers whose books, particularly her comic ones, are not largely concerned with moral issues and the instruction of a juvenile readership. Nesbit had an extra-ordinary gift for remembering her own childhood, and for putting herself inside the minds of her child-characters.... A vast gulf separates her from earlier writers who began with a *self-conscious* preference for imaginative rather than moral stories for the young: Nesbit simply does not work from the outside like this, and it shows; she is not *giving* the child reader anything, for in a sense she is that reader. (p. 111)

This special power of recall cannot readily be explained: certainly it has nothing to do with literary tradition or the time at which she wrote. To some extent it must be related to the vividness of her own childhood and character.... What her early experience certainly did enforce on Nesbit was her sense of a family, and particularly of *children:* she hardly ever writes about the solitary child, but about the interactions of brothers and sisters, and always from a position of involvement, from the children's point of view (she was one of the first to do this).

Nesbit is not a writer with a definite philosophy or moral code which unifies or gives 'purpose' to her books.... But the important point here is that she never committed herself to one thing in life (except her family), and had no fixed and narrow point of view.

One of the keys to an understanding of Nesbit is her passionate delight in life, and her wish to experience it to the full, to 'spread' herself in every direction. (pp. 111-12)

Nesbit's character—her child-likeness, her refusal to be fixed on one activity or code in life, her sheer zest—is portrayed in the character of her books. It emerges in the form of episodic narratives organized not by 'themes' or deep meanings but by comic schemata which make witty conceits out of magic.

There is no recurrent theme or motif running through the variety of stories that she wrote . . . and there is rarely a central idea in any single one of her works either. Her long stories often fall apart naturally into narrative vignettes. (p. 114)

Nesbit's books do not ask more than a literal level of reading. The search for the "heart's desire" in *The Story of the Amulet* could conceivably have been made into a metaphor of spiritual pilgrimage, but, apart from one hint, the Amulet is treated merely as an object to be secured; and at the end, when it has been restored, the heart's desire thus gained is simply the return of the children's parents from abroad. (p. 115)

There are . . . points of difference between Nesbit's and more 'philosophical' fairy-tales. For instance, her magic creatures are not inaccessible, and do not require, as they do in [George] MacDonald's fantasy [*The Princess and Curdie*], some spiritual qualification on the part of the person who wants to meet them. Pure accident often throws up the supernatural in her books. . . . There are occasional exceptions: in *The House of Arden* (1908) the children have to avoid quarrelling for first one and then three days before the door to the room with magic chests will appear. Particularly in her later magic books, Nesbit tried to move towards a more mystical and 'poetic' treatment of the supernatural, and this involved spiritual considerations: but she was a little out of her element in so reaching for the 'significant' and the portentous, and these stories are not the expression of her peculiar genius.

Nesbit's fairy-tales are perhaps not unlike other fantasies in that they usually end with the reversal of the magic. In *Five Children and It* . . ., every wish ends at nightfall and the effects, whether they be a heap of gold, wings, or a baby suddenly becoming a grown-up, are removed. In *The Phoenix and the Carpet* the magic bird may burn down the Garrick Theatre, but the audience escapes, and the theatre is restored by the phoenix that same night. The magic is often made public, but people are made to think they were temporarily mad or dreaming, or even to accept the magic as one of nature's freaks (the giant Robert in ch. 8 of *Five Children and It* is taken on as one by a showman at a fair). In this way, too, the magic can disappear without trace. Occasionally it may leave concrete effects, like the mass of gold which Edward and Gustus make out of a half-sovereign with the magic telescope in "The Mixed Mine" [*The Magic World*]: but there the enlarging takes place underground and is made by the children to appear like the discovery of a gold mine; so that the magical may be passed off as the real.

This removal of the supernatural happens at the end of many fantasies. All the disturbed magic in a Charles Williams novel returns to its origin; Tolkien's Ring is destroyed; MacDonald's Anodos and Vane return to their castles to wait. However, in these fantasies there has been one permanent change which is not generally to be found in Nesbit's tales—a change in the soul of the hero, whereby the supernatural enters and alters his spirit. But Nesbit is not usually concerned with writing fantastic *Bildungsromanen*. In her work there is rarely a permanent spiritual change, or portrayal of continued growth, in the characters:

Whereyouwantogoto in the end is Whereyoustartedfrom. Certainly her characters do gain and learn from their experiences, but the gaining and learning have nothing to do with transformation. A story may end with material profit, as in the case of the gold of "The Mixed Mine" or the valuables that Tavy finds thanks to the magic china cat in "The White Cat" [*The Magic World*]; with 'intellectual' benefit, as in the case of the fusion of the minds of the "learned gentleman" and Rekh-marā at the end of *The Story of the Amulet,* or Edwin's development as a mathematician thanks to the Arithmetic Fairy in "The Sums that Came Right" [*Nine Unlikely Tales*]. Parents return to children at the end of "Justnowland" and *The Story of the Amulet.* Annabel's dislike for her aunt is removed by her experiences in "The Aunt and Annabel" [*The Magic World*]. But however one regards them, these are not *spiritual* benefits, particularly not that entry into and transformation of the soul by the supernatural implied in the notion here. (pp. 117-18)

So far we have said what Nesbit's fairy tales are not: it is time to say rather more of what they are. The method and end of most of her fantasy is the exploitation of comic incongruities. There are several forms that this takes. For example, there is the gap between what one expects the supernatural to be, and what it turns out to be. The appearance of the Psammead is hardly one's notion of a fairy. Nesbit also plays against our notion of the remoteness of the supernatural: her magic creatures often have the hard definition and idiosyncrasy of realistic characters. The origin of the Psammead is within time, in the prehistoric past, and that past is made no more strange and remote than the everyday present. . . . The 'day's wishes' [in *Five Children and It*] is a marvellous piece of witty reduction: it shows. . . . how Nesbit's imagination works inwards to the brilliant *aperçu* rather than outward to large structures and themes. Both the Psammead and the Phoenix belong to a definite 'species,' and though the Phoenix has semi-mythical origin, it is treated almost as a household pet. Such familiarity, with the Psammead in its paper bag, or sleeping in its bath of sand, and the Phoenix roosting "on the cornice supporting the window-curtains of the boys' room" . . . is calculated deflation of mystery. (pp. 119-20)

The method here is the comic marriage of the strange and the familiar. . . .

At the same time the children in the magic books remain very real and intensely human. It is one of Nesbit's strengths as a writer of fantasy that in the midst of magic nothing is lost of realism. (p. 121)

In Nesbit's finer magic books the strangeness of the creatures, places or peoples that the children see is always to some extent reduced. This is not done by evasion, or 'drawing a veil,' because Nesbit will not insult the intelligence of her readers. Instead she often uses a technique which could loosely be called 'metaphoric' in its blending of the potentially frightening with the familiar. The strange city in which Philip and Lucy find themselves in *The Magic City* is an enlarged and animated version of the one they themselves previously built in their house out of books, finger-bowls, . . . and a host of other domestic objects, and the people in it are Philip's toys. (pp. 122-23)

What we have in this interplay of natural and supernatural in Nesbit's magic books is in part the fusion of two personal and literary impulses in her life. On the one hand she was what we may call a realist. (p. 123)

[The] various types of involvement with the 'real' world are to be contrasted with another side of her nature [: the supernatural]. (p. 124)

These two sides of Nesbit—the 'realist' and the 'supernaturalist'—are brought together in her magic books, where magic is given a colloquial and comic face, and is brought into contact with very human children. One would not claim that this makes the magic books the summit of Nesbit's achievement—the Bastable stories are as finely done—but it does show that in those books she united opposed impulses in her own nature. . . . None the less, in all Nesbit's more characteristic magic books the central aim, and the one on which her strength depends, is the production of situations or images in which maximum comic energy is generated by a clash of contents. When she veers, as she does in the later books, into a belief in the reality of the magic, the balance is upset, and we have the would-be mysticism of *The House of Arden* or *Harding's Luck,* or the mingled mysticism and horror of *The Enchanted Castle.* . . . (pp. 126-27)

At its best, this method is not purely random: it is nothing so simply as taking one context and throwing it together with one as far opposed as possible, for there is always a law which gives the bringing together of the terms a certain inevitability. . . . (p. 127)

E. Nesbit's fantasy is not what one would call great literature: it is at its best without any deeply-felt spiritual meaning, and it could be argued that the sensibility behind it is not particularly sophisticated—even that it is at times materialistic. To repeat our classification, her work is fanciful rather than imaginative. But fancy has its place: and one could claim that in Nesbit's work it reaches a high point of wit and ingenuity. She had her literary forebears—Thackeray, MacDonald, Carroll, Mrs. Molesworth and particularly F. Anstey, all of whom played magic against humdrum real life for comic effect; but she gave the 'realistic' side more vitality by her special understanding of a child's mind, and the magic more scope by her use of rules and logic. The result is that the bringing-together of opposites in her magic books is of a variety, skill and comic potential unequalled before her or since. But these books are also a picture of Nesbit's zest for life in almost any form: the 'conceited' method of juxtaposing opposites returns us to the lady who was as happy with logarithms as with Ibsen, with Shaw as with Chesterton, with Fabianism as with the *Yellow Book.* Inventive powers and wit of the kind that she shows are not often recognized by literary criticism: perhaps there might be a healthy diminution of gravity if they were. (p. 130)

> *Colin N. Manlove, "Fantasy as Witty Conceit: E. Nesbit," in* MOSAIC X/2 *(copyright © 1977 by The University of Manitoba Press), Winter, 1977, pp. 109-30.*

THE BASTABLE CHILDREN: *The Story of the Treasure Seekers: Being the Adventures of the Bastable Children in Search of a Fortune; The Would-be-Goods: Being the Further Adventures of the Treasure Seekers; The New Treasure Seekers*

[There is an] all-pervading modern theory that children's

instincts are a sure guide to what is best, in literature as in everything else. There follows, on the part of most writers, an unconcealed effort to please which can only be described as slavish. The ideal they hold up is that which requires least discipline, is most free from acquired qualities, and can be attained by children with the least effort to themselves. It seems, in short, as though the child were in future to become its own ideal; the more the natural characteristics of childhood are developed, the more do the critics admire. Mrs Nesbit's really delightful stories of *The Treasure Seekers* and *The Would-be Goods* show a decided tendency towards this state of mind. . . . The six children who play the principal parts in these stories are typically modern in other respects as well, and a thoroughly pleasant, amusing family they are. We are most grateful to Mrs Nesbit for their acquaintance; she has drawn them in the newest photographic style, whose motto is, 'I teach nothing, I relate.' (pp. 104-05)

> *Eveline C. Godley, "A Century of Children's Books," (originally published in* The National Review, *May, 1906), in* A Peculiar Gift: Nineteenth Century Writings on Books for Children, *edited by Lance Salway (copyright © 1976 by Lance Salway), Kestrel Books, 1976, pp. 92-105.*

The humor, so present in E. Nesbit's [Bastable] stories, proceeds from the contrast between the large ideas of the children and the ludicrous situations that develop as a consequence. The humor is also in the manner of writing; in the contrast between Oswald's grave, straight-forward accounts and his lapses into a grandiloquent style composed of all the phrases he has found in his reading. These stories, full of action, of humor, and of character, are written from inside the minds of children. Each character is equally childlike and believable and moves through these lively and original stories as convincingly today as when the books were written. They are the universal child, and so are timeless. (p. 145)

> *Lillian H. Smith, in her* The Unreluctant Years: A Critical Approach to Children's Literature *(reprinted by permission; copyright © 1953 by the American Library Association), American Library Association, 1953.*

Within the species 'children's story' the sub-species which happened to suit me is the fantasy or (in a loose sense of that word) the fairy tale. There are, of course, other subspecies. E. Nesbit's trilogy about the Bastable family is a very good specimen of another kind. It is a 'children's story' in the sense that children can and do read it: but it is also the only form in which E. Nesbit could have given us so much of the humours of childhood. It is true that the Bastable children appear, successfully treated from the adult point of view, in one of her grown-up novels [*The Red House*], but they appear only for a moment. I do not think she would have kept it up. Sentimentality is so apt to creep in if we write at length about children as seen by their elders. And the reality of childhood, as we all experienced it, creeps out. For we all remember that our childhood, as lived, was immeasurably different from what our elders saw. Hence Sir Michael Sadler, when I asked his opinion about a certain new experimental school, replied, 'I never give an opinion on any of those experiments till the children have grown up and can tell us *what really happened.*' Thus the Bastable trilogy, however improbable many of its episodes may be, provides even adults, in one sense, with more realistic reading about children than they could find in most books addressed to adults. But also, conversely, it enables the children who read it to do something much more mature than they realize. For the whole book is a character study of Oswald, an unconsciously satiric self-portrait, which every intelligent child can fully appreciate: but no child would sit down to read a character study in any other form. (pp. 23-4)

> *C. S. Lewis, in his* Of Other Worlds: Essays and Stories, *edited by Walter Hooper (copyright © 1966 by the Executors of the Estate of C. S. Lewis; reprinted by permission of Harcourt Brace Jovanovich, Inc.), Harcourt, Brace & World, 1966 (and reprinted by Harcourt Brace Jovanovich, 1975).*

THE BOOK OF DRAGONS (1900; also published as *The Complete Book of Dragons*, British Edition, 1972; US Edition, 1973)

[*The Complete Book of Dragons* is not] the best Nesbit, but at her second best she is still way out in front. These nine stories date from the beginning of her great period, although one appeared in book form only posthumously. The topsy-turvy humour and the blending of fantasy and the everyday are characteristic Nesbit ingredients, here applied at less than full pressure. The style is the thing, that miraculous Nesbit style which was her unique contribution to children's literature. All the stories are told in an effortlessly conversational tone which immediately engages and involves the reader. Erik Blegvad is the best of modern Nesbit illustrators. His dragons are admirable, but he might have taken his children just a little more seriously. It spoils the Nesbit jokes to underline them so obviously. (p. 386)

The Junior Bookshelf, December, 1972.

The author's fans will welcome this edition of nine dragon stories, all but one of them written for *The Strand Magazine* in 1899 and published together a year later, though as they've generally aged less gracefully than her full-length novels we wouldn't choose this as any child's introduction to Nesbit. Her mock morals now seem less amusing than they must have in 1900, her arch asides to readers verge on the precious, and that whimsical geography and natural history (as in the Kingdom of Rotundia, where the elephant, "dear little pet," is the size of a silly muff dog and the dormouse is "the biggest creature of all") can be carried to tiresome lengths. Yet her masterful, matter-of-fact juxtaposition of the ordinary, the fabulous and the wildly ridiculous is in disarming evidence throughout—whether in details such as the "universal tap room" wherein two children, the "Deliverers of Their County," turn on the rain taps and wash a horde of invading dragons off to sea; or throughout the adroitly tongue-in-cheek fairy tale of an enchanted princess, a sailor boy who overcomes a guardian dragon and nine whirlpools to rescue her from an island tower, and a witch who gives up her magic for the queen's gratitude. And even the whimsy has its redeeming triumphs—at least for those of us who can't resist an opening in which a child is summoned from his nursery blocks by Nurse's announcement: "Master Lionel, dear, they've come to fetch you to go and be King." (p. 6)

> Kirkus Reviews (*copyright © 1973 The Kirkus Service, Inc.), January 1, 1973.*

E. Nesbit had a weakness for saurian monsters, which she usually calls megatheriums—there is even one in 'The Enchanted Castle'. *The Book of Dragons . . .* has them in great variety. These short stories are interesting in their embryo themes elaborated on in later books—and for the brisk, jocular humour which takes the edge from the horror of the monstrous, without detracting from its strangeness. . . . [Ideas], often full of fascinating logic, proliferate. There are lines that one longs to produce and make into a theorem. *The Book of Beasts* has the idea which is the nucleus of *The Magic City*—that of pictures in a book, a Bestiary, full of the fabulous, jumping off the page: wonderful if the picture is of a peacock, but 'What if it had been a worm, a snake, or a revolutionary?' thinks the boy king to whom the book belongs. A dragon flies out; ten years later, in *The Magic City,* it was the Hippogriff and a giant Sloth. Lionel, the king, has to open the book again and let out a Manticora to fight the dragon; but it is a failure, rubbing its eyes with its hand and mewing pitifully. It puts its tail between its legs and hides behind the town hall, eating all the cats in the night. . . . Here is the beginning of the spell of the god Arithmos, of *The Enchanted Castle . . .*; and in 'Kind Little Edmund', Cockatrice, Dragon and Drackling have links with the Phoenix and Psammead with their stories of legend and prehistory, doubtful tempers and fondness for giving good advice.

H. R. Millar's dragons drawn for this book have infinite variety; no two appear to share similar genes. Likewise, the stories are different, not only in subject but in type, and so full of invention that the book deserves to be, and should be, reprinted with the rest. [Critic's note: "And has been: *The Complete Book of Dragons, . . .* 1972."] (pp. 120-21)

> *Margaret Blount, in her* Animal Land: The Creatures of Children's Fiction (*copyright © 1974 by Margaret Ingle-Finch; abridged by permission of William Morrow & Co., Inc.), William Morrow, 1974.*

OTHER CITATIONS

Kevin Crossley-Holland, in New Statesman, *November 10, 1972, p. 695.*

Paul Heins, in The Horn Book Magazine, *June, 1973, p. 272.*

Jean Stafford, in The New Yorker, *December 3, 1973, p. 206.*

THE ENCHANTED CASTLE (British Edition, 1907; US Edition, 1908)

It is difficult not to feel that E. Nesbit's magic sometimes gets a little out of hand in *The Enchanted Castle*, rather more poetical and mysterious than she could comfortably manage. Not that this purely fantastic magic without the humours of the Psammead is not good of its kind—but one must make the reservation that other writers have done as well and better in that field, and E. Nesbit's real excellence lay in the other direction.

However, even if E. Nesbit's magic does occasionally get out of control in *The Enchanted Castle*, and it thus comes slightly below the standard of its three predecessors, it does not come very far below them. One criticism has often been levelled against it—mistakenly, I think—that the episode of the Ugly-Wuglies is horrific. (pp. 65-6)

Certainly [they are] a less genial grotesquerie than that of the Psammead. But is it in fact frightening? Most children love a few bogies in their stories, and if deprived of them are quite likely to invent their own. The things that really frighten them are apt to lie deeper than any such description of horrors from the outside, in private, unexpected corners of the mind. . . . For most children, the Ugly-Wuglies surely come into the category of pleasurable story-book terrors. For one thing, E. Nesbit is extremely explicit about them—that full-blooded phrase, 'the ghastly crew', indicates their real story-book bogy nature—the really frightening is the half-revealed, the unexplained. One other moment in E. Nesbit's writings would, if she had done more than dwell on it very lightly and briefly, have been more likely to frighten an imaginative child. (pp. 66-7)

> *Anthea Bell, in* E. Nesbit (© *The Bodley Head Ltd 1960*), *Bodley Head, 1960.*

Good as it is compared with ordinary juvenile fiction, [*The Enchanted Castle*] is not quite in the same rank with the works that preceded it. The writing shows signs of haste, and the magic entanglements are not unravelled with that deftness she had led her admirers to expect. A certain slight falling off may be looked for almost as a matter of course, where an author produces so much and directs his energy towards so many different ends; but what comes as a surprise to the reader who has followed her career through all its phases is the absence of that sensitive touch which, in the earlier stories, constantly suggests the lovableness of the writer. In one of the principal boy characters, Jimmy, the Bastable frankness has degenerated into mere pertness. And there is a servant girl in the story whom the children treat with an unkindness which Oswald Bastable would have been quick to reprove. There is no reason why an author's heroes and heroines should be the mouthpieces of his own sentiments, but as E. Nesbit's obviously were so, or had been until now, the suspicion of hardness one gets here is a matter of some interest.

Another notable feature of the book is that it breaks a rule which she had hitherto always observed in this sort of writing—namely that she should exclude from her pages everything likely to awaken fear. The episode of the Ugly-Wuglies' coming to life, though it is from the adult's point of view one of her most original and amusing conceptions, is rather frightening to children. There is a sort of refinement of horror in the fact that these repellent creatures, whose faces are paper, whose arms and legs are covered hockey-sticks and umbrellas, and whose hands are stuffed gloves, have no roofs to their mouths and are thus only half-articulate.

The Ugly-Wuglies were invented for a game of charades at [E. Nesbit's home,] Dymchurch. One of the scenes to be acted required a larger number of players than were present, and Edith conceived the idea of hastily painting a number of grotesque faces on paper and mounting them upon coat-hangers, on which she hung clothes, and which were disposed about the room in the manner described in the story. It afterwards occurred to her that she might represent them as coming to life in the serial she was working

on, and she did so with a realism almost too convincing. H. R. Millar, though he had not seen the original Ugly-Wuglies, portrayed them with remarkable felicity, notwithstanding the great difficulty he found in giving the look of life to creatures who were intended at the same time to look unlifelike. She thought his work for this book the best that he had done.

This was the first and last time E. Nesbit ever sounded any note of horror—and perhaps the word is too strong—in writing for a juvenile audience. (pp. 212-13)

> *Doris Langley Moore, in her* E. Nesbit: A Biography *(copyright © 1966 by Doris Langley Moore; reprinted with permission of the publisher), revised edition, Chilton Book Company, 1966.*

FIVE CHILDREN AND IT (British Edition, 1902; US Edition, 1905)

Styles in writing change—for children as they do for adults. Sometimes it is tone that forces the retirement of a onetime classic. Such, it seems, may be the case in E. Nesbit's *Five Children and It,* a book that continues to appear on lists of classics but is no longer read by many children. While an occasional child today may still respond to the playful fantasy of *Five Children and It,* it is perhaps the sentimental and condescending tone that has retired it from the active shelf. Children may find it demeaning to hear themselves and their generation referred to in Nesbit's terms: Lamb, who is too old to be called a baby today, says,

> "Poor, poor." And he let the gipsy woman
> kiss him, and what is more, he kissed her
> brown cheek in return—a very nice kiss, as
> all his kisses are, and not a wet one like
> some babies give. . . .

[Robert] asks Lamb to "come and have a yidey on Yobby's back." Sentimental and stereotyped characterization combines with condescension toward gipsies, "Eyetalians," and "Red Indians."

Condescension combined with whimsy also contrasts artificially the views of children and adults on what is real and true:

> So . . . you may leave [this] book about
> quite safely, for no aunts and uncles either
> are likely to write "How true!" on the edge
> of the story. Grown-up people find it very
> difficult to believe really wonderful things,
> unless they have . . . proof. But children will
> believe almost anything, and grown-ups
> know this . . . they tell you that the earth is
> round like an orange, when you can see per-
> fectly well that it is flat and lumpy; and why
> they say that the earth goes round the sun,
> when you can see for yourself any day that
> the sun gets up in the morning and goes to
> bed at night like a good sun as it is, and the
> earth knows its place, and lies as still as a
> mouse.

While Nesbit's stories have been great favorites in the past, contemporary children might reject with disdain such talking down. (pp. 144-45)

Rebecca J. Lukens, in her A Critical Handbook of Children's Literature *(copyright © 1976 by Scott, Foresman and Company; reprinted by permission), Scott, Foresman, 1976.*

LONG AGO WHEN I WAS YOUNG (1966)

For information—in the unlikely event of any child reading this—Miss Nesbit lived in the second great era of women novelists—the first was in the 17th century, the third, so the commercials say, is now—missing Charlotte Brontë by three years and dying just before the publication of [Virginia Woolf's] *Mrs Dalloway.* Her writing had much of the wit, charm and sense of privilege of her contemporaries. This little autobiography, so gentle and remote, adds no more than a whiff of camphor to *The Railway Children* and *The Wouldbegoods.* (p. 708)

> *Penelope Mortimer, in* New Statesman *(© 1966 The Statesman & Nation Publishing Co. Ltd.), November 11, 1966.*

Edith Nesbit (known to her family as Daisy) wrote these reminiscences of her childhood in 1895-6 as a series of magazine articles; they first appeared in book form eight years ago, and here they are again, fifty years after her death, perfectly mated with illustrations by Edward Ardizzone.... It was not a common childhood. But what she's concerned with are the invariable experiences of a child: fear of the dark, for example, and the impossibility of explaining your acts and moods: periods of awful boredom ('Children are bored much more often, and much more deeply, than their elders suppose'); periods of amazing delight, especially for her in fields and gardens ('As long as I stayed among the golden buttercups and silver may-bushes, I believe I was moderately good'). About such things she writes with delicious transparency of recall and economy of prose: never a word too many.

Her father was dead; her mother moved from place to place in search of a healthy setting for a sick daughter (one of Daisy's sisters). Daisy herself was nervous, acutely sensitive, suffered from unruly hair, hands that defied soap and water, and a mortal incapacity for long division.... A loner, she was further separated from other children by those damned sums: her schoolmates 'naturally did not care to associate with one so deficient in arithmetic'....

If one sees where the Bastables came from, one sees also why Edith Nesbit gave them a firmly settled, if troubled home. 'I was tired of wandering about.' These reminiscences owe much of their charm to that sad vagrancy, but one understands that her children's books were, in this respect, an act of revenge on a childhood painfully restless. (p. 72)

> *Edward Blishen, in* Books and Bookmen *(© copyright Edward Blishen 1975; reprinted with permission), February, 1975.*

OTHER CITATIONS

Zena Sutherland, in Saturday Review, *November 12, 1966, p. 51.*

Lance E. Salway, in Children's Book Review, *Winter, 1974-75, p. 166.*

THE MAGIC CITY (1910)

The source of [*The Magic City's*] inspiration was, I conjecture, Dr. Hoffmann's story about a boy called Reinhold who built a little town of toys which grew larger and larger until it reached full size and the inhabitants were as big as himself. She had used the bare outline of it a dozen years before in a short story called *The Town in the Library in the Town in the Library,* with Rosamund and Fabian [two of her children], under their own names, as the two adventurers; and now it was dexterously elaborated.

It cannot be said that *The Magic City,* notwithstanding the competence of its style and the novelty of its matter, stands on the same high level of excellence as her eight or nine best books. The construction is somewhat loose and rambling, and there are passages which seem to indicate that the author was taking the easy rather than the interesting course. For the first time too—unless I am guilty of some oversight—she begins to obtrude personal reminiscences to the detriment of her artistry, and this was a habit which persisted and increased in nearly all her subsequent work. (pp. 242-43)

> *Doris Langley Moore, in her* E. Nesbit: A Biography *(copyright © 1966 by Doris Langley Moore; reprinted with permission of the publisher), revised edition, Chilton Book Company, 1966.*

Quite the most interesting and unusual Toyland was written about by, as might be expected, E. Nesbit in *The Magic City* ... —the only book, as distinct from her short stories, where she deals with talking toys. Nesbit children usually do not need toys—they are too busy having imaginative adventures by other means.... The Magic City, or rather series of cities, is a place that can be entered only by those who have helped to build it with books for bricks; and it is populated by creatures and people that have been put there, or have managed to escape, out of the books from which it is made. H. R. Millar's drawings give the city that slabby, Babylonian/Aztec look of any structure made of books, ornaments, chessmen and dominoes. The story has that odd, logical but numinous quality shared by *The Enchanted Castle,* when the children who enter the city find that it is greater inside than out and has a history, prophecies and laws that seem to be older than its creators. That the dragon outside it is a toy with a winding key does not make it any less fearsome; but it is still dreamlike—and one never dies in a dream. (pp. 171-72)

The Magic City is as full of invention as anything that E. Nesbit ever wrote—it almost suffers from a surfeit and the plot is breathless. But the strange, twilight atmosphere of being, so to speak, trapped inside one's imagination, however willingly, is unique. For some, it will always be rated with *The Enchanted Castle* as the best of Magic books. (p. 172)

> *Margaret Blount, in her* Animal Land: The Creatures of Children's Fiction *(copyright © 1974 by Margaret Ingle-Finch; abridged by permission of William Morrow & Co., Inc.), William Morrow, 1974.*

THE RAILWAY CHILDREN (1905)

Mrs. Bland, whose pen name is perhaps better known than

her own, has put into this book a lively and fun-loving family of children whose adventures are as amusing and as readable as those of her famous "Would-be-Goods." By a family misfortune these children are for a time deprived of their father, compelled to leave their pleasant home, and obliged to live in a little cottage close to the railway. All their strange joys and troubles are in one way or another connected with this railway and its surroundings. A jovial guard, a friendly engineer, and some curious passengers have parts in the little plot. The incidents are worked out in a decidedly original way, and the story is strong enough to hold the attention of older readers as well as of young people. The chief defect seems to us the somewhat over-melodramatic background, dealing with the father's imprisonment on false charges and final reinstatement through the unconscious agency of the children. (p. 533)

The Outlook, *October 27, 1906.*

It is arguable that a series of incidents [in *The Railway Children*] such as rescuing trains, rescuing wounded boys, rescuing babies from fires and rescuing foreign refugees constitute just as much of a fantasy as marvellous adventures on a flying carpet. The story cried out for the liveliness of the Bastables, and the pen of Oswald, to redeem it from sentimentality. One longs for a breath of Bastable fresh air, in which just one of the rescues would turn out to be superfluous. The children themselves have many good moments—even so, there is not quite the cheerful, convincing family feeling that exists between the children in most of E. Nesbit's books. She concentrates on the eldest, Roberta, who thinks a great deal about her mother. A full-scale relationship between adult and child was a new departure for E. Nesbit, and not one that suited her powers very well. There is far too much dwelling on Mother's bravery, and indeed everyone else's bravery too. Mother has to write to make ends meet; obviously this touch originated in the struggles of E. Nesbit's early married life, and she must have partly identified herself with Mother of *The Railway Children.* Perhaps this one lapse from the habit of objectivity which served her so well helps to account for the difference in quality of this story. Or perhaps, aiming at an effect of pathos more popular then than now in children's books—one thinks of the sufferings of Frances Hodgson Burnett's Sara Crewe, like the Railway Children suddenly plunged into poverty—E. Nesbit had not seen clearly that her own talents lay in a more cheerful direction.

Opinions differ about *The Railway Children;* some rank it among the best of E. Nesbit's work, and it has been successfully broadcast and televised. My own view is that it is not in the same class as the rest of her books, and without them might not have survived to the television age at all—and that a discriminating child will recognise the difference in quality subconsciously, enjoying *The Railway Children,* but not with the same satisfying kind of enjoyment as the Bastable books provide. (pp. 55-6)

> *Anthea Bell, in* E. Nesbit (© *The Bodley Head Ltd 1960), Bodley Head, 1960.*

The family depicted [in *The Railway Children*] is not, perhaps, as skilfully and beautifully drawn as the Bastable family; its adventures are less credible. Nevertheless, it is a most engaging book. To an adult the author may have seemed unduly generous in providing her child characters with opportunities of saving lives and averting disasters of

every description, but the readers for whom the tale was intended are not likely to complain about it on that score. The chapter in which the youthful hero and heroines save a train from wreck by waving flags made of red flannel petticoats is quite superbly written and a masterpiece of its kind. (pp. 211-12)

> *Doris Langley Moore, in her* E. Nesbit: A Biography *(copyright © 1966 by Doris Langley Moore; reprinted with permission of the publisher), revised edition, Chilton Book Company, 1966.*

The Railway Children was a popular story long before it was filmed and televised. It is not, all the same, the most notable in its characterization. The three children are less sharply differentiated than those in the larger families of the Bastables . . . and the 'Five Children', and an undercurrent of sentimentality over-rides the humour in the book. This seems to emanate not only from the romantically sad situation of the family but also, in part, from the understanding mother. In spite of her modest disclaimers and outgoing sympathy for others, she seems in fact to be insisting all the time on the reader's attention and admiration. Is it unfair to suggest that there is too much of the author herself in the character, that a curious secret conceit has interfered with the free spirit of the story? (p. 304)

> *Margery Fisher, in her* Who's Who in Children's Books: A Treasury of the Familiar Characters of Childhood *(copyright © 1975 by Margery Fisher; reprinted by permission of Holt, Rinehart and Winston, Publishers), Holt, 1975.*

OTHER CITATIONS

The Nation, *December 6, 1906, p. 484.*

Marcus Crouch, in his Treasure Seekers and Borrowers, *The Library Association, 1962, pp. 13-14.*

Judith Higgins, in Grade Teacher, *March, 1972, p. 100.*

THE STORY OF THE AMULET (British Edition, 1906; US Edition, 1907)

[In this essay, the critic treats the fascination with time in Ronald Welch's *The Gauntlet,* Alison Uttley's *A Traveller in Time,* Philippa Pearce's *Tom's Midnight Garden,* and E. Nesbit's *The Story of the Amulet.* These authors are intrigued by the prospect of a character's actions when transported to a different era and by the essence of time as a continuum. In each novel, an object provides the connection between two ages. The importance of objects as images of time's fluidity is stressed here. The contemplation of the object, its use in the past and the relationship between the object's past, present, and future users, impresses one with the continuity of time.]

In *The Story of the Amulet* . . . the magical nature of the journeys in time is made quite explicit. The amulet itself is a charm, a gateway to the past and other localities. The past becomes the present to the children (although . . . no time passes in their own lives) and people can be left in the past—the children find a home for a child, destitute in their own time, with an Anglo-Saxon mother. The fact that they could lose the amulet and so be lost in the past for ever, or that they could die in the past, gives the children's journeys an urgency. In either case presumably no trace of them would ever be found in their own time. For although when they go through the amulet they are moving quite outside their own duration they are in their own bodies—as Peter in *The Gauntlet,* it seems, was not.... The children leave each time and place at the height of a crisis—in the thick of a battle, or as the flood is about to engulf Atlantis. The children are not involved in the happenings just as spectators— the *presentness* of them is intense. (pp. 72-3)

And when the children return to their own duration, the scene they have left does not cease suddenly with the withdrawal of their consciousness. An apprehension of the times as somehow simultaneous is important to the story. How else, for instance, does the little girl left in pre-Roman Britain survive? But the way it all ceases for the children as they return through the amulet in each case, answers something in everyone's experience (but perhaps especially for children) which is the difficulty of being really aware of what is happening at a particular time in a different place from where one is oneself. Life continues in the place one has just left, although one is no longer there to see. Similarly, it is hard to imagine time that has no connection with one's own life and stretches before and after one's own existence. This is where E. Nesbit makes the boldest use of her time machinery by bringing the movements in time closer to the children's particular life spans. They go into the future at one point to the time when they are grown up. They do not actually see themselves (which is surely the logical conclusion of such journeys in time) but they see pictures of themselves.... (p. 73)

As the children are confronted with pictures of themselves as grown ups there is a sudden realization of time as change —though, as Anthea says in what is probably the wisest comment on time in all the books, it is so gradual you don't know it's happening. Nevertheless it's radical, and one end of the continuous process seems to have little relation to the beginning. For what adult can really feel a close relationship with himself as a child and know himself as the same person? And yet it is the same person, and throughout the development, the layers of change, there must be a coherent line. 'In my beginning is my end' and Anthea sees this for herself. It is not up to the children to regret what they are to become yet or ever; it is the learned gentleman who does that; 'You dear children! What a difference you made to that Bloomsbury house! Now you're not like you used to be.' The children rush out of this future when they hear that their Nurse is dead. They go to their own present to find her, unable to accept as yet that time is destruction, as well as change and development.

When they enter a part of the future that will be after their own deaths, again it does not touch them in relationship to themselves any more than time long before their births did. This vision of the more distant future without any suffering —not even boredom for children at school!—is used to show how grim the children's own present is. (p. 74)

E. Nesbit uses the journeys in time most specifically to provide comments on the present, although Ronald Welch did so very briefly, and Philippa Pearch does so in sad contrasts.... (p.75)

When time is considered behind and beyond a particular life span, it can be used to illustrate larger social changes and changes in the environment. For Philippa Pearce, these changes have certainly not been for the better. E. Nesbit held out hope for the social future; she could see time as bringing some improvement.

When the children in *The Story of the Amulet* meet Julius Caesar, the story hovers on the edge of making an event in the past not happen:

> '. . . we want to ask you not to trouble about conquering Britain,' said Anthea: 'it's a poor little place, not worth bothering about.'

Everything the reader suddenly realizes, would have been different if the Romans had never come. The idea of history suddenly becomes an abyss of unknown events if Julius Caesar had not had his place in the chain leading to the events we know. 'What might have been and what has been point to one end, which is always present . . .' But Caesar is persuaded by the children's description of Britain as they know it—which is not what they meant to do at all—and the invasion takes place. History rests back on its known keel. But such fantastic notions fill the book, and certainly prompt the imagination. *The Story of the Amulet* is, more than all the books, a romp with time, but it is far from being unconstructive, mere imaginative gymnastics. E. Nesbit does not tend to the accurate historical curiosity of Ronald Welch, nor the passionate poignancy of Philippa Pearce, nor even to the almost mystical imaginative power behind Penelope's adventures in *A Traveller in Time*. Instead the reader is carried robustly through from one fantastic event to another. Even something that has been destroyed in the past can be rescued from the past before that, and brought back to the present. The children do not pretend to understand how it can all happen:

> 'I don't know,' said Cyril. 'Jam, please. This about time being only a thingummy of thought is very confusing . . .'.

But a reader would take from the book, notwithstanding the joke element, perceptions about time that he might not have experienced before; and E. Nesbit's own thinking about time seems to have a positive quality—a deliberate movement forward as well as back—which is certainly missing from the [other] books. (pp. 75-6)

> *Lesley Aers, in* Children's Literature in Education *(© 1970, APS Publications, Inc., New York; reprinted by permission of the publisher), No. 2 (July), 1970.*

OTHER CITATIONS

The Outlook, *June 1, 1907, p. 256.*

Eleanor Cameron, in her The Green and Burning Tree, *Little, Brown, 1969, pp. 83-90.*

O

O'CONNOR, Patrick
   See **WIBBERLEY, Leonard**

P

PAISLEY, Tom
   See BETHANCOURT, T. Ernesto

*   *   *

PEYTON, K. M. (pseudonym of Kathleen Peyton) 1929-

A British author for young people, Kathleen Peyton published her first book at the age of fifteen. K. M. Peyton was originally the pseudonym for Kathleen Peyton and her husband, Michael; they have not collaborated since 1962. Many of Peyton's books are based on her own experiences and interests such as sailing, horseback riding, airplanes, and music. She writes using adolescents of both sexes as main characters, and accurately captures their backgrounds, actions, and feelings. Peyton studied to be a painter, and she now illustrates her own works. She won the 1969 Carnegie Medal for _The Edge of the Cloud_, and the 1970 Guardian Award for her Flambards trilogy.

AUTHOR'S COMMENTARY

I became a children's writer because I started writing as a child and naturally wrote children's books. Since then I must have suffered some sort of mental retardment, for I still write, as I did then, the sort of stories I like writing best and my audience is still young, whereas I am now gone forty. My mother asks me, 'When are you going to write a proper book?' 'They _are_ proper books,' I reply stiffly. I have thought seriously about starting on a novel about adults, but there is nothing in me that wants to do it. . . . The adult situation bores me. Characters in my mind die on me after the age of twenty. I follow them thus far, enjoying them enormously, but after that I lose interest. I don't ever even want to know what happens to them after I have finished with them. There is possibly some psychological reason for this that a trained person might be able to explain to me; I hope I haven't inadvertently revealed some highly embarrassing truth about myself of which I am still ignorant. (pp. 123-24)

One's books can only be built on one's own experiences. Which ones, at the time, one cannot always foresee. A quiet and lovely autumn afternoon searching for the grave of the Pytchley hounds drowned through the ice in 1910 in the grounds of the now derelict Fawsley Manor, eventually turned into a book, although at the time it wasn't at all what I was doing it for. I was doing it because it was what I wanted to do—and perhaps, if one wants to be analytical, it was a childlike thing to do, for it entailed struggling through a mass of brambles and going down on hands and knees under ancient laurel bushes in a wilderness of what had once been a garden, not exactly what the other visitors were doing, whose cars were parked alongside mine in the car park. I did not foresee that regularly eavesdropping on the conversation of some schoolboys on a train when I came home once a week with the shopping would grow into _Pennington's Seventeenth Summer_ (with the real-life Pennington spectacularly saving a man from drowning in the river during a Force 8 gale and being presented with a real-life medal). Nor did I realize that a dabbling in music which started with the children's recorder lessons in the village school would lead me to the complexities of following Pennington in his virtuoso career. . . . (pp. 124-25)

When I get frustrated by the demands of . . . commitments deflecting me from . . . writing, I console myself that they are the lifeblood of what I am writing about, and that the ivory tower, attractive as it may appear at times, would not suit. The male writer, quiet in his room with coffee and lunch served, the interruptions deflected by a devoted wife, is at times my great envy; but at other times I feel that the very frustrations are somehow a part of my driving force. My most difficult book to date, _A Pattern of Roses_, was written through the winter when a forty-foot boat was being built full-time in the garden and a constant stream of nautical maniacs was in and out of the house at all times. . . . (p. 125)

The fact is, I like writing very much, better than anything else. I write to entertain. . . . What it is all for, entertainment apart, I could not say. Does it have to be justified? Whether it cleanses one of one's hang-ups, a personal therapy disguised as art, or whether one is trying to wield an influence in the wide world, I could not say. I certainly do not feel it this way, but these motives are put. When a writer knows he has a juvenile audience, a certain responsibility is inevitably felt, but to think that he can 'con' his audience into what might be called correct attitudes must be doomed to failure. The writer's own attitudes probably show through, but whether these are uplifting or depressing depends on who is the judge. I feel that the only possible limitation in writing in this sphere is the necessity to write within the framework of the reader's understanding, but as this is as wide or as narrow as the writer cares to make it

..., it is scarcely to be thought of as limiting. I have not yet found this a difficulty, and when I do I suppose the time will have come to write 'a proper book'. Until then I shall continue as I am. (pp. 126-27)

> *K. M. Peyton, "On Not Writing a Proper Book," in* The Thorny Paradise: Writers on Writing for Children, *edited by Edward Blishen (© 1975 by K. M. Peyton), Kestrel, 1975, pp. 123-27.*

GENERAL COMMENTARY

At the close of Kathleen Peyton's ... most mature book [*The Edge of the Cloud*], her enchanting heroine Christina drives off to church to marry Will. This ought to be the end of a long romantic story. But Mrs. Peyton knows that stories of this kind have no end. Like Christina she is "streets ahead in experience" of the writer who, seven years ago, made her debut as an Oxford author with a magnificent yarn of sailing, endurance, heroism and villainy. Like Christina she has "grown up". (p. 153)

Hers has been a longish apprenticeship. When she settled in Essex and wrote *Windfall* [published in the United States as *Sea Fever*] she already had several books behind her. She had trained as an artist—with what success the exquisite line-drawings in *Fly-By-Night* bear witness—had taught, married and travelled the world. These experiences provided the raw materials of her art. More than some other writers she needed time to work like yeast upon them. So it is that one sees, more clearly than in many contemporary writers for children, the slow, steady development of the artist, the craftsman and the philosopher. (p. 154)

Mrs. Peyton is a born story-teller. This is not to say that she is always a good maker of plots. Most of the earlier books, breathless as they are in action and suspense, have weaknesses in the mechanics of their narrative. Like other very nice people she is not skilled in creating villains. Making due allowance for the sea-going ethics of the 1870s, it is still difficult to swallow the unqualified evil of Beckett in *Windfall*. Here, one feels, is not a bad man but a necessary factor in the plot. Much the same is true of the wicked uncle in *The Maplin Bird,* but he, in the old tradition of children's books, is merely an adult to be disposed of briskly so that the children can get on with their adventures. The two crooks in *The Plan for Birdsmarsh* are the one conspicuous defect of that remarkable book. Mrs. Peyton does better now. There are no villains in *Flambards*, only people.

Mrs. Peyton pushes the reader's credulity hard at times, another indication of her uncertainty in plotting. There are some shaky moments in *The Maplin Bird,* as well as the fundamental improbability about Uncle Gideon's tame acquiescence in the defection of cheap labour and the disappearance of 'his' boat. Surely that nasty man and his unbearable son Mark—there is another Mark later on in the Peyton canon whose nastiness is more subtle—would have been quickly after the runaways. The improbability of Sam's hitch-hike to the trenches of Flanders in *Thunder in the Sky* is harder to bear. Again the author has learnt better. There are no major improbabilities in the recent books, because she no longer needs to invent plots. The action now comes largely from within, through the interaction of

the characters and the reaction of characters to their environment.

Character-drawing has matured beyond all reasonable expectation. ... There are some brilliantly sketched portraits, like the perpetually adolescent Sydney and the professional and amateur conservationists who lead the opposition to the Birdsmarsh plan. This stops safely short of caricature but the swift impressionist line is attractive and the result memorable. The most colourful of Mrs. Peyton's minor portraits, and perhaps one from the life, is Bunyard, the old skipper of the *Flower of Ipswich* whose sanity among the madness of war is the principal delight of *Thunder in the Sky.*

The unifying factor in these books is the setting. Mrs. Peyton lives on an Essex estuary and sails the tricky waters of that deeply indented coast. She knows the sea, the creeks and the saltings, as well as the villages and the ports. She is sharply aware of the beauty of this strange and, to conventional eyes, unlovely country. She is conscious too that it is a constantly changing scene and a changing society. ... All Mrs. Peyton's books are historical stories, to the extent that in all there is a sense of change, of old ways decaying and new developing. (pp. 154-56)

So all-pervading is the Essex atmosphere of these books that it requires a conscious effort to discover how little formal scene-painting there is. The land and seascapes are present in the action. Writer and reader alike take them for granted. (p. 156)

Birdsmarsh marks the major turning-point in Mrs. Peyton's career. ... The social awareness of the book is agonizingly sharp. There is no single solution to the dilemma of Birdsmarch, which is beautiful and moribund and ripe for the kiss of death (or life) of 'development', only a compromise. Compromise is alien to young people like Paul, and it is part of Mrs. Peyton's triumph in this story that she makes the compromise tolerable, if not aceptable. There are no easy answers in any of her books; they are harder than ever in this one because the battle is fought out not on the slippery deck of a boat but in people's hearts. (pp. 156-57)

There are minor battles too in *Fly-By-Night.* This is the slightest of Mrs. Peyton's books, which is not to say the least of them. On a small scale, and in a more homely setting than usual, she works out personal problems with ruthless honesty. No one has written a better pony tale. No one else, I suspect, would have thought it worth while to devote brilliant talents to such a small theme and to devote them without stint. For Fly-By-Night, which moves uncomplainingly within the conventions of the pony story, explores unobtrusively a number of social and personal themes. And nowhere is the natural scene more discreetly and exquisitely touched in as in this little story.

The two 'Flambards' books—there is a third on the way—are Mrs. Peyton's major effort to date and her major achievement. Her sense of period is at its most delicate, especially in *Flambards* itself where she captures precisely the atmosphere of decay in a rural society committed to self-destruction. ... This is mature writing and thinking, and may push beyond the commonly accepted bounds of the children's book. No matter. There are plenty of young people who will respond to the challenge of Mrs. Peyton's wisdom and courage.

Few writers give us everything they have got. What Mrs. Peyton still holds in reserve is humour. She certainly possesses this characteristic most richly, and it is implicit in the view of life presented in *Fly-By-Night,* but she has yet to make us laugh. . . . I think she will. Her natural gaiety, so essential a part of her personality, . . . needs only to be harnessed to give a new dimension to her stories, adding fun and a touch of satire to the wisdom and tenderness of her studies of young people coming to terms with their world. This additional quality will increase the breadth of her view, which, for all that it is bounded physically by the low hills of the tidal Crouch, embraces what matters of the real world. (pp. 157, 159)

> *M. S. Crouch, "Streets Ahead in Experience," in* The Junior Bookshelf, *June, 1969, pp. 153-59*

K. M. Peyton . . . is . . . an interesting example of what we can expect for the future from writing for children. It is unlikely that she will ever write a masterpiece, but she is a sophisticated, highly intelligent, and well-organised writer making the most of her powers. . . . (p. 148)

> *Frank Eyre, in his* British Children's Books in the Twentieth Century *(copyright © 1971 by Frank Eyre; reprinted by permission of the publisher, E. P. Dutton & Co., Inc.), Dutton, 1971.*

The K. M. Peyton of today . . . is a person of action, and a writer on themes of action. She has, among many other gifts, the unusual one of writing extremely well about *movement:* about the way people move with and through and against the elements, in boats, on horseback, and—in the *Flambards* novels—in those frail, wind-buffeted early aircraft. (p. 173)

Her characters are mainly people of action, and even the gentle individualists like Will in the Flambards novels and Paul in *Birdsmarsh* show little sign of having any literary or artistic interests. Of her masculine characters, some—like Matt in *Windfall,* Sam in *Thunder in the Sky* and Dick in the Flambards books—are simple, brave, and slightly wooden; others, like the gentleman smuggler Adam in *The Maplin Bird* and the handsome cad Mark in *Flambards,* strike one as being related to the creations of feminine romantic novelists. Her two splendid heroines, Emily and Christina, are, as she says herself, 'more or less the same person'; and both of them, even in their teens, are women, not girls. The last thing a Peyton heroine would ever be is girlish.

But Mrs Peyton can deal with large themes, and construct excellent plots if she is so minded. She can tell a story with great pace and certainty. In her historical, or semi-historical, novels her research appears impeccable, but she never gives the impression of bookishness; she knows in her fingers how to handle a boat or a horse, and one feels she would manage quite well in an ancient aeroplane. She has extended her territory book by book, and undoubtedly will extend it further. And there is one vital moment that occurs sooner or later in most of her novels and accounts for much of their depth and strength: the moment of rejoicing at simply being here, to love and suffer and take what comes. (p. 178)

> *John Rowe Townsend, "K. M. Peyton," in*

his A Sense of Story: Essays on Contemporary Writing for Children *(copyright © 1971 by John Rowe Townsend; reprinted by permission of J. B. Lippincott Company), Lippincott, 1971, pp. 172-78.*

THE BEETHOVEN MEDAL (British Edition, 1971; US Edition, 1972)

Ruth Hollis, quiet, but determined, with horizons stretching no farther than the nearest stable to be 'mucked out', meets Patrick Pennington, anti-authoritarian and sensitive, but possessing a driving force towards his musical goal that is often at odds with his spontaneous actions. This tenderly written account of their interest in and then love for one another, reminds us not only of the joys and tortures of adolescence, but of the complexity of facets that contribute to the makeup of a human being.

K. M. Peyton strides confidently back and forth across the bridge between classical music and pop—making no comparisons but allowing each its weight in one person's appreciation—and for this small aspect alone I would consider the book to be of value. But it is not this alone which prompts commendation. The author is a romantic writer, and for this she has been criticised—but those who have forgotten the bitter-sweetness of adolescent love, the shattering discovery of an author or a poet who says it *for* one, only better, the choking sight of a sunset or an endearing hole in a loved one's sock, will be thankful for these reminders. (p. 161)

> *Margot Petts, in* Children's Book Review *(© 1971 by Five Owls Press Ltd.; all rights reserved), October, 1971.*

The hero of Mrs. Peyton's *Pennington's Seventeenth Summer* is older now but not a lot wiser. He still carries a very large chip and has his temper under imperfect control. In one way he has developed appreciably. He is no longer a promising beginner as a pianist; he is a promising professional. *The Beethoven Medal* is the story of his debut.

Mrs. Peyton rings the changes cleverly by varying the viewpoint. Pennington is seen through the eyes of Ruth, a sweet, rather dotty schoolgirl. . . . Slowly Ruth realises—and Mrs. Peyton shows her dawning realisation most beautifully—that this is not just a handsome oaf but a young man with a foot in two different worlds. . . . Few writers deal more convincingly with the exquisite agony of growing up than Mrs. Peyton. She is perhaps better with Ruth than Pat; her portrait of a girl trembling on the brink and then leaping boldly in is not less tender for being a little amused. The Gas Board man, at the end of the story, says "It's great to be young", and Mrs. Peyton shows that it is both great and hell. There is a tiny hint of optimism in the conclusion; Pat is going to jail and Ruth will have a long wait for him, but they are persons of character and, in their ways, they will come out all right. It is a simple message in response to a complex situation, but the author has not over-simplified the solution. She writes, as ever, delightfully, sketching in the minor characters with a sure light touch, and catching the cadences of adolescent speech successfully.

Not a great book, by the standards of this writer, but a good one. It should find its readers, mainly among girls, and should help them a little to find a way through their own problems. (pp. 322-33)

The Junior Bookshelf, *October, 1971.*

Mrs Peyton, you simply have to take my word for it, is what stumped reviewers call "compulsively readable," You *have* to turn the page, hear the next conversation, see the next bit of action. *The Beethoven Medal*, from anguished (but funny) first page to anguished (but satisfactory) last, is a love story. Ruth, the heroine of *Fly-by-Night* (to me, the only readable horse book since *Black Beauty* and *At the Back of the North Wind*) meets Patrick, the hero of *Pennington's Seventeenth Summer* (have two novels been mixed like this before, incidentally?) and falls instantly, ferociously in love. One sees it from inside and outside, from Ruth's point of view and her mother's. The respectable, lower-middle-class family becomes inextricably tangled with the wild musical genius Pennington. Take the plot and it sounds like nothing in particular; in places like romantic moonshine. Pennington is to play in the Albert Hall, *and* spend nine months in gaol for hitting a policeman. It doesn't matter. Mrs. Peyton's plots, if you look closely at them, sometimes sound unlikely, but it's the method that counts—the exactness, the psychological accuracy, the grace and humour and cool, flowing ease of it all. (p. 688)

> *Louis Claibourne, in* The Spectator (© *1971 by* The Spectator; *reprinted by permission of* The Spectator), *November 13, 1971.*

A reader who knows Pat from *Pennington's Last Term* will instantly recognize [in *The Beethoven Medal*] Pat's outstanding social qualities: his total lack of social grace, his inability to express his real feelings for fear of exposing himself, his preoccupation with situations rather than people. In short, Pat is what every adolescent sees and admires in his peers: a free spirit living a perilous existence because of adult-inspired regulations. . . .

Much of the humor of *Pennington's Last Term* has been replaced by an aching awareness of adolescent desires in *The Beethoven Medal*. Mrs. Peyton's new book is a devastating indictment of Western European and American society, a society which traps a brilliant talent within the parochial boundaries of the lower-class. Pat is willing to work hard to gain desired goals at one moment, and just as willing to bend adult rules to fit immediate adolescent needs at the next. (pp. 1261-62)

Mrs. Peyton has created a very real conflict in *The Beethoven Medal*. How does a sixteen-year-old girl from a good middle-class home react when the young man she loves is imprisoned? . . .

[The] ending is believable because Mrs. Peyton's characters are believable. Human beings are a mass of contradictions. Mrs. Peyton has the considerable literary skill to portray this. She understands the emotional turbulence of adolescents and portrays this. An adolescent reader of *The Beethoven Medal* will appreciate Mrs. Peyton's skill at portraying young people as they really are. (p. 1262)

> *John W. Conner, in* English Journal (*copyright* © *1972 by The National Council of Teachers of English), November, 1972.*

OTHER CITATIONS

Naomi Lewis, in The Listener, *November 11, 1971, p. 661.*

Kirkus Reviews, *July 1, 1972, pp. 728-29.*

Zena Sutherland, in Bulletin of the Center for Children's Books, *September, 1972, p. 14.*

Marcus Crouch, in his The Nesbit Tradition: The Children's Novel in England 1945-1970, *Ernest Benn, 1972, p. 193.*

THE EDGE OF THE CLOUD (1969)

This sequel to "Flambards" follows the eloping Christina and Will, tracing their developing relationship until their marriage on the eve of the Great War. It is no longer Christina's horses but Will's frail aircraft which dominate the tale. Against an unobtrusive background of a changing society, shortly to be thrust into the twentieth century, Mrs. Peyton vividly depicts the fanatical dedication which characterised the enclosed world of the flying pioneers, with its camaraderie and fearless acceptance of lethal risks.

Christina has to come to terms with Will's absorption in this new life which at first leaves her lonely and excluded. The maturity with which she recognises and responds to her unassuming yet demanding role in the relationship lies at the centre of the story.

Despite a less obviously dramatic plot than some of Mrs. Peyton's previous novels, the book is utterly compelling. There is no villain to add a twist to the story, only the tension of sharing Christina's constant fear of the hazards of Will's chosen way of life. Her abject terror on the occasions when she flies with him is conveyed with an accuracy made all the more painful because she can never confess it to the uncomprehending Will. It is in this facility for conjuring up powerful physical sensation that Mrs. Peyton excels—not only in her climaxes of explosive action but in descriptions of fragile craft suspended in space, the changing landscape spread out below—or the exhilaration of the pilot as he matches his skill against the violent forces which threaten to tear his plane to pieces, the ghoulish holiday crowds at Hendon, faces turned up to watch the perilous acrobatics which are to end in tragedy.

It is the conjunction of this power to evoke a world in which we experience a vivid sense of participation, together with the subtle restraint in the handling of the central relationship, which makes this such a satisfying novel. (p. 83)

> *Miss E. von Schweinitz, in* Children's Book News (*copyright* © *1969 by Children's Book Centre Ltd.), March-April, 1969.*

OTHER CITATIONS

Margaret Meek, in The School Librarian, *June, 1969, p. 199.*

Kirkus Reviews, *November 1, 1969, p. 1155.*

Zena Sutherland, in Bulletin of the Center for Children's Books, *June, 1970, p. 165.*

FLAMBARDS (British Edition, 1967; US Edition, 1968)

It is perhaps the principal limitation of K. M. Peyton's work that she lacks [the] saving grace of humour. In her very fine novel *Flambards* she rends the reader's nerves with the sufferings of her heroine, and always legitimately, for Christina grows up into a difficult world. Just possibly the picture would not have been less authentic if the author had stood back and smiled, albeit wryly, at her creation.

Mrs. Peyton is an accomplished story teller. She is also a social historian. *Flambards,* which has a country scene in Edwardian days, is a story of two worlds, one dying, one struggling in its birth pangs. Christina, an orphan, goes to live with her uncle in Flambards, a decaying mansion in the hunting belt. Uncle Russell—a powerfully drawn figure nine-tenths sinister, one-tenth pathetic—has been crippled in a hunting accident and now lives vicariously in the exploits of his elder son Mark. The younger son, Will, breaks a leg in the first chapter and retires thankfully from the field. He is a boy of the new age, dedicated secretly with all his being to the world of flight. Between the two worlds is Christina, who loves hunting but hates the mindless world of the hunters. Mrs. Peyton follows her tenderly and with affection to the final breaking of the chains binding her to Flambards.

The choice of title suggests that Mrs. Peyton sees the house as the key to her story, and so in a way it is. There is a still moment among the turmoil of the action when Christina realizes that the house is dying, a symbol of "everything that was backward and ignorant". The symbolism is not laboured, and perhaps this is right; but a firmer hand with the story might have tightened it up and strengthened its conflicts. Nevertheless it gives, in the framework of an exciting tale, a convincing view of a vanished society, and shows too the timeless spirit of courage and resolution in the young heroine growing up to love and purposeful life in the face of daunting difficulties. (p. 1155)

> The Times Literary Supplement (© *Times Newspapers Ltd., 1967; reproduced from* The Times Literary Supplement *by permission), November 30, 1967.*

It is impossible to do justice to the subtleties of this book in a review. Mrs. Peyton's marvellous economy of style allows her to convey tensions, evoke period and realize character with deceptive ease. Only a master can achieve so much in less than two hundred pages. (p. 87)

> *Pamela Royds, in* The School Librarian and School Library Review, *March, 1968.*

Flambards is that rare thing, a good 'teenage romance— and more besides. . . . The years from 1908 are brilliantly evoked in this drama of brute force against creative power, or, if you like, of the old world against the new. The author's inventiveness never fails nor does her power to describe scene and action; the cross-country race which William interrupts on wings is unforgettable. Here is one of those versions of girlhood which can stand current at any period and for any reader. (p. 1050)

> *Margery Fisher, in her* Growing Point, *July, 1968.*

OTHER CITATIONS

Naomi Lewis, in New Statesman, *November 3, 1967, p. 600.*

Virginia Haviland, in The Horn Book Magazine, *December, 1968, p. 701.*

Madeleine L'Engle, in Book World, *Part II, December 29, 1968, p. 13.*

Marcus Crouch, in his The Nesbit Tradition: The Children's Novel in England 1945-1970, *Ernest Benn, 1972, pp. 177-79.*

FLAMBARDS IN SUMMER (British Edition, 1969; US Edition, 1970)

Though K. M. Peyton's *Flambards in Summer* is the third part of a trilogy, it stands perfectly well as an experience on its own. Necessary information—the relationship between Christina and Dick and Mark—is deftly touched in without any suggestion of the Wagnerian 'story so far'. This is not to say that the book is not greatly enriched by one's having read its predecessors (*Flambards* and *Edge of the Cloud*); indeed, the whole panorama of life at Flambards before and during the First World War is a major achievement in the genre of adolescent fiction. It is sustained storytelling of an order that has all but vanished from contemporary novels.

Flambards in Summer is concerned with rebirth. Christina, widowed at twenty-one, returns to a Flambards that is likewise widowed—and dying of neglect. Then, as her dead husband's child quickens within her, she resolves that Flambards itself should be reborn. Little by little this is glowingly achieved, with every incident extending the central idea. Christina's visit to Violet, the dismissed servant, to buy Mark's illegitimate son is a marvellous scene; and the subsequent relationship of the boy with Christina and Dick—again, something new growing—is most beautifully handled. To say that the novel ends happily is to give but little idea of the deeply satisfying way in which that end is arrived at. Mrs. Peyton's great skill in completing her spacious design leaves one with admiration and gratitude. Flambards and its inhabitants will be long remembered— and often revisited. (p. 600)

> *Leon Garfield, in* The Spectator (© *1969 by* The Spectator; *reprinted by permission of* The Spectator), *November 1, 1969.*

OTHER CITATIONS

The Times Literary Supplement, *October 16, 1969, p. 1199.*

Geoffrey Trease, in New Statesman, *October 31, 1969, p. 624.*

Miss E. von Schweinitz, in Children's Book News, *November-December, 1969, p. 329.*

Margaret Meek, in The School Librarian, *March, 1970, p. 85.*

Nancy Berkowitz, in School Library Journal, *January, 1971, pp. 61-2.*

THE FLAMBARDS TRILOGY: *Flambards; The Edge of the Cloud; Flambards in Summer*

[There] is little doubt that [Mrs. Peyton's] most impressive achievement is to be found in the *Flambards* trilogy, consisting of *Flambards, The Edge of the Cloud,* and *Flambards in Summer.* . . .

Any summary of these stories, each of which can be read

quite separately by the way, though it is obviously best to read them in their published order, is bound to risk doing the books a disservice from the danger of overemphasising their richly romantic structure—they do have young orphans, handsome cousins, ponies and a passionate elopement; but the risk is worth taking, partly because it is these elements which help to make the books popular with adolescents, and also because these elements . . . are beautifully integrated by Mrs. Peyton into a serious and sustained view both of adolescence and historical movement. The opening paragraphs of *Flambards,* for example, suggest a whole way of life through the evocative images of the foxhunt across the autumn meadows. But the presence of another and contrasting way of life, creating a source of major tension within the novel, is deftly suggested by the presence of the hedger standing sardonically by. (p. 196)

It is clear that Kathleen Peyton's books deal with themes and interests of a rather wider and deeper kind than one finds in most children's books. The presence of death, the awareness of sexual love, the importance of money, give her novels an unusual texture for which their romantic structures provide a successful and accessible framework.

Even more remarkable perhaps is her moving and perceptive account of English social history over the first two decades of this century, describing society as it was, how it changed, and what the nature of the changes were. Mrs. Peyton's particular focus, of course, is on the disappearance of a landed but under-capitalised gentry, whose traditions were such an inextricable mixture of grace and boorishness, and their replacement by an, on the whole, more democratic, more civilised, social class. Indeed in the anticipated marriage of Christina and Dick one sees Mrs. Peyton looking even further into the future in a scene not unlike the conclusion of [E. M. Forster's] *Howards End.*

It is the triumph of Mrs. Peyton's art that she evokes this sense of social transformation by means of a few richly-actualised symbols in a historical romance of highly popular elements. The horse-riding and Hunt Ball of the *ancien regime,* the free-and-easy social manners of the airfield, stand out as the two supreme images, of course, the one looking back, the other to the future. Not the least of Mrs. Peyton's successes is the way in which, while she confines her characters to a particular family group, her use of resonances delicately suggests the whole social fabric beyond them, as when Christina's friend Dorothy becomes a nurse in the war, or when Christina visits Dick's mother's slum cottage in the village, or when a maid is sacked for expecting an illegimate baby.

The most potent symbol of all is Christina herself, a young romantic heroine, orphaned, isolated in a house of strange men, a heiress, not afraid to elope with the man she loves, a girl who likes riding and wearing grand party dresses, and yet sensitive and alert to all the experiences around her. . . . [She] is realised both as a growing girl with emotional problems and as a filter of the social processes. . . . (pp. 198-200)

Dennis Butts, "Writers for Children: K. M. Peyton," in The Use of English *(© Chatto and Windus 1972), Spring, 1972, pp. 195-202.*

It is my contention that the Flambards trilogy, though a lively and enjoyable story, is, if judged like any other group of novels, very definitely not of the first rank. . . . (p. 5)

We have K M Peyton's word for it that she did not plan to write two or more volumes when she started *Flambards,* but if the trilogy is viewed as it stands it does look very much like something designed to be a commercial success. Suppose we were to set out to write a story for the respectable teenage market. We must aim at three parties in particular: girls, boys and teachers. Safe subjects to choose would be horses for girls, planes for boys and some fairly reliable history for teachers (then our book will be ordered by the school library). To work all three topics into one book is not easy: a trilogy would give us more scope and would look more impressive, without having the disadvantages of one fat volume. So we put horses into one book, planes into another, and tie up our plot in the third. But that means girls will not read book two nor boys book one. Solution: the horses are part of a masculine, hunting world, though seen through the eyes of a girl; and the same girl (she'll be the connecting link then) must somehow be got up in an aeroplane. A new snag arises. If she's nuts on horses, as she must be, why does she give up a whole volume to planes? Because she's in love, of course—she's got an aviator boyfriend who attracts her away from the stables to the hangars (chance for some vivid place descriptions here). And what gets her back to the horses in book three? Death of husband (she'll have to marry him, of course) naturally—aviators are easily disposed of. As for history, there's only one period in which both hunting and aviation were open to young amateurs and that's the years around 1914, before the decay of the country landowner and the introduction of strict rules about flying. There was a war then too, so that makes it even easier to dispose of aviators. . . .

Indeed, since the aviator is going to be killed, we can marry off the heroine to the groom when she goes back to the horses in book three. (pp. 5-6)

Mrs Peyton's insight into Christina's relationship with Will 'raises issues of fundamental significance to adolescent self-awareness', according to the chairman of the Carnegie Medal committee [Colin Ray; see excerpt below for his reply]. This dusty. mouthful of clichés is supposed to be a compliment; but any book can raise an issue and far too many do. Indeed, if the old sorcerers had been as good at raising the dead as we are at raising issues, they would have left scarcely a corpse underground. (pp. 6-7)

The Carnegie committee gave its medal to the second volume only—a revealing choice. Mr Ray admits that they found the third volume too complex. Established critical practice requires us to consider the trilogy as a whole, and in terms of the whole the second volume is the weakest link while the third is by far the best. The complexity of *Flambards in Summer,* which frightened off the committee, is an essential part of the trilogy and is quite well handled; the various themes of the three books are interwoven and resolved. (p. 7)

The central character of the trilogy, Christina Parsons, is one of those tough, sensible women that have abounded in English fiction ever since Emma Woodhouse. (One only has to think of Emma to perceive Christina's flatness.) We meet her first while she is still a girl of twelve, and within a few pages we have picked up enough clues to know how much depth there is to this portrait. 'Life has already dealt her some cruel surprises'; she shows 'iron self-will' and even takes 'a long, cool look'. She enters the story in—of course—a pony trap, driven by an old retainer into the estate which will be the background of the tale, a very useful way of introducing us to her, the estate and the old retainer, and one which proved its worth often enough in the last century. However, it is startling to find her apparently capable at the age of twelve of recognizing Flambards (which she has never seen before) as a 'mid Victorian pile'. Christina's age is a sham. From the start she is a young woman, and she belongs much more to our own time than to hers. These hackneyed phrases of character description are the language of the sixties and they set a tone which Mrs Peyton never quite suceeds in changing. This opening failure to make Christina really a child seriously weakens the first volume. Indeed, it weakens all three, because she never has a chance to grow up or to learn. The young mother and widow of the third book is no more mature in her understanding of the world than the girl in the ponytrap. She's a fine young filly but Mrs Peyton always has a hand on the leading rein. . . . (pp. 7-8)

Christina, like everybody else in the book, is certainly far from cowardly, but one wishes that her intelligence had functioned at a less equine level. Her inability to foresee the certain disaster into which she leads Dick, the groom, when she persuades him to rescue favourite horse from being fed to hounds, is barely credible. As soon as the rescue is discovered, Dick is sacked. She, like us, has had frequent hints that this would happen, but she has ignored them all: as usual, she neither foresees nor learns, unless such processes are required of her by the plot. Her lack of insight into the other characters is a useful excuse for superficial portrayals of them also. Her cousin Mark, for example, is seen entirely through her eyes and remains more or less incomprehensible because Christina herself never understands him. He is thus a much more successful character than she is, because we are less tempted to question his behaviour. (pp. 8-9)

Will is a victim of Mrs Peyton's plot. He has to be disposable and the story is not his tragedy, so we must be prevented from getting fond of him. He has to be left, by us as by his fellow characters, to his own devices. Eventually, he crashes. In fact he's shot down in the war, but he might as easily have been killed in a civil accident, and his death occurs between the second and third volumes. This is, I think, the greatest single weakness of the trilogy; the worst of all the 'cruel surprises' dealt to Christina by 'life' vanishes into the formless void that lies between two outside covers. If we had been faced squarely with Will's death, we should have seen at once that it wouldn't do. The smoothness of Christina's inevitable acceptance of Dick in the last volume would have been intolerable, for one thing, and the quality of writing the crisis would have called for would have shown up Mrs Peyton's shortcomings all too clearly. . . . The reader is . . . not allowed to feel the strain of the suffering that Will's death ought to have caused. Our feelings are spared because we must be free to enjoy the rest of the book. Pain is an embarrassment in fiction of this kind; the trilogy is about events, not minds. (pp. 9-10)

[Using] the war to get rid of both Will and Mark, Mrs Peyton can pair off Christina and Dick as ushers of the new classless dawn. On a personal level, this match shows again how Christina is led by the plot. She has treated Dick throughout with remarkable insensitivity. . . .

The status of servants is a major theme in the trilogy. . . . The master-servant relationship is a bad one; servants are ignored completely and only cooperate because they have to keep alive. . . .

It is difficult not to conclude that Mrs Peyton is deliberately trying to set up a microcosm of the social history of the 1914 period. Perhaps, indeed, this is the justification for any work of historical fiction, that it should show its characters as integral parts of their time. At any rate, I believe I am not the only reader of the trilogy who felt that one is expected to take the Flambards estate as representative of its period and to suppose, perhaps rather vaguely, that most masters treated their servants heartlessly, most country estates were decaying, and so on. In fact Flambards is a rarity. Thanks to the incompetence and sadism of its old owner, patterns of relationship and economics are breaking up before the war. Old Russell has the effect on the house that the war would have done. I do not myself find him a convincing character. His dismissal of Dick, the perfect groom, is a most unlikely act from a man obsessed with horses and hunting; and Will's acceptance of violent beatings from the grotesque old cripple, whom he could escape by simply going upstairs, is strangely unexplained. (p. 11)

Whether one finds Russell credible or not, however, does not affect the fact that Mrs Peyton does not let the war play its historical part. Servants ceased to exist largely as a result of social and economic forces which the war got moving, not because they were terrorized by men like Russell; and the decay of Flambards, well under way before the war, is not the typical case that it might appear to be a young reader. Similarly, Mrs Peyton's use of the war as a means of getting rid of redundant characters is brutally misleading. We actually find ourselves *glad* when Mark goes back to the Front after discovering a suitable fiancée; we forget that he is going to almost certain death. Christina gives barely a thought, it seems, to Dick's having joined the army, and her attitudes to war, beginning with exaggerated ignorance and developing through patriotic pride in Will to her final angry feeling that she can't understand war but that it's 'mere foolishness', are little more than a vague acknowledgment of introductions to various anthologies of war poetry in which these ideas are set out and documented. Wilfred Owen said that his *Strange Meeting* was about the 'Foolishness of War'. The comparison speaks for itself. Christina's conclusion is this: 'She wanted these things to make sense, and they didn't.' Is Mrs Peyton excusing herself for failing to examine the impact of the war more closely? She and Christina abandon the whole business. (p. 12)

[When] Flambards passes into Christina's hands, the old retainers are retained and new ones are added. Christina gives orders as sharply as any Russell and only behaves better than her relations because she happens to be sane. And her engagement to Dick, which seems at last to remove the class barriers, actually does nothing of the sort; it is just the good old traditional ending when the handsome poor boy marries the heiress—an evasion of the 'issue' worthy of any Victorian sentimental novelist. Under Christian, Flambards will have servants, horses and hunting as it always did; but I fear many readers will be duped into thinking that a revolution has occurred. (p. 13)

[If] the *Flambards* trilogy is meant to be seen as a microcosm of its time, then its refusal to face urban problems and its failure to grasp the significance of the war itself are weaknesses of a pretty serious kind. And Mrs Peyton really ought not to be allowed to get away with passing off a corny Victorian ending as a revolutionary change in the social order. It may be, however, that these matters receive only accidental emphasis in the trilogy; perhaps Mrs Peyton is really not concerned with topics beyond those of the technicalities of aviation and hunting. If that is the case, we must recognize that the trilogy is not of any importance as an historical novel. (p. 14)

> *Dominic Hibberd, "The Flambards Trilogy: Objections to a Winner," in* Children's Literature in Education (© *1972, APS Publications, Inc., New York; reprinted by permission of the publisher), No. 8 (July), 1972, pp. 5-15.*

The Carnegie Medal selection committee, and its chairman, change each year. There would be no point in resurrecting that which sat in the early part of 1970, were it not for the critical article by Dominic Hibberd in *Children's literature in education 8* [See excerpt above]. . . .

Mr Hibberd's complaint of my 'dusty mouthful of clichés' is unimportant, though he may agree that more can be said, more fully, in his eleven pages than in the brief paragraph in which I had to introduce the committee's choice. But what use does he make of his space?

He objects that Mrs Peyton doesn't discuss in any great depth the problems of war, the social history of the period, the wartime urban situation. He is, of course, right: she also fails to write a treatise on prewar economics, changes in agricultural technology and so on. One good reason for these 'failures' may be that this is a novel about a young woman growing up, and about her response to the external pressures and problems to which she is exposed. Whether Mr Hibberd finds this an interesting or a rewarding exercise, whether he believes in her responses, is a matter for him: but it seems unfair to complain that it isn't a different book. . . .

Another complaint is that the trilogy has a lot of matter about horses and aeroplanes, which many young people find interesting. Is that a bad thing? Are we to have a list of topics which, because they may encourage reading, should be avoided? For myself, I should be hard put to it to decide which of these two topics holds less interest for me: and yet I enjoyed the books. Does this suggest a 'sales appeal' approach? (p. 5)

The real trouble, I think, is that we are up against Mr Hibberd's 'critical standards'. These are not defined, but appear to be those of *literary* criticism. If he will refer to the terms of the Carnegie Medal, he will find that the award is for an 'outstanding' book. I would personally criticize that adjective as being vague: but one thing it does not explicitly mean is that the Medal is a literary award. Many previous choices for the Medal have been criticized precisely because of this fallacy.

What the committee seeks, in my experience, is a book, not necessarily breaking entirely new ground, but of the highest quality in its genre. And in considering quality, literary quality is only one aspect: its potential impact on the young reader, its ideas, its chances of being read, its individual aspects which make it stand out from the rest, all are relevant. The committee, of the year in question or of any other year, would not claim infallibility: it can bring to bear

only its accumulated knowledge of children's literature and the experience of children's reading of its members. But dogmatic statements, unjustified by any argument, that 'the third (volume) is by far the best' will hardly shake their confidence. (p. 6)

> *Colin Ray, "'The Edge of the Cloud'—a Reply to Dominic Hibberd," in* Children's Literature in Education (© *1972, APS Publications, Inc., New York; reprinted by permission of the publisher), No. 9 (November), 1972, pp. 5-6.*

FLY-BY-NIGHT (British Edition, 1968; US Edition, 1969)

Any story of a girl determined to take part in a gymkhana is calculated to antagonise me; so I can't say more in praise of K. M. Peyton's *Fly by Night* . . . than that I found myself appreciative and interested by the problems of Ruth and her obstinate, unschooled pony. She's a real person, not just an animated pair of jodhpurs, and the other people in the book are at least as important to her and to the reader as the animals. (p. 592)

> *Catherine Storr, in* New Statesman (© *1968 The Statesman & Nation Publishing Co. Ltd.), November 1, 1968.*

How [Ruth] overcomes apparently insurmountable financial problems and is finally accepted by the Pony Club on her own terms, makes absorbing reading, even for those who are not pony fanatics. Mrs. Peyton presents a realistic study of the difficulties confronting a new community in its efforts to become integrated with the "old order". This is a book to extend and widen the horizons of pony-book addicts and lead them on to new interests. Mrs. Peyton's own illustrations nicely complement this quietly excellent story. (pp. 329, 332)

> *Mrs. G. V. Barton, in* Children's Book News (*copyright* © *1968 by Children's Book Centre Ltd.), November-December, 1968.*

Kathleen Peyton's *Fly-by-Night* . . . may prove to be the very last of the pony books. It is certainly one of the best.

Pony stories were from the beginning middle-class. Young riders owned their ponies by unchallenged right; there was no vulgar show of money, and Pony Club subscriptions were paid by some unseen and disembodied daddy. Kathleen Peyton made her pony book into a social novel. The Hollises are middle-class, just about, and their lives are dominated by the need for money to pay the electricity and the mortgage. Ruth buys a pony out of her savings. This is utter folly, especially as she has no reserve for tack and feed. And where in a lower middle-class semi-rural suburban house do you keep a horse? Mrs Peyton faces the problems evoked by this situation with unfailing realism and great good-humour. Ruth has a terrible time, lightened by friendship and by an increasing strength of character. Here is a very ordinary girl, not at first particularly nice or intelligent, who gets through a difficult phase of life by her 'implacable will'. It is an appealing story, to be enjoyed by readers who, far from being conversant with the grim technicalities of riding, cannot with certainty distinguish one end of a horse from the other. There is much satisfaction when Ruth survives her ordeals. It would be an exaggeration to say that she triumphs; at least the white rosette which she gains at the local pony club meeting, while the most that probability would allow her, is the least that justice demands for someone so persistently mulish in pursuit of her ends.

Fly-by-Night, although undeniably about a pony, is only marginally a pony-book. Bigger issues, personal and social, keep breaking in. When Mrs Peyton turned again to examine the fortunes of her young heroine, ponies quickly disappeared and she wrote a serious social novel. (pp. 152-53)

> *Marcus Crouch, in his* The Nesbit Tradition: The Children's Novel in England 1945-1970 *(© Marcus Crouch 1972), Ernest Benn, 1972.*

OTHER CITATIONS

Kirkus Reviews, *March 15, 1969, p. 305.*

Joyce Baumholtz, in School Library Journal, *May, 1969, p. 92.*

Diane Farrell, in The Horn Book Magazine, *August, 1969, pp. 418-19.*

THE MAPLIN BIRD (British Edition, 1964; US Edition, 1965)

Toby and Emily, orphaned by an epidemic of cholera, find life in the unkind household of their uncle too degrading to bear, and escape in their father's battered fishing-smack, "My Alice." Making harbour in Southend, Emily in particular then finds that life in a stranger's town can be degrading too. Her hard-earned respectability as a housemaid lasts only for a short time. She and Toby seem fated to be involved in the affairs of "The Maplin Bird," the fast yacht hunted without success by the revenue cutters, and in the affairs of its owner, Adam, the smuggler.

The story is an exciting one, the plot sailing along at a good round pace, but its strength lies mainly in the quality of the writing. This lifts it head and shoulders above the majority of similar sea-smuggling stories. The characters are drawn with assurance and Emily's regard for Adam treated with sensitivity—but it is almost "The Maplin Bird" and "My Alice" and the Sea herself, who are the heroines. (p. 318)

The Junior Bookshelf, *November, 1964.*

The grim conditions of fishing in the Thames estuary in the 1870's are the background of this story which has no romantic softening of the hard lot of Toby and Emily Garland.... The climax of the wellsprung plot is magnificently done. The estuary scenery and details of seafaring are skilfully woven into the texture of the relationships. It is a strong unsentimental book in good prose. The illustrations and the jacket [by Victor G. Ambrus] sensitively catch the mood. Highly recommended.... (p. 92)

> *Margaret Meek, in* The School Librarian and School Library Review, *March, 1965.*

OTHER CITATIONS

Ruth Hill Viguers, in The Horn Book Magazine, *April, 1965, p. 177.*

Chicago Tribune Book Week, *May 9, 1965, p. 29.*

A PATTERN OF ROSES (British Edition, 1972; US Edition, 1973)

Modern children's novels usually compare very badly with the conciseness, wit, and psychological power of traditional stories and fables. In *A Pattern of Roses* Tim Ingrams finds drawings by a boy whose initials are the same as his own. He is intrigued by this unknown boy who died before his 16th birthday long ago in 1910, and this leads him on a quest which ends in better understanding of himself. Instead of a job in his father's advertising agency he ends up doing manual labour, which brings him 'perfect spiritual grace' a phrase which the author, who is addicted to expressions like 'Oh cripes', describes as 'corny'. Like her book in fact. (p. viii)

> *Lavinia Marina Learmont, in* Books and Bookmen *(© copyright Lavinia Marina Learmont 1972; reprinted with permission), November, 1972.*

Although this book returns to the Essex countryside and, in part, to the Edwardian period of some of Mrs. Peyton's earlier books it is new in subject-matter and mood.... As Tim's information [about Tom] grows so the reader is taken tactfully and smoothly into Tom's life. With great sureness of touch the spirit of the Edwardian village community, the hardships of farm-labouring for a talented boy, the material gulf between cottage and vicarage are vividly presented; and the two periods are made equally alive to the reader. They are brought close together in a dramatic and moving climax.

While initially the reader may be sceptical of Tim's consciousness of Tom, his character and circumstances and the handling of events make this convincing. Characterisation, as usual, is deft and observant and one of the themes of the book is Tim's growing recognition of what he wants in life and strength to break from the pattern created by his parents. Indirectly, the book comments on the search for contentment in life, the discomforts of adolescence, the relationship of past and present. The whole is a lively, warm, at times humorous, intriguing story which is likely to stay in the minds of its readers for some time. (p. 14)

> *Judith Aldridge, in* Children's Book Review *(© 1973 Five Owls Press Ltd.; all rights reserved), February, 1973.*

The author has long proved herself a master of novels of keen social observation, both of contemporary and past times. [In *A Pattern of Roses*] she combines these, attempting to move into a more uncertain world exploring the dimension of time distantly echoing the work of more lyrical writers such as Philippa Pearce. (pp. 71-2)

Both the worlds of the Edwardian and modern teenager are, as expected, finely portrayed. The book's weakness lies in its tentative approach to the spiritual relationship between the boys. The author has sought that delicate balance between the 'real' and the metaphysical that William Mayne so successfully captured in *A Game of Dark.* Her failure has resulted in the theme of the importance in life of self-fulfilment lacking credibility. (p. 72)

> *Gordon Parsons, in* The School Librarian, *March, 1973.*

Kathleen Peyton's earlier books have been outstanding, whether set in historical or contemporary times, for their realism and conviction; here she moves into fantasy with a sure touch, knitting the story of an adolescent boy of today with episodes from the turn of the century that link the lives of Tom and Netty, children of the Victorian era, with today's Tim. . . . The plot is adroitly constructed, the characters well-defined; although the book has some introspective passages that move slowly, this deliberation contributes to the understanding of Tim's slow gathering of enough courage to make his stand for the sort of quiet life he wants. (p. 49)

> *Zena Sutherland, in* Bulletin of the Center for Children's Books *(© 1973 by the University of Chicago; all rights reserved), November, 1973.*

OTHER CITATIONS

Nicholas Tucker, in New Statesman, *November 10, 1972, p. 692.*

Kirkus Reviews, *August 1, 1973, pp. 819-20.*

Ruth Robinson, in School Library Journal, *September, 1973, p. 85.*

Margery Fisher, in her Who's Who in Children's Books: A Treasury of the Familiar Characters of Childhood, *Holt, Rinehart and Winston, 1975, pp. 348, 351.*

PENNINGTON'S HEIR (British Edition, 1973; US Edition, 1974)

With a lesser writer the Pennington stories might be thought of as written "to meet a need", so closely do they match the hopes and fears and aspirations of many young people today. Mrs. Peyton however is not just writing for young adults; she is expressing something very important which she has to say about her world and at the same time finding out delightedly more about the two characters which she created—perhaps without too much thought to their futures—some years ago. Ruth and Pat are people who refuse to stay within the covers of the book; you bump into them in the street.

I will not summarise the story. In synopsis Mrs. Peyton's novels nearly always sound like novelettes. It is not in plot but in depth of characterisation and in the evocation of society that she excels. Let it suffice to say that Pat is out of jail, that he gets Ruth pregnant and marries her, not altogether reluctantly, and that the baby is named Franz Ludwig von Pennington. Pat is as aggressive and as professional as ever, and makes his way, not always upwards, in his career with no short cuts.

Although the book is theoretically self-contained, much of the point is missed without a knowledge of what happened before. This is no drawback. Young readers will need no inducement to go back to the beginning of the Pennington story—and return to it many times. A masterly book. (p. 43)

The Junior Bookshelf, *February, 1974.*

No girl who enjoys a good read will have missed *Pennington's Seventeenth Summer* and *The Beethoven Medal* which are the forerunners of this novel in which Pennington, out of prison now, fathers a child and Ruth becomes his wife. There is enough verisimilitude in the economic struggle, the posh Hampstead and Chelsea bit, and the

fierce fight the hero has with his unruly talent, to take this novel out of the mawkishness which occasionally threatens it. The ambiguity needs further exploration to give the story genuine 'adult' status; the threats are real enough at the beginning, but somehow are arranged away. Perhaps I hanker too much for the earlier Peyton novels. (p. 82)

> *Margaret Meek, in* The School Librarian, *March, 1974.*

Patrick Pennington is probably the most attractive hero ever to appear in romantic teen-age fiction. He has that whiff of brimstone, that touch of the ruined archangel that make characters like Heathcliff and Lymond (Dorothy Dunnett's hero) irresistible to women. . . . *Pennington's Seventeenth Summer* in which we first met him was a rare, marvellous book. Penn, the seventeen-year-old rebel, hating his last year at school, arrogant and surly, butting his head against authority, getting no help from his awful, feckless parents, was a totally believable teenager. . . . The book was a complete, rounded entity and I half wish Mrs. Peyton had stopped there.

But she had not finished with Patrick Pennington. The first part of *The Beethoven Medal* (in which Penn meets Ruth from *Fly-By-Night*) portrays perfectly the horsey girl growing out of ponies and into boys and shows Penn, torn between his interest in Ruth and the nagging demands of his talent. But the second half is melodramatic. . . . (p. 20)

Pennington's Heir starts on the day he comes out of prison. It opens with no concessions to new readers: 'Ruth did not know what was going to happen when Pat came out of prison.' What in fact happens is that in their joy at being together again, they make love with no precautions taken. Six weeks later, just as Penn is about to play to a most important man, Ruth tells him she is pregnant and he plays so badly that he loses his big chance. They survive the Professor's anger, Ruth's mother's sniffs of disapproval, get married and gradually make a go of it. A rather magaziney triangle situation develops as an old girlfriend with influence in the music world sets her cap at Pat. The parts about music are good and the characters, as always in this author's books, ring true, although the baby Lud, is just too easy to handle and too perfect to be real. Both Penn and Ruth learn a lot from their marriage. Ruth learns to protect Pat's talent from the mundane and he learns to accept compromise and to control his temper. Mrs. Peyton writes beautifully and triumphs over situations which in other hands would have been trite and Penn's fans will find this an absorbing book and their hero as entrancing as ever. (pp. 20-1)

> *Pamela T. Cleaver, in* Children's Book Review *(© 1974 Five Owls Press Ltd.; all rights reserved), Spring, 1974.*

OTHER CITATIONS

Beryl Robinson, in The Horn Book Magazine, *April, 1975, pp. 153-54.*

PENNINGTON'S LAST TERM (British Edition, 1970; US Edition, 1971)

In the award-winning Flambards trilogy K. M. Peyton created a work to be re-read with ever increasing respect and love. The eight eventful years that transform Christina from an insecure girl of twelve to a young widow anxious to bring back to life the decaying reminder of a once fine house are movingly described and firmly set in the times when the twentieth century was determinedly nudging to one side the relics of the past.

Pennington's Seventeenth Summer [published in the United States as *Pennington's Last Term*] represents a new departure which is unlikely perhaps to inspire similar loyalty. It covers one term in the school life of Patrick Pennington, a seething giant of a boy very much at odds with the world around him. . . .

Many teachers have puzzled and fumed over their Penningtons, trying to adjust to their wavelength (and hair-length), often with all too little success. Unfortunately their Penningtons have not Patrick's fine gift for music to come to their rescue. Here, I think, is the book's great weakness: the essential difficulty is too easily resolved. The climax where Pennington saves the life of the music master and then goes off to win the top award at the Northern Music Festival . . . seems a disconcertingly vivid reminder of school stories of long ago when the naughtiest girl or the most unpredictable boy at last made good. This may be dramatically satisfying but it does not convince. We learn on page 178 that Pennington plays the piano in Assembly. The surprise late announcement seems only there to provide the young man with the opportunity to get his own back on Soggy Marsh, a teacher who admittedly deserves all he receives. But it does not convince. Nor does the bucket booby trap earlier on. Too many of the characters seem around only to act as a foil to Pennington; some are just a name and nothing more.

K. M. Peyton illustrated the book herself and seems happier with the drawings than with the story. Just as Pennington seems ill at ease in his surroundings, I have the impression that his creator is too. If the story is to succeed, to convince, Pennington needs to be like other Penningtons in a school like other schools. (p. 233)

> *D. L. Rees, in* Children's Book News *(copyright © 1970 by Children's Book Centre Ltd.), September–October, 1970.*

This book is not only an outstandingly good one; it is of special value because it takes us so surely and honestly into an area which has barely been touched by fiction. Pennington, unlike Casper in [B. Hines's] *A Kestrel for a Knave,* is rescued from the educational scrap-heap, but *Pennington's Seventeenth Summer* is no less devastating in its revelation of the inability of a not untypical school to come to terms with a rough, difficult, but talented boy.

Most people over twelve will like the book very much. Teachers will either hail it as one they've been waiting for, or condemn it for its subversion, according to their orientation. (pp. 449-50)

> *Alex McLeod, in* The School Librarian, *December, 1970.*

English schoolboy rebels have enchanted American readers since *Tom Brown's School Days* (1875), where Thomas Hughes gave us East, the boy who believed "rules were made to be broken." Patrick Pennington, the 196-pound "hulk of a boy" who is the anti-hero of K. M. Peyton's novel, is the contemporary version of East—bitter, defiant, and self-destructive. . . .

Mrs. Peyton's dialogue is crisp and her scenes of working-class neighborhoods vivid; but her adult characters lack the depth to offer meaningful counterpoint to her formidable adolescents. This weakness unfortunately detracts from the resolution of her story. Arriving in time to offer some hope for Penn to realize his musical talent, Professor Hampton, "the finest teacher of pianoforte in the country," is so thinly characterized he seems less a sympathetic adult than a *deus ex machina*—a device this talented author hardly intended. (p. 18)

> *Sidney Offit, in* Book World—Chicago Tribune, *Part 2 (© 1971 Postrib Corp.), May 9, 1971.*

Occasionally a surpassing adolescent novel is published. This season it is Kathleen Peyton's *Pennington's Last Term.* . . .

Patrick Pennington is bigger-than-life-size in everything he does, but a reader readily accepts this because Penn's reactions to life are honest ones. . . . He is an English school boy, but his adolescent outlook is synonymous with the outlook of youth on this side of the Atlantic.

Much of the charm in *Pennington's Last Term* can be attributed to Mrs. Peyton's syntactical style. She describes each new character in a few, precise, descriptive words, then develops the character through interaction with others in the novel. Some of her characters are stereotypes, purposefully developed that way because they are indicative of what Penn *thinks* they are like. And this is Penn's novel, page after page. Adults and adolescents move through the story with him, but as foils for his escapades.

Under the exterior bravado Penn is as insecure as any other teenager. Knowing that he is insecure, a reader applauds Penn's attempts to preserve his cool unconcerned appearance. Never does a reader doubt that Penn will succeed. He is a natural winner because he can sight his goal and concentrate on achieving it, despite obstacles and other interests which he should be attending to. Pat Pennington is charmingly unaware of his own abilities. Perhaps his most difficult super-adolescent quality to accept is his unhesitating honesty. But this quality in Penn dramatically exaggerates the adult hypocrisy under which Penn chafes.

Pennington's Last Term will be read and reread by adolescents who search for a hero who sees life in their own terms. I urge adults to enjoy his adventures too! (pp. 1156-57)

> *John W. Conner, in* English Journal *(copyright © 1971 by The National Council of Teachers of English), November, 1971.*

OTHER CITATIONS

The Junior Bookshelf, *October, 1970, p. 306.*

The Times Literary Supplement, *October 30, 1970, p. 1258.*

Sheryl B. Andrews, in The Horn Book Magazine, *August, 1971, pp. 390-91.*

Marcus Crouch, in his The Nesbit Tradition: The Children's Novel in England 1945-1970, *Ernest Benn, 1972, pp. 169-70.*

THE PLAN FOR BIRDMARSH (British Edition, 1965; US Edition, 1966)

The eastern lowlands of England have been peculiarly potent in their appeal to writers for children. K. M. Peyton has recently joined [Arthur] Ransome and others in finding adventure as well as beauty among the mud wastes and the reeds. Her latest book is *The Plan for Birdsmarsh* in which her deep feeling for the haunted creeks of the Essex estuaries is at the service of a good tale and a better study of personalities.

Birdsmarsh is a village and a farm at the mouth of the Blackwater. It means something different to each of the characters in the story. Gus sees the absurd Mr. Winnington and his wicked uncle, and indeed these are a small price to pay for so mature, wise and evocative a book. (p. 1139)

> The Times Literary Supplement (© *Times Newspapers Ltd., 1965; reproduced from* The Times Literary Supplement *by permission), December 9, 1965.*

[An] outstanding book from England about a troubled boy is K. M. Peyton's *The Plan for Birdsmarsh* . . . , a story about a boy's deep disappointment when his father sold his property for a marina. Paul had always counted on carrying on the family farm that lay between the village of Birdmarsh and the sea. The well-developed plot includes a mystery involving the life-saving suit Paul's older brother Chris had invented, and comes to an exciting climax. Even more unforgettable, however, and the turning point in Paul's maturing, is the situation when, quite by accident he—not Chris—tests the suit for thirty-three hours in a fog-bound sea. Many stories have been concerned with the changes to the landscape of England by housing and industrial developments, and by the influx of city people to English coastal farming country. Few have the interesting characterizations and the excitement of this one. (p. 596)

> *Ruth Hill Viguers, in* A Critical History of Children's Literature, *by Cornelia Meigs, Anne Thaxter Eaton, Elizabeth Nesbitt, and Ruth Hill Viguers, edited by Cornelia Meigs (copyright © 1953, 1969 by Macmillan Publishing Co., Inc.), revised edition, Macmillan, 1969.*

OTHER CITATIONS

The Junior Bookshelf, *February, 1966, p. 50.*

Lavinia Russ, in Publishers Weekly, *April 18, 1966, p. 111.*

THUNDER IN THE SKY (British Edition, 1966; US Edition, 1967)

Another Peyton for the Carnegie stakes and a remarkable book on many counts, needing no medal to show its quality. The author sees the world of a boy on a sailing barge in the early days of World War I completely and makes it into compelling reading. The youngest of three brothers, full of the spirit of the time, envies Manny in the trenches and cannot understand Gil, who is old enough to join up and in no hurry to do so. . . . [The] book is full of relish for life, especially the hard dirty life of sailing barges loaded with coal or munitions; the specialised terminology is no barrier and respect grows for the men and boys who handled such craft in such conditions. There is plenty of suspense and action here for those who want adventure first and foremost, but Mrs. Peyton's special achievement this time is capturing the truth of 1914 in terms comprehensible to readers of twelve and up. (p. 388)

> The Junior Bookshelf, *December, 1966.*

The setting of the story, chiefly on the waterways of Britain, is familiar to readers of *The Maplin Bird, Sea Fever,* and *The Plan for Birdsmarsh;* the mood and plot are, however, very different. Mrs. Peyton's ability to tell a gripping story and to create living characters is just as evident as in the earlier books. Even stronger in this one are the overtones: the delicate balance between fear and courage, so sharply defined in the minds of adolescents, can so easily in their groping hearts be weighted toward sacrifice. The rather surprising but inevitable ending, which will satisfy almost every young male reader, has the poignancy to move older ones very deeply. (p. 355)

> *Ruth Hill Viguers, in* The Horn Book Magazine *(copyright © 1967, by The Horn Book, Inc., Boston), June, 1967.*

OTHER CITATIONS

Gordon Parsons, in The School Librarian, *March, 1967, p. 86.*

Taliafero Boatwright, in Chicago Tribune Book Week, *June 4, 1967, p. 14.*

S

SCARRY, Richard   1919-

Richard Scarry is an American author-illustrator of books for children. He repeatedly combines humor and education in detailed pictures, full of activity and anthropomorphic animal characters. Although critics differ in their attitudes towards Scarry's work, his books have been internationally popular, with translations in 28 different languages. (See also *Contemporary Authors*, Vols. 17-20, rev. ed. and *Something About the Author*, Vol. 2.)

GENERAL COMMENTARY

[Roberta Miller, a former senior editor at Golden Press] has said that "the one thing merchandise books cannot do is provide just the right book for Suzy"—meaning that books which seek a common denominator for multitudes of children cannot hope to appeal to the individuality of any given one—Richard Scarry has managed to get around this problem by covering all contingencies in his books. When Scarry depicts houses, foods, trucks, boats, etc., he provides so many specific varieties within the general category that he usually manages to hit the very truck, house or boat that speaks volumes to any given small viewer. This probably explains why so many young children will pore over his busy, narrative illustrations, by themselves, for unnaturally long periods of time. (pp. 122-23)

> *Selma G. Lanes, in her* Down the Rabbit Hole: Adventures and Misadventures in the Realm of Children's Literature *(copyright © 1971 by Selma G. Lanes; reprinted by permission of Atheneum Publishers, New York), Atheneum, 1972.*

In spite of their popularity with small readers, the books of Richard Scarry are not always liked by parents or recognized by reviewers. Some form of intellectual snobbery is responsible. Many of the Scarry books are what is known as "mass market" or "merchandise" books, whose appeal is visual rather than literary. . . .

The Scarry books might be described as mass market books par excellence; they have the necessary bright covers and plentiful pictures, and they deal with such familiar subjects as supermarkets, schools, cars, trains, buses, and boats. (p. 124)

But there are delightful touches of imagination. (p. 125)

Another reason for their popularity is that the Scarry books have something of the runaway appeal of the comics. "In most of my books, you can follow the pictures one after the other, basically the same as you would a comic strip," Scarry says. Children like action and the comics give them plenty. And so does Richard Scarry. (p. 127)

> *Norah Smaridge, "Richard Scarry," in her* Famous Author-Illustrators for Young People *(copyright © 1973 by Norah Smaridge; reprinted by permission of Dodd, Mead and Company Inc.), Dodd, Mead, 1973, pp. 124-29.*

"Books are fun!" These three words, stretched out along a pink streamer flying in the wind behind Wrong Way Roger's red aeroplane (on the back cover of Richard Scarry's *What Do People Do All Day?*) are Scarry's slogan. (p. 42)

Every page of a Scarry book is crammed to capacity with animals dressed like human beings busily engaged in human activities, with words (not just text, but labels too), with fun and with good sense. Yet every page is carefully planned, every drawing absolutely clear, every character consistent, every piece of advice—"FINISH YOUR MEALS", "TRY TO BE GOOD"—the kind most parents would applaud.

Scarry is popular. Kids clamour for him because he gives them what they want: pictures, activity, words, humour— and information aplenty. How fortunate that an artist with the supreme ability to entertain is also a man who takes his work seriously: he cares about children, not in the sentimental way but, as he put it, "You have to treat a two-year-old child with as much respect as the Queen of England." His sincerity could never be in doubt, but proof of it is his resistance to the blandishments and dollars of American television companies who want to screen his stories. "We'd only take an hour of your time to discuss it," pleaded one network. "We'd do all the adaptation ourselves." But Scarry insists, "I'll spend a lot of time doing my own adaptations when the right moment comes." (pp. 42-3)

Richard Scarry is a modest man with a proper sense of perspective. Large, bear-like, deep-voiced and in deadly earnest about fun, he has a gusty laugh which wells up from the hollows of his lungs and punctuates his philosophy at the most unexpected moments. . . .

Scarry can afford to laugh. He laughs gently, with a tinge of sadness, at those librarians in the States who are reluctant to stock his books because they are available in the super-market. What kind of a policy is this? he asks. If kids want to read Scarry and Scarry is not only teaching them to read and to find out about house building, baking, farming, transport, hospitals and the postal service (just a few of the occupations covered in *What Do People Do All Day?*) but also helping them to discover that BOOKS ARE FUN, why *not* put them in libraries? (p. 43)

Scarry genuinely believes that the *A B C* with a large beau-tifully painted apple opposite 'A' 'a' is cheating the child of a huge amount of stimulating entertainment. . . . Scarry's approach is a skilful adaptation of everyman's approach and therefore deserves, I would have thought, everyman's —and that includes every librarian's—support.

To me Scarry books have a connection with the tradition of the old comics; but Richard Scarry, brought up in the States without *Chick's Own* on Tuesdays and *Rainbow*, which made every Wednesday morning one to be looked forward to, resists attempts to tie him to the comic tradi-tion. He sees comics as mainly for adolescents and adults— loves *Good ol' Charlie Brown*, admires the later *Tintin*, finds *Asterix* sophisticated but too crude for his taste—and thinks *Rupert Bear* the only acceptable strip character for kids.

Why does *he* use animals instead of people in his books? "I use animals rather than humans firstly because they're more fun and it's easier to distinguish one character from another if one is a rabbit and the other a cat than if both are boys. Also children of all races will identify more easily with a bear or a goat doing this, that or the other, than they will with a child of a different colour. If a black child sees a Japanese child in a picture of a classroom he'll say to him-self 'That's not me'. But if he sees a goat learning to read, the problem of colour and identity just doesn't arise."

Because all Scarry's books have a joyful, simple atmos-phere about them, one might imagine his use of accompany-ing words to be merely basic. Not at all. Richard Scarry is contemptuous of "controlled vocabulary" schemes. "Kids don't talk in controlled vocabulary," he says. . . . What Scarry does is to use the opportunity his pictures offer to introduce the child to as many new words as possible. (pp. 44-5)

It was in connection with the alphabet page in the middle of the *Best Word Book Ever* that Richard Scarry received an angry letter from a mother complaining that for 'X' he had used the word *Xiphias* next to a picture of a xiphias—a kind of sword-fish—instead of harnessing the letter 'X' to the well-worn, over-played *Xylophone*. It had caused a great stir in her house, she said. No one knew what a xiphias was. They had had to go to a great deal of trouble to find out. Scarry's reaction was characteristic: "Makes me really happy to think that that woman's kid will go through life till he lives to be ninety or a hundred never forgetting what a xiphias is!" (Again, the infectious laugh.)

The virtue of Scarry books is that children of almost any age look at them absorbed for hours. Very small children look at the pictures—hundreds of them, as many on one page as other artists use in a whole book. Children learning to read puzzle out the labels under the recognizable pic-tures of objects—"sand", "car", "rake", "drum",

"socks". Older children read the text and follow the mar-vellous diagrams . . . or they read the hilarious *Funniest Story Book Ever* to their younger brothers and sisters, en-joying every word of it themselves.

Totally unpretentious, bubbling with humour, alive with activity, peppered with words of wisdom and corny jokes ("All kids go through a corny joke stage," says Richard, "so I put in a few here and there"), Scarry books are a marvellous combination of entertainment, always on a child's level, and incidental instruction. They occupy a unique place in the learning-to-read process. Their bulky, ebullient presence in supermarket, bookshop, library and sitting-room (every floor should have one) indicate that for children Scarry is supreme and that he is getting his mes-sage across good and strong. BOOKS ARE FUN! (pp. 45-6)

Elaine Moss, "Richard Scarry," in Signal *(copyright © 1974 by Elaine Moss; reprinted by permission of the author and The Thim-ble Press, Lockwood Station Road, South Woodchester, Glos. GL5 5EQ, England), January, 1974, pp. 42-6.*

BEST WORD BOOK EVER (1963)

Of all the picture dictionaries on the market (and on library and preschool classroom shelves) Richard Scarry's *Best Word Book Ever* is probably the most blatant example of [the] phenomenon of erasing most of 51 per cent of the population. Since Scarry's sales have exceeded the million mark . . ., I assume he is also erasing about 500,000 of his young readers.

By using marvelously humorous animals to help define words, he does avoid the insidious racism of most of the other books which consistently show Anglo-Saxon looking people and use Anglo-Saxon names. But he does make it very possible for us to tell which animals are male and which are female. The few females that do turn up in his pages are clearly labeled with aprons, ribbons and skirts. They are found in the following numbers in these sections:

At the Playground	32 boys	11 girls
Using Tools	10 boys	0 girls
Toys	14 boys	2 girls
Boats and Ships	13 boys	0 girls
Making Music	24 boys	2 girls
Making Things Grow	4 boys	0 girls
At the Airport	11 boys	1 girl

And on and on and on. Others might come up with slightly different counts since some animals have no clothes or are very small. I won't quibble since the ratios are still very dramatic. The lexicographer's computer found that "over-all the ratio in schoolbooks of *he* to *she, him* to *her* was almost 4 to 1." Scarry usually does much worse than that.

The Best Word Book Ever can certainly leave its young readers wondering just what little girls and women do do. Well, in *When You Grow Up* Scarry shows us that females can be secretaries, singers, teachers, dancers, librarians and mommies; in *Health,* he shows us a nurse and a dental hygienist. So girls can have jobs, but they don't do much playing, planting, making things or going places. In *Things We Do,* while 32 male animals are pursuing a whole host of life-sustaining activities (riding bikes, driving cars, planting and selling food), the two females on the pages are used to illustrate the activities "sitting" and "watching." (p. 2)

> *Barbara A. Schram, in* Interracial Books for Children *(reprinted by permission of* The Bulletin—Interracial Books for Children, *1841 Broadway, New York, N.Y. 10023), Vol. 5, No. 6, 1974.*

One of the best-selling children's books today (and for the past ten years) is an identification book. *Best Word Book Ever . . .* is immodestly titled by its author, Richard Scarry, one of the world's best-selling super-stars of children's literature. Scarry has a formula and it works. But formula or no, Richard Scarry has fun with his books and his books are fun, as attested by the volume of sales of his many titles.

His format consists of pages crammed full of anthropomorphic animals engaged in all sorts of human activities. Adjoining almost every animal-person and object is a printed word defining it. The number of things and the finite detail represented on each page defy credulity. It borders on chaos and the kids love it. Richard Scarry's books tend to wear out rather than be outgrown, for each reading brings discovery of things overlooked in previous readings, and are returned to again and again.

Once asked if he was an educational writer disguised as a fun-man or a fun-man disguised as an educator, he replied that he was a fun-man disguised as an educator. The reply was an apt one; his books do educate. (p. 58)

> *Barbara Karlin, in* West Coast Review of Books *(copyright 1975 by Rapport Publishing Co., Inc.), Vol. 2, No. 1 (December, 1975).*

OTHER CITATIONS

Books for Your Children, *January, 1976, p. 14.*

BUSIEST PEOPLE EVER (1976)

"Busiest People Ever" is a hymn to employment if ever there was one, with all these little workaholics of the animal kingdom going at their specialized tasks (hay baler, hay lifter, grass mower) with a nearly obsessed vengeance. People who aren't actually involved in gainful employment get called by the name of whatever they are incidentally doing at the time—Banana Eater, Lazy Fisherman, Sandwich Eater. It brings to mind an issue of Time magazine in which a rapist was called Rapist John Smith, as though it were a job you could get from a want ad.

The two characters who travel through this vocational hothouse are Lowly Worm and Huckle Cat. Lowly has the protean ability to adopt necessary skills that retrieve each new misadventure from disaster. He catches a thief, saves a drowning hippo and averts a train wreck—but no sooner has he done these things than he is given encomiums to his paraprofessional talents. "Good work, Sea Captain Lowly," he is told. On the basis of one TV appearance he is hailed as "a television entertainer." At another point the book says, "Lowly is certainly a good railroad worker, isn't he?" And later: "Very good thinking, Policeman Lowly." After so much prodding, it is a relief to hear

Lowly tell us roguishly that when he's grown up he'd best of all like to be an apple-pie eater.

The book gives us page after colorful page of jampacked scenic activity of the familiar Scarry sort—so much so that the main characters often are hard to find in the confusion. But the message is easy to locate, and that is: Do your own division-of-labor thing or else.

The or else side of the picture is embodied in a klutzy pig called Mr. Frumble, who does every single thing wrong. He bumps into a fire hydrant, walks on wet cement and breaks the scales that weigh him. Even when he innocently tries to put out a fire, it turns out to be a chef's fire cooking some flaming bananas. Mr. Frumble's problem isn't hard to identify—he's out of work, and the devil provides a packet of failure for such people. Frumble is the odd pig out among the industrious people who have found themselves. Lowly, the achiever, scolds him: "How did you ever get your car on that new road, it's not yet ready for drivers. Get off immediately. You certainly have had a bad day, haven't you Mr. Frumble. It's about time you went home before you cause any more trouble." Also laundresses, doctors, tow-truck operators and the omniscient narrator take him to task for his failure to adjust.

But where many books help children to understand and work out their confrontations with bad luck and incompetence, Scarry leaves old Frumble in a disturbing no-pig's-land, in which he is put down as a failure by the jolly workers around him. The book doesn't allow either comfortable identification with or understanding of Frumble; rather, it teaches that it's better to set your sights on operating a forklift than to bumble around in your identity in Frumble's manner, because no one likes people like that.

As Book Reviewer, I must confess that this book left me with some doubts. Though as a Mother, a role that I play until suppertime, when I become the Cook, I could appreciate its excitement and its cuteness. My children, who sometimes wear the hats of Violin Student and Piano Student, seem to like the way the pictures put every buzzing inch of the universe in its place; and they get pleasure, even comfort, from knowing that nothing hangs in limbo, and everything has a name. Never a Zen moment in Scarry land. (p. 44)

> *Mopsy Strange Kennedy, in* The New York Times Book Review *(© 1976 by The New York Times Company; reprinted by permission), November 14, 1976.*

FUNNIEST STORYBOOK EVER (1972)

Funny perhaps to fans of Scarry's overbusy illustrations and slapstick situations, but pretty forced and foolish to the rest of us. Mr. Raccoon's Bad Day consists of such uninventive disasters as ripping his pants, getting a flat tire, stepping into a manhole, and for a finale breaking the bed when he gives up and turns in. Then there is the pig who keeps driving off in the wrong car (police car, fire truck, etc.), the gorilla who steals bananas, the rabbit who is stuck in the muck, and the incompetent Mr. Fixit who consistently aggravates the mechanical and plumbing problems he's called to fix. This might be the lamest Scarry ever—but more likely we've simply been subjected to too much of it. (p. 1095)

Kirkus Reviews *(copyright © 1972 The Kirkus Service, Inc.), September 15, 1972.*

Much as water seeks its own level, each new Richard Scarry picture-and-word compendium unerringly finds its audience—almost any child between the ages of 3 and 6. The ideal Scarry viewer can be counted on to devote from 15 to 30 rapt minutes poring over one or another of the illustrator-author's bright and busy outsized volumes. It matters little which. Like Volkswagens, this year's model looks a good deal like last year's—or next year's.

While it is true that between Scarry's first giant encyclopedia—"Best Word Book Ever," done for Golden Press in 1963—and the present shiny-covered 1972 version, their creator has ingeniously perfected the art of cramming more and more action-packed pictures onto each double-page spread, the basic formula remains unaltered. Take a surfeit of such everyday exotica as steamrollers, cement mixers, fire engines, tug boats, carpenter's tools and even household utensils; provide enough winsome animals to keep them all in constant motion within simple-minded plots; and you can't lose with the preschool set.

Ardent feminists may well scorn Scarry's retrograde attitude toward the females of almost every species. To a woman, they are apron-wearers, shopping-cart toters or passively-smiling onlookers. But any girl child with the gumption to yen for a steam shovel of her own when she grows up probably won't balk at identifying with the male pig now in the driver's seat.

Crowding Mother Goose in the affection of his admirers, Scarry has developed his own stable of familiar characters who reappear from volume to volume. There's Huckle, the lederhosen-clad cat; Bananas Gorilla, a lovable mafioso, and the indomitably resourceful and dignified Lowly Worm, among others. Even snippets of plot and locale from previous Scarry books have begun occasionally to turn up.

No child is likely to have noticed, of course, but the fact is that Scarry's lively albums are not improving year by year. The present work's 15 separate stories constantly strain, Keystone-Kops fashion, for the laughs the title promises: Cars careen and crash; boats capsize; characters walk off piers or fall into the soup—all to tickle the easily-wooed risibility of the primitive child. Yet, "Uncle Willie and the Pirates" is the single offering that comes close to being a bona fide story.

Scarry is at his best in those of his books which have some vaguely discernible didactic aim. The artist's real talent is as a compelling graphic cataloguer of the obvious, a depictor of every object imaginable to entrance small kids. "Best Word Book Ever" had the simple virtue of jam-packing 1,400 separate objects into appropriate groupings for identification. "Storybook Dictionary," too, pictures 1,000 useful words in helpful contexts. The present volume, however, relies more heavily on the author's prose, which is rather like picnic flatware—not beautiful, merely serviceable. ("She will certainly be surprised when she sees her new car, won't she?" or "He wasn't looking at the workmen, who were making a new, hot, sticky, gooey street.") Despite the fact that it is shorter than the usual Scarry collection, the work exhibits a mildly desperate quality that grows wearisome before the end is reached.

In sum, the current book is not the biggest, best, or even—

as advertised—the funniest Scarry ever. But, for those who love him—and the number grows annually—it is simply the newest, and that is probably superlative enough. (p. 8)

Selma Lanes, in The New York Times Book Review *(© 1972 by The New York Times Company; reprinted by permission), October 1, 1972.*

OTHER CITATIONS

Zena Sutherland, in Bulletin of the Center for Children's Books, *March, 1973, p. 112.*

NICKY GOES TO THE DOCTOR (1972)

Writing about Richard Scarry is like writing about a corporate entity; his books are such big-time sellers that they evoke practically ideological reactions. Many of Scarry's books have been reviewed in these pages. *Busy, Busy World* was most recently described in a letter to the editor by Debbie Stead as "a celebration of stereotypes" (Vol. 6, Nos. 3&4). Nevertheless, I think I came to this book with an open mind.

Hero Nicky [of *Nicky Goes to the Doctor*] is an anthropomorphized rabbit. Everybody in Nicky's rabbit family looks more or less the same. . . . Is all this sameness a code message for individual and racial uniformity among humans? Although it is not, in this reviewer's opinion, the obligation of every book to consciously carry a political banner, books do nevertheless embody messages. The cumulative effect of books like this may be more insidious than people realize.

The story is about Nicky Bunny's mother taking him to the bunny doctor for a physical checkup. . . . The book is a study in sexist attitudes:

1. Of course, the "Dr. Doctor" is a man; his nurse a female, referred to only as "the doctor's nurse" (no name, however inane, for her; no capital letters). She greets Nicky and his mother at the door; both she and his mother are wearing aprons. . . .

2. Nicky and his mother come home to find Mr. Bunny mowing the lawn (a traditional male role if ever there was one in America). With Nicky sitting right there, Mrs. Bunny tells Mr. Bunny what the doctor said (i.e., that Nicky had grown a great deal). And what is Mr. Bunny's response to this? He says, "Just keep it up. Some day you'll be taller than I am." This incident embodies, in my opinion, several sexist and psychologically destructive attitudes and practices: the child has contact with his father through his mother, the mother feels she is fulfilling her role as wife and mother by interceding in this way, the father relates to the child narcissistically, that is, in terms of his, rather than the child's, ego.

3. On the next to final page, the reader finds out that Nicky is only one of a family of *34* children. In the light of this over-spawned family, it becomes all the more sexist to see Mrs. Bunny taking charge of everything. . . . It is easy to believe that Mr. Bunny never helps when one contemplates the final picture in the book. Mrs. Bunny is standing in the midst of her brood, her hands outstretched, apron intact, enjoining them to be patient and wait their turn for her to take each to the doctor. Mr. Bunny, in the same picture, is

standing alone in the upper right-hand corner (a spot the eye focuses on in this culture; it is where the lead article in every newspaper is placed). He is standing with his hands behind his back, silently contemplating but not participating in his family's world.

The book does not make the most of its potential to teach. This is, after all, a slim story about a visit to a doctor, an experience many children fear. Why not include a little basic biology along with the reassurance? The two pages where the doctor uses a stethoscope are the only ones where an attempt is made to give reasons or descriptions for any physical processes, though it is by no means explained why the doctor listens to Nicky's lungs by putting the stethoscope on his back. Children are not born knowing any human biology; many parents do not have the information or ability to explain anatomy to them. Why wait until school when a book like this could so easily incorporate this kind of information? Why not, at the same time, take the obvious opportunity to demystify the expertise of the medical profession? I feel Mr. Scarry should take his educational responsibilities more seriously.

One last comment—about the drawings. They are clear, humorous and have the kind of openness, definition and animation that have so endeared Mr. Scarry to children. (p. 3)

> *Marcia Newfield, in* Interracial Books for Children Bulletin *(reprinted by permission of* Interracial Books for Children Bulletin, *1841 Broadway, New York, N.Y. 10023), Vol. 6, Nos. 5 & 6, 1975.*

OTHER CITATIONS

Elizabeth L. Miller, in School Library Journal, *February, 1973, p. 63.*

RICHARD SCARRY'S ANIMAL NURSERY TALES (1975)

Little Red Riding Hood and Goldilocks are both cats [in *Richard Scarry's Animal Nursery Tales*], the gingerbread boy's creators are pigs, the teeny-tiny woman a mouse, and in Scarry tradition all the animals—including the three pigs, three billy goats gruff, little red hen, and others—are clothed, squat and dumb looking. Though these pages aren't as frenetically cluttered as many of Scarry's, they're just as crass—only compare Raymond Briggs' 1972 *Fairy Tale Treasury* illustrations, which are just as popular in style and immediately accessible but far more expressive. (p. 710)

> Kirkus Reviews *(copyright © 1975 The Kirkus Service, Inc.), July 1, 1975.*

Scarry's cartoonish animal characters may appeal to preschoolers, but anyone over six does grow tired of seeing those placid faces in every illustration. Because the expressions never seem to change, all the stories lose their original dramatic appeal. Furthermore, Scarry includes "The Teeny-Tiny Woman" and "The Three Wishes" although neither was originally an animal folk tale, and he needlessly changes the details to suit himself (e.g., the three Billy Goats Gruff eat berries instead of grass). Scarry's books are usually available to parents at local bookstores and are readily bought as inexpensive presents; libraries should

save their money and purchase more worthwhile modern editions of folk tales. (p. 64)

> *Jill P. May, in* School Library Journal *(reprinted from the April, 1976, issue of* School Library Journal, *published by R. R. Bowker Company, a Xerox company; copyright © 1976 by Xerox Corporation), April, 1976.*

RICHARD SCARRY'S COLOR BOOK (1976)

Richard Scarry's Color Book will more than likely be a smashing success with young preschoolers. Although this book, like his others, is cleverly illustrated and enticing to preschoolers, it, like the others, is also sexist. There is no reason why Paint Pig needs to be a Mr. or why Mrs. Paint Pig should wear a dress, or, even more humiliating, ride in a back seat of a car like a second-class citizen. Today, we should be trying to avoid stereotyped roles so that young children can be aware of various lifestyles. Another criticism is that each page is too cluttered, making it confusing for reading or viewing. However, Richard Scarry's delightful way of simplifying difficult concepts makes the book appealing to teachers and parents. In addition, the book is compact and durable, and the pages are cardboard so that children can manipulate it easily. We should choose books that will arouse children's curiosity, stimulate eagerness to learn and open minds to question—all of which this book does. (p. 158)

> Science Books & Films *(copyright 1976 by the American Association for the Advancement of Science), Vol. XII, No. 3 (December, 1976).*

RICHARD SCARRY'S GREAT BIG AIR BOOK (1971)

The latest Richard Scarry, his *Great Big Air Book,* is a winner and gives credence to the astonishing fact that his books have sold twenty-five million copies in the USA alone. Naturally parents will rush to buy and children will clamour to read page after page of nattily drawn, superficial but smartly spoken facts about everything to do with air from the ailerons on the front wings of aeroplanes to the air pollution which starts with smoke from Father Cat's big black cigar. (p. 1517)

> The Times Literary Supplement *(© Times Newspapers Ltd., 1971; reproduced from* The Times Literary Supplement *by permission), December 3, 1971.*

Let's take it as read that anthropomorphism is bad for small children and no properly progressive parent would touch a book that had talking cats, foxes in headscarves and bears in pinnies. That leaves the remaining 99.9 per cent of us who, if they have to put up with Mummy and Daddy Cat, would just as well have a bit of mild instruction thrown in on the side, about the behaviour of the atmosphere, the principles of flight and the evils of air pollution. And Lowly Worm, whose moment of glory comes when he knots the airlock and saves the lives of the astronauts (Benny Baboon, Harry Hyena and no prizes at the National Aeronautics and Space Administration for guessing who is who) is a genuine original.

The illustrations are very carefully drawn: watch the changing angles of Charlie Crow's wing feathers, the remarkable collection of vintage aircraft, and also the accurate liveries of the airliners. It's a genuine puzzle, however, why children's illustrators feel a compulsion to slip in pieces of Victoriana, such as corn in sheaves and puffer trains, which are going to puzzle the toddlers of the 1970s far more than the jet engines and power shovels will. (p. 68)

> *The Economist (© The Economist Newspaper Limited, 1971), December 18, 1971.*

OTHER CITATIONS

Lavinia Russ, in Publishers Weekly, *March 1, 1971, p. 58.*

Patricia Vervoort, in School Library Journal, *November, 1971, p. 109.*

STORYBOOK DICTIONARY (1966)

Mr. Scarry has created a cast of about 70 characters who appear in numerous actions throughout the pages of this large-size book. About 700 nouns, adjectives, verbs, and conjunctions are included which are explained through action sentences and pictures rather than being defined in the usual dictionary sense. Some of the humor is adult rather than childlike, as in the case of the word *Asleep:* "Babykins [a kitten in sleeper pajamas] is *asleep.* He is such a cute little baby when he is not awake." All the drawings are in bright colors and will delight children who love books filled with small pictures. They will probably enjoy searching throughout the pages for the various characters. Each "story" is contained within the one or two sentences and a picture which illustrates a single word or group of words. The use of single sentences to show different word forms is more confusing here than in, for example, [Dr. Seuss's] *The Cat in the Hat Beginner Dictionary,* which employs simple phrases, in most cases, and less complicated verb forms. However, children may get more hours of enjoyment from Scarry's book and perhaps absorb more words because the book invites repeated browsing. A teacher or parent will probably have to read the captions to a beginning reader and provide further explanations. Purchase will depend on the individual reaction to Scarry's work or if a need for another large size picture-word-book exists. (pp. 80-1)

> *Ann Currah, in* School Library Journal *(reprinted from the November, 1966, issue of* School Library Journal, *published by R. R. Bowker Company, a Xerox company; copyright © 1966 by Xerox Corporation), November, 1966.*

Those who know Richard Scarry's "Best Word Book Ever" and "Busy, Busy World" will know what to expect from "Storybook Dictionary". . . . It is arranged like a dictionary (2,500 words) with more than 1,000 of the author's cheerfully detailed color illustrations. Mr. Scarry's humor is of a particularly nutty and winning sort. "Storybook Dictionary" makes no pretense at being practical; it offers its learning through giggles. Good for reading aloud and looking at from age 2 to 6. You either like Mr. Scarry or you don't; I do. (p. 54)

> *Eliot Fremont-Smith, in* The New York

Times Book Review, *Part II (© 1966 by The New York Times Company; reprinted by permission), November 6, 1966.*

[In] "Richard Scarry's Storybook Dictionary," . . . Scarry has used a standard list of words—there appears to be a formula for doing children's dictionaries—but what he does with the list is remarkable. With a cast of characters that includes Pickles Pig, the happy glutton who opens the refrigerator door so often he catches cold, lovable Big Hilda the Hippo, and my favorite, Brambles the Warthog who is obsessed with grooming his impossible hair, Scarry makes language what children intuitively know it is, something alive and lively.

I've known educators to take a look at a Scarry book and go into a long rage that they are too jumbled, too confusing, too much on a page. But I've met few children who would agree, and I think it is Scarry's respect for children that makes the difference. He assumes that children have curiosity, resources and intelligence that can be appealed to rather than ignored. (p. 37)

> *Jack McGarvey, in* The New York Times Book Review, *Part II (© 1973 by The New York Times Company; reprinted by permission), May 6, 1973.*

OTHER CITATIONS

David M. Glixon, in Saturday Review, *November 19, 1966, p. 49.*

Frances Nell Cheney, in Wilson Library Bulletin, *February, 1967, p. 625.*

Where: Information on Education *60, August, 1971, p. 240.*

WHAT DO PEOPLE DO ALL DAY? (1968)

What do people do all day? They keep busy and "this is Busytown" in ninety-four of the busiest (i.e. active, crowded) pages you've ever seen; the wonder is how Mr. Scarry found time to draw so many cartoons, cut-aways and animal cutups. Going about their everyday business are Stitches the (rabbit) tailor, Able Baker Charlie (a mouse), Zip the (raccoon) postman, Sawdust the (cat) carpenter, assorted pigs, bears, foxes, etc., etc., sometimes assisted by their wives and children. What's intended as a kindergarten cross between the *Occupational Outlook Handbook* and *How Things Work* [by Martin Mann] in a series of increasingly technical episodes (from mailing a letter to making electricity) is essentially a medley of fact and fancy, or a three-ring circus in the guise of a one-volume encyclopedia. Unless you're amused by such sideshows as a wild Indian raccoon (named Wild Bill Hiccup) causing traffic jams (in his Buffalomobile), you won't pay the price of admission. (p. 400)

> *Kirkus Service (copyright © 1968 Virginia Kirkus' Service, Inc.), April 1, 1968.*

Scarry's ["What Do People Do All Day?"] is as full of cute, busy detail as his previous books. In this one Captain Salty, Stitches the Tailor, Daddy Pig, and myriad others go about their business in Busytown, U.S.A. It's a big, jolly book; the multi-layered pictures make a snare for the child's eye. They can trap his full attention if he ignores the somewhat fussy lectures on behavior. (p. 52)

The New York Times Book Review, *Part II* (© *1968 by The New York Times Company; reprinted by permission*), *May 5, 1968.*

This book, which covers the activities of such workers as postmen, road builders, bakers, coal miners, sailors, grocers, etc. is characteristic Scarry. His busy pages, chockfull of animals dressed like people and going about human tasks, sell steadily in book stores but usually get sniffed at in library book selection. His bookstore sales can be traced to the fact that buyers like to get the most for their money, and Scarry gives them carefully detailed, mildly cartooned, fully colored pictures on every page. Children who have not yet learned to read can figure out what's going on from the pictures, and Scarry's text, usually made up of a series of declarative sentences, satisfies their butterfly attention spans. Not beautiful, but absorbing browsing for the preliterate. (p. 80)

> *Lillian N. Gerhardt, in* School Library Journal *(reprinted from the November, 1968, issue of* School Library Journal, *published by R. R. Bowker Company, a Xerox company; copyright* © *1968 by Xerox Corporation), November, 1968.*

OTHER CITATIONS

Zena Sutherland, in Bulletin of the Center for Children's Books, *June, 1968, p. 165.*

Mrs. J. White, in Children's Book News, *November-December, 1968, p. 313.*

*   *   *

SCHWARTZ, Alvin   1927-

Alvin Schwartz is an American author of books for adults and children. The subjects of his books vary, but he is probably best known for his work in American folklore and humor. He has researched this field extensively, producing several well-documented and amusing compilations. (See also *Contemporary Authors*, Vols. 13-16, rev. ed. and *Something About the Author*, Vol. 4.)

AUTHOR'S COMMENTARY

Scholars who study the mechanism of humor say that much of the joking we encounter involves a trick played on the mind. One expects that something rational, or normal, is going to happen—but it doesn't. Instead, something absurd happens or something nonsensical, eccentric, or untoward. Thus, a rhyme does not follow an anticipated pattern. Or a conundrum does not lead to a logical conclusion. Or a problem in arithmetic does not produce a proper answer. And if you are in a playful mood, you laugh at having been had.

Of course, not all humor involves a trick. There are times when we laugh out of the sheer pleasure of encountering the work of a humorously creative mind, whether words or illustrations are involved. In either case, what is critical is whether you are in a playful mood. Children tend to be more playful than adults; as a result, they are inclined to laugh more readily and more frequently. They also tend to laugh in situations where laughter does not seem appropriate—unless you, too, are in a playful mood. (p. 282)

One of the fascinating aspects of the humor children use and respond to is the number of discrete and surprising forms involved. Some of them are very old, and most are in use virtually everywhere, for the basic needs that humor satisfies—the needs for pleasure and for release—are universal.

A fair amount of the joking children do involves word play. One form they especially like is the tongue twister, an ancient device used to play a trick on the tongue. In this case, a pattern of consonants and vowels constitutes the trick, not a pattern of reasoning. (p. 283)

In my research with children, I also encounter what may be classified as the nonsense of humor. It ranges from the sublime to the ridiculous. Yet it often possesses a disconcertingly clear perspective of the curious nature of reality. (p. 285)

Like almost everyone, children respond to hyperbole in humor. This device has been one of the principal characteristics of American humor since the nation began to emerge as a cultural entity in the 1830s. Two intriguing forms are the tall tale, which is essentially a joke in slow motion, and the lie, a related mode. (p. 286)

But . . . there is a rich body of humor which deals with ordinary people and the extraordinary experiences they never had. I should underscore that here we are dealing with artifacts, not living material, for it is unusually difficult nowadays to collect tall tales and folkloristic lies. . . .

One Saturday as part of a book talk at the Donnell Branch of The New York Public Library, I ran a lie-telling contest. But it was hard going. The librarian later observed, correctly I believe, that few children of school age are told enough tales any more to know how to create them or tell them. Yet they are intrigued by such material. (p. 287)

> *Alvin Schwartz, "Children, Humor, and Folklore," Part I (a revision of a speech originally delivered at the conference of the National Council of Teachers of English on November 26, 1976;* © *1977 by Alvin Schwartz; reprinted by permission of Curtis Brown, Ltd.), in* The Horn Book Magazine, *June, 1977, pp. 281-87.*

I first became interested in folklore when most of us do, in childhood. But at that time I had no idea that the games, sayings, songs, rhymes, taunts, and jokes I knew; the things I wrote on walls; the superstitions I relied on; the tales I heard and learned; the customs we practiced at home; or the ways we had of doing things were all folklore. I also did not realize that much of this lore gave my life structure and continuity, that these games, songs, jokes, tales, and customs were often very old, that ordinary people like me had created them, and that all this had survived simply and remarkably because one person had told another. With each retelling the result—be it a tale or a taunt —often changed slightly to reflect the circumstances of the individual involved. . . .

It also did not occur to me as a child that the folklore we create, pass on, and change says a good deal about us, about the times in which we live, and about the needs we have. Our jests provide pleasure, but they also provide emotional release. When they deal with racial and ethnic groups and with parents and siblings, they provide weaponry. The tall tales which so amuse us spring from the vastness of a frontier wilderness where life was brutal and the people diminished and fearful. They created incredible lies in which individuals were larger and taller than life and could not fail, no matter what. Our superstitions provide answers to things we do not understand and cannot explain. (p. 474)

I am frequently asked where I obtain the folklore I include in my books for young people. Whenever it is feasible, I collect material from the folk—particularly from children, our strongest, most cohesive folk group, and from the elderly, who in many respects are as important. I do my collecting in schoolyards, in classrooms, in summer camps, on street corners, at church picnics, in city homes, in country stores, on farms, in shopping centers. . . . And clearly I rely on archives and libraries. (pp. 474-75)

We tend to think of folklore as old-fashioned. But whenever people interact and share problems, possibilities, solutions, and pain, they continue to create and use the stuff of folklore to deal with their needs. . . . Yet, for several reasons, we have come to depend less on folklore. As our technology has advanced we have come to rely increasingly on other people for goods, services, and entertainment and less on ourselves and on those we know. The extended family and the traditions it preserved have disappeared. We move about the country to an extraordinary extent. . . . As a result of such changes, we have to a serious extent become alienated from our traditions and have lost a sense of place and a sense of self. If this perception is correct, we have altered the fabric of our society, and we are changing from something we were to something we have not yet become.

In light of all this, what am I trying to say to a child who reads my books of folklore? Laugh when you can. As Josh Billings suggested, ''[O]pen your mouth wide enough for the noise to get out without squealing, throw your head back as though you was going to be shaved, hold on to your false hair with both hands and then laugh till your soul gets thoroughly rested.''

Understand that you are not very different from people who lived before you, despite the trappings of modern life. You experience the same joys, the same fears, the same anger, the same love, the same need for dignity, the same need for security.

Understand that you are part of a living tradition to which you contribute and from which you draw. You are deeply rooted in the experience of the human race and are part of something remarkable and continuous—the folk. At a time when everyone and everything seem in transit, it is good to know this. (pp. 475-76)

> *Alvin Schwartz, "Children, Humor, and Folklore", Part II (a revision of a speech originally delivered at the conference of the National Council of Teachers of English on November 26, 1976; © 1977 by Alvin Schwartz; reprinted by permission of Curtis Brown, Ltd.), in* The Horn Book Magazine, *August, 1977, pp. 471-76.*

CENTRAL CITY/SPREAD CITY: THE METROPOLITAN REGIONS WHERE MORE AND MORE OF US SPEND OUR LIVES (1973)

Eye-catching graphics and a focus on the changing charac-

ter of several typical Philadelphia area neighborhoods give this survey of urban decay above average impact. Both elements are used effectively to sketch out the results of poor planning and restrictive zoning in the suburbs, decayed housing, poverty and gang and drug related crime in the center city. Schwartz shows how the city's problems, and indeed the city itself, threaten to overtake suburbia, but he also recognizes the contradictory truth that while look-alike housing projects may be the despair of planners and bored teenagers, they still fulfill the dreams of many American adults. The text is refreshingly non-utopian, and a final chapter on the operation of regional planning boards in several cities is a concrete example of how planning at least makes urban problems comprehensible while stressing the importance of political mobilization. Little more than an outline, but one of the clearest and most accessible at this level . . . and Schwartz' bibliography—listing juvenile fiction and other popular books on urban life—may help teachers find a way to humanize a complex topic. (p. 1275)

> Kirkus Reviews *(copyright © 1973 The Kirkus Service, Inc.), November 15, 1973.*

[*Central City/Spread City* is a] depressing, yet true picture of the living and working conditions existing in most central cities and their surrounding suburbs. Although not called by name, the inner city and suburbs described are in that vast metropolitan area surrounding Philadelphia, where five million people live and work. Dilapidated and inadequate housing, lack of schools, playgrounds, health services and jobs, and the rising crime rate (especially crimes against persons) sum up the sense of futility and frustration of the seven hundred thousand predominantly black people who live in the inner city (Tioga-Nicetown neighborhood). Contrasting with this bleak picture are the conditions, different but also depressing, in the "typical" new, almost all white suburbs (Upper Merion Township) of split levels and ranch houses, apartments, vast shopping centers, industrial parks, rising crime rates (mostly crimes against property) and boredom for most young people. Some small rays of hope are offered for the future, through the possibilities of good planning to preserve adequate open spaces, through the building of new towns and through regional governmental cooperation. Reference is made to the successes of Atlanta, Indianapolis, Jacksonville, Miami, Nashville, Toronto and Minneapolis-St. Paul. The author concludes with, ". . . many of the problems of the region could be solved now. We know enough, we have the tools and the techniques, and we could find the money. The important question no longer is what to do or how to do it. It is how much we care." The book is liberally illustrated with photographs, maps and charts, and a supplementary reading list of over one hundred references is appended, including many specifically directed toward teachers. (pp. 100-01)

> Science Books *(copyright 1974 by the American Association for the Advancement of Science), Vol. X, No. 2 (September, 1974).*

OTHER CITATIONS

The Booklist, *March 1, 1974, p. 743-44.*

CROSS YOUR FINGERS, SPIT IN YOUR HAT: SUPERSTITIONS AND OTHER BELIEFS (1974)

The fourth book by this collector-artist team [Schwartz and

illustrator Glen Rounds] delves into the fascinating realm of superstition and into all the tricks, charms, amulets, talismans, and signs that people have relied upon to control the good and evil forces lurking in the cosmos. As in earlier volumes, the anecdotes and bits of information have been derived from folklore sources and have been well-annotated; but such erudition does not keep the author from presenting his material in a humorous and modest manner. . . . The book provides great entertainment as long as one doesn't take these matters seriously, but the author has imprudently included some activities for gaining money or bringing good fortune that might be rather dangerous if interpreted by a literal-minded child—biting heads off butterflies, drinking dirty water, throwing pieces of a broken mirror into the river, swallowing live goldfish. Only a few such items exist; but because of them, the project is less totally pleasing than the earlier books by the author. (p. 291)

> *Anita Silvey, in* The Horn Book Magazine *(copyright © 1974 by The Horn Book, Inc., Boston), June, 1974.*

[Julie Forsyth] Batchelor and [Claudia] Delys' *Superstitious: Here's Why* . . . offers a better presentation of the psychology of superstition for young readers, but Schwartz' title is more fun. Advice culled from American folklore and superstition is handed out with tongue in cheek (e.g., "If you eat peas on New Year's Day . . . you will have good luck all year long.") and brief information on what luck is and the origin of superstition is provided in notes at the end of the book. Although this can't be used as a reference source (the different superstitions are loosely grouped under chapter headings and no index is included), the information is intriguing and differs from the material in Maria Leach's *The Luck Book* . . . which focuses on the superstitions of other cultures. (p. 91)

> *Margaret Blue, in* School Library Journal *(reprinted from the September, 1974, issue of* School Library Journal, *published by R. R. Bowker Company, a Xerox company; copyright © 1974 by Xerox Corporation), September, 1974.*

OTHER CITATIONS

Kirkus Reviews, *May 1, 1974, p. 487.*

Christopher Davis, in The New York Times Book Review, *May 5, 1974, p. 22.*

The Booklist, *July 15, 1974, p. 1255.*

MUSEUM: THE STORY OF AMERICA'S TREASURE HOUSES (1967)

[*Museum* is a] most interesting, most useful book that gives excellent coverage of many aspects of the topic, and gives it in a straightforward style hampered only occasionally by being heavy with information. The author describes the first museums founded in this country and the proliferation of such institutions today; some of the facets of museum problems covered are financing and acquisition, others are problems to do with the collection itself (such as renovation) and still others with the problems of bringing the collection to the public (such as security or museum educa-

tion). The largest part of the book is devoted to art museums; separate sections discuss museums of history, of natural history, and of science and industry. A final chapter discusses opportunities, training, and salaries in museum careers; an index is appended. (p. 84)

> *Zena Sutherland, in* Bulletin of the Center for Children's Books *(copyright 1968 by The University of Chicago; all rights reserved), January, 1968.*

Perhaps the subtitle of Alvin Schwartz's new book, "The Story of America's Treasure Houses," best describes the theme of this straight-forward guide to and history of museums. The author feels that the public's interest in museums has risen considerably, partly because today people have more leisure time, education, curiosity and money. Mr. Schwartz collected his material for "Museum" by visiting and consulting with the staffs of 46 museums across the country. The book . . . is an historical survey of museums beginning with America's first, which was established in Charleston, South Carolina in 1773, includes the opening of the first public museum in the United States in 1784 when artist Charles Willson Peale opened part of his home in Philadelphia, and continues to the very newest institutions established just before this book saw print.

"Museum" could be categorized as a technical directory, since it includes many specifics and facts necessary in the administration of any museum. However, its simplicity and concise format makes for easy and light reading, although it never ceases to be descriptive, informative and explanatory of the subjects covered.

Of the 5000 (approximately) museums throughout America, the author separates them into categories consisting of art, history, natural history and science and industry. The author describes the function of the museum of history as one which preserves and interprets man's development, experiences, ideas and values through visual exhibits; the museum of natural history as an aid to acquiring more knowledge of man's world through the sciences of nature; and the museum of science and industry which fosters knowledge of technological advances in the world.

Mr. Schwartz informs the reader of the ownership of museums, and of the processes of acquisitions, exhibition and preservation of works of art. He cites explicit examples of processes used in the organization of exhibitions, their installation, and publicity for their success. He covers the subjects of financing of museums, the securing of foundation grants, government funds, investments and memberships. The importance of educational programs through tours, lectures, films and art courses for both children and adults is discussed.

The reader is constantly reminded that the responsibility of the museum is to teach, a theme which is demonstrated throughout the book by means of specific examples and illustrations. After reading this book, which can be done in one sitting, the unaccustomed museum-goer should develop an acute insight into the inner workings of a museum and a curiosity to investigate further.

"Museum" is a well-organized and factual publication that conveys to the reader an awareness of the complexities of museum administration. It should be in the library of a museum lover. (p. 39)

Linda H. Lichtenberg, in Museum News (© American Association of Museums, 1968), February, 1968.

OTHER CITATIONS

Allan T. Marsh, in School Library Journal, September, 1967, p. 136.

Kirkus Service, September 15, 1967, p. 1153.

Zena Sutherland, in Saturday Review, November 11, 1967, p. 50.

THE PEOPLE'S CHOICE: THE STORY OF CANDIDATES, CAMPAIGNS, AND ELECTIONS (1968)

The well chosen black-and-white photographs illustrate the American electoral process more eloquently than the anecdotal text explains it. The book's emphasis is on the conduct, strategy and financing of campaigns and the development of issues, and though it is interesting reading, it is most suitable only for attracting browsers; the book contains little information of substance that [Edmund] Lindop's *The First Book of Elections* . . . and [Duane] Bradley's *Electing a President* . . . does not cover in fuller and more orderly fashion. (pp. 141-42)

> Mary R. Sive, in School Library Journal (reprinted from the September, 1968, issue of School Library Journal, published by R. R. Bowker Company, a Xerox company; copyright © 1968 by Xerox Corporation), September, 1968.

This thought-provoking, unbiased introduction to American political campaigns and elections covers the selection of a political candidate; campaign techniques of both the past and the present, including propaganda, smear attacks and mass media; and the election itself. The author has avoided making value judgments for the reader and has done the kind of writing that will stimulate the reader to become involved with the subject. The many illustrations include current and historical photographs, political cartoons, and campaign propaganda. (pp. 462-63)

> Jean B. Lieb, in Childhood Education (reprinted by permission of the Association for Childhood Education International, 3615 Wisconsin Ave., N.W., Washington, DC 20016; copyright © 1969 by the Association), Vol. 45, No. 8 (April, 1969).

OTHER CITATIONS

Kirkus Service, May 15, 1968, p. 563.

Best Sellers, June 1, 1968, p. 114.

TOMFOOLERY: TRICKERY AND FOOLERY WITH WORDS (1973)

We can do with a little laughter. Thus a hearty welcome to Alvin Schwartz's "Tomfoolery," a collection of verbal tricks from American folklore that can be as successful with adults as with children. . . .

The material is brief, quite silly, even absurd. Some of it can deflate the pompous, raise the risibilities of the timid or

even the normally gruff. . . . [With] this collection, his notes, sources and bibliography Mr. Schwartz has elevated foolishness to a form of art. This is a dip-into book, not a volume to sit down with and read at a sitting. It has a built-in kind of permanence, a book to be shelved and saved, taken down and used as the mood demands. It is, by the way, a fitting companion to Mr. Schwartz's previous compilation, "A Twister of Twists, a Tangler of Tongues." The illustrations, scratchy and scraggly in appearance, might seem amateurish and primitive. But they have the same wit and charm as the text, and Glen Rounds is considered by many to be one of our most original and consistently underrated artists. (p. 6)

> William Cole, in The New York Times Book Review, Part II (© 1973 by The New York Times Company; reprinted by permission), May 6, 1973.

Although some of the material in the book can be found in [Duncan Emrich's] *The Hodgepodge Book* . . . , this volume has been designed to aid the trickster rather than the folklorist. But, luckily for harassed school teachers, mothers, and librarians, the tricks don't involve "nailing . . . [somebody's] sneakers to the floor. Instead they depend on words, and, at times, on a pinch or some other friendly gesture." Some of the tricks entail the perennially favorite riddles or sayings with catches—a few with foolish answers and a few with answers "no one in his right mind would give." Sentences with inflated vocabulary (tall talk), circular tales, and tales with hoax endings provide more material for the would-be buffoon; and, as in [Schwartz's] *A Twister of Twists, A Tangler of Tongues*, the humorous line-sketches should increase the giggles and groans. The perfect book for someone who wants to know "What is round and purple and hums?" or who would like to say with aplomb "Ladies and jellybeans, / Reptiles and crocodiles, / I stand before you / and sit behind you / to tell you something / I know nothing about." (p. 393)

> Anita Silvey, in The Horn Book Magazine (copyright © 1973 by The Horn Book, Inc., Boston), August, 1973.

OTHER CITATIONS

Kirkus Reviews, April 1, 1973, p. 393.

Carol A. Emmens, in School Library Journal, September, 1973, pp. 133-34.

A TWISTER OF TWISTS, A TANGLER OF TONGUES (1974)

[Until] now Dr. [Francis] Potter's two books have been the standard volumes on this rather specialized study [of tongue-twisters]. He is given proper acknowledgment in the bibliography appended to "A Twister of Twists, a Tangler of Tongues," collected by Alvin Schwartz. . . . Here, we find all our old friends, Peter Piper, Esau, Betty Botter of the tainted butter, and the unspeakable Peggy Babcock. (Unspeakable, that is, five times in a row.) It's so good to see anything done *right*, and this book is a total success: pleasing format, clear layout, amusing illustrations by Glen Rounds and a treatment of a fascinating literary bypath that is neither too short nor too exhaustive.

There are notes, sources and a bibliography. There is a section of twisters in other tongues that gives the original, a phonetic version, and the English translation. And there is a page on how to make up your own twisters. They've been around a long time—the aforementioned Mr. Piper dates to 1674—and have other uses than amusement; radio announcers employ them in their training, they're sometimes used to help people with speech problems, and Mr. Schwartz gives one fascinating example of how Polish freedom-fighters in World War II used as a password a twister that no German tongue could get around.

There *are* some I can't get through more than once: "The sixth sheik's sixth sheep's sick," and "Old, oily Ollie oils oily autos." Others come out like a troubled outboard motor. Some make revealing tests for sobriety: "Miss Smith dismisseth us." But this is a true treasury of trivial tidbits. (p. 8)

> *William Cole, in* The New York Times Book Review *(© 1972 by The New York Times Company; reprinted by permission), November 19, 1972.*

[*A Twister of Twists, a Tangler of Tongues* is an] agreeable grab bag of tongue twisters culled from a variety of sources. Most of the old favorites are represented ("If a woodchuck could chuck wood . . . ," "Peter Piper picked a peck of pickled pepper . . . ," and so forth), but many unfamiliar twisters are offered, including a few in foreign languages. The plan of the book is neatly sectional, with each twister falling under an assigned topic heading (i.e., nature, health, travel, etc.). The illustrations and a useful introduction enhance the value of the book. More varied and interesting than Esther T. Baker's *A Book of Modern Tongue Twisters* . . . and aimed at a wider audience than Charles Francis Potter's *Tongue Tanglers* . . . and *More Tongue Tanglers* . . . (both of which are designed primarily for children), the collection affords an hour or two of good fun and practice for people of all ages. (p. 3911)

> *A. J. Anderson, in* Library Journal *(reprinted from the December 1, 1972, issue of* Library Journal, *published by R. R. Bowker Company, a Xerox company; copyright © 1972 by Xerox Corporation), December 1, 1972.*

OTHER CITATIONS

Kirkus Reviews, *October 1, 1972, p. 1149.*

Patricia Tonkin, in Childhood Education, *February, 1973, pp. 258, 260.*

Margaret Blue, in School Library Journal, *May, 1973, p. 75.*

UNIVERSITY: THE STUDENTS, FACULTY, AND CAMPUS LIFE AT ONE UNIVERSITY (1969)

["University"] is an honest, brightly written account of life on a large, representative Eastern campus, the University of Pennsylvania, which has 7,000 undergraduates. While only 150 of our 2,500 halls of higher learning are universities, as the author notes, half of America's undergraduates are enrolled in them. Young men and women presently shopping college catalogues will get a practical, down-to-earth orientation course.

The author has interviewed dozens of students, faculty members, chaplains, coaches and deans at Penn, then sifted out his impressions in a book that provides information on practically any question a teen-ager could ask. Testing, admission policies, freshmen week, the quality of instruction, the grading system, study requirements, dormitory rules, fraternities, coffeehouses, athletics, costs of board and tuition—even the rash of protests and sit-ins now roiling so many campuses—this book covers every aspect of student life. Student objections to the Dow Chemical Co. and to contracts for research on germ warfare get more than a page.

One has to be brave or foolhardy these days to take on such a volatile subject as contemporary university life. If brave, Mr. Schwartz has also been wise in his choice and highlighting of the many phases of undergraduate life that are listed in a detailed index. He is particularly strong in areas of social concern, especially in what he has to say about the problems of blacks on predominantly white campuses. . . .

The author also discusses the meaning and variety of such university research programs as underwater archeology, criminology, the behavior of the K meson, etc. Scholars of the future will surely find something here to catch their attention and stir their ambitions. (p. 26)

> *Thurston N. Davis, in* The New York Times Book Review *(© 1969 by The New York Times Company; reprinted by permission), June 15, 1969.*

The author focuses on one institution of higher learning and, in this way, explores the university system in general. Emphasis is on such aspects of campus life as: the role of fraternities and sororities, expenses and scholarship aids, changing admission standards for minority youth. The discussions of research in the university, and of faculty and student activities, are especially worthwhile. The author also offers good photographs and a useful list of books describing schools and their admissions procedures. The book is weakened by the fact that no mention is made of such organizations as Students for a Democratic Society and Black Students Union, groups that have been involved in current campus unrest. Despite this omission, this introduction will give beginning high school students a helpful, though limited, birds-eye view of a university. (p. 155)

> *Claude Ury, in* School Library Journal *(reprinted from the October, 1969, issue of* School Library Journal, *published by R. R. Bowker Company, a Xerox company; copyright © 1969 by Xerox Corporation), October, 1969.*

OTHER CITATIONS

Kirkus Reviews, *June 15, 1969, p. 637.*

Zena Sutherland, in Bulletin of the Center for Children's Books, *September, 1969, p. 17.*

WHAT DO YOU THINK? AN INTRODUCTION TO PUBLIC OPINION: HOW IT FORMS, FUNCTIONS, AND AFFECTS OUR LIVES (1966)

This small but highly interesting volume sets out to demonstrate the value of individual opinion and how it can be influenced by propaganda, events, and information. How opinions form, how they influence jobs, government and politics are important facets of this book. There is an interesting chapter on teenagers and their opinions and another on methods of conducting research. This is a valuable book for teenagers on their way to taking their place in a democratic society, for it shows them not only the importance but the necessity of individual opinion. Recommended. (p. 396)

> *Sister M. Ethelreda, R.S.M., in* Catholic Library World, *February, 1967.*

[*What Do You Think?* is a] remarkably lucid and objective discussion of the factors that contribute to the formation of opinion, of the uses to which knowledge about this is put (such as market research) of the pitfalls to avoid in forming an unbiased opinion, and of the ways in which surveys and polls are conducted and questionnaires compiled. The writing is brisk, the coverage broad, the tone matter-of-fact, the examples and illustrations up-to-date. Charts, tables, and photographs of propaganda and advertising techniques are included; an index is appended. (pp. 47-8)

> *Zena Sutherland, in* Bulletin of the Center for Children's Books *(copyright 1967 by the University of Chicago; all rights reserved), November, 1967.*

OTHER CITATIONS

May H. Edmonds, in School Library Journal, *March, 1967, p. 141.*

WHOPPERS: TALL TALES AND OTHER LIES (1975)

There are few things as beguiling as a really audacious lie, and the prospect of a collection of them seems almost too good to be true. The reader better be ready for large amounts of rustic exaggeration.

Of course, there is a certain amount of variety in the subject matter: there are hunting yarns, lies about farming, about insects and animals, about the weather. Some of them have the feel of genuine tall-tale classics; others could have been culled from the humor boxes of My Weekly Reader. That they were not is made clear at the end of the book, where the compiler, who has done a few of these humorous folklore aggregations, has five pages of notes, six pages called "Sources and Related Lies," and an impressive bibliography. After reading through this documentation, the reader may scratch his head, shift the toothpick to the other corner of his mouth and go back to the stories with new respect. Instead of swamping the tales in pedantry, however, the scholarship gives them the weight of historical perspective. As Alvin Schwartz points out, the early settlers of this country took a great deal of satisfaction in making fun of grim circumstances. This humor with its illiterate dialect and whopping embellishments—was picked up by writers, journalists and advertising promoters, who used the style to create tall-tale heroes of their own. One of them, Samuel Clemens, put the stamp of his genius on American folklore. (Bob and the Child of Calamity from "Life on the Mississippi" is included in this collection.)

These lies, tall-tales and whoppers have been illustrated to

a T by Glen Rounds. His laconic-looking, often overalled figures, shamble through the pages fighting bears and panthers and outrunning cucumber vines. They embody one form of the spirit of Western Expansion. (pp. 38-9)

> *Sidney Long, in* The New York Times Book Review *(© 1975 by The New York Times Company; reprinted by permission), May 4, 1975.*

Windies, whoppers, or *gallyfloppers* are all interchangeable terms for *tall tales,* the folklorists' euphemism for outlandish and unbelievable exaggerations or harmless lies. And like the jokes, riddles, and tongue-twisters found in the compiler's four previous collections of unmitigated trickery and roguery, the lying tale is part of the folklore tradition linking our forerunners to their European ancestors. Despite this international connection, however, the tall tale has derived a distinctive flavor from the frontier experience. Sources are carefully documented; the scholarship behind the fun is thorough enough to satisfy the most pedantic reader, while the whoppers are outrageous enough to please the most demanding young liars. They will revel in "The heat was so bad . . . the farmer had to feed his hens cracked ice to keep them from laying hard-boiled eggs." The entire extravaganza is suitably embellished with the perfectly trustworthy drawings [by Glen Rounds]; a reliable index is appended—and that's the truth! (p. 393)

> *Mary M. Burns, in* The Horn Book Magazine *(copyright © 1975 by the Horn Book, Inc., Boston), August, 1975.*

OTHER CITATIONS

Publishers Weekly, April 21, 1975, p. 46.

Margaret Blue, in School Library Journal, *September, 1975, p. 111.*

Christina Carr Young, in Childhood Education, *January, 1976, p. 158.*

WITCRACKS: JOKES AND JESTS FROM AMERICAN FOLKLORE (1973)

This is the third of Alvin Schwartz's delightful folklore collections I've reviewed; I'm becoming a regular *Schwartzkopf.* I must say that I don't approve of the word "witcracks," even though it comes from Shakespeare. These are the kind of jokes that break up wise guys of 9 or 10: conundrums, knock-knocks, elephant jokes, shaggy dogs—the kind of humor that will come out in a rash for a few months, then sink away. Some are old, old classics; others have a vaguely familiar ring, yet others are new to me. "Knock, knock? *Who's there?* Little old lady. *Little old lady who?* I didn't know you could yodel." Try it on your nearest relative. There are a bunch of Little Moron jokes that reverberate with the logic of Gracie Allen: "I weighed only three pounds when I was born. *Did you live?* Did I live? You should see me now?"

There are some kinds of jokes I can't respond to: "What is black and shiny and lives in trees and is dangerous?/A crow with a submachine gun." Simply don't get the humor. Mr. Schwartz cheats once, when he has the sentence, "The girl who tied her shoelaces in a most peculiar way," which means nothing without Glen Rounds's accompanying illustration of a girl with her right foot up on a chair while she leans down to the floor to tie her left foot. Not to be offensive, Schwartz leaves blanks in his Polish and Italian jokes: "Why do flies have wings? To beat the —s to the garbage dump."

With his usual meticulousness, our author has 20 pages of acknowledgements and credits, and I have few complaints. I wish he'd given us a few of Tom Swift's original sayings, and he calls Harry Graham "Henry" Graham. The book is a beautiful job of play. Among the sources acknowledged are Mrs. Schwartz and all the little Schwartzes: John, Peter, Nancy and Elizabeth. There must be high times around the dining room table in *that* household. (p. 8)

> *William Cole, in* The New York Times Book Review (© *1973 by The New York Times Company; reprinted by permission), October 7, 1973.*

[*Witcracks: Jokes and Jests from American Folklore*] deals explicitly with folk materials and presents itself to parents and children as a collection of traditional jokes. . . . In addition to the riddles, puns, sick jokes, Tom Swifties, Confucious say, jokes featuring the elephant, little moron, and ethnic groups (with the names left blank to let the reader see how they are used for many groups), shaggy dog stories, and reverse-ethnic protest tales, Schwartz offers brief but sound comments on the backgrounds and functions of the jokes; for example, "We tell many [jokes] for the fun of it, asking only that someone laugh. But curiously we tell many others in anger. For we also use jokes to ridicule people and things we don't like, which helps us to let off steam". . . .

Schwartz does, however, make a few dated errors, such as saying that folklorists call exaggerations, such as "last winter a cow nearby caught such a cold she gave nothing but ice cream," Yankeeisms or Jonathanisms. In spite of the generalizations and brevity of discussion, Schwartz seems serious, and his comments are useful. His material does come from respectable sources (many folklore journals included), and he consulted Kenneth Goldstein and Bruce Buckley, who made material available to him. In addition, he gives a nice bibliography and notes on sources and variants of the tales he includes. The price is steep, but the book deserves some attention for its attempt to ground popular work in scholarly material and to educate while entertaining. (pp. 264-65)

> *Rayna Green, in* Journal of American Folklore *(copyright © 1974 by the American Folklore Society; reprinted by permission), July-September, 1974.*

OTHER CITATIONS

Carol A. Emmens, in School Library Journal, *December, 1973, p. 51.*

The Booklist, *December 15, 1973, pp. 446-47.*

Mary M. Burns, in The Horn Book Magazine, *February, 1974, pp. 62-3.*

*   *   *

SCHWEITZER, Byrd Baylor
See BAYLOR, Byrd

U

UNGERER, Tomi   1931-

Tomi (born Jean Thomas) Ungerer is a painter, cartoonist, and sculptor, as well as a writer and illustrator of books for adults and children. As a child in his native France, Ungerer was brainwashed by Nazi schoolteachers; it is often felt that this experience influenced the direction of his thinking. As a creator of picture books, he brings a strong graphic sense to his bitingly satirical views of animals and man, views which also reflect his affection and optimism for humanity. He has published several sophisticated collections of both his drawings for adults and his poster art, and has had worldwide exhibitions of his works in several media. Ungerer was awarded the Gold Medal of the Society of Illustrators in 1960. (See also *Contemporary Authors*, Vols. 41-44 and *Something About the Author*, Vol. 5.)

GENERAL COMMENTARY

[Tomi Ungerer's] superbly rendered satirical drawings are famous for their no-holds-barred ferocity. Ungerer's work, as if to live up to its reputation, has turned increasingly bitter and grotesque in recent years—perhaps to the point where it defeats its own purpose: rather than despise the victims of such a savage assault, one tends almost to sympathize with them. Also, the corrupt and decaying high society Ungerer frequently depicts has long since had its comeuppance at the hands of socially conscious satirists. Isn't he beating a slightly dead horse? (p. 21)

> *Martin Fox, in* Print *(copyright 1966 by RC Publications Inc.), January-February, 1966.*

[Ungerer's] particular genius is for transforming human cruelty, violence, and sadism into blackest, sickest laughter. . . . "I depict awful things in order to destroy them," says Ungerer. "Actually, the world is as cruel now as it has always been, except that people know more about it because of the vast expansion of communications." (pp. 162-63)

Ungerer makes clear that the pen is not only mightier but far deadlier than the sword. . . . Like all first-rate black humor, the end result is first-rate morality. . . . To mutilate on the drawing board [is] to heal in "real life." (p. 163)

Tomi Ungerer . . . is an overpowering satirist who, indeed, sometimes does go too far. But by going too far he heightens the effectiveness and value of black humor, giving it the bite and sharpness that are required in a world turning in ever-increasing chaos, and showing few signs of being able to effectively, or lastingly, cure its ills. (p. 164)

> *John Gruen, "Charles Addams, Tomi Ungerer" (1967), in his* Close-Up *(copyright © 1967, 1968 by John Gruen; copyright © 1963, 1964, 1965, 1966, 1967 by New York Herald Tribune, Inc.; reprinted by permission of The Viking Press, Inc.), Viking, 1968, pp. 160-64.*

[Ungerer's] work is immediately identifiable: a singular line, an intelligent, sophisticated point of view; imaginative and wry humor; bright, flat areas of color—these come to mind when describing Tomi Ungerer's work. (p. 40)

There are many facets of Tomi's work, many areas of concentration, presenting many different moods for many different purposes. If you are a parent, you have undoubtedly read some of Ungerer's books to your children, and enjoyed with them the bold drawings, his imaginative use of bright color, and the gay make-believe of the stories. (p. 42)

All of Ungerer's children's books have simple, entertaining stories yet contain a definite moral: good always triumphs over evil. . . . Tomi regards his two latest books, which he both wrote and illustrated, as among his best. Artistically and technically he is satisfied with them. One is the delightful and timely *Moon Man*, which tells the story of the lonely man-in-the-moon who sees the gaiety down on the earth and decides to descend for a whirlwind adventure. He is depicted as a portly, luminous fellow who has, of course, the power to grow and to diminish. The text is minimal; the better to savor the imaginative illustrations, bright in color and bold in line. *Zeralda's Ogre* . . . tells the story of a little girl who charms a child-eating ogre with her culinary skills. The ogre is depicted as properly "scary" (which children love) and the pen-and-ink drawings are embellished with bright color.

Tomi Ungerer's books for adults are completely different and not intended for the innocent eyes of his younger audience. They are sophisticated, sharply satiric criticisms of our social scene today. They are effective without words . . ., [and are] not for the tender-skinned nor the prudish. Ungerer's drawings vividly present his scathing contempt of those things in the world around him which he feels to be foolish and corrupt. We squirm to see our vanity and greed exposed. These illustrations are so different from the gentle charm and whimsey of Tomi's children's books that it is difficult to believe that they come from the same pen. Yet artistic talent is evident in both: in the books for young children, the wonder, magical make-believe, and imaginative innocence is dominant; Tomi's sense of fun comes to the fore. (pp. 43-4)

> *Joan Hess Michel, "A Visit with Tomi Ungerer," in* American Artist *(copyright © 1969 by Billboard Publications, Inc.; reprinted with permission; all rights reserved), May, 1969, pp. 40-5, 78-9.*

Piper Paw, the kitten hero of author-artist Tomi Ungerer's latest picture book, *No Kiss for Mother* . . . is—claws sheathed—the orneriest, most self-centered and willful hero to hit kids' picture books since the mid-nineteenth-century heyday of *Struwwelpeter*. Not only does Piper sass his mother, trample on his beautifully-ironed clothes, and spend the better part of each school day wreaking havoc with a handcrafted peashooter and an arsenal of stink bombs, but the merest hint of a maternal buss is enough to kill his appetite for herring scraps or fried finch gizzards. With the domestic world handed him on a silver fish platter by doting parents, he has the chutzpa to be in a perpetual rage. Part of Ungerer's charm in this forty-page tantrum is his instinctive grasp of the anger of impotence that grips all small children during large chunks of their early lives. It is a rage directed at the limitations of childhood itself.

In Piper's case, there are also several legitimate gripes. He is, first of all, locked in mortal combat with a mother, Velvet Paw, who persists—despite all evidence to the contrary —in labeling him "little sugar tiger," "honey pie," and "my sweet little nestling." (Some nestling! There have probably been cuddlier vipers.) No sooner does this aggressively affectionate feline bend down to "wedge" the tale's first kiss in her sleeping son's ear, than he is off and running from her relentlessly ready lips. (p. 87)

Among Ungerer's endearing qualities are a total candor and lack of condescension. The adults in his tales treat children with loving kindness and respect no oftener than they do in life. Miss Clot, the nurse at Piper's school, for example, "prefers iodine to Mercurochrome" and sews the kitten's torn ear with "the biggest needle she can find." On the other hand, Ungerer is no romantic concerning the sweet innocence of the young. "My God, children are little bastards who chew and eat you up as they grow," he said recently. "They start with the kneecaps, maybe, and slowly they devour you." Unlike Maurice Sendak, who tenderly probes the innermost fantasies of childhood, or Edward Gorey, who limns, with Arctic detachment, the horrors of being small and at the mercy of the world's unreason, Ungerer sees himself chiefly as a chronicler of the absurd. "Our world, our children, our aspirations are all absurd," he says flatly. Yet, beyond its absurdly exaggerated catalogue of childhood misconduct, *No Kiss for Mother* strikes, with therapeutic clout, at the very heart of family relationships.

The world Ungerer creates for children is one furnished for his own aesthetic and intellectual comfort. It is, in fact, here furnished out of his own childhood experience. Velvet Paw, the sugar-coated villain of the work, bears an unmis-

takable resemblance to the typical martyred 1930s mother— not entirely surprising from an author who was himself a thirties' child and remembers that, from the age of six, he could not abide any open display of maternal affection. . . . The author insists, however, that the model for Piper's intransigence is not so much himself as an impossibly stubborn Burmese cat (named Piper) he owns.

Perhaps because English is not Ungerer's native language, he prides himself on what he calls his "weird mastery" of it. "I really work at my prose style," he confesses. Oddball words like "tilbury" and "blunderbuss" delight him as collector's items to be woven into his tales. (The two mentioned appeared in *The Hat* and *The Three Robbers* respectively.) Ungerer feels strongly that children enjoy unfamiliar words and euphonious, mystifying phrases. He looks upon *No Kiss* as the first of his books in which "the specificity lies more in the words than the pictures. It is a kind of *Portnoy's Complaint* of children's books."

Graphically even more than verbally, Ungerer's picture books seem always to breathe beyond the strict requirements of plot. Though the black and white pencil drawings for *No Kiss* are as simple and direct as a comic strip's— considerably less burdened with private symbols than many a recent Ungerer work—they are nonetheless full of the sort of particulars that invests storybook events with their own internal life. (p. 88)

Ungerer has long been something of an *enfant terrible* among children's book authors, one curiously immune to the usual desire either to improve or instruct the young. . . . And if Ungerer's work for children at times contains overly sophisticated embellishments—the bathroom in which Piper sits has a douche bag hanging above the tub—there are also times when his pornographic drawings partake of a refreshingly childlike innocence. (pp. 88-9)

Ungerer grew up in a household that included his mother, two much older sisters, and a brother. "My sisters taught me to draw, my brother taught me to think, and my mother taught me to use my imagination," he says in retrospect. Other early influences included the German painters Matthias Grünewald, Albrecht Dürer, and Martin Schongauer, as well as two turn-of-the-century Alsatian illustrators, Hansi and Schnugg. His children's books, decidedly European in ambience from the outset, have frequently exhibited a kind of schizophrenia, seesawing between lighthearted Gallic charm and lugubrious Teutonic humor. (pp. 89-90)

Like many other young Europeans at the close of World War II, Ungerer developed an exaggerated admiration for all things American and came to the United States in 1956. His first children's book, *The Mellops Go Flying*—about a gentle, ingenious, and decidedly French family of pigs— was done . . . the following year. Other early books—*Crictor* . . . , about a snake sent from Africa as a herpetologist's birthday gift to his aged mother, and *Adelaide* . . . , concerning a young flying kangaroo who leaves home to seek her fortune—are equally Gallic and sanguine in outlook. But by 1967, a darker strain crept into his juvenile work. The United States was deeply involved in Vietnam, and Ungerer began turning out coruscating antiwar posters that eventually found a worldwide adult audience. One of his two children's picture books of that year, *Zeralda's Ogre*, was about a lonely monster with a big nose, sharp teeth, bristling beard, and bad temper, who liked best "of all things . . . little children for breakfast." Parents were forced to hide their progeny in the cellar when this brute was on one of his rampages, much as the Ungerer family, in real life, had hidden in their cellar during the closing months of World War II when the Allied Front reached Colmar, where they were then living. Of this period Ungerer has said: "There was plenty to see and remember, and my taste for the macabre certainly finds its roots there." The artist is, in fact, presently working on a book about war for older children, based on his own experiences as a teen-ager. . . .

Ungerer considers that his first serious juvenile work was *The Beast of Monsieur Racine*. . . . It is the story of a retired tax collector, contentedly cultivating prize pears in his own backyard (Ungerer raises sheep, geese, goats, and rabbits in Canada) until the day he discovers that his precious fruit is being pilfered by a unique and amorphous beast. Eventually, he learns that the strange predator is animated by a boy and girl secreted deep inside its skin of old blankets, a denouement that leaves many a young reader mildly disappointed. Philosophically, however, *Monsieur Racine* is a turning point in the artist's career. Its clear message—possibly as much for Ungerer as his audience—is that no one escapes the child lurking beneath the surface, so it behooves us to be on friendly terms with that hidden, motivating force. Significantly, *Monsieur Racine* was the first of his children's books Ungerer felt was good enough to dedicate to Maurice Sendak. (p. 90)

> *Selma G. Lanes, "Tomi Ungerer's Reluctant Heroes," in* The Atlantic Monthly *(copyright © 1973 by The Atlantic Monthly Company, Boston, Mass.; reprinted with permission), January, 1974, pp. 87-90.*

Tomi Ungerer is devilishly clever: the expression could have been coined for him. When he first came to the United States from his native France, his work was rejected by *The New Yorker*, reputedly, as looking too much like Saul Steinberg's. So Harper's got him, and his wiry line made its first appearance in *The Mellops Go Flying;* and children got, beginning with the Mellops, a succession of animals as civilized as the sainted Babar who inspired them.

To turn the pages of *The Mellops Go Flying* is to admire and wonder; to wonder, indeed, what it is about Mr. Mellops, "gentle pig and kind father," and his four sons Casimir, Isidor, Felix and Ferdinand constructing a plane that is so utterly absorbing—even before they take their first trip, run out of gas, and slide down a mountain to a sudden painful stop. . . . The brief artless present-tense telling, largely absent since the Thirties; the very gentleness and kindliness, the industry and resourcefulness; the interesting, varying design and the movement it engenders, Ungerer strengths from the start; the small surprises (the sun downcast when the plane falls) and consistencies (Felix always rear-first): these are sufficient reason, perhaps, but there remain the individual figures—Mother Mellops majestically bearing in a tea tray, Casimir the miserable captive. . . . (p. 544)

Another followed immediately, *The Mellops Go Diving for Treasure* . . . , a considerably more involved story with some hilariously pictured happenings (including a meeting with a menacing, music-prone octopus); and, over the years, three more. Meanwhile, however, there appeared Crictor the companionable boa constrictor, or the improbabilities of Babar extended. . . . Ungerer is a comic artist of delicate ease and Crictor is—snake and book—an exquisite creation. (pp. 544, 546)

As was said of Babar in French, it would be comprehensible and entertaining even if one didn't know the language. Indeed Ungerer, more the artist, charms us not only by what he shows us but how (the snowbank that throws Crictor's curves in relief, the seaweed that curls up as if to enclose Emile); and by the wit of his transpositions from the human norm (the seaweed potted, the fish caged), the peculiar aptness of his particular animal's adaptations (Emile the mass imbiber, Crictor the practice knot). It is incongruity elevated, an improvement on life.

He is also of course much more the designer—in [the] case [of *Emile*], the animator. From the small scene-setting vignette of the two boats . . . , indicatively light and dark, the eye moves quickly across the void to the green-toned page and the close-up of Emile finding the boxes—a natural movement from small to large, from less to more developed, from lighter to heavier weight; and a dramatic demonstration of eye movement as spatial and temporal movement, something that Ungerer has utilized as much as or more than anyone. (pp. 547-48)

The design, setting a fast pace, establishing large free rhythms, expresses the story, *tells* the story, a rampaging adventure, even as it guides us to and isolates the particulars. . . .

Ungerer has the further distinction of extreme mobility: he moves around things like a film director. We have spoken of the effect of films as regards perspective and scale, and alluded, in discussing *Emile,* to those changes of perspective and scale that set up movement. But the mobility is an expressive as well as a dynamic force, a matter of shifting his point of view (and ours) in effect as in fact—just as it is for a film maker. One has, indeed, only to compare the Ungerer sequence, and other recent work, with the differently structured sequences of [Helen] Sewell . . . and [James] Daugherty . . . , each effective in its own right, to perceive the confluence of the design influence and the film influence in the later narrative treatments. Where we have not Ungerer's mobility, we have nonetheless a new fluidity; in the aggregate, new, freely expressive forms of *picturebook* movement.

But *Emile* is composed of pictures, and it is a book. To represent the picturebook as an entity and a medium, we have elected to write the term as one word; the medium, however, remains a vehicle, capable (McLuhan notwithstanding) of diverse messages in diverse forms. So we have Emile miming in a set of drawings that are sheer drawing, as amusing in themselves as [Gene Zion's] Harry the dirty dog doing his tricks . . . or [Bernard Waber's] Lyle the crocodile doing his chores . . .; and less essential—inessential—to the story. And to bring it to a close we have a last page that is quiet, in equilibrium, bounded, contained; our eye swings around to the center of weight, the checkerboard pattern, and can go no further. . . . (p. 548)

With *The Three Robbers* . . . , Ungerer shifted to a big, bright, bold style, painting instead of drawing and filling the page with arresting forms and intense, dramatic color. There was never such an electric blue, an assertive red or, in a picturebook, so much black. The tale, fittingly, is a melodrama . . ., and its content, as well as its look, was a challenge to placid pastel juvenalia. It has, however, chiefly cliffhanger interest—there is no internal development, no struggle or comeback; and the pictures themselves are best seen, emblematically, as posters.

To the extent that *The Three Robbers* is a spoof, even a parody, of villainy, it brought into the open a strain that the depiction of the smugglers in *Emile* hints at—the satire of evil and, in time, of society's evils: gluttony, for instance, and avarice, pomposity, callousness. . . . There is real badness in Ungerer's new world and unvarnished stupidity; as there was once in the purview of [Heinrich] Hoffmann and [Wilhelm] Busch.

The object of the chase, the alarm—though no one knows it yet—is Moon Man who, envious of the people dancing on earth, catches hold of a shooting star and crash-lands. But officialdom, no better than it's shown to be, throws the 'invader' in jail; and Moon Man, crushed, languishes until—in a brilliant visual stratagem—the waning moon gives him a way out. . . . (pp. 548-49)

'Make the earth safe for Moon Man' might be the motto, and one is reminded more than once of Kurt Joos's antimilitarist ballet, "The Green Table". . . . Actually the book is a more generalized comment—or condemnation—and it has, as satire hasn't, a true hero: a gentle soul (in transport over a rose) to suffer and hope for, and an avowal that wickedness isn't quite universal.

The next blockbuster is *The Beast of Monsieur Racine,* the book that, after *Moon Man,* is as grandly conceived as executed. Ungerer is amusing doing very little (*One, Two, Where's My Shoe?*) but a slight story inflated, even if it happens to be his (*The Hat*), is no match for the combination of passion and panache that distinguishes his work today. (pp. 549-50)

M. Racine and his affection for the beast are genuine, that is the crux of it; and a cut tree, one feels, would cry if it could. (Small children, imputing their own emotions to plants will, seeing sap, assume just that.) The mysterious 'beast' is a child's joke—of larger dimension—not, uncovered, a joke on the child audience: not a figment of the imagination or some sorcerer's plaything. And just as the deception is not an unkind one, so, properly, the children are not punished—Monsieur Racine, for that matter, congratulates them "for their cleverness and endurance." It is here that Ungerer breaks with Busch who, like any good nineteenth-century moralist, would have had Max and Moritz paddled, at least, for their effrontery. But Busch did not conceive of a prank that was not in some way malicious; and it falls to Ungerer, a thorough twentieth-century man, to portray children's mischief—and mischievous children—as not, by definition, bad.

All pearly, sherberty watercolor, *The Beast of Monsieur Racine* is a lovely book, without the clangor of *Moon Man* and some of its contemporaries. More subtly colored, it is also more subtly imagined and composed—per the window flung wide, the serpentine slide, the framed swing, the trace of game. Still, there are those idiot people and, later, their 'unspeakable acts'; and there is the beast, which some took as itself something unspeakable. . . .

The Beast of Monsieur Racine [is] total theater. (p. 552)

Barbara Bader, in American Picturebooks from Noah's Ark to the Beast Within *(reprinted with permission of Macmillan Publishing Co., Inc.; copyright © 1976 by Babara Bader), Macmillan, 1976.*

Tomi Ungerer's picture books seem to prompt solicitous comments about the psyche of their creator. "Schizophrenic," "obsessive," "neurotic": all of these terms have been used to describe Ungerer's children's books. . . . (p. 26)

Ungerer's trademarks are dripping blood and severed limbs. The heroes of his children's books include a bat and a vulture and his recent works feature macabre and violent disasters, scenes of literally swinish gluttony, and, in *Zeralda's Ogre,* cannibalism. On the face of it, a kind of comic Theater of Cruelty for children and little wonder that some of Ungerer's books make some adults uncomfortable and provoke speculation about the psychology of the artist.

Those who see Ungerer's picture books as collections of personal symbols expressing the warped subjectivity of the artist take too narrow a view of things. They fail to take into account the universality of his comic images and their relevance to the child's sense of humor. For whatever Tomi Ungerer's personal demons may be—and in his children's books they seem to be, by and large, merry and agreeable fellows—his humor communicates through the traditional structure of comic grotesque imagery.

The Russian critic Mikhail Bakhtin [in his *Rabelais and His World*] has traced the sources of this structure of grotesque imagery to the festive comic forms and symbols of medieval folk humor. Ritual spectacles like the "Feast of Fools" and verbal humor of the marketplace, parodies, and the various forms of billingsgate, all contributed to the storehouse of imagery of folk humor. In this rich and vital idiom, images of the body, especially the lower body, predominate. There is great emphasis on eating, drinking, and the digestive processes. Aspects of the body—noses, mouths, bellies—are isolated and exaggerated to comic hyperbolic dimensions. Mockery, abusive language, satire, and travesty all play a part in the comic grotesque, which is an inverted version of the official culture.

Romantic and modern artists and writers have absorbed and transformed this grotesque tradition and it has become associated with personal expressions of cyncism and alienation. In the folk sources, however, images of the lower body have a deeply positive character: they are images of fertility, growth, and abundance. Images of the material body connect man with the fruitful womb of the earth. Folk humor degrades in order to renew: parody and travesty provide vital correctives to an abstract and spiritual ideology. Throughout runs the spirit of popular Utopianism, the tradition of the Saturnalia, the return of Saturn's Golden Age.

The comic forms of folk humor survive today in the oral culture of children, the lore and language collected by the Opies and other folklorists. And the utopian spirit of the folk tradition, like many forms and themes abandoned by adult literature, survives in the hopeful and regenerative endings of children's stories which are neither condescensions nor outworn conventions but rather reflections of an underlying philosophical optimism.

The comedy of Tomi Ungerer's picture books depends on

grotesque bodily realism as well as on the regenerative spirit of the Saturnalia. In *The Beast of Monsieur Racine*, imagination and the regenerative comic spirit, in the form of the two mischievous children who disguise themselves as "the Beast," triumph over the sterile rationality and perfection of Monsieur Racine and the pompousness of the French Academy. And Monsieur Racine is himself transformed from a lonely bachelor who refused to share, to a warm, giving friend of the two children.

Grotesque imagery, always present in Ungerer's adult works, surfaced more slowly in his children's books. This development has paralleled the change from the wiry line and watercolors of his earlier illustrations to the aggressive, intense colors and bold shapes of his later works. There are suggestions of the grotesque in the comic mishaps of the Mellops family but, with the exception of Felix Mellops' protruding backside, there is little of the gross bodily caricature which defines the grotesque.... The best of these earlier books is *Crictor* which, like the Mellops series, has many affinities with Babar: the French setting, the helpful little old lady, the very civilized jungle animal. The humor in this book arises from Ungerer's exploitation of the comic potential in the situation and in the line of the snake's body, much as the humor in the Babar series depends on incongruity and the use of the solid and massive shapes of the elephants. (pp. 26-8)

Zeralda's Ogre ... is the first of Tomi Ungerer's own works for children to fully employ the grotesque tradition. It is an "original" folk tale which draws on the grotesque archetype of the giant, a staple in the folk tradition. In legends and popular festive forms, giants are associated with wealth, abundance, and great appetites. Much of the humor in *Zeralda's Ogre* develops around food and eating: there is the incongruous *haute cuisine* midnight snack that Zeralda prepares for the ogre—Pompano Sarah Bernhardt indeed—and there is a riotous banquet scene with a group of neighborhood ogres pictured in various stages of demented gluttony. The story line, however, adds a gruesome twist to this eating theme. The ogre has developed a taste for small children—his crest displays a sleeping infant with crossed knife and fork superimposed—and until he is tamed by Zeralda's home cooking, he ravages the town. In the end, he is transformed and the book ends with a picture of domestic bliss: "And so, it would seem, they lived happily ever after." It would seem so, but in the final frame Zeralda holds the newest member of the family while one of the young ogres gathered around her holds a knife and fork behind his back, hidden from his parents but in full view of the reader. He stares at the infant.

I Am Papa Snap and These Are My Favorite No Such Stories ... features a gallery of grotesques: Mr. Slop Glut, young Arson Twitch, Lido Rancid. The humor here is tougher, more sardonic, the characters more aggressively vulgar. The test assumes greater importance and the humor is astringent and absurdist.... *Papa Snap* is more openly satiric. For example, Mr. and Mrs. Kaboodle, two wealthy birds, purchase a nest and eggs from a "local nidologist." The eggs turn out to be rotten and the nest falls apart—a satire on human materialism and the shoddy workmanship of modern consumer products.

The Beast of Monsieur Racine is arguably the best of Tomi Ungerer's picture books to date, a delicious blend of droll fantasy and the comic grotesque. This is not to deny the

special appeal of the later *No Kiss For Mother* which certainly has its own raucous charm, but there the text is dominant while in *Monsieur Racine* there is a perfect marriage of text and pictures. Here Ungerer indulges his sense of play totally: he plays with the borders around the illustrations, at times reflexively calling attention to artistic illusion, at times suggesting life bursting outside the confines of the illustrations themselves. He creates riotous street scenes which in the grotesque tradition suggest abundance, the cornucopia of life filled to the overflowwing.... Ungerer uses objects and people falling and severed parts of the anatomy to suggest a world exploding into pieces and being reborn. The artistic points of reference are Brueghel and Hogarth.

The text of the climactic episode reads, "Unspeakable acts were performed." And they are. But they are in keeping with a child's more innocent concept of what might be "unspeakable acts." A man's bottom is paddled with a tennis racquet, another man has hold of a woman by her ample bosom, ostensibly to keep her from falling out of a bus but is that his wife pulling him back from behind? The grin on his face speaks volumes.... All in good fun if not in good taste and very much in keeping with the carnival licentiousness of the comic grotesque. Children's humor is full of.... innocent sexual allusions and, remembering that Tomi Ungerer has some reputation as an erotic artist, perhaps it can justifiably be said that *Monsieur Racine* is the first "pornographic" book for children. (pp. 29-31)

Tomi Ungerer's favorite image is said to be that of the little boy who drops his pants in a crowd. That, in a nutshell, defines the comic grotesque tradition within which he works: the logic of "bottoms up," the liberation from restrictions, and the reaffirmation of the body and bodily processes in a world which conceals them and surrounds them with taboos. (p. 31)

> R. A. Siegel, "The Little Boy Who Drops His Pants in a Crowd: Tomi Ungerer's Art of the Comic Grotesque," in The Lion and the Unicorn (copyright © 1977 Geraldine DeLuca, Roni Natov), Vol. 1, No. 1, pp. 26-32.

ALLUMETTE: A FABLE, WITH DUE RESPECT TO HANS CHRISTIAN ANDERSEN, THE GRIMM BROTHERS, AND THE HONORABLE AMBROSE BIERCE (1974)

Though Ungerer never plays his sentimental cliches straight, he doesn't mock them so much as he wallows in their vulgarity. Here Andersen's match girl, worse off than ever in an age when everyone has lighters, lives on to help the needy through her own Matchless Light of the World Foundation. And though none of this asks to be taken seriously, the illustrations make the fairy tale squalor and the immoderate wish-fulfillment insistently palpable. Asserting themselves like Allumette and her matches against solid black backgrounds, the pictures take you in as they lead you on.... Essential Ungerer, calling for a grain of salt ... and then rubbing it in. (p. 1100)

> Kirkus Reviews (copyright © 1974 The Kirkus Service, Inc.), October 15, 1974.

The pen of Tomi Ungerer, a singularly talented illustrator, has a built-in leer. Over the years his expertly amusing drawings have taken on deeper hues, darker humors, more intricate design. In *Allumette* . . . , Ungerer has reinterpreted Andersen's "The Little Match Girl" (think of Bosch illustrating *Heidi*). She's still a wide-eyed waif in a wicked world, but here the wicked world gets top billing. The abundant visual jokes are calculated to scandalize Peoria. As for the opium-smoking mayor who sports lipstick and toenail polish, chalk up another first in children's literature. The story builds entertainingly, then searches in vain for a satisfactory resolution; then *Allumette* fizzles. Still, Ungerer haunts. (p. 108)

> *Eliot Fremont-Smith and Karla Kuskin, in* New York Magazine *(© 1974 by NYM Corp.; reprinted by permission of* New York Magazine *and Eliot Fremont-Smith and Karla Kuskin), December 16, 1974.*

Tomi Ungerer tells in trenchant tones the tale of a poor little match-girl, trodden on and spurned by greedy Christmas crowds, who gasps with her last breath a wish for someone to help her, whereupon gifts rain from the sky and she ends up as head of a huge international welfare organisation. The hideous pictures, in carefully clashing, sombre tints of jade, yellow and puce, might throttle, in some readers, any impulse to accept the moral; in any case, it is not easy to assess the degree of cynicism in the book. (p. 2648)

> *Margery Fisher, in her* Growing Point, *May, 1975.*

OTHER CITATIONS

Karla Kuskin, in The New York Times Book Review, *November 3, 1974, p. 57.*

William Cole, in Saturday Review/World, *November 30, 1974, p. 28.*

Zena Sutherland, in Bulletin of the Center for Children's Books, *December, 1974, p. 70.*

Brian W. Alderson, in Children's Book Review, *Summer, 1975, p. 56.*

THE BEAST OF MONSIEUR RACINE (1971)

[*The Beast of Monsieur Racine* is elegantly] droll and extravagantly French, from the fittingly unpossessive title to the "shiny cuirass" M. Racine dons defensively with his cavalry uniform. Because "One morning, alas! three times, alas! he found all his pears gone"—they were his pride and his joy, not for selling or sharing; now he's lying, soon sleeping, in wait for the thief . . . upon whose arrival "Our avenger jumped to his feet and grabbed his saber. '*Sapristi!*'" And voila the beast—with "long, socklike ears . . . on both sides of an apparently eyeless head," and a "shaggy, mangled mane" topping what Ungerer (forked tongue in cheek) calls a "drooping snout" but distends mistakably like an unconfigured phallus. . . . What meets the eye is at once exuberant and economical; both pictures and text are more and less sophisticated than they seem. This is funny and bright and immediate on lots of levels, a sort of rare tour de farce for the whole family. (p. 806)

> *Kirkus Reviews (copyright © 1971 The Kirkus Service, Inc.), August 1, 1971.*

Part of the purpose of any child's book is to enlarge the vocabulary—but such words as predator, marauder, Sapristi, meticulous and the like may be pushing things a bit. Nor does a child's book need to lean too heavily on logic, but when Monsieur Racine lives by the code of "no selling and no sharing," and then immediately shares everything with the monster, it seems contrived. But all in all this book has a sort of heavy guffaw appeal in its somewhat ungraceful ending. (p. B3)

> *Guernsey Le Pelley (reprinted by permission from* The Christian Science Monitor; © 1971 by The Christian Science Publishing Society; all rights reserved), The Christian Science Monitor, November 11, 1971.*

If [Ezra Jack] Keats is the sanest of contemporary American artists, Tomi Ungerer is the craziest. His hero this time is Mr. Racine, a retired French tax collector who grows, but refuses to make commercial capital out of, prize pears. These are stolen at night by a very strange beast which, armed with his sabre and in an outgrown cavalry uniform, he captures. . . . [The] emergence of two small and naughty children from the beast's skin . . . makes a splendid climax to a gorgeous tale. There are characteristic Ungerer touches in the crowd scenes: a lady scientist's gown slips perilously, another loses her wig, a professor sustains a nasty scalp wound from another's watch, scientists turn improbable colours. Some parents may be distressed by the sickness, but probably their children will be moved only to delighted laughter. The story concludes with Mr. Racine back home with his little friends, and what appropriately beastly children they look. (p. 361)

> The Junior Bookshelf, *December, 1972.*

OTHER CITATIONS

Publishers Weekly, *August 9, 1971, p. 47.*

Marjorie Lewis, in School Library Journal, *September, 1971, p. 109.*

Selma G. Lanes, in The New York Times Book Review, *September 19, 1971, p. 8.*

Eleanor von Schweinitz, in Children's Book Review, *February, 1973, p. 9.*

Robert Melville, in New Statesman, *May 21, 1976, p. 689.*

THE HAT (1970)

With two leaps (*Zeralda's Ogre* last year and now *The Hat*) Tomi Ungerer has unquestionably established himself amongst the small company capable of producing text and illustration worthy of one another. The hat, a black top hat with a ribbon of magenta silk, blows off one man's head and lands on the head of a poor veteran soldier; it changes his fortunes drastically and, when he can want nothing more, blows off his head. . . . The story is robust, often amusing, and full of side-jokes that will endear it to adults without diminishing it for children. The virile pictures are uncluttered, and yet their detail repays careful attention; and, as one might expect from this well-known cartoonist, the characterisation is superb. (p. 698)

> *Kevin Crossley-Holland, in* The Spectator *(© 1971 by* The Spectator; *reprinted by*

permission of The Spectator), *November 13, 1971.*

Here in gorgeous technicolour is another picture book from this talented author-artist which will please adults as much as children. How gratifying for instance to murmer "Potemkin" as the pram lurches down the steps to find one's associations justified on the following page. Children will like the story of a magic hat which transforms the life of an old soldier who is finally seen driving off with his bride, too rich and happy to care that the hat has blown away in the breeze. Which is where we, and the book, came in. This neatly contrived story cannot be considered apart from the pictures which are some of Ungerer's most attractive and as usual full of wit spiced with a touch of social comment. The print is large and older siblings reading to their young will enjoy pronouncing the long words and forceful (but clean) expletives. (p. 28)

The Junior Bookshelf, *February, 1972.*

OTHER CITATIONS

Polly Goodwin, in Book World, *Part 2, May 17, 1970, p. 4.*

Barbara Novak, in The New York Times Book Review, *Part II, May 24, 1970, p. 46.*

Derwent May, in The Listener, *November 11, 1971, p. 665.*

David Gentleman, in New Statesman, *November 12, 1971, p. 665.*

Brian W. Alderson, in Children's Book Review, *September, 1972, p. 9.*

I AM PAPA SNAP AND THESE ARE MY FAVORITE NO SUCH STORIES (1971)

As in Ungerer's previous picture-books, the exaggerated humor of the big, colorful illustrations will be sure to please children; however, the . . . *No Such Stories* themselves are uneven in quality and appeal. A few of the brief anecdotes are delightfully absurd (e.g., runaway Arson Twitch goes to sea in the family bathtub and downs a battleship with his slingshot); others use unusual vocabulary to amusing effect (e.g., Dr. Stigma Lohengreen tells his patient that " 'There is a PICKLE jammed in [his] vena cava/and the gangliated chords of [his] sympathetic/are all tangled up.,' "). But, the rest are either weighed down with didactic messages (e.g., the Kaboodles blow their bankroll on a store-bought nest which promptly falls apart, causing them to conclude that " '. . . that's what happens when/you start spending money.' ") or just fall flat (e.g., "Mr. Limpid is blind./Mrs. Limpid is lame./They are old./They are happy./They have each other."). Although the illustrations are more effective than the text overall, several contain gratuitous gruesome details—e.g., Mr. Slop Gut's pictured repast includes a bloody knife, sausages dripping blood, a turkey spewing water from its nether cavity, and a disemboweled intestine; Lido Rancid's sickroom features a bedpan partially filled with blood-streaked, viscous liquid; etc. On the last page Papa Snap is snatched up by a "very hungry sofa," but it is unlikely that his stories will meet a similar fate with children. (p. 62)

Pamela D. Pollack, in School Library Journal *(reprinted from the February, 1972,*

issue of School Library Journal, *published by R. R. Bowker Company, a Xerox company; copyright © 1972 by Xerox Corporation), February, 1972.*

Ungerer is one of the most brilliant illustrators at work today. His drawings are mainly European in origin, populated by delightful minor officials, stuffy pedagogues, and bacchanalian street types. His moles, dressed in overcoats, have the intrigue of bit players in the movie, "The Third Man."

If Ungerer has a weakness, it is in his story line which, in some instances, doesn't live up to his great art work. In his new book "I Am Papa Snap and These Are My Favorite No Such Stories," he generally overcomes this problem by using a short story to accommodate a single illustration, rather than a continuing narrative for the entire book. So the reader is treated to a series of "quickies" similar to blackout sketches. Some of these stories do fail, but never the accompanying illustrations.

An often heard knock against Ungerer is that many of his drawings are too violent for the eyes of children. Once in a while the charge is valid, as in "The Beast of Monsieur Racine," where, in one illustration, he has gratuitously drawn a hobo with a pack on his back that has a bloody foot hanging out. But this is a minor carp against such an artist.

In his latest work he draws a pig, Mr. Slop Glut, who devours everything on the menu at his favorite restaurant, then, exiting, falls right through the floor because of the added weight. True, Slop Glut looks like something George Grosz would have conceived, but the whole picture is darkly hilarious; and for those looking for moral messages, there is the sin of gluttony. . . .

In this book Ungerer shows a touching, gentle side to his art. He draws a loving illustration of a blind mole wheeling his lame wife in her wheelchair, and the story is simply:

> "Mr. Limpid is blind.
> Mrs. Limpid is lame.
> They are old.
> They are happy.
> They have each other." . . .

Such diverse elements are what make an artist interesting. And, of course, there is the patented Ungerer whimsy: a dragon that is used to light cigars, a steamroller in a kitchen that is used to press clothes and flatten pizza dough, a slingshot David sitting in a floating bathtub who sinks a Goliath of a battleship with a single twang of a rubber band.

But Ungerer will be Ungerer, so he closes with a scare: a great illustration of "a hungry sofa" that devours Papa Snap, Ungerer's alter ego.

I'm not complaining, mind, but I hope the sofa suffers from indigestion and coughs up Papa Snap again. Why should that damn greedy sofa have all those great future stories in his plush tummy, when they are needed to decorate the feeble table of contemporary children's literature? (p. 8)

Joe Flaherty, in The New York Times Book Review (© 1972 by The New York Times Company; reprinted by permission), *February 20, 1972.*

OTHER CITATIONS

Kirkus Reviews, *November 15, 1971, p. 1211.*

Timothy Rogers, in The School Librarian, *March, 1974, p. 109.*

THE MELLOPS' GO SPELUNKING (1963)

A family of spelunking pigs, not truffle-diggers, are the Mellops, the pigs in this fourth Mellops adventure by the author. With miners' equipment, they descend to the dreary depths of a cave, gathering useful and useless information along the way. A sudden flood—plus perfume smugglers—add to the boisterous confusion, but the pigs via perfume-filled barrels, ascend with a few cave-pieces to show for their efforts. The story would be more effective, had the author not jammed quite so many bizarre details into so small a space. But, the cartoon illustrations (in blue, peach, black and white)—especially the ones of the pigs in total blackness—have the kind of humor and exuberance which will be enjoyed. (p. 311)

Virginia Kirkus' Service, *March 15, 1963.*

What child wouldn't want to be a member of Tomi Unger-er's resourceful Mellops family? They're off on another wonderfully entertaining adventure in "The Mellops' Go Spelunking". . . . Father and sons explore an underground cavern, unearth artifacts and discover paintings done by cavemen ("or maybe cavepigs") millions of years ago. There's peril, too, when the cavern is flooded, their rubber raft is punctured by a stalagmite and they land in a perfume smugglers' den. No one can resist turning the pages to see if the Mellops come out on top. Mr. Ungerer has superbly drawn the pigs in their eerie, deep domain. (p. 4)

George A. Woods, in The New York Times Book Review, *Part II (© 1963 by The New York Times Company; reprinted by permission), May 12, 1963.*

OTHER CITATIONS

Margaret Warren Brown, in The Horn Book Magazine, *August, 1963, p. 379.*

MOON MAN (1967)

The contrast between the Moon Man, a foreshortened Uncle Fester, wistful and appealing and immaterial, and the stridency and stupidity of his tormentors is exploited by the bright, galloping illustrations, as effective as any Tomi Ungerer has done. This has some of the sting of *Dr. Strangelove*—but tenderized, the contemporary charisma of [Maurice Sendak's] *Where the Wild Things Are*: it's great. (p. 55)

Kirkus Service *(copyright © 1967 Virginia Kirkus' Service, Inc.), January 15, 1967.*

Tomi Ungerer's man in the moon is milky white, soft obese and rather slug-like. He gains sympathy only because all other characters are depicted as actively menacing. Moon Man is an earth gazer and the party he came down to join is shown as a dissolute revel. He is greeted by a very militaristic society, in which generals take charge and police are gun-happy. They seize Moon Man and jail him rather than

investigate him. He escapes through the bars by diminishing to his third quarter and is chased from the sort of wild dancing party that intrigues him to the castle of a scientist who rockets him back to the moon. The illustrations suggest more in this over-sized book than the brief text. They are painted with the facility of a most sophisticated cartoonist and violent stupidity is implicit in the faces, even in the sly, gap-toothed grin of the scientist who comes to Moon Man's aid. The jacket calls it "gentle satire." It seems more of a jeer at modern civilization. The color work is the most attractive feature, but on the whole it's an adult camp fancier's book and a malevolent stare at a decadent society. (p. 122)

Elinor S. Cullen, in School Library Journal *(reprinted from the March, 1967, issue of* School Library Journal, *published by R. R. Bowker Company, a Xerox company; copyright © 1967 by Xerox Corporation), March, 1967.*

OTHER CITATIONS

Publishers Weekly, *March 27, 1967, p. 61.*

Zena Sutherland, in Bulletin of the Center for Children's Books, *May, 1967, p. 148.*

The Times Literary Supplement, *May 25, 1967, p. 452.*

NO KISS FOR MOTHER (1973)

You can tell right away, the minute you see him glaring from the jacket: A sweetheart he isn't.

Certainly no naughtier kid (in this case a sour-pussed kitten named Piper Paw) has appeared between the covers of a picture book. He throws his clock out the window. He crumples and rumples his clothes. He has tantrums and a very, *very* fresh mouth. In school he stuffs his teacher's purse with spiders (big, black, live ones) and sprinkles itching powder on one and all.

Furthermore, his insolent ways are breaking his mother's heart, or—as in true Sophie Portnoy fashion she puts it—"Each word is a nail in my coffin." Poor lady, all she wants to do is make yummy meals for her darling, and shower her nestling, her Honey Pie, her little sugar tiger with kisses of love.

She's driving him nuts!

Kisses, kisses, who wants kisses, screams Piper. . . .

Right on the sidewalk, in front of all the people, that's how he screams at sweet Mrs. Velvet Paw. And that's when Piper's mother, for the first time in his life, slaps him—slam-whack—in the face.

Piper's disgraceful, outrageous behavior will make toes curl with horrified delight and his ooey-gooey overprotective, over-indulgent ma is bound to make young readers feel smugly superior. In one sensational illustration Piper—running the water and rubbing his toothbrush against the sink "in case Mother Snoop is listening"—sits on the toilet reading a Ratman comic book.

What kid could resist?

I don't believe for a minute that a single overdue smack is

really going to reform the terrible Piper, but that doesn't spoil the joys of this fierce, funny book.

A book that understands about boys and their parents.

A book that is also for mothers—and not just for kids. (p. 8)

> *Judith Viorst, in* The New York Times Book Review (© *1973 by The New York Times Company; reprinted by permission), June 24, 1973.*

Unlike the ebullient exaggeration of the texts and pictures of Ungerer's picture books, [*No Kiss for Mother*] has a flat and hostile tone, with no humor to relieve the acid depictions of the female characters and a climax that seems to indicate that he who gets slapped sees reason. (p. 19)

> *Zena Sutherland, in* Bulletin of the Center for Children's Books (© *1973 by the University of Chicago; all rights reserved), September, 1973.*

No Kiss for Mother is about a maladjusted kitten. . . . Full of Ungerer's usual acid wit, but somehow unattractive, partly because of the dreary monochrome illustrations, but more, I think because there is an elusive nastiness behind the story. (p. 36)

> *Valerie Alderson, in* Children's Book Review (© *1975 Five Owls Press Ltd.; all rights reserved), Spring, 1975.*

OTHER CITATIONS

Kirkus Reviews, *May 15, 1973, p. 558.*

Anita Silvey, in The Horn Book Magazine, *August, 1973, pp. 373-74.*

Diane Gersoni-Stavn, in School Library Journal, *September, 1973, p. 119.*

The Junior Bookshelf, *February, 1975, p. 28.*

ORLANDO, THE BRAVE VULTURE (1966)

Orlando's neck is not drawn with a typically vulturous menacing droop. He looks more like a bald necked, big-eyed, tipsy turkey. His story guys all the fare chaotically slapped together and filmed in living cliche for the afternoon TV children's audience—intelligent animals saving the day and creaky Western shoot-'em-ups. The story is told with a minimum of text and illustrated with cartoons in three colors. . . . [*Orlando*] is a heavy flight of fancy destined never to replace Lassie or convince TV Western fans of the foolishness of it all. (p. 178)

> Virginia Kirkus' Service *(copyright © 1966 Virginia Kirkus' Service, Inc.), February 15, 1966.*

Dad may enjoy Orlando more than the children. Satire, never far below the surface in Ungerer, that master of the sick joke, is on top here. Orlando, the only sympathetic vulture in literature, makes himself a niche in Mexican society by his energy and good works. Good fun and vigorous caricature, but the author has his eye firmly on the adults who buy books for children. (p. 26)

> The Junior Bookshelf, *February, 1968.*

OTHER CITATIONS

Publishers Weekly, *February 7, 1966, p. 90.*

SNAIL, WHERE ARE YOU? (1962)

[In *Snail, Where Are You?*, finding] the shape of a snail in a french horn, a pair of boots, a couch, a violin and a dozen more animate and inanimate objects is the task given to very young viewers whom we feel will barely be challenged. Without any progression of difficulty, the snail turns up only once in each picture—hardly enough to stimulate perceptive powers. The entire text is summed up in the title and the pictures are ordinary. (p. 105)

> Virginia Kirkus' Service, *February 1, 1962.*

"Snail, where are you?" This provocative question on the very first page will invite the young child to study these brilliantly colorful, slightly zany pictures, hunting for the snail's ubiquitous spiral. An imaginative, almost wordless picture book which should stimulate a first awareness of form, pattern, and design. (p. 150)

> *Ethel L. Heins, in* School Library Journal *(reprinted from the March, 1962, issue of* School Library Journal, *published by R. R. Bowker Company, a Xerox company; copyright © 1962 by Xerox Corporation), March, 1962.*

OTHER CITATIONS

Ellen Lewis Buell, in The New York Times Book Review, *April 8, 1962, p. 30.*

Donnarae MacCann and Olga Richard, in their The Child's First Books: A Critical Study of Pictures and Texts, *The H. W. Wilson Company, 1973, p. 109.*

A STORYBOOK FROM TOMI UNGERER (1974)

The title page shows a blue hand with a wooden ladle, bubbling up from the depths of a pot of peagreen soup; the rest of the body has already sunk, but the hand is still valiantly stirring around and around: look, no lumps, fine puree of Ungerer, as if Charles Addams were working in sunlight instead of deadly nightshade. Ungerer's tone throughout this compilation is cheerful; the most scarifying scenes are underlaid with an invisible smile.

It is, strictly speaking, not precise to call this "A Storybook From Tomi Ungerer," since he has written only one-sixth of the text; rather, it is his choice of stories to illustrate. The first is "Changing Places," an adaptation by Bernard Garfinkel of the Norwegian folk tale, "The Husband Who Was to Mind the House," familiar in its retelling by Wanda Gag as "Gone Is Gone." Garfinkel follows Gag's slight softening of the original, and it has become somewhat more wordy than need be. . . . But the sturdy folk tale still remains under the embellishments, and Ungerer's pictures are to the point, as when the farmer in a rage kicks the pig out of the kitchen: you see the iron bit on his boot and a musical note ensues as he kicks the pig so hard its pinkness turns blue before your eyes.

The second story is Andersen's "The Tinder Box" and it fares particularly well under Ungerer's auspices. The fierce dogs we see have fangs and spiked iron collars, they slaver juicily, yet become monstrously tender in the moonlight, and at the happy-ever-after ending their eyes that were large as saucers, as millwheels, as castle towers, have changed into valentine hearts. Who could resist such an image?

Bernard Garfinkel has also adapted Grimm's "Clever Gretel"; this seems, even with its extended verbiage, to be faithful to the original and a pleasure to read aloud: high marks for clever Bernard and clever Tomi, especially for his platter with the shorn chicken and a grandly choreographed chase scene.

Another Grimm follows, the fairy tale of "The Wishing Table, the Gold Donkey, and the Cudget-in-the-Sack," in an excellent adaptation by Wanda Gag; again the illustrations flourish, with the donkey coughing up gold coins before our eyes, and wicked innkeeper getting a splendid thrashing from the magic cudgel.

Jay Williams's recent "Petronella" comes next; this story of a liberated princess who wouldn't stay passive is one of the jolliest of emancipation proclamations, and it is a pleasure to have it included along with classic tales here. My favorite illustration in the whole book is of the Princess Petronella surrounded by snarling hounds, taming them by her sympathetic and glowing presence.

Last in the collection is "Little Red Riding Hood" in a version "reruminated" by Ungerer. He has chosen his phrasing well, for this is something to chew over. After a number of readings, I have come to the reluctant conclusion that it should have been omitted. Surely classic tales can be adapted to different times and circumstances; I am not objecting on purist grounds. But what we have been given here is too arbitrary a reversal of roles, with the grandmother as villain and the wolf as hero: it simply does not belong in a gathering of traditional folk and fairy tales. Jay Williams's "Petronella" works because he has kept to the fairy-tale format, whereas Ungerer has made a grown-up, slick and even snide piece out of the childhood familiar. . . .

Nevertheless, five out of six is a dandy score. (p. 28)

> *Eve Merriam, in* The New York Times Book Review *(© 1974 by The New York Times Company; reprinted by permission), November 3, 1974.*

The raison d'etre for this volume is Ungerer's illustrations, casting as usual a tinge of luridness over the whole. The six stories, almost all available elsewhere, include two Grimm tales, "The Wishing Table" and "Clever Gretel"; Andersen's "The Tinderbox"; and two tales relevant to the role of women, Jay Williams' *Petronella* and a folk tale, "Changing Places." The final touch is Ungerer's own free adaptation of "Little Red Riding Hood," in which Red abandons her crochety old grandmother to marry the wolf. Nonessential except for Ungerer cultists. (p. 573)

> The Booklist *(reprinted by permission of the American Library Association; copyright 1975 by the American Library Association), February 1, 1975.*

OTHER CITATIONS

Margery Fisher, in her Growing Point, *January, 1975, p.*

2552.

Marjorie Lewis, in School Library Journal, *March, 1975, p. 102.*

THE THREE ROBBERS (1962)

Just because [Ungerer's] illustrations for "The Three Robbers" are so effective his story is less so. His characters are, to begin with, most convincing desperadoes who rob and plunder in good old-fashioned, fairy-tale style, portrayed in pleasantly scary night scenes. When they capture a small girl, however, they quickly soften into philanthropists and protectors of orphans. It seems they had never thought to spend all that boodle. This is comfortable whimsy for the tenderhearted, but it is likely that some readers, especially small boys used to more muscular stuff, may feel cheated out of a thriller. (p. 30)

> *Ellen Lewis Buell, in* The New York Times Book Review *(© 1962 by The New York Times Company; reprinted by permission), April 8, 1962.*

[*The Three Robbers*] is certainly a calculated work of art, but the heart of the story and the pictures has a fundamental innocence.

The story is too good to be spoiled by retelling, but basically it is the story of the conversion of three wicked robbers through contact with a child's goodness. Mrs. [Frances Hodgson] Burnett told a somewhat similar story in a hundred or so tear-drenched pages, and plenty of other Victorian writers had a go. Mr. Ungerer manages in about three hundred words to be at least as moral and at the same time devastatingly funny. He is a master of the small telling detail: the robbers' eyes at their first appearance (three eyes between three robbers), the suitably irregular window in the cave fitted with an irregular frame, the drunken peasant with four xxxx on his doublet (lacings really but splendidly symbolic) among others; but detail is never allowed to interfere with the general effect. A beautifully comical nonsense story told by a master of simplicity. (p. 120)

> The Junior Bookshelf, *July, 1962.*

OTHER CITATIONS

Virginia Kirkus' Service, March 15, 1962, p. 279.

Helen Skahill, in Library Journal, *May 15, 1962, p. 86.*

The Times Literary Supplement, *June 1, 1962, p. 401.*

Diana Klemin, in her The Art of Art for Children's Books: A Contemporary Survey, *Potter, 1966, p. 105.*

ZERALDA'S OGRE (1967)

More terrifying even than *The Three Robbers,* but just as easily tamed, is the ogre who dines on little children until converted by the exquisite cookery of little Zeralda; innocent that she was, she felt only pity for the poor hungry giant and fed him so well that he hired her for the castle kitchen. . . . The illustrative style alternates between inflated ugliness in orange, black, bisque (as per *Orlando, the Brave Vulture*) and multicolor peasant picturesqueness (. . .

The Donkey Ride [written by Jean B. Shawalter and illustrated by Ungerer]), sometimes with good effect for the story, sometimes gratuitously—but children will drool over the double-page spread of delicacies, a kind of gemutlich *McCall's*. The beginning is authentic scare, the turnabout is fare play and good fun, the last is a letdown—it will repel some youngsters, probably attract more, but it's not Ungerer at his best. (p. 874)

> Kirkus Service *(copyright © 1967 Virginia Kirkus' Service, Inc.), August 1, 1967.*

This gruesome tale is told in a direct and simple prose that reads well aloud, and is illustrated in full colour with all the macabre humour so characteristic of this artist. The pictures are large and bold, and well integrated with the text, many in double-page spreads. The setting is shown as a European country in medieval times, which distances the cannibalistic horrors and aids the suspension of disbelief. Some touches cause a shiver; the caged child at the beginning, and the child's arm poking pathetically out of the ogre's sack. . . .

Most children, from about six to eight, will take the gruesome humour in their stride, and find this book hilarious, but it is not for the over-sensitive. [*Zeralda's Ogre*] is an excellent picture-book, made with energy and wit, with a direct appeal to children. (p. 16)

> *John A. Cunliffe, in* Children's Book Review *(© 1971 by Five Owls Press Ltd.; all rights reserved), February, 1971.*

In *Zeralda's Ogre,* . . . evil is directly assaulted by domestic comfort and is, for a time, triumphed over. . . . The last picture in the book is most telling. It is a family portrait of Zeralda, grown up, and the Ogre, now her clean-shaven husband, surrounded by her children who reach happily for the laughing baby on her lap. All is blissful but for the child in the lower right-hand corner with his back to us. Why does he hold a knife and fork behind him? Why are we not reassured about his intentions by a look into his eyes? Is it not possible for innocent, generous love to rid us of evil? (p. 38)

> *Welleran Poltarnees. in his* All Mirrors Are Magic Mirrors: Reflections on Pictures Found in Children's Books *(copyright © 1972 by The Green Tiger Press), Green Tiger Press, 1972.*

OTHER CITATIONS

Eve Merriam, in The New York Times Book Review, *Part II, November 5, 1967, p. 70.*

Janet Malcolm, in The New Yorker, *December 16, 1967, pp. 159-60.*

Kevin Crossley-Holland, in The Spectator, *December 5, 1970, p. xv.*

John Fuller, in New Statesman, *March 5, 1971, p. 314.*

V

VIORST, Judith

Judith Viorst is an American poet, journalist, and author of books for adults and children. In the latter she often uses her own children (Alexander, Anthony, and Nicholas) as characters and writes as a response to their problems and needs. She is a columnist for and a contributing editor of *Redbook* magazine, and won an Emmy award in 1970 for the poetic monologues written for the television special, "Annie, The Women in the Life of a Man." (See also *Contemporary Authors*, Vols. 49-52 and *Something About the Author*, Vol. 7.)

ALEXANDER AND THE TERRIBLE, HORRIBLE, NO GOOD, VERY BAD DAY (1972)

In the spiky spirit of [her] *Sunday Morning* . . . but more truly attuned to a child's point of view, Viorst reviews a really aggravating (if not terrible, horrible, and very bad) day in the life of a properly disgruntled kid who wakes up with gum in his hair and goes to bed after enduring lima beans for dinner and kissing on T.V. . . . [And] there is worse to come. It's no wonder the kid's ready to move to Australia, but in the end, "My mom says some days are like that. Even in Australia." If Alexander's mother is smart to offer casual sympathy without phoney consolation, [illustrator Ray] Cruz and Viorst accord readers the same respect. (p. 1095)

> Kirkus Reviews (*copyright © 1972 The Kirkus Service, Inc.*), *September 15, 1972.*

Will the ubiquitous Judith Viorst ever run out of zany anecdotes about her all-male household, from bullying siblings to *Alexander and the Terrible, Horrible, No Good, Very Bad Day* . . .? We hope not! In this latest thrilling installment, everything goes wrong for the brother of Anthony and Nick. Alexander's mother, alone of all parents, forgets to include dessert in the lunchbag. Only Alexander—of the three brothers—has a cavity. Only Alexander is scolded for fighting. And what with lima beans, prizeless breakfast cereal, railroad train pajamas, and his own clumsiness at father's office . . . well, his mom says comfortingly, some days are like that . . . for all of us. (p. 2)

> *Michael J. Bandler, in* Book World—The Washington Post, *Part 2 (© The Washington Post), November 5, 1972.*

No sweetness-and-light ending here, as a cruel fate pursues Alexander right up to bedtime; there is however, a consoling note in mother's last, sympathetic remark. Some days are like that—even in Australia. Small listeners can enjoy the litany of disaster, and perhaps be stimulated to discuss the possibility that one contributes by expectation. The illustrations capture the grumpy dolor of the story, ruefully funny. (p. 68)

> *Zena Sutherland, in* Bulletin of the Center for Children's Books (© *1972 by the University of Chicago; all rights reserved), December, 1972.*

Judith Viorst is an author who can enter imaginatively into a child's difficulties without being either tactless or disablingly sympathetic. *Alexander and the Terrible, Horrible, No Good, Very Bad Day* is a funny but not heartless book about a small boy whose whole day goes wrong. . . . Ray Cruz's accomplished black ink drawings do comic but sympathetic justice to the frustrations and catastrophes suffered by the unfortunate Alexander. (p. 1437)

> The Times Literary Supplement (© *Times Newspapers Ltd., 1973; reproduced from* The Times Literary Supplement *by permission), November 23, 1973.*

OTHER CITATIONS

Diane Gersoni-Stavn, in School Library Journal, *October, 1972, p. 108.*

Marilyn Willison, in West Coast Review of Books, *Vol. 2, No. 5 (August, 1976), p. 24.*

THE CHANGING EARTH (1967)

["The Changing Earth" is a] compact and readable survey of the earth sciences, geology and its various branches—petrology, geophysics, mineralogy, paleontology, etc. After some tough early chapters describing minerals and rocks in rather specialized vocabulary, the author gets down to discussing the effects upon the earth's surface of glaciers, volcanoes, earthquakes, tides, winds and rivers. The closing chapters provide an admirable summary of the geological history of the earth, from 600 million years ago to the present. (p. 79)

Lavinia Russ, in Publishers Weekly *(reprinted from the February 13, 1967, issue of* Publishers Weekly *by permission of the critic, published by R. R. Bowker Company, a Xerox company; copyright © 1967 by Xerox Corporation), February 13, 1967.*

Despite its relative brevity, this book puts across the essence of geology better than many of the regular series of introductory college texts that span the same scope. It does this through a skillful focusing on the essentials. The 18 chapters begin with a lucid history of geology followed by an introduction to the form of the earth. Next, in a usefully early position, come chapters on minerals and rocks. Then, five chapters on geomorphic processes, three on mountain building, four on historical geology, and a final chapter on the importance of geology to society. The use of jargon is minimized, yet the writing in no way underestimates the intelligence of the reader. (p. 119)

Science Books *(copyright 1967 by the American Association for the Advancement of Science), Vol. 3, No. 2 (September, 1967).*

MY MAMA SAYS THERE AREN'T ANY ZOMBIES, GHOSTS, VAMPIRES, CREATURES, DEMONS, MONSTERS, FIENDS, GOBLINS, OR THINGS (1973)

As in *Alexander and the Terrible, Horrible, No Good, Very Bad Day . . .*, Viorst deals humorously with a childhood truth; here it's the threat of imaginary monsters and a mother's reassurances that they don't exist. While wanting to believe his mother, Nick is also aware that she often makes mistakes. Each apparition . . . is wittily limned by artist Kay Chorao, as are all of Mama's mistakes. . . . Of course, it turns out that mamas *can* be trusted (most of the time). Along the way, however, Viorst presents a marvelous catalog of monsters that could terrorize an imaginative child as well as a compendium of all the mistakes that mamas make. (p. 63)

Alice H. Yucht, in School Library Journal *(reprinted from the September, 1973, issue of* School Library Journal, *published by R. R. Bowker Company, a Xerox company; copyright © 1973 by Xerox Corporation), September, 1973.*

"My Mama Says . . ." is . . . a recital which raises the question of how, in the face of the many flaws in her daily pronouncements, a mother can be depended on when she says there are no horrors in the night: "My mama says that a vampire isn't flying over my house . . . But how can I believe her when she said my wriggly tooth would fall out Thursday, and then it stayed till Sunday after lunch?" The final point is not at all a putdown of fallible parenthood, which could leave a small child anxious. It is something much more subtle, the grain of what is almost hope that maybe—since Mama is human and does make mistakes—maybe there really can be a thrilling other side to the practical realities. "My Mama Says . . ." is as sound a bit of two-way understanding as I've seen in a long time.

The plentiful black-and-white illustrations are not to be compared with [Ed] Emberley's full-color feast [in Ian Serraillier's *Suppose You Met a Witch*] and yet there is a point worth mentioning here: beauty alone can't make a picture

work. There is a further quality altogether indispensable—space, alas, does not permit an essay on the subject—that is hard to define. But whatever it is, it is present in Chorao's pictures, just as it is in Emberley's. Her pictures are warm and satisfying and—they work. (p. 8)

Natalie Babbitt, in The New York Times Book Review *(© 1973 by The New York Times Company; reprinted by permission), December 30, 1973.*

Kay Chorao's black and white pictures show both the reality of a small boy's conflict situations and the deliciously horrible creatures his imagination produces. The book has no plot line, but there are a series of amusing incidents that follow a pattern. . . . This would be only mildly amusing were it not for the yeasty style, especially noticeable in the mother-son dialogue, which captures just the right notes of plaintive child and patient-but-exasperated adult. The yes-but catalog ends on a reassuring note of maternal teasing and a loving hug. (p. 152)

Zena Sutherland, in Bulletin of the Center for Children's Books *(© 1974 by the University of Chicago; all rights reserved), May, 1974.*

OTHER CITATIONS

Kirkus Reviews, *July 1, 1973, p. 682.*

Publishers Weekly, *July 30, 1973, p. 67.*

ROSIE AND MICHAEL (1974)

With her usual acid wit, Viorst pounces on the very occasions when a good friend comes in handy [in *Rosie and Michael*]: like being voted Most Horrible Singing Voice in the Class or having someone to call up "When I cut my head and the blood came gushing out. . . ." Still and all, forty pages of such elaboration is an awful lot for anybody, and there are times when only the frenetic *Mad* magazine detail of the line drawings will revive lagging attention. And Lorna Tomei's aged looking children and enthusiastic depiction of, for example, the time when "I put a worm in his tuna salad sandwich" are fairly clever examples of that school of intentionally bilious humor which is so popular. Aggressively redundant. (p. 740)

Kirkus Reviews *(copyright © 1974 The Kirkus Service, Inc.), July 15, 1974.*

Judith Viorst and Lorna Tomei could make Genghis Khan and Attila the Hun recognize the value of friendship, if only they were around today. . . . [Rosie and Michael] are friends, and we are friends of the author and the artist forevermore for giving us this droll, pointed book. (p. 52)

Jean F. Mercier, in Publishers Weekly *(reprinted from the October 21, 1974, issue of* Publishers Weekly *by permission of the critic, published by R. R. Bowker Company, a Xerox company; copyright © 1974 by Xerox Corporation), October 21, 1974.*

Judith Viorst's humor usually sends her fans giggling through her books. But the lack of a story line, character development or tension in "Rosie and Michael" . . . stifles the giggles. R. and M.'s protestations of mutual undying devotion quickly pall. The book is a collection of one-liners waiting for a spark. That spark might have come from the illustrations, but sadly, Lorna Tomei's drawings treat us to squinty-eyed, swollen-faced children whose expressions range from grumpy to gap-toothed grotesque. (p. 8)

> *Alice Bach, in* The New York Times Book Review *(© 1975 by The New York Times Company; reprinted by permission), February 2, 1975.*

OTHER CITATIONS

Judith S. Kronick, in School Library Journal, *October, 1974, p. 108.*

The Booklist, *October 1, 1974, p. 181.*

SUNDAY MORNING (1968)

"We do not want to hear anything until 9:45 A.M.—and *we'll* tell you when *that* is," say mother and father just arrived at 12:25; what follows early Sunday morning is muffled mayhem as about-six-year-old awakens, rouses little brother, and the two innocently demolish one room after ... while mother and father try to sleep. As told by deadpan big brother, [*Sunday Morning*] is a howl (and how it is: "I walk around saying God I'm hungry, God I'm hungry because there are no grown-ups to tell me don't say God"); as drawn by Hilary Knight it is, suitably, a pantomime of black silhouettes with sharp blue detail. (In case you care, little brother undressed looks like the Little Brother doll.) But Knight's mannered, almost epicene style squelches the spontaneity, makes this a show-off, and coy where it should have been brash. Still and all, a matter of individual taste, and undeniably a home brew-haha. (p. 1108)

> Kirkus Service *(copyright © 1968 The Kirkus Service, Inc.), October 1, 1968.*

Parents enjoy Saturday night and suffer on Sunday morning, and the limbo in-between is vividly documented in this story of an active little boy suffering from acute insomnia. His father, when he wished him good night, insisted "We do not want to hear anything until 9:45 A.M.—and *we'll* tell you when *that* is," but a little after 5 A.M., operations to wake up kid brother Nick are in full swing—a successful venture which gives both boys hours of exquisite, unsupervised havoc-wreaking while mother and father work very hard at staying asleep. The delightful illustrations, marvelously detailed black silhouettes with touches of midnight blue, and the spare but lively text trace the reactions of each family member throughout the night and early morning with humor and realism. (Conservative adults may look a little askance at such lines as "I walk around our bedroom saying God I'm hungry, God I'm hungry because there are no grown-ups around to tell me don't say God" and at a profile illustration of Nick with his pajama pants down that leaves no doubt about his gender). Most parents will find the book very funny indeed, and sophisticated children may enjoy seeing themselves as others hear them. (p. 63)

> *Elinor S. Cullen, in* School Library Journal *(reprinted from the January, 1969, issue of* School Library Journal, *published by R. R. Bowker Company, a Xerox company; copy-*
> *right © 1969 by Xerox Corporation), January, 1969.*

THE TENTH GOOD THING ABOUT BARNEY (1971)

Judith Viorst, in "The Tenth Good Thing about Barney" ..., diffuses the strong emotions surrounding death with a gentle, bittersweet humor.

The message, that death is part of the cycle of life, is less distinctive than the manner in which it is presented. The style has its own message: life is not what we would have it be; it is imperfect, but nice anyway. Maybe Barney is in heaven "with lots of cats and angels, drinking cream and eating cans of tuna." But most likely, he is in the ground helping grow grass and flowers, which is "a pretty nice job for a cat." The book is charming and sympathetic but perhaps best suited to the child for whom death's sorrow is quite distant. (p. 10)

> *Sheila R. Cole, in* The New York Times Book Review *(© 1971 by The New York Times Company; reprinted by permission), September 26, 1971.*

In simple phrases narrated by a child whose cat Barney has just died, [Judith Viorst] succinctly and honestly handles both the emotions stemming from the loss of a beloved pet and the questions about the finality of death which naturally arise in such a situation.... [This is an] unusually good book that handles a difficult subject straightforwardly and with no trace of the macabre. (pp. 140-41)

> *Sheryl B. Andrews, in* The Horn Book Magazine *(copyright © 1972 by The Horn Book, Inc., Boston), April, 1972.*

The only good thing about Barney that this reviewer can discern (apart from the fact that he's dead) is that Judith Viorst's account of his obsequies is illustrated by Erik Blegvad. A more apt choice would certainly have been Miss Joan Walsh Anglund, since her human tadpoles would better have matched the invertebrate text, and it is a mark of Mr. Blegvad's skill that his restrained and slightly tousled drawings have succeeded in importing a touch of altogether alien dignity.

One is tempted to assume that Miss Viorst's impulse to write about a boy's consolation over the interment of his cat stems from the new campaign to Bring Back Death into children's literature. The (largely Transatlantic) yearning for Truth at all costs has already given us a fever of factitious sex, poverty and Human Rights, and now it is clear that envious eyes are turning in the direction of crape and coffins. (After all, the Victorians did these subjects proud in their Golden Age, so why shouldn't we?)

On the other hand, such is the unnatural coyness and false naivete of much of Miss Viorst's text, that it may be more charitable to assume that her work is propaganda for that other contemporary obsession: conservation. For 'the tenth good thing about Barney' is that he makes very rich compost so that now he's in the ground 'he's helping to grow flowers'. Even the anti-felinists should find nothing to object to in such an equable conclusion. (p. 41)

> *Brian W. Alderson, in* Children's Book Review *(© 1973 Five Owls Press Ltd.; all rights reserved), April, 1973.*

OTHER CITATIONS

Kirkus Reviews, *August 1, 1971, p. 805.*

Pamela D. Pollack, in School Library Journal, *September, 1971, p. 110.*

The Times Literary Supplement, *April 6, 1973, p. 389.*

TRY IT AGAIN, SAM: SAFETY WHEN YOU WALK (1970)

For a cautionary tale, [*Try It Again, Sam: Safety When You Walk* is] uncommonly unstuffy. When Sam sets out for David's alone, his mother has lots to say but the only thing he listens to is "come home if anything goes wrong.". . . And each time he does, his sympathetic mother says "Try it again, Sam." . . . Sprightly and, notwithstanding the appended rules, satisfactory because it's satisfying. (p. 740)

> Kirkus Reviews *(copyright © 1970 The Kirkus Service, Inc.), July 15, 1970.*

[*Try It Again, Sam: Safely When You Walk* is an] uninspired, contrived attempt at incorporating safety rules for walkers into a story format. Young Sam is finally given the opportunity to go somewhere alone. His mother's parting admonition—"If you get into any trouble on your way to David's, I expect you to turn right around and come back home"—instantly jars credibility. Equally unreal are Sam's traffic blunders and repeated returns home where he is given the comforting reassurance, "You can try it again, Sam." It would certainly seem that after one or two of Sam's major mistakes—like tying his shoelace in the middle of a busy street—Mother would justifiably be a little hesitant about letting him try again. As a book on safety this is weak; as a story it is quite unbelievable. The black-and-white drawings [by Paul Galdone], some highlighted in shades of green and orange, are humorous but cannot redeem the text. (pp. 51-2)

> *Eleanor Glaser, in* School Library Journal *(reprinted from the February, 1971, issue of* School Library Journal, *published by R. R. Bowker Company, a Xerox company; copyright © 1971 by Xerox Corporation), February, 1971.*

OTHER CITATIONS

The Booklist, *November 1, 1970, p. 231.*

W

WATSON, Clyde 1947-

Many of the poems in *Father Fox's Pennyrhymes*, a finalist for the 1972 National Book Award, were actually written as lyrics to songs Clyde Watson plays on guitar. She has also played violin professionally and has composed music. Her books for children, illustrated by her sister, Wendy, are often drawn from the memories of their childhood in New England. (See also *Contemporary Authors*, Vols. 49-52 and *Something About the Author*, Vol. 5.)

BINARY NUMBERS (1977)

[Watson] begins [*Binary Numbers*] abruptly with "Take a ball of string and a ruler. Measure off a foot of string . . ." and then has readers measuring off two-, four-, eight-, sixteen-, and thirty-two-foot lengths without a clue as to why they should bother or what she's leading up to. After more activities and some conclusions . . ., readers do at last arrive at some exercises in writing binary numbers. What then? Well, Watson suggests that you translate the alphabet into binary numbers (1 to 11010) and write secret messages —which only shows that she hasn't a mathematician's approach either. This could be used as a supplement to [Jane J.] Srivastava's *Computers* . . . or a companion to [David A.] Adler's *Base Five* . . . in the same series, but the grasp of what it's all about that Srivastava and Adler convey so naturally is hard to find. (p. 492)

> *Kirkus Reviews (copyright © 1977 The Kirkus Service, Inc.), May 1, 1977.*

Watson does a particularly effective job of explaining what the binary number system is and how it can be used. Initially, string and measured cardboard lengths help readers see for themselves the relationships within the binary sequence. Then charts are constructed (to be completed by readers), and finally Watson shows the "on-off," "one-zero" form of expression which duplicates basic computer language. [Wendy Watson's animal] characters "help out" the author but don't interfere with cuteness. (p. 1731)

> Booklist *(reprinted by permission of the American Library Association; copyright 1977 by the American Library Association), July 15, 1977.*

Binary Numbers is, I judge, . . . likely to stimulate speculation in its readers. I particularly like its activities, which take up much of the book, subtly leading up to a mathematical system. I have never had much trouble grasping and using nondecimal notation schemes, but I know some students are bothered by the problem; and Ms. Watson's approach seems as painless a one as I can recall. (p. 465)

> *Harry C. Stubbs, in* The Horn Book Magazine *(copyright © 1977 by the Horn Book, Inc., Boston), August, 1977.*

FATHER FOX'S PENNYRHYMES (1971)

A pennysworth of ditties with an old-time air, aping traditional rhymes but tending to be sugary and in fact preoccupied with confection: sassafras, ginger beer, gooseberry pie, sugar hearts and lemon tarts; "Peppermint candies are six for a penny / But true love and kisses one cannot buy any." [Wendy Watson's] fond, country style illustrations depict assorted foxes in a variety of period poses and scenes; all told, they have more flavor than the rhymes which are as interesting as Necco wafers. (p. 738)

> *Kirkus Reviews (copyright © 1971 The Kirkus Service, Inc.), July 15, 1971.*

Right now I feel that Father Fox and his pennyrhymes ought to be admitted into the select company of other great foxes. I think of Aesop, of [Thornton W.] Burgess's Reddy Fox and [Joel Chandler Harris's] Brer Fox. Reynard and Foxy-woxy from "Henny-Penny" and "The Fox Went Out on a Chilly Night" by Peter Spier, for example. Maybe I'm a little impulsive; things haven't been too grand in children's books lately.

Meanwhile I don't want to take anything away from Clyde and Wendy Watson's creation: it's an American original, inspired by their childhood home on a Vermont farm—"the seasons and the work that goes with each, the buildings, the countryside—and the atmosphere and fun of our own family." . . .

Look real hard and you can find overtones of the old standby classic nursery rhymes in sister Clyde's words. But how does anyone ever get them completely out of mind? Sister Wendy, though, sets an exuberant mood with her watercolor paintings. If there's any complaint it is that sometimes they're too diminutive; with six panels to a page details shrink. And those details are important—the calicos and ginghams, the tails and tatters and patches.

Put it all together—rhymes and pictures—and the book is like a breath of fresh country air. (p. 8)

> *George A. Woods, in* The New York Times Book Review *(© 1971 by The New York Times Company; reprinted by permission), August 15, 1971.*

It's a shame that "Father Fox's Pennyrhymes" hadn't arrived at *PW* in time to be included in our recent roundup of charming books of marvels and miracles (*PW*, August 9). This one can not only charm the birds off the trees, it will charm children away from the TV set. It's a marvel: it's a collection of wild and happy verses, happier than many in Mother Goose; its illustrations so witty they give a new dimension to the cartoon-strip format. It's a miracle: both the verses and the pictures [by Wendy Watson] of the Fox family close forever—for the lucky human family who will share the book—the generation gap. (p. 274)

> *Lavinia Russ, in* Publishers Weekly *(reprinted from the August 30, 1971, issue of* Publishers Weekly *by permission of the critic, published by R. R. Bowker Company, a Xerox company; copyright © 1971 by Xerox Corporation), August 30, 1971.*

Father Fox's Pennyrhymes, which recall the lilt and whimsy of Mother Goose verses, have the foot-stomping rhythm of an American square dance call without a missed beat or a forced rhyme: "Oh my goodness, oh my dear, / Sassafras & ginger beer, / Chocolate cake and apple punch: / I'm too full to eat my lunch." The marvelous, beautifully tinted watercolor and pen-and-ink paintings, covered with tiny, busy details and snatches of conversations in cartoon-style balloons, unfold like comic strips alongside the verse. Young children will enjoy the clap-along rhythms and nonsense rhymes; older ones will also appreciate the more sophisticated wit of the illustrations. (pp. 110-11)

> *Marjorie Lewis, in* School Library Journal *(reprinted from the September, 1971, issue of* School Library Journal, *published by R. R. Bowker Company, a Xerox company; copyright © 1971 by Xerox Corporation), September, 1971.*

At a time when the bleaker aspects of human experience seem to be poking through the surface cheer, *Father Fox's Pennyrhymes* by Clyde Watson, with illustrations by Wendy Watson . . ., romps onto the children's book scene to the lilt of . . . [the poems's] zany delights. . . . Chock-full of the joy of life, the crunch of autumn leaves and the patterns of old country ginghams, it is—text and glorified comic-strip animation—a paean to a simpler, happier day. The Watson sisters know first hand the pleasures of walking down country lanes, popping corn, gathering wild strawberries and sitting by the fire on a long winter's night. This first authentically colloquial and breezily American nursery rhyme collection may well put old Mother Goose out of business. (p. 46)

> *Selma G. Lanes, in* Life *(courtesy of* Life Magazine; © 1971 Time Inc.), December 17, 1971.*

Too much talk about 'perfection' devalues the critical currency, but it is hard to find a fitter term for Father Fox and his pennyrhymes. . . . [The poems] prove to be nursery rhymes so close to the real thing that they will eventually be taken away from Clyde Watson and assigned simply to 'trad'.

But the pleasure of such offerings . . . is doubled and redoubled by the delight of Wendy Watson's illustrations. The medium—pen and colour wash—brings the pictures into harmony with the homeliness of the verses, and there is endless enjoyment to be got from the skill and wit that have gone into each composition. Sometimes we are given a single picture—usually full of action and often with conversations going on in it . . ., or even with supplementary rhymes. Sometimes we are given strip drawings or cleverly worked out single backgrounds, divided into panels, so that a sequence of actions can be imposed upon them. Everywhere there is a humour, a warmth and a humanity that are the essence of the civilized notion of 'the family'. (pp. 39-41)

> *Brian Alderson, in* Children's Literature in Education *(© 1973, APS Publications, Inc., New York; reprinted by permission of the publisher), No. 11 (May), 1973.*

OTHER CITATIONS

The Booklist, *October 15, 1971, p. 207.*

The Times Literary Supplement, *November 3, 1972, p. 1333.*

Brian W. Alderson, in Children's Book Review, *December, 1972, p. 191.*

HICKORY STICK RAG (1976)

[In *Hickory Stick Rag*] there is at least one bird among [the] "cranky and mean" country schoolteacher's pupils; the rest are a rabbit, a raccoon, and other small animals who, when they're not playing hooky, spend their time throwing spitballs and stinkbombs, putting tacks on "her" chair, etc. . . . By June though they're all so grateful to be out of school that they give her a party "With good things galore"—a goody-goody ending that should come as no surprise after the knee-jerk nostalgia of Clyde Watson's dull jingles and [Wendy Watson's] scratchy watercolors. (p. 681)

> Kirkus Reviews *(copyright © 1976 The Kirkus Service, Inc.), June 15, 1976.*

This same Watson teaching team gave us a few years ago "Father Fox's Pennyrhymes," a brilliant lesson in Americana, for which they earned a rare A plus. Alas, these new lessons merit only a B minus. Marked down for the murkiness in the illustrations of animal expressions, for the too determinedly antic descriptions in the verses. Nothing here will replace "No more pencils, no more books, No more teacher's crosseyed looks." School dismissed. (p. 35)

> *George A. Woods, in* The New York Times Book Review *(© 1976 by The New York Times Company; reprinted by permission), July 11, 1976.*

To a roomful of energetic youngsters, add one determined

disciplinarian and place in a nostalgic schoolhouse setting. Result—a chaotic comedy. As depicted in detailed watercolor and pen-and-ink boxed illustrations accompanied by the syncopated rhythm of ingenuous four-line stanzas, the capers of the lovable animal scholars will elicit instant recognition and laughter from their human counterparts. Despite a barrage of "[s]pitballs & stinkbombs / On hot afternoons, / Peashooters, squirtguns / And water balloons," their teacher's season of discontent ends on a note of jubilation as her charges, who were only trying to" . . . liven things up / With a neat trick or two," treat her to a surprise celebration. As American as "Yankee Doodle," the book is a humorous and joyously irreverent toast to a traditional institution. (p. 497)

> Mary M. Burns, in The Horn Book Magazine (copyright © 1976 by the Horn Book, Inc., Boston), October, 1976.

OTHER CITATIONS

Publishers Weekly, June 14, 1976, p. 114.

QUIPS & QUIRKS (1975)

Clyde Watson has dusted off a lifetime supply of old insults (at least 100 years old) so that no one need ever be at a loss for words to fling at a clumsy . . . or a glutton. . . . Gross as it sounds, the Watsons have turned [Quips & Quirks, a] lexicon of vituperation into a neat, good natured enterprise, with occasional verse, notes and homespun, calicoed characters [by Wendy Watson] whose buffoonery is relatively sedate. The definitions are apt and this is one kind of word-twisting lexicon which won't require any arm-twisting. (p. 1073)

> Kirkus Reviews (copyright © 1975 The Kirkus Service, Inc.), September 15, 1975.

Derogatory monikers ad infinitum: for instance, "Stinkers, those Persons who are repulsive, loathsome, scorned . . . in short, generally objectionable and therefore disliked," are also known as creeps, crocks, crumbs, drips, humgruffins, mullipuffs, and twerps. . . . These appellations, most of which, we are told, are at least a hundred years old—some much older—are listed opposite quick verses inside Wendy Watson's framed pictures of animals who caricature the highlighted label. . . . [Prominent] footnotes in red type contribute to page design as they shed light on the meanings of obscure or unfamiliar terms. A saucy compendium. (p. 306)

> The Booklist (reprinted by permission of the American Library Association; copyright 1975 by the American Library Association), October 15, 1975.

To bring together a book of highly graphic nicknames, the author has ransacked dictionaries old and new. More than three hundred picturesque names along with explanatory comments are grouped under general headings like Pests, Spoilsports, Stinkers, Numskulls, Windbags, and Clumsies. The best of the book is contained in verses that illustrate some of the words: "Here comes Captain Cockalorum / Finest of the Fine / A puffed-up, proud & pompous Fool / He's on his way to Dine." In the strikingly designed book, the text is printed in black and red, and the black line draw-

ings humorously depict animals—not people—as the butt of all insults. (p. 606)

> Ethel L. Heins, in The Horn Book Magazine (copyright © 1975 by the Horn Book, Inc., Boston), December, 1975.

OTHER CITATIONS

Publishers Weekly, November 24, 1975, p. 52.

TOM FOX AND THE APPLE PIE (1972)

Accompanied by sharp, black-and-white scratchboard illustrations [by Wendy Watson]—with a pie and leaves in blue overlay—this animal tale forms a sequel to Father Fox's Pennyrhymes; in brief prose it tells an adventure of little Tom Fox. Tom smelled something delicious when he woke up and identified it as the sweetness of apple pie wafting in on the wind from the county fair. The completely childlike story, Potter-like in its depiction of mischief, describes the triumphs of the hungry desires of the youngest and greediest and laziest fox. Tom's escapade in getting a pie is beguiling and is presented in action-filled pictures as well as in the sound of the words of the text: "'Feathers and Foxgloves. . . . If this poor pie is cut into sixteen pieces, how tiny those pieces will be!'" (p. 459)

> Virginia Haviland, in The Horn Book Magazine (copyright © 1972 by The Horn Book, Inc., Boston), October, 1972.

Young children often express a preference for either very large or very small books and Tom Fox and the Apple Pie falls into the latter category. Author and artist have exploited the miniature in all its aspects. The story is compact and full of the lilt of American cadences, familiar to many from Joel Harris's 'Uncle Remus'. Indeed, there is a distinct transatlantic flavour to both the dialogue and the astringent black and white drawings.

The story of a delightful fox and his intention of purchasing an apple pie has a universal appeal. The road is long, the weather hot, the pie 'deelishus' and the outcome inevitable!

A welcome alternative to Aesop and Brer Rabbit. (p. 140)

> Gabrielle Maunder, in Children's Book Review (© 1973 Five Owls Press Ltd.; all rights reserved), October, 1973.

OTHER CITATIONS

Kirkus Reviews, July 1, 1972, p. 722.

George A. Woods, in The New York Times Book Review, August 6, 1972, p. 8.

*   *   *

WERSBA, Barbara   1932-

Barbara Wersba is an American author of books for children and young adults. She was a professional actress for fifteen years, and wrote her first book for children through the persuasion of a friend while recuperating from an illness. Wersba's novels for adolescents often contain sensitive, artistic characters as protagonists, and themes which advocate the individual's right to self-expression. She is a regular reviewer of children's books for The New York Times Book Review.

(See also *Contemporary Authors,* Vols. 29-32 and *Something About the Author,* Vol. 1.)

AUTHOR'S COMMENTARY

[English Journal]: You have said that writing is a process of unlearning. Would you explain that?

[Barbara Wersba]: Unlearning all of the prejudices and conventional ideas that we're taught when we're young. To be a writer you have to see the world for the first time and pretend you know nothing about it. You have to stay very fresh and open, and you have to get rid of the preconceptions formed in childhood. Writing is a very primitive and simple thing. People tend to complicate it and intellectualize it, but it's mostly a sensuous response to nature rather than an intellectual one.

Writing is a process of self-discovery. Many writers, if you read what they say about themselves, say they write a book to find out what they think. I write a book to find out who I am. It's a process of awakening; one of the richest ways of finding out what you think and who you are. Every book is yourself. You may disguise the characters, but they're all you and it's a very exciting experience for those who can stick with it. But I've discovered that most people who want to write really want to have *written,* because the labor involved is tremendous. (p. 20)

[EJ]: You have said before that writing cannot be taught. Do you believe that?

[BW]: I suppose that what I meant was that talent cannot be taught. The simple elements of craft can be taught, and I wish I had had a writing teacher when I was younger because it would have saved me years of making the same mistakes over and over. Perhaps the best thing a teacher of writing can do is to get the student in touch with his own voice: how he speaks, how he expresses himself. Every person is completely unique when he writes, even when he writes a letter. However, most young writers don't want to be themselves. They want to write intellectually, they want to write in a kind of style. The most important thing for a writer is to learn who he is.

[EJ]: What about inspiration? What role does it play in the writing process?

[BW]: If you wait for inspiration at your desk, you will wait for the rest of your life. Inspiration comes and goes at lucky moments in writing. But the whole secret of writing is to go to the desk every day of your life and put in a certain number of hours, even if you accomplish nothing. Sitting at the desk is the key.

It seems to me that inspiration comes when the door of the unconscious opens a little and light shines through. Characters begin to speak to each other, the narrative flows easily, and things suddenly become real and palpable. That fades quickly, however, and you have to go back to craft and discipline.

[EJ]: What role does the home or the school play in the creative process, or in the creative drive in a person? What about in your own life, for example?

[BW]: My parents did not encourage me to write. They were very good to me in a material sense, and there were always lots of books in the house, but I don't think anyone gave me encouragement to be an artist. Actually, I don't think the influences of home or school matter at all. I think people are born writers. I know I was, and mistakenly I decided to become an actress, which was a grave error.

I wrote from the time I went to school, and I don't think outward influences meant anything to me. If you look at the lives of many writers, you see no family encouragement, no recognition in school, no recognition from friends, but the writer seems to be the person who keeps on writing. And I know several young people like this who have no hope of publishing, but who write every day. It seems to be a drive that comes from within.

[EJ]: When did *you* know that you were a writer? How did you know it?

[BW]: I was writing fiction from the time I was in the first grade, but nobody seemed to notice. The only thing I did well in school was writing. I was a very poor student in everything except English. As a matter of fact, I wonder how I got through school at all.

I wrote throughout my adolescence and during my years in the theatre, but I had no confidence. I could never finish a piece of fiction. I could never finish a story. And I never showed them to people. The proof of it was that I was always writing—on tour with a play, waiting to go on stage for rehearsal, traveling.

At the age of twenty-seven I decided to leave the theatre. I was physically ill and recuperating on Martha's Vineyard when I wrote a book called *The Boy Who Loved the Sea.* It was the first thing I'd ever been able to finish, and within a year it was published—through beginner's luck, I might add. There is no way of overestimating what it means to be published to a young writer. It is a tremendous boost. It gives you the recognition you need to go on, the courage. And it gave me the leap into writing that I needed. From that day on I never looked back.

If a child is always playing the piano, it means something. If a child constantly paints or draws, it means something. You should do the thing that comes to you most naturally, most easily, and gives you the greatest amount of pleasure. And writing was always that for me.

[EJ]: As a writer, what do you feel you owe your readers, who, for the most part, are young people?

[BW]: I owe the reader exactly what I owe myself because I am the first reader of any book I write, and I'm a good reader. So I think I owe the reader, no matter what his age, fascination, interest, suspense, the desire to turn the page and see what happens, characters who are real and moving, and a theme that has some human value. Although I don't put much emphasis on theme, underlying any good book is a theme of great human value; it shows the potential and beauty of the human being as well as his failures and tragedies.

All good writers must be good readers first. They must know *how* to read. And I don't think you can be a writer until you are a passionate reader in the sense that you reach out for what the writer is trying to say. You understand that he has chosen a particular style and method of expression. You understand that he has done certain things to move you. Whether or not you agree with him is not important. He must move you.

I never think of the fact that I'm writing for children or

teenagers because within me is still a very active child and a very active teenager. So every book I write, I write for myself first. I do not think of audience.

[EJ]: Is young adult literature a legitimate genre?

[BW]: I think twenty years ago it would not have been, but with the change in adult literature in the past ten or fifteen years, the young adult book has become valid. People always ask me who reads these books, because any youngster who is a good reader will read an adult book. But adult books have taken a turn toward great eccentricity, toward extreme sexuality, and a pessimistic point of view. If you look at the current adult fiction, you will find amazing pessimism about life. There is a validity in the YA book in that, for some reason, perhaps because it deals with the young, there is a positive view of the world. There is sensitivity towards human values.

I think a really good young reader will read both. And the YA books seem to have a place in the schools because many teachers are reluctant to assign more sophisticated material. Oddly enough, I think some of the best writers in America are now writing for this audience. I think M. E. Kerr, John Donovan, the late Louise Fitzhugh are tremendous writers. If *Catcher in the Rye* were written today, it would be called a YA book.

When I was a child and read adult books there was a greater sense of hope, of humanity, of the goodness of life. These things now seem to be the property of the young adult novel. So I think it is a valid genre, though people ask me all the time why it should be.

[EJ]: How does Barbara Wersba see the world?

[BW]: That's a very hard question because I think I tend to see it too darkly. And yet I have always been this way. I am always the person who sees the sick cat on the side of the road, or who sees the lost child in the supermarket, or who is aware of people suffering. I have a tendency to see sadness in the world, and this is something I would like to change in myself because I know there is joy, light, frivolity.

I enter my workroom every morning to make sense of what I see. What I see comes out of what I am. What I am is the result of all the experiences that have happened to me. A lot of my writing is simply for the purpose of making *sense* of life, of bringing order to chaos. I do wish I had a lighter side, which is why I am so pleased with *Tunes for a Small Harmonica*. It is a funny book, and in many ways, a joyous book. And I loved every moment of writing it. Perhaps as I grow older I will see more light in the world, to balance the darkness. (pp. 20-1)

> *Paul Janeczko, "An Interview with Barbara Wersba," in* English Journal *(copyright © 1976 by The National Council of Teachers of English), November, 1976, pp. 20-1.*

AMANDA, DREAMING (1973)

"Amanda, Dreaming" must be examined in three quite separate ways: as a case study, as an object and as a work of fiction.

As a case study it is interesting—and baffling. It catalogues in tone poem words and fluid surreal pictures the dreams-in-series of one child on a single night, and the whole flows by smoothly and quickly. But these are, from a psychological standpoint, unlikely dreams, for Amanda is passive throughout, an observer who swims in images but is never emotionally involved in spite of the potentially disturbing statement on page 2 that "her dreams are more real than her waking."

As an object, "Amanda, Dreaming" is beautiful, a well-designed, slender book with small blocks of type and large, fascinating pictures. Mercer Mayer has gone far afield from much of his previous work to produce these muted Dali-esque paintings. As dream illustrations they are effective and satisfying both in mood and content, and they are faithful to the text in their liquid gentleness and the absence of any hint of dis-ease.

As a work of fiction, however, "Amanda, Dreaming" is a cipher. The story is over on the first page, which states that "a child named Amanda dreams every night—and she tells her dreams to no one." There should be nowhere to go after that. So this is not a work of fiction but rather a collection of images. Since dreams have a mind of their own, namely our teeming subconscious, these are dreams I doubt were ever dreamed except perhaps as prologues to other more visceral stuff. It may be that "Amanda, Dreaming" is yet another example of adult insistence on its own version of a child's mind. The truth of children's dreams is a long way from this presentation, a fact to which my own memory can painfully and vividly attest. But on the other hand, probably Miss Wersba intends this book to be a sort of lullaby, meant to induce rather than report. Used in this way it might be successful. (p. 8)

> *Natalie Babbitt, in* The New York Times Book Review *(© 1973 by The New York Times Company; reprinted by permission), October 7, 1973.*

OTHER CITATIONS

Publishers Weekly, *November 26, 1973, p. 39.*

Ruth M. McConnell, in School Library Journal, *February, 1974, p. 74.*

THE COUNTRY OF THE HEART (1975)

One wonders how tough-minded poet Hadley Norman would have evaluated this posthumous memoir written by her much younger student and sometime lover. Not that there isn't a certain depth to the portrait of an intellectually brittle, emotionally vulnerable woman who runs away from her protective former husband to face cancer alone, only to fall into a brief affair with an ardent, virginally naive, college student. And certainly the narrative—which follows Hadley's physical decline, her rejection of the young man, Steven, before he learns the truth, and his suffering—ebbs and flows in reverie-like waves of adoration and angst. Yet though the situation is more firmly grounded than that of [Wersba's] *The Dream Watcher* . . . , the perspective is just as constricted. Wersba's evident identification with both lovers and her indulgence of Steven's adolescent self-importance are simply embarrassing. And the samples of Hadley Norman's poetry make us wonder whether she's the genius she claims to be. (p. 719)

Kirkus Reviews *(copyright © 1975 The Kirkus Service, Inc.), July 1, 1975.*

Some books hurt. They give birth to an ache, a lonesome longing the reader is at a loss to define. [In *The Country of the Heart*] the pain of first love is burned 'round the edges with the cold finality of death. . . .

Tossed into the jumble of quality is a passage of pure gold. As Hadley lies dying in the hospital, there is exposed the real mystery of death. Once it is honestly accepted, the victim busies herself "beginning a journey,"—carefully gathering and packing memories, loves, thoughts—too preoccupied with this cross-over to concern herself with anyone to be left behind. Words of farewell are a mere formality, a cursory glance back; then concentration on the gentle place that lies ahead. Beautiful! and a special gift for the young adult. (p. 299)

> *Mrs. John G. Gray, in* Best Sellers *(copyright 1975, by the University of Scranton), December, 1975.*

[*The Country of the Heart* is a] lyrical, sensitive story of a young man's love for a woman old enough to be his mother. What could have been a maudlin affair becomes, with minor exceptions, a moving relationship. With fidelity the author describes the intensity and insatiability of the youth's passion. The woman's offensiveness, her irritability and feigned indifference are described with discernment. For one, the experience is a new beginning and a fresh awareness; for the other, an ending eased from the pain and loneliness of a terminal illness. (p. 618)

> *Mary Silva Cosgrave, in* The Horn Book Magazine *(copyright © 1975 by the Horn Book, Inc., Boston), December, 1975.*

It is hard for a writer to write about writers. In respect of that, at least, Barbara Wersba's "The Country of the Heart" is something of a tour de force. Here we have two writers: a famous, caustic, self-absorbed woman poet of 40 and an unformed, vulnerable, aspiring young man of 18. Steven Harper writes in the first person, retrospectively, about his brief affair with Hadley Norman, an affair both poetic and physical. (The two literary types are not new, either to fiction or to history.) . . .

The story itself is perhaps a bit of a hype. (Why do fictional young writers always turn out talented, never give up and settle for the real estate business?) Yet since we must accept the characters as the author dated them, it must be said that Wersba's deft control of tone is remarkably convincing. The voice of the narrator and the character of Steven are unmistakably one, alternately naive, self-conscious, pretentious, and, yes, talented. This is not really a book about death (we feel the affair must have ended in any case). It is a perceptive look at "growing up literary." (p. 8)

> *Georgess McHargue, in* The New York Times Book Review *(© 1976 by The New York Times Company; reprinted by permission), January 4, 1976.*

OTHER CITATIONS

Publishers Weekly, *July 14, 1975, p. 60.*

Karen Harris, in School Library Journal, *September, 1975, p. 128.*

DO TIGERS EVER BITE KINGS? (1966)

It gives me great pleasure to announce that "Do Tigers Bite Kings?" is an absolutely absurd book. An absolutely useless book. No child will find out how many teeth he has from looking at it. No child will decide, after he reads it, that he'd be happier as a horse with a milk route than as one that stuck his neck out and won the Derby. All he'll do is laugh and laugh—at an absurd Queen and her absurd King in their absurd (and wildly handsome) kingdom. Laughter *can* be dangerous—maybe you'd better play safe and read it yourself first. (p. 344)

> *Lavinia Russ, in* Publishers Weekly *(reprinted from the August 29, 1966, issue of* Publishers Weekly *by permission of the critic, published by R. R. Bowker Company, a Xerox company; copyright © 1966 by Xerox Corporation), August 29, 1966.*

This is a rollicking rhymed story of a timid king driven to participation in a tiger hunt by his shrewish Queen. A private arrangement between the King and the Tiger, somewhat reminiscent of the denouement of [Kenneth Grahame's] *The Reluctant Dragon*, provides a mutually advantageous solution. Mario Rivoli's bold illustrations in mustard, plum, and various shades of green and blue, are distinctive. Recommended for general purchase. (pp. 241-42)

> *Della Thomas, in* School Library Journal *(reprinted from the October, 1966, issue of* School Library Journal, *published by R. R. Bowker Company, a Xerox company; copyright © 1966 by Xerox Corporation), October, 1966.*

[*Do Tigers Ever Bite Kings?* is a] picture book with rhyming text and a story that has elements of humor, sophistication, and nonsense; the illustrations (some pages in black and white, some in dulled colors) are ornately stylized and quite distracting. Although the rhyme is occasionally faulty ("eyes" and "disguised," "declaim" and "brain") it has appeal for the read-aloud audience, as do the rhythm and repetition of the verses. (p. 100)

> *Zena Sutherland, in* Bulletin of the Center for Children's Books *(copyright 1967 by the University of Chicago; all rights reserved), February, 1967.*

OTHER CITATIONS

Kirkus Reviews, *August 15, 1966, p. 826.*

Richard Kluger, in Chicago Tribune Book Week, *October 30, 1966, p. 5.*

THE DREAM WATCHER (1968)

Albert liked Thoreau, long walks, Shakespeare, even gardening. He was different, and miserable because of it. Then he met one-time actress Mrs. Woodfin. . . . and she respected his ideas. What if he were different. That put him, she said, in "the company of saints and geniuses." . . . Mrs. Woodfin had been special, had believed in the important things and made him believe in them too. He would be all right.

And you know he will be. For the author, with skill and compassion, has created a good, honest human being, an individualist who needs his dreams and will have the strength, you feel sure, to be himself. She has written an unusual and very fine book about an extraordinary friendship, a book that is thoughtful, often funny and with a hero to remember. (p. 18)

> *Polly Goodwin, in* Book World *(© The Washington Post), November 3, 1968.*

"The Dream Watcher" is the story of Albert Scully, a high-school boy who says of himself, "I'm the only person in America who doesn't belong to a group. . . . And what else is there?" It is also the story of Orpha Woodfin, a marvelous old nut who helps Albert balance his doubts about himself. Like Mr. Zindel in "The Pigman," the author also finds a more sympathetic ear by skipping a generation beyond her protagonist and his parents.

"The Dream Watcher" is loaded with adult wisdom, but Miss Wersba weaves it smoothly into her over-all creation. It is not a book that will appeal to everyone—and that is no mark against it. It well may serve as reassurance to young people like Albert, who worry so much that they are "different." Mrs. Woodfin is certainly different, but despite that and what she turns out in the end to be, "She had believed the right things about what was good and beautiful." And that, the author implies, is what matters.

Miss Wersba has bravely undertaken the difficult stylistic accouterment of much quoted material from Shakespeare, Shaw, Rilke, Thoreau, and Wilfred Owen to underscore her points. Given the fantastical characters of Albert and Mrs. Woodfin, it all seems to work rather well. The old lady, living in the only remaining original house in the midst of a new development, bills herself as a bygone actress who once played Juliet to Sarah Bernhardt's applause. She also drinks a lot of sherry and burns garbage in the yard. Perhaps that gives her the right to quote Thoreau and Rilke. I think it does. (p. 2)

> *John Weston, in* The New York Times Book Review, *Part II (© 1968 by The New York Times Company; reprinted by permission), November 3, 1968.*

Miss Wersba is a very earnest American B.A. Here she explores a fine relationship between a suicidal young dropout, son of a neurotic, thwarted "House Beautiful" mother and an alcoholic father, and an octogenarian ex-actress recluse—or so we thought, for she turns out in the end to be all lies, merely an ex-schoolteacher living on relief. Well might the mind boggle! The boy is an excruciating bore, besides being just about the most unlikely character ever to slouch across a page. Had he hanged himself on page one the literary scene would not be noticably the poorer. (p. 262)

> *J. A. Morrison, in* Children's Book News *(copyright © 1969 by Children's Book Centre Ltd.), September-October, 1969.*

Can a boy in a boy's book have a mother who isn't vapid? Yes, but usually only if she's cruelly domineering or lax in her maternal obligations. In Barbara Wersba's *The Dream Watcher,* for example, there are two important women. One is a poor, alcoholic spinster on welfare whose poetic allusions and fantasized stories of her glorious past on the stage inspire the terribly normal, average Albert Scully to appreciate his own capabilities and potential: ". . . [Mrs. Woodfin] had made *me* feel different . . . I had seen myself as a person for the first time in my life." But, what about young Albert's mom, the really significant woman in his life? She is a castrator who constantly puts down her unsuccessful hard-drinking insuranceman of a husband: "'If he [Albert] had a father he could respect, he wouldn't have turned out this way.'" While Wersba treats Mr. Scully sympathetically (he had always wanted to be a pilot but his wife steered him towards business), she has little patience with the wife's own frustrations. *Why* does Mrs. Scully daydream about being a celebrity? If she's emasculated her husband, as it's implied, what in her own background limited *her* ability to relate to people and led her to cope by restructuring her reality? These questions never even come to the fore in this book; boys see only the father as immediate victim, the son as probable, long-range victim, and the mother as vulture. (p. 67)

> *Diane Gersoni Stavn, in* School Library Journal *(reprinted from the January, 1971, issue of* School Library Journal, *published by R. R. Bowker Company, a Xerox company; copyright © 1971 by Xerox Corporation), January, 1971.*

OTHER CITATIONS

Virginia Haviland, in The Horn Book Magazine, *October, 1968, p. 567.*

Zena Sutherland, in Saturday Review, *November 9, 1968, p. 69.*

Laura Polla Scanlon, in Commonweal, *November 22, 1968, pp. 288-89.*

THE LAND OF FORGOTTEN BEASTS (1964)

This delightful story could double as a fantasy and as an encyclopedia of fabulous beasts. A scholarly little boy named Andrew Peterson Smith, who . . . is opposed to anything imaginary, comes across an old bestiary in the library. To his surprise Andrew finds himself inside the book, where . . . he is introduced to [several mythological creatures, which] are all described in detail and with good humor. The excellent black-and-white illustrations [by Margot Tomes] might almost have been taken from a medieval bestiary, and readers may be as lost as Andrew in them. For those who read fairy tales, myths, and other forms of fantasy, this is an imaginative reference book, for the others it is a good introduction. (p. 651)

> Virginia Kirkus' Service, *July 15, 1964.*

[*The Land of Forgotten Beasts* is] a curious book for . . . younger children by Barbara Wersba. We have already met fantasy after Tolkien and Nesbit; now comes Lewis Carroll. The *Land of Forgotten Beasts* has a marvellous idea. Andrew, a precocious boy scientist, opens by mistake a medieval bestiary, and finds himself transported to the land of the mythological beasts where he meets, among others, the unicorn, the phoenix and more unusually, the antlion, the manticore, the amphisbena (deliciously evocative names with more reputable literary pedigrees than, say, the Mock Turtle). He returns home having learnt, no less, [these] virtues of myth and fantasy . . . : that truth can be other than scientific; and that we should be the poorer for losing our mythological inheritance.

The point is made rather too didactically—at times almost preciously. The beasts themselves, though delightfully described, come, unlike Carroll's beasts, in a kind of continuous catalogue which is monotonous as literary forms go. Andrew, too, lacks the contrast of Alice's nursery common sense—he is a bit mythological himself, like one of [Hilaire] Belloc's awful children. But there is plenty of excellent Alice-ish dialogue, even a little Alice-ish logic, and some beautiful—and individual—writing. Delectable illustrations help. (p. 1130)

> *The Times Literary Supplement (© Times Newspapers Ltd., 1965; reproduced from The Times Literary Supplement by permission), December 7, 1965.*

OTHER CITATIONS

Barbara S. Moody, in School Library Journal, *September, 1964, p. 126.*

Ethel L. Heins, in The Horn Book Magazine, *October, 1964, pp. 499-500.*

Madeleine L'Engle, in The New York Times Book Review, *October 25, 1964, p. 36.*

Margaret Sherwood Libby, in Chicago Tribune Book Week, *November 29, 1964, p. 28.*

Stella Rodway, in Spectator, *November 12, 1965, p. 631.*

The Junior Bookshelf, *December, 1965, p. 353.*

LET ME FALL BEFORE I FLY (1971)

Under a rosebush in a garden is a circus, elaborate and exquisite, with tiny lion-tamers, acrobats, bareback riders, clowns, even a fat lady two inches tall. All this exists for one "child" alone (a boy, actually, but the author refers to him only as "child"). He watches and marvels for hours on end in the grass, until he knows each feature of every performer by heart. And the more he grows to love the circus, the farther he drifts from his own, the real, world.

Then comes a storm. The circus disappears. Now both the child and the book are in terrible trouble. For the child has "lost the desire to live." And the book is up against the single subject which, to my mind, cannot be dealt with in children's literature—namely, total, unrelieved despair.

At this point the child's parents and a doctor intervene. They restore the child to normality, inconvincingly so. Meantime some highly questionable speculations have been made concerning the link between genius and alienation. Finally a resolution is attempted in the form of a dream in which the child, no longer passive spectator, takes part himself in his beloved circus. But the symbolism fails. If the circus is supposed to be the work of art, then to describe it as "both image and reality, fact and dream, fiction and longing," only adds to the confusion. And the child, who is supposed to be the artist, is still as faceless as he has been nameless all along. Functioning neither as individual nor as symbol, he remains, in the author's own words, "distant, peculiar, vague" throughout. So does the book. (p. 8)

> *Doris Orgel, in* The New York Times Book Review (© *1971 by The New York Times Company; reprinted by permission), October 17, 1971.*

Some very few times in a long landscape of books a special one is found as by magic. The experience is like a gasp. Then the delight spreads and surprise becomes joy. This is what happened to me when I opened Barbara Wersba's *Let Me Fall Before I Fly.* . . . I can't tell the story, as a critic must. It would pull off the wings of this clear flight of words. But I would like to say that when it was done I was shaken, as by reality. But this book goes beyond that which is real. It is an adventure into art where the reader, unaware, becomes a part of the strong and beautiful pattern.

There is, to me, another element in this book—that of recognition. I believe that many older people—and by that I mean non-children—will find, in truthful remembering, more than an echo of this boy's experience. The recognition may even be hurtful. And, though no grownups will ever be told, the child reader will hear his secret self speaking a response that will give him comfort and a further willingness to continue living.

Barbara Wersba is a stranger to me, but intuition tells me that she is led directly into her country of characters and listens with a very acute and musical third ear, returning to her typewriter not to invent but to record. As a writer I must rejoice in this perfect book. (p. 617)

> *Julia Cunningham, "Notes for Another's Music," in* The Horn Book Magazine (*copyright* © *1971 by The Horn Book, Inc., Boston), December, 1971.*

OTHER CITATIONS

Publishers Weekly, *September 6, 1971, p. 51.*

Kirkus Reviews, *October 15, 1971, p. 1124.*

Paul Heins, in The Horn Book Magazine, *December, 1971, pp. 616-17.*

Janet French, in School Library Journal, *April, 1972, p. 141.*

RUN SOFTLY, GO FAST (1970)

Once more into the generation gap where David rails at his just-dead father for two hundred pages: David Marks, nineteen-year-old preppie-turned-artist ("I didn't starve. I had my own show last year") living with Sarah Lawrence dropout Maggie in an East Village loft vs. Leo Marks, "the saga of the immigrant in MGM technicolor," Seventh Avenue *gelt* and Riverside Drive/Miami Beach gilt. In David's monologue, ranging back and forth over his early memories of his father as hero and comforter, disillusion, the battles up to the break, there are two fixed ideas: that Leo, in unwittingly revealing his liaison with a designer, made David impotent until Maggie "brought me home"; and that, in accusing soulmate Rick of homosexuality, he triggered Rick's refusal to fight for C.O. status, his induction and death in Vietnam. Whether or not there is any basis for David's kneejerk rejection of Leo, the book is written as if we were supposed to think there was; until suddenly, five pages before the close, he recalls a forgotten remark, realizes that he has told only half the story, and lays his father to rest. David and Leo are equally intolerant, unattractive and stereotyped, so that the ending is justice of a sort, but for the same reason none of it merits sympathetic attention. (There is also, for those who care, a descent into the bowels of hippiedom where a four-year-old is kept happy on speed and during which 'one perfect acid trip' ''had done something beautiful to my work'' and ''pot had become natural to me.'') (p. 1164)

> Kirkus Reviews *(copyright © 1970 The Kirkus Service, Inc.), October 15, 1970.*

The basic story of Barbara Wersba's new book is good— and at times moving. It is about a destructive, loving-and-hating relationship between a young man and his father. . . .

Yet the book does have failures which come from a consciousness that it was being written ''for'' young adults. It has chapters on hippie life, drugs, sex and the rest that give the impression all the currently fashionable ingredients have been duly pitched into the mixture. There's something determinedly positive about the ending (the air of ''coming to terms'' in the last chapter) that doesn't quite ring true. And the sophistication of Miss Werbsa's technique doesn't fully conceal the occasional use of hackneyed situations, machine-made characters.

There is a second, partly overlapping theme. The book can also be read as a pilgrim's progress through the teens, during which Davy moves from his suffocating home—with a detour among the hippies—to the arms of a nice girl called Maggie and early success as a painter. This last set-up appears to represent the author's chosen compromise between hip and square. A remodeled Davy rejects a cop-out —but still smokes pot and lives with Maggie in unmarried bliss.

Technically, ''Run Softly, Go Fast'' is highly accomplished. It works mainly through flashback, but with forward jumps, sudden flights of dialogue and verbatim ''repeats'' of key passages. Maybe the technique gets in the way. I do not doubt the book's underlying sincerity, but to me at least it fails to speak clearly, and only occasionally strikes a responding chord. (p. 38)

> *John Rowe Townsend, in* The New York Times Book Review *(© 1970 by The New York Times Company; reprinted by permission), November 22, 1970.*

Books about alienated youth, the drug scene, and Middle Class America seem to abound these days. And at first glance, it might appear that this book should be classified as a fluently readable story but one that dwells on what are becoming trite conventions in books for older teen-agers. Such an assumption would be a mistake. The story is told from the point of view of nineteen-year-old David Marks as he feverishly records how he once saw and now sees the deterioration of the emotional relationship between his father and himself. . . . There are no sympathetic characters in the book, with the possible exception of Maggie, the girl Davy is living with in The Village. But there are many convincing ones. And the strength of the book is that it rings true. In spite of its preoccupation with the Establishment, hippies, drugs, and sex, the book succeeds in clearly and forcefully conveying basic human weakness and blindness as well as the universal need for love and understanding, which must begin in the individual himself. A vendetta that ends in a benediction. (p. 624)

> *Sheryl B. Andrews, in* The Horn Book Magazine *(copyright © 1970 by The Horn Book, Inc., Boston), December, 1970.*

The generation gap is the impetus for another book dramatizing the conflict between a materially successful father who wants the best-out-of-life for his son and his son who is not sure what best-in-life is but is very sure that it is not what his father thinks it is. . . . *Run Softly, Go Fast* is David Marks' diary of distress.

It is overwritten. Barbara Wersba's descriptions of events tend to slow the ultimate action of the narrative. David Marks is a kaleidoscope of artistic intentions rather than a flesh and blood boy. What David Marks really is never becomes apparent because he is afraid to find out. David's father is a second generation American Jew who married a gentile, and, in David's words, swallowed the Protestant Ethic. . . .

David's mother becomes the only real character in the novel when she enters her son's East Village pad and challenges him to try to make amends with his dying father. The other characters, Maggie who shares David's East Village pad, and Rick who shared David's love for art, are really only supporting players who reflect David's current feelings.

Despite these flaws, I believe this will be a very successful book for older adolescents. The fact that the author has created types rather than characters allows a concerned adolescent reader to enter in without being totally usurped by a character. The age-old battle David Marks wages with his father, to be allowed to become himself, is of major importance to most older adolescents. Barbara Wersba has skillfully revealed the elements of conflict between David and his father. When David realizes how conservative he really is and how his father's influence really does affect his day-to-day actions, he makes his descent into the maelstrom of hard drugs. But this doesn't work. A good trip distorts David's color sense; color sense is very important to his work as a painter, and art, unlike people, can be trusted and admired without reservation.

Barbara Wersba understands the agony of establishing personal values. *Run Softly, Go Fast* is an excellent study of personal values. Long after the individual conflicts portrayed in the novel cannot be remembered, an adolescent reader will recall David's chagrin when his adult heroes revealed themselves as limited men. This is a fine book for a value-conscious older adolescent. (pp. 530-31)

> *John W. Conner, in* English Journal *(copyright © 1971 by The National Council of Teachers of English), April, 1971.*

OTHER CITATIONS

Zena Sutherland, in Bulletin of the Center for Children's Books, *February, 1971, p. 100.*

Jean C. Thomson, in School Library Journal, *February, 1971, p. 70.*

Aileen Pace Nilsen, in English Journal, *May, 1974, pp. 90-1.*

TUNES FOR A SMALL HARMONICA (1976)

Barbara Wersba writes about teenagers who are growing up in ways painfully removed from situations their parents can cope with—boys who love Shakespeare or art; girls who dress like Steve McQueen and play the harmonica. Her books are about alienation, androgyny, the individual, love, identity, pain, growth: in fact, one begins to suspect a formula. What one finds is not a rote, mechanical algebra, but deep and often beautiful derivations of theorems, carried out with care and understanding.

Tunes is shaped for us by a resourceful, brash and vulnerable girl named J. F. McAllister. She dresses in Early Tomboy. She reads books like *Homosexuality and Low Blood Sugar* to determine whether she is gay. She is not, but she is full of what we used to call masculine characteristics, which causes her perfectly coiffed mother no end of anguish. J. F. falls in love with Harold Murth, a pale poetry teacher who doesn't know she's alive. Being rich and fancying him poor, J. F. showers him with gifts which he accepts with polite astonishment, and with tentative affection which he barely acknowledges. She determines to send him to Cambridge so he can finish his thesis and raises the money for this by playing the harmonica in the street. (Shubert Alley during intermission is a lucrative spot.) Of course, when she finally presents the cash, he tells her that his poverty is voluntary, his thesis completed, and his wife is living in New Jersey. J. F. laughs "the laughter of a Wall Street tycoon who has just been wiped out" but is saved from suicide by both a Hohner Chromatic 280 in the key of C, and her anger at an exploitive film director. A survivor, J. F. learns that she can deal with her own life.

Maybe my own enthusiasm for the harmonica has influenced my feeling for *Tunes*. I don't think so. J. F.'s playing, from "Jingle Bells" to a *Brandenburg* Concerto, acts as a gentle counterpoint to the unfolding of events. It would be easy to do this crudely and to overkill, but Wersba is nothing if not a tastful and disciplined writer. J. F. was a happy if untutored piano player until forced to take lessons; her musicality is rewakened when her best friend gives her a harmonica to encourage J. F. to quit smoking.

Tunes lacks the emotional impact of Wersba's *Country of Heart*, in which a young male poet tells of his love for a now dead older woman poet. It lacks the anguished explorations of *Run Softly, Go Fast,* in which a son never forgives his father, even on his deathbed, for trying to forbid him his painting career. The writing in *Tunes* is not as emotive as in these previous books, but neither does it occasionally become saccharine or self-pitying. Wersba writes the way people talk and think—J. F. is a spunky go-getter, not an introspective romantic. She doesn't need the lessons expounded in *Country* and *Run Softly* (she doesn't know Larry Adler got his start playing harmonica outside theaters; she doesn't know or care who Larry Adler *is*.) J. F. is matter of fact and has a sense of humor about her life and hence *Tunes* is a happier if sometimes bittersweet book.

J. F. is an interesting person (which is fortunate, as no one else is developed beyond a few lines). . . .

The plot is slightly contrived, and there are problems of development. Why does J. F. fall in love with Harold Murth—does she need to fall in love that badly? Her father is curiously absent (when they meet in the hallway, she blinks, recognizes who it is, and they shake hands like

vague acquaintances). In the light of all this, why are her parents married? Why introduce a father at all? Why is the harmonica a "he"? Mine's an it, and *die Mundharmonika,* from which it stems, is definitely feminine.

The novel survives these minor flaws to create another honest, sympathetic Wersba character with real problems in today's world. I wonder what she would have written in the '50s, when androgyny wasn't discussed—and what she will write in the '80s? Most readers will enjoy knowing J. F. And if I ever meet her, I'm going to teach how to *really* play Bach on her new 280.

> *Ellen Abby Lazer, "Chromatic Fantasies,"* in Book World—The Washington Post (© The Washington Post), October 10, 1976, p. E6.

[*Tunes for a Small Harmonica*] may appeal to the junior high reader who wants a "now" situation, but to others the unreal actions which the heroine pursues may seem outlandish and corny. . . . Some of J. F.'s observations are truly humorous and universal for her age, but on the whole her efforts to find meaning in her life did not seem convincing to me. (p. 3)

> The Babbling Bookworm, *February, 1977.*

OTHER CITATIONS

Publishers Weekly, *July 12, 1976, p. 72.*

Zena Sutherland, in Bulletin of the Center for Children's Books, *February, 1977, p. 99.*

Barbara Karlin, in West Coast Review of Books, *Vol. 3, No. 2 (March, 1977), p. 47.*

*   *   *

WHITE, Robb   1909-

Born in the Philippines as the son of a missionary, Robb White is an American author of adventure stories for young people, as well as a writer of screenplays and television scripts. White attained the rank of Captain in the US Navy while serving as an aviation specialist, and has experienced many of the same types of adventures that he has brought to life for his readers. His novel *Deathwatch* won the Edgar Allen Poe Award in 1972. (See also *Contemporary Authors,* Vols. 1-4, rev. ed. and *Something About the Author,* Vol. 1.)

CANDY (1949)

[*Candy* is a] vastly entertaining and occasionally moving story but one filled with improbabilities from beginning to end. Candy lives on the coast of Florida, has a passion for boats, and is an expert sailor. A promise to a mysterious man to keep his whereabouts unknown, and her friendship with and championship of a homeless blind boy who is trying to evade institutional life, call for all the courage and resourcefulness that Candy can muster. Like all books by this author boats and sailing feature largely, narrative interest is high, and good values are mixed with bad. (p. 70)

> The Booklist *(reprinted by permission of the American Library Association; copyright 1949 by the American Library Association), October 15, 1949.*

This book has some stock characters, such as a mean millionaire and a mysterious stranger. The plot is stock, too, with Candy's wild sail through a storm made for reasons never quite convincing. None of this matters, though, since Mr. White has made Candy and her family and friends, and proud, desperate little Tony so real, warm and appealing. The dialogue is authentic and amusing, and the sailing scenes carry a feeling of freedom and fun. This is highly recommended for girls and boys. . . . (p. 20)

> *Marjorie Fischer, in* The New York Times Book Review (© *1950 by The New York Times Company; reprinted by permission), February 5, 1950.*

OTHER CITATIONS

Saturday Review, *November 12, 1949, p. 28.*

DEATHWATCH (1972)

Robb White is all-pro at the game of adventure. Like a veteran quarterback, he has mastered all the tricks and makes his moves seem like child's play. That is why this novel is a pleasure to read, either as a sizzling adventure or as an ironic allegory of our times.

The arena is the desert of the Southwest, where two men are locked in a duel for survival. Twenty-two-year-old Ben, the narrator and voice of decency, is pitted against Madec, a middle-aged villain and sadist. Ben is guiding Madec on his quest to kill a bighorn sheep when the latter accidentally shoots an old prospector. Ben refuses to cover up the killing and to continue the hunt, so Madec strips him to the buff and turns him loose in the wilderness. Then begins a lethal stalk, with the odds favoring Madec, who has the rifles, camping gear and jeep. Naked, on-foot Ben has only his knowledge of the desert, his courage, stamina and ingenuity—but he outmaneuvers Madec, hog-ties him, and carts him off to the sheriff.

If "Deathwatch" had ended at this point, with justice and Ben triumphant, it would be a whale of a tale, packed with action and heroics. But this novel is not a simple black-and-white juvenile adventure. Robb White has given it an extra, highly ironic twist. Nobody, neither friend nor relative, wants to believe Ben, the honest home-town boy with the far-fetched story. Early in the novel, Madec had warned him of such a possibility. Ben is a "nobody," a "loser," and Madec asks: "Who am I? I'm president and sole owner of a corporation. I'm married, two wonderful children."

Naturally, the people believe this shrewd, corporate man, whose age and success are certificates of virtue: it is as though a young person has to prove his honesty, while an older one can get by with an assertion. Eventually the truth comes out. Madec, the man who has it made, gets his lumps, but Ben is left sorely bruised. His friends' lack of faith is a form of betrayal, signifying the end of innocence.

None of this is spelled out by Mr. White, who prefers to end his novel on a perfect off-beat note, which shouldn't be trumpeted by a reviewer. (p. 4)

> *Robert Hood, in* The New York Times Book Review, Part II (© *1972 by The New York Times Company; reprinted by permission), May 7, 1972.*

Despite its undistinguished colloquial style and perhaps because of its straight-forward reportorial manner, [*Deathwatch*] is an exciting novel of suspense, based on a fight to the finish between an honest and courageous young man and a cynical business tycoon, who believes that anything can be had for a price. Although the locale of the desert is only vaguely situated in the American Far West, the cruel, life-draining environment forms a strong background for the dramatic struggle between two "mighty opposites." (p. 475)

> *Paul Heins, in* The Horn Book Magazine (copyright © *1972 by The Horn Book, Inc., Boston), October, 1972.*

Robb White is an acknowledged master of the adventure yarn. Books like Robb White's *Up Periscope* and *Torpedo Run* inspire adventure-loving adolescents to make return trips to library shelves seeking another book as good as the last Robb White story. *Deathwatch* is another superb Robb White yarn. The author's experience in writing screen plays is evident in this story. *Deathwatch* is extremely graphic—a reader really sees each action of the two major characters etched against the desert and the mountains. . . .

Deathwatch demands to be read in a single sitting. . . .

The characters are all too obvious: Madec is sinister, untrustworthy, and enormously wealthy; Madec's lawyers are clever and brilliant; Ben is a small town boy—virtuous to a fault. But the story entices a reader, pulling a reader into the action, immersing a reader in Ben's incessant needs: water and a chance to overpower the wily Madec.

Deathwatch would make an exciting movie because of the visual impact of the natural environment on the story. Robb White's descriptions of the setting entice a reader with half-revealed possibilities of escape for Ben. No great truths are revealed in *Deathwatch*. No thought-provoking passages are included. *Deathwatch* is good, exciting escape fiction— the kind teenagers love! (pp. 1260-61)

> *John W. Conner, in* English Journal (copyright © *1972 by The National Council of Teachers of English), November, 1972.*

OTHER CITATIONS

Kirkus Reviews, *March 15, 1972, p. 336.*

Publishers Weekly, *May 15, 1972, p. 54.*

Sister M. Constance Melvin, I.H.M., in Best Sellers, *June 15, 1972, p. 152.*

The Booklist, *July 15, 1972, p. 1000.*

THE FROGMEN (1973)

Imagine swimming half a mile or so beneath the sea before you begin disarming a prickly mine—then knowing that a slip of your hand will blow you to pieces. Navy frogmen lived with this terror during the war in the Pacific, and Robb White pays them tribute in this adventure story. Amos Wainwright, hero of "The Frogmen," is a stubborn young ensign who winds up with three other frogmen on an extremely dangerous mission. The flimsy little task force must sail several hundred miles in a tiny wooden ship, slip past Japanese patrols into a strange harbor, and disarm mines they've never seen before. They must do this before the invasion starts, radio back to Pearl Harbor, and then run for their lives—even though they suspect their skipper is a spy for the enemy. An unlikely story, far-fetched? You don't believe it can be pulled off? You don't know Capt. Robb White who takes his characters to the limits of their endurance—and then tightens the screw one-half turn. They squirm and so will you. An underwater knife fight, an exploding mine, a last-minute rescue—death, danger and suspense—the author cooks an old-fashioned chowder, and makes it delectable. (p. 12)

> *Robert Hood, in* New York Times Book Review *(© 1973 by The New York Times Company; reprinted by permission), September 16, 1973.*

OTHER CITATIONS

Kirkus Reviews, *May 1, 1973, p. 522.*

Mrs. John G. Gray, in Best Sellers, *June 15, 1973, pp. 146-47.*

SECRET SEA (1947)

[*Secret Sea* concerns the] search for a Spanish ship sunk in the Caribbean several hundred years before and the recovery of its treasure of Aztec gold. If one can accept the fact that a young ex-naval officer would undertake such an expedition, in the face of opposition from a Nazi gang, with a crew of one—and that one a fifteen-year-old boy, a typical "Dead-end kid," picked up in the harbor—and some other unlikely aspects, this is a fast-paced entertaining yarn. The writing is so graphic that the reader has the feeling of sharing adventures firsthand and the character development of the boy is convincing. (p. 158)

> The Booklist *(reprinted by permission of the American Library Association; copyright 1947 by the American Library Association), December 15, 1947.*

SILENT SHIP, SILENT SEA (1967)

War begins as calculated risk and becomes the commitment of two men to a battered hulk in Robb White's latest documentary-drama. It's 1942 and the destroyer *Caron* is off the Solomons. Aboard against his will is Kelsey Devereux.... When an enemy plane crashes against the superstructure, Kelsey calls "Abandon ship" and does; when he is fished out, all hands consider him a deserter.... In small and large ways, Kelsey emerges as a man; when he knocks out the invincible [bully] Ruddy in desperate self-defense, he is a man to look up to. And in small and large ways, the Captain and Kelsey draw closer, a relationship that is confirmed when the two find themselves on board alone after the ship passes an Australian island, and sealed with the presentation of lieutenant's bars—the Captain's own—to Kelsey. This last is almost maudlin, and the denouement is almost melodrama, but the hard core of carefully established character prevails: being who they are, this is how they might be. With a quick hook and a steady pull, divided between concern for the ship and concern for the men, this should go as well as its predecessors. (p. 888)

> Kirkus Service *(copyright © 1967 Virginia Kirkus' Service, Inc.), August 1, 1967.*

Silent Ship, Silent Sea is a sinewy, hard-bitten story of naval war and survival in the Coral Sea, full of the tension, atmosphere and sense of authenticity one expects from Robb White. The U.S. destroyer *Caron,* a victim of the disaster at Guadalcanal, sets out for refuge to Australia. An enemy torpedo reduces the ship to a helpless, drifting wreck, but the captain is grimly determined to keep her afloat, hoping that the ocean currents will ultimately carry her to safety. The drama evolves in parallel courses, for this is the story not only of a captain battling to save his ship and his men against odds which include an encounter with a submarine and, later, devastation by a typhoon, but equally of a young and bewildered seaman, Kelsey Devereux, thrown by a bureaucratic snafu into a harrowing struggle for personal survival.

If Kelsey is too patently the classic example of the underdog proving his worth to his companions, the details of his ordeal are nonetheless paralyzingly real and unflinchingly grim. Some scenes, such as his exploration of the ship's underwater compartments afloat with dead men after the attack, are not for the timid, but they deliver powerful truths about personal courage and the ugliness of war. Kelsey is nominally the hero, but the delineation of the dedicated captain and his ordeal with a dying ship is so central and so absorbing that the story assumes dimensions beyond the usual teenage adventure. The author is not inclined to explore psychological subtleties, yet the last episode is unexpectedly poignant, when the crew reaches the safety of a tropical island while the captain, loyal to the ship, and Kelsey, loyal to a dying friend, remain aboard to face the final adventure together. Boys who know *Up Periscope* or *Secret Sea* should rejoice to find Robb White in top form. (p. 20)

> *Houston L. Maples, in* Book World—Chicago Tribune *(© 1967 Postrib Corp.), October 29, 1967.*

SURRENDER (1966)

[*Surrender*] is a fiercely exciting tale of the Japanese conquest of the Philippines after the attack on Pearl Harbor, and of the almost incredible survival of a rather winning pair of children, brother and sister, whom events flick casually into the war's center. *Surrender* is an adventure yarn, pure and simple, but it's a superb one. It races along from the first Japanese assault on the Philippines to the grim resistance on the Bataan Peninsula, the final hopeless stand in the fortress of Corregidor, and the brave guerrilla operations in the jungles and swamps. It has suspense, some wild action, much good characterization, arresting drama, and quite a bit of fine deadpan humor. Juan and Juanita MacGregor, the Filipino-American boy and girl on whom the story focuses, are awesome in their resourcefulness and courage. And they display an unfailing dignity and charm that, if perhaps doomed to go unperceived by most young readers, at least delighted this older one. *Surrender* is about as inventive, appealing, and breathless an adventure story as a child—nay, anyone—could hope to plunge happily into. (p. 14)

> *Gerald Gottlieb, in* Sunday World Journal Tribune Book Week *(© The Washington Post), March 19, 1967.*

There have not been many books for children about the Second World War. Perhaps the protective blanket thrown over the young by their elders, parents, teachers, publishers, writers alike, is responsible. Robb White's *Surrender* has a rarity value, therefore, and it may be tempting to think that it is this which makes the book seem so impressive an achievement. On consideration the merits of the story are seen to be real.

Mr. White was born in the Philippines and has made them the setting of the story. It begins three days after Pearl Harbour with the first Japanese raids on the naval installations in Manila Bay. It ends four months later with the surrender of the American forces on Bataan. The events of these days are shown through the eyes of four people. There is the American petty officer Gannon, a good fighting man and still more a man of deep and genuine tenderness, as far from the war film image of the American as one could find. He makes a good contrast to George Fowler, a radar expert reluctantly launched into an alien world where courage counts for more than technology, an unattractive portrait but not an unsubtle one. Lastly there are *los dos Juanes,* two enchanting Filipino-American children whose enormous, and always credible, courage and endurance hold the action together. Their father, in the last passage of the story, calls them "indomitable". There is no other word.

There is brutality and grim tragedy in this book. Mr. White pulls no punches out of consideration for his young readers, and he is right. His story is about the ugliness of war and the beauty of the human spirit, and children who surrender to him—and with such fine narrative they are likely to do so willingly—will have no difficulty in recognizing both themes and putting the right interpretation to each. (p. 258)

> *The Times Literary Supplement (© Times Newspapers Ltd., 1968; reproduced from The Times Literary Supplement by permission), March 14, 1968.*

The picture [*Surrender*] gives of one of the beastliest theatres of an unsavoury war may be a true one, but a slight element of exaggeration in the writing, makes it seem just a little too tragic, a little too heroic, a little too grim, and a little too clean to be true; and the constant resilience and stiff-upper-lipness of the young hero and heroine in the face of unrelieved and continuous disaster, appears unrealistic. The map in the endpapers is maddening in having the places most often mentioned tucked into the fold. (p. 191)

> *The Junior Bookshelf, June, 1968.*

OTHER CITATIONS

The Booklist and Subscription Books Bulletin, *January 15, 1967, p. 531.*

Leora Oglesby, in School Library Journal, *March, 1967, p. 143.*

THE SURVIVOR (1964)

For the first half of Robb White's most recent tale of World War II the action is a little slow. In the remainder of the book he piles suspense upon suspense and winds up with a grand finale that is all fireworks. Mr. White's navy-pilot hero, Adam Land, is sent out from Pearl Harbor by submarine with a small force of select Marines. The mission: to gather intelligence on a Japanese-held island in the South Pacific slated to be the next invasion target. . . .

Land and three of his companions reach the island without equipment or means of escape. Yet escape they do, after completing their mission, in a climactic scene that must be unique even in the annals of the Marine Corps. If you don't mind the implausibility, this one has excitement aplenty. (p. 34)

> *John M. Connole, in* The New York Times Book Review *(© 1964 by The New York Times Company; reprinted by permission), September 13, 1964.*

The survivor is LTJG Adam Land, who looks into the muzzle of an enemy gun and resolves not to die so ignominiously. He survives just long enough to fly his buddies back to an American base. As in his earlier World War II dramas, the author relies again on a secret mission against the Japanese, impossible odds, and an almost indestructible hero, but the combination makes for edge-of-the-chair reading. Without resort to man-style cussing the author achieves a man-style narrative of danger and death. A Hollywood scenario will be sure to highlight the wonderful comic-relief climax in which Adam and his Marine comrades, dressed in outlandish masks and feathers, steal a plane before the very eyes of thousands of enemy soldiers. (p. 621)

> *Jane Manthorne, in* The Horn Book Magazine *(copyright © 1964, by The Horn Book, Inc., Boston), December, 1964.*

OTHER CITATIONS

Virginia Kirkus' Service, *August 1, 1964, p. 756.*

Best Sellers, *September 15, 1964, p. 235.*

Taliferro Boatwright, in Chicago Tribune Book Week, *November 1, 1964, p. 33.*

UP PERISCOPE (1960)

[This] taut, knowledgeable account of life and action aboard a submarine will most certainly earn the author a "Well done!" from any man who has ever served on a sub.

Young Lieut. (j.g.) Ken Braden is assigned an almost hopeless mission. Smuggled ashore by submarine on an enemy-infested atoll, his task is to steal a Japanese code from a radio transmitting station that is relaying top-secret United States strategy to the Tokyo High Command.

As the intensely exciting saga of the Shark builds to a smashing climax, the reader comes to know what it is like to be trapped aboard a submarine in a narrow lagoon entrance with a Jap destroyer bearing down head-on, to be "skip-bombed" by a low-flying enemy aircraft, to sneak inside a destroyer convoy and sink a carrier, then to undergo endless hours of depth-bombing so severe that the steel plates of the submarine begin to buckle. Well conceived, splendidly written, this teen-age book is one of the best yet about naval action in the Pacific after Pearl Harbor. (p. 32)

> *Henry B. Lent, in* The New York Times

Book Review (© 1956 by the New York Times Company; reprinted by permission), September 23, 1956.

OTHER CITATIONS

Heloise P. Mailloux, in The Horn Book Magazine, *October, 1956, p. 363.*

*   *   *

WIBBERLEY, Leonard   1915-
(also Patrick O'Connor)

Although Leonard Wibberley, Irish-born novelist and poet for adults and children, did not move to the United States until 1943, he has written extensively on American history in his fiction. He became a prolific free-lance writer after abandoning a long career as a newspaper man. Wibberley also makes stringed instruments, an interest evident in his *Guarneri: Story of a Genius*. His *The Mouse That Roared*, an adult novel, was filmed in 1959, as was its sequel, *The Mouse on the Moon*, in 1963. (See also *Contemporary Authors*, Vols. 5-8, rev. ed. and *Something About the Author*, Vol. 2.)

ATTAR OF THE ICE VALLEY (1968)

Neanderthal man, who disappeared about 50,000 years ago after perhaps 75,000 years of existence, could have been our ancestor. On this theme Leonard Wibberley has written an excellent book. Tightly woven, presented in deceptively simple, stark tones, it shows a way of life stripped to bare essentials. . . .

Neanderthal man may or may not have been the "first." But, as here re-created in the dawn of mankind, he might have been as the author tells it, with control so expert that the reader feels himself huddling with Attar's tribe, fearful of the unknown. (p. 30)

> *Ivan Sandrof, in* The New York Times Book Review (© 1968 by The New York Times Company; reprinted by permission), *March 31, 1968.*

Attar apparently symbolizes the emergence of man as an intelligent spirit, and as such he makes good case-book reading. However, [*Attar of the Ice Valley*] is chiefly plot, the individual characters and their relationships are not fully developed, and the ending seems curiously up in the air; the whole book reads as if it were merely a prelude to the portrayal of fully developed men living in truly organized human society. (p. 92)

> *Jean C. Thomson, in* School Library Journal *(reprinted from the May, 1968, issue of* School Library Journal, *published by R. R. Bowker Co., a Xerox company; copyright © 1968 by Xerox Corporation), May, 1968.*

OTHER CITATIONS

Virginia Haviland, in The Horn Book Magazine, *August, 1968, pp. 432-33.*

Gordon Parsons, in The School Librarian, *December, 1969, p. 405.*

Miss J. S. Jenkins, in Children's Books News, *January-February, 1970, pp. 29-30.*

THE BALLAD OF THE PILGRIM CAT (1962)

A fresh wind enlivens this ballad of the familiar voyage of the *Mayflower* and the landing of the Pilgrims, partly because its creator brings to it the same perspective he brought to the American Revolution in his Treegate stories. . . . Here is a light touch to brighten the Thanksgiving season and make the Pilgrim Fathers seem more human. Though occasional tongue-in-cheek interpolations are from an adult angle, the ballad will pass the test of being read aloud over and over by someone who enjoys its particular gusto, because of the smooth swinging of the lines and the suspenseful action.

Miss Pru is a real person, loyal to her cat, the villain of the piece, who rings true to egocentric feline nature. There is fun and a spontaneity to which boys and girls will respond as they do when they hear some of the livelier ballads from Steven Vincent Benét's "A Book of Americans." (p. 48)

> Saturday Review *(copyright 1962 by Saturday Review, Inc.; reprinted by permission), November 10, 1962.*

After all those slightly solemn stories one hears every year about the first Thanksgiving, Leonard Wibberley's "Ballad of the Pilgrim Cat" comes as a nice fillip—like a lemon soufflé after turkey and stuffing. Cheerfully irreverent, Mr. Wibberley tells in swinging lines of the friendship between a quite young Pilgrim, Prudence God-With-Us Simplicity Smith, aged 9, and a cat, "a scandalous tramp,/Missing an ear, a seaport scamp . . . A sinful, thievish, graceless knave;/An offense to God; to sin, a slave." (p. 52)

> *Ellen Lewis Buell, in* The New York Times Book Review (© 1962 by The New York Times Company; reprinted by permission), *November 18, 1962.*

OTHER CITATIONS

Ruth Hill Viguers, in The Horn Book Magazine, *December, 1962, p. 612.*

A DAWN IN THE TREES: THOMAS JEFFERSON, THE YEARS 1776 TO 1789 (1964)

[*A Dawn in the Trees*] is the second volume in a projected trilogy. Mr. Wibberley's purpose as stated in the first volume, *Young Man From the Piedmont* . . . was to create "non-fiction fiction" that would represent not only the facts of Jefferson's life but his social and political milieu as well. The first volume left off in 1776 with Jefferson working on the Declaration of Independence. This one picks up at that point and takes him through the Revolution, his governorship of Virginia, the death of his wife and to the end of his term as an ambassador to France. Again, the dialogue provided for prominent historic figures is invented or transplanted. As a re-creation of a social or political milieu, the book is not successful. For instance, Jefferson's initial and continuing ambivalence toward the French Revolution is not well analyzed. Nor, is this a sharp picture of Paris on the Eve of the French Revolution or more than a cursory examination of the issues that ignited it. In one or three volumes, this Jefferson trilogy is shaping up as another boneless juvenile biography that would bring on apopleptic fits if the same high gloss approach were tried at the adult level. (p. 744)

Virginia Kirkus' Service, August 1, 1964.

With *A Dawn in the Trees* . . . Leonard Wibberley contributes an excellent second volume to his trilogy about Thomas Jefferson. . . .

The writing is exceptionally skillful, drawing the reader irresistibly into the events of the day: the Continental Congress agonizing over the resolution for independence, George Rogers Clark's harrowing expedition to capture Vincennes and Jefferson's frustrating years as Governor of Virginia, struggling to defend his virtually defenseless land from British invasion. The later years in Europe with Adams and Franklin are no less vivid—the elegance at Versailles and the poverty in the streets of Paris preparing us for the foment that will lead to another revolution. Running in counterpoint to the tale of national violence is the healing theme of Jefferson's personal pursuit of happiness. . . . (p. 12)

> *Houston L. Maples, in* Book Week (© The Washington Post), *November 1, 1964.*

OTHER CITATIONS

Priscilla L. Moulton, in The Horn Book Magazine, *October, 1964, p. 511.*

Elnora M. Portteus, in School Library Journal, *October, 1964, pp. 227-28.*

Zena Sutherland, in Bulletin of the Center for Children's Books, *November, 1964, p. 46.*

DEADMEN'S CAVE (1954)

Mr. Wibberley's [pirates] for the most part tend to be ultra-black. His hero, however, has a sense of values and carries conviction as a person. So, too, does the fantastic evangelical pirate, God Ha' Mercy, a former divinity student whom Mr. Wibberley is to be congratulated upon making entirely credible. *Deadmen's Cave*, in fact, is not only a good average adventure story but a promise of better things to come. Few writers in this genre would have the courage to weave into a story of the sack of Panama the parable of God Ha' Mercy's life with its immemorial truths; and few would have the wit to inscribe upon their title-page this quotation from Johnson: "No man will be a sailor who has contrivance enough to get himself into a jail; for being in a ship is being in a jail, with the chance of being drowned." (p. iv)

> The Times Literary Supplement (© *Times Newspapers Ltd., 1954; reproduced from* The Times Literary Supplement *by permission), May 28, 1954.*

An apparently trivial title conceals a story of more than usual merit with an interesting and momentous historical basis. Morgan is not an unusual figure in tales of the Main but it is rare to find his notorious sack of Panama treated with such detail. There are glimpses here and there of the literary splendour of Kingsley's account of Raleigh's ill-fated Orinoco expedition and for the most part there is a firmness in the writing that would raise the book above average even if its theme were less celebrated. The more villainous characters are well drawn and local colour effectively if economically used. The narrative moves rapidly and changes of fortune are many and diverse, making a

book that will not readily be put down. For all that it is a book for more mature readers than stories of this type normally are. The illustrations [by S. Findlay] are plentiful and alive. (p. 142)

> *The Junior Bookshelf, July, 1954.*

OTHER CITATIONS

Virginia Kirkus' Bookshop Service, March 15, 1954, p. 200.

Zena Sutherland, in Bulletin of the Center for Children's Books, *July, 1954, p. 97.*

Virginia Haviland, in The Horn Book Magazine, *August, 1954, p. 253.*

ENCOUNTER NEAR VENUS (1967)

Wibberley is a good writer . . . imaginative. It's too bad that this frothy little fantasy dissipates even before it can act as a diversion. . . . There's a little morality lesson about good and evil as well as group consciousness vs. individualism fortunately de-sugarized by the author's tongue-in-cheek presentation. But like the fiberglass flying saucer, it's transparent. (p. 146)

> Kirkus Service (copyright © 1967 *Virginia Kirkus' Service, Inc.), February 1, 1967.*

Mr. Wibberley offers two novel elements in his fantasy of a sojourn in space for two boys and two girls. Firstly, there are the Lumens, small gleaming or glowing organisms that have astonishing powers of thought and communication; secondly, there are the creatures of Nede who seem to be throwbacks to the days of dragons, wyverns and similar creatures, combined with dolphins and their now recognised intelligence. The Lumens are perhaps the more difficult to accept but they are certainly interesting, although it is not quite clear what their anxiety about the existence of "fear" really means, and their positive ignorance of the ideas of "good" and "evil" is not an altogether convincing element of the story, since they seem to know about practically everything else. The illustrations [by Bernadette Watts] consist of a sort of double frontispiece and one chapter-head decoration. Perhaps the illustrator could not take the point of the story either. (p. 389)

> *The Junior Bookshelf, December, 1968.*

There is . . . innocence, shrewdness and high spirits in *Encounter near Venus* . . . by Leonard Wibberley. Wibberley's reputation rests on an extremely fine and deeply researched novel about the American Civil War. His approach to science is casual, or, to be more precise, he writes a space story out of his own exuberant fantasy, unfettered by considerations of probability. This does not make his book any the less enjoyable or exciting. If the science is innocent the writing is extremely sophisticated. In expressing his story so precisely in the idiom of the late Sixties the author courted disaster, for nothing ages more quickly than literary and oral idioms; but, if a year or two have outdated the dialogue, the sharp observation of lively and intelligent children has not.

There are moments of excitement in *Encounter near Venus*. The charm of the book comes from its gentler moments, from its skill in conveying purely physical pleasures like swimming—the children are able most conveniently to breathe the sea on the planet Nede because the water is 'super-saturated with oxygen'—and the prettiness of the lumens, light intelligences which feel 'like warm fur and ice at the same time' and which communicate with humans by Morse Code. The book is handicapped by having one of the more tedious of omniscient Uncles as its motive force, and it is enlivened by a creative imagination which never takes itself too seriously. (p. 53)

> *Marcus Crouch, in his* The Nesbit Tradition: The Children's Novel in England 1945-1970 *(© Marcus Crouch 1972), Ernest Benn, 1972.*

OTHER CITATIONS

Dorothy S. Jones, in School Library Journal, *April, 1967, p. 94.*

Alan L. Marsden, in Book Week, *July 2, 1967, p. 12.*

THE EPICS OF EVEREST (1954)

Leonard Wibberley, author of gripping adventure tales, succeeds in being . . . exciting . . . in this history of Everest expeditions. . . . [He] is at once comprehensive, sufficiently detailed, and dramatic, without seeming repetitious in his presentation of eleven different reconnaissance and climbing expeditions. His descriptions are graphic in terms of human effort and courage, individually and in team work, and in the picture of the visible and invisible defences of the perilous mountain against attack by Man. The reader is left with a clearer idea of why man must climb. Excellent maps and sketches that illustrate techniques and dangers are drawn by [Genevieve Vaughan Jackson], who is herself a mountain-climber. (p. 441)

> *Virginia Haviland, in* The Horn Book Magazine *(copyrighted, 1954, by The Horn Book, Inc., Boston), December, 1954.*

FLINT'S ISLAND (1972)

Here's what happened to "the treasure not yet lifted" from Flint's Island. Though Wibberley claims that this is not a sequel to *Treasure Island* ("Who would dare such a thing?"), it is precisely that. The return of Long John Silver is chronicled with an American accent by the youngest crew member of the *Jane,* a trading vessel out of Salem, Massachusetts. The *Jane* stops at Flint's Island to gather timber to replace the mast, but finds instead the marooned Silver who wins over the crew with promises of treasure. Even after his attempt to capture the ship is thwarted by loyal members of the crew, Long John's charisma is strong enough to cause a second mutiny and, in a manner of speaking, Silver comes out on top even though the treasure goes to the bottom of the ocean. Wibberley is not Stevenson, and there's none of the precise detail or timing which makes *Treasure Island* an archetypal adventure, but Silver's wiliness and Flint's mystique are perfectly captured and the American seamen—prudent Captain Samuels, the unimaginative Yankee carpenter Smigley, the impulsive mutineer Green and the loyal, but mean-spirited Peasbody are worthy of their *Hispaniola* counterparts. (p. 336)

Kirkus Reviews *(copyright © 1972 The Kirkus Service, Inc.), March 15, 1972.*

Writing a sequel to someone else's novel is always a risky business, especially if that work is as widely admired as *Treasure Island*. But Wibberley, long intrigued by some of the unanswered questions in Stevenson's classic, has tackled the job with remarkable success.

Flint's Island is a lean, swift adventure tale which brings a new group of seamen from Salem, Massachusetts to that fateful pirate spa and the rich treasure it still holds. Long John Silver is on hand once more, and there is a swash-buckling encounter as treacherous and bloody as any invented by Stevenson. Wibberley's knowledge of ships and the seafaring life, as well as his near-perfect attunement to the style and mood of the original, lend an air of unimpeachable authority to the whole. Some may object to a surprise ending that telescopes too many facts into too brief a space, but the expectant reader has probably been sated by this point anyhow. It is the work of a fine writer in top form. (p. 13)

> *Houston Maples, in* Book World, *Part 2 (© The Washington Post), May 7, 1972.*

Possibly *Flint's Island* is not as deep or as finished as the earlier [*The Adventures of*] *Ben Gunn* [by R. F. Delderfield] and it approaches the mystery of what happened to Flint's treasure after the close of "Treasure Island" from another point of view—the fortuitous visit of a trading brig. Events which follow bear a strong resemblance to the main skulduggery of "Treasure Island" itself and much of its atmosphere is reawakened. Silver, of course, appears as an unknown, a form of irony which has a marked effect on the already well-read. *Flint's Island* is not a great book; neither is it a mere gimmick. It is based on a good idea and competently composed. (p. 418)

> The Junior Bookshelf, *December, 1973.*

OTHER CITATIONS

Sheryl B. Andrews, in The Horn Book Magazine, *October, 1972, p. 471.*

Charity Blackstock, in Books and Bookmen, *October, 1973, p. 122.*

David L. Rees, in Children's Book Review, *October, 1973, p. 148.*

THE GALES OF SPRING: THOMAS JEFFERSON, THE YEARS 1789-1801 (1965)

First, there was *Young Man from the Piedmont*. . . . Next there was *A Dawn in the Trees*. . . . [*The Gales of Spring*] we confidently expected and profoundly hoped would be the last of a trilogy devoted to Thomas Jefferson. However, since this volume goes only from 1789 to the eve of Jefferson's election as President, it becomes apparent that the author will produce a fourth book in 1966, which we will be tempted to announce this way: "Mr. Wibberley has finally drawn and quartered Thomas Jefferson." And, we will be saying it more in bemusement than amusement. Think of it —a multi-volume, fictionalized biography, a juvenilized Jefferson in quartet, yet. (We realize that our minds boggle in solitude. The first books in this cliffhanger have been generally well-received elsewhere.) But we don't, can't believe in "non-fiction/fiction," even if Mr. Wibberley works in this form with more restraint than others. It still leads him to set this sort of invented banality sailing past George Washington's silver false teeth: "'Hmmm,' said Washington (about a noble refugee from Revolutionary France.) 'He is one of the aristocrats?'"—to set up a minute lecture from Jefferson (in quotes) on the fact that there were aristocrats AND aristocrats. *Gales* . . . is the American-based Jefferson in his transition period from diplomat to politician. Mr. Wibberley seeks to show the Renaissance Man image of Jefferson: statesman, philosopher, tinkerer, writer, farmer, father. He does better with a balanced perspective of the domestic politics of the day than he did with international affairs in *A Dawn*. . . . But, it's still surface Jefferson, serialized. (pp. 911-12)

> Virginia Kirkus' Service (*copyright © 1965 Virginia Kirkus' Service, Inc.*), *September 1, 1965.*

This third volume in Wibberley's life of Jefferson is a readable history of the post-Revolutionary period highlighting the Jefferson-Hamilton conflict which the author tries to present dispassionately, citing the rights and wrongs of each man. [It contains] truths not often found in many textbooks that tend to glorify our nation's past by glossing over its mistakes. . . . This is a book to be read cover to cover, not just for reference. Wibberley humanizes American history for young people as Handlin and Catton have for adults. Washington and his cabinet become men we can recognize rather than the legendary figures they usually seem. (p. 95)

> Therese C. Kelly, in School Library Journal (*reprinted from the December, 1965, issue of* School Library Journal, *published by R. R. Bowker Co., a Xerox company; copyright © 1965 by Xerox Corporation*), *December, 1965.*

The gradual establishment of the Federalists and the Republicans as the first American political parties is the chief theme [of "The Gales of Spring"]. For this reason, the volume is made to order for young readers beginning to delve into the American past. They will find here a superb account of one of the few political squabbles which have significantly reflected and shaped our thinking as a people.

Mr. Wibberley says he has tried to avoid making Alexander Hamilton the villain of his piece. Unfortunately, he has not fully succeeded, if only because the focus of his work is Jefferson, who is his hero. Hamilton does not come off well enough here for young people to recognize that the first Secretary of the Treasury was as indispensable as his distinguished antagonist in helping the new nation to endure what James Madison so fittingly called the "gales of spring." (p. 18)

> Henry F. Graff, in The New York Times Book Review (*© 1965 by The New York Times Company; reprinted by permission*), *December 26, 1965.*

OTHER CITATIONS

Charlotte Jackson, in The Atlantic Monthly, *December, 1965, p. 158.*

William B. Catton, in Book Week, *February 13, 1966, p. 10.*

GUARNERI: STORY OF A GENIUS (1974)

In the absence of biographical certainties, Wibberley summons from his imagination the towering personality of Guarneri del Gesu—the master violin maker worshipped by posterity but unsuccessful in his own time. . . . The presence of Guarneri, a genius with a grudge against fate, is compelling; however, one strong character does not make a novel and the persona of Guarneri's apprentice, the narrator Thomas Soli, is pleasing but altogether less imposing. . . . Wibberley's [*Guarneri: Story of a Genius*, published in England as *Guarneri: Violin-Maker of Genius*] is exceptional as a study of artistic inspiration and a remarkable view of the milieu of the Renaissance instrument maker, and the Thomas Soli subplot—though it grows out of Wibberley's characteristic lack of concentration—is carried off with his equally characteristic brio and wit. (pp. 1014-15)

> Kirkus Reviews (*copyright © 1974 The Kirkus Service, Inc.*), *September 15, 1974.*

From [G. A.]Henty onwards, writers of historical fiction for children have employed the device of presenting the lives and characters of great men through the eyes of a young observer. Such an observer, whether a page of Richard II or Drake's cabin boy, can provide a convenient witness of historical events and, at the same time, offer the reader an easily identifiable hero. Sometimes, as with Elizabeth Borton de Treviño's Juan de Pareja or Vrethiki in Jill Paton Walsh's *The Emperor's Winding Sheet*, these junior witnesses are viable characters in their own right but, all too often, they are lifeless creatures, mere devices to suit the convenience of their authors. Thomas Soli, the young narrator in Leonard Wibberley's book, falls uncomfortably between the two extremes. The author's intention has been to show the life and work of the great violin-maker Guarneri through the eyes of Thomas, taken from an orphanage in eighteenth-century Cremona to become his apprentice. And, for a time, we are indeed given a fascinating glimpse of the master, of his complex genius and changing moods. But Thomas has a life of his own: he is a gifted singer and leaves Guarneri for a more glittering career in the court of the Duke of Milan where details of court intrigues and the boy's love life replace Guarneri as the principal focus of the book. This is a pity, for Guarneri is a more rewarding and interesting character than his talented apprentice. The book is at its best when Wibberley is describing the construction of violins or the friendly rivalry which existed between Guarneri and his more eminent neighbour, Stradivari; the reader's interest flags when the author deserts these topics for a less stimulating examination of Thomas's relationships with orphan Annette and the wilful soprano Theresa de Matignon. But, as the author tells us in his Foreword, little is known of the facts of Guarneri's life and we must, therefore, be grateful for Wibberley's capable recreation of the man and his times and regret that his apprentice stole so much of the thunder in this pleasant novel. (p. 25)

> Lance E. Salway, in Children's Book Review (*© 1976 Five Owls Press Ltd.; all rights reserved*), *October, 1976.*

OTHER CITATIONS

Susan Cooper, in The Christian Science Monitor, *November 6, 1974, p. 12.*

The Booklist, *December 15, 1974, p. 427.*

The Junior Bookshelf, *October, 1976, p. 294.*

JOURNEY TO UNTOR (1970)

[In this sequel to *Encounter Near Venus*] Uncle Bill and the six kids are off again . . . on another peaches and cream puff adventure. . . . On the *Journey* Uncle Bill does his usual philosophizing about space and time while confronted by four dimensional ups and downs; some of the children get separated and end up with courtly predators determined to rob them of their past; there are freak storms and treacherous mountains and the story is, again, a gossamer maze with no real substance. (p. 105)

> Kirkus Reviews *(copyright © 1970 The Kirkus Service, Inc.), February 1, 1970.*

For the exotic drama [of *Journey to Untor*] the author has painted scenes deftly and shifted scenery with ingenuity, yet without attaining a sufficient depth of characterization and motivation for action to involve the reader quickly. A bright child may be captivated by the intricacies of "*A times b* equals nothing," and concepts of "non-matter" and four- and five-dimensional space, but many will skip the philosophical-scientific interpolations as well as the drawn-out descriptions of a psychedelic mélange of shapes, colors, and unearthly phenomena of fauna and flora. . . . [This is a] story that is rich but undisciplined, fascinating but at times unwieldily detailed. (pp. 396-97)

> *Virginia Haviland, in* The Horn Book Magazine, *(copyright © 1970 by The Horn Book, Inc., Boston), August, 1970.*

There is no menace in this gentle dreamlike story [*Journey to Untor*], only vivid descriptions of texture and colour on a strange planet. . . . Any disasters which occur are somehow muted, certainly not violent. The narrative is often held up by discussions on interpretations of time and space, and the purpose of the journey is not revealed until the end, and then only in terms which will be beyond the younger child. So the point of this sweet morality may be missed by any readers who skip from one scene of action to the next. (p. 767)

> The Times Literary Supplement *(© Times Newspapers Ltd., 1971; reproduced from* The Times Literary Supplement *by permission), July 2, 1971.*

OTHER CITATIONS

The Junior Bookshelf, *August, 1971, pp. 259-60.*

THE KING'S BEARD (1952)

It is obvious that [Leonard Wibberley] has inherited the ability of the Irish to tell a good story and that he knows his background material well. He makes people and period come alive in a spontaneous and thrilling adventure tale in which Sir Walter Raleigh and Sir Francis Drake are among the important characters. (p. 112)

> *Jennie D. Lindquist, in* The Horn Book Magazine *(copyrighted, 1952, by The Horn Book, Inc., Boston), April, 1952.*

The climax of this lively tale of Elizabethan England is based on Drake's famous raid on the Spanish fleet at Cadiz but through it runs a complicated thread of a search for information for the secret of the fabulous Eldorado. That thread not only takes John Forrester as a gunner's assistant with the expedition but leads him also into the stronghold of Cadiz itself to the rescue of his father who is indeed in possession of the secret. The opening, with its mysterious messengers and inquisitive strangers is reminiscent of *Treasure Island* but the sequel is faster moving and more briskly concluded. Mr. Wibberley still has occasional touches of self-consciousness about his writing but Miss Findlay's illustrations are often very good indeed. (p. 203)

> The Junior Bookshelf, *October, 1954.*

OTHER CITATIONS

Virginia Kirkus' Bookshop Service, *March 15, 1952, p. 192.*

Good Books for Children: A Selection of Outstanding Children's Books Published 1950-65, *compiled by Mary K. Eakin, third edition, University of Chicago Press, 1966, p. 350.*

THE LAST BATTLE (1976)

Leonard Wibberley in "The Last Battle," which concludes his Treegate family saga, works on a larger scale than the traditional sea story, and his book is a little ungainly for it. Wibberley has his characters spread over two continents and they all wind up together just in time to get into the Battle of New Orleans in 1814. As a result the credulity of even the most ardent adventure-story buff gets stretched a bit thin. Still, it's a good yarn, and reading about brave young men under fire won't hurt anybody. (p. 29)

> *Peter Andrews, in* The New York Times Book Review *(© 1976 by The New York Times Company; reprinted by permission), July 18, 1976.*

Continuing the chronicle of the Treegate family during the War of 1812, the final volume of the trilogy, preceded by *Leopard's Prey* and *Red Pawns*, spans two years and two continents, skillfully interweaving history and adventure in a fast-paced, swashbuckling manner. . . . The characters, broadly outlined rather than finely drawn, are subordinated to the events. Yet the novel succeeds as an historical adventure in the grand tradition. (pp. 409-10)

> *Mary M. Burns, in* The Horn Book Magazine *(copyright © 1976 by the Horn Book, Inc., Boston), August, 1976.*

In the concluding volume of the series about the Treegate family in the American Revolution and the War of 1812, young Peter Treegate is serving on the ship of his brother, Manly, a captain in the American navy. Peter is restive under the discipline of shipboard life, and he engages in some rather unorthodox military action along with . . . [the] leader of a band of unprincipled but patriotic pirates. . . . Some of the characters, particularly the pirates, are colorful but not convincing; their names (Gubu, Hi-Peckum, Loblolly) are an indication of the author's disparate treatment of West Indian and American characters. The writing is competent, full of drama and suspense, and the book has—although not as much as is found in preceding volumes—historical interest. (pp. 19-20)

> *Zena Sutherland, in* Bulletin of the Center for Children's Books *(© 1976 by the University of Chicago; all rights reserved), September, 1976.*

LEOPARD'S PREY (1971)

How Manly survived the brutal treatment aboard the *Leopard* and finally returned to Salem is narrated in a suspenseful sequence of events with a touch of comic relief provided by an exotic crew of Haitian pirates, who were led by one of the most inept, and surely the luckiest, of men ever to fly the Jolly Roger. A fast-paced adventure rather than an in-depth character study, [*Leopard's Prey*] deftly outlines the background of the period while maintaining the balance between history and the kind of narrative demanded by the genre. (p. 394)

> *Mary M. Burns, in* The Horn Book Magazine *(copyright © 1971 by The Horn Book, Inc., Boston), August, 1971.*

Although the pirate and his superstitious Mama Amelie seem almost comic opera characters, and the closing scene planned for a final curtain (Manly appears at the family's Christmas dinner just as Peter Treegate reads a letter from Washington saying that the boy is missing and presumed dead) the book has both dramatic and historical interest, is well written, and is strong enough to overcome such minor weaknesses. (p. 67)

> *Zena Sutherland, in* Bulletin of the Center for Children's Books *(© 1971 by the University of Chicago; all rights reserved), December, 1971.*

OTHER CITATIONS

Ruth M. Pegan, in School Library Journal, *September, 1971, p. 182.*

The Booklist, *September 1, 1971, p. 60.*

THE LIFE OF WINSTON CHURCHILL (1956)

While the biography of so complex and colorful a personality [as Winston Churchill] must be somewhat superficial when confined to a short, easily-read book, Mr. Wibberley tries to show the man behind the anecdotes, and makes Sir Winston's importance to our era apparent without becoming effusive or sentimental. Children will like the descriptions of battles, bravery and incredible escapes; older boys and girls may be stimulated to try Sir Winston's own writings. (p. 200)

> *Heloise P. Mailloux, in* The Horn Book Magazine *(copyrighted, 1956, by The Horn Book, Inc., Boston), June, 1956.*

[This is an] interesting, albeit highly laudatory biography of Churchill. Because the author has chosen to gloss over any personality characteristics of Churchill's that might have made him a difficult or even occasionally unpleasant person to the people around him, there is no depth to the characterization. For immature readers who want no more than the essential facts of Churchill's life the book is adequate. The more mature reader will find greater interest in the adult biographies or in Churchill's own writings. (p. 30)

> Bulletin of the Center for Children's Books *(published by the University of Chicago), October, 1956.*

OTHER CITATIONS

Virginia Kirkus' Service, *January 15, 1956, p. 51.*

The Booklist, *March 15, 1956, p. 297.*

PETER TREEGATE'S WAR (1960)

[*Peter Treegate's War* is the] second of a series of four books about the Treegate family during the Revolutionary War. The action of this volume takes place during the war years, starting at the battle of Bunker Hill. Peter is torn between loyalty to his father, a Boston merchant, and to the Maclaren of Spey, his foster father; both older men are on the ramparts with Peter, and Maclaren is wounded. Peter goes on to become a British prisoner, he escapes from a prison ship, crosses the Delaware with Washington, and goes back to the hills to stay with the Maclaren until the man's death. Exciting action provides a vivid picture of the American scene; Mr. Wibberley is superbly at home as a writer of historical fiction. (p. 156)

> *Zena Sutherland, in* Bulletin of the Center for Children's Books *(published by the University of Chicago), May, 1960.*

Complete in itself but closely following *John Treegate's Musket*, this exciting story gives one soldier's view of the American Revolution. . . . Since Peter is not only intensely loyal to his foster father but is also a young man of courage and ideals, his personal war has scenes as gripping as those of the larger conflict. Well told, and peopled with living characters, as Mr. Wibberley's books always are, the coincidences on which dramatic turns of the story hang are completely convincing. (pp. 221-22)

> *Ruth Hill Viguers, in* The Horn Book Magazine *(copyright, 1960, by the Horn Book, Inc., Boston), June, 1960.*

OTHER CITATIONS

Sonja Wennerblad, in School Library Journal, *May, 1960, p. 74.*

The Booklist and Subscription Books Bulletin, *May 15, 1960, p. 577.*

RED PAWNS (1973)

Nowadays no one writes the kind of boys' adventures spun by Stevenson and C. S. Forester, but Leonard Wibberley carries on the tradition with tongue in cheek. . . . The Treegates sometimes get caught between Wibberley's skeptical hindsight and their own role as committed participants, but if Peter and Manly tend to amble aimlessly from episode to episode, each new escapade revives the pleasures of old-fashioned narrative. (p. 974)

> Kirkus Reviews *(copyright © 1973 The Kirkus Service, Inc.), September 1, 1973.*

Wibberley relies heavily on caricature [in *Red Pawns*], and his protagonists are men of their time, which means that their political opinions may sometimes jar contemporary sensibilities. But the Treegates' wonderfully anticlimactic escapades—including a ride on Nicholas Roosevelt's Ohio River steamboat and a hilariously abortive duel—are intermixed with moments of painful truth, as when Manly discovers the bones of a massacred band of Mohawk Indians and sees the signature of manifest destiny firsthand. (p. 5C)

> *Joyce Alpern, in* Book World, *Part 2 (© The Washington Post), November 11, 1973.*

The red pawns of Wibberley's detailed historical novel are Tecumseh's doomed forces massed on the banks of the Tippecanoe River prior to the War of 1812. Against this setting of rising frontier tensions, the author continues the story of the Treegate family. . . . The cast of accompanying characters is vivid, and inserts of the earthy particulars of frontier life add interest as well as insight; students of history will appreciate the acute portrayal of personalities and situations behind the scenes of the War of 1812. (p. 602)

> The Booklist *(reprinted by permission of the American Library Association; copyright 1974 by the American Library Association), February 1, 1974.*

OTHER CITATIONS

Ruth Robinson, in School Library Journal, *November, 1973, p. 69.*

Beryl Robinson, in The Horn Book Magazine, *December, 1973, p. 598.*

SECRET OF THE HAWK (1953)

A dashing story of the English slave trade toward the end of the eighteenth century, ["The Secret of the Hawk"] is told as the personal history of young Peter Millet of London. . . . [This is a] wild but not improbable yarn. It is exceptionally well written—especially the first half—and if the momentum could have been maintained to the end, the story would have been outstanding. (p. 26)

> *Merritt P. Allen, in* The New York Times Book Review *(© 1953 by The New York Times Company; reprinted by permission), February 15, 1953.*

Grim realities in the dealings of English "slavers" on the African Gold Coast in 1779 furnish strong background for this gripping story of a sixteen-year-old London orphan, Peter Millet. . . . The author, an informed and skillful storyteller, has added flavor to the tale by his vivid picturing of life at sea and in Thameside London and by adept use of seaman's talk. Full-page drawings [by Christine Price] and chapter heads indicate the robustness of action. (p. 280)

> *Virginia Haviland, in* The Horn Book Magazine *(copyrighted, 1953, by The Horn Book, Inc., Boston), August, 1953.*

OTHER CITATIONS

Virginia Kirkus' Bookshop Service, *February 1, 1953, p. 72.*

The Times Literary Supplement, *November 23, 1956, p. xix.*

SOUTH SWELL (1967)

Mr. Willett, artist by profession, feeling himself out of touch with his teenage family and uninspired in his work, decides to take up surfing, practised expertly by his son, Tom, but hitherto despised by his father. Mr. Willett's decision is prompted by a desire to help his daughter, Pat, who lacks confidence in the sea. Though the exploration of family relationships is a little heavy-handed, the surfing side of the story is excellent and guaranteed to make anyone into an enthusiast. The book gives a great deal of helpful information and conveys the thrill which is the reward of the professional while in no way minimizing the hard work needed and the often discouraging results that beset the beginner. It is a pity that the only three illustrations [by Douglas Hall] are on consecutive pages at the beginning of the book. (p. 151)

> *Mrs. D. Huddy, in* Children's Book News *(copyright © 1968 by Children's Book Centre Ltd.), May-June, 1968.*

Middle-aged Mr. Willett likes sailing, but his children prefer surfing. His relations with them are as bad as can be; he is becoming estranged from his wife; and his work has gone off to the extent that he is in danger of losing his job. All these problems are triumphantly solved when he, too, decides to take up surfing; an altogether too facile solution, and one that will confirm any teenager with parent-trouble in his conviction that right is all on his own side. All members of the family are stock American film characters. When not dabbling in pseudo-psychology, the book reads like a surfing manual. (p. 249)

> The Junior Bookshelf, *August, 1968.*

TIME OF THE HARVEST: THOMAS JEFFERSON, THE YEARS 1801-1826 (1966)

Jefferson is a trifle far above it all to be a vital figure in this juvenile biography, his political and philosophical blemishes heavily powdered throughout. *A Dawn in the Trees* . . . didn't throw any light on Jefferson's French years or the influence of the French Revolution on his later thinking or decisions—but a lot about his motherless daughters, his wifeless grief. *The Gales of Spring* blew him gently into office: the author's stated intention was not to make a villain of Alexander Hamilton with the result that he didn't make him anything, thus reducing the contrast and conflict in that formative era's political development. *Time of the Harvest* recites Jefferson's Presidential accomplishments, explains the Aaron Burr contretemps, outlines but does not analyze the split with Adams (but spends space on their ultimate reconciliation) and capsulizes the final Monticello years—Jefferson among his grandchildren, long distance mentor to Madison and Monroe, still believing in the ability of an educated populace to govern themselves under democracy. Too long plus too soft equals a four volume juvenilization that has, in the first three books revealed a receptive, infatuated institutional market. (p. 910)

> *Virginia Kirkus' Service (copyright © 1966 Virginia Kirkus' Service, Inc.), September 1, 1966.*

Accurately and skillfully [Leonard Wibberley] presents a fairly complete though brief picture of the period [1801-1826], with emphasis on the Louisiana Purchase and the Burr Conspiracy and how the policies involved reflect both Jefferson's personal and political convictions. A closer acquaintance with Jefferson develops from the descriptions of his relationships with family and friends, his concern for national safety and development, and his role in establishing the University of Virginia. Using some fictional conversations, but relying mainly on direct quotations, Wibberley has produced an excellent concluding volume, showing Jefferson's faults without detracting from his greatness. (p. 68)

> *Frances Fleming, in* School Library Journal *(reprinted from the December, 1966, issue of* School Library Journal, *published by R. R. Bowker Co., a Xerox company; copyright © 1966 by Xerox Corporation), December, 1966.*

Unhappily, like many other biographers who write for young people, Wibberley is more inclined to praise than to analyze—as has been the case from the start. . . .

The "author's note" at the end of [*Time of the Harvest*] concerning his bibliographical sources provides a clue to his troubles. Though he seems not to have considered the adverse judgments of critics such as Henry Adams, he owes it to his readers to indicate that there are other opinions. Young people need help in learning the difficult trick of estimating the performance of public figures—even of immortal heroes like Jefferson. (p. 16)

> *Henry F. Graff, in* The New York Times Book Review *(© 1967 by The New York Times Company; reprinted by permission), January 1, 1967.*

OTHER CITATIONS

Joseph C. Bloh, in Best Sellers, *December 1, 1966, p. 343.*

Priscilla L. Moulton, in The Horn Book Magazine, *February, 1967, p. 86.*

Jean B. Lieb, in Childhood Education, *September, 1967, p. 54.*

TREEGATE'S RAIDERS (1962)

The fourth and last book on the exploits of the Treegate family during the Revolutionary War brings an excellent series to a grand finale. Peter Treegate, the hero, has come down from the Appalachian Mountains with a band of men ready to join Washington's forces. Clan quarrels notwithstanding, they accept the discipline of their leader and are instrumental in luring Ferguson's forces into King's Mountain where their defeat substantially weakens Cornwallis' ranks. The many subsequent battles in which the raiders participate, the capture of Peter and his narrow escape from the noose, present a realistic panorama of war in those

times. As a refreshing change from the usual black and white treatment of this subject, the treachery of Treegate's own men is never hidden from view. The preceding books in this series are recommended for further insight into the Treegate clan and greater perspective on the American Revolution. . . . (pp. 12-13)

> *Virginia Kirkus' Service, January 1, 1962.*

[*Treegate's Raiders* is fourth] in a series of books about the American Revolution, and possibly the most exciting story. . . . The book has wonderfully detailed and vivid battle scenes; it ends with the defeat of Cornwallis and touches very briefly on the match between Treegate and the daughter of that doughty character (hero of the preceding volume, *Sea Captain from Salem*), Peace of God Manly. United States history comes alive in a story replete with suspense and adventure. (p. 119)

> *Zena Sutherland, in* Bulletin of the Center for Children's Books *(copyright 1962 by the University of Chicago; all rights reserved), March, 1962.*

OTHER CITATIONS

Margaret Sherwood Libby, in New York Herald Tribune Books, *May 13, 1962, p. 5.*

THE TREEGATE SERIES: *John Treegate's Musket; Peter Treegate's War; Sea Captain from Salem; Treegate's Raiders; Leopard's Prey; Red Pawns; The Last Battle*

AUTHOR'S COMMENTARY

First of all I have always had a great interest in history—not the kind of litany of kings and presidents and knaves and heroes that is so frequently taught in schools—but the bright little incidents that gloriously illuminate a landscape which is too often mouldy with the bone dust of the dead. (p. 110)

Of all the wars of which I have any knowledge from history, it gradually became evident to me that none was as important for the Western World as the War of the American Revolution. Indeed I regard it as the most important struggle in the history of what we can call Western Man.

That is a big statement. But here are my reasons. There have been many many wars fought to overthrow tyranny. Such wars are not exclusively a feature of American history. . . . But the Revolutionary War not only sought to overthrow tyranny, it also established certain inalienable rights for people, rights which if preserved would protect mankind from tyranny in all the centuries ahead.

What was fought on the North American continent then was a war for the rights of *all* men. The scope was wider than national. It embraced all mankind who loved freedom, and its effects are felt to this very day. (pp. 110-11)

The more I read about the Revolutionary War, the more these elements came clearly to me and the more I marveled at them and wanted to bring them to the attention of others. Out of this desire came the Treegate series of books in which I have attempted to trace the fortunes and feelings of a family of Americans of the Revolutionary War period.

I asked for and was given large scope in writing these

books. I didn't want to write books in which one hero got in and out of a series of scrapes. I wanted to paint a large mural which would embrace as many of the figures of the Revolution as could be usefully depicted . . . the dissolute Earl of Sandwich, pious Peace of God Manly, the fiery Maclaren of Spey nursing the old wound of the Battle of Culloden, Gabby the seaman with his love for a piece of fat pork, a mite rancid, Benjamin Franklin, Washington himself, aging Daniel Morgan with the scars of a whip across his back, Sam Adams organizing the Boston mobs, and many many others. Some of the figures are historic—some of them creatures of my imagination. These latter came to life as I wrote, standing as it were by my elbow and telling me of the weight of their muskets and how the birds sounded in the boding woods at Saratoga and how sharp was the January frost at Morristown.

This of course is the work of the novelist in the field of history—not to instruct but to enrich that which is already known; not to distort but to listen to the insistent whisper of forgotten voices penetrating the centuries.

There were, I am sure, people like Gabby and Master Gunner Simmons and Mr. Treaser in his Queen Anne coat, and Mr. Paddock—a self-appointed traveling university, and Peter Treegate and his stubborn, enduring father, John. History has no place for them. They belong in that other wing of history called the historical novel. They are the humble builders of the world, whose names are unknown, whose graves are lost, and whose lives made no stir beyond the circle of their friends.

They are you and I and everyman, and I have tried to give them back their voices, so that they can speak across the centuries of their time on earth. (pp. 112-13)

> *Leonard Wibberley, "The Treegate Series" (originally published in* The Horn Book, *April, 1962), in* Horn Book Reflections: On Children's Books and Reading, *edited by Elinor Whitney Field (copyright © 1969 by The Horn Book, Inc., Boston), Horn Book, 1969, pp. 110-13.*

[Leonard Wibberley's books about the Treegates] are stories with muscle and spirit and make up the large mural that Mr. Wibberley wanted to paint embracing many of the historic figures of the Revolution, and including others, creatures of his imagination. . . . His Treegate books rank with [Esther Forbes's] *Johnny Tremain* in the eloquence with which they reveal the Revolutionary period and its people, known and unknown. (pp. 517-18)

> *Ruth Hill Viguers, in* A Critical History of Children's Literature, *by Cornelia Meigs, Anne Thaxter Eaton, Elizabeth Nesbitt, and Ruth Hill Viguers, edited by Cornelia Meigs (copyright © 1953, 1969 by Macmillan Publishing Co., Inc.), revised edition, Macmillan, 1969.*

Leonard Wibberley paints his stories of Peter Treegate's adventures during the Revolutionary War on a broad canvas. . . . All the books give marvelously vivid pictures not only of the Revolutionary War but of the significance of that war to the ordinary citizen of the time and to history. (p. 516)

> *May Hill Arbuthnot and Zena Sutherland, in their* Children and Books, *(copyright © 1947, 1957, 1964, 1972 by Scott, Foresman and Company; reprinted by permission) fourth edition, Scott, Foresman, 1972.*

YOUNG MAN FROM THE PIEDMONT: THE YOUTH OF THOMAS JEFFERSON (1963)

[Leonard Wibberley's] major purpose [in *Young Man from the Piedmont: The Youth of Thomas Jefferson*] has been to bring Jefferson's social/political milieu to life as well as Jefferson himself. He has invented no facts nor incidents, but he has invented dialogue. Mr. Wibberley has set himself no easy task. His subject, although a prime mover in exciting political events, was a cerebral/sedentary type who engaged in vocal rather than physical activity. This is no easier to get on paper than it is to breathe life into times past. Since Jefferson's colleagues were prominent too, the invented dialogue often has a declamatory self-consciousness. (Even on paper, dead politicians refuse to play second fiddle.) This approach shifts the spotlight around as Jefferson deals with scene stealers like Patrick Henry, Dabney Carr and others. As a biography of the whole man affecting and affected by his times, this is a brave but not entirely successful effort. . . . (p. 518)

> Virginia Kirkus' Service, *June 1, 1963.*

[*Young Man from the Piedmont* is] a convincing portrayal of the shaping of the young Jefferson against the background of the social, intellectual, and political world of Colonial Virginia. Jefferson was rooted in two worlds—the pioneer Piedmont with its independent thinkers and passion for individual liberty, and the more conservative aristocracy of the Tidewater.

Wibberley selects and develops incident carefully to show how many influences interacted in molding a young man of reason, self-disciplined, with a thirst for knowledge in many fields. Other figures of the day are also vividly characterized, especially Patrick Henry, who appears as the chief supporting actor.

This is a book to arouse interest in history, as the reader is set right down in the news of the day and sees just what such happenings as the Parsons' Cause and the Stamp Act were all about. Conversations between Jefferson and his contemporaries reveal character and the thought and discussion about serious issues leading up to the Revolution, though they occasionally serve this purpose too well to seem entirely natural. However, the author avoids that pitfall of much fictionalized juvenile biography, banality, and reveals how man and history make each other. Jefferson here comes alive as a human being, about to emerge on the world scene with the writing of the Declaration of Independence at the age of 32. (p. 34)

> *Nancy Young, in* Book Week (© The Washington Post), *November 10, 1963.*

["Young Man from the Piedmont"] is an example of juvenile biography at its best. Beautifully yet simply written, it is both thoughtful and artful. The author injects dozens of authentic details to make his scenes come to life. When Jefferson's words seem difficult for a child, he quotes them nonetheless, and then explains their meaning, helping the reader but not sparing him the effort and pleasure of grappling with historical reality. Mr. Wibberley presents a rounded and authentic portrait, carrying Jefferson down to 1776. (p. 6)

> *John A. Garraty, in* The New York Times Book Review, *Part II (© 1963 by The New York Times Company; reprinted by permission), November 10, 1963.*

OTHER CITATIONS

Elnora M. Portteus, in School Library Journal, *October, 1963, pp. 219-20.*

ZEBULON PIKE, SOLDIER AND EXPLORER (1961)

Mr. Wibberley confesses to having taken minor liberties in this biography—in the absence of complete records. This has not harmed the narrative, which is a sympathetic, full-bodied account drawing heavily on Pike's own journals of exploration. The author's performance here, like his subject's devotion to duty, is of the highest order. (p. 22)

> *George A. Woods, in* The New York Times Book Review *(© 1961 by The New York Times Company; reprinted by permission), August 27, 1961.*

[This is a] detailed biography of Pike, emphasizing his activities as an explorer who helped to open the Midwestern part of the U.S. to settlement during the early nineteenth century. Special attention is given to Pike's exploration of the source of the Mississippi and to his discovery of Pike's Peak. Wibberley brings to the biography the same swift-paced style that gives his novels appeal, and boys will find the book as exciting reading as any story of frontier adventure. (p. 37)

> The Booklist and Subscription Books Bulletin *(reprinted by permission of the American Library Association; copyright 1961 by The American Library Association), September 1, 1961.*

OTHER CITATIONS

Eunice H. Speer, in Junior Libraries, *May, 1961, p. 60.*

The Christian Science Monitor, *May 11, 1961, p. 4B.*

Y

YEP, Laurence 1948-

Laurence Yep is a Chinese-American fiction writer for adults and children. His early science fiction often dealt with the discovery of strange, new lands, which he feels expressed his first reactions to White culture, his fascination and alienation. An extension of this was *Dragonwings*, of which he says, "I finally confronted my own Chinese-American identity." (See also *Contemporary Authors*, Vols. 49-52 and *Something About the Author*, Vol. 7.)

CHILD OF THE OWL (1977)

[The] surprise ending [in *Child of the Owl*] fits seamlessly into Yep's vision, which combines the chiseled fantasy of *Dragonwings* . . . with the hard-edged anxieties of growing up poor and non-white in the early Beatles era. This is played out against a background of underheated walk-up flats, cheap souvenir shops, and memories of the old China where dream-souls wandered the earth at night. [A] beautifully transmuted Chinatown legend, and an odds-on popular favorite as well. (p. 99)

> *Kirkus Reviews (copyright © 1977 The Kirkus Service, Inc.), February 1, 1977.*

A motherless 12-year-old Chinese girl, Casey is named for Casey Stengel by her compulsive gambler father who paid off the hospital bills when she was born with money won on baseball bets. Completely ignorant of her Chinese heritage, Casey . . . [is] sent to stay in San Francisco's Chinatown with her maternal grandmother, Paw-Paw. The wisdom and sensitivity of Paw-Paw and the very fabric of life in Chinatown help Casey to come to grips with the loss of her innocent belief in her father's impossible dream and to see herself as a strong and true *Child of the Owl*. Although the early-60's setting is fuzzy, and the legend of the owl, which takes an entire chapter to tell, is strangely graceless and confusing, once again Yep creates strong and interesting characters and weaves a fascinating picture of Chinatown into an exciting and well-plotted story. (p. 73)

> *Marjorie Lewis, in* School Library Journal *(reprinted from the April, 1977, issue of* School Library Journal, *published by R. R. Bowker Company, a Xerox company; copyright © 1977 by Xerox Corporation), April, 1977.*

[In *Child of the Owl*] Casey's evolution from a vulnerable, defensive waif into an integrated, reasonably secure personality is well thought out; that, combined with a vivid sense of place and the uniquely strong personalities that people Casey's new world, gives the story strength and staying power enough to rise well above any false notes in Casey's first-person, tough-kid narrative. (p. 1173)

> *Booklist (reprinted by permission of the American Library Association; copyright 1977 by the American Library Association), April 1, 1977.*

There are scenes in *Child of the Owl* by Laurence Yep that will make every Chinese-American child gasp with recognition. "Hey! That happened to me. I did that. I saw that," the young reader will say, and be glad that a writer set it down, and feel comforted, less eccentric, less alone.

I remember at Chinese school I wrote English phonics alongside the Chinese words, just as Casey Young, the 12-year-old heroine, does. . . .

Another scene with which second-, third- and fourth-generation Chinese-Americans will identify is the painful one in which Casey Young shops in Chinatown for a dinner for her grandmother. Since she can only speak English, the Chinese push ahead of her, try to charge her extra, won't fill her orders properly, and say, "Native-born, no brains." Casey realizes they are treating her "like a tourist." (p. E1)

Like all good children's books, *Child of the Owl* can enrich an adult's life too. I had thought I was the only person with a mother who leaves the radio dial always on the station with "The Chinese Hour," afraid of losing the Chinese voices and music. Now I see that Paw-Paw, Casey's wonderful grandmother, who gives her her name and her past, handles machinery in the same way. Laurence Yep sees the old people as clearly as he sees the children:

> "All of them would at some time sit and stare emptily at the traffic passing by on the street below as if they were lost inside their own memories, trying to understand how they found themselves old and alone, sitting on a bench—with the look of people who had been left behind on some grassy shore when the ship had sailed. Only it was more than an ocean they had to cross, it was time and space itself." . . .

Perhaps in order to write straight, an "ethnic" writer needs to ignore the temptation to shock readers out of stereotypes. If we explain every misconception and joke, we would lose sight of our own original visions, and an explained joke loses all its humor. You need to know just the point at which to stop the explanations, and let the readers figure out things for themselves. Usually Laurence Yep knows where that point is. . . . The book does not get weighed down with exposition for non-Chinese-American readers. . . .

There are a few instances, however, when he succumbs to too facile solutions to stereotype-busting. A style currently popular among young Chinese-American writers is the hipster voice, a reaction—perhaps an over-reaction—against the stereotypical unctuous Confucius-say voice. At the beginning of the book Casey Young is a hip little kook like the heroines in American movie—throughout the book, one of Casey Young's main references is the movies—which give individuality to women by characterizing them as oddballs, like Streisand characters, like Liza Minnelli characters. Barney and Casey Young remind me immediately of Ryan and Tatum O'Neal in *Paper Moon*. Fortunately, as Casey grows up, she wisecracks less, and she does seem to find new ways of speaking.

Laurence Yep himself has at least two voices, and I was enchanted that he tells a story-within-a-story about the owl totem of the Young family. It disconcerted me, however, when he adds an afterword in which the "I" is no longer Casey Young as in the rest of the book but apparently the author. He tells us that he has not actually seen an owl charm nor heard the owl story but made them up himself. Now in that afterword I believe Laurence Yep to be anticipating those critics—both Caucasian and Chinese-American—who will question whether his work is "typical" of the rest of us Chinese-Americans. So to all those ethnocentric villagers, he in effect says, "No, I'm not misrepresenting Chinese customs. This is fiction." Good art is always singular, always one-of-a-kind, and an artist certainly has the right to make things up to write fiction—but somehow we expect Chinese-American artists to represent all Chinese-Americans in a way we do not expect of Caucasian-American writers. I hope that when more of our work gets into print that this burden—"Speak for me! Speak for me!"—we lay on each of our writers who gets published will become lighter. Laurence Yep has written a lovely novel that needs no apologies. (p. E8)

> *Maxine Hong Kingston, "Middle Kingdom to Middle America," in* Book World—The Washington Post *(© The Washington Post), May 1, 1977, pp. E1, E8.*

OTHER CITATIONS

Zena Sutherland, in Bulletin of the Center for Children's Books, *April, 1977, p. 136.*

Georgess McHargue, in The New York Times Book Review, *May 22, 1977, p. 29.*

DRAGONWINGS (1975)

AUTHOR'S COMMENTARY

Once some anthropologists found a primitive tribe whose artists carved statues of powerful simplicity. When the scientists questioned the artists about their art, the artists would not say that they had sculpted the statues; rather they claimed that the statue already lived within each block of wood and told the artist how to free it.

Something similar happened to me when I tried to write my novel, *Dragonwings*. The story of the early Chinese-American aviator seemed to tell itself to me, but it was possible largely because I kept children in mind as the main reading audience.

But before I can begin to talk about the story of *Dragonwings,* I have to explain my general situation six years before when I first began my general research. Trying to research Chinese-American history—that is, the history of men and women of Chinese ancestry who had been influenced by their experience of America—can be difficult. . . .

I tried to understand the background that shaped me. It took some six years of research in the libraries of different cities to find the bits and pieces that could be fitted into Chinese-American history. (p. 359)

Most of the Chinese who emigrated to America were from Southern China. . . . Because of immense troubles at home, these Southern Chinese came to America since they could send large amounts of money to their families and clans back home. And for a variety of reasons, including prejudice and fear, it was mostly men who came over. . . . [From] the 1850s to the 1930s, it was largely a society of bachelors, for when the original men grew old, they sent for their sons, brothers, cousins, and nephews to take their place.

But a small number of men were able to . . . [bring] their wives over to join them and start families in America. They created a family society within the shell of the older, larger bachelor society. And this family society, with its determination to sink its roots in America, survived psychologically by selectively forgetting the past history of the bachelor society and the often violent record of confrontations between Chinese and Americans. Ignoring acts of discrimination . . ., the Chinese-Americans still maintained a discreet distance between themselves and white Americans, choosing to imitate their white counterparts within the confines of Chinatown. . . . (pp. 359-60)

The third generation, my generation, grew up in households in which little or no Chinese was spoken and Chinese myths and legends were looked upon largely as a source of embarrassment. . . . I found that I was truly like Ralph Ellison's Invisible Man—without form, without shape. It was as if all the features on my face had been erased and I was simply a blank mirror reflecting other people's hopes and fears. . . .

[When] I did find material on [my ancestors], I found that the Chinese-Americans had been a faceless crowd for most writers, providing statistical fodder for historians or abstractions for sociologists. I could give the Chinese population in each of California's counties for a fifty year period; but I could not have told you what any of those Chinese hoped for or feared. (p. 360)

One of the few early Chinese-Americans in my notes to have a name was Fung Joe Guey who flew a biplane of his own construction over in Oakland in 1909. The scene of his flight seemed so vivid to me that it was easy to put it on paper, but trying to explain how he got to that field with his biplane was difficult because I could only find two newspaper articles, the September 23, 1909 issues of the San Francisco *Call* and the San Francisco *Examiner*.

Since I wanted to respect his historical integrity, I used his flight as the basis for my novel, *Dragonwings;* and to make my own fictional aviator, Windrider, seem real, I had to recreate the bachelor society itself. However, to do that I discovered that a writer must not be like the anatomist who dictates a record of facts and figures after an autopsy; instead, a writer must be like a necromancer speaking to the shadows of the dead. . . .

If I wanted to write about the Midwest, I would have the work of writers like Hamlin Garland and Sinclair Lewis to show me how to create that space and time. If I wanted to write about New England, I would have Hawthorne and Thoreau to guide me. In their writings, I could find guidelines not only for setting up a fictional world but also its population. . . . But I have no such guidelines for creating the Chinatown of seventy years ago, which is the time in which *Dragonwings* is set.

So in trying to recreate the world of the past, I was like a child myself who must have the most basic things explained to it. (p. 361)

I had grown up as a child in the 1950s so that my sense of reality was an American one. Now I had to grow up again, but this time in the 1900s, developing a Chinese sense of reality. Milk and cheese had to become exotic to me. . . . The turning point in writing *Dragonwings* came when the checkered tablecloth on a table suddenly seemed strange to me, as if it were too cold and abstract a design because I was used to designs that usually filled up space. So when I chose to describe things from the viewpoint of an eight year old Chinese boy, it was more than simply choosing a narrative device; it was close to the process of discovery I myself was experiencing in writing the story.

But at the same time . . ., I would also have to discover what relationships would be like within that bachelor society—that lonely group of men who spent most of their adult years apart from family and home. So again, it was natural to write about this experience with children as the audience. What were personal relationships like among men who would work for five to ten years or longer before they could visit their families back in China? . . . I would have to project myself back into the past and see how I myself would react to others in that same situation.

And the relationship with which I would most easily empathize would be the most elemental relationship, the relationship between parent and child. And since most Chinese-Americans were men at this time, it would be easiest to describe the relationship between father and son—with the mother present only in the emotions and memories of the man and boy. It was within the strong emotional context of this evolving father-son relationship that the boy's relationships to others would unfold.

Then, too, it would be easier for me to describe the relationship between the boy and his father if I could use the most honest and direct terms. I couldn't be like D. H. Lawrence who described a parent-child relationship in "The Rocking-Horse Winner" by telling the story of a little boy who sat on a rocking horse all day until he rocked himself to death trying to win money for his mother. To be able to write about the relationship in this symbolic way requires a thorough grounding in the basic ways a culture expresses love and affection; but I was unsure of even that much for the early Chinese-Americans. (pp. 361-62)

[If] I kept children in mind as the reading audience, I would keep myself from wandering off into conceptual tangents such as the existential alienation of Chinese-Americans. The important thing, after all, was to give emotional form to the people of that world and not to play intellectual games. (p. 362)

[When] I speak of selecting children as the audience for *Dragonwings,* much of that was intuitive, occurring at a preconscious . . . level. But I had another reason in writing *Dragonwings* for children. Because children are inexperienced and new to the world in general, their . . . ability to handle complex grammatical structures [is] as limited as their ability to handle abstract concepts; yet this same inexperience is also a source of special strength for children's stories. To write for children, one must try to see things as they do; and trying to look at the world with the fresh, inexperienced eyes of a child enables the writer to approach the world with a sense of wonder. (I think I can say this without necessarily sentimentalizing childhood if I add that the sense of wonder produces as many terrors for a child as it does beauties.) Adopting the child's sense of wonder is the reason why—at least for me—the texts of so many picture books approach the lyricism that eludes so many modern poets today with their jaded, world-weary tastes.

I wanted to utilize this sense of wonder when I wrote *Dragonwings* since I wanted to base a large part of the father's motives upon Chinese dragon myths. I could have given the father more ordinary motives. I could have said he was compensating for feelings of inadequacy by proving he could do anything that white Americans could do. Or I could have left the novel simply as a story of . . . a far-sighted person among shortsighted people. But the invention with which I was dealing was . . . a flying machine, a machine that most people were convinced was impossible to build even several years after the Wright Brothers' original flight. When I wrote of the aeroplane, called Dragonwings, I was actually dealing with the reach of our imagination. . . . (pp. 362-63)

[In] *Dragonwings,* Windrider's former life as a dragon symbolizes [the] imaginative power in all of us. And so Windrider and his son, Moon Shadow, are engaged not only in the process of discovering America and each other, but also in a pilgrimage, or even a quest for a special moment when they can reaffirm the power of the imagination; that power in each of us to grasp with the mind and heart what we cannot immediately grasp with the hand.

Moreover, children's stories retain a sense of wonder not only toward the world but toward the act of writing itself. . . . [Children's writers] are still in touch with the magical power of words and pictures to capture the world in a way that many who write for adults are not. Adult writers often seem too self-conscious of their own technique. With all the splendid and terrible spirits of myth or of past history to choose from, they would rather conjure up the necromancers of the past in order to talk shop, mistaking an overwhelming self-absorption for a sophisticated complexity.

I am not trying to claim that adult Chinese-American stories are impossible to write; but given my general situation and certain types of story material, it was best to write *Dragonwings* for children. Growing up as I myself did without form or shape, I felt as ghostly as the spirits of the dead and so by giving them form, I was also giving form to myself. And it was only by feeling and seeing and hearing and interpreting things as a child that I could do so. (p. 363)

> *Laurence Yep, "Writing 'Dragonwings'," in* The Reading Teacher *(copyright 1977 by the International Reading Association, Inc.; reprinted with permission of Laurence Yep and the International Reading Association), January, 1977, pp. 359-63.*

The plot [of "Dragonwings"] seems occasionally forced, and at times the language seems more ornate than that which a young immigrant would be likely to use; but never mind. If it were only a fantastic story of high adventure, "Dragonwings" would be a success, but as an exquisitely written poem of praise to the courage and industry of the Chinese-American people, it is a triumph. (p. 30)

> *Ruth H. Pelmas, in* The New York Times Book Review *(© 1975 by The New York Times Company; reprinted by permission), November 16, 1975.*

Here is a book that consciously attempts to counter Asian American stereotypes.... The book tries and in some ways succeeds in showing that the Chinese in America were, and are, ordinary as well as extraordinary people. (p. 8)

Chinatown's secret societies, prostitution, and opium dens are depicted, a bit luridly perhaps, but this is offset by warm characterizations of Moonshadow's family and friends....

Windrider and his son meet a white woman and her niece who befriend them and respect their dreams. They are atypical whites and are strongly drawn feminist characters as well. The relationship with the women is important to the father and son, but it is not essential to them in the paternalistically racist way that is common in so many children's books.

The book, though highly recommended, does have a weakness. While oppression and racism are well described, blame is not placed squarely on the economic system which then, as now, exploited non-white labor for maximum profit. (p. 9)

> Interracial Books for Children Bulletin *(reprinted by permission of* Interracial Books for Children Bulletin, *1841 Broadway, New York, N.Y. 10023), Vol. 7, Nos. 2 & 3, 1976.*

Yep's *Dragonwings* is not a yellow man living in white society, because that is not his way of seeing Chinese Americans. What Yep has produced is the first book to capture the arrogant style of spoken Cantonese and create out of it a new American English. He's not telling a white sobsister's minority success story. Yellows don't think of themselves as particularly minor in this book. His story is about a Chinese man who came to America to start a family and challenge the unknown in a new country. His life here somehow brought the best out of him, and he had big ideas, daring plans and a Chinese American son to help him take to the air. In *Dragonwings,* Yep has written an Asian American myth that will someday be as deeply rooted in American folklore as Paul Bunyan and Johnny Appleseed. The lives of Yep's people suggest that there is a spirit of adventure which is uniquely Chinese American and which smacks of legend, both in the language and in the sense the language makes. (p. 25)

> *Frank Chin, in* Interracial Books for Children Bulletin *(reprinted by permission of* Interracial Books for Children Bulletin, *1841 Broadway, New York, N.Y. 10023), Vol. 7, Nos. 2 & 3, 1976.*

OTHER CITATIONS

Publishers Weekly, *June 16, 1975, p. 82.*

Jane E. Gardner, in School Library Journal, *September, 1975, p. 129.*

Paul Heins, in The Horn Book Magazine, *October, 1975, pp. 472-73.*

SWEETWATER (1973)

Fantasy/science fiction has always seemed to be at least a second-cousin to the authentically visionary. The very spring of its conception would appear to be a dissatisfaction with the merely ordinary, with the generally verifiable, the mundane. In short, it has, at its best, a yearning for more, for "other." Laurence Yep's *Sweetwater* reflects and embodies that yearning. And at moments the feeling for it is truly present in the bitter-sweet tone of the book, as these future descendants of the human residents of earth struggle to perpetuate a dying way of life and its system of values on another planet, which has for generations been their home. Nostalgia, loss, regret, even the sense of the largeness, the vastness of life (human and nonhuman) in which they participate—these emotions anchor this writing in the firm substance of loss-longing that is involved in the quest for the unknown.

But *Sweetwater* shares a major problem of fantasy/science fiction whenever it leaves the familiar terrain of this world, earth. It has to introduce the reader to another literal world. It has to convince him of its physical presence. It's a difficult task, particularly if the setting is to be not only another world, but even a change from a dry-land existence to a life on and in the water. Yep almost succeeds in making this existence come fully alive, but the life remains somehow alien, for all its sympathetic beauty. And that fact may well keep readers from going back to this book a second time, to relive the experience. Still, *Sweetwater* does have the energies of authentic emotions, and that is a considerable strength. (pp. 173-74)

> *Wayne Dodd, in* Children's Literature: Annual of The Modern Language Association Seminar on Children's Literature and The Children's Literature Association, *Vol. 4, edited by Francelia Butler (© 1975 by Francelia Butler; all rights reserved), Temple University Press, 1975.*

Sweetwater is, I suppose, a juvenile novel, although the

only clue to this is the fact that the ads on the back flap are for other juveniles. But as in the case of so many good juvenile SF books, *Sweetwater* is a good deal better written, and more mature, than the commonplace mass-produced *genre* novel.

Apart from the trivial point that it features a juvenile protagonist there are several aspects of the book that mark its appeal to young readers. It is a very conservative book, placing high value on tradition, on patriarchal authority, on family and community loyalty, and it presents these values in a manner loaded with nostalgia, for the secure world which all these things represent is, in the plot, slowly and irrevocably decaying. Nostalgia is something which is always attractive to adolescents, who are trapped in a situation of rapid and inevitable change, moving out of security into uncertainty. This is also a book much concerned with darkness and loneliness and learning and modest creativity —all characteristic adolescent preoccupations. On top of all this; as the title suggests, *Sweetwater* is a book steeped in sentimentality. It has a powerful emotional voice. . . .

Neither the plot nor the set of values it carries would normally attract my admiration. But *Sweetwater* has one powerful thing going for it, and that is the fact that its writing is, in every sense of the word, beautiful. The saccharin is too strong at just one point, when the protagonist's alien mentor is described as "the Ultimate Uncle". Otherwise, this is prose of a quality far too rarely seen in science fiction. (p. 37)

> *Brian Stableford, in* Vector 78 *(copyright © Christopher Fowler, 1976; reprinted by permission of the critic), November-December, 1976.*

Laurence Yep's *Sweetwater* is an exciting story of the future. The hero, Tyree, belongs to an invented minority group called Silkies, descendants of space-ship crews which were long ago stranded on the planet Harmony and now inhabit the half-flooded ruins of a city by the sea. The novel traces simultaneously the boy's growing up and the destruction of the Silkies' communal life-style after the intrusion of a greedy capitalist and a vast sea dragon. The themes here are strong and contemporary—the rights of minorities, the necessity for courage, the utility of art, and the interdependence and sacredness of all life—themes woven into a unit of immediate socio-ecological thrust. And Yep evokes the warm and complex relationships between the members of Tyree's family. Why, then, is the book less successful than [L. Frank] Baum's [*The Master Key*] or [Nancy] Willard's [*Sailing to Cythera*]? To some extent the very transparency of the themes may be blamed; but I think the principal difficulty lies in Yep's handling of point of view. The story is told by Tyree, and the narrator's boyish diction and frequent intrusions may account for the diffuseness and lack of immediacy in action sequences, for the fact that wonders such as the sea dragon are only partially realized in their enormity. Tyree is no Huck Finn. Nevertheless, the book is a rich piece of imagination and a well-constructed story. (p. 290)

> *William H. Green, in* Children's Literature: Annual of the Modern Language Association Seminar on Children's Literature and The Children's Literature Association, *Vol. 5, edited by Francelia Butler (© 1976 by Francelia Butler; all rights reserved), Temple University Press, 1976.*

OTHER CITATIONS

The Booklist, *October 15, 1973, p. 243.*

Z

ZIMNIK, Reiner   1930-

Reiner Zimnik is a German writer and artist. His first writing experience came when he was asked, as an art student, to illustrate a book which he disliked. Instead, he substituted his own story and pictures, thus creating his first book, *Xaver der Ringelstecher*.

GENERAL COMMENTARY

Reiner Zimnik spells out in line what most people have to spell out in letters. For this reason his first books, where text and illustration are a unity, were his best. He reels off incidents like a child prodigy. . . . But one cannot be a child prodigy for ever and Reiner Zimnik has today become one of the most productive creators of picture-books, having in the meantime come to a fuller understanding of colour work. His books all retain a sense of humour which conceals a profound seriousness, and they still have this very individual unity of text and picture. So far he is to be seen at his best when he is given generous scope to bring to life his most personal thoughts and imaginings. (p. 222)

> *Bettina Hürlimann, in her* Three Centuries of Children's Books in Europe, *translated and edited by Brian W. Alderson (English translation © Oxford University Press 1967; reprinted by permission), Oxford University Press, 1967.*

Reiner Zimnik has taken an entirely new direction with his picture-books, using the same pen both for drawing and writing and spontaneously elaborating his own very original ideas. From an international viewpoint his picture-stories, particularly those in black and white, are perhaps Germany's most individual contribution to the world of picture-books. There is also a marked strain of the moralist in Zimnik, holding as he frequently does a mirror up to the human species. . . . His most recent picture-books in colour are by no means so original as his earlier volumes in line only. (pp. 11-12)

> *Bettina Hürlimann, in her* Picture-Book World: Modern Picture-Books for Children from Twenty-Four Countries, *edited and translated by Brian W. Alderson (copyright © 1965 by Oxford University Press; reprinted by permission), Oxford University*

Press, 1968 (and reprinted by World Publishing Co., 1969).

Zimnik accomplishes miracles with his agile line drawings. He suggests movement, busyness, quietness, mass, humor, flight—all in an immensely ingenious manner. In *Jonah the Fisherman* . . . twenty-nine assorted, striding fishermen are drawn on the frontispiece. The men and their fishing rods make a delicately moving curve of repeated line patterns on the lower third of the picture page. . . . Zimnik brings many objects forward from a distance: ships, nets of fish, buffaloes, and a page of twenty-two tractors, the last of which recedes to a dot on the horizon.

Some of Zimnik's recurring textural delineations are seen in his clouds, sky, beards, foliage, and always in smoke—pipe smoke, car smoke, boat smoke, city and building smoke, bonfire smoke, and so forth. Sometimes he masses line to create a value contrast, as in trouser cloth differentiated from shirt fabric, or in hatbands, or spots on horses. Often he creates interest in clothing, animals, and architecture with decorative pattern.

Zimnik's compositional arrangements are inspired. No matter how much or how little space remains after the type is accommodated, he can treat this space ingeniously. On some pages he competes with a sizable block of type and one's eye goes to the dynamic line first. There is a humorous quality in his line that suggests the spontaneity and rhythmic feeling of some of the Paul Klee drawings. (pp. 68, 70)

Zimnik alters his linear style to accommodate color in *The Bear on the Motorcycle* (1963). He is more the cartoonist here and less the designer. It seems he cannot design poorly nonetheless. His line is still tidy and precise but colored shapes predominate—larger shapes used with fewer groupings. The work is more gross, with more obvious substance and mass, and although efficient and full of style, it lacks the special inventive quality Zimnik shows in his feeling for line. (p. 71)

> *Donnarae MacCann and Olga Richard, in their* The Child's First Books: A Critical Study of Pictures and Texts *(copyright © 1973 by Donnarae MacCann and Olga Richard; reprinted by permission of The H. W. Wilson Company), The H. W. Wilson Company, 1973.*

THE BEAR AND THE PEOPLE (German Edition, 1954; translation published in US, 1971)

The bear, a dancing bear, is the protagonist in this tender story, a creature more humane than human around whom revolve the people, the animals, the seasons in prose as peaceful and remote as the stars in the Bearman's nightly tales. Events are like whirlpools in a quiet river—sudden, violent, brief: a fight with the jealous Dudas, an attack by fierce dogs, a dreary trek with gypsies. . . .

The jacket flap says that this book "celebrates the power of goodness over all that is wicked in the human soul." Surely it is more than that. The Bearman is not above pride, rage, competitiveness and name-calling, in spite of his friendship with Dear God. The fights are bloody, there is a bit of top-less dancing, there are some startling curses. But it goes well beyond emotion into stoic philosophy: yes, this is the way life is, my dear, no use to be other than calm about it. Here is no moralistic fable, but a folktale, humble and pro-found, about a love which exists of and for itself as a gentle counterpart to indifferent nature and endless time.

Only a European could create a book like this, I think. Will American children understand it? Impossible to say. If they don't, and if there is a fault to assign, I would say that the fault lies with us. We want, and we train our children to want, quite another kind of story, brisk and well-plotted, where illusion improves on reality and stars are to hitch your wagon to. We do not seem to want stories that tell of the journey as if there were no destination, stories that smell of time and slow roots. We are perhaps too new.

And yet, this is such a lovely book—we need this kind of thinking just as a ghetto child needs a summer in the coun-try. As the Bearman says of the bear's dancing, "Very good, Brown One, and so harmonious."

Casual ink line sketches sprinkled throughout neither add nor detract. "The Bear and the People" needs only its words and a receptive ear. (p. 4)

> Natalie Babbitt, in The New York Times Book Review, Part II (© 1971 by The New York Times Company; reprinted by permis-sion), May 2, 1971.

[Of the German fantasy novels written for children, the] most important work in narrative prose is Reiner Zimnik's The Bear and the People in which text and drawings form a unit. With his bear a juggler is traveling on the high roads. He holds dialogues with his bear and with God and he is involved in conflict with the evil in our world. I don't like giving forecasts, but I think this book will last. And if it happens that there are good translations, it will be world literature. (p. 350)

> Walter Scherf, "Across the Rhine: Juvenile Literature in German-Speaking Countries" (reprinted by permission of the author), a revision of a speech delivered at Loughbor-ough in 1969 (and reprinted in Children and Literature: Views and Reviews, edited by Virginia Haviland, Scott, Foresman and Company, 1973, pp. 345-54).

OTHER CITATIONS

Publishers Weekly, April 19, 1971, p. 47.

Virginia Haviland, in Children's Book World, Part II, May 9, 1971, p. 15.

Sylvia Mogg, in Children's Book Review, February, 1973, p. 11.

BILLY'S BALLOON RIDE (German Edition, 1972; translation published in US, 1974)

Of all the world's picture-book artists, Reiner Zimnik is the least predictable. Even his most devoted admirer would not have expected Bill's Balloon Ride [British title], and most of us would rather not have had it. The book, about a boy who had balloons for birthday presents and so realised his ambition to fly, is brilliantly clever, drawn with easy mas-tery, and most uncomfortably nasty. Perhaps it is the horrid hero who makes the whole thing so hard to bear. This is an adult reaction. The book may well prove a smash-hit with children, who will enjoy the exactly realised detail of each picture, the uncompromising colour, and the wide streak of vulgarity. (pp. 239-40)

> The Junior Bookshelf, August, 1973.

The aggressive cartoon ugliness of Zimnik's people and the routine realism of his scenery make an unusual contrast to the soaring fantasy suggested by the balloons [in Billy's Balloon Ride], and such sights as the fire truck ladders reaching vainly to the rescue take humorous advantage of the juxtaposition. Still, Billy's unimaginative descent—when he gets hungry next day he simply follows the note dropped onto his bed by a police helicopter and cuts off one balloon at a time—is a letdown indeed, and the book's dime store construction and appearance doesn't encourage par-ticipation. (p. 1250)

> Kirkus Reviews (copyright © 1974 The Kirkus Service, Inc.), December 1, 1974.

OTHER CITATIONS

Janice P. Patterson, in School Library Journal, January, 1975, p. 42.

THE CRANE (German Edition, 1956; translation published in US, 1970)

Illustrations are still of the utmost importance for children under nine. The visual orgy of modern picture-books isn't far behind them, and children want pictures they can read, pictures that really elaborate on the text. This is exactly what Reiner Zimnik provides in The Crane. Every page has a line drawing of some kind. Most are both sketchy and inventively witty. . . .

The story itself appears at first to be yet another uncon-vincing tale from the Continent about small-town bureauc-racy, with faceless town councillors and cardboard mayors. But there is much more to The Crane than this. The crane-driver is in love with his crane and his entire life is spent looking after it. He doesn't leave his high perch until the end of the story, when as a tired old man he disappears be-hind the mountain. This is a very moral story. The crane-driver is simple, happy and good. He values friendship and work, and he cheerfully survives war, famine, flood and isolation with only an eagle for company. . . . This could have been all rather tedious and pious, but the wittiness of the drawings also pervades the text. On the whole, the moral is handled lightly, and the story itself is absorbing. A book for a thoughtful child. (p. 1200)

> The Times Literary Supplement (© *Times Newspapers Ltd., 1969; reproduced from* The Times Literary Supplement *by permission), October 16, 1969.*

The Crane . . . bears about as much resemblance to other children's books as Kafka bears to most British novelists, being the recurrent European allegory of some puny anon (here the cranedriver) struggling to preserve his identity—symbolised presumably by the crane—in face of the most cataclysmic pressures; an allegory to which I am not normally susceptible. Yet I was seduced by this—an extraordinary dreamlike book, without formal pacing of narrative. The way the action almost floats, slips past, might have become irritating had it not been framed by such precise understandings; of the cranedriver himself and of his obsession with the crane; of the crane itself, how it is constructed and how it works (this, though, without recourse to endless technicality). The author's accomplished and witty illustrations are integral to his text, and at times send it up most beautifully.

Reiner Zimnik understands the real world and creates from it, imaginatively, his own. (p. 625)

> *Penelope Farmer, in* New Statesman (© *1969 The Statesman & Nation Publishing Co. Ltd.), October 31, 1969.*

This book is totally beyond the experience and comprehension of most children. The theme—war, destruction and rebirth—is handled with too much sophistication and subtlety. The Craneman, a modern Everyman, is the allegorical custodian of the human condition; he lacks both humor and humanity. Black-and-white ink drawings, which look like bizarre, sometimes macabre cartoons, superbly catch and sustain the mood and message of the story. (p. 113)

> *Mary E. Ballou, in* School Library Journal (*reprinted from the November, 1970, issue of* School Library Journal, *published by R. R. Bowker Company, a Xerox company; copyright © 1970 by Xerox Corporation), November, 1970.*

There are certain books, like people one meets at cocktail parties—that provoke immediate distrust, and I regret to say that "The Crane" is such a book. The first suspicious note is the jacket reference to "biblical power." The second is the sheer mass of words and illustrations we must wade through to learn what the plot is about. (p. 26)

Granted, there's a kind of fable here—perhaps about the endurance of man. Granted Mr. Zimnik's imagination is as well-lubricated as the giant machine of his title. The reader's trouble is that the forest cannot be seen for all the wordy trees that inhabit it. (p. 28)

> *Barbara Wersba, in* The New York Times Book Review, *Part II* (© *1970 by The New York Times Company; reprinted by permission), November 8, 1970.*

OTHER CITATIONS

B. W. Alderson, in Children's Book News, *November-December, 1969, pp. 323-24.*

Aidan Chambers, in Signal, *May, 1977, p. 78.*

JONAH, THE FISHERMAN (German Edition, 1954; translation published in US, 1956)

When a bright little idea slipped into Jonah's garret room in Madame Dupoint's house on the Street of the Fishermen, Jonah's whole life changed. Now, instead of catching little fish in the Seine, like all the other fishermen, he learned how to catch a fish as big as a hog.

The enchanting story of Jonah's further fortunes when he is forced by angry fishermen to leave Paris and of his travels all over the world rollicks along in melodious prose. The author touches upon religion, geography, foreign customs, but so easily that the reader is not unduly aware that facts are woven through the fantasy. The descriptions are pungent and vivid, the pictures superbly imaginative. This is the first book [published in English] by a young German author-artist; one hopes there will be many more. (p. 16)

> *Olga Hoyt, in* The New York Times Book Review (© *1956 by The New York Times Company; reprinted by permission), July 22, 1956.*

This most unusual picture-book could have come only from a continental country with a long tradition. (p. 195)

Although *Jonah the Fisherman* comes from Germany it belongs to the French school of picture-books. The drawings are in line. They are full of tremendous vitality and are comical but with great virtuosity. Each opening gives real pleasure for its happy balance of line and word and for the gay humour of the conception. But the appeal of the book is to the sophisticated taste, and it will be the exceptional child who will appreciate its subtlety and the gently satirical tone of its writing and drawing. (pp. 195-96)

> The Junior Bookshelf, *October, 1957.*

OTHER CITATIONS

Helen M. Brogan, in Library Journal, *July, 1956, p. 1721.*

Ruth Hill Viguers, in Saturday Review, *September 22, 1956, p. 35.*

THE LITTLE ROARING TIGER (German Edition, 1960; translation published in US, 1961)

[*The Little Roaring Tiger* is a] very German little book, which shows life and humans as ugly and stupid and yet has a kind of poetry to it. Impossible to guess its effect on children here, but, somehow, it seems likely to intrigue those who attempt it. The robber gang will undoubtedly appeal, but their mistreatment of the tiger *should* appal the reader, but it is difficult to know just what the effect will be. Typical Zimnik drawings include a human-faced tiger. (p. 168)

> *Janice H. Dohm, in* School Library Journal (*reprinted from the October, 1961, issue of* School Library Journal, *published by R. R. Bowker Company, a Xerox company; copyright © 1961 by Xerox Corporation), October, 1961.*

So much of the best of American art is continental in origin that it is interesting to compare the American picture-books with their European contemporaries. Of all modern author-artists the most provocative is Reiner Zimnik. *The Little Roaring Tiger* is not his best work. He has not succeeded in establishing the character of his hero pictorially, and there is little here of the fine symmetrical design of a book like *Jonah the Fisherman*. The story, however, is excellent. The Black-Hat Gangsters are a delightful invention. One cannot help admiring the ingenuity with which they sell the tiger every morning to a different zoo and every evening steal him away again; one almost regrets their ultimate downfall, however thoroughly deserved. Zimnik is a master of the subtle moral, but this time he seems to have written his story purely for fun. (p. 268)

The Junior Bookshelf, November, 1961.

OTHER CITATIONS

Olga Hoyt, in The New York Times Book Review, *September 17, 1961, p. 36.*

The Times Literary Supplement, December 1, 1961, p. 160.

THE PROUD CIRCUS HORSE (German Edition, 1956; translation published in US, 1957)

Although Mr. Zimnik's [*The Proud Circus Horse*, published in Britain as *The Proud White Circus Horse*] is not so original or full of humor as his *Jonah the Fisherman*, it will, I think, be more appealing to most children. It is a shorter, less complicated story with a subject of universal interest—a proud circus horse who runs away "in order to live freely in God's free nature." Mr. Zimnik writes well, with an economy of words that is refreshing. His pen-and-ink sketches, which have been given plenty of white space to set them off, are a delight. (pp. 32-3)

> *Jennie D. Lindquist, in* The Horn Book Magazine *(copyright, 1958, by the Horn Book, Inc., Boston), February, 1958.*

Herr Zimnik's drawing is not so aggressively stylised as it was in *Jonah the Fisherman*, and English children, more conventional in their art education than German, may like it the more. I hope so, for this story has great charm and individuality. The pictures are technically brilliant and vigorous in execution. Let anyone who thinks this kind of drawing is easy look at the Saint Leonard's day procession or at the white horse's last homeward journey and recognise the genius of pure simplicity.

It is rare to find a real story in picture-books today. This tale of the performing horse who grew proud and abandoned the circus is excellent, unexpected in its development, and fundamentally true. It is told with great spirit and style, and is pervaded by a genuine and kindly humour.

It should be added that, although this looks like a book for very small children, it makes considerable demands both on reading ability and on concentration. (pp. 209-10)

The Junior Bookshelf, October, 1958.

OTHER CITATIONS

The Times Literary Supplement, November 2, 1958, p. xxiv.

ZINDEL, Paul   1936-

Paul Zindel is an American screenwriter, playwright for adults, and novelist for young adults and children. At the urging of Harper & Row editor Charlotte Zolotow, who was impressed by the perceptive rendering of children in his play *The Effect of Gamma Rays on Man-in-the-Moon Marigolds,* **he began to write for young adults, producing** *The Pigman* **in 1968. His fiction is characterized by its insightful portrayal of the personalities and problems of teenagers, insight partly obtained by ten years of experience as a high school chemistry teacher. Zindel's** *Gamma Rays,* **which was produced on and off Broadway and filmed, was awarded the 1971 Pulitzer Prize for Drama. (See also** *Contemporary Literary Criticism,* **Vol. 6.)**

GENERAL COMMENTARY

Adult literature today tends often to be depressive simply because ours is an optimistic culture, and optimism is so often betrayed. In other cultures which are perhaps more melancholy, or fatalistic, other sorts of children's literature might be written, but optimism is ingrained in our habits and traditions of thought. This is why I think that the newer sub-Salinger writers, such as Zindel, despite their virtues of freshness and an authentic teenage voice are on the whole unsuitable for children. There is such an overall cynical depressive quality about Zindel's books, which seems to me to be destructive of values before values have properly had time to form. It is the depression I would want to protect emergent minds from, rather than the promiscuity. For even the sexual adventures of his young heroes and heroines are presented in a depressive light, and this presentation of sexuality arguably is as potentially harmful as direct licentiousness. So though Zindel obviously understands the confusion and amorality of teenagers and their frequent failure to associate consequences with actions, rather better than does K M Peyton, I feel the work of the latter is preferable because of its underlying optimism, even if it is sometimes clumsily handled (the professor, deus ex machina, of *Pennington's Seventeenth Summer,* for example), although Peyton's language does not have the same adolescent ring as Zindel's. (pp. 59-60)

> *Myles McDowell, in* Children's Literature in Education *(© 1973, APS Publications, Inc., New York; reprinted by permission of the publisher), No. 10 (March), 1973.*

Why are we so cruel to each other? Ever since man appeared on the scene and learned to write, literature has reflected a preoccupation with this question. And today's society suffers prodigiously more than previous generations from an inability to find satisfying answers. Apparently, some people don't want to think about the question. Like the businessman of the fourth planet in Antoine de Saint-Exupery's *The Little Prince,* they are "interested in matters of consequence" only. Unfortunately, some people have evolved some rather strange and myopic definitions of "matters of consequence."

Paul Zindel is one writer who speaks to young people about man's cruelty and "matters of consequence" in three novels, *The Pigman* . . . , *My Darling, My Hamburger* . . . , and *I Never Loved Your Mind.* . . . In these amusing, provocative, and very-much-of-our-time works, Zindel presents questions to his readers, and if they care (and they do), they will search for answers. Their own answers.

And how does he do this? He looks at the world through the eyes of adolescents, many kinds of adolescents, all trying to find some meaning in a world apparently gone mad, all concerned with man's cruelty and "matters of consequence." By selecting an adolescent point of view, Zindel forces the reader to look at the world as if he were awakening to it for the first time, a kind of rebirth. (p. 941)

Several themes run through all [these] works. The search for identity and meaning. The theme of youthful questioning of traditional values. The theme of the loneliness of the individual in the crowd. The theme of man's inability to communicate in a world of instantaneous communication. All these themes are universal and most of them classic. Zindel makes these primordial themes believable and relevant and significant to young people. . . .

[The] theme of loneliness [is] the dominant theme of all [these] works. In each story, the protagonists are basically lonely because they are unable to establish communication with their parents. Ironically, the adolescents themselves seem to understand *why* the parents behave as they do and to forgive them while the parents are too self-centered to make any real effort to establish any communication link with their teenagers. The instinctive wisdom of youth seems superior to the learned wisdom of adults.

The results in each book? In *The Pigman,* John and Lorraine first try to escape through beer drinking and mischievous games. Then they find a "substitute parent" in Mr. Pignati, a childless widower, who becomes the parent neither has ever known, as they become the children he has never had. Their situation reminds the reader of a lamentable but obvious fact of our society, that it is denying young people the uniquely vital child-parent and child-grandparent relationship typical of previous generations.

In *My Darling, My Hamburger,* Liz turns from her mother and her new stepfather to try to find meaning through relating to her boyfriend and her best girlfriend. When she becomes pregnant, her boyfriend vacillates between protecting and abandoning her. First, he dangles before her lonely eyes the promise of marriage and love and security she has never found in her own home, but ultimately he succumbs to his father's "buddy" advice and offers her only money for an abortion. Maggie, Liz's best friend, has a more stable homelife, but even she cannot really communicate with her parents. All four adolescents in this novel are insecure and lonely, but at the end of the story Maggie and her boyfriend Dennis show some promise of maturing into positive young people.

In *I Never Loved Your Mind,* Yvette and Dewey have dropped out of school and left their homes in their loneliness and inability to communicate with their parents. Yvette seeks her answer in communal life, but her moving from one place to the next, never really finding what she is searching for, makes clear Zindel's point that merely moving from one unhappy situation does not necessarily imply any happiness. Dewey is torn between what Yvette believes in and what the "establishment" represents. He comes close to communicating with and caring about two people, Yvette and the "senior citizen" invalid Irene, but even with them he fails. In an atmosphere of old age, death, and illness in the hospital where Dewey works and plays, Dewey stands near the brink of discovering what life means to him. (p. 943)

The duality and paradox of the theme of loneliness is that in a crowded, urban society with instant and inescapable communication, loneliness has become a major source of other problems. "In the midst of plenty, the masses are starving" in terms of warmth and love and understanding.

Some of the values most highly regarded by tradition are questioned in these . . . works. Is the "establishment" always right? Is motherhood a "holy" institution? Can mothers do no wrong? . . . Are adults necessarily wiser than young people? Are sex and drinking moral wrongs? Is the family unit the best way for people in our society to learn communication? Is the well-adjusted life *the* worthwhile goal of young people? (p. 944)

Paul Zindel examines our society, realizes the pathos and sometimes the bathos of its condition, and finally presents an affirmation of his faith in people, particularly young people, of the basic worth of the individual human being and the collective human spirit. . . .

Why are we so cruel to each other? Because the world whirls too rapidly about us and we will not take time out to look at each other and love each other. Because the world (or society) seems to give lip service to values it does not truly accept or act on.

What are "matters of consequence"? That any action has consequences and each person must be and will be known by his willingness to accept responsibility for his actions. That we love one another, not because love conquers all, but because all understanding and communication begin with love. (p. 945)

> *Beverly A. Haley and Kenneth L. Donelson, "Pigs and Hamburgers, Cadavers and Gamma Rays: Paul Zindel's Adolescents,"* in Elementary English *(copyright 1974, by The National Council of Teachers of English), October, 1974, pp. 941-45.*

Since the appearance of *The Pigman* in 1968, the novels of Paul Zindel have been the objects of a good deal of contradictory discussion and evaluation. These works, *The Pigman, My Darling, My Hamburger,* and *I Never Loved Your Mind,* have been hailed as delightfully humorous, refreshingly honest attempts to deal with a number of the classic themes of modern literature. On the other hand, they have been condemned, with equal fervor, as squalid pieces of trash, as slick "con jobs," and as simple-minded hack work.

Obviously, the resolution of such controversy, if indeed any resolution is possible, is an undertaking far too ambitious for a single essay. Therefore, in this discussion my goals will be much more modest. First, I will sketch one thematic approach to Zindel's novels and then attempt a brief evaluation of the literary worth of each. In so doing, I anticipate that, rather than providing a resolution, this discussion will intensify the Zindel debate. (p. 130)

When [John, Lorraine, and Mr. Pignati, the major characters of Zindel's first novel, *The Pigman,*] meet quite by accident, their lives are changed, but not in the way critics generally assume. For instance, Haley and Donelson write: "Then they [the children] find a substitute parent in Mr. Pignati, a childless widower, who becomes the parent neither has ever known, as they become the children he has never had." [See excerpt above.] Although close, this is not quite on the mark. None of Zindel's heroes and heroines is seeking a surrogate parent. Quite to the contrary, all of Zindel's paired protagonists (and the reader encounters these boy-girl teams in all three novels) have rejected the subordinate role of child and are seeking to assume for themselves the dominant identity of parent. In other words, what they attempt to do is in various ways to create their own families in order to successfully fulfill the role of parent, a role at which their own parents have failed so miserably.

Thus, in *The Pigman* John and Lorraine are not searching for a substitute father. Without the remotest awareness on their part, they are searching for a surrogate child, and Mr. Angelo Pignati, the aging widower, becomes that child. (p. 131)

[Lorraine] is clearly the surrogate mother and the old widower her child, and although she never seems completely to grasp this psychological reality, she is at least partially aware of it. Later, just before the Pigman's first heart attack, she reflects on the significance of her and John's relationship with the old fellow: "The longer he knew us, the more of a kid he became. It was cute in a way". . . .

But it is not really cute; it is tragic. Mr. Pignati's regression indirectly costs him his life. While he is in the hospital, John and Lorraine take over his house and, *sans* sex, act out the role of man and wife. They masquerade in adult clothes, enjoy a candlelight dinner, and even throw a cocktail party. The fantasy is shattered, however; for at the party John gets drunk, the guests become unruly, and Mr. Pignati's cherished collection of pig figurines is smashed—just as Mr. Pignati returns home unexpectedly from the hospital.

The Pigman forgives John and Lorraine. He forgives them as only the adoring child can forgive those parents who have inexplicably caused him pain. Yet they know and the reader knows that their betrayal is partially responsible for the death of their surrogate son. (pp. 132-33)

In Zindel's next novel, the theme of adolescent aspirations to parenthood is once again traceable, but, perhaps because *My Darling, My Hamburger* concerns two teenage couples instead of one, the idea is less central than in *Pigman*. In *My Darling,* the story focuses as much upon the maturation of Maggie and Dennis as upon the young lovers Sean and Liz. Moreover, in this second book the author seems to get tangled in a rather superficial examination of such fashionable topics as teenage premarital sex, illicit pregnancy, and abortion, and in so doing partially to slight the theme he first introduced in *The Pigman.* Nevertheless, the idea is there and merits examination. . . . [For] the parents of Sean and Liz, Zindel once again creates stereotypically "bad" parents, not unlike those which appear in *The Pigman.*

In this second book, then, the reader again encounters a teenage couple attempting to escape the harshness of their respective family lives by creating a third family in which they assume the parental roles. Now, however, the protagonists are older and are no longer content to "beget" surrogate children. Sean and Liz, high school seniors, become lovers and soon Liz becomes pregnant.

Like John and Lorraine in *The Pigman,* these young people also botch their new parental roles. With a premeditation lacking in John and Lorraine, they kill the life that they have created. Sean, who had promised to marry Liz, reneges under pressure from his father and the girl gets an abortion.

What is interesting here is not the love story itself, but the elaboration upon a Zindel stance not fully developed in *Pigman.* In *My Darling* the author suggests the reason why these adolescents fail in their prematurely assumed parental roles is that contemporary society is so brutal and so sterile itself that it deliberately seeks to corrupt the greatest parental duty, which is not simply to create life, but to cherish it. (p. 133)

That Zindel does indeed share with his adolescents their view of contemporary society becomes . . . apparent in his last novel, *I Never Loved Your Mind.* In this first-person narration by Dewey Daniels, the seventeen-year-old high school dropout, the family, which in the earlier novels stood as the chief symbol of a sterile society, has all but disappeared. On one occasion when Dewey asks Yvette Goethals, the heroine of the book, why she does not live with her parents, she responds: "Because they're bastards. My mother's a dumb one. My father's a mean one". . . . But this is virtually the only time they are mentioned. To Yvette, they seem to be merely a part of the general corruption and brutality of society, a society for which her own neighborhood becomes a kind of malignant biopsy sample blighted by such as a crooked judge, a cheating doctor, a thieving cop, and a host of other parasites. . . . Rather than parents, then, in this last novel, the principal symbol of a degenerate society is the hospital in which both Dewey and Yvette work, a hospital steered by a vacuously authoritarian administrator, staffed by indifferent nurses, and stocked with deformed or dying patients.

In the midst of this pain and despair, Dewey discovers Yvette, another high school dropout. The girl, who once waged a futile battle with bulldozers to save a plot of woods in her old neighborhood, becomes a symbol of new life. In fact, Yvette Goethals appears to be a twentieth-century, adolescent reincarnation of the Greek goddess Demeter, the Earth Mother and Goddess of Grain. . . . [Throughout] the narrative, Dewey, with what appears to be unconscious intuition, speaks of her in such a way as to link her with all things natural. For instance, when he first meets her, she appears to him to "look like an owl with a thyroid condition". . . . On their first date Yvette wears a huge, furry mouton coat which, Dewey tells the reader, makes her look like a grizzly bear, a "wolf-woman" . . . , and a "koala cub". . . . At the end of this first date, he walks her to Clove Lakes Park, but she will not allow him to take her home. As Dewey describes it: "She just took off into the brush, like a bear at Yellowstone National Park . . .". Probably, she is headed for her house on "Van Pelt" street. This house Dewey will later see and will describe as being surrounded by "landscaping that resembled an acre of overfertilized rain forest". . . .

Even more than the narrator's intuitive descriptions, however, the actual events of the story suggest that Yvette is a twentieth-century version of the Earth Mother, who, in addition to her role as fertility goddess, is also a goddess of rebirth. That Zindel does indeed intend to endow the girl symbolically with the Goddess' power of rejuvenation is apparent in the fact that Dewey first actually meets his love in the autopsy room, as he awakens from a fainting spell to see her bending over him. The symbolic significance of this episode is underscored some eight chapters later when Dewey describes his thoughts and emotions on the morning after he and Yvette have made love: "When I woke up in my own room on Saturday morning, I felt like I had just been born.... I kept myself in a luxurious somnolent state, trying to relive everything all over again.... I remembered her gently nursing me back to health in the autopsy room"....

This, then, is symbolic rebirth, but before complete rebirth Dewey had had to ply his Demeter with "sacrificial offerings." When he first courts Yvette, he gives her flowers and candy. However, she tells him that instead of these she would prefer bags of seed, especially wheat and barley (both grains are traditionally associated with Demeter). Moreover, on the night they make love, Dewey brings her a fifty pound bag of Burpee radish seed.

Nevertheless, even though he thinks himself born anew, the goddess ultimately rejects him. Although she loves him, she feels that he has been corrupted by society, and she flees.... (pp. 134-35)

Does Dewey follow? Zindel does not tell the reader. He lets him see only that Dewey has indeed undergone a rebirth of sorts. In the final pages of the novel, having learned the address of Yvette's commune, the hero resigns his position at the hospital and closes his story: "I don't really know what I'm going to do.... I'm not going to give civilization a kick in the behind, because I might need an appendectomy sometime. But I'm going to do something, and I have a strange feeling it's going to be phantasmagorically different"....

Zindel's final novel, then, presents a mythically translated and exalted treatment of the theme of the adolescent aspiration for parenthood. After all, while John and Lorraine become surrogate parents and while Sean and Liz almost become real parents, Dewey may have the chance to embrace the family of the Earth Mother. And because, as Yvette has told him several times, her relationship with the Stallions [the rock band with whom she lives] is platonic, if the hero is accepted as being worthy of the honor, he will become the goddess' consort and patriarch of the communal family.

But Zindel may be hinting at much more here. Should the Earth Goddess mate, the result would be a general rebirth of nature. Thus, the author may be telling the reader that from the zest for life, from the compassion for nature of such young people as Dewey and Yvette a new order is possible. Such vital young parents may beget not just children, but a whole new world.

The question is whether or not one must turn his back on contemporary society to create this world. Here, perhaps, Zindel's attitude toward contemporary society may soften. Although Yvette has fled, Dewey has resolved not to do so completely. He is not, as he says, "going to kick civilization in the behind." Maybe this is just a cowardly evasion on Dewey's part. Or maybe Zindel is saying that society can be rejuvenated and purified by the union of the hero, who will not forsake it, and the goddess: the one representing the rebirth of civilized humanity's love for nature, the other representing the lifegiving forces of nature itself.

Is this a Pollyannic interpretation of Zindel's meaning? Perhaps. But before we dismiss it, we ought to remember that in the hospital, that symbol of a dying society, both Dewey and Yvette worked in the inhalation section. Their jobs were to resuscitate patients with oxygen, literally to revive them by providing a breath of fresh air. We ought to remember, too, that when Yvette leaves the hospital and heads for the covered wagon that will take her to a new world, Dewey tried to stop her. In the struggle, her mouton coat flaps open, and Dewey sees that the girl has strapped a "Byrd" machine to her waist. At first, this detail may seem insignificant, since Yvette previously has pilfered medical supplies from the hospital. Still, on second thought, we must wonder: after all, the function of a Byrd machine is to resuscitate patients dying of asphyxiation. In other words, literally and symbolically Yvette has the means to revive and restore life; all that remains now is for Dewey to have the courage to go after her and teach her how to use it.

This, then, is a sketch of the treatment of one of Zindel's themes, an overview which we can use as background for a rough evaluation of the author's individual works. So, let us return to *The Pigman*.

Paul Zindel's first novel is rich in provocatively suggestive metaphor and symbol, only a small part of which is noted in our previous discussion. For instance, Mr. Pignati's beloved zoo is a symbol of the plight of modern man in our impersonal society. Each of us, so Zindel says, lives in his own cage of indifference, boredom, or self-absorption. As do the creatures in the zoo, we may live in close proximity, but we do not live together. At the zoo, Mr. Pignati delights in tossing peanuts to Bobo the gorilla, and John delights in teasing Bobo by attempting to "speak" like an ape. Both acts, one pathetic, the other comic, are symbolic of modern man's need to communicate with someone, something, anything.... (pp. 136-37)

In *The Pigman* even stereotypes are functional. Although John's and Lorraine's parents may remind the reader a bit of Cinderella's stepmother, the author puts their stereotypical nature to good use as a yardstick against which to measure the final actions of their children. Consider, for instance, the drunken cocktail party which wrecks Mr. Pignati's house. Inadvertently, without malice, John and Lorraine betray the trust of their "child." Surely, the reader is meant to compare their selfish thoughtlessness with that of their own parents. They have failed their "child," as they themselves have been failed. Thus, the stereotyped parents stand as an indictment of the actions of their children, while at the same time the stereotype of the "bad" parent is given greater depth by those actions, which suggest that John's and Lorraine's parents abuse their children, not out of brutality, but out of thoughtlessness. Finally, the rigid parental stereotypes, when compared with the protagonists' final contrition, serve to emphasize John and Lorraine's moral superiority: they are capable of moral growth; their parents are not.

About Zindel's second novel, *My Darling, My Hamburger*, I wish I could be as enthusiastic. This appears to have been a hastily written book whose stereotypical characters and actions manifest little of the functional utility of those in *Pigman*.... [In] this story the reader also encounters parents whose wickedness is as unmotivated as is that of Cinderella's stepmother. In fact, Liz's father, a particularly vicious and insensitive type, is really her stepfather, *a la* Cinderella. The story reads like a mushy episode from *Peyton Place*.

Still, *My Darling, My Hamburger* does have interest as a transitional link between *The Pigman* and *I Never Loved Your Mind.* Indeed, *My Darling* could prove very useful in the classroom. Paired with *The Pigman,* for instance, it could be used to demonstrate to young readers the limitations of slick, pat literature, and at the same time, to demonstrate the provocative richness of the other work.

Finally, Zindel's last novel, *I Never Loved Your Mind,* is both his most ambitious and his most difficult. The craftsmanship here is painstaking, but it is often obscured by the narrator Dewey's cloyingly fatuous prose style, perhaps best described by his own favorite adjective "puerile." Nevertheless, Zindel clearly intends the style to be functionally suggestive. The overused technique of alliteration, the often-inappropriate diction, and the generally inflated rhetoric suggest both the immaturity of Dewey's intellect and the fact that he does possess a vigorous, perceptive intellect capable of growth. In one sense, we should see Dewey as an embodiment of the intellect, of the mind paired with but at the same time contrasted to the unbridled spirit of the flesh, Yvette Goethals.

The danger with this novel is that because Zindel chooses to tell the story through the limited, first-person narration of a hero who does not yet understand either his own or Yvette's role, the inexperienced reader may confuse the story's meaning and accept the girl's flight from society as the intelligent way to deal with evil. But this is not Zindel's meaning. The phoniness of the Loveland commune, to which Zindel devotes an entire chapter, and Yvette's illiteracy, evidenced in the note which Zindel inserts toward the close of the story, suggest both her own very limited intelligence and the impossibility of realizing the pastoral dream. This impossibility is further emphasized by the plight of Irene. In the hospital Irene, eighty years old and dying of emphysema, writes a poem entitled "Let's Go Back." But just as she cannot return to childhood, so neither can society return to an agrarian Eden.

As her covered wagon pulls away from the hospital gate, Yvette screams at Dewey: "I never loved your mind." Certainly. The business of the Earth Goddess is not the intellect, but the spirit and the flesh. Zindel seems to be telling his youthful readers that only by a combination of common-sense intelligence (one that appreciates the virtue of civilization represented by the appendectomy Dewey may some day need) and passionate spirit can society be saved.

The final evaluation, then? Paul Zindel is a fine craftsman, a genuine literary artist. Whether, as many have questioned, his novels are appropriate for the adolescent audience, I will leave to others to decide. I am certain of one thing, however: I will not be the last critic to attend to those novels. (pp. 137-39)

> *James T. Henke, "Six Characters in Search of the Family: The Novels of Paul Zindel," in* Children's Literature: Annual of The Modern Language Association Seminar on Children's Literature and The Children's Literature Association, *Vol. 5, edited by Francelia Butler (© 1976 by Francelia Butler; all rights reserved), Temple University Press, 1976, pp. 130-39.*

I LOVE MY MOTHER (1975)

As I see it, we have too many mood pieces for young children today. But I make an exception for this book and, anyway, it is more than straight impressionism. John Melo's double-spread pictures are strong in color and character, and in imagination, too, and pick up the flights of thought by which the little boy expands the realistic ways his mother loves him. We see her only in the final picture—and wonder a little about the present status of the family. (p. 401)

> *Ethna Sheehan, in* America *(© America Press, 1975; all rights reserved), December 6, 1975.*

"She showed me how to kick a football. She has a nice nose and taught me judo. When I told her I was swallowed by a shark she believed it. But she bought me an aquarium. I love my mother." This hymn of praise goes on in a repeat pattern, etching a picture of a wise and loving woman with a sense of humor; it ends, "When I tell her I miss my father she hugs me and says he misses me too. I love my mother. I really do." All of the pictures, lavish with color, show almost photographic representations of the boy with large out-of-scale pictures of brilliant butterflies or marine creatures or zoo creatures; only in the last picture is mother seen, sad-faced, hugging her child, with a remembered father looming above them. The text has the exaggeration, the non-sequential prattle, the enthusiasm of a child's talk—but the ending is out of key. Realistic, but there's nothing in the text to prepare a child for the poignant hopelessness of the last pages. (p. 88)

> *Zena Sutherland, in* Bulletin of the Center for Children's Books *(© 1976 by the University of Chicago; all rights reserved), January, 1976.*

OTHER CITATIONS

Publishers Weekly, *October 20, 1975, pp. 71, 74.*

I NEVER LOVED YOUR MIND (1970)

This is the hardest review your reviewer has ever had to write: the hardest because, after finding Paul Zindel's first two books, his "The Pigman" and "My Darling, My Hamburger," two great reasons for unqualified paeans of praise, I can't praise this, his third novel. I could be chicken—complain of its form (I found the use of footnotes very distracting); or I could say, as its non-hero does every time he is faced with a choice, "what the Hell," and skip reviewing it all together. But Paul Zindel's talent is too big to ignore. He has used it this time to write an ugly book. The ugly words don't bother me, but the ugly hopelessness of the story they tell does. As a social document, a reflection of the young who are disenchanted, it may be of some value to adults. As a novel for anybody of any age, it doesn't work. (p. 85)

> *Lavinia Russ, in* Publishers Weekly *(reprinted from the April 13, 1970, issue of* Publishers Weekly *by permission of the critic, published by R. R. Bowker Company, a Xerox company; copyright © 1970 by Xerox Corporation), April 13, 1970.*

"I Never Loved Your Mind" is a sweet and sour mash of old boy-meets-girl pulp, poured into a contemporary hippie flask. (p. 14)

On surface, "I Never Loved Your Mind" seems "phantasmagorically different" from its usual juvenile fiction peers. Zindel knows how to make all sorts of cutesy moves. His style is breezy and brash, almost self-consciously slipstreams Salinger. He uses the old four letter words of the new dictions and un-selfconsciously trots out as new high school humor the old college humor. ("One girl at the bar did look highly respectable. She looked like she might have been a school teacher but never had any principal.") His characters go topless and bottomless, drink and fornicate, and seem to take far-out, anti-Establishment poses. But that's just it. They're only poses.

To be sure, Zindel allows his hero and anti-heroine to voice anti-Establishment knocks, particularly against such easy marks as high school teachers. But in the end he stacks his value deck completely by making the hippie commune—the only alternative he offers—and all of the hippie characters seem gross, grotesque, and terribly unattractive. Indeed, finally one can't quite understand why Dewey was attracted to Yvette in the first place—except for slender plot line on which an author could hang some arch jokes.

How do you reach the young, the teen-agers? In books, as in life, I do not know. But neither, I think, does Mr. Zindel. For I do know that fiction must offer truth in the guise of illusion, not illusion instead of the truth. And the one thing our Now children can sense most assuredly, as they peer across that well-known gap at their generators, is the scent of adult con.

So for openers, I would submit, you have to treat them with the respect that comes of love. Especially when it comes to their minds. (p. 15)

> *Josh Greenfield, in* The New York Times Book Review, *Part II (© 1970 by The New York Times Company; reprinted by permission), May 24, 1970.*

The action in "I Never Loved Your Mind," by Paul Zindel . . ., takes place chiefly in a hospital, so the protagonist, a seventeen-year-old high-school dropout and one of the most offensive young blatherskites to be found in all of fiction, is given every opportunity to feast upon what is unfortunate but vile, pathetic but hideous, and to report his unspeakable findings. Under the publishers' label of an "intensely funny, insanely serious novel," there is a brew so venomous and cruel that an honest bookseller should hang over it a placard reading "Caveat Emptor." (pp. 218-19)

> *Jean Stafford, in* The New Yorker *(© 1970 by The New Yorker Magazine, Inc.), December 5, 1970.*

On first reading Paul Zindel's *I Never Loved Your Mind* I felt very strongly that it was not for me. I retain an in-built puritanical streak which mentally and emotionally inhibits my acceptance of four-letter words in any kind of public utterance. Originally, the book had already got up my nose by the end of Chapter 2 where Dewey Daniels challenges the vegetarian virago, Yvette Goethals, over her insistence that she can always tell if someone has slipped meat into her sandwich:

"Well," she started, slowly, carefully, "beef makes my stomach churn—".
"Is that so?"
"—and pork makes me fart".

If you share this sort of resentment over a character's language you can always resort to Chaucer's apology in his *Prologue*—that he must set down the story as it is told, or he would be telling the tale unfaithfully and, in any case, the fault is not in him. At the same time you need to bear in mind that context can make a world of difference to the degree of resentment you feel. In *All Quiet on the Western Front* (if memory serves) a fussy body in the hospital is descibed as "frigging about like a fart on a curtain rail". The difference is that the latter is witty and not merely crude and conveys an impression which is probably not to be conveyed in any other words.

Perhaps what is most to be resented about the language in *I Never Loved Your Mind* is that the worst of it comes from the lips of the girl, and it is she who is the more a-moral of the two main characters. Zindel doesn't make concessions in any department of his writing. Dewey and Yvette meet when Dewey goes to work as an orderly in what he describes as "a penicillin pleasure palace called Richmond Valley Hospital" where he is allocated a job in the inhalation therapy department. The place is full of rich people dying with varying degrees of indignity, and Yvette and Dewey perform for them the dreary and soul-depressing personal chores, and these are described in graphic detail; but whereas Dewey to the end retains his basic humanity Yvette has already become a clincally cynical shrew when they meet. It would need a great deal of space to discuss the book in detail. I shall just add that I have re-read it with lessening resentment and, unhappy as I still feel about it, it has begun to seem a necessary book and worth writing when all is said. Dewey and Yvette are portraits of young people adrift in their society and in the confusing world of today. One can think of them as not truly nasty—more pragmatic, more clinical and less sentimental than we are accustomed to in juvenile literature. (pp. 294-95)

Whether you like the story or despise it, you cannot deny that Zindel lightens the gloom and disgust with the pithiness of his language, if only to remind you that laughing at life is what makes it bearable. (p. 295)

> *Aneurin Rhys, in* The Junior Bookshelf, *October, 1972.*

OTHER CITATIONS

Kirkus Reviews, *May 15, 1970, p. 560.*

John W. Conner, in English Journal, *December, 1970, p. 1305.*

Margot Hentoff, in The New York Review of Books, *December 17, 1970, pp. 11-12.*

The Junior Bookshelf, *June, 1971, p. 194.*

MY DARLING, MY HAMBURGER (1969)

When Paul Zindel's first book "The Pigman" appeared, it was so astonishingly good it made your reviewer feel like some watcher of the skies when a new planet swims into his ken. When his second book arrived and topped his first, even Keats could offer no poetry to express the joy it brought, the assurance that Mr. Zindel was no one-book writer. Mr. Zindel is well on his way to being one of the brightest stars in the children's book sky. For this story of four high school seniors, the emotional crises they face and the way they face them is told with such compassionate and loving awareness that the reader is swept immediately into the illusion that no outsider is recording their story: they are talking it out loud themselves. And that, my friends, is *writing*. (p. 85)

> *Lavinia Russ, in* Publishers Weekly *(reprinted from the September 22, 1969, issue of* Publishers Weekly *by permission of the critic, published by R. R. Bowker Company, a Xerox company; copyright © 1969 by Xerox Corporation), September 22, 1969.*

[*My Darling, My Hamburger* is a] skillfully written story of four high school seniors . . . that has tremendous appeal on the entertainment level, but that totally cops out on the issues raised: sex, contraception, abortion. The action in the story happens to Liz and Sean; Maggie and Dennis, there to register and transmit what's happening emotionally, are sensitive, insecure alter egos for those glamorous, hip loners. The teenagers here are the most realistic of any in high-school novels to date: they have appropriate feelings and relationships; smoke, drink, swear; have refreshingly normal sexual thoughts and conflicts. The dialogue and description are so natural and entertaining (and often very funny) that the author disarms his audience (anyone who writes so convincingly must be a friend) while planting mines of moralism: *pot and sex are destructive*. . . . Yesterday's ideas seductively disguised for today's teens. (pp. 137-38)

> *Marilyn R. Singer, in* School Library Journal *(reprinted from* School Library Journal, *November, 1969, published by R. R. Bowker Co., a Xerox company; copyright © 1969 by Xerox Corporation), November, 1969.*

Second books are disappointments almost by definition, but "My Darling, My Hamburger" . . . seems to me to be a better novel than "The Pigman." And I'm sure it will take off with the kids—which isn't quite the same thing, but is always nice for authors and publishers. . . .

It proves for the millionth time that you can get along quite well without a brilliant plot. The book is concerned single-mindedly with sex and growing up; more precisely, it's about the predicament—funny, bitter and nerveracking—of men and women who are also children. The hamburger of the title comes from the advice of a teacher in the first chapter to girls whose boyfriends are getting out of hand: why not suggest going for a hamburger? The first half of the book is called "The darling," the second half "The hamburger." In the first half, Liz is flitting, mothlike and perilously, round the flame, and a light, edgy humor is the keynote. In the second half she falls, scorched; it is dark comedy, and more dark than comedy.

True, the story is value-laden; but then, the subject is value-laden. It's made plain, without being pointed out in so many words, that the girl still pays and that abortion is what it is, not just a fashionable talking-point. The writing is professional in the extreme. Some of the important action

takes place offstage—for instance, Liz's telling the boy of her pregnancy and her parents' discovery of what's happened. We don't need these scenes; they're standard; we can picture them well enough. But it's not so obviously sound to skip (between parts one and two) from Liz's capitulation to the news, months later, that she's pregnant. We've seen the flitting and the scorching; what about the flame? This is too near the heart of the story to be skipped; this is where the author's quick leap is an evasion, and he misses the chance to supersede at last the row of asterisks or the strictly-clinical account or the romantic euphemisms. We could have done to see these two as lovers. (Happy lovers? Perhaps.)

The facsimiles of letters and announcements and whatnot that decorate the text strike me as gimmickry, and here and there, especially at the end of the book, there's a patch of sogginess where we want it to be crisp. As a work of literary art this is more a promise than an achievement, but it's quite a big promise and it's not a negligible achievement. (p. 2)

> *John Rowe Townsend, in* The New York Times Book Review, *Part II (© 1969 by The New York Times Company; reprinted by permission), November 9, 1969.*

Paul Zindel's first teenage novel to reach this country [England], *The Pigman*, was concerned with the friendship between an old man and two teenagers who unintentionally, but irrevocably, come to abuse this relationship. *My Darling, My Hamburger* delves into the private worlds of two teenage girls at the point where they are beginning to explore sexual relationships. One girl has a comparatively secure home background and she provides the 'norm' against which to observe the second girl, who is driven, by the total breakdown in communications between herself and her parents, to indulge in a series of promiscuous affairs which inevitably lead to pregnancy terminating in backstreet abortion. It is as a study of the breakdown in communication between generations that this book may be singled out from its contemporaries. The author's development of his theme is wholly sympathetic, engaging the good will of the reader throughout, and yet, so honest is his treatment that no surer way could have been found for underlining the moral issues. As a book it may shock those who still believe innocence to be synonymous with ignorance, but at a time when teenage promiscuity is giving cause for concern and abortion is much in the news, it can only be a healthy shock. The book is using *effect* to underline *cause*. (p. 9)

> *Valerie Alderson, in* Children's Book Review *(© 1971 by Five Owls Press Ltd.; all rights reserved), February, 1971.*

OTHER CITATIONS

John W. Conner, in English Journal, *January, 1970, p. 1305.*

Diane Farrell, in The Horn Book Magazine, *April, 1970, p. 171.*

PARDON ME, YOU'RE STEPPING ON MY EYEBALL! (1976)

The bizarre list [in *Pardon Me, You're Stepping on My*

Eyeball!] occupies the position of overture to the story, the petty and smart-alecky items scarcely disguising [Marsh's] problems: his alcoholic mother, his nonexistent father, and his own psychological difficulties. In the second chapter, the female protagonist appears. Edna Shinglebox, too, is fifteen and has problems with her parents—chiefly her mother—because no boys seem to be anxious to date her. The meeting and the interaction of the two adolescents, however, transcend the realistic details and the contemporaneous idiom of the story and come to a climax in a weird but spectacular scene in which they set off a three-stage American flag firework rocket in Arlington Cemetery. The final paragraph of the book not only ends spectacularly but resolves—in a symbolic way—the boy's psychological tensions, accomplishing a genuine literary catharsis. (p. 19)

> *Paul Heins, in* Bookbird, *Vol. XIV, No. 4 (December 15, 1976).*

Two members of a high school therapy group run by the school psychologist grope toward real friendship and understanding, in a story that is ebulliently zany, at times seeming exaggerated, at times very funny. . . . The story is sophisticated, candid, not quite believable in what happens —but it is more than convincing in its perceptiveness and its sensitivity to the anguish of the unhappy adolescent. In their own way, Edna and Marsh, for all the abrasion they feel at times, help each other move toward self-acceptance and stability. (p. 136)

> *Zena Sutherland, in* Bulletin of the Center for Children's Books (© *1977 by the University of Chicago; all rights reserved), April, 1977.*

Pardon Me, You're Stepping On My Eyeball! is, like its title, a long and unwieldy book which tries very hard indeed to present an engaging and sympathetic picture of ''Marsh'' Mellow and Edna Shinglebox and their tentative relationship. But, if one takes away the parade of wisecracks and brand names and if one ignores the gratuitous eccentricities of the characters, a very shallow and insubstantial core is left. Zindel takes a great many words to lead his characters to their climactic acknowledgement of the truth about themselves, and this book seems a far cry from the more concise, convincing and compassionate *Pigman* and *My Darling, My Hamburger.* And, despite the self-consciously comic setpieces, his . . . book lacks the compensation of humour. Even the spectacular party sequence is writ too large to amuse. (p. 94)

> *Lance Salway, in* Signal (copyright © *1977 Lance Salway; reprinted by permission of the author and The Thimble Press, Lockwood Station Road, South Woodchester, Glos. GL5 5EQ, England), May, 1977.*

[*Pardon Me, You're Stepping on My Eyeball!* is an] extravagant send-up of the whole teenage genre. The two main characters are traditional—the lonely boy and girl whose maladjusted parents insist that they attend psychiatric sessions. 'Marsh' Mellow's problem is that he won't accept his father's death, although he keeps his ashes under his bed, and so he has become a compulsive liar and fantasist. Edna Shinglebox is more 'normal', though her mother, in hilarious scenes abounding in Jewish-type humour, persecutes her because she hasn't ever had a boyfriend. Other caricatures include: the enormous school psychiatrist; the

crazy fortune-teller who's infested with cockroaches; the freaky religious cult-leader God Boy. The climax—a fire at a friend's party with parents away—recalls the end of *The Pigman,* but is much more disastrous, and from then on the book careers to its conclusion where Marsh Faces the Truth, via the death of his pet raccoon, and a car smash by the cemetery where Kennedy is buried.

One can't avoid the feeling of repetition. It's ground welltrod, and even though Zindel is outstanding in the genre, it is not sufficiently different from his others to mark a real advance. (p. 163)

> *Jessica Kemball-Cook, in* The School Librarian, *June, 1977.*

THE PIGMAN (1968)

[This] book is headline news because, though it may be a first book, it is so remarkable that it automatically shows its writer to be a professional. Paul Zindel tells a story of a boy and a girl and their meeting with an old man. He has written the boy's version as a boy would write it, and the girl's version as a girl would write it. He has written a story that will not be denied. I hope he's very proud of it. He should be. (p. 61)

> *Lavinia Russ, in* Publishers Weekly *(reprinted from the September 30, 1968, issue of* Publishers Weekly *by permission of the critic, published by R. R. Bowker Company, a Xerox company; copyright © 1968 by Xerox Corporation), September 30, 1968.*

The Pigman is Mr. Angelo Pignati, dupe, patron, playmate, responsibility of high school sophomores John Conlan and Lorraine Jensen, who take turns telling what happened . . . ''but you really can't say we murdered him.'' Hooked like that, you really can't stop reading either, although this echoes the current preoccupation with floundering kids and niggling parents and the abyss between, underlined. . . . Insistently rebellious as this is (John smokes, drinks, plays practical jokes deliberately), it's not churlish like some of its sort. And though the kids miss coalescing as individuals, there are moments when you know just what they're talking about. (pp. 1123-24)

> Kirkus Service *(copyright © 1968 The Kirkus Service, Inc.) October 1, 1968.*

''The Pigman'' is a ''memorial epic'' told, chapter-in-turn, by two high school sophomores, John and Lorraine. They are an engaging pair, nicely iconoclastic, who suspect nearly everyone else of congenital brain damage. Their ''epic'' makes a very funny book at one level because Mr. Zindel catches the bright, hyperbolic sheen of teen-age language accurately and with humor. It is a serious book as it reveals their touching and sad, yet happy, acquaintance with a lonely old man, Mr. Pignati, The Pigman, to whom they give some moments of joy and hurt, in exchange for another piece of knowledge gained in the puzzle of growing up.

At odds with their harassed parents, not much interested in school, John and Lorraine find in The Pigman a kind of consanguineous spirit, an aged simile for themselves. Mr. Pinati has lived beyond the cares of the stock exchange and has returned to the myths of childhood. Unfortunately, the boy and girl do not recognize the symptoms of senility—or that an old man may be hurt as well as pleased by life, as easily as they. His defenses are down while theirs are daily battered and strengthened.

"The Pigman" is in most ways a thoroughly successful book with the right combination of the preposterous and the sensible. Only at the end does Mr. Zindel find it necessary to patronize his young readers by spelling out the moral; surely any kid bright enough to read the medium will be bright enough to get its message. (p. 2)

> *John Weston, in* The New York Times Book Review, *Part II (© 1968 by The New York Times Company; reprinted by permission), November 3, 1968.*

[The younger generation] may recognize themselves in the problems [in *The Pigman*] but they will not I fear be able to identify themselves with the two characters, Lorraine and John. . . . The world of psychoanalysis and sex-starved mums fearing for their daughters at every turn is as yet a strange one for the average European teenager. . . .

[How] far do European readers of between thirteen and sixteen really appreciate this new genre of specialized American fiction? For me at least a great deal of it reads as fantasy and I should suspect this to be the reaction of the average English reader. Remember that the intelligent child will by fifteen be reading Hemingway and James Baldwin, Harper Lee and Mary McCarthy, therefore these novels should, if they are to succeed, appeal to the non-academic reader, and this I very much doubt. (p. 307)

> *Joan Murphy, in* The School Librarian, *September, 1969.*

[*The Pigman*] focuses on a lonely, old man, Mr. Pignati, whose story is told in odyssey-like movement. The terminus of the journey in the characters' intention is carefree enjoyment of life. The terminus of the journey in actuality becomes a beginning for the teenagers and an end for Mr. Pignati.

With the opening words "The Oath," the author gives himself over to his main characters to tell the story. . . . They weave a multi-stranded story of interactions with other characters and between themselves at the writing level itself. . . . Tied in with this level but separate from it, there is the sexual level of interaction between the two which is sustained to the end of the novel. This dual first person narrator produces two fully developed relationships to the Pigman as well as to the individual sets of parents. Each of these strands is unique to each of its writers, yet each separate relationship is meshed into what seems like a single narrator formed by the personalities of Lorraine and John.

Along with the intimacy that naturally results from the first person point of view, there is the added insight given by their interactions with each other. This establishes the environment for a literary double exposure of the Pigman himself. I think this exposure is essential since he functions not only in his own right, but also as contrast for John's father and mother, for Lorraine's mother, and in a lesser degree, for the librarian. This seems to be the reason Zindel called the book *The Pigman* and not *John and Lorraine.* (p. 1164)

The two young authors call their writing a "memorial epic," in the opening oath, "The truth and nothing but the truth, until this memorial epic is finished, So Help Us God!" The scant invocation perhaps attests to the epic intention. The story opens *in media res* and it isn't until chapter four that we meet Mr. Pignati, the Pigman. Because Zindel puts the term *epic* into the mouths of the adolescents, it cannot be taken as a serious literary attempt. It may be more hyperbolic than actual; although the quality of tragedy attendant upon an epic is present, it does not dominate. This story fits Aristotle's first of four kinds of tragedy: "The Complex, depending entirely on Reversal of the Situation and Recognition." Within the story, the Pigman, Lorraine, and John experience grief as a result of their experience of childhood carefreeness; and recognition comes to Pignati in awareness that his relationship with the young people was unstable and impermanent and that he is totally alone when Bobo is dead. It comes to Lorraine and John in Mr. Pignati's death when John writes, "There was no one else to blame anymore". . . .

The entire movement in the book builds toward the recognition scene. The pain, concomitant with a recognition scene, is reciprocal for the two sets of lives involved. Lorraine and John mature at the expense of the Pigman; the Pigman recaptures joy at the expense of a heart attack and of later trauma on his return home.

It seems obvious that the Pigman is not an epic hero in the classical sense, but he has his struggle with life and closes his role in the story with what Aristotle calls the "Scene of Suffering." His painful or destructive action is his death in the zoo. I am not saying that Zindel consciously fits his story into Aristotle's descriptive analysis. Aristotle's perception of tragedy is so broad that he creates a universal description to which individual tragedy relates in some way. It is at this abstract level that Zindel's story relates to the description quoted. I think it is fair to say that the novel is written toward that moment of recognition experienced by all three during the scene of Mr. Pignati's death. From the beginning of the story, there is this characteristic of a larger-than-life quality which stands out in the power the facts have had to urge these two young people to write their story in the first place. Whether we look at *King Lear* or at *Crime and Punishment,* at [John R. Tunis's] *His Enemy, His Friend,* or at *The Pigman* itself, we find a relationship among them in that each one shows us a human being struggling to come to terms with a force identifiable within himself that seems beyond his own ability to overcome. It is this struggle that eventually leads to the moment of recognition where one sees *what is,* against the possibility of what could have or should have been. The more complex the struggle and its involvements, the greater the impact of the story.

Certainly, the Pigman is not a tragic hero in an epic sense; he is a pathetic figure, bearing symbolic weight with the name given him, who shuffles through the pages of the book trailing two teenagers to what to him looks like a glory of joy but which ends as the final seal to his testimony of loneliness. The Pigman is the focus of the story which, symbolically, can be represented as a circle. The center is the Pigman; the circumference consists of two 180° arcs representing John and Lorraine. These arcs are not discrete, but continuous in movement around the center. Without the center the circumference would not be defined; likewise, without the circumference the center would be undefined.

One of the notable features in the telling of the story is the almost indistinguishable shift from one author to the other across the chapters. Although the momentum of the action moves the story, the writing could easily snag as the narration moves from John to Lorraine. Zindel masters this movement so artfully that at times the chapters merge and the shift has to be worked back upon to discover where it occurred. (pp. 1165-66)

This effect would not always be desirable, since the interaction of the two writers is part of the artistic shape of this work, but the dramatic action does not suffer because it is in the hands of alternate writers, the creative conception the artist had of the story he wanted to write. He wanted to tell three stories—not in an obviously separate manner. He saw the three lives bound together in that moment of self realization, the last for the Pigman, and in a sense, the first for the two young writers. What better way is there to present the adolescent and his world in a story than to let him present it himself? And despite the wide range of difference between the male and female approach to life, the telling of this story comes off as one continuous story told by two different people with neither overlapping nor repetitions, as one constantly moving development which is seen from separate viewpoints that merge only in the telling, but not in the personality or temperament of either one.

Another notable feature of the narrative technique of this work is that despite the episodic nature of the story—"let it be known that Lorraine Jensen and John Conlan have decided to record the facts, and only the facts, about our experiences with Mr. Angelo Pignati"—the story is not cumulative. By this I mean that with the oath, Zindel generated (in contradistinction to accumulated) a literary organism that grows through character motivation and interaction. With only "the facts" Zindel creates the Pigman in rather broad strokes at first. . . . By the end of the book the reader has come to know [him] quite intimately. . . . Each detail builds into the reality of the Pigman's loneliness. Concomitant with this growth is the creation of an awareness of what life really ought to mean; with these two young people he experiences again some brief moments of it.

Because it is only through Lorraine and John that we come to observe and listen to the Pigman, they had to be so created that one could accept their "epic" as true. Credibility lends itself to this eye-witness type of writing as the two writers speak of their interactions and thoughts both in the structured situations of the home scenes with Lorraine and her mother, or with John and his parents, and in the free association moments like the one where Lorraine speaks about the librarian and her outgrown clothes and associates that idea to another. . . . (pp. 1166-67)

These associations are not confined to interior monolog. Many of the associations are made through a presentation in dramatic form. John, the future actor, recreates his scenes with an immediacy that fits a drama-oriented person. . . . [Eye-witness] drama is one of the narrator's way of making a comment about his life's situation in such a way as to share the experience with us. (p. 1167)

The image of Lorraine's mother is formed more sharply through the language the mother uses than through the language Lorraine uses to describe her. (p. 1168)

Zindel . . . depicts the working mother (one time divorced, now widowed), judging all of life by the limitations and experiences of her own. He shows us the talented daughter trying to understand her mother's loneliness, yet realizing that there is no communication between them.

John's parents, too, are defined by language—John's language. The Bore and the Old Lady are his names for them. In fact all the characters in the story come through John and Lorraine's limited view of fifteen years of living. This view is what contributes to the thinness of the story itself. By thinness I mean an obvious lack of perception into personalities and situations outside the interactions of their own lives. By thinness I mean the superficial character development which consists only in the telling of happenings, never in the inner struggle outward to some moment of pain or peace. The story is meant to be a fast told narrative—"record the facts, and only the facts"— and the book achieves what it has set out to do. True, the framework set out in the "Preface" permits the facile story development, but genuine character development is missing. The doubt about how seriously to take the Pigman's plight rests on this point. Had his anguish been rooted in his personality, had we some insight into the nature of his past loneliness, had we seen some struggle to come to grips with his life, we would not wonder just what it is he represents. This is not meant to imply that each writer must attempt to develop character in the same way. But character insight must be actively engaged within the story so that this insight authenticates itself.

The use of the zoo, no doubt, was meant to intensify the loneliness of the Pigman. However, the zoo seems more like a stock place for old men to go for visits than an integral part of the Pigman's character presentation in the story. Had he been visiting Beckman's or some place more consonant with the relationship he had with his wife, there would be more credibility. Bobo lessens the dignity of the old man; he does not, as the author intends, intensify the aloneness of his life. Even the final scene in front of Bobo's cage, where death overtakes the Pigman, strains toward the pathetic. Genuine tragedy isn't present; simulated tragedy played through the death of the baboon and paralleled by the death of the Pigman creates the strain. And this is so, despite the objectified symbolizing of the baboon in the last three lines of the book:

> Baboons.
> Baboons.
> They build their own cages, we could almost
> hear the Pigman whisper, as he took his children with him. . . .

These three lines intrude upon the story. The use of the phrase "his children" strains or, perhaps more accurately, intrudes upon the consciousness of the adolescents writing. It is true that Lorraine and John posed as his children to visit him in the hospital, and to validate their presence in his home after his first attack. But no mention is made of this fact again until the above quoted sentence.

Despite these weaknesses, Zindel has reflected through his adolescent writers an adolescent view of life. It represents a small population of precocious students, but the existence of such a population cannot be denied. The fictional adolescents relate episodes in their life which lead to a tragedy of death, which in turn becomes their moment of recognition. As a swift moving narrative, the story works well. Its lack of complexity fits the statement of intent made by the narrators in the opening oath "to record the facts, and only the facts." (pp. 1169, 1175)

Loretta Clarke, in English Journal *(copyright © 1972 by The National Council of Teachers of English), November, 1972.*

OTHER CITATIONS

B. W. Alderson, in Children's Book News, *May-June, 1969, p. 136.*

CUMULATIVE INDEX TO AUTHORS

CUMULATIVE INDEX TO TITLES

CUMULATIVE INDEX TO CRITICS

APPENDIX

THE EXCERPTS IN CLR-3 WERE REPRINTED FROM THE FOLLOWING PERIODICALS:

AB Bookman's Weekly
Algol
America
American Artist
Appraisal
The Atlantic Monthly
The Babbling Bookworm
Best Sellers
Black Books Bulletin
Black World
Book Week
Book World
Book World—Chicago Tribune
Book World—The Washington Post
Bookbird
Booklist
Books and Bookmen
Books for Your Children
Bulletin of the Center for Children's Books
Cambridge Review
Canadian Children's Literature
Catholic Library World
Chicago Sunday Tribune Magazine of Books
Childhood Education
Children's Book News
Children's Book Review
Children's Book Review Service
Children's Literature

Children's Literature in Education
Choice
The Christian Century
The Christian Science Monitor
Commonweal
The Economist
Elementary English
English Journal
Growing Point
The Horn Book Magazine
In Review
Instructor
Interracial Books for Children Bulletin
Journal of American Folklore
The Junior Bookshelf
Junior Libraries
Kirkus Reviews
Language Arts
Library Journal
Life
The Lion and the Unicorn
The Listener
MOSIAC
Museum News
Natural History
Negro History Bulletin
The New Republic
New Statesman
New York Magazine

The New York Review of Books
New York Sunday Herald Tribune Book Week
The New York Times Book Review
The New Yorker
North Carolina State Library Book Review
The Outlook
Print
Publishers Weekly
The Reading Teacher
Saturday Review
The School Librarian
School Library Journal
Science Books
Science Books & Films
Scientific American
Signal
The Spectator
Sunday World Journal Tribune Book Week
Teacher
The Times Literary Supplement
Top of the News
The Use of English
Vector
West Coast Review of Books
Wilson Library Bulletin
Young Adult Cooperative Book Review

THE EXCERPTS IN CLR-3 WERE REPRINTED FROM THE FOLLOWING BOOKS:

Arbuthnot, May Hill and Zena Sutherland, Children and Books, *fourth edition, Scott, Foresman, 1972.*

Bader, Barbara, American Picturebooks from Noah's Ark to the Beast Within, *Macmillan, 1976.*

Bader, Barbara, Betty Binns, and Alvin Eisenman, Children's Book Showcase, *Children's Book Council, 1977.*

Bell, Anthea, E. Nesbit, *Bodley Head, 1960.*

Blishen, Edward, ed., The Thorny Paradise: Writers on Writing for Children, *Kestrel, 1975.*

Blount, Margaret, Animal Land: The Creatures of Children's Fiction, *Morrow, 1974.*

Bova, Ben, Notes to a Science Fiction Writer, *Scribner's, 1977.*

Cameron, Eleanor, Crosscurrents of Criticism: Horn Book Essays 1968-1977, *selected and ed. by Paul Heins, Horn Book, 1977.*

Crouch, Marcus, The Nesbit Tradition: The Children's Novel in England 1945-1970, *Benn, 1972.*

Crouch, Marcus, Treasure Seekers and Borrowers: Children's Books in Britain 1900-1960, *The Library Association, 1962.*

Egoff, Sheila, The Republic of Childhood: A Critical Guide to Canadian Children's Literature in English, *second edition, Oxford University Press, 1975.*

Egoff, Sheila, G. T. Stubbs, and L. F. Ashley, eds., Only Connect: Readings on Children's Literature, *Oxford University Press, 1969.*

Eyre, Frank, British Children's Books in the Twentieth Century, *Dutton, 1971.*

Field, Elinor Whitney, ed., Horn Book Reflections: On Children's Books and Reading, *Horn Book, 1969.*

Fisher, Margery, Who's Who in Children's Books: A Treasury of the Familiar Characters of Childhood, *Holt, 1975.*

Fisher, Margery, Roger Lancelyn Green, and Marcus Crouch, Henry Treece, C. S. Lewis and Beatrix Potter, *revised edition, Bodley Head, 1969.*

Georgiou, Constantine, Children and Their Literature, *Prentice-Hall, 1969.*

Gibb, Jocelyn, ed., Light on C. S. Lewis, *Harcourt, 1976.*

Green, Roger Lancelyn, Tellers of Tales, *Watts, 1965.*

Gruen, John, Close-Up, *Viking, 1968.*

Higgins, James E., Beyond Words: Mystical Fancy in Children's Literature, *Teachers College Press, 1971.*

Hoffman, Miriam and Eva Samuels, eds., Authors and Illustrators of Children's Books: Writings on Their Lives and Works, *Bowker, 1972.*

Hürlimann, Bettina, Picture-Book World: Modern Picture-Books for Children from Twenty-Four Countries, *trans. and ed. by Brian W. Alderson, World, 1969.*

Hürlimann, Bettina, Three Centuries of Children's Books in Europe, *trans. and ed. by Brian W. Alderson, Oxford University Press, 1967.*

Huttar, Charles A., ed., Imagination and the Spirit: Essays in Literature and the Christian Faith, *Eerdmans, 1971.*

Kilby, Clyde S., The Christian World of C. S. Lewis, *Eerdmans, 1964.*

Lanes, Selma G., Down the Rabbit Hole: Adventures and Misadventures in the Realm of Children's Literature, *Atheneum, 1972.*

Lewis, C. S., Of Other Worlds: Essays and Stories, *ed. by Walter Hooper, Harcourt, 1975.*

Lukens, Rebecca J., A Critical Handbook of Children's Literature, *Scott, Foresman, 1976.*

MacCann, Donnarae and Olga Richard, The Child's First Books: A Critical Study of Pictures and Texts, *Wilson, 1973.*

Meek, Margaret, Aidan Warlow, and Griselda Barton, eds., The Cool Web: The Pattern of Children's Reading, *Bodley Head, 1977.*

Meigs, Cornelia, ed., A Critical History of Children's Literature, *revised edition, Macmillan, 1969.*

Moore, Doris Langley, E. Nesbit: A Biography, *Chilton, 1966.*

Moss, Elaine, Children's Books of the Year 1974, *Hamish Hamilton, 1975.*

Poltarnees, Welleran, All Mirrors Are Magic Mirrors: Reflections on Pictures Found in Children's Books, *Green Tiger Press, 1972.*

Rose, Jasper, Lucy Boston: A Walck Monograph, *Walck, 1965.*

Sagar, Keith, The Art of Ted Hughes, *Cambridge University Press, 1975.*

Salway, Lance, ed., A Peculiar Gift: Nineteenth Century Writings on Books for Children, *Kestrel, 1976.*

Scholes, Robert, Structural Fabulation: An Essay on Fiction of the Future, *University of Notre Dame Press, 1975.*

Smaridge, Norah, Famous Author-Illustrators for Young People, *Dodd, Mead, 1973.*

Smith, Lillian H., The Unreluctant Years: A Critical Approach to Children's Literature, *American Library Association, 1953.*

Streatfeild, Noël, Magic and the Magician: E. Nesbit and Her Children's Books, *Abelard-Schuman, 1958.*

Townsend, John Rowe, A Sense of Story: Essays on Contemporary Writing for Children, *Lippincott, 1971.*

Townsend, John Rowe, Written for Children: An Outline of English-Language Children's Literature, *revised edition, Lippincott, 1974.*